Official

Microsoft®

Intranet
Solutions

Using Microsoft Office 97 and FrontPage™ 97

*Micro Modeling
Associates, Inc.*

PUBLISHED BY
Microsoft Press
A Division of Microsoft Corporation
One Microsoft Way
Redmond, Washington 98052-6399

Library of Congress Cataloging-in-Publication Data
Official Microsoft Intranet Solutions / Micro Modeling Associates,
   Inc.
       p.   cm.
   Includes index.
   ISBN 1-57231-509-1
    1. Intranets (Computer networks)   2. Business enterprises--
Computer networks.   3. Client/server computing.   I. Micro Modeling
Associates.
   HD30.385.037   1997
   005.368'2--dc21   97-7687
                                             CIP

Printed and bound in the United States of America.

2 3 4 5 6 7 8 9 MLML 2 1 0 9 8 7

Distributed to the book trade in Canada by Macmillan of Canada, a division of Canada Publishing Corporation.

A CIP catalogue record for this book is available from the British Library.

Microsoft Press books are available through booksellers and distributors worldwide. For further information about international editions, contact your local Microsoft Corporation office. Or contact Microsoft Press International directly at fax (206) 936-7329.

Acquisitions Editor: Casey D. Doyle
Project Editor: Sally Stickney
Technical Editor: Jean Ross

Table of Contents

Foreword .... *ix*
Preface .... *xi*
Acknowledgments .... *xiii*
Using the Companion CD .... *xv*

1   What Is an Intranet? 3
    The Needs of Business 4
    How an Intranet Can Help 6
    Components of an Intranet 7
    How an Intranet Differs from a Regular Network 9
    Microsoft's Intranet Tools 10
    Summary 21

2   Developing Your First Web with FrontPage 97 23
    What Can FrontPage 97 Do for You? 24
    And Now...Let's Make a Web 28
    Web Views 33
    The FrontPage Explorer Toolkit 35
    FrontPage Wizards and Templates 44
    Webs Within Webs 53
    Wisdom Born of Experience 53

3   Creating Intranet Pages with FrontPage 97 57
    FrontPage Editor Page Wizards and Templates 59
    Saving Pages to Webs 65
    Customizing Page Templates 66
    Imported HTML: Open with Care 67
    What You See Ain't All You Get 68
    (Almost) Effortless Editing 71

4   Building the Sample Web 87

     Creating a Boilerplate Web Page Template 88

     Creating a Cascading Style Sheet 94

     Including the Footer 102

     Adding Script Shells 105

     Saving the Master Page Templates 108

     There's No Such Thing As an Empty Web 112

     Toolbars and Menus 113

     What's on the Menu? 122

     Bringing It All Back Home 125

     Advanced Projects 136

     You've Taken the First Step 161

5   Internet Information Server 163

     Requirements for Setting Up Internet Information Server 164

     Installing Internet Information Server 166

     Configuring Internet Information Server 169

     Access Control, Security, and Other Important Information 175

     Publishing Your Web to IIS from FrontPage 180

6   Microsoft Internet Explorer 183

     Viewing ActiveX Documents in Internet Explorer 186

     Customizing Internet Explorer for Your Intranet 187

     Don't Forget Your Cache 188

     The Internet Explorer Scripting Object Model 189

     The Web Browser Control's Object Model 194

     Programming Internet Explorer 194

7   Creating Dynamic Pages with VBScript and ActiveX 205

     Visual Basic, Scripting Edition 205

     ActiveX Controls 227

8   Using the Intranet Tools of Microsoft Office 97 253

     User-Side Web Page Tools 254

     Under the Hood: The Microsoft Office Web Object Model 261

HTML Made Easy 266

Posting Your Microsoft Office Files Online 266

9 Creating Web Documents with Microsoft Word 97 269

The Three Faces of Word 270

The Shared Tools: Hyperlinks and Backgrounds 271

Building and Editing HTML Files in Word 275

Converting a Word Document to HTML 290

Converting HTML to Word 292

Word Template Architecture and Intranet Files 293

Posting Word Documents Online 296

Automating Your Web Page Building with Word VBA 306

Building the MMA Intranet 315

Going Forward 328

10 Microsoft Excel 97 331

Integration and Microsoft Excel 97 332

Microsoft Excel 97 and External Data 339

Building Your Intranet 347

11 Microsoft Access 97 361

Hyperlinks 363

Linking and Importing External Data 370

Saving in Web Format 374

Internet Replication 397

Building Your Intranet 398

12 Creating Web Slide Shows with Microsoft PowerPoint 97 411

Posting Online Presentations 413

Getting Started with Microsoft PowerPoint 414

Posting PowerPoint Files on Your Intranet 416

Converting Presentations to HTML 420

Using Graphics and Multimedia Features 425

Working with Hyperlinks 432

Intranet Programming in PowerPoint 438

Building the MMA Intranet 450

Combining Your Talents 454

13 Microsoft Outlook 97 457

The Outlook Bar 459

Integration 469

The Six Degrees of Customization 470

A Customized View 471

Public Folders 475

Customized Outlook Forms 484

Rules 496

The Outlook Object Model 499

Web Browsers and the Internet 502

Really Cool Things in Outlook 504

Sample Application 504

14 Web Site Search 527

The FrontPage Search WebBot 528

Web Find Fast 529

Microsoft Index Server 537

Using Index Server on Our Intranet 543

15 Extending Internet Information Server 551

CGI 552

ISAPI 555

Active Server Pages 558

DCOM and Transaction Server 562

16 Integration with Microsoft SQL Server 569

Advantages of Web-Based Solutions 570

Microsoft SQL Server Web Assistant 571

Handling Dynamic Requests 572

SNA Server and the AS/400 573

Building Sample Web Pages That Utilize SQL Server 574

17 Web Administration 597

FrontPage Administration 598

FrontPage Server Administration 619

Document Management with Visual SourceSafe 622

18 Putting It All Together 637

Building an Intranet Site Framework 638

Delivering Content: HTML and Office Documents 639

Database Integration 643

Other Application Development Tools 645

A The FrontPage File/Folder Structure 651

What Is All That Stuff? 651

A Few Simple Rules 653

The Belly of the Beast 653

Creating "Hidden" Pages and Directories 654

B Where to Get More Information 657

Books 657

Magazines 658

Internet Resources 659

Etcetera 661

Index 663

Foreword

Since its introduction, the World Wide Web, or the graphical arm of the public Internet, has taken the computing world by storm—and for good reason. The Web appeals to end users partly because it employs intuitive technologies, such as searching and hyperlinking, that make it easy to find information. The Web excites the folks behind the scenes because it takes advantage of open, platform-independent standards that reduce administrative complexity and costs on both the client and the server.

Recently, private organizations have been deploying the open technologies invented for the World Wide Web across their existing network infrastructures. These infrastructures, called intranets, hold great promise for internal publishing and collaboration. Intranets are relatively inexpensive and easy to establish, and most companies can run their intranet on existing local area or wide area networks (LAN/WAN) without the security concerns of the public Internet. Intranets also provide companies with a low-cost, low-maintenance, convenient way to share information with employees and clients no matter where they are or what types of PCs they use.

No doubt about it, intranets today are hot. If your job has anything to do with your company's network, chances are that you've either been considering developing an intranet yourself or have been asked to look into creating one. If you're reading this, you've probably already decided that an intranet is in your future. So what's next?

That's where this book comes in. To prepare yourself for this exciting new world, you'll need to take some time to find out exactly what intranets are all about and to ask some important questions: What kind of things will I expect our intranet to do? What exactly is a "Web site," and how do I set one up? What kind of software do I need to install on my servers? And what about the clients?

Before you start planning where you want to go with your intranet, one of your most critical tasks will be to determine exactly where you are now. Chances are that your organization has established certain software standards. You'll want to keep those standards in mind when you're planning your intranet. It would be counterproductive to throw away everything already installed on the client desktops just to use this new technology. If you're one of the millions who have already adopted Microsoft Windows and Office as their desktop standard, you're probably a lot closer than you think to having your intranet up and running. Your organization can take advantage of the new built-in technology and intranet features of Office 97 and FrontPage to build and deploy robust intranet solutions incredibly quickly. And because intranets require the use of tools such as Microsoft Internet Explorer and Office, both of which users are already familiar with, you won't have to spend a lot of time or money training staff on how to use the intranet. Administrators will appreciate the power of the new FrontPage 97 Explorer to help them manage the intranet and keep this "private" Web from becoming tangled.

In *Official Microsoft Intranet Solutions,* you'll first learn the basics of building and implementing intranets quickly and economically using Office 97 and FrontPage 97. You'll then explore such topics as how Office 97 and FrontPage integrate with Microsoft's BackOffice products to make even advanced Web-based applications easy to create and administer. By the time you've finished this book, you'll see that your own intranet is well within reach.

So relax, enjoy, and read on. We think you'll be pleasantly surprised by how easy it is to create your very own intranet using Office 97 and FrontPage.

Jon DeVaan, Vice President,
Desktop Applications Division
Microsoft Corporation
March 1997

Preface

We jumped at the chance to write this book because the advent of the intranet has been so core to our business. Intranets will soon be nearly as common as local area networks. One reason for this boon in intranets is that they are relatively inexpensive and easy to establish, and most companies can run their intranet on their existing LAN/WAN infrastructure (without the security concerns of the Internet). Intranets also provide companies with a low-cost, low-maintenance, easy way to share information with employees and clients no matter where they are or what type of PCs they use.

At Micro Modeling Associates, Inc., we frequently use this phrase to describe what it is that we do: "We develop applications that make it easier to *retrieve, analyze, present, and share* critical business information within a department, a division, or throughout an entire firm." Over the past ten years, the pace of change in software applications has been rapid but evolutionary. The primary focus of new software releases has been to increase the number of features. These new features have tended to focus on making it easier to retrieve, analyze, or present information. Relatively little progress has been made on making it easier to *share* information—until now. Intranets are revolutionizing the way companies share information, providing a single point of entry into a universe of corporate information and business applications.

Many custom intranet applications that we are building today are changing the way companies do business in compelling ways. Intranets are now so much more than the linking of static HTML documents. With ActiveX Documents and ActiveX Controls, you can now access native document formats and full applications through your browser. These browser-based applications allow you to do much more than simply view and disseminate information. They allow you to have full-blown business applications that can be easily distributed to your company's users. We demonstrate how to use these technologies as we build a sample intranet throughout the book.

Who Should Read This Book

Two broad audiences should read this book. *Technical managers* responsible for planning, designing, and supporting intranets should read with an eye toward understanding what technology is available and what it can do. As you will find out, more tools than ever are now available to create intranets, each tool with unique value. This book will help you understand what to apply where, how to leverage what you already have, and what you can promise to your users. *Developers* responsible for implementing intranets should read with an eye toward honing their technical skills in this new area. This book provides valuable insight into how to apply Microsoft tools to solve problems. Complete sample applications and code are provided. As you will find out, much of intranet development is simply an extension of the skills you may already have.

What Is Covered in This Book

This book covers a wide range of topics. We start with an overview of the value of intranets and the technology behind them. From here, we learn to build the basic framework of an intranet site using Microsoft FrontPage, Microsoft Internet Information Server, and Microsoft Internet Explorer. With this as a base, we quickly move on to using ActiveX controls, client-side scripting, and server-side scripting to add more "application"-like sophistication to a site. Next we examine using Microsoft Office 97 itself as a platform for intranet development. This includes using Microsoft Excel, Microsoft Word, and Microsoft PowerPoint documents as content, database publishing with Microsoft Access, collaboration with Microsoft Outlook, and application development with Visual Basic for Applications. Following this, we learn how to integrate the intranet with corporate databases such as Microsoft SQL Server, message stores such as Microsoft Exchange, and mainframe data through Microsoft SNA Server. Finally, we provide an overview of sophisticated techniques for extending the intranet and building large-scale distributed applications. And all along the way, we'll build a sample intranet site that uses all of the technology explained in the book.

Many debates rage today about what technologies will "win" the Internet/intranet wars—what browsers, what programming languages, what hardware. But what can't be debated is that millions of business users are using Microsoft products every day to conduct business. Word processors, spreadsheets, and databases have become as important to many business users as the telephone. Recognizing this, Microsoft has enhanced many of their applications so that they integrate well with intranets and take what you can do with intranets to new heights. By the end of this book, you will understand how to leverage these technologies (many of which you have probably used for years) into the new world of the intranet.

I hope you get as much out of this book as we did in writing it.

Roy Wetterstrom
President, Micro Modeling
Associates, Inc.

Acknowledgments

As project manager and internal editor of this book, I will certainly breathe a huge sigh of relief seeing it in print. When we agreed to do this book, we thought it would be a piece of cake. We are, after all, the Microsoft Office experts. By splitting up chapters among our incredibly talented employees, no one person (*except me*) would have too much on his or her shoulders. And with Microsoft promising to support us technically, what could go wrong? Well, suffice it to say that writing this book was a more difficult task than we ever imagined.

Heartfelt thanks to:

The entire Micro Modeling team of authors and contributors. You sacrificed personal time and billability to deliver quality work under tight deadlines with limited support. I promise not to hold anything you said or did to me during this project against you.

The rest of Micro Modeling for putting up with unavailable resources, lower realization, the "quiet room," and cranky people.

Bryna Hebert, System Engineer in Microsoft's Boston office, for providing valuable feedback and additional real-world perspective.

Bob Crissman, FrontPage Product Manager, for flying out to demo FrontPage for us when we were desperate for information; Randy Forgaard, FrontPage Senior Program Manager, for providing technical assistance up to the eleventh hour.

David Streams of the Microsoft SourceSafe team, who gave us the advance information we needed for the book.

Casey Doyle, Sally Stickney, Jean Ross, Robert Lyon, Xavier Callahan, Dail Magee Jr., and everyone at Microsoft Press, and Sybil Ihrig and all the people at VersaTech Associates, for getting the book out in record time.

Eric Wells, formerly of Microsoft Office Marketing, a long-time friend to Micro Modeling and an incredibly talented and prolific author in his own right, for recommending us for this project. We have new-found appreciation for his ability to publish so many books while keeping his day (and night) job.

And most especially John Vail of Microsoft Office Marketing, for helping us get this plum assignment, coordinating the support effort, sending us beta, and not hating me for all the extra work I made him do on our behalf.

Lenore Michaels
michaelsl@micromodeling.com

Using the Companion CD

The CD attached to the inside of the back cover of this book contains the Micro Modeling Associates, Inc., sample intranet. This sample demonstrates all the techniques and processes discussed throughout this book. The files for the sample intranet are contained in the SAMPLES folder on the CD. They are organized according to the chapters in the book in which they are discussed. The CHAPTER2-DEVELOPING WEB folder contains the samples discussed in Chapters 2 through 5 and Chapter 7, and it is the folder that contains the starting point for the entire sample Web site (DEFAULT.HTM). CHAPTER6-MICROSOFT IE contains the samples discussed in Chapter 6; CHAPTER9-WORD contains the samples discussed in Chapter 9; and so on.

You can browse these files on the CD, or you can install them on your hard drive. Keep in mind the fact that these files were created to run on a Web server. Running them from the CD will not work correctly in all cases.

Installing the files requires approximately 14 MB of disk space. To install the sample files on your hard drive, place the CD in your CD drive and follow these steps:

1. Open the CD drive in your Microsoft Windows Explorer.

2. Double-click SETUP.EXE in the root of the CD.

Or you could do this:

1. Select Run from the Start menu.

2. Type *d:\setup* in the Run dialog box (where *d* is the drive letter of your CD drive).

Note that if you try to browse the files on the CD and you're unable to read anything in the SAMPLES folder, your CD driver software does not support long filenames. If this is the case, you must run the setup program to install the sample files on your hard disk in order to browse them.

To uninstall the sample files, take the following steps:

1. Open the Control Panel and select Add/Remove Programs.

2. On the Install/Uninstall tab, select Official Microsoft Intranet Solutions.

3. Click Add/Remove.

4. Click Yes when prompted.

If you have trouble running any of the sample files, please review the text in the appropriate chapter or chapters in the book. You can also refer to the README.TXT file in the root of the CD.

Also contained on the CD are the installation programs for Microsoft Internet Explorer, ActiveX Control Pad, and the Microsoft Excel Web Connectivity Kit. These are on the CD in the folders IE30, ACTVXCP, and WEBCK, respectively. Run the EXE file in the appropriate folder to install the applications you need.

CHAPTER 1

What Is an Intranet?

Steve Harshbarger

Ask someone to describe an intranet or the Internet, and the answer could whisk you into a strange new world of technology and terminology. You might hear odd-sounding abbreviations such as *HTML, TCP/IP,* and *HTTP.* You could hear hip-sounding terms like *web surfing, cyberspace,* and *virtual reality.* You might hear about new technologies like *browsers, controls,* and *scripting.* With all the new lingo, it can be hard to discern what the technology can actually do for a business.

Key to understanding an intranet's role in business is understanding the success of its close relative, the Internet. The Internet is a mass-communication medium whose importance is on a par with that of the printing press, the telephone, and television. In the past two years, we've seen the Internet grow into a major public platform for conversation, communication, commerce, entertainment, advertising, and news. People are drawn to it for several reasons.

CHAPTER 1

First, the Internet is incredibly simple to browse. The only skills needed for exploring the World Wide Web are the ability to use a mouse (so you can click on what are known as *hypertext jumps,* or links to other electronic documents) and the ability to remember Web site addresses (which are becoming as common and accepted as phone numbers).

Second, the Internet is increasingly engaging. People enjoy experiencing textual information combined with graphics, sound, and other multimedia elements.

Third, the Internet is empowering. People can share information and views with others via newsgroups, and customers can provide direct feedback to companies via e-mail.

Finally, the Internet is completely integrated. From one public source, you can browse through literally a whole world of information with a click of the mouse.

If the Internet is mass communication for the public, an intranet is a mass-communication medium for business. An intranet can offer a single point of entry into a corporate world of information and applications, and the same facets of the Internet that are so compelling to the public can drive an organization to communicate and collaborate at a new level. The simple, consistent interface literally draws people in.

This book is about using Microsoft technology to create intranet solutions which do just that. As you'll see, intranets are not exclusively a new technology. In fact, they are more like a great integration of the best existing technology. By the time you reach the end of the book, you will understand how to combine new and established technologies into solutions that can truly transform your organization.

The Needs of Business

Information is the key to making decisions that drive customer satisfaction, profitability, and stock values, so every business can benefit from more efficient use of information. This concept is not new, and businesses have been applying information technology to their challenges for decades. The effective use of information boils down to four concepts:

- Finding information
- Getting current information
- Manipulating information
- Sharing information

4

Finding Information

Finding information might seem like a simple step, but it can be anything but in a large organization. Information can exist in legacy mainframe applications, client/server applications, and departmental databases, spreadsheets, and documents. It can exist in printed documents sitting in binders on a shelf in an obscure corner of the office. It can exist in people's heads. The point is that information can exist anywhere, and knowing how to locate what you are looking for can be a daunting task.

The typical technological solution to finding information is to build specific applications that provide certain types of information to interested subsets of the organization. Many such applications are very effective in this regard. But what is always missing is a high-level road map from which to move between sources. The problem is compounded by the existence of all the information *outside* these "real" applications.

Getting Current Information

If all goes well and you find the information you need, how do you know that it's current? If you are looking at sales information in an online client/server application, chances are the information is up to date. But if you are reading a printed document on employee benefits, how do you know the information is not six months out of date? The fact is, most of the information in unstructured documents (especially printed ones) is chronically out of date, given the typically high cost and overhead expenses of printing and distributing such information. Most of the time, only highly structured information—the kind best suited to a database—can readily be accessed in its most current form.

Manipulating Information

Let's say you've been fortunate enough to find the most current information you need for making a decision. What are the chances that it is in the exact form you need to make your decisions, or in the exact form you need to present it to others? Too often, the focus of application developers is more on the entry and storage of information than on its delivery and use, which means that too much information is delivered in the form of static reports, which people can only *read*. But people need to receive information in the format best suited to its further manipulation. For example, financial information is best delivered in spreadsheets because further analysis can be done with spreadsheet formulas, charting, and database features.

5

Sharing Information

Suppose that, with significant effort, you have found pertinent information that is current and have managed to manipulate it into a useful form. How can you share it with others in your organization? Certainly you can circulate it via e-mail or printed output, but what if you want to publish it for a wider audience? What if you need to collaborate with colleagues who have complementary information? An intranet can help you address this need and each of the others we have just discussed.

How an Intranet Can Help

Let's examine each of the four business needs—finding information, getting current information, manipulating information, and sharing information—in terms of how an intranet can help.

Finding Information

A corporate intranet offers a single point of entry into information stored in diverse ways. People can locate information quickly and intuitively through a combination of hierarchical organization, search capabilities, and unstructured links between sources. Because the intranet serves as the "road map" application, it can integrate everything from unstructured documents to large traditional applications. It can unify information that is stored in physically separate places. Suddenly the task of finding information becomes less daunting, and the outcome seems more likely to be successful.

Getting Current Information

An intranet can eliminate the barriers to distributing unstructured, document-centric information. When documents are on line, the need to print is reduced (and, fortunately, so is the cost of printing). Moreover, because documents can be stored centrally, updates can be applied at a single location instead of at locations all over the organization. People can view the most current documents right from their desktops, at virtually no distribution cost to the information publishers.

Manipulating Information

As this book will show you, an intranet solution built with Microsoft tools can deliver information in a variety of formats. Financial data can be delivered in spreadsheets. Narrative information can be delivered in word-processed documents. Graphical information can be delivered in presentation-graphics documents. People can receive information directly via their familiar desktop tools. Despite the varied formats, the information can be linked and managed within a single intranet application.

Sharing Information

An intranet can foster the sharing of information in many ways. For example, an intranet can include public discussion groups set up to share ideas on particular projects, customers, or products. Publishers of information can be contacted easily via integrated e-mail. Perhaps most important, potentially anyone in the organization can publish information on the corporate intranet.

Components of an Intranet

From the technological standpoint, an intranet consists of several components: a network infrastructure, servers, documents, browsers, and applications.

Network Infrastructure

A network is the backbone of any intranet. The network provides the necessary connectivity that allows access to information from anywhere within the organization. Like the Internet, an intranet uses a network protocol, called *TCP/IP* (Transmission Control Protocol/Internet Protocol), to effect communication. TCP/IP provides for the unique naming of machines on the network (via what is called an *IP address*). It also provides a mechanism by which machines can locate and communicate with each other. An intranet uses a second protocol, called *HTTP* (Hypertext Transfer Protocol), on top of TCP/IP. HTTP is used to transmit the text, images, and *hyperlinks* (that is, links to other electronic documents) associated with Web pages. You can think of TCP/IP as the generic way in which machines communicate over the network, and of HTTP as a special superimposed layer that allows machines to transfer Web information.

Most companies will find that an intranet can be built on the existing network infrastructure. If the user community is already connected, the network itself is probably ready to support an intranet.

Servers

With the network in place, the next piece of the intranet is a place to store information. Typically, information is stored on a computer running what is usually referred to as a *Web server*. The server stores documents, and it responds to users' requests to locate and view the documents. On the Internet, each Web site is hosted by a separate server, and the servers are situated all over the world. On an intranet, corporate information can be stored on one server or on many servers throughout the organization. Web servers can also provide access to information stored on other types of servers. For example, a Web server can be integrated with a database server, a messaging (e-mail) server, or a mainframe data source.

Documents

The actual content of an intranet—that is, the information that you view—is stored in documents. The default format for these documents is called *HTML* (Hypertext Markup Language), a text-file format consisting of content text and *tags,* which control formatting and hyperlinks to other documents. If you ever visited a Web site and used your browser's View Source feature, you were looking at the HTML that was used to render the document you saw on the screen. HTML has been successful for several reasons:

- HTML documents are small and therefore easy to transmit over a network.

- HTML's text-based format is not tied to any specific platform, so servers and clients alike can be running on any number of operating systems.

- The HTML format is more or less a public standard that has spawned tools from a variety of companies.

Although HTML documents are a key component of any intranet solution, other document types can play an important role as well (at least in a Microsoft solution). You can read more on this topic in the section titled "Microsoft's Intranet Tools" (page 10).

Browsers

People use an application called a *browser* to explore the intranet and view documents stored on servers. The browser performs several functions:

- It locates Web servers and communicates with them.

- It reads the HTML format and displays the stored documents, including their formatting and graphics.

- It reads the hyperlinks that are embedded in the documents and "jumps" to related documents.

- It provides such standard tools to the user as Back and Next buttons, Favorites folders, and History folders.

Beyond offering these basic features, a browser also renders such multimedia elements as sound, video, and 3D images. As you'll see, a browser can also host controls (see the following section), which greatly extend the browser's functionality.

Applications

Applications are written by developers to solve specific business problems. There are many tools available to the intranet developer for writing applications. These tools include controls, scripts, and server components.

Controls are parts of applications that can run inside a browser. Controls, by extending the functionality of the browser, enable the construction of solutions that are closer in nature to traditional applications than to mere document-viewing functionality. Controls can be written in tools like C++, Java, and even Microsoft Visual Basic. Once written, they are embedded directly into HTML documents and other types of documents.

Closely related to controls are *scripting languages,* which are used to bring the controls to life or to generate content dynamically, on the fly. These simple programming languages can manipulate controls, respond to events, and interact with server-side databases. Microsoft Visual Basic Scripting Edition (VBScript) is an example of a scripting language, as is JavaScript. Scripts are also embedded directly into HTML documents and, as we'll see later in the book, can run either on the server or in the browser as the client.

How an Intranet Differs from a Regular Network

It may seem to you that an intranet is not significantly different from a typical network application. After all, it consists of servers, which contain data; client applications, which view and manipulate the data; and a network infrastructure, which keeps everything connected. From the technical point of view, there's not a whole lot that's new except for the browser and the new HTML document format.

The key difference between an intranet and a traditional network is not really technical. It's in the presentation. The combination of the common entry point (that is, the browser) with the graphical nature of the documents is what distinguishes the intranet. Compare the traditional network with this new way of locating and using information. The new way is a lot more compelling than mapping a drive to a particular server that has an odd name, traversing a complicated directory structure, and browsing through lists of cryptic filenames. You can find the same information that way, but let's face it—people prefer clicking on pictures to hunting through directories, long filenames or not.

9

To be fair, however, there are some important technical differences. For example, the platform-independent nature of HTTP and HTML makes it much easier to support diverse clients on an intranet than a typical network application does. But here's the main point: add a little Internet technology to an existing base of technology, and, from the user's point of view, you've just made possible a great leap forward in presentation.

One last important difference is related to application installation and maintenance. Intranet applications can be designed to run largely from the server and to install any necessary client components automatically. This can significantly reduce the burden of distributing, configuring, and upgrading applications throughout an organization.

Microsoft's Intranet Tools

Microsoft's intranet tools are specifically designed to leverage current investments in several crucial areas. The tools build on existing networks, thus obviating the need to build an expensive new infrastructure. They incorporate legacy (non-HTML) documents, a feature that opens the door to using the most appropriate document format for the job. They can be integrated with Microsoft Office applications to make use of accrued knowledge, training, and experience. Finally, they extend existing development tools, to take advantage of developers' current skills.

The following tools for building intranet solutions are available from Microsoft:

- FrontPage 97
- Internet Explorer
- Office 97
- Microsoft Internet Information Server (IIS) and other BackOffice products
- Custom ActiveX technologies

FrontPage 97

Microsoft FrontPage 97 will typically be the focal point of an intranet development effort. This tool not only authors individual documents but also creates and manages the complex webs of documents that usually comprise an intranet solution. FrontPage and the Bonus Pack included with it provide the following distinct services:

- 🌐 Web management
- 🌐 Document authoring
- 🌐 Image authoring
- 🌐 Site testing

Web management

To an intranet developer, Web management means creating and managing scores of links between individual documents. In fact, it is useful to think of a Web as a single "metadocument." FrontPage provides a graphical tool, FrontPage Explorer (Figure 1-1), which makes it easy to view everything from the entire Web to the relationships among a few select documents. The tool not only manages traditional HTML documents but also covers the Office documents that are part of the Web. Links can be created and viewed, and broken links can be diagnosed and repaired. You can even perform spelling checks and search/replace functions across all the documents in the Web!

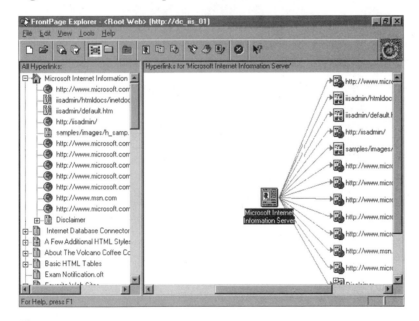

Figure 1-1
FrontPage Explorer.

To get you started quickly, the FrontPage Wizards, such as the Corporate Presence Wizard and the Frame Wizard, help you create shells—the basic framework, if you please—of common types of sites. There is even a wizard to help you import an existing Web into FrontPage for editing. Advanced intranet developers will appreciate the ability to write custom FrontPage Wizards (typically in C++) with the FrontPage Software Development Kit (SDK) available from Microsoft.

FrontPage, once you have used it to create a Web, will automatically post your entire Web to a Web server. To help you manage changes to your Web over time, FrontPage can even be integrated with Microsoft SourceSafe, a version-control tool. This feature allows you to maintain tight control over changes made and new documents added to your Web.

Document authoring

Not only does FrontPage manage the web as a whole, it also lets you create individual HTML documents complete with embedded controls and scripts. FrontPage Editor (Figure 1-2) is designed to lay out pages in a graphical manner. Included features add text, apply styles, insert images, create tables, manage frames, identify hot spots, and add links. FrontPage takes care of generating the resulting HTML for you (although you are always free to modify the generated HTML, as necessary). To make sure the document looks good on all target platforms, you can preview it from within FrontPage at different screen resolutions, and in different browsers.

Figure 1-2

FrontPage Editor.

FrontPage Editor also lets you insert components and scripts into your documents. With a simple menu command, you can place ActiveX components, Java applets, and Netscape plug-ins anywhere in a document. There are Properties dialog boxes to help you view and set the properties of inserted components. You can even write VBScript and JavaScript code in response to events raised by these components, all in a graphical interface similar to that of Visual Basic. The one thing you cannot do from within FrontPage, however, is run and debug this code. Figure 1-3 shows the insertion of a control and the viewing of its properties with the FrontPage Editor.

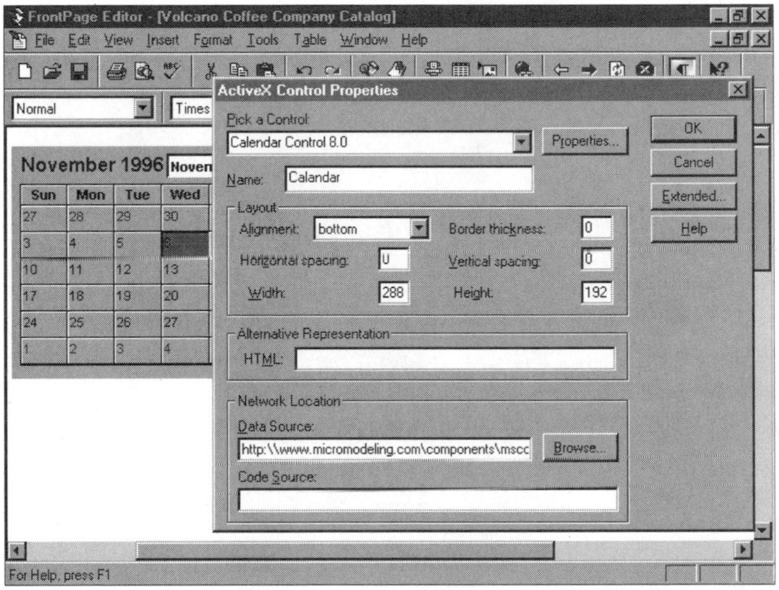

Figure 1-3
Inserting a control and viewing its properties and event procedures.

In addition to handling ActiveX and other controls, FrontPage also provides the ability to add Microsoft FrontPage WebBot components to your Web pages. WebBots implement such useful functionality as site searches. (If you need a hint about where the syllable *Bot* comes from, think of *robot*.) A WebBot is typically inserted into a particular page via a simple menu command, and then it communicates with a server application (supplied with FrontPage) that provides the specific functionality.

Image authoring

The Bonus Pack that ships with FrontPage includes a terrific image-authoring tool called Microsoft Image Composer (Figure 1-4). This tool helps developers create professional-looking artwork without having to rely on professional artists. It provides all the functions necessary for arranging and manipulating images, applying a broad spectrum of special effects, and incorporating the resulting artwork into a Web page. It also includes a great library of images, which you can use as a starting point from which to build images of your own.

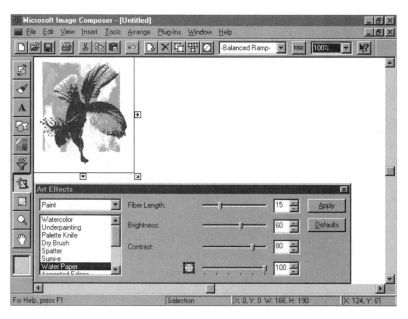

Figure 1-4
Microsoft Image Composer.

Site testing
Front Page includes Personal Web Server, which lets you develop and test your Webs off line. In other words, you can run a Web without actually posting it to a Web server. Personal Web Server is 100 percent compatible with IIS, and this compatibility makes for a very effective test platform.

Internet Explorer
The Microsoft Internet Explorer (Figure 1-5) is a browser used to view and explore the content of an intranet. Its basic features include the ability to display HTML documents, including all popular HTML extensions (frames, tables, animations, sound, and so on). Internet Explorer also provides a whole set of features beyond the basics, and these features are critical to an intranet.

Figure 1-5

Microsoft Internet Explorer.

First, Internet Explorer can display non-HTML documents, including any Microsoft Office document, right in the browser window (see Figure 1-6). This feature gives you the option of publishing information by using the most appropriate type of document, and it gives users the option of manipulating information right in that document.

Second, Internet Explorer can host controls (ActiveX controls, Java applets, and Netscape plug-ins) and run VBScript and JavaScript code to integrate them. Internet Explorer includes all the functionality necessary for dynamically downloading and installing controls and vouching for their authenticity via electronic certificates. Figure 1-7 shows Internet Explorer displaying a page with embedded ActiveX controls.

Third, Internet Explorer itself provides an OLE Automation interface, which allows other applications to control it with Visual Basic, Microsoft Visual Basic for Applications (VBA), C++, and other programming languages. Even the browser itself is available as an ActiveX control, so you can incorporate it directly into a custom application.

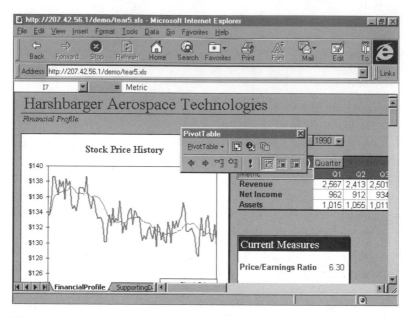

Figure 1-6

Internet Explorer displaying an Office document.

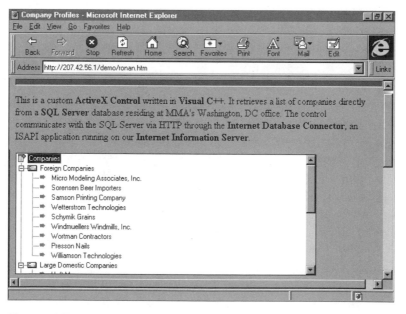

Figure 1-7

Internet Explorer displaying a page with embedded ActiveX controls.

Office 97

Each of the member applications of Microsoft Office 97—Excel, Word, Power-Point, Access, and Outlook—provides specific features for intranet solutions, and the member applications offer common features as well.

Common Office 97 features

As already mentioned, Internet Explorer can be used to view Office documents. To complement this capability, all Office documents can contain hyperlinks to other Office documents, HTML documents, or external Web sites. A Web-browser toolbar, available in each application, also provides for browsing from within Office.

All the Office applications can save Office documents in native HTML format (see Figure 1-8). And, of course, Office documents can host ActiveX controls and entire applications written in VBA.

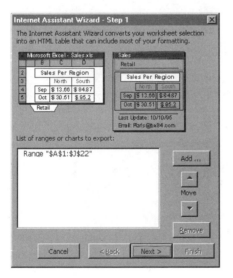

Figure 1-8
Microsoft Excel Internet Assistant Wizard.

Microsoft Excel features

Microsoft Excel provides a feature called *Web queries* (Figure 1-9) that allows Excel to retrieve data from a remote or local Web site directly into a spreadsheet. Excel ships with predefined Web queries that retrieve information from sites such as that hosted by *PC Quote, Inc.*

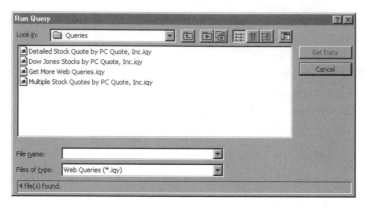

Figure 1-9

The Web Query feature in Microsoft Excel.

Word features

Microsoft Word provides a new document view, called *Document Map,* which is designed to ease movement through large documents. The Document Map view presents an outline of your document on the left side (according to its headings) and the document itself on the right. Figure 1-10 shows the Document Map view in Internet Explorer.

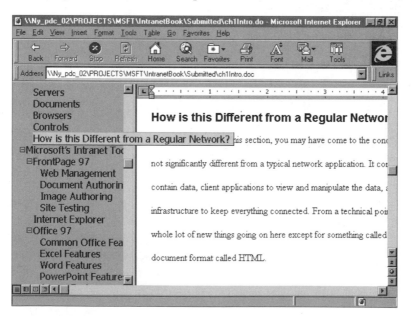

Figure 1-10

Word's Document Map view as seen in Internet Explorer.

PowerPoint features

Microsoft PowerPoint provides a tool called the *PowerPoint Animation Player,* which lets you run presentations from within a Web page. This procedure can be far more effective than simply saving a presentation as HTML: when you run a presentation from within a Web page instead of just saving it as HTML, such features as sound and animation are not lost. The PowerPoint Animation Player itself is an ActiveX control that you embed in a document. The control reads the presentation from a special compressed-file format into which PowerPoint can save any presentation.

Microsoft Access features

Microsoft Access can publish data as tables, queries, forms, and reports right in HTML documents (see Figure 1-11). It can also import and create links to data contained in HTML tables. You can store hyperlinks as data within a table, embed hyperlinks in forms, and even specify a Microsoft Access database or object as the target of a hyperlink from another document.

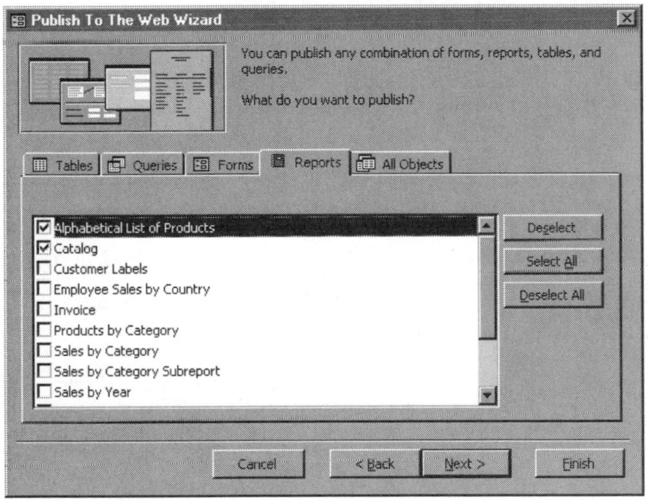

Figure 1-11

Publish To The Web Wizard in Microsoft Access.

Outlook features

As the new mail client, Microsoft Outlook (Figure 1-12) provides e-mail services to intranet applications. Outlook provides an object model against which you can write VBA or other code and integrate its functionality into a custom solution. In conjunction with Microsoft Exchange, Outlook can serve as a front end for discussion, collaboration, and support applications using Exchange's public folders.

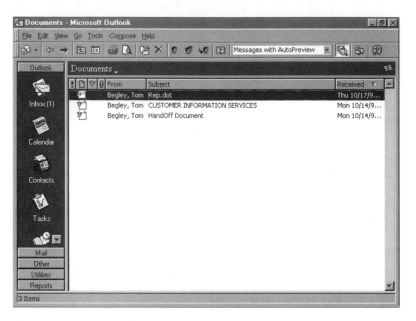

Figure 1-12
Microsoft Outlook.

BackOffice

On the server side, Microsoft BackOffice provides several tools to host intranet sites and connect to corporate data stores. These tools include IIS, Microsoft SQL Server and SNA Server, and Exchange Server.

Internet Information Server

Internet Information Server is Microsoft's Web server product. IIS runs on Microsoft Windows NT Server and is used to host and store intranet documents (both HTML and Office). It provides a search engine to locate HTML and Office documents. It also functions as a platform for running powerful server (ISAPI) applications that can be called remotely from a browser. IIS provides a connection point to other BackOffice products and to corporate data sources in many formats and locations.

IIS also has the ability to run server-side scripts written in VBScript or TrueScript. These scripts, embedded directly into HTML documents, can be used to create content dynamically by querying databases, calling other applications, or creating custom HTML on the fly for each individual user.

Microsoft SQL Server and SNA Server

Microsoft SQL Server is Microsoft's enterprise-level database server product. There are tools available for integrating SQL Server data into an intranet, either by "pushing" it out on a scheduled basis or by letting users "pull" it by request from the browser. Microsoft SNA Server provides connectivity to host-based (mainframe) data stores. Host data can also be incorporated into the intranet via IIS.

Exchange Server

Microsoft Exchange Server is a platform for messaging and workgroup applications. In addition to providing e-mail services, it can be used to implement Web-based public folders and discussion forums, often with Outlook as a front end.

Custom ActiveX Technology

Although tools like Visual C++, Visual J++ (Java), and Visual Basic are beyond the scope of this book, you can use them to write your own ActiveX controls and server applications. This is an ideal way to extend the capabilities of an intranet solution so that it incorporates specialized or business-specific features and functionality.

Summary

In this chapter, we discussed the need of businesses to find, manipulate, and share current information for the purpose of making better decisions. We examined how an intranet can address these needs and drive an organization to use its information assets to best advantage. We examined the components of a generic intranet, and then we considered the specific Microsoft tools for implementing intranet solutions. In the chapters to come, we'll be delving into the specifics of each tool.

CHAPTER 2

Developing Your First Web with FrontPage 97

Jeffrey M. Jones

This chapter presents an overview of Microsoft FrontPage 97. When you've finished reading it, you will be familiar with FrontPage 97's principal components and additional utilities. The chapter focuses mainly on one of those components—the FrontPage Explorer—and takes you through the process of creating a simple intranet with standard FrontPage features. You will also learn how to use the FrontPage Wizards to help you create a Web.

Before we begin, however, it might be a good idea to establish what we mean by the term *Web*. Semantic purists claim that this term should be used only to denote the World Wide Web, and that any group of related files hosted by a server should be called a *Web site*. That may be the LC (linguistically correct) way to go, but it also makes sense to adopt Microsoft's terminology if we're discussing a Microsoft product. There's also a subtle but significant difference between the browser-oriented perspective of an Internet surfer going from site to site and a FrontPage author who can—and, in this

CHAPTER 2

chapter, will—create Webs *within* Webs. Using the term *Webs* for those wondrous things that spin out with a click of the mouse just seems—well, more poetic.

What Can FrontPage 97 Do for You?

Think of FrontPage 97 as a minisuite of applications and utilities for creating and maintaining Webs. Its principal components and additional utilities provide all the basic tools you'll need for authoring and publishing Web pages.

Principal FrontPage Components

FrontPage has three principal components: the FrontPage Explorer, the FrontPage Editor, and the FrontPage Personal Web Server.

The FrontPage Explorer

The *FrontPage Explorer* is a Web-maintenance tool that comprises three main functions:

- 🌐 Building Webs
- 🌐 Creating new Webs, either with FrontPage Web templates or your own contents
- 🌐 Doing work on Webs (that is, opening, closing, refreshing, renaming, publishing, copying, pasting, and deleting existing Webs, as well as importing and exporting files into and out of existing Webs, and even doing spelling checks and find/replace operations on selected text pages within Webs)

The Explorer not only displays a Web's file structure graphically, it also displays links between Web pages (including image references and hypertext

---

To Backslash or to Forward Slash?

Depend on it: slashes can drive you crazy. The *backslash* (\) is the MS-DOS and Microsoft Windows delimiter. The *slash mark,* or *forward slash* (/)—that is, The Symbol Formerly Known as the Virgule—is the UNIX-based URL delimiter. If you're authoring in HTML, most browsers will let you get away with using either \ or /, but the FrontPage Editor will display an error if you try to save a page to a subfolder by using backslashes. This book uses slash marks (/) to refer to Web URLs, and backslashes (\) to refer to the corresponding file directories.

24

jumps) and lets you verify and recalculate broken links. The Explorer also allows you to control such Web properties and settings as passwords, permissions, and proxy server configurations. (If you don't know yet what all these terms mean, keep reading—we'll get to them.)

The FrontPage Editor

The *FrontPage Editor* is a WYSIWYG Web page authoring tool. Obviously, it lets you write Hypertext Markup Language (HTML) without having to know (or look up) tag syntax, but it can also show you a page's underlying HTML, with color coding for easier under-the-hood editing. The Editor automates all the HTML 3.2 advanced features, such as tables, forms, and frames—you can even create clickable image maps directly in a page. It also lets you see how your pages will look in any browser you've installed on your PC. The Editor includes a number of default page templates but allows you to create your own as well. More important, the Editor provides automation tools, called *WebBots* (you may recall the discussion of WebBots in Chapter 1), which can insert updatable timestamps, Search and Contents pages, even the entire contents of other Web pages. But the most powerful feature of the Editor is its support for Microsoft ActiveX controls and the scripting that you'll need to make your pages dynamic. (Just try doing all that in Notepad!)

NOTE

The client/server paradigm is often applied to the World Wide Web because every basic transaction involves a browser's request and the server's response. FrontPage extends this metaphor to cover any applications that query a server and receive HTML in response. In FrontPage, the Explorer and the Editor are both client software.

The FrontPage Personal Web Server

The *FrontPage Personal Web Server* is a separate software package that lets you or anyone else with access to your Internet Protocol (IP) address use Hypertext Transfer Protocol (HTTP) to view your Web through a browser. The ability to do this is crucial: it's true that you can use most browsers to view HTML documents and other files directly, but you won't get all the automation (such as the FrontPage WebBots) that is essential to Web forms and messaging until you browse a document that a server has sent in response to an HTTP request. Of course, the Personal Web Server server isn't as robust as the Microsoft Internet Information Server (IIS). But even though you probably won't use the Personal Web Server to host your intranet, it's a great way to mount a test site while you work. (It's always a good idea to work on a test site, anyway.) The FrontPage Personal Web Server is compact enough for laptop use, so it's ideal for Web demos.

CHAPTER 2

Additional FrontPage Utilities

In addition to its three principal components, FrontPage offers several utilities that can make your life as a Webmaster even easier.

🌐 **An editable, sortable To Do list that displays tasks, work assignments, and priorities by Web page.** Some tasks are generated automatically when you use a Web wizard, but you can also add and edit tasks manually. You can keep the FrontPage To Do list visible while you work. You can also hide or view completed tasks. In fact, the To Do list can even take you directly to the Web page or task that needs completion. (Note, however, that there are no plans to automate the To Do list in upcoming releases of FrontPage so that it will also do your work for you!)

🌐 **FrontPage Server Extensions, which let you use FrontPage Webs on non-FrontPage servers.** The extensions not only support FrontPage WebBots and other automation but also allow you to upload your Web to the specified server by using the Publish FrontPage Web command of the FrontPage Explorer.

What's in a Domain Name?

You and I prefer to communicate with words, whereas computers prefer to communicate with numbers like *192.9.200.19*. Therein lies the source of a certain amount of woe in this world. To make life easier for human beings who don't like to type long strings of numbers, the FrontPage Domain Name System (DNS) server translates domain names like *jonesj* or *microsoft.com* (which FrontPage, confusingly, calls *host names*) into IP addresses. Unless you're using a dynamic IP address system, you can use domain names and IP addresses interchangeably. By convention, the IP address *127.0.0.1*, which FrontPage calls the *local host,* is always assigned to the computer you're currently using. This means that if the FrontPage Personal Web Server happens to be running on your own machine (as it would be in a standard FrontPage installation), you can use the IP address *127.0.0.1* in your browser as well. By the way, during the installation process, FrontPage prompts you for an administrator name and password. If, like some of us, you're password-impaired, you would do well to write the password down, since there's no easy way to retrieve it later. Without this name and password, you won't be able to open your FrontPage Webs. Write it down!

Again, you probably won't want to use the FrontPage Personal Web Server server for your intranet, so you probably *will* want the FrontPage Server Extensions. At this writing, they are absolutely free and downloadable from

http://www.microsoft.com/frontpage/softlib/fs_fp_extensions.htm.

Isn't a Web just a bunch of HTML files? Yes, in a sense—the same sense in which you are mainly a bunch of water, with a few trace elements thrown in for good measure. If you're of a philosophic bent, you might think of your Web as the manifestation of the data in your files (just as you probably think of yourself as a particularly interesting manifestation of water and various trace elements). From your browser's standpoint, though, the crucial, practical difference between a Web and a bunch of HTML files has to do with whether a server is using HTTP to transmit those files. This distinction is even more important from the standpoint of FrontPage. The FrontPage Explorer will let you move or copy an HTML file to a designated directory in your Web—but even though the file will then exist in that directory, you won't actually be able to *see* it in the FrontPage Explorer until you refresh your Web and transmit the file via HTTP. That's why you should always use the FrontPage Explorer to access the FrontPage Editor when you're working on your Web. Avoid the temptation to move, copy, or edit files directly with other applications. Sure, you might be able to make a few quick changes with WordPad or Windows Explorer, but if you rely on them for ongoing Web authoring or maintenance, you'll come to grief sooner or later. Remember: a Web is more than just a bunch of HTML files.

- 🌐 **A Server Administrator (for MS-DOS and Windows) exclusively devoted to the care and feeding of your Personal Web Server.** You'll use the FrontPage Server Administrator to load and upgrade FrontPage Server Extensions on your Web server. The Server Administrator also displays essential information about your server configuration (the port number, FrontPage configuration filename and path, and so forth) and sets Web security restrictions.

- 🌐 **The FrontPage TCP/IP Test, which ensures that your TCP/IP network connection is running properly**. The TCP/IP Test is normally run from the Server Administrator, but you can also run it by choosing About Microsoft FrontPage Explorer from the FrontPage Explorer's Help menu and clicking the Network Test button. The TCP/IP Test determines whether a 32-bit WINSOCK.DLL

2 CHAPTER

is running (if not, FrontPage won't work, since it configures your TCP/IP connection to your client applications), and then it returns your host name, IP address, and local host. Better yet, you can click the Explain Results button and see a long and informative message that tells you, among many other things, how to fix or disable your Domain Name Server (DNS) configuration when you're using a laptop and your browser hangs for 90 seconds. (For a description of what the DNS does, see page 26, "What's in a Domain Name?")

And Now...Let's Make a Web

Now let's take a quick tour of the package. We'll be moving fast, since this is a package tour—but, as you'll see, the Web creation process is easy and intuitive. First we'll create a new demo Web with one of the FrontPage Explorer's Web Wizards. Then we'll take a closer look at the Explorer interface and a few more tools before we do an in-depth examination of the wizards themselves. Finally, we'll take a very quick glance at the FrontPage directory/file structure.

Ladies and Gentlemen, Start Your Servers

Right now, before you do anything else in FrontPage, launch your Personal Web Server. You'll need it for saving and refreshing your Web. Even though the Explorer and the Editor launch the Server if it isn't running, it's important to understand that you can't *have* a Web unless you have a server hosting it.

You launch the Personal Web Server in the standard way, by choosing it from your Start menu or double-clicking its icon. Once the Server is running, you'll see its icon on your Microsoft Windows 95 taskbar, with a message indicating whether the Server is idle or busy. Other than this icon and the message, there's not much of a user interface for the Server.

TIP Check the status of your Personal Web Server whenever FrontPage appears to hang. If the Server is busy, it may simply be responding to a request.

Of course, you can also use the FrontPage Explorer and Editor directly with other servers, such as the IIS network server that will ultimately host your intranet. As long as a network server is running and its TCP/IP address is available to you, it will appear in the FrontPage user interface, and you will be able to work with the FrontPage Webs that it's hosting.

Webward, Ho!

After your Personal Web Server is up and running, the next step in a FrontPage session should usually be launching the FrontPage Explorer. Even if all you're planning to do is edit Web pages, you still need to create or open the Web that they're part of. To do that, you need the FrontPage Explorer to be running against your Personal Web Server.

The very first time you launch the Explorer, you'll see the Getting Started With Microsoft FrontPage dialog box. (You can suppress this dialog box thereafter by checking the designated box; if you've already suppressed it, just choose New from the File menu, and then choose FrontPage Web.) In the Create A New FrontPage Web section, select the From A Wizard Or Template option and choose OK. The New FrontPage Web dialog box will then display a list of available Web Templates and Wizards, as shown in Figure 2-1. For now, just to see how the FrontPage interface works, select Corporate Presence Wizard and choose OK.

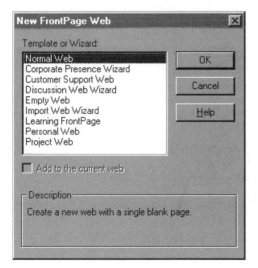

Figure 2-1
New FrontPage Web dialog box.

When you start the Corporate Presence Wizard, you'll be prompted for the host server and Web name. All servers currently available to you will be listed in the drop-down list and FrontPage, using the Web name you provide, will create the Corporate Presence Web in a subdirectory of your <Root Web> directory. Although HTML supports uniform resource locators (URLs) containing spaces, FrontPage does not, so your Web name must be a continuous string of characters, with no spaces. You will then be prompted to

29

2
CHAPTER

enter the administrator user name and password that you established during the installation of FrontPage 97. (You did write them down, didn't you?) FrontPage confers Web-creation rights only on the administrators, so if you forget the password, you'll have to reinstall FrontPage (when you do, however, you can perform a custom installation and select only the client software).

NOTE This chapter uses <Root Web> to designate the Web (or, if you prefer, the corresponding directories) that FrontPage 97 creates as the primary Web for your Personal Web Server. You can have only one <Root Web> per server. All other Webs hosted by your server will be sub-Webs (and also subdirectories) of <Root Web>. When you install FrontPage 97, you also establish the name and password of the <Root Web> administrator, from whom all permissions flow.

After you launch the Corporate Presence Wizard, you'll select Web page options in a succession of screens. For the purposes of this demonstration, you can accept the default options. When you're prompted to choose a presentation style, you can choose to be Conservative, Flashy, or Cool; just don't be Plain, or your Web won't have any graphics. As you move through the screens, you'll see that the Wizard lets you specify four different kinds of Web attributes:

- The *content* of various predefined types of Web pages, some containing specialized information, and others performing specialized functions (such as doing searches and displaying feedback forms)

- The *layout* of all pages, an attribute that includes color schemes, common graphical elements (such as toolbars and rules), and standardized data (such as revision dates and the e-mail links that appear at the top or bottom of every page)

- *Parameters* or *configuration variables,* which are standard bits of information (such as the Webmaster's e-mail address) that are maintained in a common source and are automatically updated throughout the Web in the pages where they appear

- The *behavior of the To Do list* while you are working on your Web

When you're done, you should have the Web of ACME Industries, Inc., at 123 Web Way, Cambridge, Massachusetts, a company that has been shipping dangerous and defective merchandise to coyotes since the late 1950s.

In a moment, we'll use the ACME Industries Web to get a quick overview of the FrontPage Explorer itself as we look at the different views of your Web that are displayed in the Explorer interface. We'll examine links between pages, and we'll look at the FrontPage Explorer's file/folder structure, as well as at some of its other features. We'll also examine the FrontPage Explorer toolkit, which includes commands for Web building and maintenance. Now let's take a look at the ACME Web in all its glory.

Viewing your Web

You view Webs in your browser—which, for a number of reasons, we hope is the Microsoft Internet Explorer. Launch Internet Explorer, and point it to

http://HostServer/WebName/

(where *HostServer* and *WebName* correspond to the equivalent values you entered when you started the Corporate Presence Wizard). Note that you do not need a fully qualified URL. The FrontPage Personal Web Server knows that *HostServer* actually refers to a directory called, for example,

C:\FrontPage Webs\Content

and it knows that if you haven't specified a file, you must want the Home page, which is a file called INDEX.HTM in the *WebName* folder.

The Corporate Presence Wizard not only creates your Web and its initial contents, it also adds active internal links to the text and graphics. For example, to jump to the ACME Industries Table of Contents page, from which you can easily browse the whole Web, click the TOC button on your Cool, Conservative, or Flashy exploration bar. (See Figure 2-2.) It's worth your while to spend some time browsing the site, just to appreciate how much FrontPage does for you.

In addition to the automatically created Table of Contents page, there's a working Search form and a Feedback form (with a confirmation screen) for users' comments. On all pages devoted to products and services, there's an Information Request form (and a confirmation screen) that generates a separate thread for information requests. As you work, you'll also appreciate the Wizard's eye for design. The Wizard, by using relative URLs throughout, makes it easy to customize the site by linking pages to a simple, noncascading style sheet (*WebName*_private\style.htm) and a common set of images (including a placeholder for the company logo) that the FrontPage Editor's Include WebBot will update throughout your Web. If you send yourself Information Request or Feedback forms, you can read your messages in the INFOREQ.HTM and INFOREQ.TXT files, respectively, of the _private directory. It will even be worth your while to take a look at the underlying HTML source code.

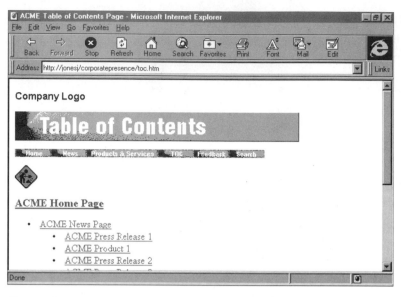

Figure 2-2

The ACME Web Table of Contents as viewed in Microsoft Internet Explorer.

What to do, what to do?

If you selected the default options, the To Do List (Figure 2-3) will be open, showing the seven tasks that the Corporate Presence Wizard initially adds. You manipulate the task list with the buttons at the bottom—for example, you click the Add button to add your own user-defined tasks; the Do Task button even launches the FrontPage Editor and can take you to the page that is linked to the selected task.

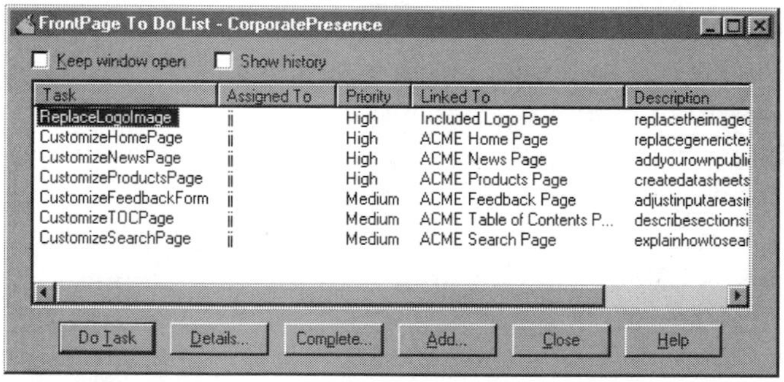

Figure 2-3

The FrontPage To Do list, showing tasks added by the Corporate Presence Wizard.

Web Views

The FrontPage Explorer interface consists of a single window with a menu bar, a toolbar, and a status bar. This window has two panes, one on the left side and one on the right, which display your Web from various points of view. Commands on the Explorer's View menu can hide or reveal the toolbar and the status bar and let you see the different Web views in the left and right panes.

Links Between Pages

Select Hyperlink View from the FrontPage Explorer View menu to see the links between Web pages (this is also the view that appears by default when you launch the FrontPage Explorer). The left pane shows an expandable hierarchy of pages, starting with the Home page (see Figure 2-4). Remember that the hierarchy is based on links, so it won't initially show you *all* the pages in your Web unless they're linked to the Home page. Of course, you can eventually reveal a Web's contents if you continue to click on pages and expand the hierarchy outline, but keep in mind that you'll be better off switching to the Folder View when you want to see the overall structure of a Web.

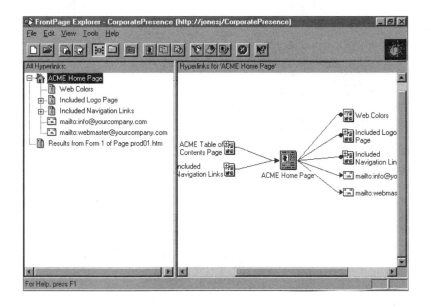

Figure 2-4
The Acme Web Home page in Hyperlink View.

CHAPTER 2

Click any page in the left pane of the Hyperlink View, and in the right pane you will see a graphical display of all the links into and out of that page. Point to the icon of any linked page in the right pane, but don't click. In a moment, you'll see a pop-up display with the name of the target and the nature of the link. WebBot links, internal links, and external links are all displayed differently, as are broken links.

Using the right pane to move through a Web is a breeze once you figure out that you need to select a linked file, right-click the mouse, and choose Move To Center. (Double-clicking a file icon, as you might have discovered, launches the FrontPage Editor and loads the corresponding page.) You can also control the number of displayed links by choosing options on the FrontPage Explorer View menu that let you show or hide hyperlinks to images, show or hide repeated hyperlinks, and show or hide hyperlinks inside pages.

The File/Folder Structure

Select Folder View from the View menu to see the file/folder structure of your Web. The left pane of the Folder View provides an expanding outline view of the folder structure. The contents of the active folder are displayed in the right pane. In other words, the Folder View isn't terribly mysterious (see Figure 2-5). For more information about your Web's file/folder structure, see Appendix A at the back of this book.

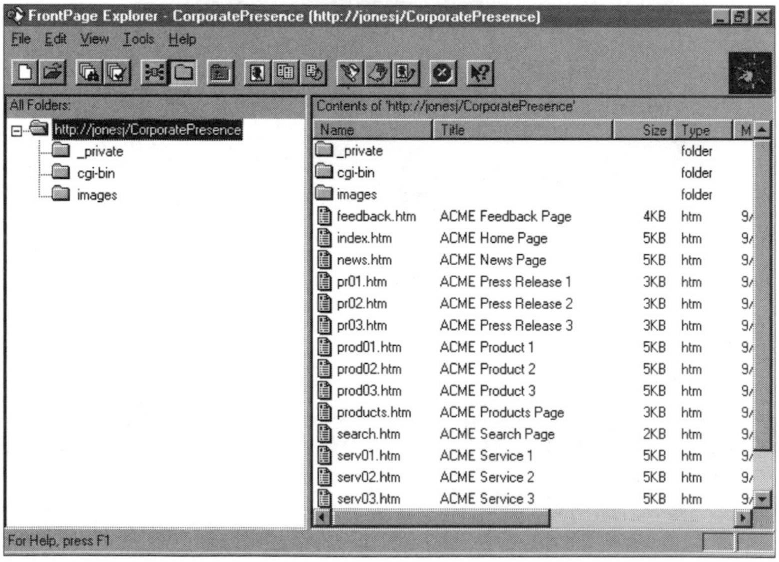

Figure 2-5

The ACME Web in Folder View.

Other Features

Since the functionality of the FrontPage Explorer in Folder View resembles that of Windows Explorer in Windows 95 and similar file utilities, only two unique features need to be mentioned:

🌐   If you select a file in the right pane of the Folder View and right-click the mouse, you can choose Show Hyperlinks to see the page in Hyperlink View. This feature is incredibly useful when you're trying to figure out how or whether a file is being used; clicking through the Hyperlink View to find the file could take forever.

🌐   By default, the Folder View does not show files in hidden directories—that is, directories whose names have an underscore as the first character (for example, _PRIVATE). If you want to see the contents of such directories, choose Web Settings from the Tools menu, click the Advanced tab, and check the Show Documents In Hidden Directories box. (For more information about this point, see Appendix A.)

The FrontPage Explorer Toolkit

Besides showing you different views of your Web, the FrontPage Explorer provides all FrontPage Web-building and maintenance commands, including shortcuts to the FrontPage Editor, the To Do List, and your image editor.

Building Your Web

Most of the FrontPage Explorer's File menu commands are pretty self-explanatory. For example, the only thing that might not be completely obvious about the Open FrontPage Web dialog box is that you won't actually be able to open a FrontPage Web until you select a server from the drop-down list box and click the List Webs button (see Figure 2-6).

The FrontPage Explorer lets you work on only one Web at a time. And since the Explorer is a client application receiving Web data from the server you've specified, you won't be able to run multiple instances of the Explorer (or of the FrontPage Editor) simultaneously. To *close* the Web that is currently open, choose Close FrontPage Web from the FrontPage Explorer's File menu. To permanently *remove* the open Web, choose Delete FrontPage Web from the File menu.

!   Remember that deletion of an open Web is irreversible. A deleted Web is not simply moved to the Recycle Bin.

CHAPTER 2

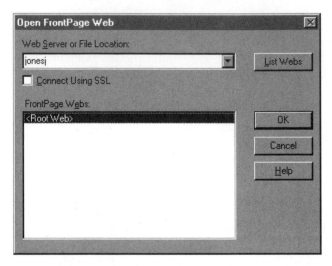

Figure 2-6

The Open FrontPage Web dialog box.

In addition to new pages created via a FrontPage Wizard or Template, your intranet will most likely incorporate existing and reworked pages that will come either from previous incarnations of your own Web or from other sources (surely you're not the *only* person in your company feverishly scribbling HTML). The FrontPage Explorer gives you three ways to move existing HTML files (and other kinds of files) around:

- 🌐 You can *move files within an open Web* by dragging and dropping their icons in the FrontPage Explorer's Folder View. You can also cut, copy, and paste pages with Edit menu commands.

- 🌐 You can *import and export selected files* between an open Web and some other directory (which may or may not be in a Web).

- 🌐 You can *publish* the open Web, which entails copying everything (HTML files, GIF files, JPEG images, Microsoft Office documents, and WebBots) to another Web or server.

> When you open an imported file in the FrontPage Editor, FrontPage imposes a standard HTML structure on it, which may or may not change the underlying HTML and file data.

Moving between folders and webs

When you drag and drop Web pages in the FrontPage Explorer's Folder View, FrontPage automatically updates the relative URLs. You can even use all the usual Windows keyboard shortcuts, such as copying, by pressing the Ctrl key while dragging.

Importing and exporting

Strictly speaking, there are only two ways to import files into your active Web, but there's nothing to prevent you from exporting files from the active Web to a directory that is part of another Web. Here are the two methods of importing followed by the export method:

🌐 To select the files or whole directories to be imported into an open Web, choose Import (Figure 2-7) from the FrontPage Explorer's File menu. (You can also use Windows Ctrl and Shift key combinations to select multiple files.) Once you add a file to the Import list, you can also click the Edit URL button to specify the name and location you want the file to have in your Web. The interface is actually somewhat confusing: the main dialog box and the Edit URL button refer to *URLs* (which are delimited with forward slashes), but the Edit URL dialog box prompts you for a *file path* (which would be delimited by the backslash). Either forward slashes or backslashes will work. If you use backslashes, however, your imported files will go immediately to their destinations, whereas if you enter a URL, you'll need to refresh your Web if you want to see your imported files in their true locations.

🌐 To quickly import the contents of selected directories, select New from the FrontPage Explorer's File menu, choose FrontPage Web, and select Import Web Wizard. This is probably the best way of importing a large number of files from a common location. But if that location also contains a significant number of files that you *don't* want to import, deselecting them in the Import Web Wizard is somewhat tedious. (There is a more expanded discussions of Wizards later in this chapter, in the section titled "Wizards and Templates," page 45.)

🌐 Unless you have a background in economics or foreign trade, you might not see the Export command as an import tool, but it's really all the same process. In the FrontPage Explorer, select the file you want. Then choose Export from the Explorer's File menu, and specify the destination filename and directory. The greatest limitation of the Export command, of course, is that you can export only one file at a time.

CHAPTER 2

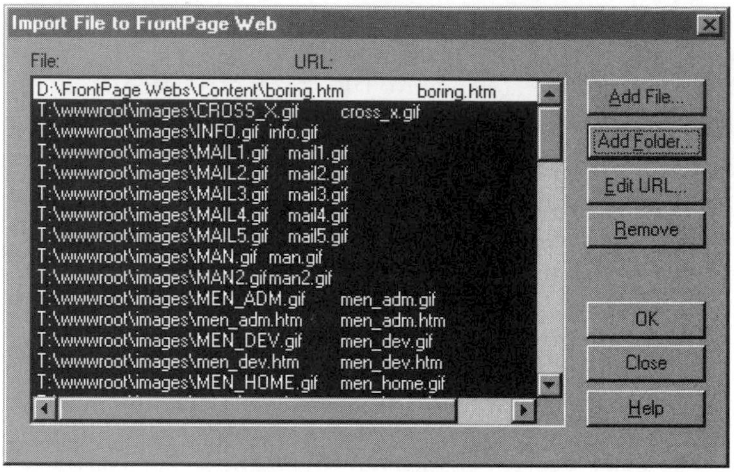

Figure 2-7

Using the Import command in the FrontPage Explorer's File menu to bring data from external sources into an open Web.

TIP

You can use long filenames in FrontPage, but you can't use spaces. If you decide to use long and informative filenames, so you won't get totally lost six months from now, throw in a mix of UpperAndLowerCaseLetters to aid legibility.

Publishing

The Publish command is designed to let you mount your Web to a host server, but there's no reason why you can't use it to *add* an open Web to another Web on the same (or a different) server—or to any available directory, for that matter. In fact, this command used to be called Copy Web, and there are several advantages to using it:

🌐 All the essential non-HTML data will sort itself out automatically (and a Web, as you know, is far more than just HTML files).

🌐 If you're copying the <Root Web> directory, you can include all the Webs within it (known as *child Webs*).

🌐 You'll be prompted when files with identical names exist in the source and target directories.

There is, however, a small price to be paid for such power: it's an all-or-nothing proposition; you can't pick and choose files.

Maintaining Your Web

The FrontPage Explorer Toolkit includes a number of Web maintenance tools that you will find helpful after you've built your Web. You can use these tools to refresh your Web, validate and refresh links, make global text edits, choose Web settings, configure Web permissions, and perform tasks related to password administration and other options.

Refreshing your Web

Sometimes—if several authors are working simultaneously, or if you designate an Import destination with a URL—the FrontPage Explorer may not show you an accurate, current view of your Web. To be sure you're always getting up-to-date information, get in the habit of regularly choosing Refresh from the FrontPage Explorer's View menu. Like the Internet Explorer's Refresh command, refreshing your Web constitutes an explicit HTTP request for FrontPage server data from a client application (in this case, the FrontPage Explorer).

Validating and refreshing links

The FrontPage Explorer has two powerful tools for checking links:

1. From the Tools menu, you can choose Verify Hyperlinks to see a list of all internal and external hyperlinks in the Verify Hyperlinks dialog box (Figure 2-8). If you don't see any links in the dialog box, don't worry; it only means you have no external hyperlinks or broken internal links. At first, all links display the yellow status icon, meaning they're unverified. Once you click the Verify (or Resume) button, FrontPage changes the status icon for each tested link to green or red, indicating whether the link is valid (green) or broken (red). You can repair broken links on the spot by clicking the Edit Link button, and you can display the linked page in the FrontPage Editor by clicking the Edit Page button. You can even *postpone* the edit: you do this by clicking the Add Task button to add the updating of the selected link to the To Do list (with a link to the relevant page).

2. You can also choose Recalculate Hyperlinks to update all the links in your Web. Updating not only verifies all internal hyperlinks but also runs the TOC and Search WebBots to regenerate new tables of contents and text indexes (and may even repair some broken links, as when you've renamed a file outside of FrontPage Explorer). When you've added, modified, or deleted Web pages (especially if you haven't used FrontPage), you should always recalculate hyperlinks; otherwise, your Table of Contents and Search forms will show incorrect information.

CHAPTER

2

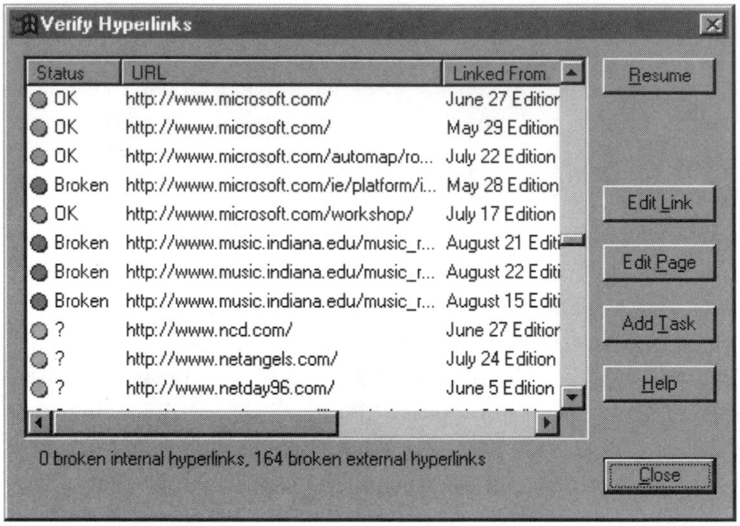

Figure 2-8

The Verify Hyperlinks dialog box.

NOTE

FrontPage verification tests only whether links exist and, if so, whether they will work in your browser. You will have to test the *placement* of any internal hyperlinks in Web pages yourself.

Editing text globally

The FrontPage Explorer lets you perform three global text operations on some or all of the pages in an open Web:

1. You can choose Spelling from the Tools menu to generate a count of misspelled words (see Figure 2-9).

2. You can choose Find from the Tools menu to generate a count of matching instances of the text being searched for.

3. You can choose Replace from the Tools menu to generate a count of matching instances of the text being searched for (see Figure 2-10).

All the commands work in essentially the same way. The Explorer runs a process against the entire Web, or against a selected range of pages. Then it displays a dialog box that shows a status icon next to each page in the range, to indicate the results of the process. In all cases, you must then click the Edit Page button and, in the FrontPage Editor, complete the process on each individual page. If you are working on a range of pages, you'll be prompted

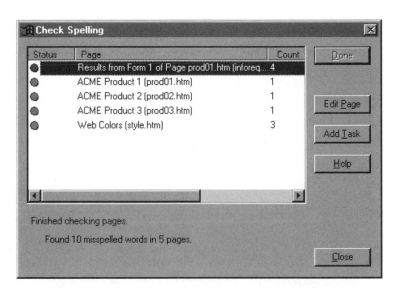

Figure 2-9
The Check Spelling dialog box.

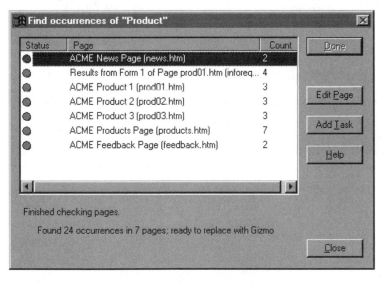

Figure 2-10
The Find dialog box.

for each new page in a dialog box like the one shown in Figure 2-11. Thoughtfully, FrontPage also makes it easy for you to procrastinate: you can add tasks to the To Do list simply by clicking the Add Task button.

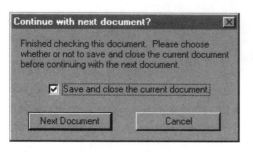

Figure 2-11

Continue With Next Document dialog box.

Editing web settings

From the FrontPage Explorer Tools menu, you can choose Web Settings to edit four very different kinds of settings:

1. To add, modify, or remove the parameters or configuration variables inserted by the Substitution WebBot, click the Parameters tab. A picture is worth a thousand words: to see how the Substitution Bot decides what to substitute where, take a look at Figure 2-12, which shows the default parameters that FrontPage creates for ACME Industries. Obviously, you can create your own parameters for company slogans, product prices, the names of department heads, or any other modifiable phrases you'd like to be able to use throughout a Web.

Figure 2 -12

FrontPage Web Settings for the ACME Web.

2. To change your Web's name and title, or to view server configuration data, you can click the Configuration tab. You can change a Web name only if you have Administrator privileges and if your server supports changing names. You should avoid adding spaces to a Web name, since the name forms part of the Web's URL. Web *titles,* however, are used only in the FrontPage Explorer title bar, so they can contain spaces.

3. To configure the type of image map you want FrontPage to generate for your Web, click the Advanced tab. Here you can also configure the default validation script for your browser and determine whether the contents of "hidden" directories will be displayed in the FrontPage Explorer. ("Hidden" directories have an underscore as the first character of their names; see Appendix A for more information about creating "hidden" pages and directories.)

4. Click the Language tab to establish the default Web language (that is, the language the server will use to return error messages to the browser), and the default HTML encoding language, if you want to save HTML pages in a character set other than the default character set for your system. If you want to write HTML in *several* different languages, use one language as the default HTML encoding language, and establish others on a page-by-page basis with the Page Properties command on the FrontPage Editor's File menu.

Configuring Web permissions

From the Tools menu, choose Permissions to establish Web passwords, maintain a list of authorized users and the access rights assigned to them, and restrict access to specific computers (as designated by their IP addresses). Select Change Password from the Tools menu to reset your own password. (Sorry, you can't use this command to *retrieve* your password—but the good news is that if you forget your password, you won't have access to this command in the first place!)

Working with other settings

From the Tools menu, choose Options to view or change three unrelated groups of settings:

1. Click the General tab to hide or suppress the Getting Started dialog box, as well as the warnings that are displayed when page dependencies or text indexes are out of date.

2. Click the Proxies tab to establish a proxy server. A proxy server typically establishes a firewall to prevent outside access to an Internet site, but you might also want to establish proxies to create

2 CHAPTER

internal firewalls and limit access to certain departments or IP addresses.

3. Click the Configure Editors tab to enter or edit the applications that FrontPage uses to edit files that have designated file extensions. (For example, you might want to use the CSS extension for style sheets and always edit them in WordPad, to be sure that FrontPage doesn't add tags and reformat them as standard HTML documents.) Once you associate an application with an extension, FrontPage will always use that application to open files with that extension when you double-click them in the FrontPage Explorer.

Editing Web properties

If you choose Properties from the Explorer's Edit menu, you can click the Summary tab and then enter or edit comments (such as author's notes) for the selected page. These comments won't become part of the page's contents; they're actually added to the data stored in the HTML file, in the _VTI_CNF directory, that is named for the page. But you might prefer to add your comments here, instead of letting them become HTML comments, because FrontPage often reformats multiline comments as run-on lines, making them hard to read.

TIP
You can't really edit Web pages from the FrontPage Explorer. But, as you've probably discovered, double-clicking a Web page in any of the views launches the FrontPage *Editor* and displays the page. Remember, always use the FrontPage Editor to work on your Web. Moving, copying, or editing files directly with other applications is asking for trouble. Why? That's right: because a Web is more than just a bunch of HTML files.

FrontPage Wizards and Templates

The FrontPage Explorer has *Web* Wizards and Templates; the FrontPage Editor has *Page* Wizards and Templates. The distinctions between Web Wizards, Web Templates, Page Wizards, and Page Templates, might not be obvious:

- 🌐 **Templates** are the master patterns that FrontPage uses to create Webs and pages in your <Root Web> folder.

- 🌐 **Wizards** are the series of screens that provide options during the creation process (in other words, no Wizard, no options).

Web Wizards and Templates

Any Web Wizard, of course, starts by creating a Web, but the primary purpose of most Web Wizards is really to add a specified series of pages. You can also use the Web Wizards to add different pages to the same Web.

To use one of the FrontPage Explorer's Web Wizards or Templates, choose New from the FrontPage Explorer's File menu, and select one of the wizards or templates listed in Table 2-1. The table contains short descriptions of what several of the wizards and templates do; the rest of the wizards and templates are described at greater length in the remainder of this section. The Learning FrontPage Wizard is a tutorial and is discussed in the FrontPage documentation. The Import Wizard is a file-import utility, which was already discussed in the section of this chapter titled "Importing and Exporting" (page 37). For the most part, you'll use the Empty Template or the Normal Template to build your intranet, and then you'll add custom pages, but you can also create a bulletin board with the Discussion Web Wizard, and you can customize the Project Template to create a developer knowledge base.

Table 2-1   FrontPage Explorer Web Wizards and Templates.

Wizard	Template
Learning FrontPage (tutorial; see FrontPage 97 documentation)	Normal (creates a Web containing one blank Home page, called INDEX.HTM)
Import (file-import utility; see page 37)	Empty (creates a Web containing no HTML pages)
Corporate Presence	Customer Support
Discussion	Project
	Personal (creates a single page, called INDEX.HTM, containing hypertext links to preformatted topics about an individual's occupation, preferences, and so on; page can also contain a response form for user input)

45

Wizards always use identical names for pages from identical Webs, even though identically named pages might have different features in different Webs. If you use a Wizard to add pages to a current Web, you'll have to choose which version of the Home page (INDEX.HTM) you want, and you won't be able to add more than one instance of a Web (or page type). You can also *rerun* a wizard to change page options. If you select different options, however, be aware that existing pages will not be deleted, and the exploration bar will include only the buttons for the pages selected in the latest run of the wizard.

Corporate Presence Wizard

The Corporate Presence Wizard creates a sample business Web that contains the following elements:

- A required Home page (INDEX.HTM), with optional topics (Introduction, Mission Statement, Company Profile, Contact Information).

- A Search page (SEARCH.HTM).

- An optional What's New page (NEWS.HTM), with optional topics (Web Changes, Press Releases, Articles & Reviews).

- An optional Products/Services page (PRODUCTS.HTM) linked to a user-defined number of Products pages, each with optional topics (Product Image, Pricing Information, Information Request Form), and to a user-defined number of Services pages, each with optional topics (Capabilities List, Reference Accounts, Information Request Form).

- An optional Feedback form (FEEDBACK.HTM), with optional items (Full Name, Job Title, Company Affiliation, Mailing Address, Telephone Number, Fax Number, E-mail Address). This form is also used to specify whether returned data will be maintained on the server in tab-delimited or Web page (HTML) formats (in either _PRIVATE\INFOREQ.TXT or _PRIVATE\INFOREQ.HTM, respectively).

- An optional Table of Contents page (TOC.HTM), which automatically generates a list of HTM files in your Web, with options for automatic updates, showing or hiding pages not linked to any other Web page, and bullets for top-level pages.

- Standard page formatting options, including specification of whether the company logo, page title, and/or links to the Home page will appear at the top of each page and whether Home page links, Webmaster e-mail links, copyright notice and/or the Last Modified date will appear at the bottom. (Note that at least one Home page link option is required.) If the company logo is included, FrontPage uses the Include WebBot to add a file (_PRIVATE\LOGO.HTM) that references the logo graphic (IMAGES\LOGO.GIF). When you update the graphic, be sure to change the image, not the hidden HTM file.

 Graphic style options (Plain, Conservative, Flashy, or Cool). If one of the latter three options is chosen, corresponding exploration-bar and page-heading GIF files will be added to the IMAGES directory. The Home page header graphic, for example, is always named IMAGES\HHOME.GIF, regardless of the style chosen. (If you have selected client-side image maps, FrontPage also constructs a shared exploration bar, _PRIVATE\NAVBAR.HTM, incorporating button graphics for only those pages selected for the Web.)

 Custom or default page-color schemes, including background, text, and link-text options. FrontPage creates a file called _PRIVATE \STYLE.HTM with these values and adds a custom attribute (stylesrc="_private/style.htm") to the <BODY> tag of all other Web pages, to reference the file.

 Options to designate whether a graphic symbol (IMAGES\UNDER-CON.GIF) will or will not be used to indicate that a page is "under construction." FrontPage can automatically add this symbol to unfinished pages and remove it from pages marked as completed on the To Do list. (You, as the Webmaster, should consider whether you even *want* unfinished pages to appear on your intranet, or whether pages should be added only when they're complete.)

 Configuration variables for the company name (full-length and one-word variants), street address, telephone and fax numbers, e-mail address of the Webmaster, and general information.

Customer Support Template

This template creates a Web with the following elements, all linked to an Included Page header (HEADER.HTM) and an Included Page footer (FOOTER.HTM):

 A Welcome page (INDEX.HTM).

 A What's New page (WHATSNEW.HTM) that is linked to a Tech Note #1 page (TN001.HTM) with a dummy screen shot (IMAGES \SCRNSHOT.GIF).

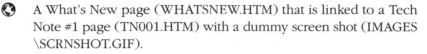

- 🌐 A FAQ (frequently asked questions) page (FAQ.HTM).

- 🌐 A Bug Reports From Customers form (BUGREP.HTM), which writes data to the Bug List From Customers page (BUGLIST.HTM).

- 🌐 A Suggestions From Customers form (SUGGEST.HTM), which writes data to the Suggestions From Customers page (FEED-BACK.HTM).

- 🌐 A Download page (DOWNLOAD.HTM).

- 🌐 A Search page (SEARCH.HTM).

- 🌐 A series of pages that make up a Discussion Group, including the Discussion page (DISCUSS.HTM), an Article Post form (CUSUPOST.HTM), a Confirmation form (CUSUCFRM.HTM), a Table of Contents page (CUSUTOC.HTM), and a Search page (CUSUSRCH.HTM), all linked to an included header (CUSU-HEAD.HTM) and an included footer (CUSUFOOT.HTM) for customer support. The discussion-group Table of Contents is generated from the _CUSUDI\TOC.HTM and _CUSUDI\TOC-PROTO.HTM files. Postings are individually maintained in sequentially numbered files named _CUSUDI\00000001.HTM, and so forth. Each numbered file is linked to an Included Article header (CUSUAHDR.HTM) and an Included Article footer (CUSUFTR.HTM).

Discussion Wizard

This wizard creates threaded discussion groups containing the following elements, all linked to an Included Page header (HEADER.HTM) and an Included Page footer (FOOTER.HTM):

- 🌐 A required Home page (INDEX.HTM), which optionally can be a frameset in which the Navigation Ledge (DTFWNAV.HTM), the Table of Contents page, and also the Welcome page (DTFWWELC.HTM) are displayed. You can also make INDEX.HTM the Table of Contents page. You can even create a discussion group without a Table of Contents page, in which case you will see no page called INDEX.HTM; instead, FrontPage will generate a virtual Table of Contents page from the _PRIVATE \TOCPROTO.HTM file.

- 🌐 A required Submission form (DTFWPOST.HTM), with the following options:

  - 🌐 Subject and Comments

  - 🌐 Subject, Category, and Comments

  - 🌐 Subject, Product, and Comments

- More fields can be added later with the FrontPage Editor. Articles posted in the discussion will not show up in FrontPage views, and this is desirable if there are to be other pages in the Web besides the discussion. To change this behavior, go back and deselect the TOC option.

- An optional Confirmation form (DTFWCFRM.HTM) for submissions.

- A suggested Table of Contents page (DTFWTOCF.HTM), with articles listed Oldest to Newest or Newest to Oldest. You can also make the Table of Contents page the Web Home page, but if you're adding the discussion group to an existing Web, you will over-write the current page named INDEX.HTM. The discussion group's Table of Contents page is generated from the files _DTFW\TOC.HTM and _DTFW\TOCPROTO.HTM. Postings are individually maintained in sequentially numbered files named _DTFW\00000001.HTM, and so forth, and these files are linked to an Included Article header (_PRIVATE\DTFWAHDR.HTM) and an Included Article footer (_PRIVATE\DTFWAFTR.HTM).

- A Search form (DTFWSRCH.HTM), with one of the following four optional criteria:

  - Subject
  - Subject and Size
  - Subject, Size, and Date
  - Subject, Size, Date, and Score

NOTE

With the Discussion Wizard, if you do not include a Table of Contents page, Web filenames and directory names will begin with DISC instead of DTFW.

The Discussion Wizard also lets you make the choices about the following elements:

- The page-color scheme, maintained in _PRIVATE\DTFWSTYL.HTM and referenced in all other pages with a custom attribute (stylesrc="_private/dtfwstyl.htm") to the <BODY> tag.

- Whether frames will be used to display contents and articles and, if so, the relative placement of contents and articles. Although the Internet Explorer (and most other current browsers) do support frames, there's an option for creating a dual interface so browsers that don't support frames can still view the Web properly.

2
CHAPTER

- Whether replies will be threaded.

- The Discussion Group title that appears on all pages.

- Whether Web protection will be enabled, limiting participation to registered users and automatically including the author's name in each article.

NOTE

If threaded replies are *not* implemented, the Web created by the Discussion Wizard may appear to behave strangely. You won't find an INDEX.HTM Home page; instead, FrontPage will use the _PRIVATE\TOCPROTO.HTM file to generate a virtual Table of Contents page that lists all the contents of this Web.

Project Template

This template creates the following pages and elements, all linked to an Included Page header (HEADER.HTM) and an Included Page footer (FOOTER.HTM):

- A Home page (INDEX.HTM)

- A Members page (MEMBERS.HTM)

- A Schedule page (SCHEDULE.HTM)

- An Archive page (ARCHIVE.HTM)

- A Discussions page (DISCUSS.HTM)

- A Status page (STATUS.HTM)

- A Search page (SEARCH.HTM)

The Project Template also creates the following series of elements, which make up the Knowledge Base:

- The Table of Contents page (KNOBTOC.THM).

- The Submissions form (KNOBPOST.HTM).

- The Confirmation and Search (KNOBSRCH.HTM) forms (KNOBCFRM.HTM and KNOBSRCH.HTM, respectively), which are linked to an Included Page header (KNOBHEAD.HTM) and an Included Page footer (KNOBFOOT.HTM) for the Knowledge Base.

The Table of Contents for the Knowledge Base, generated from the _KNOBAS\TOC.HTM and _KNOBAS\TOCPROTO.HTM files. Postings are individually maintained in sequentially numbered files named _KNOBAS\00000001.HTM, and so forth, which are linked to an Included Article header (KNOBAHDR.HTM) and an Included Article footer (KNOBAFTR.HTM).

In addition, the Project Template creates the following elements, which make up the Requirements discussion:

 The Table of Contents (REQDTOC.THM) page.

 Submissions (REQDPOST.HTM), Confirmation (REQDCFRM.HTM), and Search (REQDSRCH.HTM) forms, linked to an Included Page header (REQDHEAD.HTM) and an Included Page footer (REQDFOOT.HTM) for the Requirements discussion. The Table of Contents page for the Requirements discussion is generated from the _REQDIS\TOC.HTM and _REQDIS\TOCPROTO.HTM files. Postings are individually maintained in sequentially num bered files named _REQDIS\00000001.HTM, and so forth, which are linked to an Included Article header (REQDAHDR.HTM) and an Included Article footer (REQDAFTR.HTM).

Page Wizards and Templates

The FrontPage Editor's Page Wizards and Templates will be described at greater length in Chapter 3. For now, keep in mind that you can use the FrontPage Editor to add the preformatted elements shown in Table 2-2 directly to any Web. Since many of these elements also occur in various FrontPage Web Wizards, it shouldn't come as a surprise to learn that they're actually files saved in the TEM and WIZ subdirectories of the FrontPage program directory's Pages directory. The FrontPage Software Development Kit (SDK), available from Microsoft, provides some information on customizing Page templates. Fortunately, as you'll see in the next chapter, you can create individual Page templates much more easily by using standard FrontPage Editor commands.

2 CHAPTER

Table 2-2 FrontPage Editor Page Wizards and Templates.

Wizards	Templates
Database Connector	Bibliography
Form	Confirmation Form
Frames	Directory of Press Releases
Personal Home Page	Employee Directory
	Employment Opportunities
	Feedback Form
	Frequently Asked Questions
	Glossary of Terms
	Guest Book
	Hot List (contains URL links)
	Hyper Document Page (for creating "documents" made up of linked individual pages)
	Lecture Abstract
	Meeting Agenda
	Normal Page
	Office Directory
	Press Release
	Product Description
	Product or Event Registration
	Search Page
	Seminar Schedule
	Software Data Sheet
	Survey Form
	Table of Contents
	User Registration
	What's New

Custom Wizards

You *can* build custom wizards, but only in Visual Basic or Visual C++. If you want to know more, you'll need the FrontPage SDK and an iron constitution (not included), but first make sure the juice is worth the squeeze. FrontPage Web Wizards are great for providing fully functional sites to newbie Webmasters, but they may be less applicable to your intranet, where you can achieve consistency of page formatting simply by using custom Page templates, and where WebBot functionality can be replaced with ActiveX controls and other scripts. Typically, you'll need only one or two instances of a Search form or a Table of Contents page, so it might take you less time to generate the FrontPage version and customize the results than to build your own wizard simply to create a few pages from scratch.

Webs Within Webs

You're probably still thinking of your intranet as a single Web, but there are several reasons why FrontPage actually favors the implementation of multiple, interconnected Webs:

🌐 WebBots are Web-specific. If you want a Help Desk in your Web, with a Search form limited to Help Desk topics, you'll need to create it as a separate Web. Similarly, if you want to create several different discussion groups, each one will need a Web of its own.

🌐 Administrator, Author, and User permissions are set at the Web level. If you want one set of rules for authors in Human Resources and another set of rules for authors in Marketing, you might want to consider creating separate Webs.

🌐 FrontPage always imposes a fixed subdirectory structure on Web directories. If you want to use a frame-based graphical Web exploration system (in other words, clickable image maps and Visual Basic Scripting Edition) with content in nested subdirectories several levels down, you might find that maintenance is less of a headache if you move your data to new Webs.

All sub-Webs, of course, will be subdirectories of the designated <Root Web> directory, but FrontPage will not consider them *subfolders* of that Web—that is, you will not see your sub-Webs from the <Root Web> directory in the FrontPage Explorer's Outline View, and you will be able to create hyperlinks to them only by entering a URL to an external Web.

Wisdom Born of Experience

🌐 To put it succinctly, there is no such thing as too much design time. Every hour you spend designing your site to maximum efficiency will save you hours of building time, and tens of hours of revision time.

🌐 Map out your folder hierarchy before you create your first Web. Otherwise, you might waste a lot of time updating relative URLs.

- Consider your basic page layout before you begin editing. It's much easier to create a basic page template by using style sheets, configuration variables for standardized data, and Bot links to headers and footers than it will be to update a few hundred separate pages a month from now.

- You can control what's displayed in your Table of Contents page and your Search page only if you deploy them in parent Webs and child Webs. Changing your mind in midstream can mean extra work, and Web maintenance is enough of a chore without that.

- Design your Web with maintenance in mind. Web building, like empire building, eventually grinds to a halt; maintenance is forever. And remember, no matter how brilliant you think your ideas are, somebody (if not you) will surely want to change them all six months from now, so consider not only who will be editing your Web (and possibly undoing all your handiwork) but also how you yourself would go about ripping up your Web and starting over from scratch—just in case you ever have to.

- If the purpose of your intranet is to disseminate information, you should pay more attention to indexing and to the logical grouping of related information than to snazzy graphics. When it comes to your employee manual, for example, a picture probably isn't worth a thousand words, so spend as much time as you can tweaking your style sheet. Text counts. Content matters.

- Volume, volume, volume. Take a wild stab at how many files your Web will eventually accommodate—and then double that number. You simply would not *believe* how much stuff is going to accumulate there! Long filenames can help you remember what files are *for,* and a logical directory structure can be almost as useful as a search engine when you want to locate material. But you should also plan from day one how authorship and maintenance will be delegated and implemented. For example, if Ken, in your Washington office, is in charge of the industry newsletter, he may need a separate page template and style sheet—and possibly even his own Web.

- Reuse and recycle. The Include WebBot makes it easy to incorporate common file "headers" and "footers," and the Substitution Bot can be configured to insert all kinds of data as configuration variables. If you're going to use an exploration bar or a construction sign or even a graphical bullet throughout your Web, why have more than a single instance? FrontPage replicates the same set of subdirectories within each Web directory, so if you use nested folders to separate pages by topic, be sure to adopt consistency and symmetry throughout your site.

🌐 To the extent that WebBots drive your Web, they dictate its structure. If you want an automatic Table of Contents page that lists only the back issues of your company newsletter, you'll need to create a separate Web.

🌐 We live in a relative universe, so you'll be much happier if you use relative instead of absolute (or "fully qualified") URLs in your Web. Absolute URLs will need to be updated if you author on a different server (or in a different <Root Web> from your intranet server's). Relative URLs make it easier to move files between subfolders within a Web. FrontPage uses relative URLs by default and is pretty good at managing URLs for you, but if you map your test site to match your Web site, you should be able to publish with a minimum of edits to the finished product.

🌐 Let your GUI reflect your architecture. An intuitive interface mirrors the layout of a good Web. If your exploration bars or menus aren't clear, maybe the structure of your Web needs rethinking.

🌐 Work with dummies—that is, with perfectly intelligent people whose familiarity with browsers and other Webby things just happens to be considerably less than your own. They will instantly find each broken link and gravitate toward every less than obvious feature of your Web, thereby sparing you unpleasant encounters with senior management later on.

CHAPTER 2

CHAPTER

3

Creating Intranet Pages with FrontPage 97

Jeffrey M. Jones

In this chapter, you'll go right to the nitty-gritty: using the Microsoft FrontPage Editor to build custom Web pages (with a little help from the FrontPage Explorer). You'll start by seeing how to create your own basic page template and Web style sheet, and then you'll go step by step through building the following custom elements:

- A Home page, with frames for exploration bars, section menus, and Web contents
- A shared exploration bar using tables and inserted graphics
- Graphical menus with clickable hot spots
- A simple Download page for company templates and forms
- A Product Catalog consisting of hyperlinked documents
- A Newsletter Web using the TOC and Search WebBots
- A Product Knowledge Base using the Form Page Wizard and Confirmation Form Template

This chapter assumes that you're already familiar with the FrontPage Editor and will show you how to put its advanced features to work. If you've never used FrontPage, you might want to open the Learning FrontPage Wizard in the FrontPage Explorer and follow the tutorial in the documentation before plunging into this chapter.

Before we get started, though, a word about (*gulp!*) HTML. Maybe you purchased Microsoft FrontPage 97 because of its promise to shield you from the arcana of HTML code. Can you now rest assured that you—and, more important, the elves and munchkins to whom you'll surely be delegating most of the ongoing maintenance of your intranet—will be able to author 99.99 percent of your Web pages through the user interface and never (knowingly) write a single tag?

In a word, no.

You can't be a Webmaster without mucking about in HTML from time to time, so if you've ever harbored dreams of building your intranet without learning HTML, forget it. Not only is this book going to show you HTML from time to time, but it's also going to assume that you understand it.

Don't panic.

Back when dinosaurs roamed the earth (and some of us were young), people still talked about a universal language called Esperanto. It was supposed to be easy to learn. It wasn't, which is part of the reason why you're not reading it in this book. But HTML, which is a *functional* universal language, is RL EZ 2 LRN. Y? BCUZ ITSO beautifully DUM. And in the cross-platform, multibrowser World Wide Web, dumb is beautiful. As of this writing, the Microsoft Internet Explorer supports a grand total of 83 HTML tags—that's all, folks. The tags all have attributes, but still—it's a pretty small dictionary. And the grammar's not exactly rocket science, either. Look:

```
<p><SMALL>What, you expected maybe <I>big</I> text?
</SMALL></p>
```

Still, you're going to need a ready reference, and here are three dandy places to get one:

http://www.microsoft.com/workshop/author/newhtml/default.htm

http://www.microsoft.com/workshop/author/howto/novice-f.htm

http://www.ncsa.uiuc.edu/General/Internet/WWW/
HTMLPrimer.html

These are the URLs of, respectively, Microsoft's HTML guide, the Novice HTML tutorial, and the National Center for Supercomputing Applications (NCSA) tutorial. For an absolutely free HTML library in compiled online help format, courtesy of the invaluable Stephen Le Hunte, you can browse the following site:

http://subnet.virtual-pc.com/~le387818/

OK, are you ready? If so, launch the FrontPage Explorer, choose Open Existing FrontPage Web from the Getting Started dialog box (or choose Open FrontPage Web from the File menu), select your Personal Web Server, click the List Webs button, select <Root Web> . . . and go! From the FrontPage Explorer's Tools menu, select Show FrontPage Editor—or click the Show FrontPage Editor button on the FrontPage Explorer toolbar—to launch the FrontPage Editor without opening a page.

TIP

Once you start working on your intranet, you can launch the FrontPage Editor by selecting a page in the FrontPage Explorer and double-clicking (or by right-clicking, and choosing Open from the menu). However you launch the Editor, get in the habit of launching the FrontPage Explorer (and, by extension, your Personal Web Server) first.

FrontPage Editor Page Wizards and Templates

The FrontPage Editor has an extensive set of Page Wizards and Templates that create preformatted HTML pages (refer again to Table 2-2, page 52). Unlike the FrontPage Explorer's Web Wizards and Templates, however, the Page Wizards and Templates do *not* create Webs. When you use a FrontPage Editor Template, you must *save* the new page back to a Web. This is one reason why you'll always want to work with the FrontPage Explorer and the Personal Web Server running in the background: if you don't, you won't have an open Web.

Most Page Wizards and Templates produce static, preformatted HTML documents. That ain't chopped liver, but you can also learn how to create your own custom templates, so unless your intranet's design exactly matches the FrontPage formats, the Page Wizards and Templates are only a marginal improvement over what you could build on your own.

CHAPTER 3

You can use the FrontPage Explorer's Normal Web Template to create a simple Web, and then you can use the FrontPage Editor to create and save an instance of each page in the Web. If you want the Table of Contents page to be displayed by default when you browse the Web, use the FrontPage Explorer to delete the original INDEX.HTM file and rename the Table of Contents page INDEX.HTM. Once you jump to a sample page, use the Back button of Microsoft Internet Explorer to return to the Table of Contents page (unless you include navigation elements such as a toolbar with clickable buttons or hypertext links to other pages).

The Page Wizards and Templates outlined in the following paragraphs create boilerplate documents, which are described briefly. If these documents sound useful to you, you can create your own instances of them by choosing New from the FrontPage Editor's File menu and then choosing a Template or Wizard from the New Page dialog box. Unless there are indications to the contrary, each Wizard or Template creates a single, unnamed HTML page in the FrontPage format (often with comments in purple text, which are generated with the FrontPage Comment WebBot). Any of the pages you create in this way can be edited manually and saved to a Web or a directory.

Page Wizards

The FrontPage Editor has four Page Wizards: the Database Connector Wizard, the Form Page Wizard, the Frames Wizard, and the Personal Home Page Wizard.

Database Connector

The Database Connector Wizard helps you create an Internet Database Connector (IDC) file. The Wizard prompts you for an ODBC source and an HTX file where the query results will be stored. You can set some advanced ODBC options and then continue on to specify query information.

Form Page

The Form Page Wizard is an extremely powerful tool that manages the configuration of custom forms for user input. You can use the Form Page Wizard to add a form to the current page; if no page is currently open in the FrontPage Editor, the Form Page Wizard creates a new, blank one.

Frames

The Frames Wizard, a tool that automates the process of making frames, creates an HTML frameset page containing not only the frame definitions but also all the additional HTML pages you'll need for supplying the contents of each frame. You use the FrontPage Editor to work on content pages, but be aware that you cannot work directly on any HTML page containing <FRAMESET> tags. Instead, when you edit a frameset page in FrontPage 97, you'll see the same series of options for editing grids that appear when you use the Frames Wizard to create a new page and choose the Make A Custom Grid option instead of the Pick A Template option.

NOTE

Unfortunately, the Frames Wizard does not give you access to all frame-formatting options—specifically, you can only specify exact frame dimensions or hidden frame borders directly in the underlying HTML, by using an ASCII text editor. You should also be aware that the Frames Wizard only generates boilerplate Table of Contents pages. For instance, it generates a nested TOC page, but you have to add the table of contents to the page manually with the TOC WebBot.

Personal Home Page

The Personal Home Page Wizard provides a wide range of options for creating a single HTML page with customizable informational sections and a Comments form, which can deliver user feedback as e-mail. It can also deliver user feedback to a designated text file (_PRIVATE/HOMERESP.TXT) or HTML file (_PRIVATE/HOMERESP.HTM). The settings in the Personal Home Page Wizard are "sticky"—that is, they retain the user's most recent selection by default. You can find those settings in the \TEMP\VTIHOME.INI file in the Microsoft FrontPage directory.

Page Templates

The most interesting templates incorporate FrontPage WebBot components— dynamic objects that appear in the page (and can be configured with FrontPage Editor commands) but ultimately reference automated routines that run on the server. You can, of course, customize any template-based WebBot component, but later in this chapter we'll cover in detail how each of the significant WebBots works.

Bibliography

The Bibliography Template creates a short boilerplate bibliography page, with three dummy alphabetic-listing paragraphs, each with a dummy bookmark (that is, in HTML, a <A NAME="*ALastName*"> tag).

CHAPTER 3

Confirmation Form

The Confirmation Form Template creates a short boilerplate Confirmation page, with editable text and six possible Confirmation Field WebBot entries.

Database Results

The Database Results Template creates a page designed to store database information. This template corresponds to an IDC file created with the Database Connector Wizard.

Directory Of Press Releases

The Directory Of Press Releases Template creates a simple page with internal hyperlinks to three boilerplate sections where press releases can be listed on a monthly basis. You can use this template in conjunction with the Press Release Template.

Employee Directory

The Employee Directory Template creates a long HTML page with internal links to boilerplate alphabetic entries for employees. Each of the four sample entries contains a different combination of employee-data options, but the bottom line is that you'll still have to enter all employee data manually. Even the dummy Company Logo is an inert GIF file rather than a dynamic Include WebBot reference.

When you save a page with references to graphics that are not part of your Web, the FrontPage Editor prompts you to save them, too, but you will *not* be prompted for unsaved graphics when you close the file. If you reopen a file that you closed with unsaved graphics, the graphic references might be invalid. As a rule, you should either save graphics when you create new pages or delete the references before you save.

Employment Opportunities

The Employment Opportunities Template generates a long HTML page with internal links to dummy job listings and a Personnel file data submission form at the bottom. Remember that the form itself is static; the script that captures the data and writes it to the FrontPage Personal Web server is the Save Results WebBot.

Feedback Form

The Feedback Form Template creates a short page with a sample Submission or Post form. (It's a good basic form, but you can build *any* such form from scratch with the Form Page Wizard, described on page 60.)

Frequently Asked Questions

As its name suggests, the Frequently Asked Questions Template creates a short HTML page with internal links to categories of frequently asked questions, or FAQs.

Glossary Of Terms

The Glossary Of Terms Template creates a long template with a text-only exploration bar linked to alphabetic sections. The boilerplate glossary entries are also bookmarked. The glossary you create uses Defined Term styles, which are discussed briefly later in this chapter, in the section titled "Making a List" (page 76).

Guest Book

The Guest Book Template creates a form for capturing user comments and adding them to a guest log that appears below the form. The form itself uses a Save Results WebBot configured to the file GUESTLOG.HTM. The same file name is referenced in the Include WebBot below the form. Be aware that unless you tweak your guest log page, the user's comments will be anonymous (unless the user thoughtfully appends her name to her comments).

Hot List

The Hot List Template creates a short HTML page with internal links to various categories of Web sites.

HyperDocument Page

The HyperDocument Page Template is intended to create a page that's part of a "document" made up of a number of independent pages. If you use the HyperDocument Page Template, you have to supply all the links manually.

Lecture Abstract

The Lecture Abstract Template creates a very simple page with boilerplate references to an event. You can use such a page in conjunction with the Seminar Schedule Template (described on page 65), but you will have to supply all the external links manually.

Meeting Agenda

The Meeting Agenda Template creates a very simple boilerplate agenda page.

CHAPTER 3

Normal Page

The Normal Page Template creates a new blank page. Just remember that even a new blank page is an HTML document. Here's the standard FrontPage "blank page" HTML code:

```
<!DOCTYPE HTML PUBLIC "-//IETF//DTD HTML//EN">
<html>

<head>
<meta http-equiv="Content-Type"
content="text/html; charset=iso-8859-1">
<meta name="GENERATOR" content="Microsoft FrontPage 2.0">
<title>Untitled Normal Page</title>
</head>

<body bgcolor=" FFFFFF">
</body>
</html>
```

You can ignore most of this stuff, but be aware that whenever you open an imported HTML file—say, from a previous Web, or from an author who is not using FrontPage—the FrontPage Editor writes, reads, and wraps the same HTML shell around its contents, with potentially disastrous results (see "Imported HTML: Open with Care," page 67).

Office Directory

The Office Directory Template creates a short HTML page with internal links to office location descriptions.

Press Release

The Press Release Template creates a very short boilerplate for a press release.

Product Description

The Product Description Template creates a simple page with internal links to categories describing a product.

Product Or Event Registration

The Product Or Event Registration Template provides a form for capturing many kinds of user input, with controls (a drop-down list box and check boxes) that you can easily modify. Note that in order to use the form, you must customize the Save Results WebBot by specifying a Results file on your Web, and that the form also returns hidden data with each submission (including the date, time, IP address, domain name, and browser type).

Search Page

The Search Page Template lets you add a Search page to your Web. The FrontPage comment at the top of the page indicates that no customization is required, but you *will* have to change the Search WebBot properties if you want to limit the search range or change how search results are returned.

Seminar Schedule

The Seminar Schedule Template creates a short page with internal links to conference or seminar descriptions. You can also use the Seminar Schedule Template as a master page, adding hypertext links to pages for each event created with the Lecture Abstract Template.

Software Data Sheet

The Software Data Sheet Template creates a page with boilerplate descriptions of software products' characteristics.

Survey Form

The Survey Form Template creates a long HTML page that incorporates all Form controls supported by FrontPage. The Survey Form Template is worth studying if you plan to work with FrontPage forms. Just save it to your Web and view it in your browser. When you click the Submit Form button, your entries will be displayed in a Confirmation form and will be appended to an HTML file. (By default, this file is called _PRIVATE\SURVRESP.HTM.)

Table Of Contents

The Table Of Contents Template creates a Table of Contents page with the FrontPage TOC WebBot component and includes instructions for both the end user and the Webmaster. Be aware that the table of contents itself is WebBot-generated and is displayed only in your browser. The table of contents will include all pages in your Web except those in "hidden" directories. If you want a table of contents configured to a limited subset of directories, you'll have to create a sub-Web.

User Registration

The User Registration Template is a form that incorporates the FrontPage Registration WebBot component and requires users to register passwords for sub-Webs that you have designated as protected.

What's New

The What's New Template creates a simple page with a boilerplate you can customize to create a listing of new features added to your intranet.

Saving Pages to Webs

Use the FrontPage Save or Save As command (shown in Figure 3-1) to add a new page to a Web or file directory. If you have launched the FrontPage Personal Web Server and opened a Web in the FrontPage Explorer, the default

CHAPTER 3

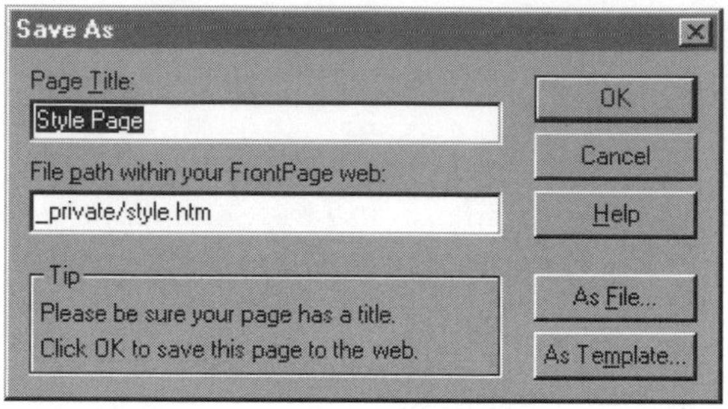

Figure 3-1

The Save As dialog box of the FrontPage Editor.

option will be the active Web. If you do *not* have an open Web, you'll have to save the file to a specified directory. You can also save the file as a template, which you'll learn how to do in Chapter 4.

If you create a new document from a template that contains graphics—which are really HTML <IMG> tags specifying valid URLs for image files—FrontPage will prompt you to save them, too. If you do save them, accept the default /IMAGES subfolder URL that FrontPage proposes. If you don't save the images used in a page, be sure to delete them (and their <IMG> tag references). Otherwise FrontPage will keep prompting you each time you save, until you close the file—at which point you will *not* be prompted, but you will see error messages the next time you open the file, since it will contain links to images that are outside your Web.

> FrontPage is designed to store all the images belonging to the pages of a given folder in that folder's /IMAGES subfolder. Unless you have a truly compelling reason for storing images elsewhere, you will only be courting unnecessary confusion if you monkey with this default.

Customizing Page Templates

Every Page Template is maintained as a pair of files in a .TEM subfolder of the FrontPage program folder's PAGES folder. The Bibliography Template, for example, consists of BIBLIO.HTM (an HTML file containing the boilerplate text and WebBot references) and BIBLIO.INF (a short text file configured like an INI file and containing the template title and description entries that appear in the FrontPage Editor's New Page dialog box). By default, these files are saved to the folder C:\PROGRAM FILES\MICROSOFT FRONTPAGE\PAGES\BIBLIO.TEM; drive and folder names might be different on your PC, of course.

You can customize any FrontPage Template by opening and changing the file in the FrontPage Editor. You can do this in any other text editor, too, but only FrontPage properly displays WebBot information (such as the purple Comments text).

Imported HTML: Open with Care

The FrontPage Editor is aptly named: when it opens an HTML file imported from an outside source (whether from another Web or from another HTML editing application), the FrontPage Editor automatically reviews the document and brings it into conformity with the FrontPage Editor's default structure. Here, for example, is how the FrontPage Editor renders a simple one-line sample of HTML (and note the "helpful" <FONT SIZE> tags):

```
!DOCTYPE HTML PUBLIC "-//IETF//DTD HTML//EN">
<html>

<head>
<meta name="GENERATOR" content="Microsoft FrontPage 2.0">
<title>Bunged Up Page #1</title>
</head>

<body>

<p><font size="2">What, you expected maybe </font><font
size="4"><i>big</i></font><font
size="2"> text?</font></p>
</body>
</html>
```

This *might* be what you want—but it almost certainly *won't* be what you want in the case of valid HTML files with Microsoft Visual Basic, Scripting Edition (VBScript) code within the <HEAD> tag. FrontPage will overwrite the imported <HEAD> tag, and in the process it will strip out all the HTML it considers "nonstandard." In many cases, however, the scripts that have been stripped from the <HEAD> tag have simply been moved to a different location in the file. But the possibility still exists that your pages won't work properly. (Grrrrrrrr.)

CHAPTER 3

What You See Ain't All You Get

No matter what you do in a Web page, the end result is HTML. You might choose to ignore the HTML code itself, but you should never forget the *function* of the code: it provides a generic description of a document's structure.

Now, if you wanted to revive the thrilling Nominalist debates of the Medieval era, you could argue that a <MARQUEE> tag is as much document *content* as it is *form*. I don't care! All I want you to care about is the distinction between the *description* of a thing and the *thing itself*. The function of HTML is to provide the information that all browsers use to render a document in a similar way. Exactly how a given browser renders a given document, however, depends on the browser type, the browser's settings, the user's operating environment, and even (or so it can seem around two o'clock in the morning) the flight path of some random butterfly in a garden in Peking.

Still, an intranet is a heck of a lot easier to work with than the Internet is. In principle, you have control over the user's browser. You may not know the user's screen resolution, but you can be reasonably confident they he or she won't try to view your masterpiece through an Archie or Lynx browser. We'll assume (with rare exceptions, which will be noted) that you are authoring solely for an Internet Explorer 3.0 audience. (And if you're not, you should cultivate some friendships in your Information Systems department.) Just be sure that, before you start using the FrontPage Editor, you install a copy of *every* browser that will be used to render your intranet.

Browsing for Browsers

If anyone were to claim that the FrontPage Editor is a WYSIWYG HTML authoring tool, you would know that this claim was patently absurd, since HTML is specifically designed to allow *different* renderings of the same source code. All that the FrontPage Editor can do, at best, is render HTML in its own intuitive and inimitable way, just as any other browser would do. Moreover, some WebBots display their results only in a browser, not in the FrontPage Editor, so if you care *at all* about design—heck, even if you just want to be sure that the HTML equivalent of your slip isn't showing—you must regularly view your work in *all* the browsers that are being used in your environment. But don't worry—FrontPage makes this a breeze.

During its Setup procedure, FrontPage registers every browser on your PC, and you can view the page you're currently editing by choosing Preview In Browser from the FrontPage Editor's File menu and selecting the browser you want (see Figure 3-2). You should preview your work often,

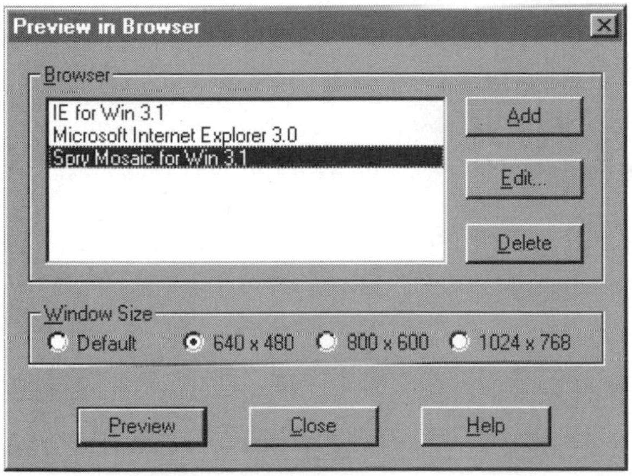

Figure 3-2

The FrontPage Editor's Preview In Browser dialog box.

partly to be sure that the results are to your liking, but also because you always want your browser's cache to contain a recent copy of any HTML that you're working on.

NOTE

You can't preview a frameset from the FrontPage Editor because the Frames Wizard prevents you from opening it in the FrontPage Editor. You also can't preview your work in browsers that won't run on your PC. This limitation can be a problem for Webmasters who want to author for the Macintosh in the Microsoft Windows environment. But you can add new, *compatible* browsers from the FrontPage Editor's Preview In Browser dialog box, and you can select different screen resolutions, too.

A Quick Peek Under the Hood

Let's say there's some funky expanse of empty space in your Web page that you want to remove and, try as you might, there seems to be no way for you to grab it in the FrontPage Editor (let alone delete the darn thing). Has this ever happened to you? If not, it will—and you will be very, very grateful to FrontPage for letting you choose HTML from the View menu. Case in point: the default DISCUSS.HTM page created as part of the Included Page Header of the Project Web template has some lovely indented paragraphs below each hypertext link, and you decide you don't want the paragraphs indented. With the HTML viewer, you can see that this effect is created with <BLOCKQUOTE> tags. (See Figure 3-3.) (This is just an example. The easy way to remove the indents is to select the paragraph and click the Decrease Indent button on the Format toolbar.) Even if you've promised yourself never to learn a lick of HTML, do yourself a favor and use the HTML command from the FrontPage Editor's View menu when you're stumped about what you're seeing in the FrontPage Editor. If there's only a simple HTML tag to blame for an error, you might be able to fix it.

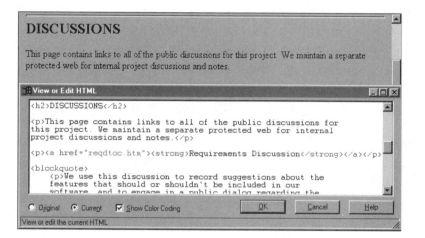

Figure 3-3
View or Edit HTML window showing the HTML code behind the DISCUSS.HTM page.

The View or Edit HTML window might fool you into thinking it's only a simple window on the subterranean world of Hypertext Markup Language, but it's actually a sophisticated tool that evaluates and adjusts your code after you close the window. The aim of all this extra effort is to minimize the possibility of mistakes, but the results can be surprising. For a demonstration, open a new, normal page and select HTML from the View menu. On a new line following the <BODY BGCOLOR="FFFFFF"> tag, type *<LI>This is a list item*. Then click the OK button to close the window. As you'll see in the FrontPage Editor, FrontPage has recognized that list elements belong within list-definition tags, so it has turned your entry into a bulleted entry within a definition list. A second look at the HTML code shows that additional <DIR>, </LI>, and </DIR> tags have been added to turn your intentional mistake into valid HTML syntax.

(Almost) Effortless Editing

Perhaps you caught the inference that the FrontPage Editor works just the way any other browser works. Don't believe me? Try this: choose Open from the FrontPage Editor's File menu, click the Other Location tab, click the From Location button and enter a valid URL for the World Wide Web (say, *www.microsoft.com*) in the From Location dialog box, click OK, and wait a moment. If you have a valid Internet connection, you'll eventually load the Home page of the Microsoft Corporation into your very own FrontPage Editor. From there, if you want to, you can add the Home page of the Microsoft Corporation to your very own active Web.

You know now that the FrontPage Editor works the same way any other browser does, so you can understand that when you edit a page in your active Web (which is open in the FrontPage Explorer), you're actually working on data that a server has generated in response to an HTTP request from the FrontPage Editor—you're *not* working directly on the Web page itself. The situation is analogous to what you're used to in Microsoft Word: the data in your active Word document isn't saved to a file until the Save command is executed.

You'll also encounter various FrontPage Editor messages having to do with functionality such as the Original and Current options in the View Or Edit HTML window, or messages like the one shown in Figure 3-4, which appears when you try to close a page with unsaved changes in the FrontPage Editor. If you have unsaved changes in the current page and you open the page directly from your browser, you won't see them because the server won't be able to display them in response to an HTTP request. If you want to see your changes, you must first save your Web pages back to the server with one of the Save commands. When you choose Refresh from the FrontPage Editor's View menu, you're doing just the opposite: making an HTTP request to the server to *replace* the current data in your Web page with the server version, and you will be prompted to save. FrontPage also saves changes automatically when you choose the Preview In Browser command.

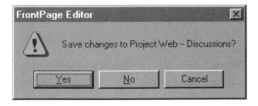

Figure 3-4

Unsaved changes alert.

If you have unsaved changes and choose Refresh from the FrontPage Explorer View menu, you will lose your changes, and you won't even be prompted to save them.

The majority of the FrontPage Editor commands let you *write* HTML without *knowing* HTML. Because those commands are well documented in the FrontPage 97 manual and the online Help, I won't waste time on them here (with one exception). Instead, I'll focus on some advanced FrontPage Editor functionality, as well as on processes that are less obvious in the FrontPage Editor because of underlying HTML issues or because of the ways in which the FrontPage Editor manipulates HTML to conform to its standards.

Working with Defaults

Here's the exception I just mentioned—I'm going to tell you how to add a 5-pixel gray horizontal rule to a Web page:

1. Choose Horizontal Line from the FrontPage Editor's Insert menu.

2. Now do it again (that's right, make two of them), and select the second one.

3. Double-click with the left mouse button, *or* single-click with the right mouse button and choose Horizontal Line Properties from the Context menu, *or* choose Horizontal Line Properties from the FrontPage Editor's Edit menu, *or* press the Alt-Enter key combination.

   Any way you slice it, you'll come up with the Horizontal Line Properties dialog box (see Figure 3-5).

4. Change the Height value to 5, and then select Gray from the Color dropdown list. Click OK.

Now move your cursor and type some text, and then choose Horizontal Line from the FrontPage Editor's Insert menu. Just like magic, FrontPage remembers your last request and serves you up another 5-pixel gray rule. The same settings will apply even if you open a new page; the inherited default (inherited from the previous instance) applies throughout your current FrontPage session.

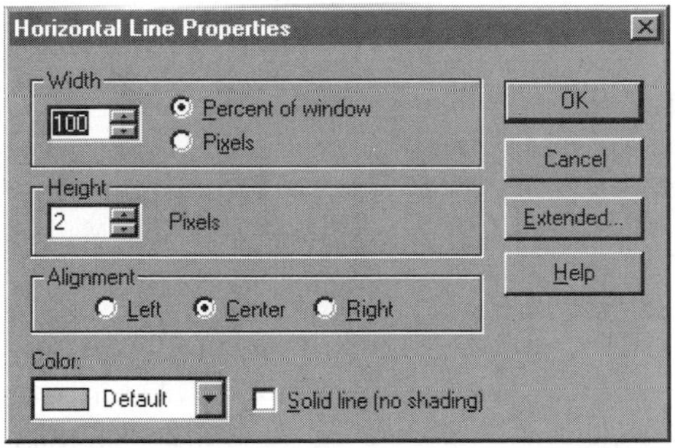

Figure 3-5

Horizontal Line Properties dialog box.

Paragraph and font formats also exhibit a kind of "local" inheritance in the FrontPage Editor, much as they do in Microsoft Word. In both applications, the current paragraph and font settings are applied to a new blank paragraph when you press the Enter key. If you know HTML, you might assume that the <P> tag, which establishes the new paragraph, has simply been inserted within the existing formatting tags (that is, *before* whatever closing tag FrontPage generated as part of the original reformatting). I mention this only because this assumption would be wrong. FrontPage *always* resolves that tag pairing within the current paragraph before starting a new one, and then it writes fresh instances of the attributes inherited from the preceding paragraph. Such inheritance is always localized to the preceding or "parent" paragraph but also applies to extended attributes (which we'll cover in the section that follows this one).

TIP

FrontPage does revert to its original defaults for each new session, but if you've already added a 5-pixel gray rule to any open page, all you have to do is double-click the rule and then click the OK button on the Horizontal Line Properties dialog box to reestablish the default for your current session.

Session-specific inheritance in the FrontPage Editor is also accepted by marquees and certain table formats, including borders, padding, and spacing.

Extending HTML

Extended HTML is simply HTML whose attribute values aren't supported in FrontPage 97, and you must set these values manually.

Yes, yes, I know— you're planning never to write a lick of HTML in your life, and that's why you bought FrontPage 97 in the first place. And the few times you *might* have to write HTML, you're going use the HTML Markup WebBot (which is about to be demonstrated). In a pinch, maybe you'll fire up the HTML command from the FrontPage Editor's View menu.

But suppose you'd like to create a table that has only horizontal rules above and below each row, with no vertical rules between columns. You could do this by selecting table elements and applying the formats you want, but there's an even easier way: adding the FRAMES and RULES attributes, which FrontPage doesn't support, to the <TABLE> tag. (I'm using table as an example, but the technique is the same for all elements of a Web page— paragraphs, fonts, lists and so forth—that can be assigned unique properties when selected in the FrontPage Editor.) Here's how you add these extended attributes:

1. Select the table you want to format, and then right-click the mouse and choose Table Properties from the Context menu (or choose Table Properties from the Table menu—it's all the same to me). Set your properties to match those in the Table Properties dialog box shown here:

2. In the Table Properties dialog box, click the Extended button. You'll see the Extended Attributes dialog box on page 75, with the value of the underlying HTML tag. (In this case, the tag is <TABLE>.)

The underlying HTML tag

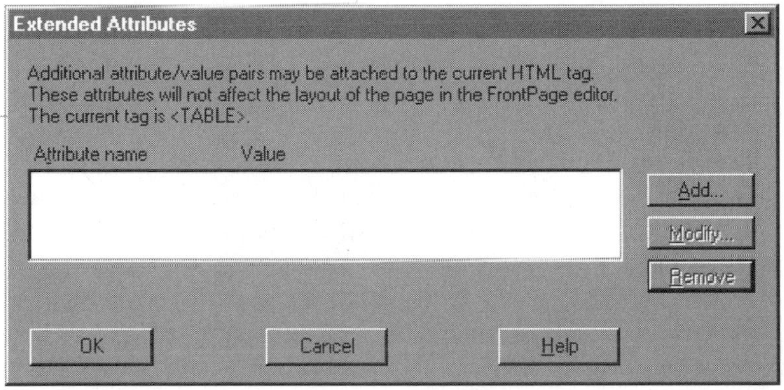

Extended Attributes

Additional attribute/value pairs may be attached to the current HTML tag.
These attributes will not affect the layout of the page in the FrontPage editor.
The current tag is <TABLE>.

Attribute name   Value

Add...

Modify...

Remove

OK   Cancel   Help

3.   In the Extended Attributes dialog box, click the Add button to
     display the Name/Value Pair dialog box, shown below, where you
     enter the name and value of the attributes you want to add. In
     this case, we'll add the "Rules" attribute with a value of "Rows."

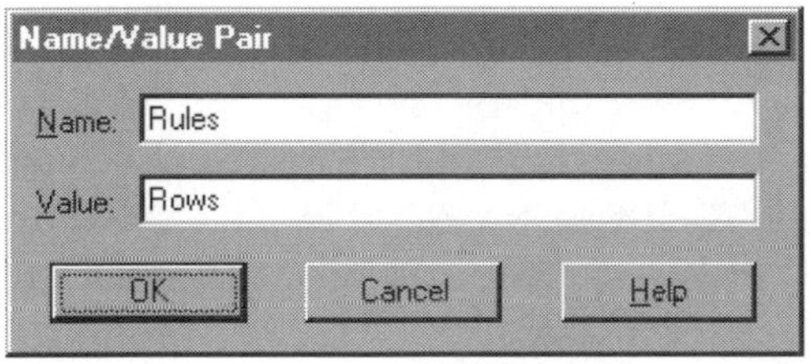

Name/Value Pair

Name: Rules

Value: Rows

OK   Cancel   Help

4.   Click the OK button to see your extended attribute and its value in
     the Extended Attributes dialog box as shown below. (Note that we've
     previously added the Frame attribute with a value of "HSides.")

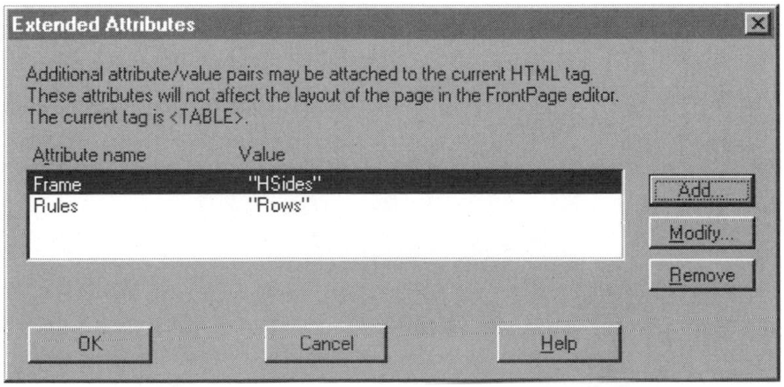

Extended Attributes

Additional attribute/value pairs may be attached to the current HTML tag.
These attributes will not affect the layout of the page in the FrontPage editor.
The current tag is <TABLE>.

Attribute name   Value

Frame   "HSides"
Rules   "Rows"

Add

Modify...

Remove

OK   Cancel   Help

Don't be surprised when you return to the FrontPage Editor and see that your table still has vertical borders. Extended attributes are not displayed in the FrontPage Editor precisely because they fall outside the FrontPage command set. (In fact, FrontPage displays an error message when you try to set an attribute that *isn't* considered to be "extended." That's why you can't use this technique to center-align a paragraph, for example, because FrontPage supports the attribute of center alignment through its regular command set.) To see your extended attributes in action, you have to pre-view your page in your browser; refreshing your page and your Web won't do the trick.

NOTE By default, FrontPage uses vanilla HTML—that is, the applicable HTML tag with the fewest possible attributes—but some FrontPage commands add attributes "under the hood" when you select an option in a dialog box. For instance, when you choose to center-align a paragraph on your Web page, FrontPage generates the <p align="center"> tag.

Getting Rid of Blank Space

Sometimes you'll find blank space inexplicably cropping up in your Web pages where it doesn't belong. Before you do anything, preview your work in your browser: some FrontPage WebBots, for example, have space around them in the FrontPage Editor that will not be apparent in a browser. If there is indeed unwanted space, however, try choosing the HTML option from the FrontPage Editor's View menu. Often you can easily spot and delete some garbage HTML.

Making a List

Every list—whether it's a bulleted, definition, directory, menu, or numbered list—consists of a pair of HTML tags for every list item, and all those pairs of tags are nested within a pair of tags that defines the list type. When you apply the Bulleted List style, for example, FrontPage inserts an HTML struc-ture that looks (schematically) like this:

```
<UL>
<LI>You are here</LI>
</UL>
```

FrontPage manages lists aggressively for you, and it gets them right 99 percent of the time. For example, if you press the Enter key in a blank para-graph at the end of a list, FrontPage automatically closes out the list for you.

Nevertheless, it's still possible for FrontPage to drop a stitch—by, say, deleting everything in a list but an initial <UL> list-definition tag, which will cause the paragraphs that follow the deleted list items and tags to be mysteriously indented. Bulleted, numbered, menu, and directory lists have a list-item tag in common: <LI></LI>. If you're using style sheets (as we do in the sample intranet that we'll build over the course of this book), the characteristic that you assign to this tag will apply to the entire list, which might not be what you want. In a common ASCII text editor, you could easily apply a Class attribute to each instance of the <LI> tag. FrontPage won't let you do this, however (except in the FrontPage Editor's View Or Edit HTML window, where you won't be able to do a global replace). In the FrontPage Editor, extended attributes can be applied only to list-definition tags, not to list-item tags.

Creating Tables

There's nothing terribly complicated about a table—until you try to create one in HTML. Then it becomes a grisly thicket of unruly tags, and you'll need a machete to hack through them. Any number of HTML editors can do a graceful enough job of making a table—that is, they display a grid that you can drag around in the interface. But lurking underneath are some HTML-related issues that you should know about.

First, in its simplest form, a table is a series of nested tags that take the following generic form:

```
<TABLE>
    <TR>
        <TD>
        </TD>
        <TD>
        </TD>
    </TR>
</TABLE>
```

<TABLE> defines the table structure, <TR> defines each row, and <TD> defines each cell in the row. Simple enough, so far—but there's no *requirement* that each row have the same number of cells, and this is a situation that different browsers handle differently. There are also some formatting attributes, such as alignment, that can be assigned (differently) at any level. Some, like font size, must be assigned to every single <TD> element in a table. FrontPage handles all this fairly gracefully, but just try reformatting a spreadsheet that's been Saved As HTML in Excel, or a table created with Word, and you'll see what I mean: everywhere you look, the thing is littered with <FONT SIZE=2> tags, and if that's not what you want, you'll have to clean them all up.

Second, most browsers won't display blank cells. If you've applied borders to a table, they also won't be displayed around blank cells, which can make for a pretty strange-looking table. FrontPage manages this situation for you by adding a nonbreaking space (" " in HTML) to all blank cells.

Third, HTML lets you stipulate table dimensions either absolutely (in units such as pixels) or proportionally. Since you can never be sure of your user's screen resolution, you will almost always want to define table dimensions proportionally, which the FrontPage Editor lets you do from the Cell Properties and Table Properties dialog boxes.

Fourth, HTML 3 and 3.2 have introduced advanced table-definition tags for table headers, the table's body text, and table footers, so you can break a table into distinct parts by using the following generic syntax:

```
<TABLE>
<THEAD>
<TH>
    <TD>
    ⋮
    </TD>
</TH>
<TBODY>
<TR>
    <TD>
    ⋮
    </TD>
</TR>
<TFOOT>
<TR>
    <TD>
    ⋮
    </TD>
</TR>
</TABLE>
```

I'm telling you all this because the Microsoft Internet Explorer supports these tags, but FrontPage 97 does not as of this writing, so if you're planning to use a style sheet, don't bother creating custom <TH> styles: you'll get the equivalent result from header and footer variants for the <TD> tag, applied as extended attributes to a whole row.

Finally, the Internet Explorer family of browsers supports background images in individual table cells. In fact, these browsers support them quite elegantly: images larger than the cell are automatically scaled to fit, and images smaller than the cell are automatically tiled. In the FrontPage Editor you add images by selecting the cell (or cells) and changing the cell (or table) properties, which you do by choosing Cell Properties (or Table Properties) from the Table menu. When you add a background image to a *group of cells,* you'll see the cell borders between the images in the selected cells (even if you've set cell borders to 0); when you add a background image to a *table* or a group of *merged* cells, you won't. You can also confuse your browser by adding images to various groupings of cells within a table: in effect, you're sending the browser contradictory information at various levels of the nested HTML tags that make up your table. For instance, if you add IMAGE1.GIF to the whole table, IMAGE2.GIF to the top row, and IMAGE3.GIF to the third column, you might not see the IMAGE4.GIF that's referenced in the <TD> tags for cells 2 and 3 in row 4. The solution for this, as for so much else in corporate life, is to KISS (Keep It Simple, Stupid).

Working with Frames

Some HTML authoring books treat frames and <FRAMESET></FRAMESET> tags as if they were potentially as confusing as tables. There are indeed some issues to be addressed, but since there are far, far fewer frames on a page than there are cells in a table, frames are not really hard to puzzle out, even in HTML.

NOTE The FrontPage Editor doesn't exactly make it difficult to work with frames. It just requires that you work in only one way—with the Frames Wizard. Trouble is, the Frames Wizard (as of this writing) doesn't support borderless frames through the user interface, which are what you'll find all over the Microsoft Web site, and which we'll be using in our intranet.

Frames work in much the same way as tables do. There's a pair of frame-definition tags <FRAMESET> </FRAMESET>, within which you define individual frames (and subframes). The initial <FRAMESET> tag takes the place of a <BODY> tag (that is, you can't have frames coexisting with text outside the frame on the same Web page). But since frames are not supported by all browsers, you can add a <NOFRAMES> tag within the parent <FRAMESET> tag to stipulate how the page will be displayed in nonframe browsers, and that's where you'll add a <BODY> tag. The net result creates three frames, as shown in Figure 3-6. The first frame, TargetName1, spans the entire width of the page, in a row that is 89 pixels high. It is followed by the second frame, TargetName2, a row 120 pixels wide that falls to the left of the third frame, TargetName3, which takes up the rest of the page's

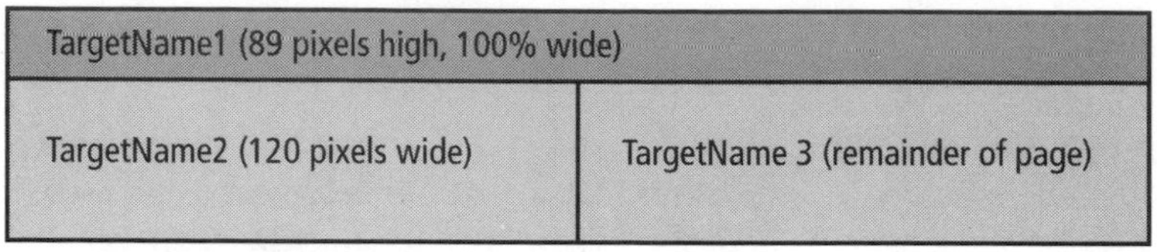

| TargetName1 (89 pixels high, 100% wide) | |
| TargetName2 (120 pixels wide) | TargetName 3 (remainder of page) |

Figure 3-6

Web page created with <FRAMESET></FRAMESET> tags.

width, regardless of the user's screen resolution. The following code generates the page shown in the figure:

```
<HTML>
<HEAD>
⋮
</HEAD>
<FRAMESET FRAMEBORDER="0" FRAMESPACING="0" ROWS="89,*">
    <FRAME
        SRC="webpage1.htm"
        NAME="targetname1"
        NORESIZE
        SCROLLING="No">
        <FRAMESET Cols="120,*">
            <FRAME
                SRC="webpage2.htm"
                NAME="targetname2"
                NORESIZE
                SCROLLING="Auto">
            <FRAME
                SRC ="webpage3.htm"
                Name="targetname3"
                NORESIZE
                SCROLLING="Auto">
        </FRAMESET>
<NOFRAMES>
    <BODY BGCOLOR="FFFFFF">
    <BASEFONT SIZE = 2>
    <FONT FACE="Arial">
    <p>MMA OnLine uses frames, which your browser doesn't support.
        To view MMA Online, contact ITOPS for the latest version of
        the Microsoft Explorer.</p>
    </FONT>
    </BODY>
</NOFRAMES>
</FRAMESET>
</HTML>
```

You can enter a frameset definition with these attributes by selecting HTML from the FrontPage Editor's View menu, but you'd better get it right the first time: the next time you try to open it, the FrontPage Editor will recognize the <FRAMESET> tag and summon up the Frames Wizard, blowing out your FRAMEBORDER=0 attribute in the process. Inserting the frameset with the Markup WebBot doesn't work any better: the FrontPage Editor recognizes the <FRAMESET> tag inside the Markup WebBot and launches the Frames Wizard, which then displays a message that there are no frames to edit!

Working with FrontPage WebBots

WebBots are actually chunks of code (C++ code, if you're curious) that execute various functions. They're the FrontPage version of CGI (Common Gateway Interface) scripting, which is a generic term for the server-side processes that extend functionality. In simple terms, CGI scripts process user-driven name/value pairs (that's really what's being captured in an HTML form and passed back when you click the Submit button) and generate a result.

But FrontPage WebBot components are more like CGI scripts on steroids, since they generate dynamic objects in your Web pages that you can configure directly from the FrontPage Editor interface. You insert WebBots directly with FrontPage Editor commands, and when you click an inserted WebBot in the FrontPage Editor, you'll see a dialog box where you can modify the underlying functionality.

There are eight WebBots that you insert by choosing the WebBot Component command on the FrontPage Editor's Insert menu:

- The **Confirmation Field WebBot** generates an object that displays the name of a form field in bracketed text in the FrontPage Editor, but it displays the *contents* of the referenced form field in your browser when the page in which it appears has been configured as a Confirmation form.

- The **Include WebBot** generates an object that displays, both in the FrontPage Editor and your browser, the contents of any other Web page that you can reference with a URL. The FrontPage Editor interface, however, prevents you from browsing files that don't have an HTM(L) extension or are not part of the active Web. You can enter *any* URL in the WebBot Include Component Properties dialog box, including a reference to a file you haven't created yet. But since the WebBot needs to work in conjunction with the FrontPage Personal Web Server, including a reference to a non-existent file is not recommended.

CHAPTER 3

◉ The **Scheduled Image WebBot** is like an Include WebBot for graphics, but with a start and expiration date. In your browser, it displays any graphic in your Web that you can reference with a URL during a stipulated time period, and it allows you to reference a graphic to be displayed before and after the stipulated period. In the FrontPage Editor, it also displays the graphic during the stipulated period but replaces it with the bracketed text *[Expired Scheduled Image]* before or after that. You might use the two WebBots together for new listings, highlighted by an animated GIF file.

◉ The **Scheduled Include WebBot** is just the Include WebBot with the start and expiration date functionality of the Scheduled Image WebBot.

◉ The **Search WebBot** generates an object that displays, in both the FrontPage Editor and your browser, the Search For text input form, the Start Search button, and the Clear button, which are the warm, beating heart of any FrontPage search form.

◉ The **Substitution WebBot** generates an object that displays the value of a selected configuration variable in both the FrontPage Editor and your browser. If the variable currently has no value, you'll see the variable name in square brackets in the FrontPage Editor; you won't see anything in your browser.

◉ The **Table of Contents WebBot** generates an object that, in your browser, displays an automatically generated list of all (nonhidden) HTML pages in the Web but displays only a generic table of contents in your FrontPage Editor.

◉ The **Timestamp WebBot** generates an object that displays the time of the last edit or update, in several formats, in both the FrontPage Editor and your browser.

Three more WebBot objects are inserted when you choose other commands from the Insert menu:

◉ Choose Comment to generate a WebBot object that displays user instructions in purple text in the Editor. These instructions will *not* appear in your browser, so they are useful only for intranet authors.

🌏 Choose HTML Markup to generate the WebBot object shown here:

This object contains HTML code that the FrontPage Editor *won't* be able to interpret. You use this WebBot to insert tags that the FrontPage Editor doesn't support—such as <IFRAME>, for floating frames, or the <LINK> tag, which enables style sheets. You can also use this WebBot to insert HTML that you want to make sure the FrontPage Editor won't re-edit "under the hood."

🌏 Choose Script to generate a WebBot object like the object for VBScript shown here:

This type of object contains VBScript, JavaScript, or any other client-side code the FrontPage Editor won't know what to do with (and will therefore try to strip away if you insert it directly by using the View Or Edit HTML window).

NOTE

If you add a Scheduled Image, Scheduled Include, or Timestamp WebBot, you'll receive a message alerting you that a WebBot has been modified for each instance of these WebBots every time you open the page (which it has, since the CGI script component of the WebBot has had to do a time check). Ignore these messages. Everything is working properly.

A Word to the Wise

A few other FrontPage Editor features deserve comment, not because they're hard to implement, but because they use HTML tags and attributes that aren't supported by all browsers. For example, marquees and table cell backgrounds are not displayed in the Netscape Navigator, and the <BLINK> font formatting doesn't show up in the Microsoft Internet Explorer family. But this will be only a minor inconvenience, since you're going to be previewing your work in all the applicable browsers.

Other c-o-o-o-l features, like background sound, AVI video clips, and third-party ActiveX controls, might make your users pay a price in terms of download time. Just to show you the problem, a spinning ONLINE.AVI file from an early incarnation of our intranet is included in the Images subfolder of the Chapter2 folder on this book's CD. It looked way cool for a few days, and then the performance hit that it caused every time we loaded up the page got to be a bit of a drag.

You've undoubtedly also gathered that the FrontPage Editor takes a very aggressive attitude toward HTML, changing code to meet its own standards. All in all, this is a great convenience, but there's one aspect of this ruthless editing that you must be aware of: the FrontPage Editor accepts *only* <TITLE> and <META> tags in the <HEAD> section of your document. We'll be putting our style-sheet links and VBScript in the body, which isn't quite up to international HTML Consortium standards but has the singular advantage of being stable in FrontPage.

CHAPTER 4

Building the
Sample Web

Jeffrey M. Jones

If you've read this far, you're probably itching to get started building a Web. And if you jumped ahead because you couldn't wait, that's OK, too—but there's information in the previous chapters about how Microsoft FrontPage 97 works, and you might want to go over it.

In this chapter, I'll provide hands-on explanations of how we built the sample intranet that you'll find on this book's CD. You'll find the samples relating to this chapter in the Chapter2 folder on the CD. I won't tell you everything (there isn't space), and I'm going to summarize the obvious stuff. (The FrontPage documentation is your best resource if stuff *doesn't* seem obvious.) But for best results, fire up your PC and follow along.

The first major section covers the basics. The first step will be to create a set of custom templates we'll use for all body text in our intranet. We'll then create the shell around the content: a framed home page with exploration bar and menus. You could stop right there and still build a fully functional intranet, but I'll also show you how to create a simple download page for corporate forms and templates.

CHAPTER 4

Then, in the next section, I'll show you three advanced projects, in which we'll use the full resources of FrontPage:

🌐 A news archive

🌐 A marketing catalog

🌐 A developer knowledge base

Since each of these advanced projects will actually be a sub-Web of our intranet main Web, we'll start at the top, in the <ROOT WEB> directory.

Creating a Boilerplate Web Page Template

If you're working with a clean, default FrontPage 97 installation, you'll see some subfolders and a file in the <ROOT WEB> directory in the FrontPage Explorer's Folder View. INDEX.HTM is a customizable home page created by default. We're not going to use this file, so you might want to delete it, along with the GIF files in the /IMAGES subfolder and anything else you don't need. Then add a new blank page to the <ROOT WEB> directory by opening a new Normal Page in the FrontPage Editor and saving it back to the <ROOT WEB> directory. Call the page STYLE.HTM.

Creating the Page Properties Style Sheet

The Page Properties command on the FrontPage Editor File menu invokes the Page Properties dialog box shown in Figure 4-1. The Page Properties dialog box lets you set the following characteristics of the current page:

🌐 General properties

    🌐 Location (URL)

    🌐 Title

    🌐 Base Location and Default Target Frame (the two attributes of the <BASE> tag)

    🌐 Background Sound (if any)

    🌐 HTML Encoding

🌐 Background

    🌐 Background colors or image

    🌐 Watermark

    🌐 Text and hyperlink colors

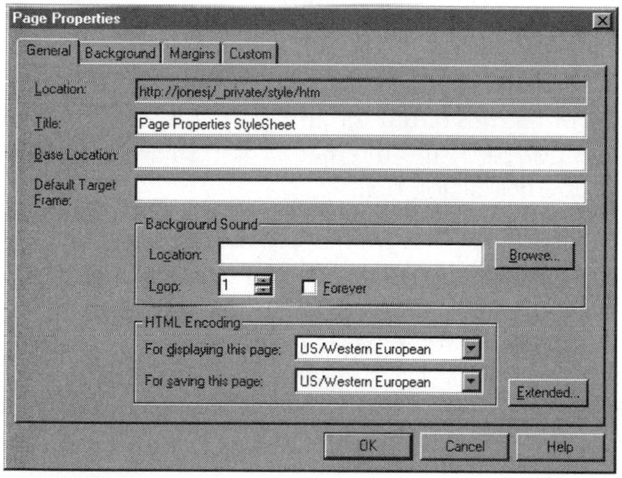

Figure 4-1

The Page Properties dialog box.

- 🌐 The URL of another page from which to copy these attributes (This is a custom feature of the FrontPage server that we'll use to establish a Page Properties style sheet for our intranet.)
- 🌐 Margins (in pixels)
  - 🌐 Top margin
  - 🌐 Left margin
- 🌐 Meta Information (two kinds of attributes of the <META> tag that appears in the <HEAD> section)
  - 🌐 System variables
  - 🌐 User variables

System variables use the HTTP-EQUIV=*value* and CONTENT=*value* attributes. You'd use this tag to assign keywords that some Webcrawlers look for to index URLs on the World Wide Web, or the ratings the Microsoft Internet Explorer supports. It's also used in client-pull, where the syntax is:

```
<META HTTP-EQUIV="refresh" CONTENT=5 URL="http://SecondPage.htm">
```

Unfortunately, you can't browse to the URL from the FrontPage interface, and without it you're only reloading the same page over and over. So if you want to use client-pull, you'll have to enter the URL of the second page manually.

User variables use the NAME=*value* and CONTENT=*value* attributes. They're principally added by HTML editing tools as a kind of signature. You could create user variables for authoring information, such as the name of your department, that might otherwise appear as HTML comments in your <HEAD> tag.

We're going to set the page properties for STYLE.HTM and then use it as the basis for the page properties of our intranet Page Template. All the standard <BODY> tags supported by the Internet Explorer can be configured through the Page Properties dialog box:

1. Select Page Properties from the File menu, click the Background tab, and change the background color to white and set the color of visited hyperlinks to match the unvisited hyperlink color. In an intranet, users are likely to visit some pages over and over. I find it distracting to have those links displayed in different colors in the table of contents. If you don't find this distracting, keep the colors different.

2. Click the Margins Tab, and click both check boxes. Set the top margin to 10 and the left margin to 15. I've added space at the top and left because ultimately all our content is going to appear within a borderless frame, and this gives the (pleasing, to me) effect of a margin.

3. The next step is to save the page again and move the file to the _PRIVATE subfolder. FrontPage Search and TOC WebBot components won't read the contents of directories with an underscore as the first character of their name, and since the FrontPage Explorer adds a _PRIVATE subfolder to any new Web you create, you can use relative URLs throughout your Webs as long you add a copy of the Page Properties style sheet to every _PRIVATE subfolder. The easiest way to move STYLE.HTM is by dragging and dropping in the FrontPage Explorer's Folder View. When you do, you'll see a message similar to the one shown here:

This message indicates that FrontPage is not only renaming the file but updating any links to the Web page. In fact, you should always use the FrontPage Explorer to move files between folders because it updates all links when you do. Once you've moved the file, make sure you can see it in the Folder View. If you can't, choose Web Settings from the Tools menu, click the Advanced tab, and check the Show Documents In Hidden Directories box. Once you do, the contents of _PRIVATE and other hidden subfolders will also be displayed in the FrontPage Editor, so you'll be able to create hyperlinks.

4. Return to the page in the FrontPage Editor, and view the General tab of the Page Properties dialog box. Even though users will never open the document directly in your Web, you still might want to add an identifying title in the Title field that will be displayed in the Explorer interface, such as "Page Properties StyleSheet."

> FrontPage applies Page properties by replacing the <BODY> tag in all documents linked to the style sheet with the style sheet's <BODY> tag. Once you link a page to the Page Properties style sheet, you will not be able to add modifications to the <BODY> tag in the linked page, including the Extended Attributes needed for Microsoft Visual Basic Scripting Edition (VBScript). Instead, you must make all such modifications in the Page Properties style sheet itself.

Creating the Boilerplate Template

Now that we have a Page Properties style sheet, we can attach it to a Web page with the standard text elements (or "boilerplate") we want to appear on every content page in our Web. You might want other elements, but here are the ones we're including:

- **Sample elements and basic page structure,** added as a guide to (or convenience for) subsequent authors. A well-designed boilerplate template will have enough elements to provide consistency without cluttering up the page.

- **Instructions for authors** (best practices, as well as warnings for objects that users must not delete).

- **A standardized footer with the timestamp.** Depending on the design of your intranet, you might want other elements (such as a watermark, a company logo, or an exploration bar) to appear on every page.

- **Default frame target names.** You might add other exploration elements (such as links to your home page, or exploration bars).

◉ **A boilerplate VBScript object and the extended <BODY> tag attributes needed to run the code.** Don't worry—I'll show you how to set up the page to run VBScript. You might also want to add JavaScript or ActiveX objects to your page.

It goes without saying (though I'll say it anyway) that every hour spent in template design can save you tens if not hundreds of hours later on. Be sure your design has all the necessary approvals before you roll it out. Your firm might be impatient to see an intranet up and running, but if hasty approval means you're going to change your collective minds later on, that just means extra work. One page template may not do the job. Remember, too, that I'm only showing you how to add basic features here. In practice, before you begin designing the page template, you'll need a good understanding not just of advanced features (such as scripting or ActiveX controls) but also of your overall Web and sub-Web structure. In an ideal universe you'd probably build the ideal template after the Web was complete. (Of course, in an ideal universe you'd live forever, and you wouldn't have a boss, either.)

We'll start building a boilerplate template by creating a new Normal page in the FrontPage Editor and then following these steps:

1. Choose Page Properties from the File menu, and click the Background tab. Choose Get Background And Colors From Page, click the Browse button, and choose _PRIVATE/STYLE.HTM.

2. Click the OK buttons until you return to your page in the FrontPage Editor. If you view the page in the View Or Edit HTML window, you'll see that the custom *stylesrc="_private/style.htm"* attribute has been added to the <BODY> tag. You won't, however, be able to see any changes to your page background in the FrontPage Editor. For that, you must preview your work in a browser, and you won't be able to do *that* until you save your page to your <ROOT WEB> directory.

3. Choose Save from the File menu. While you're at it, you might as well provide a page title (such as "Page Template") and filename (such as IntranetTemplate.htm). FrontPage will propose up to the first eight letters of the first word of your page title as the filename—but there's nothing to prevent you from using long filenames (just don't add any spaces). Don't save your file as a template yet. We have more boilerplate text to add, and a footer to create and include, before we're done. (In fact, the only way to see the page properties is to choose Preview In Browser from

the File menu, and that command is not available until you save.)
Click OK to save the page.

Figure 4-2 shows you what the completed boilerplate template will look like.

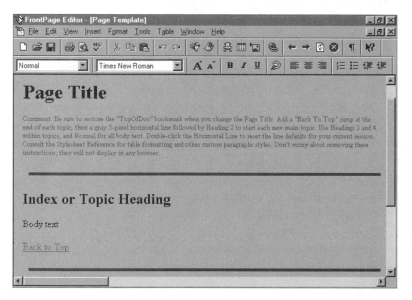

Figure 4-2

Boilerplate Page Template.

Here's a summary of what needs to be done to create the boilerplate template in Figure 4-2:

 Use Heading 1 for the page title, Heading 2 for the index or first heading paragraph, and Normal for the body text. The horizontal line has been reformatted to a 5-pixel gray line. It's there so users can reset the inherited defaults for each session.

 Add a bookmark (TopOfDoc) to the page title, as well as a hyperlink (Back To Top) to the bookmark.

 Insert a comment for the purple user instructions, and format the results in an 8-point font so it takes up less screen space. The Back To Top jump text is also too large, but we won't use the Format Font command to set the font to 8 points because the FrontPage Editor actually adds the <FONT SIZE=1> tag, which browsers won't necessarily render as 8-point text. Instead, we'll explicitly reformat the text once we've added the cascading style sheet, which is the next step.

Creating a Cascading Style Sheet

The FrontPage server uses the Page Properties style sheet to apply a single set of page and text-color definitions across all referenced pages in a Web. All Internet Explorer versions 3.0 and later can also use cascading style sheets to apply a single set of paragraph and font definitions across Web pages.

Cascading style sheets are just text files (not necessarily HTML files) that contain definitions for the attributes for most (but not all) HTML text tags. Not only can you set the size, color, alignment, indentation, and other characteristics of <H> (header) and <P> (paragraph) styles, you can also define these characteristics *differently* in classes of substyles for each tag, such as the P.8 and P.7 classes we'll use in our style sheet. In short, style sheets make it possible to achieve some of the precision in layout and formatting that your users have come to expect from their Microsoft Word documents. Nevertheless, you can't define the characteristics of certain tags (such as the horizontal line <HR>) at all. A complete rundown of all style sheet–related syntactical rules and limitations is far beyond the scope of this chapter. You'll find everything you need at the following location:

http://www.microsoft.com/workshop/author/howto/cssf.htm

In the meantime, here are a few points to watch out for when you're using cascading style sheets on your intranet:

- Only Microsoft Internet Explorer 3.0 and later support style sheets and the related <STYLE> blocks and inline style definitions that use the same syntax. If you're using an earlier version of Microsoft Internet Explorer or Netscape Navigator 3.0, you might want to skip style sheets altogether or consider supplementing style sheets with <BASEFONT> tags.

- Style-sheet definitions are rendered by the browser. If you've specified a font that isn't available to a user's browser, the browser will substitute as best it can. As a rule, then, use only standard Microsoft Windows fonts in addition to a few other fonts (such as Verdana) that are part of Internet Explorer itself.

- Style-sheet syntax is buggy. Some definitions, for example, work in one order but don't work in another order.

- Style sheets "cascade" because style definitions are inherited— that is, attributes established in a parent tag (such as <BODY>) apply to all child tags within the parent tag unless further definitions have been applied (either in the definition of the child tags or via style classes or direct formatting in the HTML of the page itself). As much as possible, limit style-sheet definitions to the standard HTML tags, since they will take effect without any additional coding. You might, however, want to define several classes of tables with different font sizes because once the style class is applied to the <TABLE> tag, the font specifications will affect the nested <TR> and <TD> tags within the table. Similarly, you can define different classes of <OL> (ordered list) and <UL> (unordered list) tags, which all share the common <LI> (list item) tag.

🌐 You apply style-sheet classes as extended attributes in FrontPage. FrontPage does not support extended attributes for some HTML tags, such as <LI> and <TH>. Be careful to test all your style definitions in FrontPage before rolling out your style sheet, and provide your authors with a style-sheet reference, since they'll have to enter extended attributes manually.

🌐 Style-sheet definitions can be overridden by explicit style definitions in your pages, which applications like the FrontPage Editor and Microsoft Word sometimes supply automatically (and as part of some commands, too). Provide your authors with best practices to minimize the introduction of explicit style formatting in source documents.

Oh, yes—you'll need a good, up-to-date HTML reference.

Configuring Your Style-Sheet Editor

In theory, you could add cascading style sheets to your Page Properties template. There are, however, two very good reasons why you don't want to use the FrontPage Editor to work with cascading style sheets:

🌐 Style sheets are even simpler than HTML files. They don't even use HTML tags. Since you're just writing lines of code, the FrontPage Editor confers no special advantage.

🌐 You *will* be using punctuation such as quotation marks, however, which the FrontPage Editor is quite capable of converting into HTML as """ and thereby screwing up your style sheet.

We'll use Microsoft WordPad as our style-sheet editor and assign the special file extension CSS to WordPad so that FrontPage will always use that application to edit style sheets:

1. Choose Options from the FrontPage Explorer's Tools menu, select the Configure Editors tab, and click the Add Button.

CHAPTER 4

2. Enter the file type, editor name, and the path and command to run the editor in the Add Editor Association dialog box so it looks like this:

Add Editor Association

File Type: .css

Editor Name: Word Pad

Command: C:\Program Files\Accessories\Wordpad.exe   Browse...

OK   Cancel   Help

3. When you click the OK button, you'll see the new association in the Configure Editors tab of the Options dialog box, as shown here:

Options

General | Proxies | Configure Editors

Type: Editor:

htm	FrontPage Editor (C:\Program Files\Microsol
html	FrontPage Editor (C:\Program Files\Microsol
htx	FrontPage Editor (C:\Program Files\Microsol
asp	FrontPage Editor (C:\Program Files\Microsol
frm	FrontPage Frames Wizard (C:\Program Files
idc	FrontPage Database Connection Wizard (C:
	Text Editor (notepad.exe)
.css	WordPad (C:\Program Files\Accessories\W

Add...

Modify...

Remove

OK   Cancel   Help

4. Click OK, then return to the FrontPage Editor, create a new Normal page, and save it with the CSS extension to the _PRIVATE folder. As you can see, you can type the relative URL (folder and page name) directly in the Save As dialog box:

5. When you click OK, FrontPage displays a warning that the URL is not valid. This warning occurs because pages with custom file extensions don't display in the FrontPage Editor; but since you won't be using the FrontPage Editor to open the file, you can ignore this warning and click Yes to save the page.

6. Return to the FrontPage Explorer, and double-click the file to open the style sheet in WordPad. You'll see that FrontPage has inserted default HTML Web page tags, all of which you can delete. Now you're ready to start typing style-sheet definitions.

Let's Go to the Code!

Here's the style sheet used in the sample intranet that you'll find on this book's CD. It's pretty simple and should make sense even if you know nothing about style-sheet syntax. We defined the six heading styles as Verdana, with Arial as the substitute. (Because Internet Explorer 3.0 and later is currently the only browser that supports both style sheets *and* Verdana, the substitute style is actually redundant.) We defined the default <P> tag as 10-point Arial and created three subclasses, which we'll use for Back To Top jumps, footer text, and internal hyperlinks, respectively. There are four classes of tables and three table heads. Note that the table subhead and heads have reversed text and background colors and can be defined as classes of either the <TH> or the <TR> tags. We created two classes of numbered and bulleted lists. Each of these two classes has a second-level nested indent, but the Compact class has defined line spacing. Finally, we created our own custom definitions for the <CITE>, <BLOCKQUOTE>, and Definition List tags. You might also want to use rare tags like <XMP> or <TT> differently from the way they were originally intended to be used. Here's the code:

```
H1 {font: 18pt "Verdana, Arial";}
H2 {font: 16pt "Verdana, Arial";}
H3 {font: 14pt "Verdana, Arial";}
H4 {font: 12pt "Verdana, Arial";}
H5 {font: 11pt "Verdana, Arial";}
H6 {font: 10pt "Verdana, Arial";}
BODY {font: 10pt "Arial";}
P {font: 10pt "Arial";}
P.8 {font: 8pt "Arial";}
P.7 {font: 7pt "Arial";}
P.HREF {font: extra-bold 8.5pt "Arial"}

TABLE {font: 8pt "Arial";}
TABLE.10{font: 10pt "Arial";}
TABLE.85 {font: 8.5pt "Arial";}
TH, TR.HEAD{font: bold 9pt "arial";color: white; background: gray}
TH.10, TR.HEAD10 {font: bold 11pt "arial";color: white;
                  background: gray}
TH.8, TH.HEAD8 {font: extra-bold 8pt "arial";color: white;
            background: gray; text-align: left}
TH.SUBHEAD, TR.SUBHEAD {font: bold 9pt "arial";color: black;
                  background: silver}

UL, OL {font: 9pt "Arial";}
UL.Compact, OL.Compact {font: 9pt/11pt "Arial";}
UL.1 OL.1{font: 9pt "Arial";text-indent: ".25 in";}
UL.1Compact OL.1Compact{font: 9pt/11pt "Arial";
                  text-indent: ".25 in";}

CITE, BLOCKQUOTE{font: 9pt "Arial";}

DT {font: extra-bold 10pt "Verdana";}
DD {font: 9pt "Arial";}
```

> **!** When you edit your style sheet by launching a text editor, FrontPage actually opens a separate copy that it creates in the TEMP subdirectory of its program files. You can save all you want, but your changes won't take effect until you choose Save As and save the file back to its location on your Web. Be sure to save it as a text document.

Attaching the Style Sheet

Now that we have a style sheet, we need to attach it to our template. You attach style sheets with the HTML <LINK> tag, typically in the <HEAD>

section of your template page. Unfortunately, FrontPage doesn't support the <LINK> tag from its interface; but don't despair—there are at least three easy workarounds.

The World Wide Web Consortium (W3C) implements the <LINK> tag in the <HEAD> section of the Web page, and there are a couple of good reasons to conform to their standards. If you add the style-sheet link to the head, it will load in your browser—thereby making its style definitions available—before the <BODY> text is rendered. And on a more prosaic level, tags in the <HEAD> don't appear in the FrontPage Editor and are therefore less likely to be accidentally clobbered.

Because you have no fear of HTML (heh heh heh), just choose HTML from the FrontPage Editor View menu and type a <LINK> tag with the appropriate attributes directly in the <HEAD> section of your template page. As an example, here's how the first few lines of our sample content page template would look with the <LINK> tag added:

```
<!DOCTYPE HTML PUBLIC "-//IETF//DTD HTML//EN">

<html>

<head>
<meta name="GENERATOR" content="Microsoft FrontPage 2.0">
<title>Untitled Intranet Content Page</title>
<meta name="FORMATTER" content="Microsoft FrontPage 2.0">
<LINK REL="STYLESHEET" TYPE="text/css" HREF="../_private/css1.css">
</head>
```

A style-sheet <LINK> requires three attributes, two of which—REL and TYPE—must always be "stylesheet" and "text/css," respectively. The HREF attribute, of course, supplies the URL of your style sheet, which in this case is the most common *relative* URL, since pages created from the template will be in subfolders of the Web root, parallel to the _PRIVATE subfolder. Just be aware that you will always have to edit this URL manually to change it. Because FrontPage doesn't support style-sheet links, it won't automatically update the HREF attribute when you move pages up or down subfolder levels.

Alternatively, you can always insert your style-sheet <LINK> in an HTML Markup object in the body of your template page. The syntax of the tag is the same, and you'll want to add it at the top of the page so that it loads as quickly as possible. Because the Markup object is visible and vulnerable, it's a good idea to add a FrontPage comment, too, as shown in Figure 4-3.

If you want a style-sheet link that *will* update automatically, though, you might want to consider the truly baroque option of adding *all* your style-sheet definitions within a <STYLE> tag in an HTML Markup object at the top of an included header (that is, a document you then add to your page

CHAPTER 4

HTML Markup object

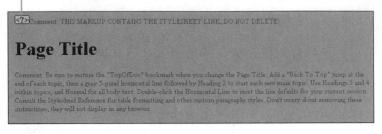

Comment: THIS MARKUP CONTAINS THE STYLESHEET LINK, DO NOT DELETE!

Page Title

Comment: Be sure to restore the "TopOfDoc" bookmark when you change the Page Title. Add a "Back To Top" jump at the end of each topic, then a gray 5-pixel horizontal line followed by Heading 2 to start each new main topic. Use Headings 3 and 4 within topics, and Normal for all body text. Double-click the Horizontal Line to reset the line defaults for your current session. Consult the Stylesheet Reference for table formatting and other custom paragraph styles. Don't worry about removing these instructions; they will not display in any browser.

Figure 4-3
Page Template with HTML Markup for style sheet link.

template with the FrontPage Include WebBot). True, there's a bit more work at the outset, but in exchange, you'll be able to maintain all your definitions in a single source, which will update automatically yet still be edited from the FrontPage interface. If you're interested, you can examine INCLUDEDHEADER.HTM in the Chapter 2 folder of our sample Web on the book's CD to see how it's done.

Just be aware that regardless of the method you use to create your stylesheet link, the style definitions won't appear in the FrontPage Editor (or indeed, in any other browser that doesn't support style sheets). Instead, save your page to the Web, and then choose Preview In Browser from the FrontPage Editor File menu. As you'll see in Figure 4-4, the styles have changed the appearance of the <H1>, <H2>, and <P> tags, without any additional HTML attributes.

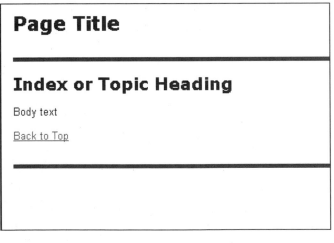

Page Title

Index or Topic Heading

Body text

Back to Top

Figure 4-4
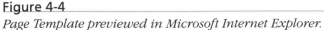
Page Template previewed in Microsoft Internet Explorer.

Adding Styled Text to Your Template

Of course, our style sheet also has classes, which have to be added as extended attributes of existing tags. I'll show you how easy this is to do by styling the Back To Top hyperlink:

1. With the template page open in the FrontPage Editor, select the Back To Top paragraph, and choose Paragraph from the Format menu.

2. In the Paragraph Properties dialog box, click the Extended button to invoke the Extended Attributes dialog box.

3. Click the Add button in the Extended Attributes dialog box, and enter the name CLASS and the value of the style class you want. In this case, we'll use a value of 8 to designate the P.8 class, which is defined in our style sheet as 8-point Arial.

Again, you won't see the style take effect in the FrontPage Editor. Figure 4-5 shows what it looks like when you save your page and preview it in Internet Explorer 3.0.

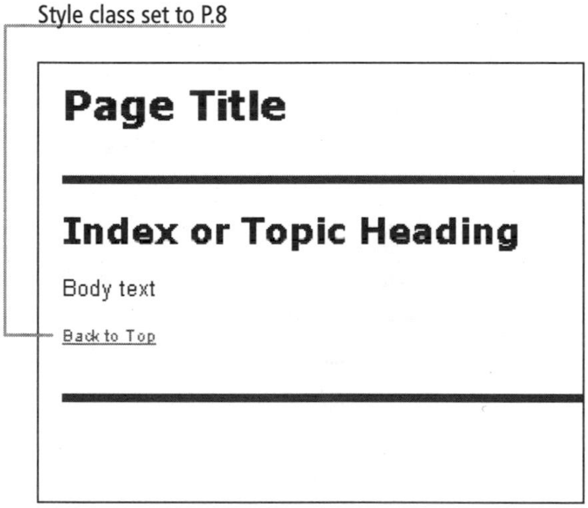

Style class set to P.8

Page Title

Index or Topic Heading

Body text

Back to Top

Figure 4-5

Page Template previewed in Internet Explorer after setting the style class for the Back To Top paragraph.

You apply other style classes in the same way. For instance, if you select a table and apply the extended 85 class attribute, all the text in the table displays as 8.5-point Arial. To add a gray background and change the font to bold, 9-point Arial, white, select the top row and apply the extended HEAD9 attribute.

Including the Footer

You'll often see standard information at the bottom of Web pages. In our intranet, we're going to start by inserting the Web name and the date of last modification. We could, of course, add these as boilerplate, but if we ever changed the name of our Web, we'd have to go back and edit every single page.

Fortunately, there's a better way. The FrontPage Substitution WebBot lets you define parameters (or "configuration variables"), which can be used throughout your Web but will update automatically when you redefine a parameter in the FrontPage Explorer. And since we might want to change the content or layout of the footer itself, we'll create a single instance of the footer as a separate page and then use the Include WebBot to insert it in our template. That way, all we'll have to do is change the footer page, and FrontPage will automatically update every page on the basis of the template in which the footer has been included.

We'll start by defining a new parameter:

1. Choose Web Settings from the FrontPage Explorer's Tools menu, and click the Parameters tab.

2. Click the Add button, and then enter the name and value of each Web parameter in the Add Name And Value dialog box. As shown here, we're assigning the value *MMA OnLine!* to the Web Name parameter.

Add Name and Value dialog box showing Name: Web Name and Value: MMA OnLine! with OK, Cancel, and Help buttons.

3. Click OK until you've returned to the FrontPage Explorer.

Many FrontPage Web Wizards create Web parameters for you, but since we're working in the <ROOT WEB> directory, we'll have to create them all from scratch. Later on, we'll add parameters for section names, and these will appear in the footers of custom templates for some sections of our Web. We'll also add parameters for product information, which we'll use later in this chapter in the Marketing Catalog project.

Now we'll create the Included Footer page and insert the parameters and other footer data in a table:

1. Create a new Normal Web page in the FrontPage Editor.

2. Insert a one-row, two-column table that is 100 percent the width of the page, with border size set to 0. To apply the footer style from the cascading style sheet, click the Extended button and add an extended attribute named *CLASS* with the value *Footer.*

3. With your cursor in the left table cell, choose WebBot Component from the Insert menu. Choose Substitution from the Insert WebBot Component list, and click OK. The WebBot Substitution Component Properties dialog box appears.

4. Choose Web Name from the Substitute With list and click OK. The value of Web Name, MMA Online!, is inserted in the first column.

5. Enter a colon and the word *modified* in the first column immediately following MMA Online! Once again choose WebBot Component from the Insert menu, and then choose Timestamp from the Insert WebBot Component list. This brings up the WebBot Timestamp Component Properties dialog box.

6. Change the Date Format field to display the date as Month day, year (April 23, 1997). Click OK.

7. We use Microsoft Exchange as the e-mail client for our intranet, so we can't create an e-mail link from the FrontPage interface (which only allows you to create Mailto hyperlinks to a URL, in the World Wide Web tab). Instead, we'll add the link with the HTML Markup WebBot, using the Exchange post office address of the Webmaster. Click in the right-hand column of the table. Select HTML Markup from the Insert menu, and enter the Mailto HREF, as shown here:

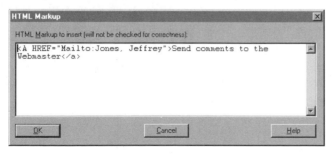

Click OK.

8. With your cursor in the right-hand cell of the table, choose Cell Properties from the Table menu. In the Cell Properties dialog box, choose Horizontal Alignment Right and Vertical Alignment Top, and then click OK.

9. Click in the left-hand cell, again choose Cell Properties from the Table menu, choose Vertical Alignment Top, and then click OK.

10. Add a comment and a 5-pixel gray horizontal rule at the top of the page. The final result as it appears in the FrontPage Editor is shown here:

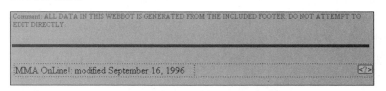

11. Save the footer as INCLUDEDFOOTER.HTM in the _PRIVATE subfolder so it won't appear in any WebBot-generated Table Of Contents or Search pages.

Once a page has been saved to your Web, you can include it in any other page by choosing WebBot Component from the FrontPage Editor's Insert menu, choosing Include from the Insert WebBot Component list, and either clicking the Browse button or entering the URL directly in the WebBot Include Component Properties dialog box. When we include the footer in our Page Template, we should also delete the gray horizontal line above the included footer. The final result of including our Intranet Footer as a WebBot component into our Page Template, as previewed in Internet Explorer, is shown in Figure 4-6. As you look at the figure, notice that the page properties in STYLE.HTM, as well as the style definitions in CSS1.CSS, which have been applied to the page template, are also automatically applied to the included footer, even without direct links to either style sheet in INCLUDEDFOOTER.HTM itself.

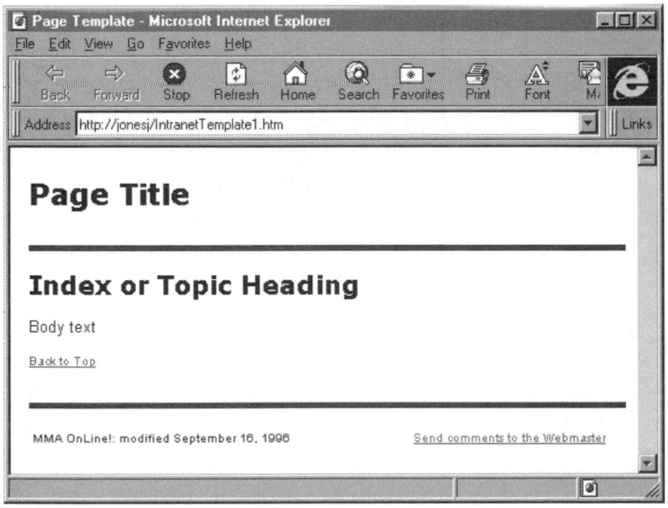

Figure 4-6

Page Template with the included footer as previewed in Internet Explorer.

Adding Script Shells

In our intranet, the default Home page consists of two frames, called Content and Menu. All content is displayed in the Content frame, which is to the right of the smaller Menu frame. The Menu frame displays the menu of all the other documents in the section. What if we want the section menu in the frame on the left to be updated whenever a user jumps to a new document in the Content frame on the right? What we can do for now is add the elements that are needed in order for content pages to work in the framed environment:

1. From the FrontPage Explorer's Tools menu, choose Web Settings, and then choose the Advanced tab and select VBScript from the Validation Scripts drop-down list. Now you can be sure that Microsoft Visual Basic, Scripting Edition is the default scripting language for your Web. Once you've configured your Web for VBScript, you can add VBScript to individual pages.

2. In the FrontPage Editor, place your cursor at the top of the Page Template, and choose Script from the Insert menu. Check the VBScript option, and add the first and last lines of a "shell" Onload routine in the Script input box, as shown here:

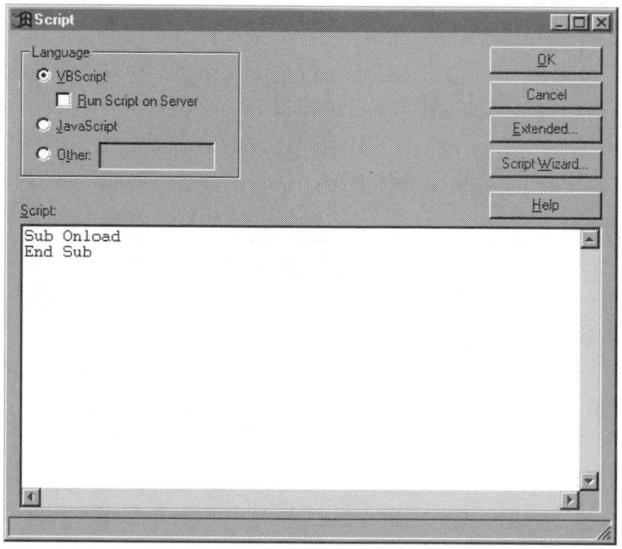

Okay, even if you've never seen a line of Visual Basic before, you can probably guess that our little subroutine isn't going to do much yet. But you could add all the nifty code in the world, and it would still just sit there like a good dog, waiting until you *call* it. In this case, calling our subroutine to run when the page is first loaded is as easy as adding two extended attributes to the <BODY> tag.

1. Choose Page Properties from the FrontPage Editor File menu.

2. In the General tab of the Page Properties dialog box, click the Extended button.

3. In the Extended Attributes dialog box, click the Add button.

4. In the Name/Value Pair dialog box, shown here, add the name "Language" and the value "VB Script," and then click the OK button.

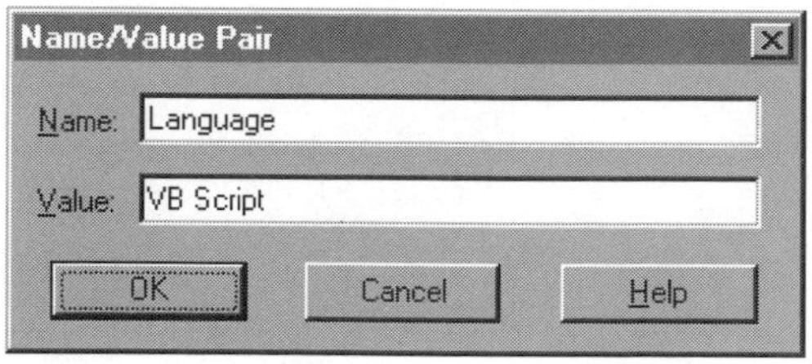

5. In the Extended Attributes dialog box, click the Add button.

6. In the Name/Value Pair dialog box, add the name "Onload" and the value "Onload," and then click the OK button. The Extended Attributes dialog box shown here has these two additions to the Body tag:

7. Click the OK button to return to the Page Properties dialog box.

All subroutines have to be called—that is, explicitly told when to begin. Routines can be called directly through code statements that say, in effect, "Call the routine named XYZ" or that associate the routine with generic Windows events such as button clicks. Technically speaking, our extended attributes associate the Onload subroutine with an Onload event that fires when the Internet Explorer *window* loads the document. But you can think of it this way: as Internet Explorer interprets the HTML of the <BODY> tag, the Language attribute warns it to look for VBScript code, and then the Onload attribute tells Internet Explorer that it's time to call the designated subroutine . . . which just happens to be named Onload.

As long as you've got the Page Properties dialog box open, you can also designate the Default Target Frame for content documents. Select Page Properties from the File menu to open the Page Properties dialog box. On the General tab you can designate the Default Target Frame for content documents. (You can always enter the name even if you haven't created or named the frame yet.) Just be aware that the target is the default frame that Internet Explorer uses to load all the links on the current page—that is, when you jump to another page. (The default target frame will be the frame in which the current page loads only if it's also the default target of every page *from which you jump* to the current page.)

You could assign an explicit Default Target Frame name, but the Internet Explorer also recognizes four relative names:

- **_blank,** which loads the link to a new blank, unnamed window (and, in effect, jumps out of the framed environment)

- **_parent,** which loads the link into the immediate parent of the current document (if any)

- **_top,** which removes all frames and loads the link into the full body of the window

- **_self,** which loads the link in the same window in which the link was clicked, and is the option we used

Saving the Master Page Templates

Once you've created and added all the elements to your master page, the last step is to save it as a template. You should always be sure that this *is* in fact the last step, since it's a little more difficult to open a template and make further edits once you've saved the template.

To save your master page as a template, choose Save As from the File menu, and then click the As Template button. In the Save As Template dialog box (see Figure 4-7), enter both the title you want users to see in the New Page dialog box and the name of the template file and subdirectory (without the HTM extension), and then click the OK button.

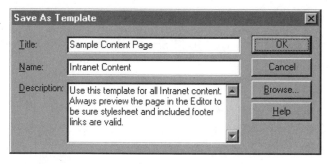

Figure 4-7
Save As Template dialog box.

When you save a Web page as a template, FrontPage creates a new subfolder called *YOURTEMPLATENAME*.TEM in the PAGES subfolder of the Microsoft FrontPage folder. You can easily determine the full path in your environment from the Most Recently Used file list at the bottom of the

FrontPage Editor's File menu. Inside the folder you'll find two files: *YOUR-TEMPLATENAME*.HTM (the Web page) and *YOURTEMPLATENAME*.INF (a text file with the title and description that appear in the New Page dialog box). If you want to make further edits to a template, open the file and save it under the same name and title.

That's all you'd have to do to create a simple boilerplate template, but our template has several kinds of links. You'll have to decide how you want to handle them before closing the file in the FrontPage Editor.

Launch the View Or Edit HTML window by selecting HTML from the View menu, and scroll down in the document to where you see the HTML markup for the Back To Top hyperlink, above the markup for the Include WebBot that generates the included footer, as shown in Figure 4-8. Depending on how you inserted the Back To Top hyperlink, you might have included an absolute reference to the HTML file (as in Figure 4-8), as well as the fragment identifier (#TopOfDoc) that refers to the bookmark (technically, an anchor tag using the Name attribute). Obviously, when we create new pages from the template, we don't want the Back To Top hyperlink to take the user back to the original INTRANETTEMPLATE1.HTM file (if it even exists), so use the HTML Editor to review all hyperlink jumps in your template. Make sure that each one points to a relative URL, and save your changes if you need to.

Figure 4-8
HTML markup for template references.

The Include WebBot reference—like the Stylesrc attribute in the <BODY> tag that creates the Page Properties style-sheet link—is more problematic. FrontPage, in saving the file, converts the relative URL to an absolute URL, using the HTTP protocol. The good news is that this reference will continue to work for the current Web. The bad news is that in any other Web, the URL "http://jonesj/_private/pagestyle.htm" will still be valid but won't display the footer, because the Personal Web Server, which interprets the WebBot code at browse time, won't have access to the referenced subfolder. When you choose Validate Hyperlinks from the FrontPage Explorer's Tools menu, the link will be displayed as valid (which it is, after all), but when you preview the page in your intranet browser, you'll simply see the URL. As you can see in Figure 4-9, the link to the Page Properties style sheet also can't be found. (The *cascading* style sheet, however, does attach because no Personal Web Server functionality is required to generate the link.)

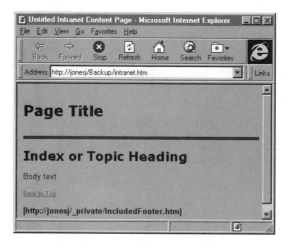

Figure 4-9

Invalid Include WebBot links.

Since this issue arises only in sub-Webs, and since you're *always* going to preview your work in the FrontPage Editor, you'll be able to fix the problem quickly when and if it occurs by taking the following steps:

1. Be sure that you have copied the necessary style sheets and included documents to your sub-Web.

2. Choose HTML from the FrontPage Editor's View menu, and convert all absolute references to relative references, removing the HTTP protocol as well. (You can also select any Include WebBot and change its properties in the FrontPage Editor, but the <BODY STYLSRC> attribute can be changed only in the HTML itself.)

3. Choose Save from the FrontPage Editor's File menu to update the server, and then choose Preview In Browser from the File menu.

4. Return to the FrontPage Explorer, and choose Recalculate Hyperlinks from the Tools menu.

NOTE Even if you update the references in the Web page, you won't see changes that affect FrontPage server processes until you recalculate the hyperlinks in your Web. Refreshing the document in your browser won't work, either.

If you don't like this kludgy approach, consider the following alternatives:

🌐 Use a text editor to create relative (or invalid) references in the template. You will not be able to do this in the FrontPage View Or Edit HTML window, which corrects these "mistakes" for you. (Of course, when you create new pages from the template, you'll get an error message for each Include WebBot, but both the included document and the style-sheet references *will* be displayed as broken links in the FrontPage Editor.) Choose Verify Hyperlinks from the FrontPage Explorer's Tools menu, and click the Verify button. Then select each broken link, and click the Edit Link button. The only real advantage to this approach is that all broken links can be fixed at the same time, but against this you must weigh the disadvantage of generating confusing error messages whenever a new page is created.

🌐 Instead of using the Page Properties style sheet, set the equivalent attributes in the <BODY> tag of the template itself, and then replace included documents with document write-ins, using VBScript. The advantage of this approach is true portability across Webs and sub-Webs. Against this, weigh the maintenance disadvantage of having to update each page if you want new properties or footer data.

🌐 Create a simple Web Template by copying your custom template subfolder and its contents to the WEBS subfolder of the Microsoft FrontPage folder. Add any style sheets to the new subfolder. (Do *not* create subfolders within your template subfolder.) Change the referenced file names so they start with the underscore character (for example, _INCLUDEDFOOTER.HTM), and use a text editor to create relative URLs for each link in the template. Unlike Page Templates, Web Templates also copy all files with valid local references from the template folder to the target folder on your Web. Against this advantage, weigh the disadvantage of being able to add new pages only from the FrontPage Explorer (and having to remember to check the Add To The Current Web option when you first create a new Web).

CHAPTER 4

🌐 Save your template to a template subfolder in your Web. Of course, you won't be able to access it with the File New command; you'll have to open the file and save it under a new name.

🌐 Create a custom FrontPage Wizard in Visual Basic or C++. Against the advantage of this, the only true nonkludge approach, consider the relative poverty of the available methods (all are listed in the FrontPage Software Development Kit, available from Microsoft), and the disadvantage of having to learn C++ and Visual Basic if you don't already know them.

There's No Such Thing As an Empty Web

Now that you've created a template, you can delete it from your Web, in which case you might (momentarily) have an empty <ROOT WEB> directory. If so, what will you see when you point your browser to it?

Remember that a Web is a response made by a server to a client. If your browser requests a specific file that doesn't exist, the FrontPage server displays an error message. When your browser requests a Web for which FrontPage has no default Home page, however, the server generates a clickable list of all files and subdirectories in the Web's root. The example shown in Figure 4-10 includes the _PRIVATE, _CGI_BIN, and IMAGES

Figure 4-10
A list of folders and files in the <ROOT WEB> displayed in Internet Explorer.

subfolders of the <ROOT WEB> directory, as well as the ARCHIVE, BACKUP, EDITORTEMPLATES, and INTRANETDEMO *directories* that represent sub-Webs. Since the "page" is actually generated on the fly, there's not much you can do in the way of formatting; you might use the functionality as a mock-FTP (File Transfer Protocol) Template Download site, but later in this chapter I can show you a much classier way of doing the same thing.

Toolbars and Menus

Now that we have a way to create consistent content, we need to examine the problem of navigation—or (since hyperlinks are essentially the only way to navigate) we need to examine ways of mapping our content. Anyone who has ever spent five minutes on the World Wide Web (make that ten minutes, since five minutes were probably spent just downloading images) knows how quickly the thrill of jumping from site to site leads to bewilderment, confusion, boredom, irritation, frustration, and, ultimately, ALT+F4 (shut down). Almost from the beginning, to alleviate this problem, Webs have provided users with structured hyperlinks: a map of jumps displayed throughout a Web to impose a system of exploration based on a hierarchy of content.

With the advent of graphical browsers, text maps gave way to images: buttons, bars, and (for a while, though this trend seems to be waning) the Home page, where an elaborate picture contained multiple hot spots. But the idea remained the same: users need an intuitive map that not only makes it easy to move through a Web but also tells them what they can expect to find.

If we don't spend much time on graphics in this chapter, it's not because the issues are trivial. Even such issues as image size, image format, and palette matching quickly become arcane, and whole books have quite properly been devoted to design, the use of advanced graphical tools—and don't even *start* with VRML (Virtual Reality Modeling Language)! In fact, Microsoft is introducing its own suite of advanced drawing and image-manipulation applications, including the Microsoft Image Composer and the Microsoft Internet Studio (long known as "Blackbird"), for high-end users. But high-end graphics are also labor-intensive and might be more appropriate as an advertising element in a commercial Web site than they are in an intranet devoted to disseminating information. We're going to rely on graphics only sparingly, and I'll show you how to get the job done effectively with very simple methods.

TIP   Microsoft's recommendation is to keep total page size, including graphics, to 40 KB or less.

Our navigational system will consist of a common exploration bar and a series of menus. The exploration bar will contain links to all sections of our intranet. Each section will also have a menu that lists all the documents in that section. The exploration bar will always be displayed above any document. Each section menu will always be displayed to the left of any document in that section. Clicking a button on the exploration bar will display the section menu to the left and a section-content or "Home" page, both of which will have links to documents in the section.

First I'll show you how to build a simple, colorful set of buttons and menus. Later in this chapter, I'll explain how they fit together with content pages. Later on in this book, you'll learn how to add VBScript to create a truly dynamic site in which menus are refreshed automatically as users jump *between* pages.

Client-Side Image Maps

What's a client-side image map, and why would you want one? You probably know that a hyperlink is just an HTML anchor (<A>) tag containing a valid URL, wrapped around some additional text that your browser displays as a hot spot. In other words, it looks something like this:

```
<A HREF="www.microsoft.com">Where do you want to go today?</A>
```

The magic (what magic there is) lies in the fact that your browser can render the HTML as a hot spot and interpret the HTML so that a mouse click over the hot spot generates an HTTP request to the specified URL. Image hot spots aren't significantly more magical, but the magic can occur in other places.

In order to create hot spots in an image, you must first create an image map, assigning various regions of the image, as defined by coordinates, to various URLs. The image map, then, is just a text file listing coordinates and associated URLs. In the case of image hot spots, the map is separate from the image, so a really interesting question comes up: Where does the click meet the map? Surprisingly, the answer until not so long ago was "On the server." The client browser would simply pass back coordinate data from the mouse click, and the server would look up the URL in the map—a process known as server-side image mapping. Obviously, client-side image mapping would require the map to be sent with the image to a browser capable of making its own mappings. But even very large image maps are small in comparison to Web pages, so there is a significant net speed advantage in processing image clicks locally, which is why state-of-the-art browsers like Internet Explorer support client-side image mapping, and why we'll use it in our intranet.

NOTE

Would you be terribly surprised to learn that there are several different types of image maps, all working more or less the same way but all incompatible with the others? Not if you've encountered the vast array of incompatible graphics formats: format incompatibility is evidently a natural law of computer graphics.

The FrontPage Editor comes with its own built-in image-mapping utility, but you configure the image-mapping format for each Web from the FrontPage Explorer. Choose Web Settings from the FrontPage Explorer's Tools menu, and click the Advanced tab (see Figure 4-11). You'll see a list of various Image Map styles, but since our intranet will be running on a server with FrontPage extensions, there's no reason not to choose the FrontPage style. Be sure to check the Generate Client-Side Image Maps box, too. That's all there is to it; the FrontPage Image Editor will do the rest for you.

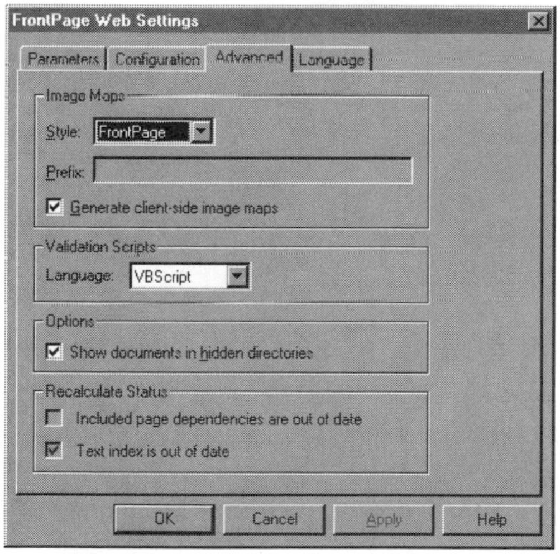

Figure 4-11
Image Map settings in the FrontPage Explorer's Web Settings dialog box.

Building the Exploration Bar

There are two ways you could build an exploration bar: as a single image with clickable hot spots, or as an HTML file with smaller graphics for each button (this is the way the FrontPage Wizards build an exploration bar). If you want to use complex graphics, the single-image approach is best; the advantages of the composite table-and-button approach include smaller overall file size and "tool tips," and Internet Explorer gives you enough control over cell formatting to create the graphics effects.

Before creating any Web graphics in our sample intranet, which you'll find on this book's CD, we established a simple 256-color palette for our Web, which we saved as a PAL file. Our two graphics tools—the Microsoft Image Composer and PaintShop Pro IV—required separate palettes, but we made sure that both had the custom colors in the same numeric sequence. We needed only five colors, but we used Stephen LeHunte's Color Wizard to convert the RGB (red, green, blue) values used by our graphics tools to the hexadecimal values used on our Web pages. Table 4-1 shows our custom palette.

Table 4-1 Custom Palette Settings for MMA's Intranet.

Color	RGB Value	Hexadecimal Value
MMA blue	0,51,102	#003366
Dark red highlight	153,0,1	#990000
Dark gray	153,153,153	#999999
Light gray	204,204,204	#CCCCCC
Terracotta	239,214,198	#EFD6D6
Mustard	255,255,204	#FFFFCC
Ochre	231,231,214	#E7E7D6

To give our color scheme some logic, we'll use the pastels to distinguish different sections, and we'll reserve the remaining four colors for the exploration and menu framework. The most important color choice, however, will be to replace the default gray background of our Web pages with white. We'll add white space liberally throughout our intranet, to keep the pages easy to read.

We'll start by creating a new page in our <ROOT WEB> directory, using the Normal Page Template, and we'll save the new page to the _PRIVATE subdirectory as NAVBAR.HTM. Don't attach the page to the Page Properties style sheet—since the exploration bar will be displayed in a frame, we don't want the style sheet top and left margin settings—but do choose Page Properties from the FrontPage Editor's File menu, set the page background color to the custom dark gray (153,153,153), and set the top and left margins to 0. Then choose Insert Table from the Table menu, and create a two-row, six-column table with left alignment, Border Size at 0, Cell Padding (the space around the table) set at 5, and Cell Spacing (the space between the cell border and its contents) set at 2. Since we'll resize our table to fit the buttons later on, be sure the Specify Table Width option isn't selected.

We used the Microsoft Image Composer to create the template for our rectangular exploration buttons, placing a solid-color rectangle on top of a larger gradient ramp, which created the blue shading in the lower right corner, and we saved the image as a GIF file. If your server is running and you have an open Web in the FrontPage Explorer, you can also choose Save To FrontPage from the Image Composer File menu and save your selection directly to the active Web, but you'll probably want to change the default name that the Image Composer provides. We used PaintShop Pro, however, to crop the image and add the pastel shades and text to individual buttons because the Image Composer dithers the colors and text boundaries when saving to the GIF format. (GIF and JPEG are the two preferred Web graphics formats because they both use compression formulas to reduce file size.) The Image Composer converters also changed some of the gray pixels in the background gradient, so we also replaced these with our dark gray color (153,153,153) in Paintshop Pro.

FrontPage lets you import graphics from a variety of sources, but we created a new ADD-INS subfolder on the MICROSOFT FRONTPAGE \CLIPART folder, for buttons and other standard interface elements so they would always be easy to find. To add them to your exploration bar, place your cursor in each of the table cells, and then choose Image from the FrontPage Editor's Insert menu, click the Clip Art tab, choose Add-ins from the Category list, and select the button you want from the dialog box. Once you've added buttons to each cell, save the exploration-bar page to your server. FrontPage will also save the selected graphics to your Web, proposing the IMAGES directory as a default. Unless you have a compelling reason to save images elsewhere—say, for specialized pages with graphics that will need regular updating—you might as well save all your graphics in a common directory, and IMAGES is as good a name as any.

Although we've added cell spacing and padding to separate the buttons, we want the toolbar to be as compact as possible. Since your images have a fixed size, you can specify the cell widths in pixels as well. You can figure out the size of your graphics in FrontPage by selecting an image and

CHAPTER 4

choosing Image Properties from the Edit menu—if you don't see it, you haven't selected an image—and reading the pixel dimensions of the image on the Appearance tab in the Image Properties dialog box. You can then select the cell (or, if your buttons are the same size, the entire row), choose Cell Properties from the Table menu (see Figure 4-12), and specify a minimum width equal to the image size plus the cell padding (in our case, 75 + 2 = 77).

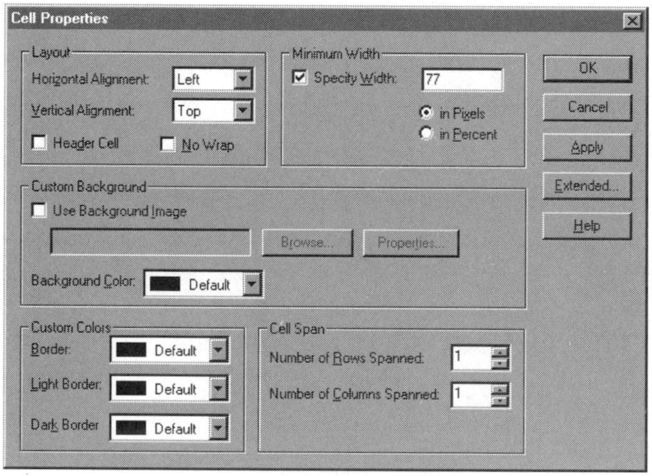

Figure 4-12
Cell Properties dialog box.

Forging the Links

Now that we've created the exploration bar, the next step is adding hyperlinks. When the user clicks a button, we want the Overview or Contents page for the specified section to display in the Content frame below the exploration bar. Of course, we haven't created those pages yet, but FrontPage will let us do that on the fly, as part of adding the links.

Select an image in your exploration bar, and then choose Image Properties from the FrontPage Editor's Edit menu. If you wanted to draw hot spots within an image, you would click buttons on the Image toolbar. Since our buttons are small, however, it's easier just to make the whole image a single hot spot. You could enter a link to a nonexistent page in the Default Hyperlink Location input box at the bottom of the Image Properties dialog box, but if you click the Browse button in the Default Hyperlink section, FrontPage will actually let you create the new page as well.

Once you click the Browse button, click the New Page tab in the Create Hyperlink dialog box, and then enter a page title and relative URL, as shown in Figure 4-13. Note the URL syntax. We want to create separate subdirectories for each section of our Web, but since we are adding the link to _PRIVATE/NAVBAR.HTM, we use the partial URL syntax "../" to indicate that WELCOME is a subdirectory of the *parent* of the current directory. We can also enter the default Target Frame, since any jumps from the exploration bar should display new documents in the Content frame. With the Edit New Page Immediately option selected, when you click the OK button, you will see the FrontPage Editor's New Page dialog box, where you select the template you want for your new page. In our intranet, we selected the Contents Page template, even though (as you'll see) we wanted to change some of the template features.

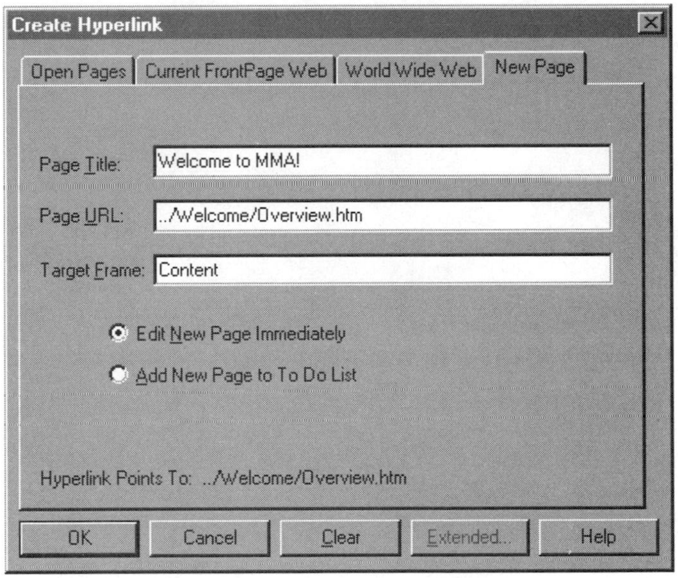

Create Hyperlink	☒

Open Pages | Current FrontPage Web | World Wide Web | **New Page**

Page Title: Welcome to MMA!

Page URL: ../Welcome/Overview.htm

Target Frame: Content

⊙ Edit New Page Immediately

○ Add New Page to To Do List

Hyperlink Points To: ../Welcome/Overview.htm

| OK | Cancel | Clear | Extended... | Help |

Figure 4-13
Create Hyperlink dialog box.

Before you can save the page to your Web, you must create the new subdirectory by returning to the FrontPage Explorer and choosing New from the File menu. If you don't like receiving error messages, you can create the subdirectory *before* you create the link, or you can save the page in an existing subdirectory and use the FrontPage Explorer to move it later. Any way you slice it, though, you can create new subdirectories only in the FrontPage Explorer.

After you save the page to your Web, be sure to check the style sheet and included document links. In the case of an Overview page like ours, you'd apply a background color matching the button color by choosing Page

Properties from the FrontPage Editor's File menu, choosing the Custom background option from the Background tab, and entering the RGB values in the Color dialog box, as shown in Figure 4-14.

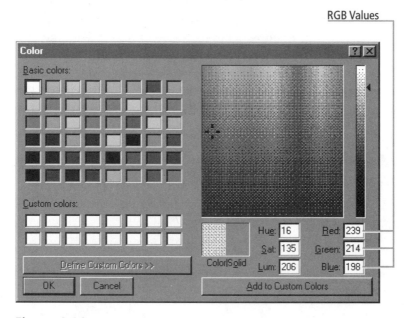

Figure 4-14

Color dialog box.

When you set specific page properties, FrontPage eliminates the STYLESRC link to the Page Properties style sheet, so you'll need to add any other style-sheet settings that you want in the current page, including top and left margin values, Visited Hyperlink colors, and the Default Target "_self". Since you're saving the page to a subdirectory, you'll also need to update the partial URL in the style-sheet link at the top of the page—in this case, to ../_PRIVATE/CSS1.CSS—and make a similar change to Included document references by using the View Or Edit HTML window. (If you only change the WebBot properties in the FrontPage Editor, FrontPage automatically restores the HTTP:// link created from the template.)

Once you save the exploration bar, you can test your links by previewing the page in the browser. Each time you click, the pages will be displayed in a separate instance of the browser because that's how the application treats an unresolved target frame reference (in this case, Content). It may be a little irritating, but it's worth it to make sure that your links and style-sheet references are valid before going further.

ToolTips and Other Graphics Tricks

When graphical browsers were relatively new, it was important to provide an alternative, text-based description of an image for text-only browsers. We hope this is a nonissue for your intranet, but one advantage of creating a toolbar of separate images is that Microsoft Internet Explorer displays text alternatives as ToolTips when the user moves her mouse over the image. As you can see in Figure 4-15, we chose to deviate from traditional GUI design and provide supplementary information instead of simply repeating the name of the button. If your primary image is a large graphic, you can also add a second, low-resolution graphic for the browser to load first, but it's hardly necessary at 1.3 KB per button.

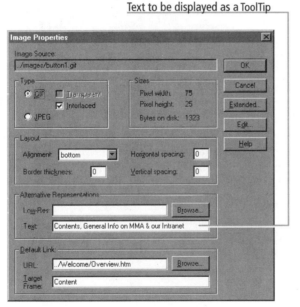

Text to be displayed as a ToolTip

Figure 4-15

Image Properties dialog box.

There are in fact two different GIF formats—GIF87a and GIF89a, invented by CompuServe in 1987 and 1989, respectively—each of which comes in two "flavors": interlaced and noninterlaced. The interlaced formats load sequentially, in increasingly high resolution with each pass. Noninterlaced-format images load only once, but because the image isn't completely rendered until the load is done, there's often the perception that noninterlaced-format images take longer to load (they don't). If you're going to use large images *against our sound advice,* you might want to use the interlaced format. Should anyone question your judgment, you can always point out that even large images will redraw more quickly after the initial load, since the browser will have a copy in the cache.

The GIF89a format has two additional tricks. Some graphics applications (such as Microsoft Image Composer) will let you designate one color as "transparent" when you save. In FrontPage, you select the image, click the Make Transparent button on the Images toolbar, and then move your cursor over the color you want to be transparent and click again. When the graphic is loaded in a compatible browser (such as Internet Explorer), the color of the underlying page or image replaces the designated color in the graphic. (We could have used this to blend the gray edges of the button-shading gradient into the page background instead of actually matching the colors in PaintShop Pro.)

The GIF89a format also supports animations, which are multiple image files that essentially loop out of your browser's cache. You need a special tool to create them—one common product is the GIF Construction Set, by Alchemy Mindworks (http://www.mindworkshop.com)—but since Microsoft doesn't currently provide a special tool of this kind, we're not going to go over this process step by step. As in any other kind of frame-based animation, the process is tedious but easy to learn. We've included a sample "exploding logo" in our *MMA Industry News,* on this book's companion CD (PULSE1MMA.GIF). If you want moving images in your site, GIF animation is far preferable to AVI files, which typically take up hundreds of kilobytes and can create baffling error messages if the user's PC isn't properly configured to handle them. We've included a spinning logo from our earliest intranet. If you're tempted to use AVI animation, try adding the file to a page that you browse daily. At first, you might think the effect is way cool. After a week or two, though, we're guessing you'll agree that it looks—well, kinda stupid.

What's on the Menu?

The last exploration element of our interface is a series of menus, one for each section, containing hyperlink jumps to all the pages in the section. We could have created these menus as graphics, to ensure complete control over their appearance, but experience has taught us that section menus are revised fairly frequently, and editing text in a drawing application is slow and tedious. So even though the section menus are a strong design element of our intranet, we created them as text because they'll be easier to revise that way. In fact, since there will be relatively few menus in our intranet and only a handful of authors will ever edit them, we added the body and text styles directly to each Web page instead of referencing style sheets. Changing them will be a little more work, but we want our menus to load as quickly as possible.

All section menus are Web pages with custom page properties, and inline styles in an HTML Markup WebBot, which are stored in the _PRIVATE subfolder to exclude their text from the results of the Search WebBot. Since our menu design might not be applicable to your intranet, let's just go over the main points here; you can examine the source files on this book's companion CD if you're interested in more detail.

We chose Page Properties from the FrontPage Editor's File menu to set the page background color to the custom dark gray color (153,153,153), and the left and top margins to 0. We eliminated page margins so that the logo at the top of each menu would be flush with the frame. (Later on, we'll establish text indents to offset menu entries.) Since all menu jumps take the user to content pages, we set the default hyperlink target to the Content frame. We also changed the Hyperlink color, Visited Hyperlink color, and Active Hyperlink color to white.

We wanted the menus themselves to have a fixed width, and we used 100 pixels as the working dimension. (In fact, it was easier to make the final adjustments through trial and error rather than exact calculations, so this dimension was simply used as a benchmark.) To control the width of the document, as well as spacing between the menu entries and subheads, we created a borderless, one-column table for all menu content. We chose Table Properties from the Table menu, set the cell padding to 2, and set the cell spacing to 0.

We inserted the company logo as a GIF file in the first table cell—but if we'd inserted it as a BMP file, FrontPage would have converted it to a GIF when we saved it to the Web. (Incidentally, if you copy or move a GIF file into a Web folder with a file utility, it won't appear in FrontPage dialog boxes until you refresh your Web in the FrontPage Explorer.) FrontPage 2.0 also lets you scale inline graphics by dragging. For greater precision, however, we used the View Or Edit HTML window and entered absolute pixel dimensions for the WIDTH and HEIGHT attributes directly in the HTML. By trial and error, we determined that a width of 96 pixels sized the logo flush to the vertical scrollbar without creating a horizontal scrollbar. Then we applied the fixed width of 96 pixels to the table as well. (A cell containing an image is always sized to the graphic; we just wanted the text to match.) We then selected the cell containing the logo, and we applied a white background and added a hyperlink from the logo to the intranet's table of contents.

Instead of linking our menus to a cascading style sheet, we entered the menu styles directly into an HTML Markup WebBot at the top of the page.

CHAPTER 4

Since everything in the menu was in a table cell, the style sheet needed only one selector:

```
<STYLE>
<!--
TD {font: extra-bold 10px/13px Verdana;margin-left: 4px;
text-decoration: none;color: #ffffff;}
-->
</STYLE>
```

Because the <STYLE> tag is supported only by Internet Explorer, we enclosed the actual style definition between the HTML comment tags (<!--, -->) so that other browsers won't include the TD definition as part of the menu page text. (Of course, other browsers also won't be able to see our styles or interpret the VBScript we'll be adding in our script shell, so it's really just a courtesy.)

The TD definition starts by grouping four font characteristics: font weight, font size, line height (in pixels), and font family. Bear in mind that, as of this writing, the order of grouped style definitions was sometimes critical and that certain definitions were not available in certain contexts. (For example, "extra bold" had no effect coming after "Verdana," nor was there any apparent difference between "demi-bold" and "extra bold" Verdana.) Setting the text decoration to "none" removed the underscore that is applied by default to text hyperlinks; the same effect could have been achieved if the <A> tag had been redefined.

We then added the menu entries and subheads and chose Cell Properties from the Table menu to apply our custom red as the subhead background color. We created space between the last menu entry in a subsection and the following subhead by pressing the Shift-Enter keys to insert a line break and then pressing the Shift-Ctrl-Spacebar keys to add a nonbreaking space *after* the line break. The FrontPage Editor won't let you create space with the spacebar after a break at the end of a line, and without empty space, Internet Explorer will interpret your line break as the end of a paragraph and won't display the empty line.

Finally, we selected menu entries and for each one chose Hyperlink from the Insert menu to add hyperlinks. As of this writing, FrontPage displays a list of bookmarks only for open pages. If you want to create a hyperlink to a bookmark in an unopened page, you must enter the bookmark name directly in the Create Hyperlink dialog box. Most important, be sure to designate the Content frame as the Target Frame of all menu hyperlinks. If you don't, the server will load the specified document in the Menu frame when you click the link.

Since there are so few menus in our intranet, we didn't create a separate template. Instead, we simply saved our initial page under new names to create the remaining menus.

Bringing It All Back Home

Once you have the basic elements of your intranet, you can assemble them in a common interface. Traditional Webs—anything created before, say, 1995—only displayed one page at a time in the browser. But the advent of browsers (like Internet Explorer) that support frames now makes it possible to display several pages simultaneously.

Even with an intranet that will always be viewed with frame-enabled browsers, it's still worth considering the nonframed alternative, if only because frames make exploration more complex. It's not just a matter of writing scripts to make sure that frames are properly updated when you jump to a new page: Internet Explorer treats each frame as a separate window, so if you change the section menu as well as the Web page when you jump, clicking the Back button may not immediately take the user to the previous content page. Another issue is that frames take up screen space, and ActiveX documents and the PowerPoint Viewer don't always look their best in a framed environment. Still, once you've established frames in a Web, moving the user in and out of the framed environment can quickly get tricky if not downright confusing.

On the plus side, frames are an ideal way to incorporate an exploration system like the one we've built, so we'll display our intranet in a framed Home page with the exploration bar always across the top, the current section menu to the left, and the current page taking up the rest of the window. We'll name our frames Navbar, Menu, and Content, respectively, so we can use their names as targets for hyperlink jumps and in manipulating frame updates with Visual Basic, Scripting Edition. We'll specify exact dimensions for the height of the exploration bar and the width of the section menu (using the relative unit of pixels) and prevent the user from dragging the frames to resize them. Finally, we'll provide scrollbars for the Content frame, suppress them in the exploration bar, and add a vertical scrollbar to the section menu only as needed. Here's a schematic of how it should look when we're done:

Menu	Navbar
	Content

CHAPTER 4

Unfortunately, we won't be able to do all this by using the FrontPage Editor's Frame Wizard. Instead, we'll use the FrontPage Editor to configure the basic shell. Since the FrontPage Editor does not allow us to edit the HTML for the frames directly, we'll make final adjustments with an ASCII text editor. The adjustments need to be made only once, and there are only three frames, so it's all fairly easy to do.

First choose New from the FrontPage Editor's File menu. Then select Frames Wizard from the list.

There are two ways to create the basic layout we want. The easiest way is to choose the Pick A Template option in the Frames Wizard's Choose Technique dialog box and then select Nested Three-Level Hierarchy in the Frames Wizard's Pick Template Layout dialog box and drag the bottom screen to enlarge it. (See Figure 4-16; we'll set the exact dimensions later.)

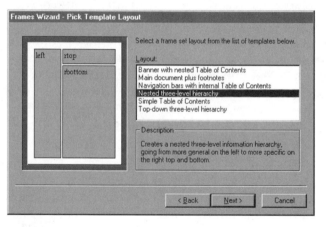

Figure 4-16

Nested Three-Level Hierarchy option in the Frames Wizard's Pick Template Layout dialog box.

The other way to create the basic layout we want is to choose the Make A Custom Grid option in the Frames Wizard's Choose Technique dialog box and then, with the entire grid selected, specify 1 row and 2 columns in the Frames Wizard's Edit Frameset Grid dialog box. Press the Shift key while clicking the left mouse button to select the right-hand column, and click the Split button to create a four-frame grid. Then, with only the four frames in the second column still selected, change the settings in the dialog box to 2 rows and 1 column to merge the grid into two rows. Again, you can drag the frame borders to approximate the final result (see Figure 4-17).

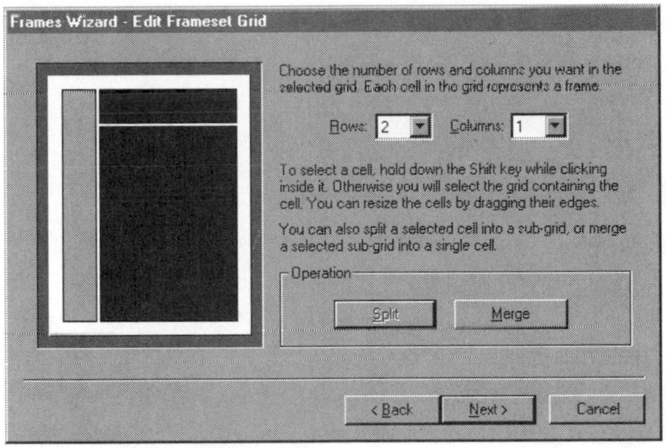

Figure 4-17

Frames Wizard's Edit Frameset Grid dialog box.

If you chose to make a custom grid, the next dialog box in the Frames Wizard lets you assign frame target names, as well as margin and scrolling options and the page that loads by default in each frame. If you picked a template, you won't have these options, and you'll have to change existing names in a text editor. Both versions of the dialog box let you assign an alternate page URL for browsers that don't support frames.

In our sample intranet, we called the left-hand frame Menu, and we assigned the Welcome Section menu (_PRIVATE/MENU1.HTM) to load by default. If you don't stipulate a default URL for each frame, FrontPage creates a boilerplate Web page so that at least your frame will be displayed without server errors. Since menus are of variable length, we chose the autoscrolling option for this frame—which means that scrollbars will appear only when the page is larger than the frame. (Later on, we'll manually set the frame width to the widest text element to prevent a horizontal scrollbar from appearing.) We didn't choose the Yes scrollbar option because a horizontal scrollbar is unnecessary; but if you want a vertical scrollbar to appear consistently in all menus, you'll have to add blank paragraphs to lengthen shorter menus. We called the lower right frame Content and also selected auto scrollbars. Figure 4-18 at the top of the following page shows the options for the attributes of the top frame, which, like the other frames, is not resizable.

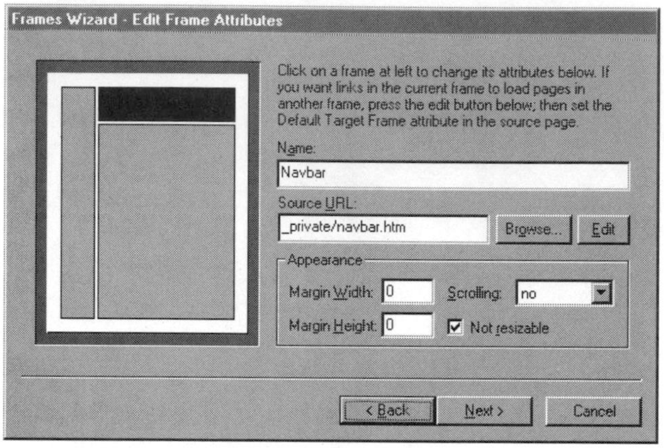

Figure 4-18

Frame Wizard's Edit Frame Attributes dialog box.

Both frame-construction methods let you assign an alternate page for browsers that are not frame-enabled, a situation that is more relevant to the Internet, where you must accommodate a wide range of browsers, than to an intranet. If you don't choose an alternate page, however, the Wizard adds a message in the <NOFRAMES> tag of your frameset, which you may want to change with an ASCII text editor. (You could also write a simple JavaScript routine to test for Internet Explorer, and you could extend it to include browsers that are not frame-enabled.) Both methods also let you give your page a title and save it to a URL. For now, we'll give it the name originally given to the FrontPage Personal Web Server's default Home page, in the Web root: INDEX.HTM. If you were following in our footsteps and pointed your browser to our <ROOT WEB> directory, you'd see something like what is shown in Figure 4-19.

The exploration-bar buttons should load the different Overview pages for each section. If you've added jumps to the section menus, you should be able to go to those pages, too. There are two obvious problems, however: we haven't provided a way to change the section menus, and the frames still don't look right. I'll show you how to fix the frames in this chapter, and then we'll go on to examine other kinds of pages and sub-Webs that you can build with FrontPage.

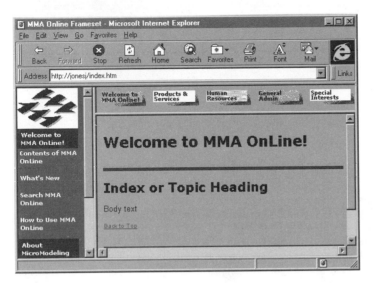

Figure 4-19

MMA Online Frameset seen in Microsoft Internet Explorer.

Massaging Your Frame

No, it's not a New Age thing—it's just HTML; but it's the only way you'll be able to set exact frame dimensions or remove those unsightly frame borders. Of course, if you're not using Microsoft Internet Explorer, you're stuck with frame borders, so maybe they don't look unsightly to you. But you still have to peek under the HTML hood to massage your frameset.

Fire up your favorite ASCII text editor (we prefer WordPad for its TrueType fonts), and open your frameset. You should see something like this:

```
<!DOCTYPE HTML PUBLIC "-//IETF//DTD HTML//EN">

<html>

<head>
<title>MMA Online Frameset</title>
<meta name="FORMATTER" content="Microsoft FrontPage 2.0">
</head>
```

(continued)

CHAPTER 4

```
<frameset cols="23%,77%">
    <frame src="_private/menu1.htm" name="Menu" noresize>
    <frameset rows="16%,84%">
        <frame src="_private/navbar.htm" name="Navbar"
        scrolling="no" noresize>
        <frame src="Welcome/Overview.htm" name="Content"
        scrolling="yes" noresize>
    </frameset>
    <noframes>
    <body>
    <p><!--webbot bot="PurpleText"
    preview="INSTRUCTIONS: The frameset on this page can be edited
    with the FrontPage Frames Wizard; use the Open or Open With
    option from the FrontPage Explorer's Edit menu. This page must
    be saved to a Web before you can edit it with the Frames Wizard.
    Browsers that don't support frames will display the contents of
    this page, without these instructions. Use the Frames Wizard to
    specify an alternate page for browsers without frames."
    s-viewable=" " --> </p>
    <p>MMA OnLine uses frames, but your browser doesn't
    support them. Contact ITOPS for the latest version of the
    Internet Explorer.</p>
    </body>
    </noframes>
</frameset>
</html>
```

There are two framesets. The first defines two columns. The second (corresponding to the second column of the first frameset) defines two rows. Note that both frameset dimensions are proportional, whereas we want to stipulate the width of the first column (at 118 pixels, in our sample site) and the height of the first row (at 39 pixels, ditto), replacing the percentage value of the second dimension in both framesets with the asterisk wildcard. You can also poke around in your handy HTML reference to find the attributes that make frame borders disappear, but we'll save you the trouble:

```
frameborder="0" framespacing="0"
```

(If you don't set the spacing to zero, you'll still see a thin band.) A few edits later, and you're good to go:

```
<frameset cols="118,*" frameborder="0" framespacing="0">
    <frame src="_private/menu1.htm" name="Menu" noresize>
    <frameset rows="39,*" frameborder="0" framespacing="0">
        <frame src="_private/navbar.htm" name="Navbar"
        scrolling="no" noresize>
        <frame src="Welcome/Overview.htm" name="Content"
        scrolling="yes" noresize>
    </frameset>
```

Now, that wasn't so painful, was it? And see how much better your Home page looks? You can now run down the hall and invite everyone to come and view your Web page. Just don't try viewing it in the FrontPage Editor: you won't be able to see the page (or use the Preview In Browser command). If you try to open it from the FrontPage Explorer, the Frames Wizard will be invoked.

Default with Indexes

We called our Home page INDEX.HTM because that's the default name the FrontPage Personal Web Server recognizes when it receives a request from a browser for a valid URL that doesn't include a Home page name (for instance, good old http://www.microsoft.com takes you right to http://www.microsoft.com/default.htm).

Most servers recognize a default Home page name, but they don't all use INDEX.HTM. The Microsoft Internet Information Server (IIS), for example, uses DEFAULT.HTM instead. It's easy to rename your Home page in the FrontPage Explorer, but you'll also need to reconfigure your FrontPage Personal Web Server to recognize the new default. Here's how:

1. Use Notepad or WordPad to open the SERVER\CONF\SRM.CNF file in your FRONTPAGE WEBS (*not* PROGRAM FILES\MICROSOFT FRONTPAGE) folder. It's the same folder that's the parent of the CONTENT folder, which your server calls its <ROOT WEB>.

2. Find the commented-out Directory Index section, and add a new DirectoryIndex line, with the filename you want to use. The following example uses DEFAULT.HTM:

```
#DirectoryIndex: Name of the file to use as a prewritten HTML
#directory index. This document, if present, will be opened
#when the server receives a request containing a URL for the
#directory, instead of generating a directory index.
#
#DirectoryIndex index.htm

DirectoryIndex default.htm
```

3. Close the file, and relaunch your FrontPage Personal Web Server.

Of course, you've only changed how your FrontPage Personal Web Server behaves; your intranet server won't be affected at all. Be aware that the change will now apply to any Web hosted by your server and that previously valid URLs may now display a simple index of the Web rather than the designated Home page (if it is still named something other than DEFAULT.HTM or another filename that you chose). That's because, as we saw earlier in this chapter ("There's No Such Thing As an Empty Web"), the FrontPage server, rather than choking with the dreaded Server Error 404, generates an FTP-like index when it can't find the Home page.

Creating a Simple Download Page

One of an intranet's most useful functions is distributing company forms and templates to employees. You'll see that we've included Template and Form Download pages on several section menus, and you can also create them very easily just by adding hyperlinks to the downloadable templates:

1. In the FrontPage Explorer, create template subdirectories of the _PRIVATE directory, and import the files and templates you want. Storing the templates in a subdirectory of a hidden directory not only makes version control easier but keeps the templates from appearing on WebBot-generated Table Of Contents and Search forms. You can use compressed files with the ZIP or EXE extensions, or you can use standard Microsoft Word and Microsoft Excel file formats—that is, you can use any format but HTML. You should decide whether you want your templates to be in read-only format, too.

2. In the FrontPage Editor, create a new master Download page from your Contents template, and save it to the Web root as TemplateDownload.HTM. This time we want the Template Download page to be included in searches, since employees might know the name of the template they want but not where to find it. Note, incidentally, that each download subsection on the page is referenced with a "bookmark" (that is, a <NAME> anchor tag), which is included in any hyperlink jump to the subsection. It just makes sense to include all your downloads in a common page.

3. Enter instructions to the user, as well as the text you want for hyperlink anchors. Select an anchor, and choose Hyperlink from the Insert menu to bring up the Create Hyperlink dialog box. Then click the Current FrontPage Web tab. (See Figure 4-20.) Select the file you want the user to download.

In our sample page, we entered all the hyperlinks in a centered table, with borders and cell padding set to 1 and cell spacing set to 2. We did not specify a dimension for the table, so that we could specify percentage dimensions for each column. Finally, we selected the top row and chose Cell Properties from the Table menu, and then we checked the Header Cell box in the Cell Properties dialog box, clicked the Extended button, and applied the style Class named subhead to the <TH> tag, as shown in Figure 4-21.

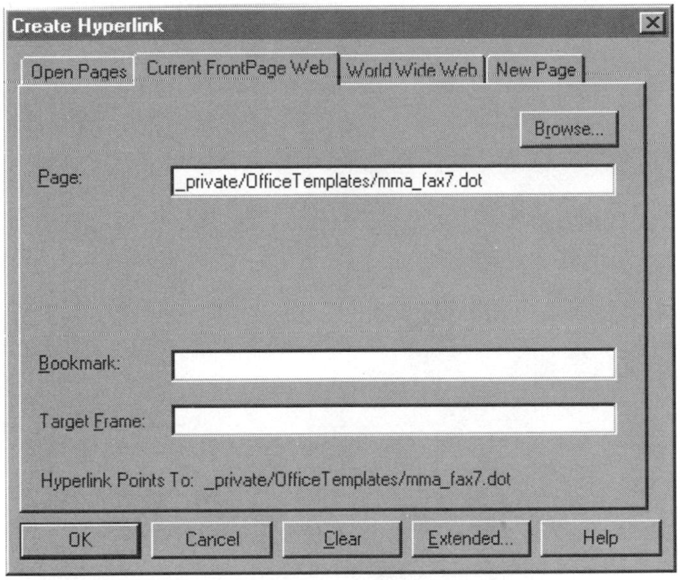

Figure 4-20

The Create Hyperlink dialog box.

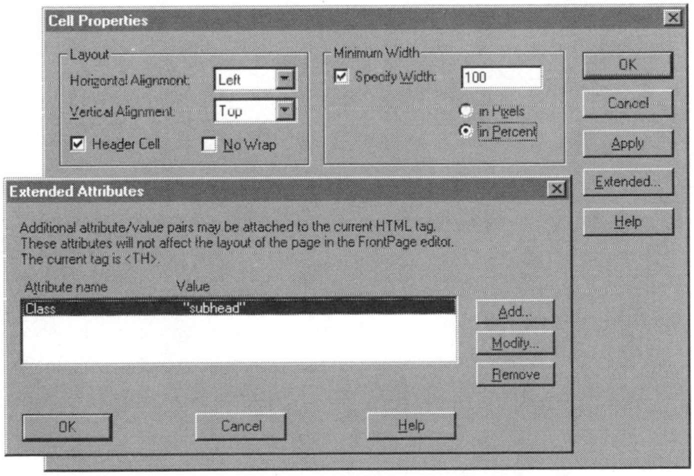

Figure 4-21

Extended Attributes for the Cell Properties.

So far, all you've done is create a garden-variety http:// link to a non-HTML document. The rest is up to your browser. When the user clicks any hyperlink, the browser requests a specified URL, and the server responds by sending back a file. This is the point where a modern browser typically

133

recognizes that the file format is "unknown" and offers the user several choices, including saving to disk and attempting to open the file anyway. Figures 4-22, 4-23, and 4-24 show how different browsers deal with unknown file formats.

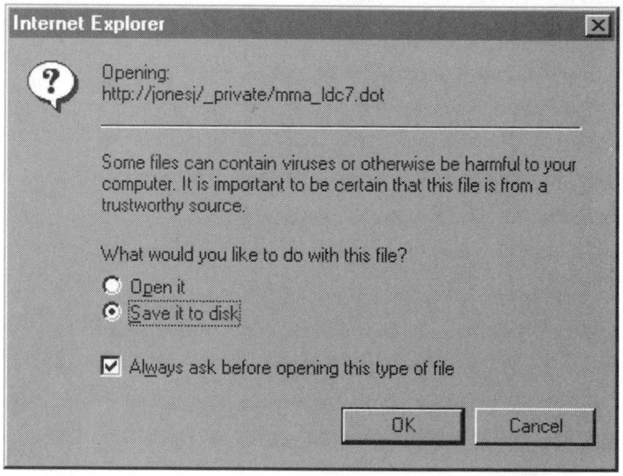

Figure 4-22

Opening an unknown file format in Internet Explorer.

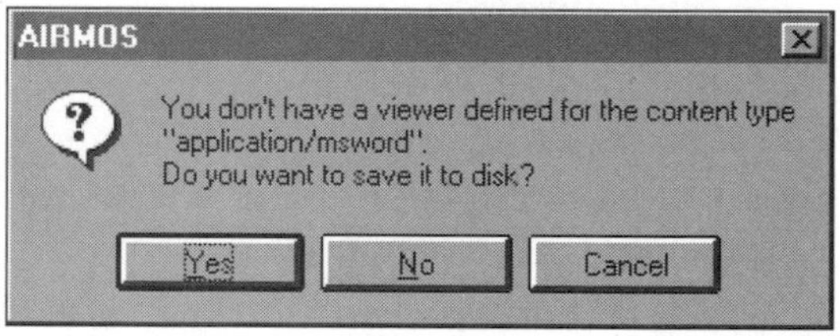

Figure 4-23

Opening an unknown file format in Mosaic.

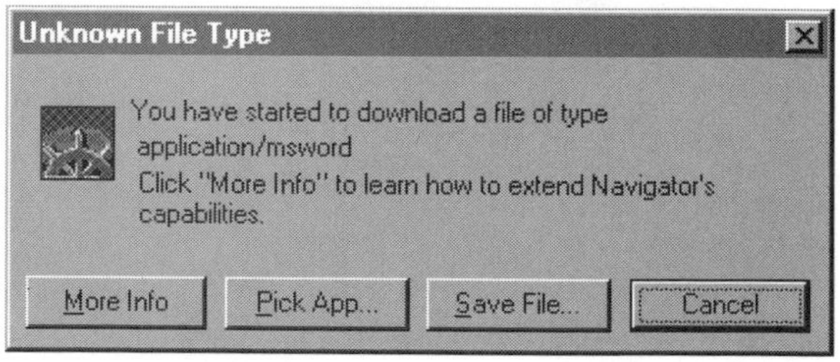

Figure 4-24

Opening an unknown file format in Netscape Navigator.

If you create HTTP downloads, however, you should be aware—and make your users aware—of a peculiarity unique to Internet Explorer for Windows: Internet Explorer version 3.0 and later can open Microsoft Office documents, but if the user unchecks the innocuous Always Ask Before Opening This Type Of File box (see Figure 4-22), Internet Explorer will open *all* Office documents with the same extension *from that point on*—until, of course, the user resets the option. You can do this in Internet Explorer, but it isn't easy; we found this whole rigmarole sufficiently baffling to give it pride of place in our How To Use MMA Online section, with a hot link to any Template Download page:

1. Choose Options from Internet Explorer's View menu, and then choose the Programs tab and click the File Types button to bring up the File Types dialog box:

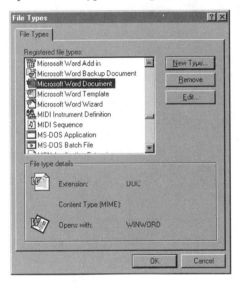

2. Select the file type from the list, and then click the Edit button.

3. Lo and behold, there's the little culprit, lurking at the bottom of the Edit File Type dialog box at the top of the next page and masquerading as Confirm Open After Download. Yes, yes, I know—what you really want to confirm is the *save*, but just play along, OK?

Edit File Type

[Change Icon...]

Description of type: | Microsoft Word Document

Content Type (MIME):

Default Extension for Content Type:

Actions:
New
open
print
printto

[New...] [Edit...] [Remove] [Set Default]

☐ Enable Quick View   ☑ Confirm open after download
☐ Always show extension   ☐ Open web documents in place

[Close] [Cancel]

Advanced Projects

In this section, I'm going to show you how to use FrontPage 97 to build three advanced projects, which combine multiple pages in a common subfolder or sub-Web:

🌐 The marketing catalog is a *hyperdocument,* consisting of a series of similar, interlinked pages. (See the MARKETING subfolder of the Chapter2 folder on the companion CD.)

🌐 The *Industry News* archive is a sub-Web with its own Table of Contents and Search form for previous editions of our *Industry News.* (See the NEWSARCHIVE subfolder of the Chapter2 folder on the companion CD.)

🌐 The developer knowledge base is a sub-Web containing multiple threaded discussion groups, each with its own Search form and index. (See the DEVELOPERKNOWLEDGEBASE subfolder of the Chapter2 folder on the companion CD.)

The Marketing Catalog

There are really only two ways to create long intranet documents. One way is by creating a single long page with hyperlink cross-references. The marketing catalog is an example of the other way: creating a series of interlinked

Web pages that collectively make up a hyperdocument. A document becomes "hyper" by virtue of a system of hyperlinks that take you through the pages one after another—replicating, in effect, the structure of the Web itself. FrontPage does have a boilerplate template for creating hyperdocuments, and it does provide you with basic instructions, but you're not much better off than you would be starting from scratch.

You could take many approaches to hyperdocument exploration, including the following two methods:

🌐 **Using the Back and Next buttons.** These buttons move you along in a linear sequence. When supplemented by text or graphical information, they give you an idea of where you are in the document.

🌐 **Using a graphical map of clickable hot spots.** With this method, the user can jump freely to any page. You can use a common map on all pages, or you can use a different map on each page, showing the current page location.

Our marketing catalog uses the new inline (or "floating") frame tag, which Internet Explorer supports, to create a scrolling catalog index within every page. You have to insert the code for an inline frame directly in the HTML Markup WebBot, but the attributes are fairly straightforward:

```
<IFRAME
    ALIGN=TOP|MIDDLE|BOTTOM|LEFT|RIGHT
    FRAMEBORDER=1|0
    HEIGHT=height
    MARGINHEIGHT=height
    MARGINWIDTH=width
    NAME=name
    SCROLLING=yes|no
    SRC=address
    WIDTH=width
    [NORESIZE]
/IFRAME>
```

You'll find the syntax explained in detail in any up-to-date HTML reference. In broad terms, however, here's how it works:

🌐 You can align surrounding text to the top, middle, or bottom of the frame, or you can let surrounding text wrap to the left or right.

🌐 You can add or suppress frame borders and/or scrolling.

4

- 🌐 You can set the size of the frame and its internal margins in pixels.

- 🌐 You can (and should) provide a target name, if only to avoid any confusion between the inline frame and other active frames.

- 🌐 You must display another document (or graphic) in the frame.

We created a separate subfolder for the marketing catalog—mainly for ease of maintenance—and, within that, we created a boilerplate template containing the frame, style-sheet links, and other standard layouts, and we saved it to a hidden directory in the FrontPage Explorer. We created each new page by opening the template and saving it to the parent directory under a new name. From that point on, everything was simply a matter of entering content and editing it.

The *Industry News* Archive

The *Industry News* archive is a self-indexing repository of previous editions of our *Industry News,* compiled daily by our Washington office and distributed within the firm over our intranet. The current edition of the *Industry News* is always a page in our main Web, but the archive is maintained in a separate sub-Web in which there is a page containing a FrontPage Table Of Contents WebBot. The WebBot contents are updated whenever the Web (or, for that matter, any Web page) changes. Because the sub-Web contains only previous editions of the *Industry News,* that's all that appears in the table of contents. Building the sub-Web involved five main steps:

1. Creating and configuring the sub-Web
2. Importing and configuring previous editions of the *Industry News*
3. Creating the table of contents
4. Creating the Search page
5. Validating hyperlinks

Creating and configuring the sub-Web

You create a new sub-Web by choosing New from the FrontPage Explorer's File menu and then choosing FrontPage Web (or by choosing Create A New FrontPage Web From A Wizard Or Template in the Getting Started dialog box when you first start FrontPage). We selected Empty Web from the Template Or Wizard list and then entered the name NewsArchive in the Empty Web Template dialog box (Figure 4-25). Whenever you create a new Web, you'll also be prompted for your administrator ID and password.

Figure 4-25
Empty Web Template dialog box.

Importing and configuring previous editions

If you are importing a large number of files into a Web from a common source, you can choose New from the FrontPage Explorer's File menu and then choose FrontPage Web and select Import Web Wizard from the list of options (you can also select it directly from the Getting Started dialog box). If you want to import files into the current Web, make sure you check the Add To The Current Web box.

After you specify the name and location of the new Web and click OK, the Import Web Wizard takes you through the necessary steps.

1. In the first dialog box of the Import Web Wizard, Choose Directory, click the Browse button to find the source directory. Click OK to return to the Choose Directory dialog box.

2. If you want to see a list of subdirectories later, check the Include Subdirectories box.

3. Click the Next button on the Choose Directory dialog box to bring up the dialog box shown at the top of the next page.

4. In our case, we had more than 30 previous editions of the *Industry News* on file in various formats, so we decided to start our archive with editions dated later than September 1. Therefore, to refresh the list, we selected all other files, and then we clicked the Exclude button:

In the end, we imported only four previous editions, a style sheet, and the animated GIF file used in our header.

If you're importing a number of files with referenced graphics, you may not know which graphics go with which files, so just import them all, and use the FrontPage Explorer's Hyperlink view to track down unused images.

After importing the source files, we renamed the style sheet "NEWSSTYLE.CSS" (which is simply an identical copy of CSS1.CSS), and we changed the style-sheet links in each of the previous editions. We also imported the Included footer from our <ROOT WEB> directory and replaced the reference to a Page Properties style sheet with direct page formatting. We moved the image file to the IMAGES folder by dragging the icon in the FrontPage Explorer's Folder view; FrontPage automatically updated the references in the document files. Finally, we opened each of the archived editions in the FrontPage Editor, previewed them in our browser to be sure the text formats were all correct, and chose Page Properties from the FrontPage Editor's File menu to set the default target frame to Content and review the page title that would appear in our Table of Contents and Search page results.

You can simplify the task of archive maintenance by using identical frame targets and relative style-sheet URLs for the current edition in the <ROOT WEB> directory and creating a template with the same references.

Creating the table of contents

Once we had the previous editions, style sheet, and Included footer, we chose New from the FrontPage Editor's File menu and selected Table Of Contents from the Template Or Wizard list to create a default table of contents page. We then saved the page in the root of our Archive sub-Web as DEFAULT.HTM (see Figure 4-26) because that's the filename that Microsoft Internet Information Server (and the reconfigured FrontPage Personal Web Server) recognizes as the default Home page.

The Table Of Contents WebBot generates an object representing a schematic table of contents in your Web page. Since the actual table of contents is generated at browse time, you won't see it until you preview the page in your browser. You can configure the WebBot properties, however, by selecting the object, choosing WebBot Component Properties from the FrontPage Editor's Edit menu, and choosing the options you want in the WebBot Table Of Contents Component Properties dialog box. In our sample

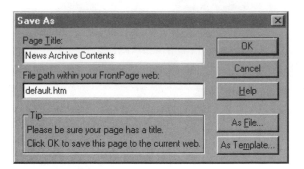

Figure 4-26

Saving the Table Of Contents page.

intranet, we set the Contents page as the starting point of the table (which simply means it's the first listed item), and selected the other options as shown in Figure 4-27.

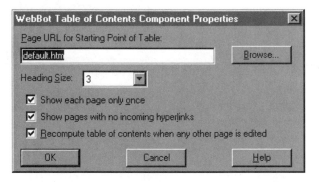

Figure 4-27

WebBot Table Of Contents Component Properties dialog box.

Finally, of course, we added an HTML Markup WebBot containing the style-sheet link, a VBScript shell to update the menus in the Home page frame, an Include WebBot reference to the Included footer, and our own custom text.

OK. In the FrontPage Editor, in the WebBot Table Of Contents Component Properties dialog box, you selected Recompute Table Of Contents When Any Other Page Is Edited. You've edited lots of pages. You even refreshed your Web in the FrontPage Explorer. How come your Table of Contents still isn't updated?

It's because a Table Of Contents doesn't update itself automatically. It's a two-step process performed in the FrontPage Explorer. First you choose

Refresh from the View menu to update your Web contents. (If you've added new pages by using the FrontPage Editor, you should be able to see them now in the FrontPage Explorer.) Then you choose Recalculate Hyperlinks from the Tools menu. Since the Table Of Contents WebBot uses hyperlinks, you do need to perform this second step.

Creating the Search page

To create the new Search page from the FrontPage Editor's Search Page Template, we followed essentially the same sequence that we used for creating the Table Of Contents page. We chose New from the FrontPage Editor's File menu, and then we selected Search Page in the New Page dialog box.

Once the page was created, we saved it to the _PRIVATE subfolder of our Web, to exclude it from the WebBot-generated Table Of Contents. (We added a text hyperlink to the Search page instead.) We chose the Page Properties command on the FrontPage Editor's File menu to apply a custom background color and margin and make Content the default target frame. We added a VBScript shell to control frame updates, but because the Search page contains internal hyperlinks, we added inline styles in the HTML Markup WebBot at the top of the page, using the <STYLE> tag instead of a <LINK> tag referencing a style sheet.

OK. Let's say you fire up your browser. Let's say you enter some text in your Search form. Let's say you even click the Start Search button. You get . . . nothing. How come your Search form isn't working?

It's because the Search WebBot doesn't actually browse your documents. It browses special text indexes that FrontPage creates for each folder and subfolder of your Web. (When you limit a search, you're actually specifying the subfolder indexes to be searched.) To update the text indexes, you need to choose Recalculate Hyperlinks from the FrontPage Explorer's Tools menu. Sure enough, there in the status bar you'll see the message "Updating hyperlinks and text indices."

You need to recalculate your hyperlinks whenever you edit your Web. If you don't, you may continue to see references to long-deleted pages in your search results.

Validating hyperlinks

Since the imported editions of the *Industry News* were created before our intranet was, some of the links inevitably changed. For example, the archive index from the source Web (ARCHIVE.HTM) is now the default Home page (DEFAULT.HTM) in our Archive sub-Web. Other links (such as the "placeholder" link to the "Under Construction" page) also require updating, whereas some of the external hyperlinks might have gone stale.

143

You can easily determine the status of all the hyperlinks in a Web by choosing Verify Hyperlinks from the FrontPage Explorer's Tools menu. This command generates a list of all the hyperlinks in your Web, initially displayed with the yellow, question mark status icon, which indicates that they are unverified (or changed), as shown in Figure 4-28.

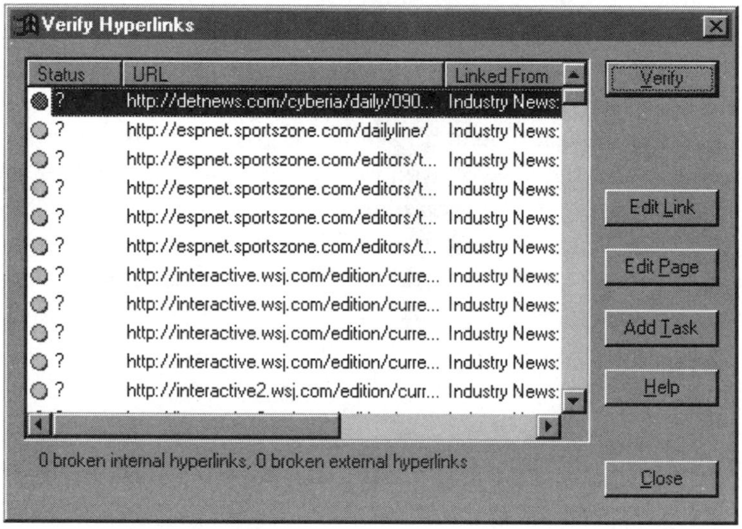

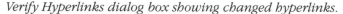

Figure 4-28

Verify Hyperlinks dialog box showing changed hyperlinks.

Click the Verify button to launch the process that tests whether each link is still valid and then changes the icon for each tested hyperlink, indicating that the hyperlink is Broken (red) or OK (green), as shown in Figure 4-29.

The verification process can be quite lengthy, but you can halt the process in the middle by clicking the Stop button. In our case, we had decided as a matter of policy not to verify external links. That meant we had only a few links to change.

When you select a broken link in the Verify Hyperlinks dialog box and click the Edit Link button, you see the Edit Link dialog box, which contains a list of all the pages with that link. You can replace one or more of these pages simultaneously by selecting the appropriate option in the Edit Link dialog box. As it turned out, we needed to replace not only the underlying HTML references but also the hyperlink text in the documents themselves. Of course, we could have opened each page individually in the FrontPage Editor, but there's an easier way: you choose Replace from the FrontPage Explorer's

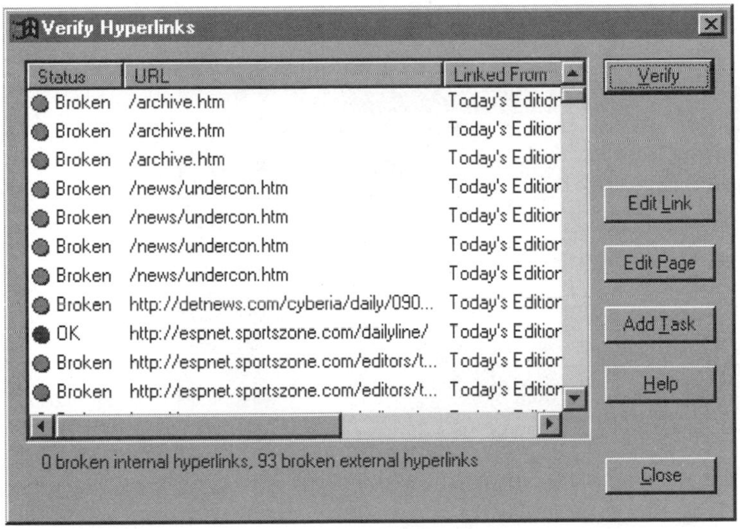

Figure 4-29
Verify Hyperlinks dialog box showing Broken and OK hyperlinks.

Tools menu, and enter a search string and a replace string in the Replace In FrontPage Web dialog box, as shown in Figure 4-30.

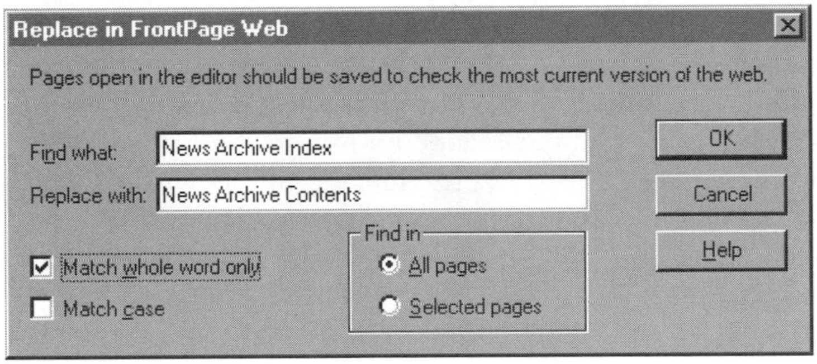

Figure 4-30
Replace In FrontPage Web dialog box.

When you click the OK button, you see a list of all the pages in which the search string occurs displayed in the Find Occurrences Of dialog box, as shown in Figure 4-31.

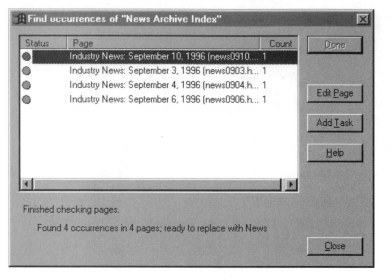

Figure 4-31

Find Occurrences Of dialog box.

Using this command does give you a list of all the pages, but you still have to click the Edit Page button and change each one individually.

So far, we've created an autonomous sub-Web with its own internal hyperlinks and external links to the World Wide Web, but ultimately our goal is to incorporate this sub-Web into the <ROOT WEB> framed Home page. There isn't much to it, as long as you remember to use target frames. For example, in our main Search page we added a link to the News Archive Search page by opening the <ROOT WEB> directory in the FrontPage Explorer and then opening the Micro Modeling Associates (MMA) OnLine Search page in the FrontPage Editor, selecting the relevant text, and inserting the hyperlink shown in Figure 4-32.

Note that even though the Web is a subdirectory of the <ROOT WEB> directory on our hard disk, the link uses the HTTP protocol and the absolute URL of our sub-Web. Choosing Content as the target frame, however, ensures that even though the page is coming from a different Web, the content will always be displayed in the lower right frame of our Home page.

If you don't stipulate a target frame (or specify a valid target), when you click a hyperlink, the browser opens the Web page in a new window. You can think of each frame as a separate browser window within the Home page. Like any browser window, a frame can contain valid HTML from any server, so a frame with multiple frames can contain pages from different servers. But because the frames are contained on a common page, such frame

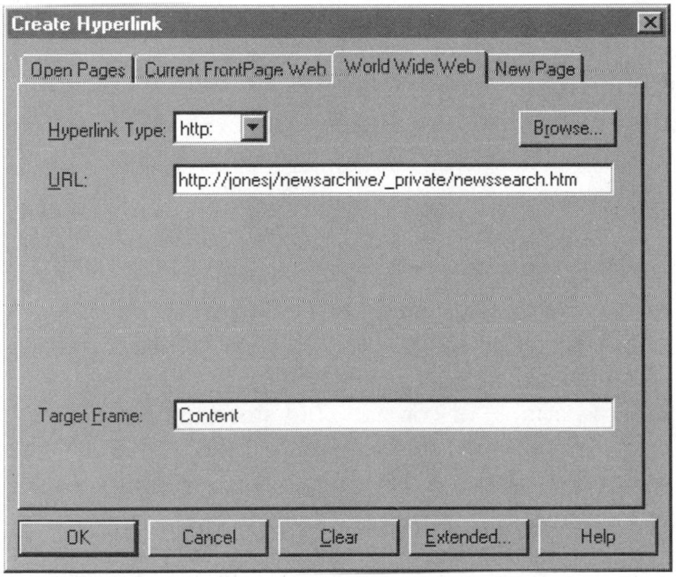

Figure 4-32

Inserting a hyperlink to the World Wide Web.

properties as target names remain constant, regardless of changes to the frame contents. Therefore, it's absolutely essential that you designate a default target frame for every page in your Web. If you don't, and if by some mistake you allow users to jump out of the framed environment, you'll find it mighty difficult to get them back in.

The Developer Knowledge Base

Arguably, the strongest feature of FrontPage 97 is its automation of HTML forms. Unfortunately, the various tools and components are not integrated on the interface. There are a number of powerful wizards and templates in both the FrontPage Editor and the FrontPage Explorer that configure forms and message handlers for you. You can also use related tools in the FrontPage Editor to build most (but not all) of the wizard-generated features by hand. Deep down under the hood, however, the commands all operate on three basic Form WebBot components:

🌐 The **Save Results** WebBot component captures input that the user enters in a form, and it writes the input to a text file in your Web. You have considerable control over the nature of the data and output formats, but the process is essentially one-way: from the user to the data repository on the server. While this type of

CHAPTER 4

form has many applications on a commercial Internet Web, it's less useful on an intranet, where e-mail and other messaging alternatives are available.

- The **Registration** WebBot component allows users to designate passwords for access to restricted sub-Webs. The security isn't terribly tight: validation is performed only upon initial entry, and nothing prevents anyone else from (for example) entering your user name and password, if they are known.

- The **Discussion** WebBot component manages a threaded discussion group, in which user postings are logged as articles in a separate subfolder and listed in a self-generating index. (FrontPage refers to this index as a table of contents, but since the mechanism by which it is generated does not rely on the Table Of Contents WebBot, we'll refer to it for the sake of clarity as the index.) I'm concentrating on this WebBot here because it's the most complex and the most difficult to configure. Even though you won't learn everything about FrontPage WebBots in this section, I hope you'll learn enough to create your own custom forms with ease.

The Developer Knowledge Base is essentially a Web containing a series of parallel threaded discussion groups, each with its own Submission and Search forms and table of contents. Each knowledge base could have been incorporated as a subfolder of our main Web (or as its own sub-Web), but we implemented the Knowledge Base as a common sub-Web for ease of maintenance so that we could keep the data separate from our main Web but still make common pages available to all discussion groups. Here, we're going to use a hybrid approach—creating an initial set of pages with a Web Wizard and then customizing them with FrontPage Editor tools—but if you're interested in advanced form handling, you owe it to yourself to spend some time experimenting with all the following FrontPage features:

- The FrontPage Explorer's **Discussion Web Wizard** is the easiest way to set up a threaded discussion group and the only way (short of typing directly in a dialog box) to hook up various undocumented FrontPage WebBots. Other FrontPage Explorer Web Wizards include form pages, but you can build them just as easily from the FrontPage Editor.

- The FrontPage Editor's **Form Page Wizard** is the easiest way to configure the Save Results WebBot. Other FrontPage Editor Page Templates—Feedback Form, Guest Book, Product Or Event

148

Registration, and Survey Form—automate the process of creating various configurations of the Save Results WebBot, but the Form Page Wizard is so easy to use that you might as well go right to the source.

🌐 The FrontPage Editor's **User Registration Template** creates a Web page with the Registration WebBot and boilerplate user instructions. The instructions are probably the main reason for using this template.

🌐 The FrontPage Editor's menu commands let you add Form components. For example, choose WebBot Component from the FrontPage Editor's Insert menu to insert a Confirmation Field WebBot in a Confirmation form. If this sounds like mumbo-jumbo to you at this point, don't worry. I'll show you how to use this WebBot in customizing our confirmation page. You can also choose Form Field from the FrontPage Editor's Insert menu (or choose Forms Toolbar from the View menu, and click toolbar buttons) to add individual form components, such as text boxes, radio buttons, drop-down menu boxes, and so forth.

🌐 Many form functions are available only (or most readily) if you right-click a selected object on the Web page, in the FrontPage Editor interface. For example, if you select a drop-down menu in a FrontPage form and right-click, you'll see menu commands for Form Properties (where you configure the settings for the whole form itself, including how user input is handled), Form Field Properties (where you configure the selected element of the form), and Form Field Validation (where you configure how user input will be validated before it's written to the data repository on the server).

Building forms becomes time-consuming rather quickly. Not only that, it typically requires an approach based on the nature of the data and the desired results—both of which, of course, tend to be unique in every situation. I'm not going to show you every last step (you can examine the sample CD for that), but I'll certainly review the procedures involved in each of the following four basic steps:

1. Creating a new sub-Web with the Discussion Web Wizard

2. Moving the main pages to a new subfolder and updating the links

3. Reconfiguring components of the Submission form and the Confirmation page

4. Changing standardized pages to custom formats

149

Creating a new sub-Web

We'll use a Web Wizard to create the basic pages of each discussion group, and then we'll move them to another location in our Web and customize them in the FrontPage Editor. To begin the process, choose New from the FrontPage Explorer's File menu, and then choose FrontPage Web and select Discussion Web Wizard. In creating the first discussion group, give the Web the name of this discussion group (in this case, DeveloperKnowledge-Base) when you save it; thereafter, choose the Add To The Current Web option to add each new discussion group to the Web. The Discussion Web Wizard takes you through a series of fairly self-evident screens in which you make the following selections:

- **The standardized Web pages that will be included in the discussion group.** We selected all options for our knowledge base.

- **The descriptive title that will appear in the Included headers.** The screen also shows the name of the hidden directory the Wizard will create for articles.

- **The Input fields on the Submission form.** Don't worry if you don't see the exact options you want; as the screen indicates, you can add more later in the FrontPage Editor.

- **Whether the Web is protected.** If so, users will be required to register. (We chose not to protect our Web.)

- **The rank order of articles.** This question applies only if a table of contents is selected. (We chose newest to oldest.)

- **Whether the table of contents will be the Home page.** (We chose not to have the table of contents be the Home page.)

- **Search Results criteria.** Specifies what information will be reported by the Search Form for matching documents.

- **Page properties.** This includes background colors and patterns as well as text colors.

- **Whether frames will be used to display contents and articles simultaneously.** There are already a number of frames in our intranet, and since the discussion-group interface is clean and intuitive, we chose the No Frames option. There are also some bugs in the Wizard, as of this writing, which caused the contents not to update automatically when the Dual Interface option was selected.

When the Wizard is done, here is what you will find:

 Up to four pages in the DeveloperKnowledgeBase Web root (for the Index (TOC) form, the Search form, the Confirmation form, and the Submission form)

 Up to five more pages in the _PRIVATE subfolder (the Included headers and footers for the Discussion Group forms and articles, and the "Web Colors" Page Properties style sheet)

 A new hidden subfolder, where articles are stored (as sequentially numbered HTM files)

 Two hidden WebBot-driven pages (TOCPROTO.HTM and TOC.HTM) that generate the index

We could keep adding discussion groups to the Web root, but our Web will be less cluttered if we move the Search, Submission, and Index forms for each group to a separate subfolder. This operation will require us to customize some internal links. We also want to move the Confirmation form to the _PRIVATE directory and customize it to be shared by all discussion groups. We'll maintain specific headers for each discussion group, using separate forms and article headers within each group so that the article headers will have additional buttons for replying to and moving through messages. We'll only use one footer per discussion group, however, and a common Page Properties style sheet for the entire knowledge base. There are, however, a couple of things to do first in the Web root:

 From our Internet Content template, create a new page named DEFAULT.HTM (or INDEX.HTM), to serve as the knowledge base's Home page. You'll need this page to hook up the Home button in each toolbar of the knowledge base.

 Choose Import from the FrontPage Explorer's File menu, and import the Included header and Included footer from the <ROOT WEB> directory.

 Choose Web Settings from the Explorer's Tools menu, and then click the Advanced tab and check Show Documents In Hidden Directories.

You can also select pages at any time in the FrontPage Explorer, and then choose Properties from the Edit menu to perform an ad hoc error check. If the FrontPage Explorer detects errors, you'll see them listed in the Errors tab of the Properties dialog box. As you can see in Figure 4-33, our new Home page has two template settings that we need to update: an invalid style-sheet reference and a parameter that we have yet to define for our Web. This tab is displayed in the dialog box only when the FrontPage Explorer detects errors.

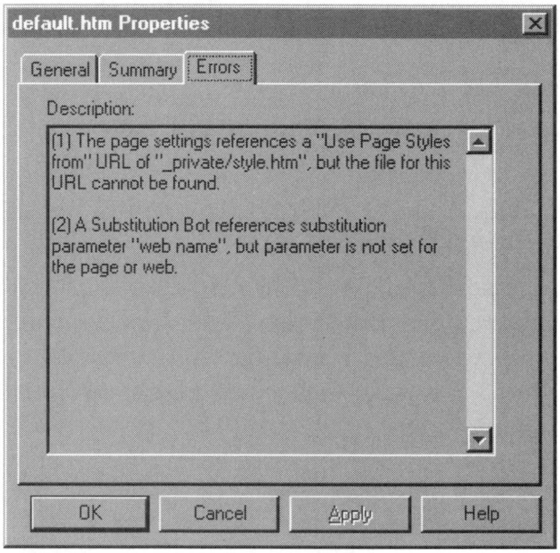

Figure 4-33

Errors tab of the Properties dialog box.

Moving pages to a new subfolder and updating links

Moving the pages to a new subfolder in the FrontPage Explorer is the easy part. Choose New from the FrontPage Explorer's File menu, and then choose Folder and enter the subfolder name you want for your discussion group. (In our intranet, the first subfolder was XLKB.) Now move the Submission, Search, and Table Of Contents forms to the new subfolder by dragging them in the FrontPage Explorer's Folder view. Move the Confirmation form to the _PRIVATE subfolder, and delete the Wizard-generated Included footer and Included Article footer. Don't forget to choose Refresh from the View menu— you won't see your pages in their new locations until you do.

Updating the hyperlinks will be a little trickier, for two reasons: we want to substitute some common files (such as our imported Included footer for the Wizard-generated equivalents), and we'll have to update all relative URLs that reference undocumented WebBots (which can only be done manually).

First, however, let's see where we stand. Choose Recalculate Hyperlinks from the FrontPage Explorer's Tools menu. When that's done, choose Verify

Hyperlinks from the same menu. Figure 4-34 shows the broken links that remain after the main pages of a second knowledge base have been moved to a new subfolder. It's easy to fix the Page Properties style-sheet links from the template and the links to deleted footers: just select the link, click the Edit Link button, and substitute the URL of a valid file. In our intranet, within each knowledge base, we replaced all links to Included footers and Included Article footers with a link to the common Included footer imported from our <ROOT WEB> directory. For consistency, however, we changed the name of one of the Wizard-generated "Web Colors" Page Properties style sheets to _PRIVATE/STYLE.HTM, and we updated all style-sheet links in each knowledge base to this common file. The broken link to the undocumented --WEBBOT-SELF-- is trickier to fix: it requires not only a manual entry in the Submission form but also some understanding of what the link represents.

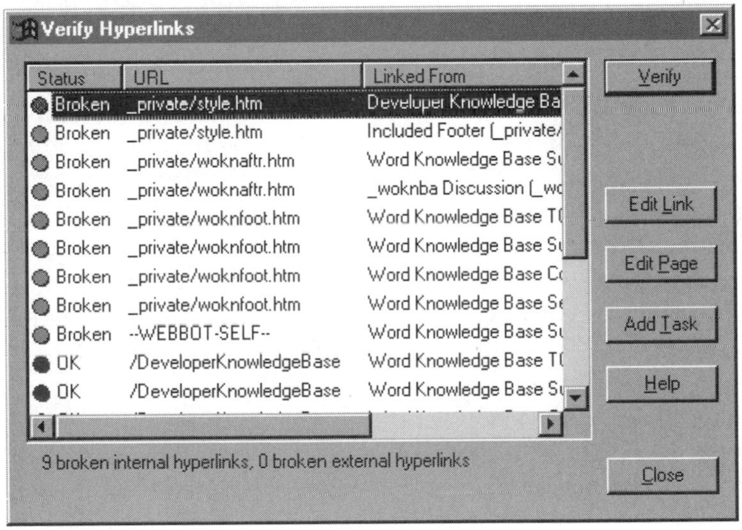

![Verify Hyperlinks dialog box showing a list of broken internal hyperlinks with Status, URL, and Linked From columns, and buttons for Verify, Edit Link, Edit Page, Add Task, Help, and Close. The status bar reads "9 broken internal hyperlinks, 0 broken external hyperlinks".]

Figure 4-34
Broken links as shown in the Verify Hyperlinks dialog box.

All HTML forms are basically structures for capturing and labeling various kinds of user-defined input. (Remember—although you're creating the page on your server, it's the copy in the user's browser that will be sending information back to the server.) When the user clicks the Submit button, the browser transmits a text stream of captured and labeled data to the server, via HTTP. Included in the stream is an additional bit of information (one of many, actually) containing the name of the server-side routine (or form handler, action, or CGI Script) invoked to process the data. The

FrontPage CGI scripts (to give the WebBots their generic name) reside in the CONTENT folders of the Webs themselves.

Launch the FrontPage Editor, open one of the Wizard-generated Included headers, and review the underlying code in the View Or Edit HTML window. You'll be looking at something like this:

```
⋮
<h1>Excel Knowledge Base</h1>
<p class="Href">[ <a href="../default.htm" target="_top">Home</a> |
<a href="--VERMEER-TOC-../XLKB/exkntoc.htm--">Contents</a> |
<a href="../XLKB/exknsrch.htm">Search</a> |
<a href="../XLKB/exknpost.htm">Post</a> |
<a href="--WEBBOT-REPLY--" name="disabled">Reply</a> |
<a href="--WEBBOT-NEXT--" name="disabled">Next</a> |
<a href="--WEBBOT-PREV--" name="disabled">Previous</a> |
<a href="--WEBBOT-UP--" name="disabled">Up</a> ] </p>
⋮
```

The preceding code (EXKNAHDR.HTM) shows the text that generates the toolbar in our Microsoft Excel knowledge base's Included header—and, sure enough, if you look at the anchor tags for the Contents button, you'll find that the reference includes the WebBot followed by a relative URL, representing instructions to the server to run the CGI script named --VERMEER-TOC on the relative URL for the Index page. (If you're curious about how the Index is generated, there's part of your answer.) In other words, the toolbar hyperlinks are instructions to the server to run a designated server-side routine on a target page that can be designated with a relative address because it's *in the current Web*.

Equipped with this knowledge, let's open the Submission form and view it in the View Or Edit HTML window. Lo and behold, there at the top of the code (EXKNPOST.HTM) defining the form itself is the reference to --WEBBOT-SELF--:

```
⋮
<form action="--WEBBOT-SELF--" method="POST">
    <!--webbot bot="Discussion" s-dir-name="_exknba"
    s-article-format="HTML/BR"
    u-style-url="_private/exknstyl.htm"
    b-reverse-chronology="TRUE" s-toc-fields="Subject From Date"
    u-header-url="../_private/exknahdr.htm"
    u-footer-url="../_private/includedfooter.htm"
    s-builtin-fields="Date Time REMOTE_NAME"
    u-confirmation-url="exkncfrm.htm" --><p><strong>Subject:
    </strong><br>
     <input type="text" size="50" name="Subject"> <br>
```

```
<strong>From:</strong><br>
<input type="text" size="50" name="From"> <br>
<select name="Category" size="1">
    <option selected>Category 1 </option>
    <option>Category 2 </option>
    <option>Category 3 </option>
    <option>Category 4 </option>
    <option>Category 5 </option>
</select> <!--webbot bot="PurpleText"
preview="Customize these drop-down menu selections." -->
<strong>Comments:</strong><br>
<textarea name="Comments" rows="6" cols="50"></textarea> <br>
<br>
<input type="submit" value="Post Article"> <input type="reset"
value="Reset Form"> </p>
</form>
⋮
```

So where's the relative URL? You'd be forgiven for assuming that this WebBot doesn't require a URL. If that were the case, however, why would moving the page from the Web root to a subfolder *break* the link? If every WebBot reference requires a relative URL, and if the page worked fine in the Web root, then perhaps the link is broken because it still references the original URL—and only one page could have a relative URL of "": the current page when it's in the Web root! Hence the name --WEBBOT-SELF--.

Now, if we work backward by deduction, we see that repairing the link involves nothing more than updating the URL of the current page, which is now in a subfolder of the Web root: an address designated relatively as two dots and a slash:

```
<form action="--WEBBOT-SELF--../" method="POST">
```

If you are the obsessive type, you may decide to revisit your edit after closing the FrontPage Editor, at which point you will see that the FrontPage Editor has removed the additional URL. Panic ensues, along with muttered curses and gnashing of teeth. But *do not despair:* if you rerun the FrontPage Explorer's Verify Hyperlinks command, you will see that the link is no longer broken. A simple one-time direction was enough to reorient the FrontPage Server (which, after all, is running in the background on the open Web) to the new relative address of --WEBBOT-SELF--. The rest of the HTML for the Submission form isn't terribly hard to decipher (the Category menu being particularly obvious), but it's much easier to edit the form with FrontPage Editor functions than to plunge around in raw code.

CHAPTER 4

In addition to the undocumented WEBBOT-SELF and WEBBOT-TOC, you'll find
WEBBOT-REPLY, WEBBOT-NEXT, WEBBOT-PREV, and WEBBOT-UP referenced in
the respective text buttons of the Wizard-generated Included Article toolbar. You
can't really control these WebBots, but you can copy the hyperlink references and
use them to create your own Discussion Group toolbars.

Reconfiguring components of the Submission form and the Confirmation page

You configure the elements of the form, as well as the form itself, by right-clicking on elements in the FrontPage Editor window and then choosing commands from the pop-up menu. To replace the boilerplate menu entries with useful categories, right-click the drop-down menu in the FrontPage Editor, and then choose Form Field Properties. You'll see a dialog box displaying the current values, as well as the controls that let you change them. Figure 4-35 shows the changes we made to the Category menu.

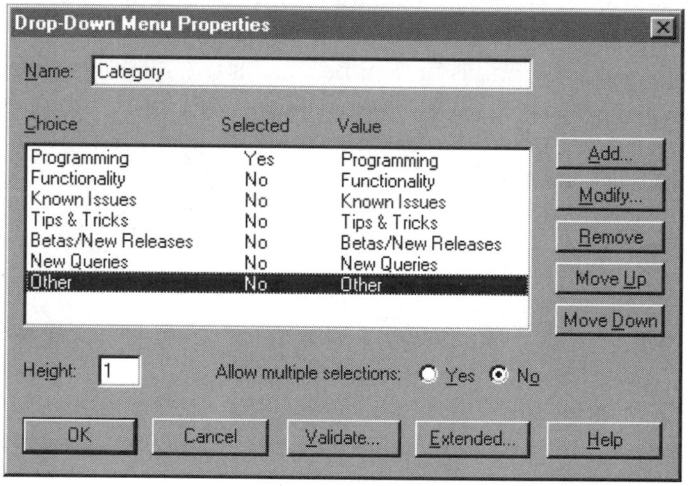

Figure 4-35

Changes made to the Category menu in the Drop-Down Menu Properties dialog box.

You add form elements by choosing Form Field from the FrontPage Editor's Insert menu and then choosing the form you want from the pop-up menu (or clicking the appropriate button on the Forms toolbar). In our knowledge base's Submission form (WOKNPOST.HTM), for example, we added a text box for user input, and then we right-clicked the text box and chose Form Field Properties to display the Text Box Properties dialog box (Figure 4-36), where we entered the field dimensions and the name that will be given to the data in this field when it's passed back to the server.

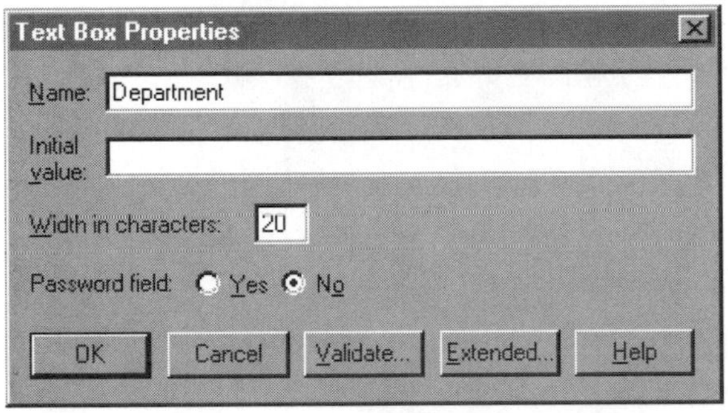

Text Box Properties

Name: Department

Initial value:

Width in characters: 20

Password field: ○ Yes ● No

OK   Cancel   Validate...   Extended...   Help

Figure 4-36

The Text Box Properties dialog box.

To select rules governing the user's input, you click the Validate button (or you right-click the form element in the FrontPage Editor and then choose Form Field Validation from the menu). We didn't want to allow the user to leave the department blank in our Submission form, so we applied the desired settings to the Text Box Validation dialog box shown in Figure 4-37. The actual options and the full title of the dialog box will change according to the form element selected.

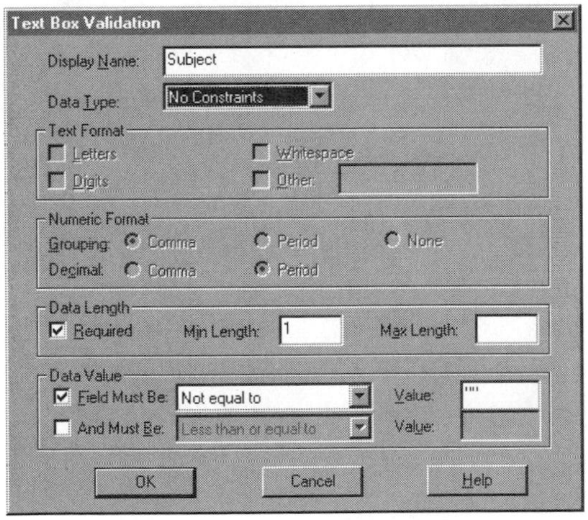

Text Box Validation

Display Name: Subject

Data Type: No Constraints

Text Format
☐ Letters   ☐ Whitespace
☐ Digits   ☐ Other:

Numeric Format
Grouping: ● Comma   ○ Period   ○ None
Decimal: ○ Comma   ● Period

Data Length
☑ Required   Min Length: 1   Max Length:

Data Value
☑ Field Must Be: Not equal to   Value: ""
☐ And Must Be: Less than or equal to   Value:

OK   Cancel   Help

Figure 4-37

The Text Box Validation dialog box.

157

To configure the overall form, right-click anywhere within the dashed-line box that represents the form, and then choose Form Properties. Figure 4-38 shows the hidden field KBName, which we created as an extended attribute by clicking the Add button.

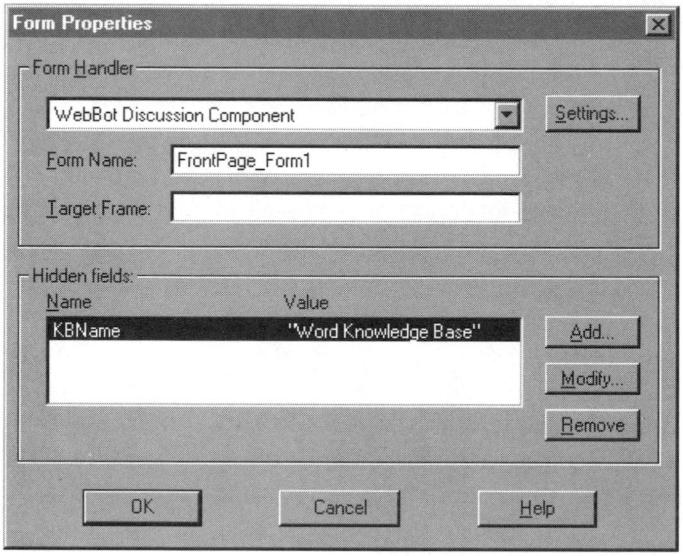

Figure 4-38
The Form Properties dialog box.

If you want to, you can also change the server-side CGI script used to process the form data by selecting a new WebBot from the Form Handler drop-down list, but this will usually entail a great deal of additional work to ensure that all the data in the form finds its proper place on the server. You'll usually be better off creating a new form with the appropriate wizard or template than switching WebBots in mid(data)stream.

Click the Settings button in the Form Properties dialog box to see tabs with options for configuring how the WebBot will handle data from the form. In the case of the WebBot Discussion Component, the Discussion tab lets you edit the title that appears on all articles, the subfolder to which articles are posted, the data that appears in the index, and the Page Properties style sheet that will be used for all articles (which is what FrontPage calls the HTML file generated from the user's posting). Figure 4-39 shows the values we used in our knowledge base.

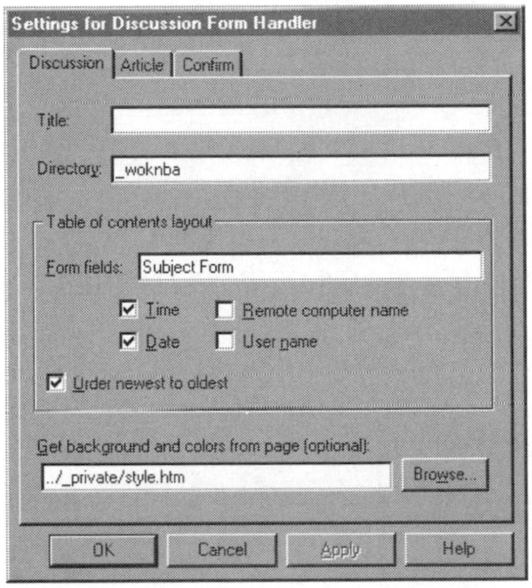

Figure 4-39

The Discussion tab of the Settings For Discussion Form Handler dialog box.

The Article tab is unique to the WebBot Discussion Component. It lets you enter or edit the URL of the Included header and Included footer and select additional system-generated data to include in each article. In our knowledge base, we didn't select User Name (which is the FrontPage user ID), since we are capturing the user's name in the From field.

The Confirm tab lets you designate the URLs of optional Confirmation and Validation Failure pages, which (if selected) are displayed after the user clicks the Submit button in the form. In our intranet, we clicked the Browse button and selected the common Confirmation page, as well as a common Validation Form page that we had created previously by using the FrontPage Editor's Confirmation Form Template.

A Confirmation page is basically a Web page in which confirmation variables, named for a corresponding form field, have been inserted with the Confirmation Field WebBot, much as configuration variables are inserted with the Substitution WebBot. If the URL of the Confirmation page has been entered in the dialog box generated by the Confirm tab (and if all the variables have been named correctly), the page will be displayed when the user clicks the Submit button in the Submission form, and the Confirmation Field WebBots will display the value of the named form field.

You can create a Confirmation page by using the FrontPage Editor's Confirmation Form Template, or you can do the same thing almost as easily from scratch. In our sample intranet, we wanted a common Confirmation page for all knowledge bases. Therefore, to distinguish the destination of each posting, we created a hidden field, called KBName, for each submission form. This field contains the name of the specific knowledge base.

You insert a Confirmation Field WebBot at your current cursor position by choosing WebBot Component from the FrontPage Editor's Insert menu and then selecting Confirmation Field from the list. You'll see the dialog box shown in Figure 4-40, where you enter the name of the corresponding form field. Alas, you'll have to *know* the name you want in advance; there are no menus or Browse buttons to make your job easier.

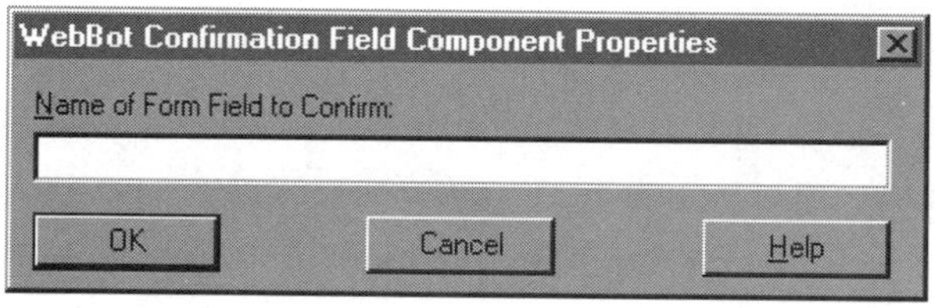

Figure 4-40
The WebBot Confirmation Field Component Properties dialog box.

Applying custom formats

The last step in completing our knowledge base was to apply custom styles and formats where they were needed, to supplement the FrontPage template layouts and our style sheets. Nothing terribly tricky or mysterious here:

- We aligned the elements of each Submission form by placing them in a table.

- We applied the HREF style from our style sheet and added FrontPage Clip Art to the toolbars for our Included header.

- We adjusted column widths in our Included footer to accommodate the longer Web Name configuration variable.

- We converted image links and Page Property style-sheet links that referenced absolute URLs by using the HTTP protocol to relative references.

- We added links to our Developer Knowledge Base on the system menus of our <ROOT WEB> directory by using the World Wide Web tab of the Create Hyperlink dialog box and making sure to stipulate Content as the Target Frame. Each Wizard-generated knowledge base also uses the generic target *_top,* which means "Load the link to the full body of the window." Internet Explorer interprets this to mean the full body of the *current frame.* To be on the safe side, however, it's a good idea to change any such reference to the actual name of your Content frame. That way, you avoid ambiguity and make sure that the user has no way to pop out of the framed environment by mistake.

You've Taken the First Step

By now, you should have not only the makings of a pretty impressive and complex intranet but also a deep appreciation of the structural issues involved in creating an intranet and an appreciation of the capabilities of FrontPage. Of course, as a Webmaster, you'll find that your work has only just begun, since the task of filling out and revising content, tedious though it may be, is endless in theory—and almost endless in practice.

5

CHAPTER

Internet Information Server

Peter Mueller and Jason Harper

The purpose of this chapter is to lead you through the steps for installing and administering Microsoft Internet Information Server (IIS) 2.0. IIS 2.0 for Microsoft Windows NT Server contains all the software you'll need if you want to publish on your corporate intranet or on the World Wide Web. The tight integration of IIS with NT Server allows you to take advantage of NT's built-in security and administration. IIS includes the following features:

- 🌐 Reduced administrative overhead, thanks to the above-mentioned integration with Windows NT Server

- 🌐 Remote management

- 🌐 The ability to access existing database information from the Web by using ODBC gateway (Microsoft SQL Server, Microsoft Access)

- 🌐 The availability of tools (SQL Server, Microsoft Access) for Web-use tracking and analysis

CHAPTER 5

🌐 Integration with the Microsoft Internet Explorer browser

🌐 Support for standards (common gateway interface, or CGI) for extending server functionality

Requirements for Setting Up Internet Information Server

The four basic requirements for setting up IIS involve hardware, software, infrastructure (setting a communication protocol), and security.

Hardware

Table 5-1 shows both the minimum and recommended configurations for your IIS server.

Table 5-1   IIS Configurations.

Minimum Hardware	Recommended Hardware
Intel i486 (33 MHz)	Pentium (90 MHz)
16 MB RAM	32 MB RAM
1-GB hard drive	2-GB hard drive
2x CD-ROM	4x CD-ROM
VGA monitor	SVGA Monitor

Software

Setting up an Internet or intranet server is really quite simple. All you need are Microsoft Windows NT 4.0 or later, with the latest service pack; Transmission Control Protocol/Internet Protocol (TCP/IP); and the Internet Information Server software included on the NT 4.0 disk.

NOTE   Microsoft Windows NT 4.0 service pack upgrades are available through the Microsoft Network (MSN), CompuServe, and Microsoft's Internet site at http://www.microsoft.com.

Infrastructure

When information is transmitted over the Internet or an intranet, the information is broken down into packets that travel across the network. TCP/IP is the communication protocol used to route the packets across the network. Use of this protocol allows computers running different operating systems to communicate with one another. Each computer communicating over the Internet or over an intranet has an IP address. A machine can be assigned an IP address in two ways:

1. Dynamic Host Configuration Protocol (DHCP) is a client/server program that automatically assigns IP addresses to computers configured to use DHCP. You can use DHCP to configure your intranet to run inside your organization, reducing the administrative burden of manually assigning IP addresses.

2. If you plan to extend your intranet out to the Internet, you will need to obtain an IP address from your Internet service provider.

Both of these actions can be accomplished using the Network dialog box shown in Figure 5-1. Select Network from the Control Panel, and then click the Protocols tab. Select TCP/IP Protocol, and click the Properties button. In the Microsoft TCP/IP Properties dialog box, you can select from the two options described above.

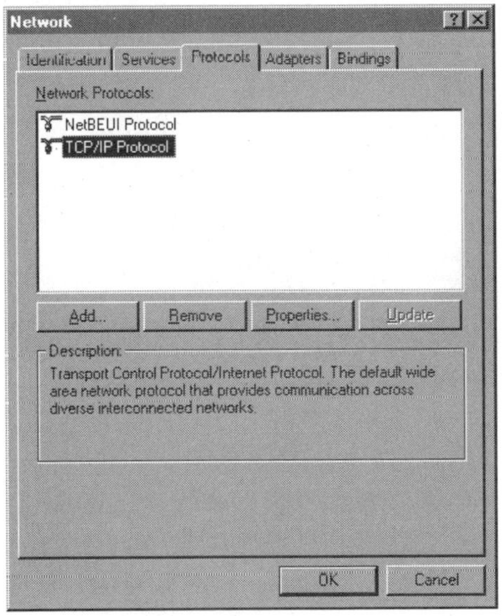

Figure 5-1
The Protocols tab of the Network dialog box.

165

Security

Windows NT provides many features to help you secure your Internet Information Server. Here are some basic guidelines:

- 🌐 Use NT File System (NTFS) as your file system. With NTFS, you can set access control permissions to your files and directories.

- 🌐 Choose and protect passwords. Use passwords with a mix of 12 or more alphanumeric characters.

- 🌐 Limit the guest account to specific directories on the server.

- 🌐 Run only the services and protocols that your system requires.

- 🌐 Check permissions on network shares.

- 🌐 Enable auditing.

Installing Internet Information Server

When you install Windows NT 4.0, you have the option of installing IIS. (For now, we'll assume that NT is already installed.) Let's begin:

1. Log on, using an account with Administrator privileges. (If security has been implemented correctly on your NT server, you should never have to log on as the administrator but rather under an *account* that has *Administrator privileges;* the Administrator account should be renamed and/or deactivated.)

2. In the Control Panel, double-click the Network icon. Under the Services tab, click Add and then select Microsoft Internet Information Server 2.0. Read the information in the Microsoft Internet Information Server 2.0 Setup dialog box, and click OK. The following installation options will appear. (Note that the World Wide Web service, the File Transfer Protocol service, and the Gopher service, listed here, are automatically started at the end of setup.)

   - 🌐 *Internet Service Manager.* Select this option to install the administration program for managing the services.

   - 🌐 *World Wide Web Service.* Select this option to create a World Wide Web publishing server. This is the core element of your Web server.

   - 🌐 *WWW Service Samples.* HTML Internet Database Connector, and ActiveX samples to help you design your Web site.

   - 🌐 *Internet Service Manager (HTML).* This is an HTML version of the service manager (not selected by default).

- *Gopher Service.* Select this option to create a Gopher publishing service.

- *FTP Service.* Select this option to create a File Transfer Protocol (FTP) publishing service.

- *ODBC Drivers & Administration.* Select this option to install ODBC drivers. These are required for logging on to ODBC files and enabling ODBC access from the Internet server.

3. Click OK to accept the default installation directory (or click Change Directory, and enter a new directory).

4. When prompted to create the C:\WINNT\System32\Inetsrv directory, click Yes.

5. The Publishing Directories dialog box shown here appears with a list of the default directories:

Publishing Directories	✕
World Wide Web Publishing Directory	
C:\InetPub\wwwroot	Browse...
FTP Publishing Directory	
C:\InetPub\ftproot	Browse...
Gopher Publishing Directory	
C:\InetPub\gophroot	Browse...
OK Cancel Help	

You can accept the default directories for the publishing services that you have installed, or you can change them. Click OK.

6. When you are prompted to create the directories, click Yes.

7. When the dialog box with the Internet Domain Name warning appears, click OK.

8. If you are prompted to close the Control Panel, click OK.

9. When you are prompted to install the ODBC drivers, click SQL Server, and then click OK. If you have a newer version of the SQL Server ODBC driver already installed, you will be asked if you want to replace it. Click No.

10. When setup is complete, click OK.

167

There is no need to start Internet Service Manager unless you want to make advanced configurations.

Installing the Microsoft FrontPage 97 Extensions

You will need to install the FrontPage extensions in order to move your FrontPage intranet into IIS:

1. Install the Microsoft FrontPage 97 client software on your Windows NT Server. Follow the steps in the setup procedure to perform a typical installation of FrontPage from the installation disks or CD you received with FrontPage. Details on setting up the FrontPage client can be found in the FrontPage manual. If you want to install only the minimum required software to work with the Server Extensions for IIS, you should run FrontPage setup, select Custom Install, and install only the Server Extensions.

2. Configure the Server Extensions as follows:

   🌍 If the FrontPage Server Administrator is not yet running, start it by double-clicking the Microsoft FrontPage Server Administrator shortcut in the \Program Files\Microsoft FrontPage folder in Windows NT Explorer.

   🌍 If you have server ports already configured, select a server port (typically 80), and then click the Uninstall button to remove any older server extensions that might be installed.

   🌍 Click the Install button, select Microsoft Internet Information Server, and click OK.

   🌍 Click OK to confirm the server port and type information.

   🌍 In the Administrator Setup dialog box, type *Administrator* in the name field and a password in the password field.

   🌍 Click Yes to restart the WWW Service.

3. Configure IIS for use with FrontPage. After installing IIS, but before running FrontPage, run the Internet Service Manager. From the Start menu, select Programs, and then select Microsoft Internet Server (Common). Select WWW Service, and choose Service Properties from the Properties menu. On the Service tab, check Basic [Clear Text]. Click Yes to continue when prompted.

4. Set up access control to assign permissions to your server. Be sure to read the "Controlling Web Access with FrontPage" section later in this chapter. It contains important information about setting up and managing access to FrontPage Webs. Because Web security

is such an important issue, it is very important that you read the instructions in this section.

5. Run FrontPage. To do so, choose Programs from the Start menu, and then choose Microsoft FrontPage.

Configuring Internet Information Server

Microsoft Internet Service Manager is the tool you can use to configure and enhance the performance of your information server. Internet Service Manager is located on the Microsoft Internet Server menu of the Programs menu.

Internet Service Manager

Internet Service Manager displays the running Internet services of any NT Server–based computer in your network. The information can be displayed in several formats:

🌐 **Report View** lists the running services for each computer on the network. You can sort the entire list by clicking the various column headings.

🌐 **Servers View** displays a list of running services by computer name as shown at the top of the next page. If you expand the listing, you see the services that the server is running.

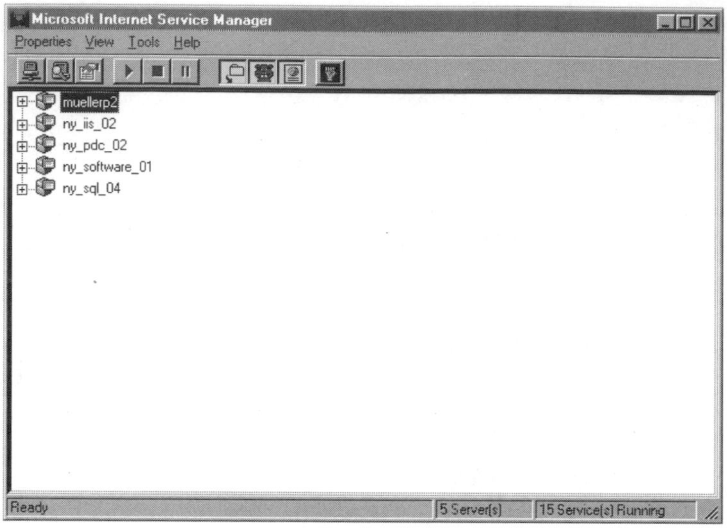

🌐 **Services View** displays a list of running computers by service, as shown below. If you expand the listing, you see the computer names running the service.

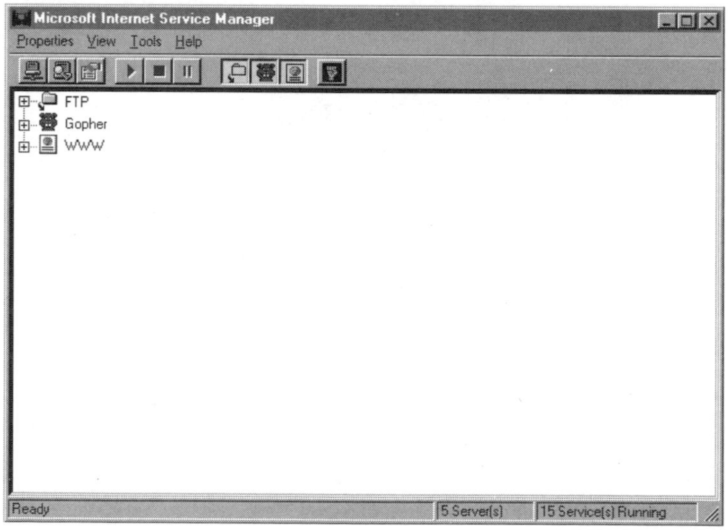

The Service Properties Dialog Box

The Service Properties dialog box of the Internet Service Manager can be used to configure and manage the WWW, Gopher, and FTP services. Double-click on a computer name or service (depending on the view) to display the Service Properties dialog box.

The Service tab

The Service tab of the Service Properties dialog box shown in Figure 5-2 sets user connections and user logon and authentication requirements. It also sets the comments used in the main Microsoft Internet Service Manager window.

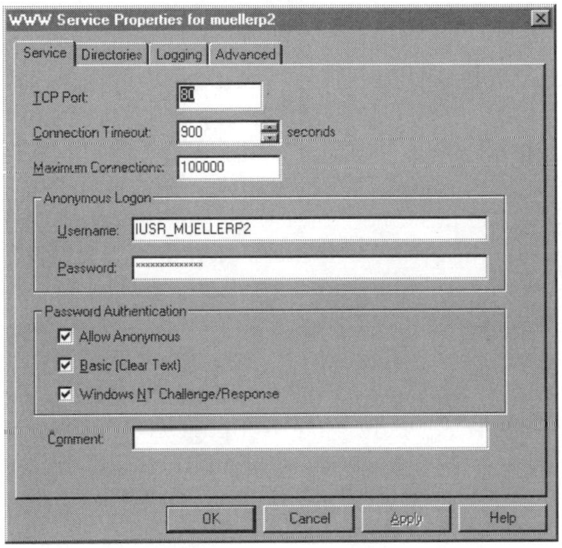

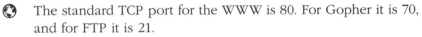

Figure 5-2
The Service tab of the WWW Service Properties dialog box.

Note the following facts and features about the Service tab:

- The standard TCP port for the WWW is 80. For Gopher it is 70, and for FTP it is 21.

- Microsoft Internet Information Server does not have a truly Anonymous logon. Instead, it allows for an Internet guest account. The password for the Internet guest account is randomly generated when the product is installed.

- An Advanced Security feature is the Windows NT Challenge/Response, which requires the guest account to have a valid Windows NT account on the computer.

- Connection timeouts should always be set so that connections are not wasted by idle users. An average setting for a connection time is 300 seconds (5 minutes). After 300 seconds, the connection is terminated.

The Directories tab

Every server must have a home directory, and each of the three services we have been discussing—WWW, Gopher, and FTP—has its own root directory:

```
\INETPUB\WWWROOT
\INETPUB\GOPHROOT
\INETPUB\FTPROOT
```

The home directory and all subdirectories are available to all users. IIS also allows you to add other directories that will appear as subdirectories of the home service. These are called *virtual directories*. An administrator can specify the physical locations of virtual directories and have them appear as subdirectories of the home directory. The published directories can be located on local or network drives. If a virtual directory is located on a network drive, you should also specify the user name and password that allow access to that drive. You can create an unlimited number of virtual directories. Performance may deteriorate, however, so use them only when they are required.

On the Directories tab (shown in Figure 5-3), the Default Document settings are for directing the user to a default page if a page has not been specified. The Directory Browsing Allowed setting provides the remote user with an HTML directory listing if the default document is not specified.

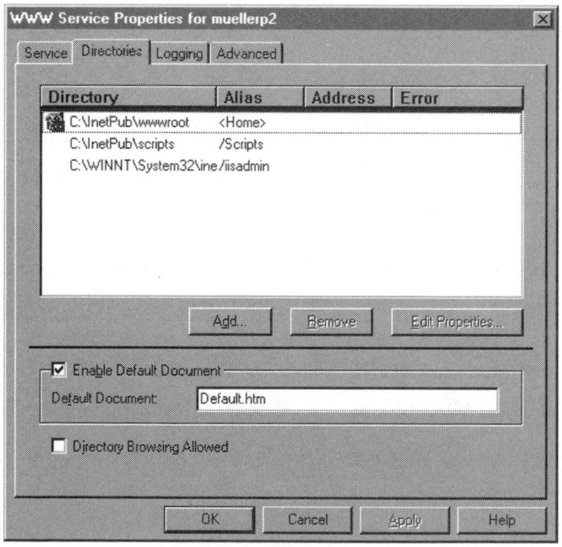

Figure 5-3

The Directories tab of the WWW Service Properties dialog box.

The Logging tab

Each service can log user activity (see Figure 5-4). Logging is important in finding out what services are being used. You can send log data to files or to an ODBC database. If you have multiple servers or services on a network, you can log all their activity in a single file or database on any network computer.

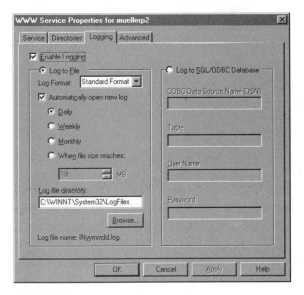

Figure 5-4

The Logging tab of the WWW Service Properties dialog box.

The Advanced tab

You can use the Advanced tab of the Service Properties dialog box (see Figure 5-5) to prevent access to certain users/IP addresses and set the maximum bandwidth for outbound traffic. That way, you can regulate the amount of traffic on your server. In most cases, you will allow almost everyone access to a service. In general, explicitly denying access will only work if IP addressees are fixed and not randomly generated by a DHCP server.

5

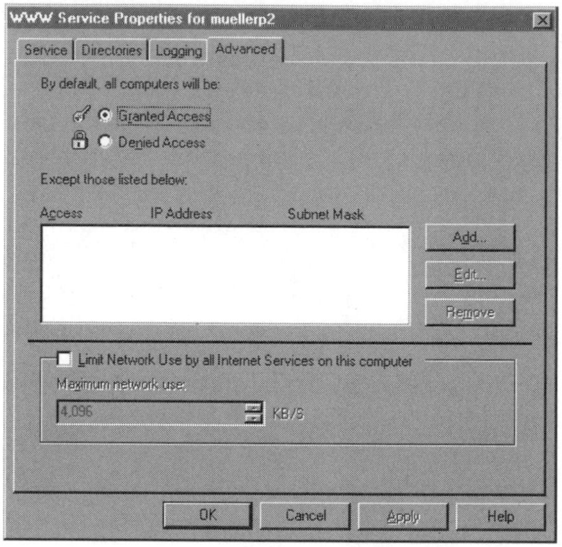

Figure 5-5

The Advanced tab of the WWW Service Properties dialog box.

Tips for Configuring Services

This section offers you some tips for configuring services when using the WWW and FTP services.

WWW

🌐   Set the Default Document as DEFAULT.HTM so that clients who are browsing always receive the main page.

🌐   Disable directory browsing by unchecking the Directory Browsing Allowed box on the Directories tab of the WWW Service Properties dialog box.

🌐   Set logging to record who has visited your page. This will give you excellent information on your users and how often pages are accessed.

🌐   Always configure timeouts for idle connections.

FTP

🌐   Always add an information file to each directory to help describe the files in that directory.

🌐   To enable FTP clients to view files on NTFS partitions, you must select UNIX as the directory's listing style. This setting is on the Directories tab of the FTP Service Properties dialog box.

Access Control, Security, and Other Important Information

The most common questions on FrontPage and IIS have to do with the way that security and access control are managed. For more specific documentation on running IIS, point your browser at the following URL:

http://localhost/winnt/system32/iisadmin/htmldocs

Controlling Web Access with FrontPage

When running with IIS, FrontPage uses the Windows NT security system instead of the FrontPage-specific security model that is used for other Web servers. Here are some tips to remember:

🌐 To add or remove FrontPage administrators, you must add or remove them from the NT Administrators group by using the NT User Manager or User Manager For Domains in the Administrative Tools program group. When you are using IIS as your Web server, do not set administrators by choosing Permissions from the FrontPage Explorer's Tools menu.

🌐 The easiest way to control Web access in FrontPage is to create an Authors group under Windows NT and then add the Authors group to the Authoring Permissions list by choosing Permissions from the FrontPage Explorer's Tools menu. From then on, just use the User Manager For Domains to add and remove users to the Authors group when you want to add or remove FrontPage authoring permissions for users.

🌐 FrontPage requires users to have local logon rights under Windows NT. You can set these rights by choosing User Rights from the User Manager's Policies menu.

Restricting browse access

If you want to restrict access to a Web, create a local Windows NT group for the Web's end users, or use a group that is already on the Windows NT system. In the FrontPage Explorer, choose Permissions from the Tools menu. In the Users tab of the Permissions dialog box, select Only Registered Users Have Browse Access, and then remove all Windows NT groups that have the IIS Anonymous user logon (IUSR_<machine_name>). Add the user group you created, and then click OK. Then, to update who has browse access to the Web, update the users and groups in the Windows NT Users group, using the User Manager.

CHAPTER 5

Allowing unrestricted access

Adding the Anonymous user or adding a group containing the Anonymous user to the list of users on a Web allows all users access to that Web. Note that you must use the same password for the IUSR_<machine_name> account in the User Manager and in the Internet Service Manager's Service Properties dialog box.

Giving access to users from other domains

To add administrators, authors, or end users (or groups of administrators, authors, or end users) from domains that are outside the local host's domain, you must add the users or groups by using the User Manager so that they have the right to log on locally. To do this, open the User Manager, and select the local domain. Select User Rights from the Policies menu. From the Right drop-down list, select Log On Locally. Scroll down the Grant To field to see if the user or the group you want to add is listed. If not, add the group or user with the Add button.

Allowing access without user names and passwords

Check the Allow Anonymous box on the Service tab in the Internet Service Manager's Service Properties dialog box.

Controlling the list of users in the Permissions dialog box

You can choose Permissions from the FrontPage Explorer's Tools menu to control which users and groups can be added to the lists of authors and end users. To do this, open the FRONTPG.INI file in the WINNT35 folder, and under the [Port N] section, where N is the port number for the IIS server, add the variables shown in Table 5-2 to modify the contents of the list of users and groups. (Note that setting both GroupsOnly and UsersOnly to 1 defaults to listing only groups, and no users.)

Table 5-2   Variables for Modifying Lists of Users and Groups.

Setting	Meaning
GroupsOnly=1	List only groups (no users).
UsersOnly=1	List only users (no groups).
LocalComputerOnly=1	List only the users and/or groups from the local computer instead of from the local computer and the primary domain.
ListDomains=DOMAIN1 DOMAIN2 DOMAIN3	List users and/or groups from domains listed here, as well as from the local computer and the primary domain. The list of domains should be space-separated.

Security Notes

This section contains a few pointers about how some FrontPage WebBot components work and about using FrontPage on a FAT file system.

The Save Results WebBot component

Save Results WebBots produced by FrontPage Wizards place their output files in the _PRIVATE directory of the Web. Because end users of a Web on an Internet Information Server must have access to these files to write to them, they also have access to browse them. Therefore, an end user who guesses the name of the output file can have access to the results of your form.

NOTE

The name of the output file is not listed where an end user could see it, nor can an end user list the files in the _PRIVATE directory.

To work around this potential problem, change the location of the Save Results WebBot's output. Open the Form Properties dialog box by right-clicking on a form page and selecting Form Properties from the menu. Click the Settings button. In the File For Results field of the Results tab, change the output file or page. To keep the results within the Web, use the root Web's _VTI_LOG directory. No one (including authors and administrators) can browse to this directory. To save the results to a file, supply the absolute filename of a file that is writeable by end users of the Web.

Access control under FAT

Under the FAT system, all access control is turned off. However, all FrontPage administrators are required to be Windows NT administrators. This level of access control is still enforced because FrontPage administrators update the server's configuration, which requires Windows NT Administrator privileges. If you try to do a FrontPage administrator operation and you are not a Windows NT administrator, you will get a message that ends with "Error Code 5."

When authoring a Web under the FAT system, you should turn off the Allow Anonymous option in the Service Properties dialog box in the Internet Service Manager. This forces authors to log on to create and edit documents.

When you've finished authoring the Web, turn Allow Anonymous back on in the Service Properties dialog box in the Internet Service Manager. This enables users to browse the Web without password authorization.

To protect your Web from authoring while it is in this state, use the FrontPage Server Administrator to disable authoring. Open the FrontPage Server Administrator, click Authoring, select the Disabled option, click OK, and click Close to close the FrontPage Server Administrator.

Troubleshooting

This section offers tips for tracking down problems you might have in using FrontPage and IIS and explains how to solve these problems.

Logon problems

If you aren't being recognized as a valid user on the Web site, try specifying *domain\account_name* instead of just *account_name* in the FrontPage logon dialog box. If that doesn't work, make sure the permissions are properly set for that user and that the user is in fact a registered author, administrator, or end user with local logon rights.

Problems opening a Web not on the primary domain controller

When the FrontPage Explorer is being used to open a Web from an Internet Information Server that is not on the machine that is the primary domain controller for your user name, the Internet Information Server requires that you enter *domain\username* as your user name. This limitation also affects browsers. You can specify the default logon domain that validates a clear-text logon when no domain is specified in the User Name field. Use the Registry Editor (REGEDT32.EXE) to add the following registry value of data type REG_SZ:

```
HKEY_LOCAL_MACHINE\SYSTEM\CurrentControlSet\Services\W3SVC\
Parameters\DefaultLogonDomain={domain name}
```

> Using the Registry Editor incorrectly can cause serious, systemwide problems that might require you to reinstall Windows NT to correct them. Microsoft cannot guarantee that problems resulting from the use of the Registry Editor can be solved. Use this tool at your own risk.

Problems with server authentication

Let's say you receive the following error message when you attempt to open a Web:

```
"Unable to complete transaction - the server requested
authentication information (userid/password) using an authentication
scheme (ntlm) that is unsupported by this tool."
```

This means that you have not selected the Basic [Clear Text] password-authentication option in the Internet Service Manager. To do so, run the Internet Service Manager. Select the WWW Service, and choose Service

Properties from the Properties menu. In the WWW Service Properties dialog box, click the Service tab. In the Password Authentication section, check Basic [Clear Text].

Error 5

If you try to do a FrontPage Administrator operation, such as creating a Web, and if IIS is running on the FAT file system, or on NTFS with Access Control disabled, an error message ending in "Error 5" indicates one of the following two problems:

1. You did not turn off Allow Anonymous on the Service tab of the WWW Service Properties dialog box in the Internet Service Manager.

2. You are currently logged on under an account that does not have Windows NT Administrator privileges on the IIS host machine. To log on as administrator, quit FrontPage to flush the password cache, and then reconnect to the server with a Windows NT Administrator user name and password.

Error 500

If, after supplying your name and password to the FrontPage Explorer, an error message beginning with "500" appears, it indicates one of the following two conditions:

1. You are logging on from a domain that is not recognized by the IIS host machine.

2. You are logging on from a domain that is recognized, but you do not have privileges on the IIS host machine.

Problems caused by Port 80

Let's say you get the following message:

```
httpd: could not bind to port 80
```

This means that you are trying to start the FrontPage Personal Web Server while another server (like the Internet Information Server) is running on port 80.

Problems with the WebBot registration component

The User Registration Page Template, the WebBot Registration component, and in general, on-the-fly registration of new users through the Web browser are not supported by the FrontPage Server Extensions for IIS. Additional information on using FrontPage and IIS can be found in Microsoft Online Support at the following URL:

```
http://www.microsoft.com/FrontPageSupport/
```

CHAPTER 5

Publishing Your Web to IIS from FrontPage

Now that you have installed and configured Microsoft Internet Information Server, as well as the FrontPage and ActiveX extensions, you are ready to copy your HTML files to your home directory to make them available to the Internet or your intranet. FrontPage includes a command that makes it easy to publish any FrontPage Web or sub-Web to another server. The Publish FrontPage Web command in FrontPage Explorer's File menu was originally created so that FrontPage users wouldn't have to use FTP to send their Web pages to the independent service provider hosting their Webs on the Internet. But there's also every reason to use this command to move your FrontPage data from a local, authoring server to a corporate IIS server. Be sure to use the FrontPage commands Recalculate Hyperlinks and Verify Hyperlinks when you do this. Otherwise, some relative URLs may be rewritten as absolute references to your source server.

To publish a Web, launch FrontPage Server, and then open the Web in the FrontPage Explorer. Select Publish FrontPage Web from the FrontPage Explorer's File menu, and enter the Web name and URL of the destination server in the Publish FrontPage Web dialog box shown in Figure 5-6.

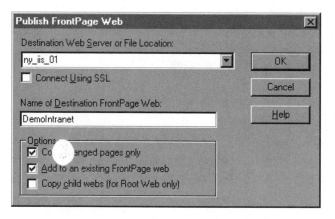

Figure 5-6
The Publish FrontPage Web dialog box.

The Options are the only remotely tricky aspect of the process, and they're tricky only if you're publishing your <ROOT WEB> directory. If you are, FrontPage will allow you to publish your <ROOT WEB> directory only if you also select the Copy Child Webs option. Otherwise, nothing will be

saved *unless* you provide a destination name for your <ROOT WEB> directory, in which case it will be published as a sub-Web of your server root.
Be aware, too, that publishing overwrites identically named files on the server
without prompting.

CHAPTER 5

CHAPTER

6

Microsoft Internet Explorer

Brian Stanton and Jeffrey M. Jones

You probably know that Microsoft Internet Explorer is Microsoft's Web browser. (If you don't, and your name is van Winkle, call home immediately.)

Internet Explorer supports nifty features like floating frames, style sheets, Secure Sockets Layer 3.0, Private Communication Technology, and other cool stuff. But that's only the beginning. In fact, what we know as Microsoft Internet Explorer 3.0 is really a "wrapper" for several smaller COM (Component Object Model) objects originally bundled inside Internet Explorer 2.0. The most important of these are the *Web browser object* (SHDOCVW.DLL), a fully implemented Microsoft ActiveX control that can be hosted by any Visual Basic–based application (version 4.0 or later) and is a complete ActiveX Document host; and the *Web browser host* (IEXPLORE.EXE), which provides a message pump and the shell window (class name IEFrame) for the actual browser object. The shell window works with the Web browser object to become a complete ActiveX Document container (or *shell document viewer*); therefore the Internet Explorer as a whole is an ActiveX Document container.

6
CHAPTER

What the *heck* am I talking about? Remember Object Linking and Embedding (OLE)? Sure you do. That was the container/object technology that allowed you to plop a Microsoft Excel spreadsheet into a Microsoft Word document and create a compound document. When the term OLE began to encompass more than compound documents, a new term, ActiveX, was created to describe the additional features. The actual mechanics of OLE and ActiveX are far too complex for this discussion, but the basic idea is that a container document (such as Word) hosts a server object (Microsoft Excel, in our example) that doesn't do much more than sit around and look pretty until the user wants to edit the server object—at which point the server takes over the Windows user interface and becomes (more or less) the active application. The user then sees Microsoft Excel menus and toolbars replace the Word menus and toolbars. More important, the user then has access to Microsoft Excel functionality from within a Word document.

The ActiveX model is simply an extension of the original OLE model, with specific implications for the Internet (or, to be more specific, for browsers like Internet Explorer, which can be containers or "shells" for ActiveX Document objects). The most significant difference is that in OLE the container determines the document-level behavior (as, for example, when Word header or footer data is applied to an embedded Microsoft Excel spreadsheet), whereas an ActiveX container is merely a frame and document-level behavior is determined by the ActiveX Document itself.

And what is an ActiveX Document, you might ask? Well, the technology originated within the Microsoft Binder application, which shipped with Microsoft Office for Windows 95, so for now you can think of all Office documents as being ActiveX Documents. Does that mean Internet Explorer can host any Office document? In the long run, the answer will be yes: Internet Explorer as we know it will effectively disappear, and you'll have read/write access to all ActiveX Documents—be they Word, Excel, or HTML documents on local drives, network drives, or the Internet—through a common browser host, the enhanced Windows Explorer. In the long run—a year at most—Web browsing in the Windows environment will be no different from file, network, or printer browsing. But for now, the answer is a qualified yes: Internet Explorer 3.0 can open, view, and edit Office documents directly (see Figure 6-1), though some commands (such as Mail Merge in Word) are not available on the Internet Explorer interface.

The implications for your Office 97 intranet are profound. Internet Explorer is a complete implementation of an ActiveX Document container, so you can maintain, browse, and edit data in all native Office formats (Microsoft Excel, Microsoft Access, Microsoft PowerPoint, Microsoft Outlook,

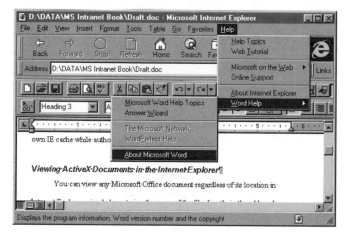

Figure 6-1

Microsoft Word running in Internet Explorer.

and Microsoft Word) as well as in HTML. And don't forget that you can use these other applications to control browsing programmatically, either through Internet Explorer or by directly manipulating the Web browser control (CLSID_IExplorer, implemented in SHDOCVW.DLL). Internet Explorer and the Web browser control both have their own (and, obviously, quite similar) object models; if you want to get technical, the IWebBrowser interface, exposed by the Web browser control, is implemented as a dual interface, one of which represents the base interface for InternetExplorer (the InternetExplorer.Application object being the implementation of the Web browser control for that instance of Internet Explorer). For example, the following lines of Microsoft Visual Basic code—which can be run as Microsoft Visual Basic, Microsoft Visual Basic for Applications, or Microsoft Visual Basic, Scripting Edition (VBScript)—will create a running instance of Internet Explorer 3.0, display it, and jump to the Microsoft Web site:

```
Set obj = CreateObject("InternetExplorer.Application")
obj.Visible = True
obj.Navigate URL="http://www.microsoft.com"
```

Internet Explorer, of course, also supports other ActiveX controls and a COM interface known as ActiveX scripting, which allows plug-in scripting engines. Microsoft has provided VBScript (and, for compatibility, JScript, Microsoft's implementation of JavaScript) for this interface, and because scripts can be contained within their own HTML <SCRIPT> tags, you can in fact use *both* scripts on a common page, as we do on our sample Home page (DEFAULT.HTM in the Chapter2 folder of the book's CD). Internet Explorer also supports Java applets with high performance by using a just-in-time (JIT) compiler, which converts Java byte-codes into native machine instructions on the fly. Internet Explorer, however, does *not* support Dynamic Data Exchange (DDE)—and if you've ever debugged a DDE routine, you might even be grateful for this.

Later in this chapter, you'll find a brief overview of the Internet Explorer object model and then a discussion of some advanced Automation. First, though, you need to learn how to view ActiveX Documents in Internet Explorer and how to preconfigure options for your end users' Internet Explorer interface and make effective use of your own Internet Explorer cache while authoring.

Viewing ActiveX Documents in Internet Explorer

In Internet Explorer, you can view any Microsoft Office document, regardless of its location, simply by entering the name of the file directly in the address box. For example, if you enter *C:\XYZ\ABC.DOC,* Internet Explorer loads a local Word document; enter *www.yourcompany.com/PublicDocs/ sales96.xls,* and Internet Explorer will allow you to download the Microsoft Excel workbook and open it (assuming, of course, that the URLs are valid and the relevant source applications have been installed on your machine). You can even browse local folders in Internet Explorer. When you enter a path like *C:\Windows* in the address box, Internet Explorer loads the Windows Explorer List View of that folder (see Figure 6-2). When Internet Explorer hosts the Windows Explorer, its View menu includes all standard Windows Explorer views: Large Icons, Small Icons, List, and Details.

Double-clicking a folder in the Windows Explorer's List View launches an instance of the relevant file in its own application window. Even if you've selected Options from the View menu of the My Computer window and checked the setting to open folders in a single window, the Windows Explorer window doesn't recognize that it is embedded inside Internet Explorer, and so it doesn't open the file within the current Internet Explorer window. This "feature" is scheduled to be fixed in Internet Explorer 4.0.

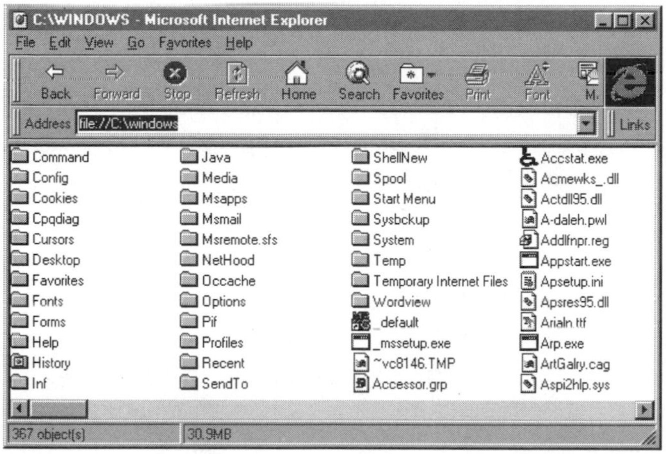

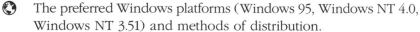

Figure 6-2

Windows Explorer List View in Internet Explorer.

Customizing Internet Explorer for Your Intranet

The Microsoft Internet Explorer Administration Kit (IEAK) lets organizations create and distribute a customized version of Internet Explorer, which can include the following features:

 Versions localized by language.

 The preferred Windows platforms (Windows 95, Windows NT 4.0, Windows NT 3.51) and methods of distribution.

 Optional components such as Internet Mail, Internet News, NetMeeting, ActiveMovie, and the HTMLLayout Control and Comic Chat, all of which will be installed automatically or available to select individually on an installation menu. You can also specify default options for some of the components, such as the addresses of Mail and News servers.

 Up to two additional custom components (that is, self-extracting and self-installing programs) that will be part of the distribution package.

 Default Start and Search pages and custom Toolbar Quick Link buttons that allow you to move around your intranet.

CHAPTER 6

- An Online Support page.
- A custom default Favorites list.
- A custom CD Auto-Run screen (the HTML page that displays in Kiosk mode when you insert a CD in your compact disk drive).
- The Window title ("The Acme Exploding Internet Explorer") and a custom bitmap to replace the static logo in the upper right corner of Internet Explorer ("Bang!").
- The settings for any proxy servers.
- Installation, configuration, and security settings, such as the default installation folder, commands that will be unavailable to users, and the file paths and command lines for custom commands.

The IEAK is available to any organization that has an Internet Explorer distribution agreement and complies with the Microsoft Internet Explorer usage guidelines. For more information, or to download the IEAK, point your browser to the following address:

http://www.microsoft.com/ie/ieak

Don't Forget Your Cache

Internet Explorer, like virtually any other browser nowadays, creates a local copy of everything it received through HTTP (though not, for example, local files that you open and view). The accumulated files are stored in a cache (typically, the Temporary Internet Files subfolder of your Windows folder), and, as the old joke goes, there's some good news and some bad news.

The (not-so) bad news is that you should be mindful of the accumulated cache size. As the Webmaster, you'll probably be browsing and caching a great many Web pages, and a megabyte here and a megabyte there can add up to real disk space. You can limit the size of the cache and purge the cache by choosing Options from Internet Explorer's View menu, selecting the Advanced tab, and clicking the Settings button in the Temporary Internet Files group. The Settings dialog box, which is shown in Figure 6-3, contains a slider control for setting the maximum cache size and an Empty Folder button to purge the cache.

And now the (really) good news: the cache can sure save a Webmaster's . . . bacon. Suppose that after a hard day's authoring, the PC gremlins (or good old operator error) cause some horrendous damage to your Web site. Before you resign yourself to ordering pizza and working through the night,

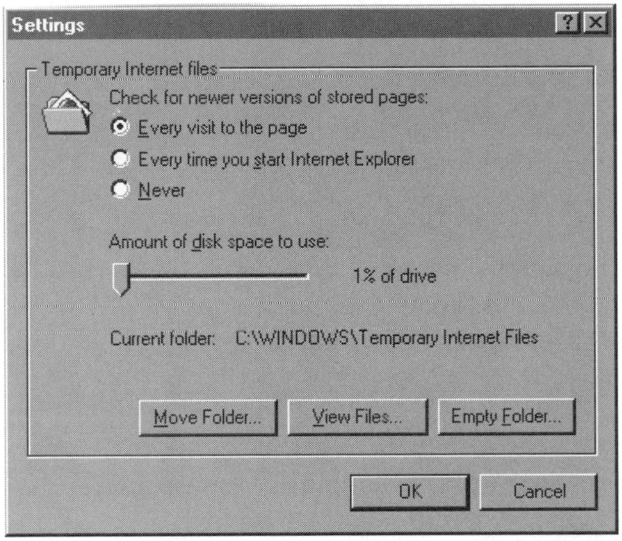

Figure 6-3

Internet Explorer's Settings dialog box for cache settings.

remember—if you've been checking your work in Internet Explorer as you go, *there's an intact copy in your cache of everything you've browsed!* You can open the cached versions, save or copy them back to your Web site, and go home singing (unless you take the subway, of course).

The Internet Explorer Scripting Object Model

The Internet Explorer scripting object model is a structure of objects, properties, methods, and events that allow the browser to be controlled with embedded HTML VBScript and JavaScript routines as well as Visual Basic code. The model consists of a hierarchy of eleven objects, some of which can have multiple instances, as shown in Figure 6-4.

Overview of the Model

This section will provide you with an introductory overview of the model and sample code that shows how it works. The complete Microsoft Internet Explorer scripting object model can (and should) be downloaded; here's the current address:

http://www.microsoft.com/intdev/sdk/docs/scriptom/

Figure 6-4

The Internet Explorer Scripting Object hierarchy.

The Window object and Frame object

The Window object is the top-level object. In a sense, it corresponds to the browser itself. Every Window object contains a Frame, History, Navigator, Location, Script, and Document object. Some of the most useful Window methods are Alert, Confirm, and Prompt (which display dialog boxes) and Navigate, which lets you move to a new URL. Because the *location* property (different from the Location object shown in the model) returns the URL of the current Web page, you can also navigate by setting the Window object's *location* property to a different ULR, as follows:

    window.location="http://jonesj/welcome/overview.htm"

A Window object, of course, can also contain multiple frames, in which case each Frame object is itself considered a Window object, with its own properties (including a *Document* property). In a framed environment, you can use the Window object's *self, parent,* and *top* properties to return the Window objects of the current window, the window containing the current frame, and the window containing *all* frames in the current browser instance (which might not be the same as the parent), respectively. The Window object's *frames* property (usefully, if somewhat confusingly) returns an array of frames for the specified window. When the following code is run on a content page in our current sample Web, it displays five message boxes with the frame name ("Content"):

```
alert window.name
alert self.name
alert name    'NOTE THAT "WINDOW" IS IMPLICIT WITHIN THE WINDOW SCOPE
alert parent.Frames(2).name
```

To display messages, you can also set the Window object's *Status* property to be equal to a text string.

The History object

The History object resides below the Window object, and it provides access to the browser's history list. It currently supports only three methods (*forward, back,* and *go*) and a property (*length*) that is not implemented in the current release.

The Navigator object

The Navigator object also resides below the Window object. It provides information about the browser application.

The Location object

The Location object resides below the Window object, and it corresponds to the current URL. Its various properties—*href, protocol, host, hostname, port, hash,* and so forth—correspond to various parts of the URL. Setting the location to a new URL causes Internet Explorer to browse the specified address.

The Script object

The Script object resides below the Window object. Although the Script object has no methods, properties, or events, you can use it to call scripts in other windows. For example, the following statement would run the script Myscript in the topmost window:

```
top.myscript()
```

The Script object also exposes your VBScript to Automation.

The Document object

The Document object resides a level below the Window object and corresponds to the Web page (or ActiveX document, graphics file, or what have you) currently loaded in the browser. Its properties include the page color scheme (bgColor, fgColor, linkColor, and so forth) and arrays for the anchors, links, and forms on the page. The *lastModified* property returns the date the page was last saved to the server directory; the *write* and *writeLn* methods insert a specified text string in your document. The *Cookie* property is an editable text file associated with the page. The Document object also contains the Link, Anchor, and Form objects.

The Link object

The Link object resides below the Document object, and it generates a read-only array of links in the currently loaded page. The object supports three events (*onMouseMove, onMouseOver, onClick*) and a number of properties (*href, protocol, pathname,* and so forth) that return the link target, as well as part or all of the link URL.

The Anchor object

The Anchor object also resides below the Document object, and it generates a read-only array of anchors (<A NAME=*text*> tags) in the currently loaded page. The object supports only one property, *name,* which returns the anchor name.

The Form object

The Form object resides at a level below the Document object and corresponds to a <FORM> tag in the currently loaded document. Forms are collectively maintained in the Document object as an array and individually, by name; if the second form in your document were named SubmissionForm, you could refer to it either as document.SubmissionForm or as document.forms(1). The Form object has only one method (*submit*) and related event (*onSubmit*). To write a conditional routine that submits the form only if the function evaluates to True, you can use the Return statement with a function:

```
form.onsubmit = "return IsItValid()"
```

The *action, encoding, method,* and *target* properties refer, respectively, to the ACTION, ENCTYPE, METHOD, and TARGET attributes of the <FORM> tag. The Form object's *elements* property returns an array of the elements of the form in the order in which they have been declared in the HTML file.

The Element object

The Element object resides at the level below that of the Form object, and it corresponds to an intrinsic HTML control (such as <INPUT>) or to an ActiveX control that has been placed with the <OBJECT> tag. It supports four methods: *click, focus, blur,* and *select.* It also supports five related events: *onClick, onFocus, onBlur, onSelect,* and *onChange.* The properties of the Element object get or set the name, value, or state of the control (different properties being available for different controls). The *options* property returns an array of <SELECT> tag menu items, and the *selectedIndex* property returns the index value (starting with 0) of a menu selection. If the first element in the first form in your document were a <SELECT> tag, the following code would display the value of the selection in a message box:

```
n = document.forms(0).elements(0).SelectedIndex
alert document.forms(0).elements(0).options(n).text
```

Limitations of the Model

You'd think the Internet Explorer object model would allow a programmer to use Automation to do anything the end user can do with the application, but this isn't the case. The most glaring examples of missing functionality can be seen in the Options dialog box (shown in Figure 6-5), invoked by selecting Options from Internet Explorer's View menu. Several tabs have settings that would correspond to objects, properties, and methods in the object model—if only they existed!

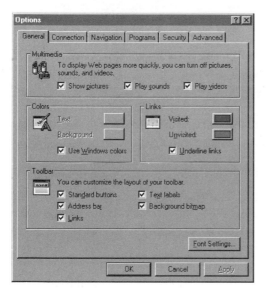

Figure 6-5
Internet Explorer's Options dialog box.

The fact that this functionality is missing is both good and bad. It's good because it involves many properties that are likely to change in future versions of Internet Explorer as well as some properties that are quite powerful and dangerous to change (so you probably shouldn't be messing around with them anyway). As long as they're missing, you won't need to worry about backward compatibility in the future. Still, the bad news is that many features currently missing from the object model *are* likely to be added in

CHAPTER 6

future releases, so they should be accessible. For instance, if you're using a custom setup program instead of the IEAK, you might well need to set properties such as proxy settings, which you can currently do only by hacking at the Registry settings—and these, by the way, are undocumented, hard to decipher, and subject to change. In Windows 95 you can find the global settings in

```
HKEY_LOCAL_MACHINE\SOFTWARE\Microsoft\Internet Explorer\...
```

For user settings, they're in

```
HKEY_CURRENT_USER\Software\Microsoft\Internet Explorer\...
```

The Web Browser Control's Object Model

This object model is similar to Internet Explorer's object model and is fully documented on the Microsoft Web site. The control can be embedded in a Visual Basic form or a C++ dialog box and manipulated through Automation to browse Internet sites as well as directories on the local machine and on network servers. However, since the Automation would have to be written in Visual Basic or C++, it falls outside the scope of this book. Nevertheless, in the next section, you'll see one example of how you can use Visual Basic with the Web browser control to automate Internet Explorer.

Programming Internet Explorer

Has this ever happened to you? You're surfing the net, and almost every site has some interesting software that you'd like to download. There's just one tiny little catch: they all expect you to fill out a request form first. Now, since you've already filled out about a million of these (and your name hasn't changed in the process), you figure there has got to be a better way; if only your computer or some kind of software (Are you listening, Microsoft?) were smart enough to do it for you.

Until then, let's suppose you're also a lousy typist, so it takes you a minute or two to fill out each form (always the same basic information), and then you have to proof the darn thing, and—hey, wouldn't it almost be more efficient to figure out a way to have Internet Explorer fill out these forms for you? In fact, you could probably do it with Automation. But there's just one more catch. How do you know what's being displayed in Internet Explorer?

You'd think, given the Source option of Internet Explorer's View menu, that a Source property or a ViewSource method or something useful like that would be in the object model. Well, there isn't. OK. So now you say to yourself, "But the Internet Explorer scripting object model exposes the information in the HTML page. Why can't I use that?" Here's why you can't: because the Internet Explorer scripting object model is not exposed to Automation.

Then you remember the Web browser control—the "guts" of Internet Explorer, which *is* exposed to Automation. Specifically, you remember reading this very paragraph and learning about the Web browser control's Document property, which is an object reference to the active document being viewed. Since Internet Explorer can display any ActiveX document as well as HTML, text, GIF files, and heaven knows what else, you can't assume that the active document is HTML. And only HTML documents have a scripting object model in the first place. But if your browser is displaying a Microsoft Excel sheet, the Web browser control's Document property refers to a Worksheet object. For Word documents, Document will be an object reference, and you can use the following syntax to get to the WordBasic object:

```
Document.Application.WordBasic
```

For HTML pages, Document will have an IHTMLDocument object reference.

If you have Visual Basic 5.0, you can determine the Document reference yourself with the following procedure:

1. Launch Visual Basic 5.0.

2. Add a reference to the Microsoft Internet controls by choosing Components from the Project menu and then selecting Microsoft Internet Controls, or by browsing to:

   C:\Windows\System\SHDOCVW.DLL

3. Add a WebBrowser control to a Visual Basic form.

4. Enter the code in the Form_Load event procedure to move to any Web page. (*WebBrowser1.Navigate "www.microsoft.com"* will do just fine.)

5. Run the program. Once the Web page loads, press Ctrl-Break to enter Break mode.

6. Press Control-G to open the Immediate pane.

7. Enter *? TypeName(Form1.WebBrowser1.Document)* and press ENTER. You'll see the class IHTMLDocument.

6
CHAPTER

You can inspect this undocumented class by adding a reference to it to the project, launching the Object Browser, and then selecting the library you're interested in—which, in this case, is "Internet Explorer Scripting Object Model," located in MSHTML.DLL. You can see that the IHTMLDocument object has only one property: Script (see Figure 6-6). You can also view OLE information by running the OLE View or OLE/COM Object Viewer utility (Figure 6-7), a very handy application that lets expert users browse the world of OLE as it relates to software installed on their computers. You can download this utility from the Microsoft Web site at:

http:/www.microsoft.com/oledev/olecom/oleview.htm

"Hmmmm," you say to yourself as you look at the following characters on your screen:

```
?TypeName(Form1.WebBrowser1.Document.Script)  IOmWindow_class.
```

"What type of object is Script?" Except for the *IOm* prefix and the *_class* suffix, it looks a lot like the Window object in the scripting object model—and it is! From this object you can move right into the scripting object model and retrieve details about the HTML document currently being viewed.

If you're interested in filling out a form, you'll be dealing with the form elements in the scripting object model: text boxes, mostly. And, specifically, you'll want a way to set the Value property of those text elements that have recognizable names (such as FirstName, Address, Company, Email, and so

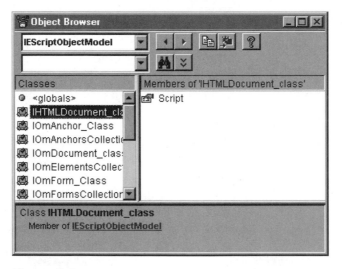

Figure 6-6

The methods and properties of the IHTMLDocument class in the Visual Basic Object Browser.

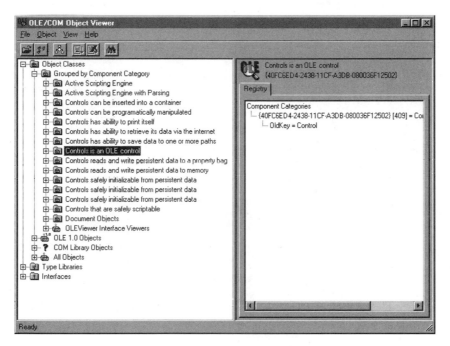

Figure 6-7
The OLE/COM Object Viewer utility.

forth) to the specific values of *your* first name, address, company name, e-mail address, and so forth. Listing 6-1 shows you some Visual Basic code that'll do just that. (The code from the listings in the rest of this chapter can also be found on the book's companion CD in the Chapter6 folder.)

```
Dim sFirstName As String
Dim sLastName As String
Dim sMiddleInit As String
Dim sCompany As String
Dim sAddress1 As String
Dim sAddress2 As String
Dim sCity As String
Dim sState As String
```

Listing 6-1
Internet Explorer Form Update Code

(continued)

Listing 6-1 *(continued)*

```vb
Dim sZip As String
Dim sAreaCode As String
Dim sEmail As String
Dim sPhone As String
Dim sFax As String

Sub UpdateHTMLDocument(InternetExplorer As Object)
    With InternetExplorer.Document.Script
        Dim frameIndex As Integer
        For frameIndex = 0 To .Frames.Count - 1
            With .Frames(frameIndex).Document
                Dim formIndex As Integer
                For formIndex = 0 To .Forms.Count - 1
                    UpdateFormElements .Forms(formIndex)
                Next   ' formIndex
            End With    ' .Frames(frameIndex).Document
        Next   ' frameIndex
    End With    ' InternetExplorer.Document.Script.Document
End Sub

Sub UpdateFormElements(Form As Object)
    Dim elemIndex As Integer
    For elemIndex = 0 To Form.Elements.Count - 1
        With Form.Elements(elemIndex)
            If Len(.Name) > 0 And _
                TypeName(Form.Elements(elemIndex)) = "Text" Then
                Select Case LCase$(.Name)
                    Case "first name", "firstname", "first_name"
                        .Value = sFirstName
                    Case "last name", "name2", "lastname", _
                    "last_name"
                        .Value = sLastName
                    Case "name"
                        If Len(sMiddleInit) > 0 Then
                            .Value = sFirstName & " " & _
                                sMiddleInit & " " & sLastName
                        Else
                            .Value = sFirstName & " " & _
                                sLastName
                        End If
                    Case "mi", "reg_middleinitial"
                        .Value = sMiddleInit
                    Case "company", "reg_companyname", "co_name"
                        .Value = sCompany
```

Listing 6-1 *(continued)*

```
                        Case "address", "reg_address"
                            If Len(sAddress2) > 0 Then
                                .Value = sAddress1 & ", " & _
                                    sAddress2
                            Else
                                .Value = sAddress1
                            End If
                        Case "address1", "reg_address1", "addr"
                            .Value = sAddress1
                        Case "address2", "reg_address2", "addr2"
                            .Value = sAddress2
                        Case "city", "reg_city"
                            .Value = sCity
                        Case "state", "st", "reg_state"
                            .Value = sState
                        Case "zip", "zipcode", "reg_postalcode"
                            .Value = sZip
                        Case "country", "ctry"
                            .Value = "US"
                        Case "email", "e-mail", "reg_email"
                            .Value = sEmail
                        Case "phone", "telephone", "telno"
                            .Value = sAreaCode & "-" & sPhone
                        Case "reg_phonenumber"
                            .Value = sPhone
                        Case "reg_area"
                            .Value = sAreaCode
                        Case "fax"
                            .Value = sFax
                        Case Else
                            ' MsgBox "Don't know how to handle " & _
                            ' "field: " & .Name & "'"
                    End Select    ' LCase$(.Name)
                End If    ' Len(.Name) > 0
            End With  ' .Element(elementIndex)
        Next    ' elementIndex
End Sub

Private Sub Form_Load()
    Me.Move (Screen.Width - Me.Width) * 0.5, _
        (Screen.Height - Me.Height) * 0.5
    sFirstName = "John"
    sLastName = "Public"
```

(continued)

Listing 6-1 *(continued)*

```
        sMiddleInit = "Q"
        sCompany = "Micro Modeling Associates, Inc."
        sAddress1 = "115 Broadway"
        sAddress2 = "14th Floor"
        sCity = "New York"
        sState = "NY"
        sZip = "10006"
        sAreaCode = "212"
        sPhone = "233-9890"
        sFax = "212-233-9897"
        sEmail = "publicj@micromodeling.com"
        URL.AddItem "www.microsoft.com"
        URL.AddItem "www.micromodeling.com"
        URL.AddItem "www.yahoo.com"
    End Sub

    Private Sub WebBrowser1_DownloadComplete()
        On Error Resume Next
        frmEvents.List1.AddItem "DownloadComplete"
    '   UpdateHTMLDocument WebBrowser1
        If Err Then MsgBox Error$
        Err.Clear
    End Sub
```

There's only one more little catch (I promise): the code in Listing 6-1 works only if the Web browser control is embedded in a Visual Basic form. This might be okay for you and me, but some people actually prefer Internet Explorer's interface. They don't really need a customized browser; they want to be able to run Internet Explorer by itself. So how do you get Visual Basic to "interface" with an already running instance of Internet Explorer? By using Visual Basic's GetObject function—and Listing 6-2 shows you how that's done.

OK, OK, there's only one more little catch—really. Since no events are fired in Visual Basic when you use external objects, how can you tell if and when the user jumps to another page? You could use a Timer control to regularly poll Internet Explorer's status and look at the Busy property for signs of change, as shown in Listing 6-3. It's not a perfect method, but if you poll fast enough it will do the trick. (Just don't poll too often, or other applications won't get a chance to run.)

```
Private objInternetExplorer As Object

Private Sub Form_Load()
    :
    On Error Resume Next
    Set objInternetExplorer = _
        GetObject(, "InternetExplorer.Application")
    If objInternetExplorer Is Nothing Then
        If MsgBox("Start Internet Explorer?", vbYesNo) _
            <> vbYes Then
            Exit Sub
        End If
        Set objInternetExplorer = _
            CreateObject("InternetExplorer.Application")
        If objInternetExplorer Is Nothing Then
            MsgBox "Cannot start Internet Explorer.", _
                vbOKOnly + vbExclamation
            Exit Sub
        End If
        objInternetExplorer.Visible = True  ' normally starts up
                                            ' hidden
    End If
    Err.Clear
    ' At this point objInternetExplorer contains reference to a
    ' running app
End Sub

Private Sub Command1_Click()
    On Error Resume Next
    Dim i As Integer
    For i = 0 To URL.ListCount - 1
        If StrComp(URL.Text, URL.List(i), 1) = 0 Then Exit For
    Next
    If i = URL.ListCount Then URL.AddItem URL.Text
    WebBrowser1.Navigate URL.Text
    If Err Then
        MsgBox Error$
    End If
    Err.Clear
End Sub
```

Listing 6-2

Controlling Internet Explorer Application

201

```
Private bWasBusy As Boolean
Private Sub Timer1_Timer()
    On Error Resume Next
    If objInternetExplorer Is Nothing Then Exit Sub
    If objInternetExplorer.Busy Then
        If bWasBusy = False Then
            OnStartBusy objInternetExplorer
        End If
    Else
        If bWasBusy Then OnStopBusy objInternetExplorer
    End If
    bWasBusy = objInternetExplorer.Busy
    If objInternetExplorer.Visible = False Then
        MsgBox "User quit"
        Set objInternetExplorer = Nothing
    End If
    Err.Clear
End Sub

Sub OnStartBusy(InternetExplorer As Object)
    ' get current form element values and update our database
    ' hopefully it's not too late
    frmEvents.List1.AddItem "Start Busy..."
End Sub

Sub OnStopBusy(InternetExplorer As Object)
    ' loop through form elements
    ' update their values from our database
    frmEvents.List1.AddItem "Stop busy."
    UpdateHTMLDocument InternetExplorer
End Sub
```

Listing 6-3

Automatic Form Updating Using a Timer

You'll notice that Listing 6-3 handles only one instance of Internet Explorer—and, ideally, you'd want additional routines to deal with users who are running more than one instance of Internet Explorer—but this should be enough to give you the basic idea.

CHAPTER 7

Creating Dynamic Pages with VBScript and ActiveX

Jeffrey M. Jones

In this chapter, you'll see how easy it is to write Microsoft Visual Basic, Scripting Edition (VBScript) routines that can update frames, enter text into your Web pages on the fly, and validate data on the client side before it's sent back to the server. You'll then learn how to add Microsoft ActiveX controls to your pages and hook them up to VBScript routines.

Visual Basic, Scripting Edition

VBScript is the newest, most portable member of the Visual Basic family of programming languages developed by Microsoft. The family includes Visual Basic for Applications (VBA)—now common to all applications in the Microsoft Office Suite—as well as Visual Basic in Standard (or Learning), Professional, and Enterprise editions. VBScript contains only a subset of Visual Basic features. For example, it will not let you create user interfaces, call external dynamic-link library (DLL) functions, or create instances of OLE objects. Most frustrating of all, it does not currently ship with a debugger. Yet what it will do—in conjunction with Microsoft Internet Explorer and Microsoft Internet Information Server (IIS)—is let you write simple and robust routines that can execute on either the client or the server side. At this writing, no other programming language can make such a claim.

Scripting languages need not be mutually exclusive. Java, Visual J++, VBA, Visual C++, and even older CGI scripts, such as Perl, might all have a place on your intranet. But there are at least four reasons why you should consider VBScript before turning elsewhere:

1. VBScript, unlike Java, can provide server-side functionality on IIS and can also be integrated with the ISAPI DLL to run back-end applications.

2. Because VBScript is a subset of both VBA and Visual Basic, it is forward-compatible with development throughout your Microsoft Windows environment.

3. It's relatively simple and easy to learn.

4. It's free.

A Bit of History

Some of the most exciting recent advances in Internet and intranet technology have been in the area of Web programming. By 1995, the server-side routines—collectively known as CGI scripts and written in languages such as C, AppleScript, and Perl—had been supplemented by interpreted objects known as Java Applets, which were written in the Java language developed by Sun Microsystems. (Java was originally developed in 1991 as a compact, device-independent language for automating small appliances like toasters and microwaves. It was only in 1994, when Sun unveiled its Java-enabled HotJava browser, that Java hit the Web. The rest, as they say, is history.)

Java not only allowed startling new effects, such as animation and real-time stock tickers, but also was a totally new approach to Web programming. In fact, the Java system required three main components: the programming language (Java), a Java compiler to convert the language into processor-independent objects written in byte-code, and a Java run-time interpreter. When a system with the Java interpreter (read "Java-compliant browser") encountered an embedded Java object in a Web page, executable code was downloaded from the server and run on the client side.

Java was revolutionary because for the first time HTML could deliver not just data but also the software for manipulating the data, thereby challenging the supremacy of operating systems in providing application support. But Java was also C, and C was and is an advanced programming language. The next major advances involved refinements of the Java approach, creating far simpler languages (or "scripts") for browser control while greatly expanding the class of compiled objects (now called ActiveX controls) to run on the server or be downloaded to the client, as needed.

VBScript and the Internet Explorer Object Model

For the most part, we'll be using VBScript embedded directly in the Web page HTML code to manipulate the Internet Explorer object model: providing instructions, let's say, to write data into the file as it is rendered or to check whether the contents of a designated frame need refreshing. When Internet Explorer renders a page with embedded script at browse time, it loads the local copy of the VBScript at run time, which in turn compiles and executes the code on the fly. You should bear in mind, however, that advancing technology involves an ever-expanding server-side role for VBScript.

The ISAPI DLL, which resides on the server, can be used to load other DLLs for performing additional server-side functions. This mechanism, for example, allows ISAPI to call VBScript routines through intermediate DLLs known as Visual Basic Script shims. Instead of executing the VBScript code themselves, the shims launch other applications, which then run the VBScript routines. The first release of IIS, for example, contained an ISAPI shim that launched and passed variables to a server application and then closed the server application, after receiving data back, and then passed the data on to ISAPI itself. (For an example of this functionality in action, browse our Micro Modeling Web site at http:/www.micromodeling.com.) At this writing, shim DLLs cannot maintain persistent connections to server applications, nor do they strip out and restore HTTP parameters in the passed variables. (Currently, the server applications require code to do this.) Nevertheless, server-side scripting with VBScript under the open ActiveX Server Pages (ASP) represents one of the newest frontiers of Web technology.

Scripting Basics

If you're a seasoned Visual Basic programmer, you can skip directly to the examples (and even they won't detain you for long). But if you're not, stay tuned for an orientation to your Basic training. The training itself is up to you, so brace yourself and point your browser to http://www.microsoft.com/vbscript.

Any Visual Basic routine requires two generic components:

 A named subroutine or function (the code)

 A context in which the code is invoked (a call to the named routine, associated with an event or a control)

7

C
H
A
P
T
E
R

The code itself is inserted into a Web page HTML file between <SCRIPT> </SCRIPT> tags. It's also good form to add <COMMENT></COMMENT> tags (or <!-- -->) bracketing the code; that way, browsers unable to interpret your code won't misinterpret it as text to be displayed. Launch the Microsoft FrontPage 97 Editor, select Script from the Insert menu, and check the VBScript option; at least the command will do that much for you. (Alas, there's currently no tool that saves you the trouble of writing the script itself!)

The following illustration shows yet another contribution (as it would appear in the FrontPage Editor's Script dialog box) to the series of inane "Hello, World!" routines used by programmers to explain programming to nonprogrammers:

The beginning of the routine is defined by the Sub statement, followed by the routine name: NoBigDeal. The next line of the routine is actually the second, third, and fourth lines of code in the window; indents and the line-continuation symbol (a space followed by the underscore, or _) were used to break up the line so the graphic would be smaller, but it's executed as a single line of code. This line is a call to the MsgBox function, which in this example generates a message box titled "Hello, World!" that displays the message "Are we having fun yet?" and the Yes and No buttons (that's what the value 4 means). The MsgBox function also performs a calculation: its result, in this case, is the preassigned value of the button that the user clicks. The Yes button is assigned the value of 6, and a click on the No button returns a value of 7. You could assign the value of the function (that is, the result of its calculation) to a variable. In this case, however, it's assigned to the status property of the Internet Explorer's Window object, which gets or sets the status text in the lower left of the status bar. Here's a pseudocode rewrite of the subroutine:

```
The subroutine named NoBigDeal...
    Displays a Yes/No message box that reads "Are we having fun yet?"
    Captures the value of the button clicked by the user
    Assigns that value to the status bar text in the current
        Internet Explorer window
And ends
```

Not bad—but you won't see any of this magic until you assign the subroutine to an event. One easy way to do that is to create a button on your Web page and assign the routine to the OnClick event associated with clicking the button. Here is how you create the button in the FrontPage Editor:

1. Click the Push Button button on the Forms toolbar.

2. Select the button on the form and choose Form Field Properties from the Edit menu to bring up the Push Button Properties dialog box.

3. Select the Reset button type. (Submit buttons require an action, which we're not providing.)

4. Click the Extended button and add the Extended Attribute named OnClick with the value of our VBScript routine: NoBigDeal.

FrontPage will insert the button in an HTML form, but for now that's okay. If you look at your page in the View Or Edit HTML window, you should see something like this—the routine within <SCRIPT> tags; the button within the <FORM> tags:

```
<!DOCTYPE HTML PUBLIC "-//IETF//DTD HTML//EN">
<html>

<head>
<meta name="GENERATOR" content="Microsoft FrontPage 2.0">
<title>VBScript test Page</title>
</head>

<body>

<p><script language="VBScript"><!--
Sub NoBigDeal
    window.status = _
    MsgBox("Are we having fun yet?",4, _
    "Hello World")
End sub

--></script></p>
```

(continued)

```
<form method="POST">
    <p> <input type="reset" name="B1" value="Reset"
    onclick="NoBigDeal"> </p>
</form>
</body>
</html>
```

Go ahead—save the page and preview it in Internet Explorer. When you click the Reset button, you should see the "Hello, World!" message box. When you click the No button, you should see the number 7 in the status bar. (Numbers persist even after the routine ends, which is why if you click Reset again you'll see the value of the previous run, as in Figure 7-1.)

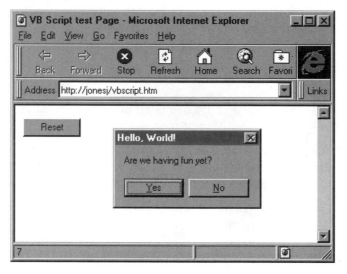

Figure 7-1

"Hello, World!" in Internet Explorer.

NOTE Even though OnClick is valid within an <INPUT> tag, you'll search your HTML reference in vain for any mention of an OnClick attribute. That's because it's an *event*. Confused? Internet Explorer interprets the HTML <INPUT> tag as an Element object within the Document object. The Internet Explorer object model allows different events for different elements; for example, buttons support OnClick and OnFocus, while text elements support onFocus, onBlur, onChange, and onSelect. Technically speaking, the HTML OnClick attribute is nonstandard HTML, supported only by the Internet Explorer object model, but you can also think of it as VBScript dressed like HTML.

You can associate a VBScript routine with an event in several other ways as well. In our example, you could associate it directly with the button's OnClick attribute; here's an example using the same MsgBox function:

```
<p> <input type="reset" name="B1" value="Reset"
onclick="window.status=MsgBox('Are we having fun yet?',36,'Hello,
World!')"> </p>
```

The VBScript is essentially the same; the only difference is that double quotes were replaced with single quotes so that the statement could "nest" within the quotes that define the value of the OnClick button attribute. The 32 was also added to the original button value of 4 to display the Warning Query icon in the message box. But there would obviously be real problems in using this approach to create extended routines. Worse yet, without designating VBScript as the script language somewhere on the page (as in the <SCRIPT LANGUAGE="VBScript"> tag, which is interpreted at browse time, regardless of whether any of the routines it contains are executed), Internet Explorer tries to interpret your code as JavaScript—and fails.

A far, far better approach is to create subroutines and functions that are event procedures—that is, Visual Basic procedures that are uniquely associated with the manipulation of a specified object. As long as you get the naming right, Internet Explorer and the VB engine are collectively smart enough to figure out the rest. In our example, all you have to do is change the name of the subroutine from NoBigDeal to B1_OnClick, which converts it to an event procedure for the object that is named B1.

Taking a conceptual leap, it's also possible to use VBScript to assign the results of a function to an HTML object instead of to an Internet Explorer object. The following example shows how to add a text area next to the button, which will display a different message according to which button the user clicks in our message box. (We added a third button by changing the value to 3, as well as adding 32 to generate the Warning Query icon.)

```
<p><script language="VBScript">
<!--
Option Explicit          'REQUIRES ALL VARIABLES TO BE DEFINED.
Dim sGlobalVar1          'EXPLICITLY DEFINES A VARIABLE; THE NEXT
                         'LINE ASSIGNS A VALUE TO GLOBALVAR1.
sGlobalVar1="Don't enter text, just click that big button...!"
Sub B1_OnClick           'DEFINES AN EVENT PROCEDURE FOR BUTTON 1.
Dim nRetVal, sMessage    'EXPLICITLY DEFINES TWO LOCAL VARIABLES;
                         'THE NEXT LINE SETS ONE VARIABLE TO
                         'MSGBOX RESULTS.
```

(continued)

211

```
        nRetVal=MsgBox("Are we having fun yet?",35,"Hello, World!")
        Select Case nRetVal      'EVALUATES THE VARIABLE.
        Case 6                   'IF THE USER CLICKS 'YES'
          sMessage="Get a life, Zippy!"
        Case 7                   'IF THE USER CLICKS 'NO'
          sMessage="Goodbye, cruel world..."
        Case Else                'IF THE USER CLICKS 'CANCEL'
          sMessage=""
        end select

                                 'THE NEXT LINE ASSIGNS THE MESSAGE
                                 'VARIABLE TO THE VALUE (or contents) OF
                                 'THE TEXT1 OBJECT.

        Form1.text1.value=sMessage
        window.status=""         'CLEARS THE STATUS BAR.
End sub

sub Text1_OnFocus            'ANOTHER EVENT PROCEDURE.
        window.status="Don't enter text, just click the button...!"
End sub
-->
</script> </p>

<form name="Form1">
    <p>
        <input type="button" name="1" value="Reset">
        <input type="text" size="20" name="Text1">
    </p>
</form>
```

What happens in the B1_OnClick event procedure is that the results of the MsgBox function are captured in a variable (nRetVal) that is then evaluated by a Select Case statement, which assigns different text strings to a second variable (sMessage) according to the value of the result. The initial value of the text input "Text1" is blank (we could just as easily have created an initial default text entry by stipulating a value), but the event procedure assigns it a new value that is equal to the string variable generated by the Select Case structure. Finally, the routine clears the Window Status bar (it might be better programming practice to display a success message), which cleans up after a *second* event procedure that displays a status bar message when the user clicks, tabs to, or otherwise selects the text box. Note also that the Option Explicit statement is outside any routine or procedure. It is loaded at browse time, and it causes a VBScript messaging error to display when the user tries to execute a routine containing a variable that hasn't been previously defined with the Dim statement. Adding the Option Explicit statement might at first seem like making more work for yourself, but because it's the only way to track down misspelled variable names and other kinds of human error, it's actually a real time-saver (and very good programming practice).

Simple as these examples might seem, they already illustrate the power that VBScript can bring to a Web page: capturing user input, performing calculations, and manipulating HTML or browser objects.

Creating OnLoad Routines

As you've seen with the Option Explicit statement, VBScript is loaded at browse time, when the <SCRIPT> tag is first evaluated by Internet Explorer. In fact, loading the page causes all executable statements within the Script tag that aren't contained within a subroutine or function to run. That's how, in the last code sample, we were able to define a *script-level* global variable (sGlobalVar1), which will be available as long as the page is in the browser (unlike the *procedure-level* variables, which are available only when you run the procedure in which they're defined). Script-level global variables are also the closest you'll ever come to true constants in VBScript.

You can, if you like, create de facto OnLoad routines simply by adding "naked" VBScript within the <SCRIPT> tag. There are, however, two good reasons for writing an explicit OnLoad procedure:

1. You'll find it somewhat easier to track down and debug errors if all your script is contained within an explicit routine (and, of course, you'll get an error if you accidentally *delete* the routine).

2. When you create the OnLoad event that triggers your routine, you can also establish VBScript as the default scripting language for the whole page.

You create an OnLoad event by adding an extended attribute to the HTML <BODY> tag. The only tricky aspect is that a FrontPage Page Properties style sheet, if implemented, overwrites the <BODY> tag of every Web page attached to the template. What to do? Add the attribute to the Page Properties style sheet, of course:

1. Launch the FrontPage server and open your <ROOT WEB> directory in the FrontPage Explorer.

2. Open the Page Properties style sheet in the FrontPage Editor.

3. Choose Page Properties from the File menu, and click the Extended button.

4. Click the Add button in the Extended Attributes dialog box, and then enter the name of your OnLoad subroutine as the value of the OnLoad attribute. (The example given here is perhaps a little

confusing in that the value of the OnLoad attribute is also "OnLoad"; just remember that the attribute value is always the *name* of a Visual Basic routine, while the attribute name represents an event recognized by Internet Explorer.)

You must explicitly declare VBScript (or VBS, which is the same thing only shorter) as the scripting language *somewhere* on the page. If we were planning to use a bewildering variety of scripts on a single page (keeping in mind that there are currently, in all the world, only two), there might be a reason to declare the language locally—but we're not, and we won't. Instead, we'll add a second extended attribute to the <BODY> tag of the Page Properties style sheet, named Language, with the value "VBScript"; when you click the OK button, you should see something like this in the Extended Attributes dialog box:

You have, at one stroke, created the event that will trigger, throughout the pages on your Web, the separate instances of the OnLoad procedure.

TIP

In our example, we created blank OnLoad routines. You might prefer to include one more innocuous line—such as *window.status="Running Onload Routine"*—to make sure that the routines actually do run once you hook them up.

Evaluating and Updating Frame Contents

Here's a problem: Suzanne decides to use our company intranet to find out about our vacation policy. When Suzanne launches MMA Online, she sees a window with three frames. They contain the exploration bar, section menus, and Web contents, respectively. At first, she sees the Welcome section menu and the Table Of Contents page; but when she clicks the Human Resources button on the exploration bar, what happens? Suzanne jumps to the Our Human Resources page in the Contents frame. Why? Because the anchor tag in NAVBAR.HTM contains an HREF to ..\HUMANRESOURCES\OVER-VIEW.HTM and the Target attribute "Contents." Plain vanilla HTML can do all that—but what about the Section menu? The Our Human Resources page (OVERVIEW.HTM) is in the Human Resources section, and HTML alone cannot update an adjacent frame. But VBScript certainly can, and here's all the code you need:

```
sub Onload
  If self.name="Content" then
    If LCase(Right(parent.Frames(0).location.href, 9)) <> _
        "menu3.htm" then
      parent.Frames(0).location.href="../_private/menu3.htm"
    End if
  End if
End Sub
```

In pseudocode, the first line simply means "If I'm in a frame named Content. . . ." In any other circumstances (that is, if the current page is loaded in a frame with a different name, or if it isn't in a frame at all), the rest of the routine doesn't run. But if it does, the next line of code determines the name of the document in the adjacent frame.

The code for the second test ("Is menu3.htm located in the next frame?") could have been written more directly, but the direct path is not always a virtue in programming, especially if it requires the use of explicit values and references instead of variables and functions that return values dynamically. For instance, the Frames property of the Internet Explorer's Window object does just that—it returns an array of frames contained in the designated window (which in this case can also be designated dynamically as "parent," since all frames are contained in the Frameset window and this line will run successfully only if the current page is framed; if the current page is *not* framed, there won't be any way to update a menu).

If you aren't familiar with arrays, don't worry too much—they're just a collective variable representing a list of individual variables, all of which are similar, and all of which are designated as numbered elements within the array. Arrays are convenient not just because you can collectively refer to (and manipulate) the group of items by using the array variable but also because the variable can be mathematically manipulated to spit out the value of a given item in the list. The screwy thing about arrays in Basic is that the first item is always numbered 0; that's why our default Home page frameset

CHAPTER 7

contains the following array of three frames, numbered in the order in which they are defined in the HTML:

```
Frame(0)="Menu"
Frame(1)="NavBar"
Frame(2)="Content"
```

Bear in mind that VBScript controls Window objects as well as their methods, events, and properties. If parent.Frames(0) designates the Menu frame, the location.href property returns the URL of the contents of the Menu frame. We only want to test the last nine characters in the string—that's what the Right(...,9) function does—and make sure that the test doesn't fail because some careless system administrator accidentally changed the case of the menu filename, which is what the LCase( ) function does. We compared a lowercase test string ("menu3.htm") against the results of the LCase( ) function, which converts the last nine characters of the URL of the frame contents to lowercase.

The rest of the code should be pretty clear sailing. The second test is a negative—after all, if menu3.htm is already loaded, there's nothing to do—and, if it's successful, it *assigns* the relative URL of the appropriate menu to the designated frame. If and when that line is executed, VBScript updates the object in Internet Explorer, and voilà: the Human Resources Section menu is updated in Suzanne's browser.

You might be wondering why the Web page updates the Section menu, whereas it would seem more logical if things happened the other way around. Once again, the answer is economy of code. All pages in a section share the same menu, but if we wrote the code in the Section menu, we would have to add (and update!) *all* the page names in the section. Moreover, instead of writing the VBScript directly into each page, you might want to diverge from our example and create Included Header pages for each section, with each of these pages containing the VBScript for that section. It's a little more initial work, but if you ever need to add or rename frames (or move your content to a different Web), you'll have far fewer scripts to change later on.

Those Last-Minute Write-Ins

This subject is easy: the Internet Explorer Document object supports two methods—Write and WriteLn—that, at browse time, insert a specified string at the current position on the Web page. The only difference between the two methods is that WriteLn appends a new-line character and Write doesn't; and even that ain't necessarily so. Turns out you have to bracket your write-in between the <PRE> </PRE> tags in order for your browser to render the new-line character. How's that for valuable information?

Writing is the easy part; figuring out *what* to write is always a little more difficult. You could conceivably capture user input and write it in the document, or you could use the technique to create a VBScript-generated Confirmation form, but some of the most useful information you can write in has to do with the page itself. For example, the LastModified property of the Internet Explorer's Document object represents the file save date, so the VBScript

```
document.writedocument.lastmodified
```

statement will write that information into the current page.

Similarly, the Location property of the Document object returns the URL of the current page, which includes the filename as well as the protocol and the directory path on the server. The following VBScript shows how you can convert the URL to uppercase, assign it to a variable, then parse the string to remove everything but the filename:

```
sParseString=UCASE(document.location)
do while Instr(sParseString,chr(47))> 0
    sParseString=Mid(sParseString, 2)
Loop
```

Parsing is such a useful technique that it's worth a little further discussion. The act of parsing—a fancy word for looking through a string and getting rid of the stuff you don't want—involves four procedures:

1. Analyzing the structure of your string to determine the thing (known as a "delimiter") that always separates the stuff you want from the stuff you don't. Parsing depends upon structure. Without a completely reliable delimiter, such as a slash (/) in Web addresses, you'll never be able to separate what you want from what you don't.

2. Starting from the beginning (or the end) and looking for the first instance of the delimiter in the string. Because parsing is so completely dependent upon structure, where you start makes all the difference.

3. Lopping off the delimiter together with all the stuff to one side of it you don't want.

4. Evaluating the contents of the resulting string and, usually, repeating the process until there are no more delimiters.

We decided to look for the slash character (/), represented as chr(47) because the chr() function returns the ASCII character represented by the number used in the function. In our example, the Instr() function returns a number representing the first instance in sParseString of chr(47), and as long as it isn't zero, there's a slash in the string somewhere, and we want to lop off all the characters coming before it. In fact, there will initially be at least three slashes (http:://webroot/page.htm). The MID( ) function starts at the second character of the sParseString variable, and it returns everything to the right; assigning the results of this calculation to the same variable means the first character has been lopped off the string. The DO...WHILE...LOOP structure means this operation continues until the Instr( ) function equals zero, at which point the variable contains just the filename. Several more elegant lopping-off approaches could have been used, but the brute-force method was used because it's simple, and computers are good at simple, brute-force calculations.

You can also use Document write-ins to insert HTML markup into your Web page at browse time. The following code is an example of a longer VBScript routine that writes the filename and date of last modification into an HTML table structure. For clarity, the statement "document.write" is used somewhat redundantly; note the following elements as well:

- The use of <SPAN></SPAN> tags to create in-line styles using the CSS (which is short for "Cascading Style Sheet") syntax

- The use of a single quote *within* HTML markup

- The concatenation of text and text variables with the ampersand (&) character

Here's the code:

```
sParseString=UCASE(document.location)
do while Instr(sParseString,chr(47))> 0
    sParseString=Mid(sParseString, 2)
Loop
document.write "<HR SIZE='5' COLOR='808080'>"
document.write "<SPAN STYLE='font: 7pt Verdana';>"
document.write
"<TABLE BORDER='0' CELLPADDING='0' CELLSPACING='0' WIDTH='100%'><TR>"
document.write "<TD WIDTH='55%'>"
document.write sParseString & ":  " & document.title
document.write "</TD>"
document.write "<TD WIDTH='45%' ALIGN='RIGHT'>"
document.write "LAST MODIFIED: " & document.lastmodified &""
document.write "</TD>"
document.write "</TR></TABLE>"
document.write "</SPAN>"
```

Validating Client-Side Input

Evaluating the effects that a user's selection will have on the browser, before any action is performed, is called *client-side validation*. Even on an intranet, it's a lot slower to pass data back to the server and run error handling on the server side. Breaking a task down into components and writing separate procedures for each one is known as *modular programming* (or *modular coding*). Not only is modular code easier to debug, but it also forces you from the outset to analyze the logic of the problem you're trying to solve.

The sample code that follows shows how an HTML form can be integrated with VBScript routines to evaluate the user's selection and then either download the selected file or display a message that the file will not be available until a specified date. You'll find this code in the VBSCRIPT.HTM file in the Chapter2 folder of the companion CD. Here we'll go through the principal components of the code step by step.

In our example, Micro Modeling Associates has developed a suite of office templates, some of which have custom headers with our office address. Our code sample begins by defining a standard HTML form named DLOADFRM, inside of which is a table that aligns the following elements:

- 🌐 A menu for template selection
- 🌐 A menu for office selection
- 🌐 A checkbox to indicate that the user wants the online help file for the selected template
- 🌐 A control button

Because Internet Explorer lets you download only one file at a time, we did not allow multiple selections on the Template menu. We added a background image from the Microsoft MultiMedia gallery to give the table a little pizzazz, and we added <SPAN></SPAN> tags with the HTML Markup WebBot to create the effect of a hanging indent for the checkbox label:

```
<form name="DloadFrm">
    <table border="0" background="../images/BACKGD03.JPG">
        <tr>
            <td width="10%"><font size="2"
            face="Arial"><strong>Template:
            </strong></font></td>
            <td width="10%"><font size="2"
            face="Arial"><strong>Office:
            </strong></font></td>
```

(continued)

219

```
    </tr>
    <tr>
        <td valign="top" width="10%"><font size="2"
        face="Arial"><select name="TemplateSelection"
        size="1">
            <option value="ltr">Letter Template</option>
            <option value="fax">Fax Template</option>
            <option value="mem">Memo Template</option>
        </select> </font></td>
        <td valign="top" width="10%"><font size="2"
        face="Arial"><select name="OfficeSelection" size="1">
            <option>New York, NY</option>
            <option>Morristown, NJ</option>
            <option>Washington, D.C.</option>
            <option>Minneapolis, MN</option>
            <option>Chicago, IL</option>
            <option>Boston, MA</option>
        </select> </font></td>
    </tr>
    <tr>
        <td colspan="2"><input type="checkbox"
        name="HelpOption">
        <span style="FONT: bold 8.5pt arial; line-height: 10pt;
        margin-left: 22px">
        Check this box if you want the online<br>
        help file for the selected template.</span></td>
    </tr>
    <tr>
        <td align="center" colspan="2"><font size="2"
        face="Arial"><input type="button" name="btnDLoad"
        value="Download..."> </font><font size="2"><script
        language="VBScript">
```

The VBScript routine is contained within the table structure. For ease of maintenance, we made the availability date for new-office templates one of the global variables initialized at the top of our routine. Notice that the event procedure, below, associated with the button click is actually quite short; most of the actual work is done by the fEvaluateResults function—in fact, if the function doesn't return a value of -1, the event procedure doesn't do anything:

```
<!--
'INITIALIZE GLOBAL VARIABLES
Dim sFileToOpen
Dim sURLstub
Dim nIndex
```

220

```
Dim sAvailableDate
sAvailableDate="January 1, 1997."

    Sub btnDLoad_OnClick
        sURLstub="../_private/OfficeTemplates/"
        if fEvaluateResults()=-1 then
            sFileToOpen=sURLstub & sFileToOpen
            window.status="Opening " & sFileToOpen
            navigate sFileToOpen
        end if
    End sub
```

The fEvaluateResults( ) function analyzes the user's menu selections and either constructs the name of the selected file or displays an error message. You already know that a function returns a value, and you can set the value of functions with a statement making the function equal to a value or variable. You're allowed only one such statement per function. Nevertheless, by defining a variable (nretVal) whose value changes when the user accepts the confirmation message (MsgBox(sMessage,4,"MMA OnLine")=6) and then assigning the variable to the function at the end, we were able to have the function return one of two possible values.

```
Function fEvaluateResults()
    'DECLARE RETURN VARIABLE
    Dim nretVal
    nretVal=0
    'DECLARE VARIABLES FOR FORM SELECTIONS AND MESSAGING
    Dim nOfficeSelection
    Dim nTemplateSelection
    Dim nHelpOption
    Dim nNotAvail
    nNotAvail=0
    Dim sMessage
```

We manipulated the index values of the two menus, office and template, to create a single, two-digit number assigned to a variable, nIndex, and then we used two Select Case structures to evaluate the variable. The first structure uses the integer value of one-tenth of the index variable to test the first character, which represents the office selection. If the user selects an office without using a template, a variable known as a *flag* is set (nNotAvail); otherwise, part of the confirmation message string is built up:

```
'CALCULATE VARIABLE VALUES FROM FORM SELECTIONS
nOfficeSelection=document.dLoadFrm.OfficeSelection.SelectedIndex
nTemplateSelection=document.dLoadFrm.TemplateSelection.SelectedIndex
```

(continued)

```
nIndex=(nOfficeSelection*10)+(nTemplateSelection+1)
if document.dLoadFrm.helpOption.checked then nIndex=nIndex+3

'EVALUATE OFFICE SELECTION
Select Case Int(nIndex/10)

Case 0
    sMessage="for the New York Office?"
Case 1
sMessage="for the New Jersey Office?"
Case 2
    sMessage="for the Washington, D.C. Office?"
Case 3
    sMessage="for the Minneapolis Office?"
Case else
    nNotAvail=-1
End Select
```

The second Select Case structure is set within a conditional statement that tests whether the nNotAvail flag has been set. If it has, a message is displayed to the user that shows the date that the template will be available. If the flag has not been set, the last number in the index variable is tested to determine the template type and, when there are different office-specific versions of a template, a third-level Select Case structure determines the filename:

```
'EVALUATE TEMPLATE SELECTION IF THEY ARE AVAILABLE
If nNotAvail = -1 then
    MsgBox "Templates for this MMA Office will be" & Chr(13) _
    & "available after " & sAvailableDate
Else
    Select Case Right(nIndex, 1)
    Case 1
        sMessage="the Letter Template " & sMessage
        Select Case nIndex
        Case 1
            sFileToOpen="mma_ltr7.dot"
        Case 11
            sFileToOpen="mma_lnj7.dot"
        Case 21
            sFileToOpen="mma_ldc7.dot"
        Case 31
            sFileToOpen="mma_lmn7.dot"
        Case else
        End Select
    Case 2
        sMessage="the Fax Template " & sMessage
        Select Case nIndex
```

```
        Case 2
            sFileToOpen="mma_fax7.dot"
        Case 12
            sFileToOpen="mma_fnj7.dot"
        Case 22
            sFileToOpen="mma_fdc7.dot"
        Case 32
            sFileToOpen="mma_fmn7.dot"
        Case else
        End Select
    Case 3
        sMessage="the Memo Template " & sMessage
        sFileToOpen="mma_mem7.dot"
    Case 4
        sMessage="the Letter Template Online Help?"
        sFileToOpen="mma_ltr.hlp"
    Case 5
        sMessage="the Fax Template Online Help?"
        sFileToOpen="mma_fax.hlp"
    Case 6
        sMessage="the Memo Template Online Help?"
        sFileToOpen="mma_mem.hlp"
    Case else
    End select
```

So far, the validation function has constructed only a concatenated text string and a filename from the user's selection. The last step is to display a message box with the string and then reset the variable for the return value of the function if the user clicks the Yes button. The rest of the HTML includes the FrontPage Confirmation WebBot and the end of the table and form structures:

```
        'DISPLAY CONFIRMATION MESSAGE
        sMessage="Do you really want to download " & sMessage
        If MsgBox(sMessage,4,"MMA OnLine")=6 then
            nretVal=-1
        end if
    End if
    'ASSIGN RETURN VALUE TO FUNCTION
    fEvaluateResults=nretVal
End function

--></script></font> <!--webbot
        bot="PurpleText"
        preview="This code controls the download menu." --></td>
    </tr>
    </table>
</form>
```

It's possible, by the way, to pass variables *between* functions, and you might wonder why we didn't pass the filename into the evaluation function as an empty string and then retrieve it as the fully articulated name. The problem is that in VBScript you can pass variables only by value. (*Passing by value* is a method that prevents the variable itself from being redefined in the function to which it is passed.) You can't change the value of a variable passed into a subprocedure, but you can redefine a global variable, so that's the approach we took.

Have a Cookie. . .

Web technology involves various components—in this case, the server and the browser—that talk to each other from time to time but don't maintain a state of constant communication. Servers, after all, are in the business of dishing out Web pages to all comers, whereas browsers need to be free to jump from server to server via hyperlinks. For example, once you request and receive the Home page of www.microsoft.com, you and the Microsoft server go your separate ways; each of you has lost track of what the other is doing, so you are said to be in a stateless condition.

Being stateless makes it easy to travel but hard to shop. By looking at the current page, you can tell where you are. By looking at your browser's History list, you can even tell where you've been in the last few days. But you can't go shopping—that is, picking up data from page after page and carrying it all over with you as you go along—unless you can keep track of things *between* pages.

The ability to keep track of data in your browser between successive HTTP requests is known as a *persistent client state,* and the term *cookie* is a generic name for various mechanisms (usually CGI scripts) that create a persistent client state. In other words, if you have a persistent client state, you have a cookie.

But there are cookies and there are cookies. The broadest definition of the term covers *any* mechanism that maintains a persistent client state, including state information that a server can send to your browser (via a CGI script) and later read back. Those cookies are mighty good cookies, but those are not the cookies we're talking about. Our cookie is a property of the Internet Explorer's Document object. Essentially, it's just a string variable that is available throughout your current browser session, but you can add data to the cookie and extract data from the cookie by using simple string manipulation.

We unabashedly cribbed our code from the VBScript samples on the Microsoft Web site so that you'd have an idea of what cookies can do. Here's all it takes to capture text from an Input box and write it to your cookie:

```
Option Explicit
Dim sCookieName
Dim sCookieValue
Dim sDBXTITLE
sDBXTitle="MMA OnLine"
sub CookieNamer_OnClick
    sCookieName=""
    sCookieValue=""
    sCookieName=InputBox("What's the Cookie's name?",sDBXTitle)
    sCookieValue=InputBox("What's the Cookie's value?",sDBXTitle)
    If sCookieName="" OR sCookieValue="" then
        MsgBox _
            "You must enter both a Cookie Name and Cookie Value.", _
            64, sDBXTitle
    else
        document.cookie=sCookieName & " = " & sCookieValue
    end if
end sub
```

And reading the cookie is even easier:

```
sub CookieReader_onClick
    MsgBox document.cookie,,"Here is your cookie"
end sub
```

You can't really get the full effect of what cookies are about until you jump to the associated COOKIES.HTM page in the Chapter2 folder of the companion CD. Everything on the page (except the lovely yellow background) is generated by VBScript at browse time. If your cookie is empty, you'll get a message to that effect; otherwise, your current cookie will be displayed in a marquee. This means that you can get up one fine morning, launch Internet Explorer, write yourself a cookie, spend the entire day surfing the Internet with abandon, and, just before bedtime, open your Cookie page. Your cookie should be there. Unless, of course, there's been a power failure.

. . . And a Sip of Java

As long as Internet Explorer is the only browser that supports VBScript, there will always be at least one task for which you'll need another scripting language. That task is to detect the user's browser type. Of course, if you're able to enforce 100 percent browser-type compliance from the user's desktop, you might never have to deal with this problem in building your intranet.

CHAPTER 7

Still, with all those Netscape Navigator browsers floating around out there, it's nice to know how to solve the problem, should the need arise. Both Internet Explorer 3.0 and later and Netscape Navigator 2.0 and later support JavaScript, and the code itself is fairly straightforward:

```
<SCRIPT LANGUAGE="JavaScript">
{
  var ver = navigator.appVersion;
  if (ver.indexOf("MSIE") == -1)
    {
    Alert("You must use Internet Explorer 3.0 Release 2.0 to browse
          MMA OnLine! successfully.")
    }
}
</SCRIPT>
```

The appVersion property of the Navigator object returns a string containing the version of the current browser application. If the string does not contain the letters MSIE in it somewhere (in other words, if the IndexOf( ) function does not return a true value), you're not using Microsoft Internet Explorer. It's that simple.

But nothing's ever *really* simple. If you needed a more comprehensive way to test the user's browser type—so that you could send, say, a curt dismissive note to the odd Lynx browser stumbling onto your intranet—you'd need to write a server-side CGI script to capture and evaluate the identifying HTTP_USER_AGENT field that's part of the browser's request.

That's Computing, Folks!

What's to prevent A. Datum Corporation from including MSIE somewhere in its appProperty string and thereby passing the A. Datum Corporation Web Browser off as Internet Explorer? Something like that has already happened with the Internet Explorer's UserAgent property. After Netscape came up with the string Mozilla—a name derived from *Mosaic* and *Godzilla* and carrying the implication that the Navigator would soon be tossing its rival browser around like so many scale-model railroad cars—Internet Explorer incorporated Mozilla into its own UserAgent property so that Microsoft's new rival browser would also be welcome at Netscape Navigator–enabled sites.

ActiveX Controls

The term *ActiveX* is hard to define. You can take your pick from this sampling of Microsoft's own attempts at a definition:

🌐 "ActiveX is a set of technologies from Microsoft that enables interactive content for the World Wide Web. With ActiveX, Web sites come alive using multimedia effects, interactive objects, and sophisticated applications that create a user experience comparable to that of high-quality CD-ROM titles. ActiveX provides the glue that ties together a wide assortment of technology building blocks to enable these 'active' Web sites." ("What is ActiveX?"—Microsoft Web site: www.microsoft.com/activex/actx-gen/awhatis.htm)

🌐 "ActiveX is the Microsoft technology that bridges the Internet/intranet and desktop applications. It provides you with the tools and components you need to create active Web pages, Internet/intranet enhanced desktop applications, or traditional desktop applications with advanced functionality." (*Microsoft Component Builder's ActiveX Sampler CD*)

🌐 "ActiveX controls, formerly known as OLE controls or OCX controls, are components (or objects) you can insert into a Web page or other application to reuse packaged functionality someone else programmed." ("ActiveX Controls"—Microsoft Web site: www.microsoft.com/intdev/controls/controls.htm)

🌐 "ActiveX controls are reusable software components developed by software vendors. These controls can be used to quickly add specialized functionality to Web sites, desktop applications, and development tools." ("ActiveX FAQ"—Microsoft Web site: www.microsoft.com/activex/actx-gen/faq.htm)

🌐 "The term ActiveX refers to any technology that serves to 'activate' your computer, especially with regard to the Internet." (*Microsoft Interactive Developer,* October 1996)

Underneath all the verbal fuzz are two basic, very powerful ideas:

1. ActiveX technology consists of reusable controls, or *objects*.
2. ActiveX embraces the full spectrum of HTML pages and desktop application documents.

227

CHAPTER 7

The reality is a market frenzy of software developers pushing new ActiveX controls out the door, with Microsoft proposing certification standards and digital signatures to keep track of all those downloaded components. No doubt about it, ActiveX controls can do very cool things, things like playing multimedia files, generating data-driven charts, managing credit-card transactions, and creating database connectivity. Over time, ActiveX will likely emerge as a leading technology in Microsoft's projected Windows environment, where the browser becomes a container for desktop applications and your desktop merges with the World Wide Web. As you begin to work with ActiveX controls, however, you need to keep in mind a few other considerations:

🌐 **Weigh that load.** Unless you install the ActiveX Server extensions and run your controls on the server side, most of the ActiveX controls will require the user to download a local copy before they will work.

🌐 **Caveat vendor.** Unless you have resources to build your ActiveX controls for you, you'll have to license and purchase them from third-party developers. A great many of the ActiveX controls that are listed on the ActiveX Control Pad (included on this book's companion CD) turn out to be third-party products. Use them, by all means. Until you pay for them and register them, however, you'll get an irritating message every time you load the page.

🌐 **It's terra incognito out there.** ActiveX is an emerging technology, which is a polite way of saying that you can expect plenty of things not to work, or at least to work differently from the way they're supposed to; and you'll be lucky if there's documentation of any kind—even incomplete, inaccurate, and/or outdated documentation.

So far, ActiveX controls fall into two general camps:

1. Those that enhance basic Web page functionality by adding buttons, tabs, and so forth

2. Those that perform specific, complex functions, such as displaying animated vector graphics

For your intranet, you'll probably be most interested in the second category. To give you an introduction to ActiveX methodology, however, we'll concentrate here on controls in the first category.

Internet Explorer ActiveX Controls

Advanced controls typically require licensing, and they can involve issues that aren't relevant to other controls or situations. Nevertheless, the ActiveX controls that come with Internet Explorer are an ideal way to start learning because they're free, easy to understand, and don't require a client download.

The list of Internet Explorer ActiveX controls shown in Table 7-1 on page 230 is adapted directly from the Microsoft Web site (www.microsoft.com/intdev/controls/ctrlref-f.htm). The section of the Web site devoted to ActiveX components also includes a page with a working sample of each control and, more important, a page listing the properties, methods, and events associated with the control. Some of these controls, as you will discover, have significant limitations. Others, like the Timer control, are extremely powerful and useful. We'll concentrate on the Label and Menu controls in our first examples because their functionality is both intuitive and broadly applicable. Additional Microsoft controls come with the ActiveX Control Pad, which we will examine a bit later.

Anatomy of a Control

You will often read of controls or objects being "inserted on" a Web page. Actually, what's inserted is good old HTML, which references the object itself by using the unique alphanumeric identifier associated with that object in the Windows Registry (the system registration database that keeps track of objects in the Windows environment). All ActiveX controls are referenced with the <OBJECT> tag, which must include the appropriate identifier from the Registry in the CLASSID attribute, as well as the name by which the control will be referenced on the page in the ID attribute. Here, for example, is what the HTML for a pop-up menu (the PopUp Menu object) looks like:

```
<OBJECT
    ID="PopUpMenuObject"
    WIDTH=0
    HEIGHT=0
    CLASSID="CLSID:7823A620-9DD9-11CF-A662-00AA00C066D2"
>
<PARAM NAME="Menuitem[0]" VALUE="Blackberries">
<PARAM NAME="Menuitem[1]" VALUE="Blueberries">
<PARAM NAME="Menuitem[2]" VALUE="Boysenberries">
<PARAM NAME="Menuitem[3]" VALUE="Raspberries">
<PARAM NAME="Menuitem[4]" VALUE="Strawberries">
</OBJECT>
```

CHAPTER 7

Table 7-1 Internet Explorer ActiveX Controls.

Control	Description
Animated Button	Uses the Microsoft Windows Animation common control to display various frame sequences of an AVI, depending on the button state.
Chart	Enables you to draw various types of charts with different styles.
Gradient	Shades the area with a range of colors, displaying a transition from one specified color to another.
Label	Displays given text at any specified angle. It can also render the text along user-defined curves.
Marquee	Scrolls, slides, and/or bounces URLs within a user-defined window.
Menu	Displays a menu button or a pull-down menu. This control acts like a tri-state button when no menu items are specified, or it displays a pull-down menu when one or more menu items are specified. It can also display a pop-up menu if the Popup method is used.
Popup Menu	Displays a pop-up menu whenever the Popup method is called, and fires a Click event when a menu item is selected.
Popup Window	Displays specified HTML documents in a pop-up window. This control can be used to provide ToolTips or previews of links.
Preloader	Downloads the specified URL and puts it in the cache. The control is invisible at run time and starts downloading when enabled.
Stock Ticker	Continuously displays changing data. The control downloads the URL specified at regular intervals and displays that data. The data can be in text format or XRT format.
Timer	Invokes an event periodically. It is invisible at run time.
View Tracker	Generates OnShow and OnHide events whenever the control falls inside/outside the viewable area.

The ID and CLASSID attributes are required to create an instance of the object when the page is loaded in the browser; everything else just configures this particular instantiation. But notice that within the <OBJECT> tag there are additional <PARAM> tags with the familiar NAME and VALUE attributes, which include additional information—in this case, the contents of the menu itself, defined as terms in an array.

That CLASSID thingamajig, though: looks a little...*gnarly* doesn't it? Oh, what fun it must be to while away those long winter nights, keying in 36-digit alphanumeric strings before a roaring fireplace! Well, relax. You won't even have to remember the darned things, thanks to the ActiveX Control Pad (which we'll get to momentarily). But suppose you took the time to write out, on some greasy slip of paper, all the 36-character CLASSID strings of all the ActiveX controls you wanted to use. The HTML code still wouldn't tell you anything about how the gizmo behaves. For that, you'd need to know the properties, methods, and events associated with the object—in short, the *object model*. (And, yes, the ActiveX Control Pad will even be able to show you the object model, too—we'll get to it, we'll get to it!)

The ActiveX Control Object Model

If it walks like an object, it's bound to have properties, methods, and events like an object. Finding out what they are can be another matter altogether. In the case of our PopUp Menu object, however, relief is just a mouse click (or two) away. The object model for every Microsoft control is listed in a separate page of the ActiveX Component Gallery on the Microsoft Web site; here's what the PopUp Menu Control object model looks like.

Properties

- The ItemCount property is the number of menu items in the current menu (read only).

Parameter tags

- Menuitem[] is the menu item to be displayed.
- Caption is the caption to be displayed.

Methods

- The AboutBox method displays the About dialog box.
- The PopUp ([in] int x, [in] int y) method pops up the menu. If no value is passed for the x or y position (or both), the current mouse position is used to display the pop-up menu. The x and y values are relative to the window, not to the screen.
- The Clear method clears off all menu items.
- The RemoveItem ([in] int index) method removes the specified item. If the menu item does not exist, nothing is done.
- The AddItem ([in] String, [in/optional] int index) method adds the passed menu item at the specified index. If no index is passed, the item is appended to the menu.

CHAPTER 7

These methods, properties, and events, when manipulated with scripting language, determine how the PopUpMenu object behaves on your Web page. Once you've got the CLASSID attribute and object model for a control, there's nothing to stop you from creating full functionality with WordPad alone; it's just an awful lot easier to use the ActiveX Control Pad.

The ActiveX Control Pad

In general terms (and we'll get to the specifics *in a moment*), getting an ActiveX control up and running involves three steps:

1. Inserting the HTML <OBJECT> tag to create a reference to the object in the page

2. Configuring the control (its size, its color, and so forth) by setting its <OBJECT> attributes and <PARAM></PARAM> tags

3. Writing the scripting routines that constitute the event procedures associated with the control

The ActiveX Control Pad is an application that makes it (relatively) easy to do all three tasks from a common interface. It's available as a stand-alone application (http://www.microsoft.com/workshop/author/cpad/), but it also comes bundled within the FrontPage 97 application. Visual Basic programmers will recognize the ActiveX Control Pad as a modified version of the Object Browser. For the rest of us, the application consists of the following elements:

🌐 An HTML editing pane (in the FrontPage version, this is replaced by the FrontPage Editor). Everything you add or edit with any other Control Pad utility can also be changed directly in the HTML code.

🌐 The ActiveX Control Menu, listing all controls installed locally and registered on your system database.

🌐 The Properties Table Editor, where you configure the control.

🌐 The Script Wizard, where you create VBScript routines that manipulate all object models available on the page (window, controls, and so forth).

🌐 The HTML Layout control, which lets you control the placement of other controls and page elements (and reposition elements from user input, such as mouse movements).

We're going to use the stand-alone version of the ActiveX Control Pad to illustrate these tools because it has the greater functionality. If you're using the FrontPage version, you'll be able to do almost everything shown here except use the HTML Layout control, edit the HTML directly, view the

Properties tables of some controls, and view the downloadable VBScript reference. Nevertheless, the stand-alone version lets you edit HTML to your heart's content—and, as you know, that's always the way we prefer to go.

Installing the ActiveX Control Pad

As of this writing, you install the stand-alone ActiveX Control Pad by downloading and running an executable file from the Microsoft Web site. The file is self-extracting, and it also launches a setup wizard that guides you through the rest of the installation process. The ActiveX Control Pad is also available for downloading from this book's companion CD. If your version doesn't have a VBScript reference, you can download and expand another self-extracting executable from the VBScript section of the Microsoft Web site and then rename a copy of the Table Of Contents page with the name of the short VBScript page created by the ActiveX Control Pad. (You want to rename a copy and retain the original because the internal HREFs of the scripting reference use the URL of the original page.)

Inserting controls

Once you have everything up and running and have launched the ActiveX Control Pad, you'll see a blank, boilerplate Web page in all its resplendent, glorious HTML. By now, we trust, a window like this will hold no terrors:

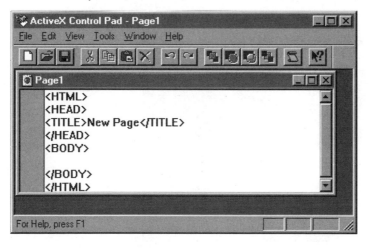

And here's all you do to insert a control:

1. Place your cursor on a blank line in the page. (Because the end result of the command is going be HTML markup written in at the current cursor position, you don't want your cursor to be in the middle of other HTML or you'll louse up your page. This is probably the most difficult part of the whole procedure.)

233

2. Choose Insert ActiveX Control from the Edit menu, and select a control from the Insert ActiveX Control dialog box, as shown here:

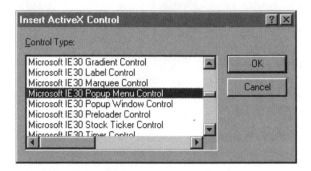

NOTE If you're using FrontPage 97 rather than the stand-alone ActiveX Control Pad, you won't see the HTML editing pane, of course, but cursor placement is still critical. You'll choose Other Components from the FrontPage Editor's Insert Menu, and then you'll choose ActiveX Control and select a control from the Pick A Control List, as shown here:

It's critical, however, to enter a control name before clicking the OK button. The stand-alone ActiveX Control Pad names each control by default, but FrontPage doesn't, and unnamed controls won't be displayed in the Script Wizard—for the very good reason that you need a name (or ID) to refer to an object in script.

If you're using the stand-alone Control Pad, you'll see two dialog boxes once you insert your control, as shown here:

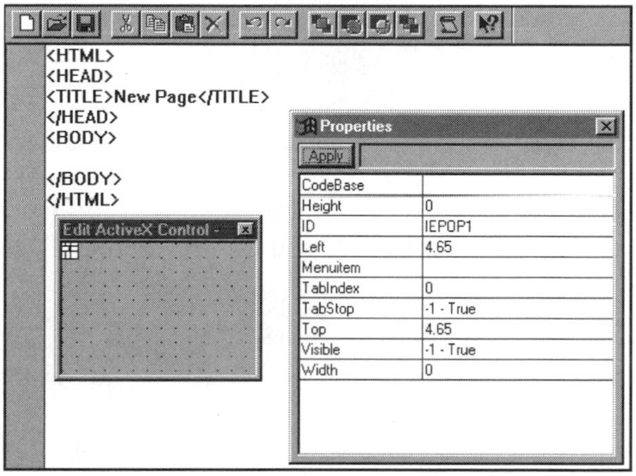

These are the tools you use to configure your control...and we'll get to them in a moment. For now, click the Close button in both dialog boxes, and you'll see the HTML <OBJECT> tag in your page, as shown here:

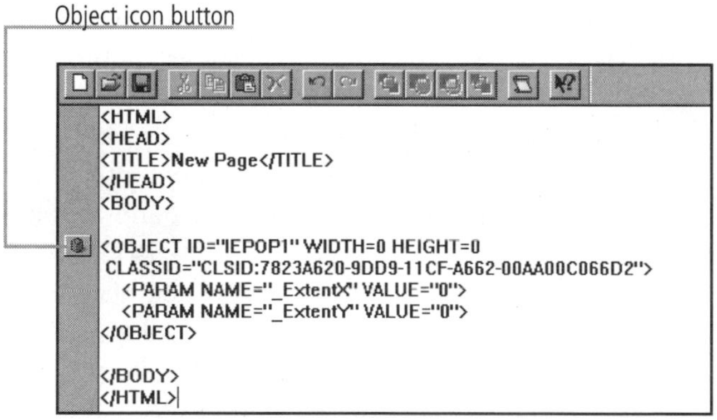

Object icon button

In addition to the HTML, notice the small button with the cube (or "object" icon) to the left of the screen. Click that button to display the two dialog boxes for the selected control that we just closed: the Edit ActiveX Control dialog box and the Properties table.

CHAPTER 7

NOTE   FrontPage users will once again have a somewhat different experience. Once you select a control and click the OK button in the ActiveX Control Properties dialog box, you'll see a *graphical* representation of the control in the FrontPage Editor. To configure the control, double-click the control (or select it, and choose ActiveX Control Properties from the Edit menu), and click the Properties button in the ActiveX Control Properties dialog box.

Configuring controls

Once you have a control in your Web page, you can configure its properties in two ways:

- Drag the representation of the control in the Edit ActiveX Control dialog box to move and resize the control, and set other properties in the Properties table.

- Add <OBJECT> attributes and <PARAM> tags directly in the HTML.

Of course, you'll probably find one of these methods considerably simpler and easier than the other (although, as of this writing, some <PARAM> tags can be entered only manually, alas). You open both dialog boxes at the same time by clicking the Object button associated with the control in the stand-alone ActiveX Control Pad (or double-clicking the object in the FrontPage Editor and then clicking the Properties button in the ActiveX Control Properties dialog box).

The Edit ActiveX Control dialog box lets you size the control. In the case of the PopUpMenu control, however, the size of the control has nothing to do with the size of the menu (the control simply generates a menu, which is sized to fit its entries). Therefore, there's every reason to make the control as small as possible so that it won't displace other, visible page elements. The easiest way to do that is to enter zero as the value of the height and width in the Properties table (just try doing *that* with your mouse). In the case of our PopUp menu, we've used the Properties table to change the ID from the default (IEPOP1) to PopUpMenuObject.

TIP

The Properties table lists all available properties of the control (or attributes of the <OBJECT> tag; it's the same thing) even if they aren't part of the initial markup. For example, the CodeBase property is initially blank, but it's a critical attribute for the object that the client will have to download and install locally. When the page is first loaded, each client browser checks its system registry for a local instance of the control; if one isn't found, it then uses the CodeBase property to locate and download an original instance of the control from somewhere else, so you need to be sure the URL is valid. An intranet gives you far more leeway, because you have greater control over the end user's directory/URL structure. But it's still a good idea to use a relative URL, referencing an instance of the control in a subfolder on your Web.

Some properties can accept user-defined values; other properties have only predefined values. The Properties table performs validation of user-defined entries (you'll get an error message if you try to enter a height of "five pts."), and it displays a drop-down menu of predefined choices, as for the Alignment property of the Label object (Figures 7-2 and 7-3).

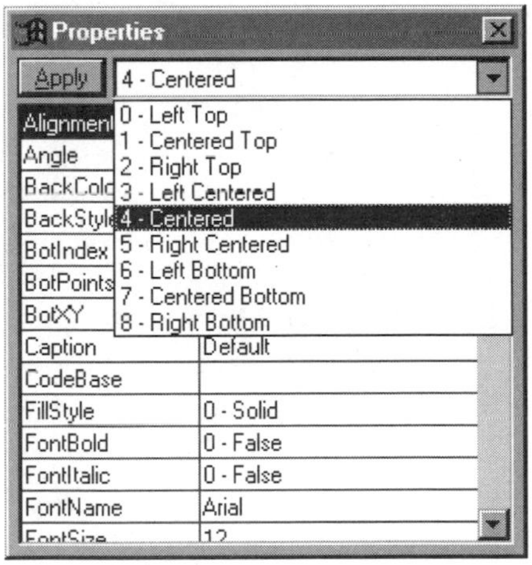

Figure 7-2
Properties table showing the drop-down menu for predefined values for the Alignment property.

CHAPTER 7

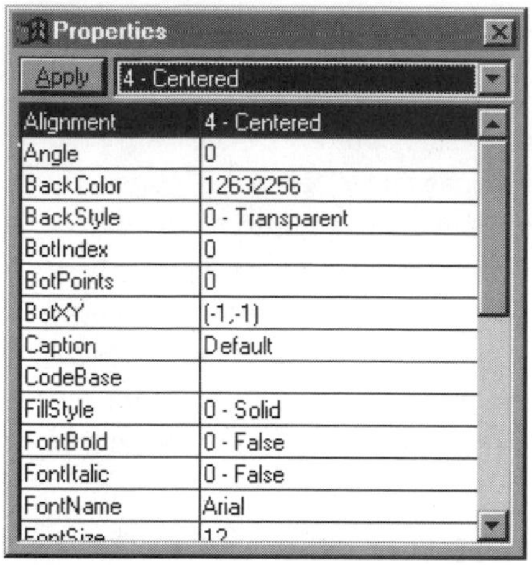

Figure 7-3

Result of selecting a predefined value in the Properties table for the Alignment property.

Does this mean that you'll be using the Properties table to enter *all* your attribute values and <PARAM> tags? Well, not exactly. For some ungodly reason, the Properties table displays color values in the decimal version of the hexadecimal number. (If this sounds like gobbledygook, bear with me.) Colors are defined by RGB (red, green, blue) values, each of which can range from 0 to 256. The hexadecimal (base 16, for you new-math folks) version uses a two-character alphanumeric representation of each color value, rendering 255,255,255—which is white—as FFFFFF. A little bizarre, perhaps, but at least there's a correspondence between the hexadecimal value and the RGB original. The decimal version, however, is 16777215, and if that makes perfect sense to you, perhaps you need to spend a tad less time around your computer.

So here's the trick: you enter hexadecimal color values in the Properties table with an "&H" prefix. Once you click the Apply button, &HFFFFFF is displayed as 16777215—but at least you got it in there. Perversely, the ActiveX Control Pad still writes the HTML value of the color in hexadecimal notation, so if you're used to hex values, you'll probably maintain colors directly in the HTML. Either way, you can live with the results.

The problem is that, as of this writing, some valid <PARAM> tags (such as the array of values that make up menu entries) cannot be entered in the Properties table. If you want to add something like this within your <OBJECT> tag, you'll have to do it by hand. And note the square brackets: parentheses are valid for delineating the index value of array items in VBScript but not in HTML:

```
<PARAM NAME="Menuitem[0]" VALUE="Blackberries">
<PARAM NAME="Menuitem[1]" VALUE="Blueberries">
<PARAM NAME="Menuitem[2]" VALUE="Boysenberries">
<PARAM NAME="Menuitem[3]" VALUE="Raspberries">
<PARAM NAME="Menuitem[4]" VALUE="Strawberries">
```

You can enter menu arrays in other ways, but there's more to say about the ActiveX Control Pad. It won't let you write your MenuItem <PARAM> tags, and if you key them in manually and open the Properties table, the Control Pad strips them out when you close the table. As of this writing, the ActiveX Control Pad writes the BackStyle property of the Microsoft Label control as "FillStyle"—first time, every time—leaving you with *two* values for the foreground color and no way to set the background color by using the Properties table. Sooner or later somebody's going to get around to fixing this bug—we hope by the time you read this book—but the larger point is that a user-friendly interface doth not always valid markup make—not, at least, in an emerging technology.

NOTE

FrontPage users configure controls by double-clicking the object in the FrontPage Editor and choosing the Properties button in the ActiveX Control Properties dialog box. Some controls don't have properties that can be set in FrontPage. When you click the Properties button for these controls, you'll see the Extended Attributes dialog box. Otherwise, your experience will be the same as with the standalone version of the ActiveX Control Pad.

Writing scripts

Both the FrontPage and stand-alone versions of the ActiveX Control Pad come with a Script Wizard, which provides a graphical interface for using VBScript. You can always write code the old-fashioned way, but the Script Wizard exposes all available object models in the page and proposes the proper syntax for actions and procedures, so it can save you a great deal of time. (The tool is not without its peculiarities, but you should be getting used to that by now.)

In the stand-alone version of the ActiveX Control Pad, you launch the Script Wizard by choosing Script Wizard from the Tools menu, by clicking the Script Wizard button on the toolbar, or by right-clicking anywhere in the page and choosing Script Wizard from the resulting menu. Once you've written a script—that is, once you have inserted a <SCRIPT> tag—you can also launch the Script Wizard by clicking the Edits Script button. It's at the left of the screen and looks like this:

Edits Script button

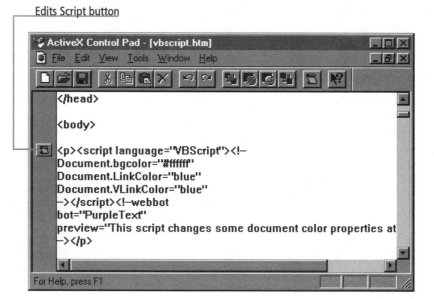

In the FrontPage Editor, you can launch the Script Wizard only by choosing Script from the Insert menu and clicking the Script Wizard button or by right-clicking an ActiveX control and choosing Script Wizard from the resulting menu.

When you first launch the Script Wizard, you're in List View. All the named objects in the page—that is, a combination of some (not necessarily all) of the Internet Explorer objects (the Window object, such Element objects as buttons, and so forth)—plus all the ActiveX controls will be displayed in the clickable Select An Event list, on the left. The same objects, along with properties, global variables, and the Go To Page action, appear in the clickable Insert Actions list, on the right. Click any of the objects on the left to expose the events associated with those objects. Click any of the objects on the right to expose some (not necessarily all) of the methods and properties associated with those objects. Got it? Figure 7-4 shows what the Script Wizard for our ActiveX demo page (contained in the ACTIVEX.HTM file in the Chapter2 folder on the book's companion CD) looks like in List View, with the events exposed for all the objects, and with the methods and properties of the PopUpMenu object (named BtnMenuObject) exposed. (The

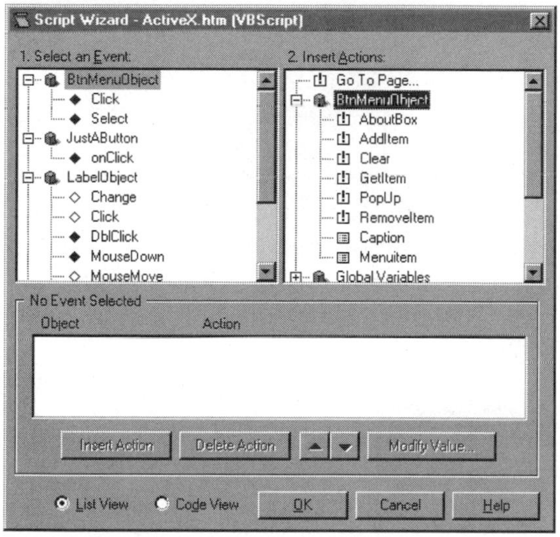

Figure 7-4
The Script Wizard in List View exposes object events on the left, object methods and properties on the right.

ACTIVEX.HTM file on the CD will look a little different because of some custom procedures, which will be explained in a moment.)

NOTE

You would be forgiven for thinking that the Click event associated with the PopUpMenuObject control is what makes the menu pop up, but you'd still be wrong. It turns out that the PopUp method is what makes the menu pop up, and the Click event is triggered when the user chooses an item from the menu. In order to pop the menu up, you have to invoke the PopUp method in another event or procedure—which is why, in our ActiveX demo page, we've added a plain-vanilla HTML <INPUT> button called JustAButton.

In principle, the Script Wizard lets you write scripts with a click of the mouse. (In practice…well, we'll get to that in a moment; principles first.) Here's how you'd use the Script Wizard to write an event procedure for the JustAButton object and manipulate the PopUpMenu Object:

1. Click to expand the JustAButton object in the Select An Event list to expose the onClick event.

2. Select the JustAButton onClick event in the Select An Event list.

241

3. Click the PopUpMenuObject in the Insert Actions list.

4. Select the AboutBox method for the PopUpMenuObject.

5. Click the Insert Action button.

And voilà: an event procedure in which the user clicks the JustAButton button and sees...what you see in Figure 7-5? Hey, what happened to the PopUp method? Dear reader, for reasons that we cannot presume to fathom, the List View of all current versions of the ActiveX Control Pad (both the stand-alone and FrontPage flavors) does not display *all* the methods and properties of an object.

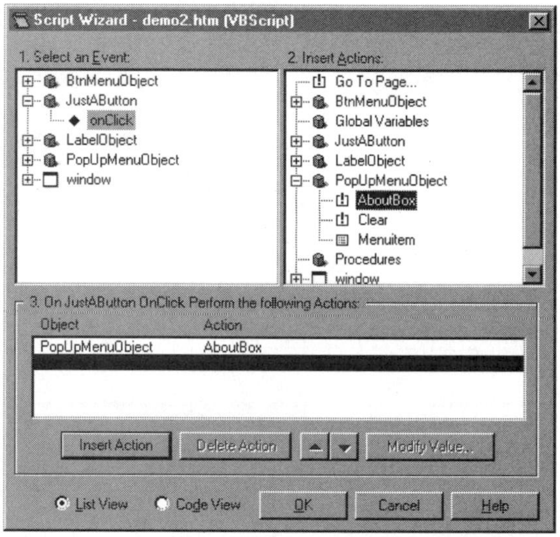

Figure 7-5

The Script Wizard List View might not *show all methods and properties.*

But the Code View (Figure 7-6) does. Clicking the Code View option gives you not only all the methods and properties but also the proper VBScript syntax, as well as a pane in which you can write your own code—which you'll need to do if you want to manipulate variables, use most VBScript functions, and, in fact, write most of your code. The Script Wizard isn't a snare and a delusion—exposing the object models and showing you the proper statement syntax are invaluable assets—but it certainly isn't going to write all your code for you. You will write it yourself, using the Code View as a kind of run-time online reference. Just be aware that once you write one statement in the Code View, the whole routine is considered a custom procedure, and it won't be displayed in the List View—a small price to pay for good syntax.

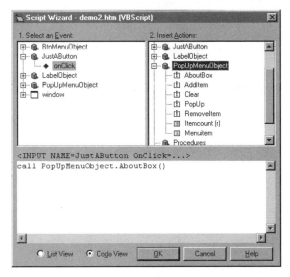

Figure 7-6

The Script Wizard Code View docs show all methods and properties.

You can add VBScript statements in Code View by double-clicking the method or property of the object you want to manipulate in the Insert Actions list, to the right. For example, to create the JustAButton_Onclick event procedure, which displays the PopUp menu as shown in Figure 7-7, you switch

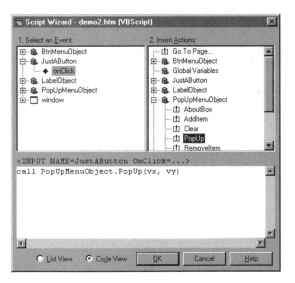

Figure 7-7

The Script Wizard writes code with the full syntax.

to the Code View and double-click the relevant method in the Insert Actions list. The syntax—including arguments for the x and y positions of the upper left corner of the menu, passed by value—comes at no extra charge. There's only one slight problem: you can run this code till the cows come home (and they do, they do; just be patient), but you won't see a menu pop up until you create menu entries. And, as already noted, there seems to be no way to do that short of keying the array in by hand.

At this point, let's jump ahead to the finished ActiveX demo page so you'll understand how we approach writing scripts. We wanted to include both the BtnMenuObject and the PopUpMenuObject so that you could see the differences between them. Both controls require the definition of a menu, however. It would have been possible to invoke the AddItem method separately for each control, but it made sense to write a common routine for both objects.

More Peculiarities of the PopUpMenuObject

Although it looks as if there ought to be a way to manipulate the MenuItem property with the ActiveX Control Pad, there really isn't; but you can get the same effect with the AddItem method—called once for each item, preceded by the Clear method or you'll just keep repeating the entries every time you pop the menu up—with the added advantage that the ActiveX Control Pad won't trash your code every time you return to the HTML Editing View. Hey, it's an emerging technology; that's part of the fun. But the code looks something like this:

```
call PopUpMenuObject.Clear()
call PopUpMenuObject.AddItem('Blackberries', 1)
call PopUpMenuObject.AddItem('Blueberries', 2)
call PopUpMenuObject.AddItem('Boysenberries', 3)
call PopUpMenuObject.AddItem('Raspberries', 4)
call PopUpMenuObject.AddItem('Strawberries', 5)
call PopUpMenuObject.AddItem('Gooseberries', 6)
call PopUpMenuObject.AddItem('Loganberries', 7)
call PopUpMenuObject.AddItem('Lingonberries', 8)
```

Why the single quotes? When you use the ActiveX Control Pad to write code for an HTML button, everything winds up inside the ONLOAD=" " attribute of the <INPUT> tag. The ActiveX Control Pad inserts your text quite literally, and since the ONLOAD attribute itself is bracketed by double quotes, you need to use single quotes in your VBScript or you'll get garbage.

Common routines are called *procedures*, and they're just like event procedures except they're not associated with any specific event. It certainly would have been possible to add a series of PopUpMenuObject.AddItem statements to the JustAButton_Onclick event procedure, but then it would have been necessary to repeat them for the BtnMenuObject. It's just far more elegant to write a procedure that both menus can use, and here's how you'd do that:

1. Choose Code View.

2. Right-click on Procedures on the Insert Actions list, and choose New Procedure from the resulting menu. (To edit an existing procedure, right-click on the procedure in the Insert Actions list, and choose Edit from the resulting menu.)

3. Rename the new procedure, and then continue writing script in the Code pane, as shown here:

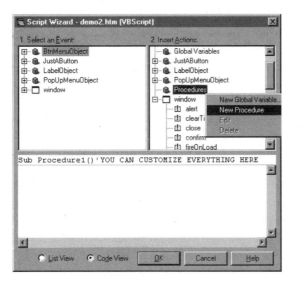

In our completed page, we took the process one step further and created a function called fPopulateMenu, which uses the MenuName variable to invoke the Clear and AddItem methods that both Menu controls share. As you'll see from the code, first the array is dimensioned (with a global variable defined at the top of the routine, for ease of maintenance), and then an AddItem statement within a For...Next loop uses the *i* variable to increment the array through all the menu items. (Remember that the array in-

dex is always one less than the AddItem index because the numbering of
Basic arrays starts at 0.)

```
function fPopulateMenu(MenuName)
    LabelObject.Caption=""
    MenuName.clear
    ReDim MenuItems(ITEM_COUNT)
    MenuItems(0)="Blackberries"
    MenuItems(1)="Blueberries"
    MenuItems(2)="Boysenberries"
    MenuItems(3)="Raspberries"
    MenuItems(4)="Strawberries"
    MenuItems(5)="Gooseberries"
    MenuItems(6)="Huckleberries"
    MenuItems(7)="Loganberries"
    MenuItems(8)="Lingonberries"

    for i = 1 to ITEM_COUNT
        call MenuName.AddItem(MenuItems(i-1), i)
    next
end function
```

The LabelObject.Caption statement simply clears the Label object, which
displays the results of the user's selection. You can examine the code of the
fEvaluateMenuMessageString shared procedure in our ActiveX demo page
to see how the results message is generated. While you're at it, take a look
at the procedures that use the LabelObject MouseDown, MouseUp, and
DblClick methods to clear the object and display instructions to the user.

If you think about it for a minute, you can see that assigning objects
and properties to a variable poses a special problem. You can't use the
variable=textstring statement because object and property names aren't
considered text strings in VBScript (any more than VBScript statements are
text strings). Placing an object name within quotation marks makes it a text
string, all right, but text strings aren't object names, either—they're just given
sequences of ASCII characters with no deeper meaning or significance
whatsoever. The Dim, Redim, Public, and Private statements won't do the
trick, either. You have to use the Set statement to assign an object reference
to a variable, as we've done in the JustAButton_Onclick event procedure in
our finished page:

```
Sub JustAButton_Onclick
    Set MenuName=PopUpMenuObject
    Call fPopulateMenu(MenuName)
    Call MenuName.popup(x+10,80)
end sub
```

246

It's worth spending a little time with the page in your browser as well to see the differences in how the controls behave. Finally, download the Menu sample page from the Microsoft Web site at http://microsoft.saltmine.com/ activexisv/msctls/ie/menu.htm for a completely different code strategy that uses the Timer object.

The HTML Layout Control

The HTML Layout Control is an ActiveX control that defines and positions other ActiveX controls. Think of it as a control container—or, if you have a background in Visual Basic, as the closest thing you'll find to a VB form. The control lets you create individual groupings of specified ActiveX controls known as layouts, which are saved as .ALX files. The Layout Control lets you overlap the objects in the layout, control the "front-to-back," or z-order, of objects, and make some objects transparent so background objects show through. And once you've created a layout, you can then insert it into any Web page just as you would any other ActiveX control, with one important difference: while you have to provide a URL reference to the .ALX file, your user's won't be aware of a separate download because Internet Explorer reads and renders the layout from the server along with the rest of the page. Pretty cool, you say? But wait, there's more.

If you open an .ALX file in a text editor, you'll see it's really just HTML—with the standard <OBJECT> and <PARAM> tags as any other Web page. You won't see the HTML in the ActiveX Control Pad, of course, but you *will* be able to use the Script Wizard to write the procedures that activate your controls. So the long and short of it is that HTML Layouts are HTML pages containing ActiveX Controls and VB scripts, which can themselves be referenced by ActiveX controls in other pages. *Tres* cool, you say? No, wait—there's more!

In addition to forms elements like buttons and list boxes, Layout Controls can contain objects that display text and images. Such objects also support methods that can capture the x,y coordinates of the user's mouse position, which in turn can be manipulated to change the x,y coordinates of the objects themselves. Which is geektalk for drag and drop. That's right, you heard correctly, the Layout Control allows you to create pages in which users can actually drag and drop page elements in their browser; and if you want further proof, just point your Internet Explorer to:

http://www.microsoft.com/ie/most/howto/layout/eggplant/ eggplant.htm

and check out Mr. Eggplant Head! He's waaaaaaay cool.

CHAPTER 7

We're not going to take you that far. But we will take you quickly through the process of recreating the Office Template Download menus in the Layout Control to give you an idea how it works.

Creating an HTML layout

You create a new layout in the stand-alone version of the ActiveX Control Pad by choosing New HTML Layout from the File menu. As of this writing, you can't create a new layout in the FrontPage version—in fact, you'll only be able to see an instance of the Layout Control as a large, empty frame.

Once you run the command, you'll see a new window—named Layout*n* by default, instead of Page*n*—with a grid of dots and a floating Toolbox dialog box (see Figure 7-8). If you've ever created a form in Visual Basic, you'll know exactly what to do; even if you haven't, it won't take long for you to get the hang of it.

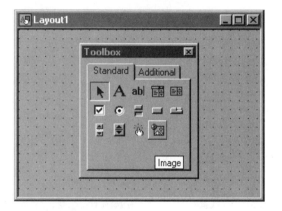

Figure 7-8
HTML Layout window.

1. Click controls in the toolbox to select them.

2. Drag them into the layout, and then size and position them.

3. Double-click objects in the layout to configure their properties in the Properties table. You'll quickly discover that HTML Layout controls support a great many more methods and properties than Internet Explorer ActiveX controls do.

4. Choose the commands from the Format menu to align and order objects and to set the spacing between objects as well as to enable or disable the snap-to-grid functionality.

5. Choose the commands from the Edit menu to select all items and to group or ungroup selected items.

6. Size the Layout window to configure the size of the inserted Layout control as it will appear in your Web page.

We created a new layout named TEMPLATEDOWNLOAD.ALX (available on the CD in the _PRIVATE subfolder of the Chapter2 folder) with two list boxes, a check box, a command button, and three labels (the third label is the second line of the check box text). Here's what it looks like:

We then wrote two event procedures, reusing much of the code from our VBScript demo page:

- A Layout1_OnLoad event procedure that runs when the page is loaded and that calls the fPopulateMenus( ) function to generate the menu items

- A BtnDLoad_Click event procedure that calls the fEvaluate-Results( ) function

We saved the file to the _PRIVATE subdirectory of our <ROOT WEB> directory, and then we opened the ActiveX Control demo page in the ActiveX Control Pad, chose Insert HTML Layout from the Edit menu, and selected _PRIVATE\TEMPLATEDOWNLOAD.ALX. Here's what the Layout Control looks like in the HTML code for the Web page in the ActiveX Control Pad:

```
<OBJECT CLASSID="CLSID:812AE312-8B8E-11CF-93C8-00AA00C08FDF"
ID="TemplateDownload_alx" STYLE="LEFT:0;TOP:0">
<PARAM NAME="ALXPATH" REF VALUE="_private\TemplateDownload.alx">
</OBJECT>
```

Because all the VBScript and layout control configurations are contained in the .ALX file, no additional configurations or scripting are needed for the Control object in this page. You can examine the sample on the companion CD if you want to learn more about how it all works.

CHAPTER 7

The coolest, least documented commands

Sometimes you wonder if the people who cook up the Microsoft "Easter eggs"—those nifty product-team credits that pop up magically once you perform some arcane combination of commands and procedures—also moonlight in GUI design. The innocuous little ToolBox window that opens with the HTML Layout has two very neat tricks, but it will perform them only if you happen to right-click somewhere in the toolbox. (These commands are otherwise unavailable on the interface.)

🌐   If you right-click on the tab titles, you'll see a menu with commands for adding, deleting, renaming, moving, importing, and exporting pages:

🌐   If you right-click on a control icon in the toolbox, you'll see a menu with commands for deleting and renaming the selected control as well as for adding any other control in your Registry to the toolbox:

That's right: by selecting Additional Controls you can add timers, common dialogs, document objects, and third-party custom controls to your HTML layout, just like a real Visual Basic Enterprise Edition developer:

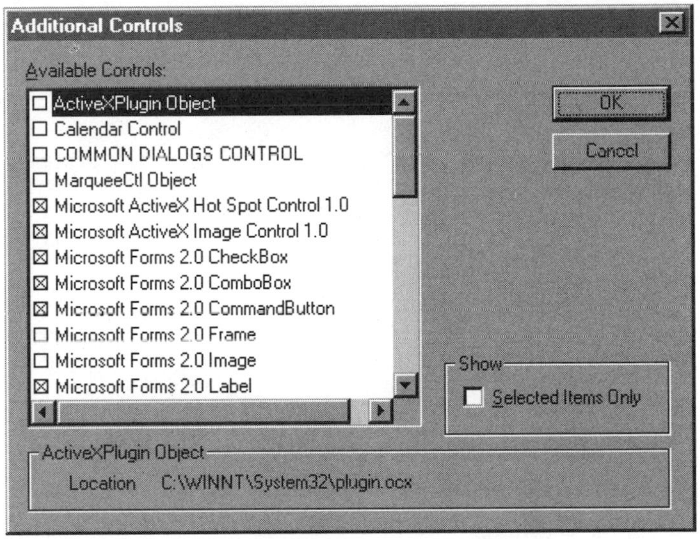

Nice of them to tuck away this functionality, don't you think?

CHAPTER 8

Using the Intranet Tools of Microsoft Office 97

Donna Jensen

For years, Microsoft has been building and strengthening a fundamental consistency among Microsoft Excel, Microsoft Access, Microsoft PowerPoint, and Microsoft Word, the applications that make up its Microsoft Office suite. If you know how to save a file in Microsoft Word, you know how to save a file in Microsoft Excel; if you press CTRL-P in any of the applications, you know that your document—or presentation, or workbook—is going to print. The evolution of consistency among applications continues in Office 97 in general and in Office's intranet capabilities in particular. The intranet tools available throughout Office 97 look and work in much the same way regardless of which particular application you are in, often because many of the intranet tools are shared components, and you can leverage your skills in one application across the whole suite. This chapter will give you a road map for doing just that by surveying the intranet features that all the Office applications have in common.

Microsoft Office 97 includes utilities to build Web pages on both the user-interface and programming sides:

🌐 **User-side Web page tools.** The Office 97 applications give you a basic toolkit for building and setting up Web pages and hyperlinks, including the Insert Hyperlink dialog box, the Web toolbar, and easy file-management interaction with HTTP and FTP sites.

🌐 **The VBA Web object model.** The lifeblood of an intranet is the hyperlink, and Visual Basic for Applications (VBA) Hyperlink objects drill down in the same way and use the same methods throughout the Office suite.

In addition to the tools they provide for working with Webs, the Office 97 documents, workbooks, presentations, and databases are designed to interact with the Web in ways that are straightforward and powerful. Microsoft had two basic goals here: make it easy for users to create HTML files in all the Office applications, and make Office files themselves powerful carriers of information when posted online in their native formats.

🌐 **Easy HTML.** Microsoft Office applications and HTML are comfortable with each other. You can create an Office document and save it in HTML format or convert an HTML file to an Office document. You can also open and edit HTML files in your Office application.

🌐 **Powerful online Microsoft Office files.** Easy as Office makes it to work with HTML, you might want to take a different approach and post your Office files themselves on your intranet. Each application has built-in document- and information-sharing features designed especially for intranet use. On top of that, Microsoft Internet Explorer can in effect "run" Office applications, displaying the files faithfully and making the applications' full functionality available to your intranet users.

User-Side Web Page Tools

You can do a lot of your Web page building in Office 97 without touching code. As part of the user interface, Office offers several utilities to work with hyperlinks, file formatting, and Web sites.

Hyperlinks

With Office, you can quickly create a hyperlink to any file or document with a recognized address—to local or network folders, URLs, or FTP sites. Each Office application ships with the same straightforward interface for inserting hyperlinks—open the Insert Hyperlink dialog box from the Insert menu or from the Insert Hyperlink button on the standard toolbar.

The Insert Hyperlink dialog box, which is shown in Figure 8-1, is the same across the Office suite. In the example in Figure 8-1, the hyperlink will resolve to a Microsoft Excel worksheet on the company intranet. The hyperlink will also select a named range in the worksheet, "NYOffice," but you could create a hyperlink to an unnamed range and use the range's row:column cell references instead.

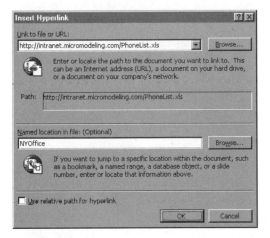

Figure 8-1
The Insert Hyperlink dialog box.

Linking to ranges

Once you choose a target file for the hyperlink, you can view a list of ranges within that file and have the hyperlink resolve to a specific location in the file. The named locations you link to can be text, graphics, tables, or ActiveX objects such as MS Graph charts or WordArt. If your hyperlink is to a Word document, the location can be anything you create a bookmark for, such as a paragraph or a heading. For PowerPoint presentations, you can link to a particular slide. With Microsoft Excel workbooks, you can link to a specific worksheet, a cell, or a range of cells by row:column labels or by defined name ranges. In Microsoft Access, you can link to a table, query, report, or form.

CHAPTER 8

Pasting clipboard content as hyperlinks

In all of the Office applications, you can paste the content of the clipboard into your Office file as a hyperlink. To do this, you must first save the source file. Copy a selection from the source file to the clipboard, and then select Paste As Hyperlink from the Edit menu in the destination file. The clipboard content will paste into your file in the format in which you copied it to the clipboard. For example, a copied table will paste in as a table, but it will also be formatted as a hyperlink to the source file you copied the content from.

Dragging and dropping

Another way to put hyperlinks in your file is by dragging and dropping them in with the mouse. Right-click the selected object, drag it to the destination file, and then select Create Hyperlink Here from the context menu. The dragged object can be text or graphics from a Word file or PowerPoint slide, a cell range in Microsoft Excel, or a database object in Microsoft Access.

If you like working with mouse buttons, this method is the easiest and quickest way to make hyperlinks to specific locations in destination files. Although you're setting up the hyperlink to jump to a specific location, you don't need to create a bookmark or name the range in the destination file. Office will generate a unique identifier for you.

If your dragged selection was text, that text will appear as the display text in the hyperlink. If the selection was a picture, then that picture will be displayed as the hyperlink. You can change the hyperlink's display text or image by selecting it and then typing or inserting an image over it.

Available Internet protocols

The Microsoft Office Setup program automatically installs and registers the files you need to jump to any Office document or file on an HTTP or FTP server. In addition, if you have the appropriate files installed and registered, Office will recognize the protocols listed in Table 8-1.

Table 8-1   Internet Protocols

Protocol	Name	Description
cid	CompuServe® Internet Dialer (CID)	Establishes a point-to-point protocol (PPP) connection with the Internet through CompuServe's network.
file	File	Opens a file on a local hard drive or local area network (LAN).
gopher	Gopher	Displays information on a Gopher server.

Table 8-1 *(continued)*

Protocol	Name	Description
https	Hypertext Transfer with privacy	Establishes an HTTP connection that uses Secure Sockets Layer (SSL) encryption.
mailto	MailTo	Opens your electronic mail program to send a message to the specified Internet e-mail address. Uses the format *mailto:username@domain*.
mid	Musical Instrument Digital Interface (MIDI)	Plays MIDI sequencer files if the user's computer has a sound card.
mms	Microsoft Media Server (MMS)	Plays media such as ActiveMovie streaming format files (.asf) from an MMS server.
msn	Microsoft Network	Jumps to a location on The Microsoft Network.
news	News	Starts a newsreader and opens the specified Usenet newsgroup. Uses the format *news:newsgroupname*.
nntp	Network News Transfer	Performs the same function as the News protocol, except that two slashes follow the colon. Uses the format *nntp://newsgroupname*.
pnm	RealAudio	Plays RealAudio streaming audio from a RealAudio server.
prospero	Prospero	Opens files on the Prospero distributed file system.
rlogin	Rlogin	Starts an Rlogin terminal-emulation program.
telnet	Telnet	Starts a telnet terminal-emulation program.
tn3270	TN3270	Starts a TN3270 terminal-emulation program.
wais	WAIS	Accesses a Wide Area Information Servers database.

The Web Toolbar

The Web toolbar, shown in Figure 8-2, turns Microsoft Office applications into virtual browsers. You can test the navigation of your hyperlinks in any

Office file without having to open the file in Internet Explorer, because the Web toolbar provides standard browser functionality.

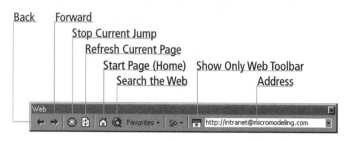

Back   Forward
        Stop Current Jump
        Refresh Current Page
        Start Page (Home)   Show Only Web Toolbar
        Search the Web   Address

Figure 8-2

The Web toolbar.

- 🌐 **Navigation buttons.** The Back, Forward, Stop, Refresh, Start(Home), and Search functions work just as they do in a "real" browser.

- 🌐 **Favorites list.** A Favorites list is fully operational, letting you not only jump to favorite sites but also add to and edit the list. This list is shared, so any updates appear universally across the Office suite and in Internet Explorer.

- 🌐 **Go button.** The Go button duplicates, as menu items, the functions of the other buttons on the toolbar, but it also contains handy items to manage your Web start and search pages. (See the next section, "Changing the Web Start and Search Pages," for details.)

- 🌐 **Show Only Web Toolbar button.** This toolbar button hides all other toolbars in the application except the Web toolbar, completing the virtual browser effect.

- 🌐 **Address history list.** The Address history list tracks the ten sites you have visited most recently. The list is shared, so updates are universal across the Office suite and in Internet Explorer. For example, if the last site you jumped to in Microsoft Excel was http://intranet.micromodeling.com/PhoneList.xls, that same site will also appear at the top of the history lists in Microsoft Access, Word, PowerPoint, and Internet Explorer.

Each Office application has its own Web toolbar that is bound to it. To avoid clutter, however, the only Web toolbar that will display at any time will be the toolbar that belongs to the active application. You can customize the Web toolbar in the same way you customize any Office toolbar, but your customizations will be local to the toolbar's application. For example, a button you add to the Microsoft Access Web toolbar won't appear on the Microsoft Excel Web toolbar.

Setting the Web start and search pages

You use the Set Start Page and Set Search Page items under the Web toolbar's Go button to set new defaults for your start and search pages. The procedure is the same for both the start and search pages:

1. Open the file you want to set as the start or search page.

2. Click Go on the Web toolbar, and then select Set Start Page or Set Search Page.

You'll see a message box reporting the current start or search page. Click Yes to change the default to the active file.

The file(s) you select for the start and search pages will be adopted universally: all the Web toolbars in all your Office applications will use those pages, and so will Internet Explorer when you launch it independently.

Basic File Management

The Office applications supply some handy file-management aids for hooking into intranet files and sites.

Using the Hyperlink Base and Title properties

The Properties dialog box has a new field, Hyperlink Base, that you can use to specify a hyperlink base for all the hyperlinks in the active file or database. In addition, for Microsoft Excel, PowerPoint, and Word, the dialog box's Title field does double duty in Office 97, supplying display text for the Internet Explorer title bar. For Microsoft Access databases, the title bar text will be the name of the form, table, or report that you've published to the Web. The Properties dialog box is available by selecting Properties from the File menu (in Microsoft Access select Database Properties) and is shown in Figure 8-3.

Opening and saving files to Web sites

You can use Office's standard dialog boxes to open and save Office and HTML files to intranet locations. In the dialog box, just type the full intranet address of the file. For example, to open Policies.html on your company intranet, type http://intranet.micromodeling.com/policies.html in the File Name text box in the Open dialog box. To save the file directly back to your Web, enter the address again in the Save dialog box.

Interacting with FTP sites

You can add, modify, and interact with FTP sites from within the Office applications.

🌐 **Add an FTP site to the list of intranet sites** from the File/ Open dialog box. In the Look In drop-down list, choose Add/Modify FTP Locations to bring up the dialog box shown in Figure 8-4, and then enter the name of the site and its logon properties.

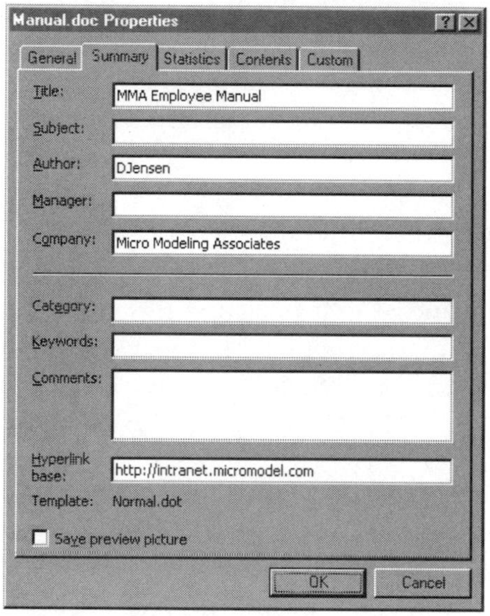

Figure 8-3
The Properties dialog box.

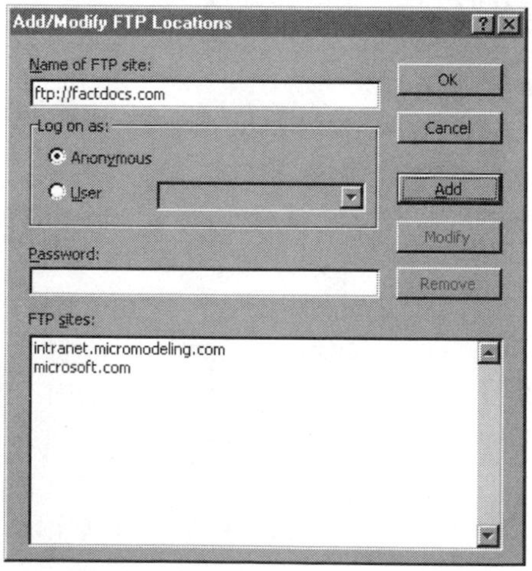

Figure 8-4

The Add/Modify FTP Locations dialog box.

Save a document to an FTP site by choosing File/Save As and then selecting one of the FTP sites in the Save In drop-down list, as shown here:

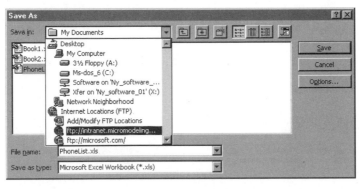

 Open a document at an FTP site from the File/Open dialog box's list of intranet locations. You can also just type the address in the File Name box as described above.

 Change the logon name or password for an FTP site from the File/Open dialog box. Choose Add/Modify FTP Locations from the Look In drop-down list to open the Add/Modify FTP Locations dialog box shown in Figure 8-4. Select an FTP site, change the Log On information, and then select Modify.

Under the Hood: The Microsoft Office Web Object Model

The Microsoft Office 97 applications share the same programming language, Visual Basic for Applications (VBA), and the same approach to automating intranet features, the Web object model. The Web object model for the Office applications revolves around two basic elements:

 Hyperlink collections and objects

 New intranet-oriented methods for file objects

Hyperlinks Collections

For Microsoft Excel, Word, and PowerPoint, the relationship of the Hyperlinks collection to the objects above it in the object model hierarchy is fundamentally the same. Hyperlinks collections now exist as properties of the applications' file objects: worksheets or cell ranges (Microsoft Excel), documents

CHAPTER 8

or text ranges (Word), and slides (PowerPoint). Figure 8-5 shows the Hyperlinks collection and the Hyperlink object in the object hierarchy for these applications.

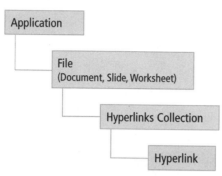

Figure 8-5

The Hyperlinks collection and Hyperlink object in the application hierarchy.

You can use the standard properties and methods of collections—such as Item and Count—on hyperlink collections. To create a hyperlink programmatically in Microsoft Word and Microsoft Excel, use the Add method on the collection.

NOTE Microsoft Access does not use hyperlink collections; rather, it refers to individual Hyperlink objects as properties of controls. In Microsoft Access, you would specify properties for a control's hyperlink to create the hyperlink. Microsoft PowerPoint uses a Hyperlinks collection, but to add a new hyperlink you must assign it as an object's Action Setting. The Add method is unavailable for hyperlinks.

The Add method on hyperlink collections takes three arguments:

- 🌐 **Anchor** determines the location and display text of the hyperlink.
- 🌐 **Address,** an optional argument, gives the destination path and file name for the hyperlink.
- 🌐 **SubAddress,** an optional argument, points the hyperlink to a specific range in the target file.

Aside from differences in file type, the Add method is the same for Microsoft Excel, Word, and PowerPoint. The following code samples add hyperlinks to Micro Modeling's intranet home page at the insertion point in the active document, worksheet, and slide.

In Word, add this code to the Document object's collection:

```
ActiveDocument.Hyperlinks.Add Anchor:=Selection.Range, _
    Address:="http://intranet.micromodeling.com"
```

In Microsoft Excel, add this code to the Worksheets collection:

```
ActiveSheet.Hyperlinks.Add Anchor:=Selection, _
    Address:="http://intranet.micromodeling.com"
```

Working with Hyperlink objects

Hyperlink objects have many properties and methods in Office, but you'll probably find yourself working primarily with a small suite of them. Five properties are especially useful and apply to hyperlinks in Microsoft Excel, Word, and PowerPoint: Address, SubAddress, Name, Range, and Type.

- **Address** returns the destination file or URL of the hyperlink.

- **SubAddress** returns a range—such as a bookmark or a cell range—within the hyperlink's destination file.

- **Name** returns the display text of the hyperlink.

- **Range** returns the range of text to which the hyperlink is attached.

- **Type** indicates whether the hyperlink is attached to a Range or Shape object. This property can return one of the following constants: msoHyperlinkInlineShape, msoHyperlinkRange, or msoHyperlinkShape.

These properties are read-only and return strings, except for Type, whose constants are long integers. The Address and SubAddress properties also apply to hyperlinks in Microsoft Access, and they work the same way there.

The following example reports the basic properties of the second hyperlink in a Word document in a message box:

```
With ActiveDocument.Hyperlinks(2)
  sMsg = "Address: " & .Address & vbCr
  sMsg = sMsg + "SubAddress: " & .SubAddress & vbCr
  sMsg = sMsg + "Name: " & .Name & vbCr
  sMsg = sMsg + "Range: " & .Range & vbCr
End With
MsgBox sMsg, vbOKOnly,"Hyperlink Info"
```

Figure 8-6 shows the dump of the hyperlink properties that can result from this code sample.

Figure 8-6

Hyperlink properties dump.

Using Hyperlink object methods

In general, you can apply the basic object methods—such as Cut, Copy, Select, and Delete—to hyperlinks. There is some variation among the Office applications as to how the methods operate; the online documentation supplies details on application-specific differences. In addition, Office supplies two especially handy methods specifically for the Hyperlink object:

- 🌐 **AddToFavorites** adds a shortcut to a specified hyperlink to the Favorites folder.

- 🌐 **Follow** makes the hyperlink connection, downloading (if necessary) and displaying the target file.

The AddToFavorites method is a simple command and takes no arguments. For example, the following line of code adds the first hyperlink in the active Word document to the Favorites list:

```
ActiveDocument.Hyperlinks(1).AddToFavorites
```

The Follow method can take five optional arguments:

- 🌐 **NewWindow,** if set to True, will display the file in a new window.

- 🌐 **AddHistory,** if set to True, will add the hyperlink to the History list.

- 🌐 **ExtraInfo** is a string that supplies additional information to resolve the hyperlink.

- 🌐 **Method** is a variant that tells how the ExtraInfo string should be used. It can be either the msoGet value, which appends the information to the URL address, or the msoPost value, which supplies the extra information after the address has been resolved.

- 🌐 **HeaderInfo** is a string that can supply header information for the HTTP request. Its default value is an empty string.

The following example runs the first hyperlink in the active Microsoft Excel worksheet, opening the hyperlink's target in a new window and adding it to the History list:

```
ActiveSheet.Hyperlinks(1).Follow NewWindow:=True, _
AddHistory:=True
```

Using hyperlinks and shapes

Microsoft Excel, Word, and PowerPoint now host a shared drawing utility that can place a wide variety of graphic elements in your files. In the VBA object models, these drawing elements are Shape objects.

In addition to being a member of a Hyperlinks collection, an individual Hyperlink object can also be a property of a Shape object. (As described above, you can determine if a hyperlink is attached to a shape by returning the hyperlink's Type property.) The following example for PowerPoint displays the Address property of a shape's Hyperlink property:

```
MsgBox ActivePresentation.Slides(1).Shapes(1).Hyperlink.Address
```

Web Features for File Objects

Office 97 offers some intranet-oriented methods that apply to the Office applications' fundamental information vehicles: documents in Word, presentations in PowerPoint, and workbooks in Microsoft Excel. (The method isn't available for Microsoft Access data containers.) Two handy methods for working with file object hyperlinks are AddToFavorites and FollowHyperlink.

🌐 **AddToFavorites** allows you to add a shortcut to any file currently open in your application to the Favorites folder.

🌐 **FollowHyperlink** performs a hyperlink jump.

As with its counterpart that acts on the Hyperlink object, the AddToFavorites method on a file object doesn't take any arguments. This example adds the currently active PowerPoint presentation to the Favorites list:

```
ActivePresentation.AddToFavorites
```

What is appealing about the FollowHyperlink method is that it gives you a way to perform a hyperlink jump without a hyperlink actually existing in your document or worksheet or presentation. The VBA command itself performs the hyperlink. For example, a watchful administrator might add a routine to the Document Close event in a global Word template that notices whenever a user closes a document with the word "Resume" in its name

CHAPTER 8

and then automatically sends the user to a pertinent file on the company intranet:

```
Sub Document_Close()
If InStr(1, ActiveDocument.Name, "Resume", vbTextCompare) <> 0 Then
  '/Uh-oh. The user is typing a resume!
  MsgBox "Perhaps you'd like to see company policy on personal" _
          & " use of your computer?", _
          vbOKOnly & vbQuestion, "Personnel Department"
  '/Make the hyperlink jump:
  ActiveDocument.FollowHyperlink _
    "http://intranet.meancompany.com/termination.html"
End If
End Sub
```

HTML Made Easy

In Office 97, working with HTML is easy, whether you're creating and editing HTML content or converting files between Office and HTML formats. You can save any file created in an Office application in HTML format by selecting Save As HTML on the File menu. You can also open HTML files in Office applications. Your Office application—with the help of the Web toolbar—serves as a virtual browser that lets you do more than browse, because you can view Web files in a WYSIWYG setting and edit them too. You can also view, edit, and save HTML source text within Office. Finally, you can easily convert HTML files to Office format by selecting Save As from the File menu.

In addition, the individual applications add specific features, such as Microsoft Access's Web Page Wizard, to make HTML conversion and creation easy.

Posting Your Microsoft Office Files Online

All of the Office applications' files can be published online in their native format and opened in Internet Explorer with their full functionality intact. Each Office 97 application also has new features that exploit the interactive nature of the intranet:

🌐 **Collaborative editing in Microsoft Excel.** Multiple users can view and edit Microsoft Excel workbooks over the intranet.

Microsoft Excel will track the changes, allow administrators to accept or reject changes, and display the files' editing history— when changes were made and by whom. Word 97 offers those features, too, but Microsoft Excel goes a large step further and lets users edit workbooks simultaneously.

- **Document maps in Word.** In the Document Map display mode, you can view Word documents' headings as an outline in a frame-style layout running down the left side of the screen. When you click on one of the headings, it acts like a hyperlink and takes you to that heading's location in the document.

- **Action buttons in PowerPoint.** On an intranet, there's obviously no one to give a slide presentation, so PowerPoint has added action buttons that can make presentations interactive. The 3-D buttons are part of the presentation, and they let users access different slides, presentations, files, or URLs at their discretion.

- **Hyperlink data type in Microsoft Access.** Because hyperlinks are now native data types, Microsoft Access databases can be more interactive and powerful as gatherers of information with very little effort on the developer's part. Users can jump to supplemental documents and external Web sites using command buttons, labels, and images as exploration controls.

This chapter has provided just a sampling of the intranet tools and options available to you in Microsoft Office 97. As intranets evolve into serious information-sharing vehicles, Office is also evolving into a powerful and integrated resource for developing intranet content.

So far, you've seen how to apply the same intranet features and code across the Office suite, and your awareness of those shared features will help you choose and effectively use the right Office application for each facet of your intranet. The chapters that follow will build on the basic capabilities outlined here and show you how to take advantage of the intranet features of the individual Office applications.

CHAPTER 9

Creating Web Documents with Microsoft Word 97

Donna Jensen

When it comes to developing content for your intranet, Microsoft Word is a powerful and versatile member of the Microsoft Office 97 family. Not only can you take advantage of Word's traditional word processing and formatting features, but now you can also wield the might of Visual Basic for Applications (VBA) to speed your work along.

On top of that, Word 97 has many new features designed specifically for intranet developers. In this chapter you'll get a thorough grounding in all of those features. You'll also learn some strategies for using Word's traditional tools to help you build Web pages. You will find examples of the information covered in this chapter in the Chapter9 folder on the companion CD.

TIP   You can take advantage of the general intranet tools available in Microsoft Office 97 as you work in Microsoft Word. See Chapter 8 for details on those tools.

When planning Word's role in your intranet, you have a few basic options:

- Use Word to create and edit HTML pages directly.

- Create and work on your files as Word documents and then convert them to HTML.

- Post your Word documents on your intranet without converting them to HTML.

Word 97 has been designed to give you as many tools and as much flexibility as possible as you work with and move between the two file formats.

The Three Faces of Word

Because of that flexibility, Word is a chameleon. Its interface can change markedly depending on the type of file you're working with. If you're working on a native Word document, you have one universe of menu commands and toolbar buttons available to you; but the moment you open an HTML file (or convert your Word document to an HTML file), the menus and toolbars will alter, and you'll be in an HTML file-editing environment. Although there is a lot of overlap, many features available to Word documents aren't available to HTML files, and vice versa, and the menus and toolbars change to reflect the available features.

Beyond that interface split is another split: you can edit HTML files in two ways in Word—in a browser-like WYSIWYG (what you see is what you get) setting (usually referred to as Word's HTML authoring mode) or as tagged HTML markup in a plain text editing window. This chapter will help acquaint you with Word's different editing modes and the features that are and aren't available in each one.

The first part of the chapter introduces you to Word's new intranet tools. It falls into four basic parts:

1. First it covers two fundamental intranet utilities that are available and work the same way regardless of whether you're working on a Word document or an HTML file: hyperlinks and graphic backgrounds.

2. It then describes Word as a building and editing utility from an HTML perspective.

3. Next it covers the factors you'll want to consider when you convert Word files to and from HTML and delves into Word templates and how they affect the conversion process.

4. Finally, it examines strategies for posting Word documents on your intranet without converting them to HTML.

The second part of the chapter deals with Word and intranets from a programmer's perspective. It describes Word's object model in depth as the model relates to intranet elements and suggests VBA coding strategies for developing intranet content. Finally, you'll see how to build some sample applications using many of the features described throughout this chapter.

The Shared Tools: Hyperlinks and Backgrounds

Hyperlinks and backgrounds are two basic intranet features that you can insert into your document in either its Word document or HTML file incarnation. Although you'll see that the two features have some minor differences depending on your file type, they share most of the same functionality.

Inserting Hyperlinks

You can insert hyperlinks in your document in four ways:

- 🌐 Using the Office 97 Insert Hyperlink dialog box
- 🌐 Pasting clipboard content as a hyperlink
- 🌐 Dragging and dropping the hyperlink with the mouse
- 🌐 Using Word's AutoFormatting option

You learned about the first three options in Chapter 8. The fourth option, though, is particular to Word.

Using Word's AutoFormatting option

If you have file paths and URLs in your document, you can have Word's AutoFormat utility convert them all to hyperlinks. Word recognizes the characters "http://www" as the prefix to a Web address and also recognizes network file names and URLs such as "www.microsoft.com" and "\\Server\Archive." The AutoFormat utility will search through the document, and when it finds a text string with characters or a syntax that it recognizes, it will convert the string to a hyperlink.

To set up AutoFormat for hyperlinks, select AutoCorrect from the Tools menu, and then select the AutoFormat tab. The dialog box will appear as shown in Figure 9-1.

In this dialog box, check the Internet And Network Paths With Hyperlinks box. The AutoFormat option will turn all network paths and URLs in your document into hyperlinks. This feature is a good batch process for existing documents or text.

9
C H A P T E R

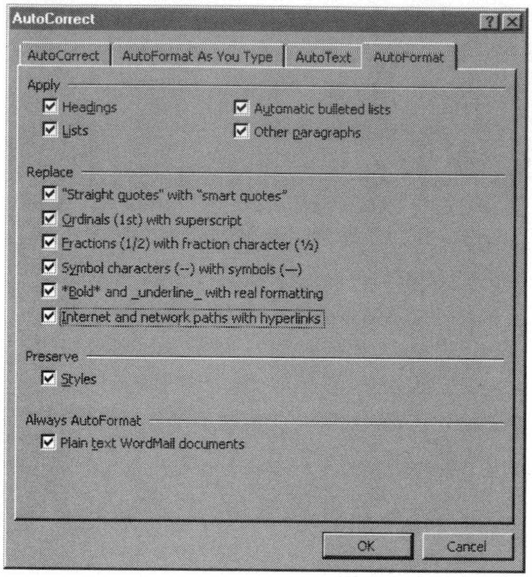

Figure 9-1

The AutoFormat page of the AutoCorrect dialog box.

You can also have Word automatically reformat file names and URLs into hyperlinks as you type them. Simply select the AutoFormat As You Type tab in the AutoCorrect dialog box and then check the Internet And Network Paths With Hyperlinks box. From this point on, whenever you type a recognizable string of text and then press the space bar or Enter, Word will convert the text into a hyperlink for you.

How Word stores hyperlinks

When you're working with hyperlinks in Word—whether the file you're working on is a Word document or an HTML file—Word inserts and stores the hyperlinks as fields. Fields are essentially formulas embedded in the page, and they reevaluate as conditions change. For example, whenever you open a document with a Date field, Word will reevaluate the result of that field so that it displays the current date.

Fields have two display modes: field code, which displays the formula; and field result, which displays the user-friendly outcome of the formula. The right mouse menu Toggle Field Code option and the key combination ALT+F9 are the handiest ways to toggle between the two display modes.

Hyperlink field codes can vary significantly depending on the type of hyperlink and how it was created. For example, the code for a hyperlink to MMA's home page is simply "{HYPERLINK "http://intranet.micro-modeling.com"}." On the other hand, the code for a dragged-and-dropped hyperlink, because of all the internally generated information it contains, could look something like this:

```
{ HYPERLINK "http:\\\\My Documents\\\\PageOne.html"
\\l _H1k365620979 \\s "1,10,15,0,,Label"\}
```

You can use Word's standard features for fields on hyperlink fields. For example, if you've changed the field code, you'll want to update the field so that the new formula takes effect. Select the field and press the F9 key to update the field. Or you might want to convert a hyperlink into plain text. In that case, select the hyperlink and unlink it (the shortcut key combination is CTRL+SHIFT+F9) as you would any field in Word.

Editing hyperlink fields

If you click on any hyperlink with the right mouse button, you'll see a Hyperlink entry with a submenu containing several options for editing and refining the hyperlink, as shown in Figure 9-2.

Figure 9-2
Context menu options and the Hyperlink submenu.

You can also edit the hyperlink field directly. Clearly, it's not a good idea to revise the code of a field like the drag-and-drop hyperlink shown above. But on a humbler scale, you should feel free to do some tweaking of your hyperlink fields.

You can change both the result and the code for the field.

🌐 **Change the field result.** If you've selected some text and then inserted a hyperlink using the Office shared Insert Hyperlink dialog box, your selection will become a hyperlink field and Word will set up the original text you selected as the field's result. But if you've selected nothing before inserting the hyperlink, Word will display the field's code, such as "http:/www.microsoft.com/", as its display result also. To change "http:/www.microsoft.com/" to the more agreeable "Click here for the Microsoft Home Page", in field result view, highlight the hyperlink, and then type in the new text. The new text will replace the field code while maintaining the correct hyperlink.

🌐 **Change the field code.** When you're in the field code display mode, the hyperlink is inactive, so you can select and click on the field without jumping to its destination. In this mode, for example, you can fix basic errors such as typos in the field. Select the problem text, such as "{ HYPERLINK "http://www.macrosoft.com/" }", and change it to "{ HYPERLINK "http://www.microsoft.com/" }".

TIP

If you find yourself inserting certain hyperlinks frequently, you might want to store them as Word AutoText entries. (Select New from the AutoText submenu in the Insert menu.) You can assign a short name for them, and every time you type that name and press F3, Word will insert the hyperlink.

Creating Background Effects

You can make online files more exciting by using background colors and textures. Backgrounds work with both HTML files and Word documents, but in Word documents they're not visible unless you're viewing the document in Online Layout display mode. (For more information on Online Layout mode, see the "Online Layout View" section on page 297.)

To add a background color, select Background from the Format menu. The palette shown in Figure 9-3 will appear. (If you're working on an HTML file, you can also click the Background button on the Drawing and Formatting toolbars.) Choose a color from the palette by clicking on it.

Figure 9-3

The background color palette.

You can also view a more delineated palette or even mix your own background color by clicking More Colors at the bottom of the palette. If you want to use a texture for your background instead of a solid color, display the background palette and choose Fill Effects.

If you want to choose another image for your background, click the Other Texture button in the Texture tab of the Fill Effects dialog box and browse for the file you want to use. You can also use any bitmap (a .BMP or .DIB file), metafile (a .WMF or .EMF file), or graphics file for which you have an import filter as your background texture.

Textures (including custom images) are the only available background fill effect for HTML files. Word saves the image as a separate file in the folder where your HTML file is located. With Word documents, you can also use patterns, gradients, or pictures as your background fill.

Building and Editing HTML Files in Word

When you're developing intranet content in Word, you have access to all the Office 97 intranet features—the Web toolbar, Insert Hyperlink dialog box, file management utilities, and easy crossover between native document format and HTML.

On top of that, Word has its own features that make it an alluring vehicle for building intranet pages:

🌐 **HTML right off the bat.** You can create HTML files in Word directly without having to create and convert Word documents as an intermediate format.

- 🌐 **Windows WYSIWYG.** You can use the traditional Windows WYSIWYG nature of Word to design your HTML page as your intranet users will see it.

- 🌐 **Word processing power.** Exploit Word's word processing power to edit, format, and spell check HTML files.

- 🌐 **Special utilities for Web page building.** Word adds some special features just for intranet developers, such as the Web Page Wizard and an array of graphical and multimedia effects.

- 🌐 **Macros.** You can't save macros in HTML files, but you can *run* macros on HTML files to automate some of your frequent Web page tasks. Just create and store the macros in a template.

In this section you'll learn how to create HTML files in Word and use Word's custom graphic features to bring them to life.

Ways to Create HTML Files

Word provides two roads to HTML pages: the Web Page Wizard and a blank Web page template so you can build your own HTML file from scratch.

Using the Web Page Wizard

The easiest way to create HTML files is through Word's Web Page Wizard, which will help you produce different types of HTML pages and apply graphic formats to them.

The Wizard is one of Office 97's Web Page Authoring tools, so you'll need to make sure you install those tools when you set up Office. To start the Wizard, choose New from the File menu, then select the Web Pages tab in the New dialog box. Select Web Page Wizard and click OK. As Figures 9-4 and 9-5 show, Web Page Wizard lets you choose among several layouts and styles. As you click on different items in the dialog box lists, you'll see your page change to reflect your choices.

When the Wizard finishes, save your new HTML file. The layouts included in the Wizard are optimized for online viewing: fonts, backgrounds, and tables will fit well and read easily in your browser.

Starting from scratch

If you prefer to work from a clean slate, choose New from the File menu, click on the Web Pages tab, and select Blank Web Page instead of the Web Page Wizard. Your new document will be an empty HTML file based on the template HTML.Dot. The blank Web page contains style definitions that call for larger font sizes and so are more suited to online viewing than new files based on Word's standard Normal.Dot.

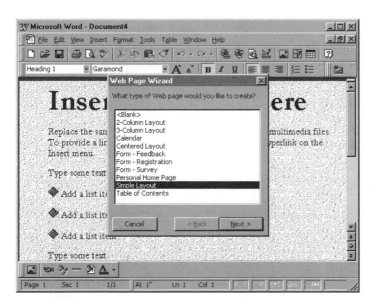

Figure 9-4

Web page layouts available in the Web Page Wizard in Word.

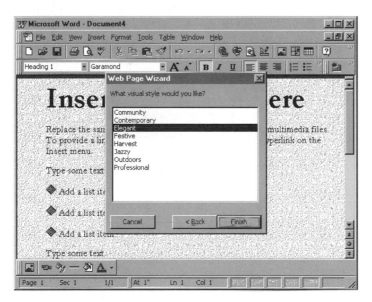

Figure 9-5

Web page styles available in the Web Page Wizard in Word.

Once you've developed a standard look for your Web pages, you might want to create your own Web page templates and base all your new files on them. See the "How to Create HTML Templates" section later in this chapter for details on creating and working with templates.

Word as an HTML Editing Environment

As you build HTML files in Word, you can exploit most of Word's word-processing features, and you have the added benefit of seeing your Web page as your intranet users will see it. Several of Word's features, such as bullets, are much more powerful in HTML authoring mode; other features aren't available at all. The rule of thumb is that if a feature isn't supported by HTML, you won't have access to it in HTML authoring mode. See the section "What's Kept, What's Lost in the Conversion Process" later in this chapter for a list of Word document elements that aren't available for HTML files in Word.

Web Page Preview

The Office 97 Web toolbar is an easy way to simulate a browser-like display of your HTML files within Word. But you can also go a step further and view your files in Internet Explorer as you work on them in Word. Word's File menu has a new entry, Web Page Preview, that launches Internet Explorer and displays the HTML file, while keeping the file active and open in Word. Make your editing changes in Word and then save the file. To preview the file with the new changes, switch to Internet Explorer and just refresh the screen.

HTML the old-fashioned way

As you format text, apply styles, and insert graphic objects and tables in your file, Word maps them—when it can—to their counterpart HTML tags. Although it's easier to edit HTML files in Word's HTML authoring mode, Word will also let you do your HTML work the old-fashioned way, as tagged plain text.

To edit your file's HTML markup in Word, choose HTML Source from the View menu. You'll notice that Word's interface changes: any toolbars you might have open become hidden except for the Standard toolbar, which Word alters significantly, showing only those buttons that are more likely to help you in editing the HTML text. (See Figure 9-6.)

Figure 9-6

The Standard toolbar in HTML Source mode in Word.

When you finish editing the text, save it and click the Exit HTML Source button. You'll immediately see the changes you made.

Word's Design Tools for HTML Files

Word 97 ships with easy-to-use and powerful design features that let you add graphics and multimedia objects to your HTML files. In all cases, when you insert a graphic or multimedia image into an HTML file, Word will by default store the image in the same folder as your HTML file. One way to simplify image storing is to use Office's Hyperlink Basc document property. (See Chapter 8 for more information on this property.)

Graphic elements

With Word's graphics tools, you can create graphical bullets and horizontal lines and insert pictures in HTML files.

Word's META HTML Tags

When you create an HTML file, Word adds custom properties to it. Those properties are represented in HTML as META tags. For example, the following lines are from an HTML file newly created in Word:

```
<HTML>
<HEAD>
<META HTTP-EQUIV="Content-Type" CONTENT="text/html;
charset=windows-1252">
<META NAME="Generator" CONTENT="Microsoft Word 97">

<TITLE>Doc33</TITLE>
<META NAME="Version" CONTENT="8.0.3410">
<META NAME="Date" CONTENT="10/11/96">
<META NAME="template" CONTENT="C:\Program Files\Microsoft
Office\Office\HTML.DOT">
</HEAD>
```

Two of the tags are especially relevant to Word:

🌐 The "Generator" tag identifies Word as the application used to create the page. This tag is something of a Microsoft standard, used by Microsoft Publisher, Microsoft FrontPage, Microsoft Excel, and Microsoft Access.

🌐 The "Template" tag provides for custom HTML templates. With this information, Word can correctly reassociate the custom template with the document upon reopening it in Word.

Bullets   To insert a bullet, place the cursor in the paragraph you want to bullet. You can also select and bullet multiple paragraphs. Then choose Bullets And Numbering from the Format menu to bring up the Bullets and Numbering dialog box shown in Figure 9-7.

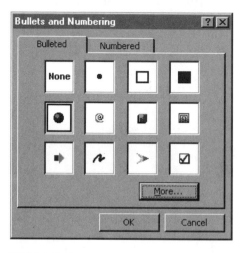

Figure 9-7

Bullets And Numbering dialog box for HTML files in Word.

The bullet selection for HTML files includes more graphically sophisticated bullets than the selection for Word documents. The bullets in the top row of this dialog box are Wingdings characters. The other bullets are .gif images.

In HTML authoring mode, you can work with the graphic bullets in much the same way you would work with standard bullets in Word documents. For example, if you're typing in a graphic-bulleted paragraph and then press Enter, the next paragraph will also be bulleted with the graphic image. Also, the graphic image becomes Word's default bullet, so that later on if you click the Bullets button on the Formatting toolbar, Word will bullet the paragraph(s) you've selected with the graphic bullet.

The supply of graphic bullets to choose from is limitless. Click the More button to open the Insert Picture dialog box, where you can find a list of graphic bullets included with your Office installation, as shown in Figure 9-8, or you can search for other image files to insert.

To insert an image into your file, choose an image from the list on the left side of the dialog box and then click the Insert button. You can download more images from Microsoft's World Wide Web site or add your own images to the set. Store your new bullet images in the Microsoft Office \Clipart\Bullets folder, and the dialog box will add them to its display list.

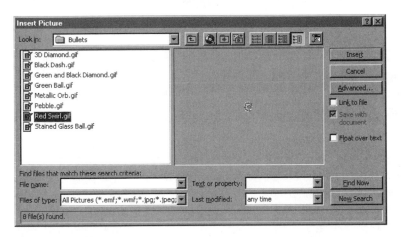

Figure 9-8

Insert Picture dialog box with default Office bullet images for HTML files in Word.

Horizontal lines   Because HTML files don't support page or section breaks, horizontal lines can be a useful way to segment thematically discrete sections of your page. Word 97 includes a set of colorful lines designed to help organize your HTML files and keep them visually interesting.

To insert a horizontal line, place the cursor where the line should appear and choose Horizontal Line from the Insert menu. The dialog box shown in Figure 9-9 will appear.

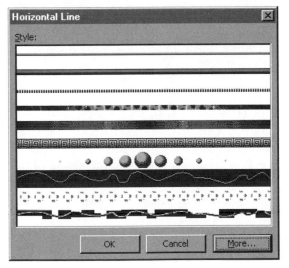

Figure 9-9

The Horizontal Line dialog box for HTML files in Word.

The top line in the dialog box is a Word line shape that takes on an HTML <HL> tag when you insert it. The rest of the lines are .gif files. If you click the More button on the dialog box, you'll be able to see a list of the available additional lines in your Microsoft Office\Clipart\Lines folder. Just as with bullets, you can add to the collection with downloads from Microsoft or with your own graphics.

TIP The horizontal line you insert becomes something of a default. You can repeatedly insert it elsewhere in the file by clicking the horizontal line button on the HTML page's Formatting toolbar:

Pictures   From the Insert menu, choose Picture to add clip art, scans, and charts to your file. Word inserts the pictures in INCLUDEPICTURE fields, which in turn become HTML <IMG> tags. From this cascading menu, you can also hook into Microsoft's World Wide Web site and download more images.

Embedded objects   When you're working on an HTML file in Word, you can embed the whole gamut of OLE objects into your file, including Paintbrush pictures, graphs and charts, and maps. After you've inserted the objects, you can still manipulate them—for example, you can double-click on a graph and change its data and its chart type. It's a good idea to do your manipulating immediately, though, because there's a small catch: when you close your file, Word will convert all the updateable objects to .GIF image files.

Multimedia features

You can also enhance your HTML files with video and sound by using Word's multimedia features.

Video   It's easy to liven up your HTML files with video clips, and Word provides you with options to customize their playback. To insert a video clip, choose Video from the Insert menu. The dialog box in Figure 9-10 will appear.

In the top part of the dialog box, enter the location and name of the clip in the Video box. Or use the Browse buttons to search for files. In the Alternate Image box, you can also specify an image to show if for some reason Internet Explorer can't find the clip. The Alternate Text box provides a second line of defense, displaying a text message if neither the video nor the backup image is available or if the user's browser does not support more advanced features.

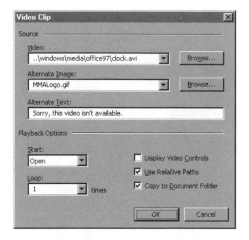

Figure 9-10

The Video Clip dialog box for HTML files in Word.

The controls in the lower part of the dialog box let you customize the clip's playback:

- The Start list offers three options—Open, Mouseover, and Both—that dictate the events that will launch the video playback.

- The Loop box sets the number of times the video will play when it is launched. You can choose one of the values from the drop-down list or type in your own.

- The Display Video Controls check box lets you include Start and Stop play controls with the clip.

- The final two check boxes—Use Relative Paths and Copy To Document Folder—are designed to help you manage your files, shortening the clip's address in its HTML tag by using a relative reference and storing a copy of the clip with the host document.

Once the video clip is in your HTML file, you can change the properties you set in the Video Clip dialog box. Click on the clip with the right mouse button for a menu with several play control options. If you select Properties, you'll return to the Video Clip dialog box, and you can make more revisions there.

Sound   You can add background sound to your HTML file that will play every time a user activates the file, whether he or she is loading the file for the first time or returning to a cached version of it.

*Official
Microsoft
Intranet
Solutions*

To add the sound, choose Properties from the Background Sound submenu of the Insert menu. The dialog box shown in Figure 9-11 will appear.

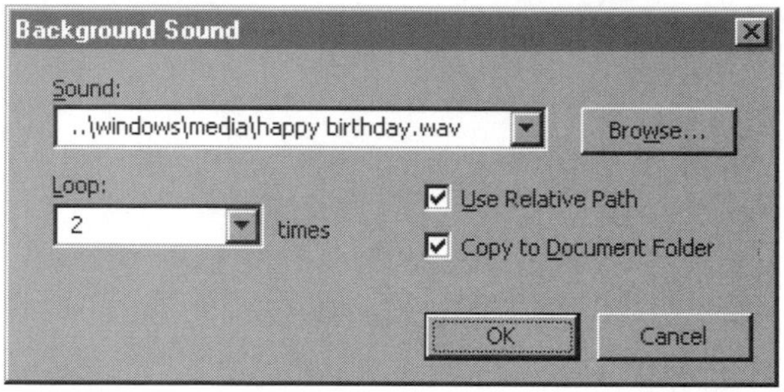

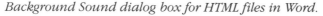

Figure 9-11
Background Sound dialog box for HTML files in Word.

Type the address of the sound you want to use in the Sound box, or choose the Browse button to search for a file. The Loop, Use Relative Path, and Copy To Document Folder controls work the same way they do in the Video Clip dialog box. You can insert sound files in .wav, .mid, .au, .aif, .rmi, .snd, and .mp2 (mpeg audio) formats.

Graphic objects and their HTML tags   Whenever Word can recognize a graphic object, it will assign an appropriate HTML tag to it. Table 9-1 summarizes the graphic elements in an HTML file and the HTML tags that Word applies to them.

Table 9-1   Graphics and the HTML Tags Word Assigns to Them.

Object in Word	HTML Tag
Bullets, graphic lines, OLE objects	<IMG>
Simple horizontal line drawing objects	<HR>
Backgrounds	<BODY BGCOLOR=...>
Video clips	<IMG DYNSRC=...>
Audio clips	<BGSOUND SRC=...>

Text formatting

A lot of the basic text formatting you take for granted with Word documents isn't available to HTML files. Such standards as line spacing, margins, kerning,

284

and tabs won't be picked up by Internet Explorer; and neither will Word's fancier features such as shadowing, embossing, and animated fonts.

You can still choose from a wide range of formatting options, however, including these:

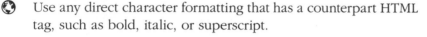

- Select text and change its font size, and your HTML file will retain and display your settings. The formatting toolbar for HTML files in Word has two buttons—Increase Font Size and Decrease Font Size—that can speed up your font resizing by increasing and decreasing the size in 2-point increments.

- Use any direct character formatting that has a counterpart HTML tag, such as bold, italic, or superscript.

- Change the font color. Word provides an easy way to do this. Just select the Font Color button on the Formatting toolbar, and Word will display a color palette. Choose a color from the palette, or drag the palette and use it as a floating toolbar (as shown in Figure 9-12).

- Control the alignment and indentation of your text. Left-, right-, and center-aligned paragraphs will display correctly in Internet Explorer, and you can work around the lack of tabs by increasing your text indents. Change the indents by selecting text and then clicking the formatting toolbar's Increase Indent or Decrease Indent button.

- Use bullets and numbering. These work fine in your HTML files. Again, you'll find buttons for them on the Formatting toolbar.

- Use styles to format your text, although they won't be retained in HTML. Word will pass along their formatting to HTML as direct font formatting.

The Formatting toolbar in Word's HTML authoring mode, shown in Figure 9-12, does a good job of presenting your text formatting options.

Marquee text   You are not totally doomed to static text formats. You can easily add scrolling marquee-style text to your HTML files.

To use scrolling text, choose Scrolling Text from the Insert menu to bring up the dialog box shown in Figure 9-13. The controls in the dialog box will help you set virtually all aspects (except the font!) of your scrolling text. Type your text, and as you apply different options to it, you can see their effect in the Preview window at the bottom of the dialog box.

285

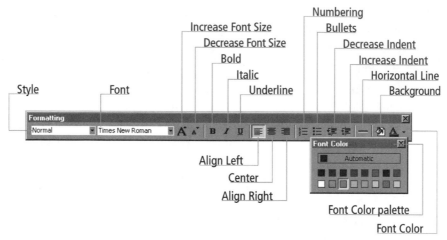

Figure 9-12

The Formatting toolbar in Word's HTML authoring mode.

The Behavior list gives you three choices:

🌐 Scroll, which will move your text across the screen in the direction you specify in the Direction list for the number of loops you specify in the Loop list

🌐 Slide, which will send your text from one side of the screen to the other—again, in whichever direction you specify—just once

🌐 Alternate, which will send your text ping-ponging back and forth across the screen

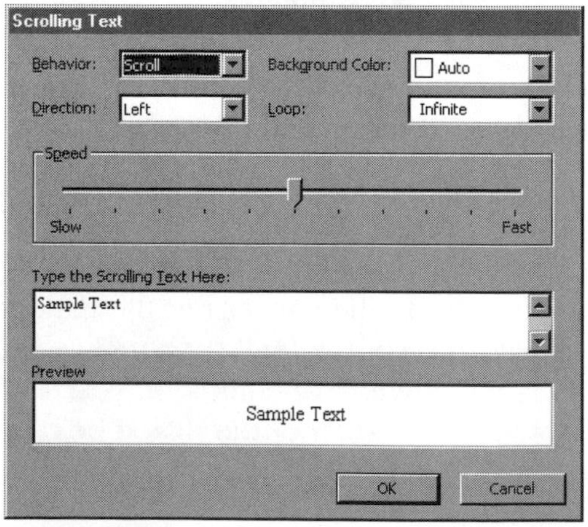

Scrolling Text

Behavior: Scroll Background Color: ☐ Auto

Direction: Left Loop: Infinite

Speed
Slow _____ Fast

Type the Scrolling Text Here:
Sample Text

Preview
Sample Text

OK Cancel

Figure 9-13

The Scrolling Text dialog box for HTML files in Word.

In the Speed section, you can set the text's scrolling speed.

When you create scrolling text, Word places the text in a frame at your cursor position.

TIP

You can change the properties of your scrolling text by clicking on the frame with the right mouse button and selecting Properties from the drop-down menu.

Word's text formats and HTML tags   Table 9-2 shows common text formatting options in Word and their HTML tags.

Table 9-2   Basic Text Formats in Word and Their Corresponding HTML Tags.

Text Formatting in Word	HTML Tag
Title (first words of document or Title document property)	<TITLE>
Numbered list	<OL>; each paragraph gets an <LI> tag
Bulleted list	<UL>; each paragraph gets an <LI> tag
Table	<TABLE>, <TR>, <TD>
Bold	<B>
Italic	<I>
Underline	<U>
Strikethrough	<STRIKE>
Superscript	<SUP>
Subscript	<SUB>
Paragraph mark	<P>
Line break	
Scrolling text	<MARQUEE>
Center-aligned paragraph	<P ALIGN="CENTER">
Right-aligned paragraph	<P ALIGN="RIGHT">

Creating HTML Forms

Using Word, you can create online forms in three ways:

🌐   Post Word documents with Word's traditional form fields on your intranet. Internet Explorer will display them accurately, and your users will have an interface they're probably accustomed to.

287

CHAPTER 9

🌐 For an enormously powerful form, use ActiveX controls in a Word document that you then post on your intranet.

🌐 For a form in an HTML file, use Word's HTML form tools.

Compared with ActiveX, HTML forms are, well, quaint. But if your assignment is to create an HTML form, you might consider creating it in Word and taking advantage of Word's user-friendly Windows environment rather than coding HTML markup.

The best way to access Word's HTML form controls is to show the Control Toolbox toolbar, which appears in Figure 9-14.

Figure 9-14

Control Toolbox toolbar for HTML forms in Word.

Select a control, and Word will create a form area on your page. Word will mark the beginning and end of the form in your file with specially styled paragraphs labeled "Top of Form" and "Bottom of Form" and place your control between the paragraphs.

You can manipulate your control's properties within Word. Select the Properties control on the Control Toolbox to bring up the Properties window. The Properties window lets you format basic aspects of the control in a Visual Basic-like manner. The window for each control displays the appropriate attributes for that control. For example, the Properties window for the Submit button, shown in Figure 9-15, lets you set the control's Value attribute (note that the attribute is referred to by the Visual Basic-esque "Caption" property in the window), the CGI script for its Action attribute, and its Method and Encoding attributes—all without touching the HTML source code.

The form controls go into the HTML file as special HTML control fields. To display the HTML source for the form, Word interprets the styles and the HTML control fields as HTML tags.

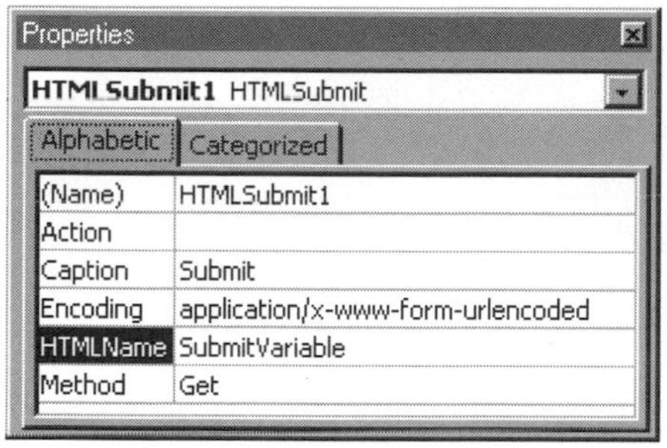

Figure 9-15

The Properties window for a Submit control.

Form controls in Word and their HTML tags

Table 9-3 summarizes the mapping of the Word style or toolbar control to the HTML tag.

Table 9-3   HTML Form Controls and Tags.

Control or Style in Word	HTML Tag
"Z-TopofForm" Style	\<FORM>
"Z-BottomofForm" Style	\<\FORM>
Checkbox control	\<INPUT TYPE="CHECKBOX">
Option button	\<INPUT TYPE="RADIO">
List box	\<SELECT SIZE="3">
	\</SELECT>
Text box	\<INPUT TYPE="TEXT">
Large text box	\<TEXTAREA>
	\</TEXTAREA>
Submit button	\<INPUT TYPE="SUBMIT">
Reset button	\<INPUT TYPE="RESET">
Hidden Text control	\<INPUT TYPE="HIDDEN">
Password control	\<INPUT TYPE="PASSWORD">

HTML Encoding Options

Word includes encoding options as properties of HTML files so that you can specify the language character set of the files as they'll appear in Internet Explorer. Choose Properties from the File menu and set the HTML encoding options in the dialog box that appears (Figure 9-16).

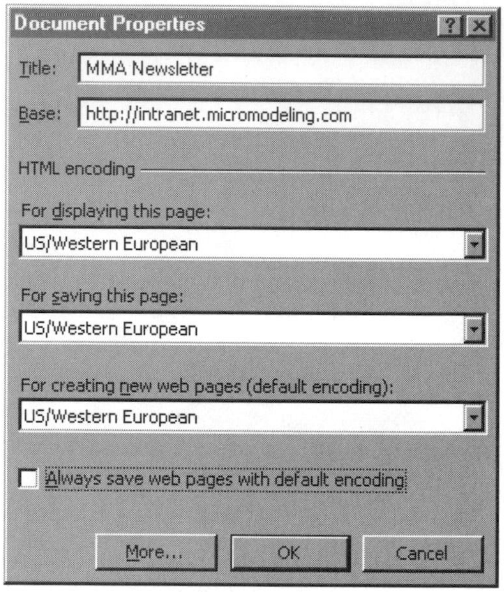

Figure 9-16

The Document Properties dialog box for encoding options for HTML files in Word.

In the dialog box, specify the language code you want Word to use for displaying and saving the current Web page and for creating new pages. To have Word always save your pages using a default language encoding, select the Always Save Web Pages With Default Encoding check box. This setting affects the current page and future pages that you save.

Converting a Word Document to HTML

Creating an HTML file from a Word document could not be much easier: just choose Save As HTML from the File menu. Word will point the document to a special template, HTML.Dot, designed for Web pages (see the "Behind the Scenes: HTML Template Attachments" section later in this chapter for details on that part of the process) and examine the document for those elements in it that can map to HTML tags. The result will be an HTML version of your Word document that's quite faithful to the original.

What's Kept, What's Lost in the Conversion Process

Before you convert a Word document to HTML, you should face the fact that not all elements of your document will survive the transition. Some, such as OLE objects, will mutate. Others will disappear.

Here are some of the mainstays of printed documents that aren't available for HTML files:

- Page and section breaks
- Columns
- Paragraph formatting such as spacing, leading, indents, and borders
- Tabs
- Fields (except, of course, the hyperlink field)
- Tables of contents and authorities
- Indexes
- Styles
- Comments
- Revision marks
- Cross references
- Headers and footers
- Footnotes and endnotes
- Drawing objects ("Drawing objects" here does not mean graphic images or clip art. The drawing objects not supported in HTML are those you create with Word's Drawing toolbar. There is one exception here: Word *will* accept simple horizontal line drawing objects and format them with <HL> tags in HTML.)

The conversion process will also strip out some of the more sophisticated elements in your Word document, including these:

- Macros
- Updateable OLE objects
- Advanced text effects such as shadowing, embossing, highlighting, and animation
- Master documents
- Mail merge

Before Converting

You can make the conversion much more successful if you prepare your document ahead of time. Here's a checklist of tips:

- **Keep a backup Word document.** Make this a rule. You might need important elements—a comment or footnote, for example—after the conversion. Also, you can continue to update your data-driven charts in your backup Word document and then incorporate them into the HTML file.

- **Examine fields.** Only hyperlink fields survive the conversion. Other fields are unlinked—that is, they're converted to plain text. Make sure conversion to plain text is appropriate for all your fields.

- **Use AutoFormat to change paths to hyperlinks.** Exploit Word's powerful AutoFormatting feature to change all file path and URL references in the document to hyperlinks. This isn't a necessity, but it will add a nice interactive touch to your HTML files.

- **Change your cross references to hyperlinks.** All cross references are converted to plain text. Later in this chapter you'll find a handy VBA routine that will replace all the cross references in your document with hyperlink fields.

- **Preserve comments and notes.** Go through your document and incorporate comments, footnotes, and endnotes into the document's body.

- **Examine graphics.** Update your data-driven OLE objects, because they will become static images in HTML. Any drawings you create with the Office drawing toolbar will disappear from your HTML file completely, so consider searching them out and converting them to images with a screen-capture utility.

- **Review table formatting.** Tables whose border color is black will take on the standard Internet sculpted look. Those that used colored borders will retain the border as a solid thin line.

- **Convert columns.** Use table formatting to create a column-like appearance.

- **Replace paragraph borders.** HTML won't retain borders around paragraphs. Use plain horizontal lines or tables instead.

The VBA samples in the second part of this chapter will give you some additional tips on preparing your document for conversion and show you how to employ automation techniques to speed up the process.

Converting HTML to Word

You'll find that Word does a very good job of converting HTML files to Word documents. Your part in the conversion process is easy: open the HTML file in Word, select Save As Word Document from the File menu, and you're done. Your new Word document will retain any styles it was using in HTML, and it will also retain manual text formatting. Images in your HTML file will convert faithfully, as will backgrounds and multimedia objects such as background sounds and video clips.

Word Template Architecture and Intranet Files

If you've spent much time working with Word as a user or as a developer, then you're aware of the critical role that templates play. Templates are especially important in a business environment, where you must be concerned with consistency in the look and feel of your documents.

Text content may vary from document to document, but three basic building blocks should underlie all your documents: styles, formatting, and macros. Although you can store all three elements in individual documents, in general they're more appropriate in templates.

Behind the Scenes: HTML Template Attachments

The template attachment architecture for HTML files is more complex than that for Word documents. When you create a new HTML file by choosing Blank Web Page on the Web Pages tab in the New dialog box, Word creates a new document based on the HTML.Dot template. It is the presence of HTML.Dot that causes the menu and toolbar changes you see when you work with HTML files.

HTML.Dot also contains its own set of about forty macros, which handle file saving and formatting utilities specifically for HTML files. But the macros are not self-contained. When you create or open an HTML file, Word loads the global add-in HTML.WLL. HTML.Dot's macros are only calls to functions within the WLL.

When you choose HTML Source from the View menu, Word closes the HTML file and reopens it attached to another template—HTMLView.Dot— and displays the file's content in tagged plain-text form. HTMLView.Dot's presence dictates the changes you now see in the menus and toolbars. Like HTML.Dot, it contains its own set of macros, but they too are simply calls to the WLL's functions.

The role of templates in the conversion between Word and HTML

When you convert a Word document based on Word's Normal template to HTML, Word removes the document's attachment to Normal.Dot and attaches the document to HTML.Dot. It then loads the HTML.WLL add-in.

CHAPTER 9

If the Word document you convert is not based on Normal.Dot, you'll still see the HTML file's attachment to its Word template in Word's Templates And Add-Ins list, (available from the Tools menu) as shown in Figure 9-17. Because your new file is not attached to HTML.Dot, Word will create the HTML authoring environment by loading both HTML.WLL *and* HTML.Dot as global add-ins.

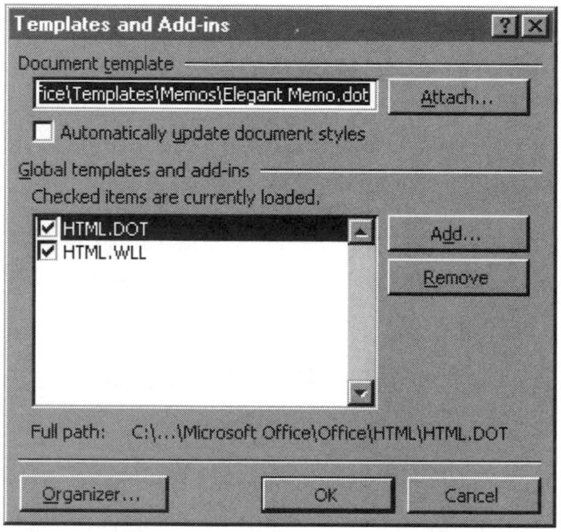

Figure 9-17

The Templates and Add-ins dialog box from Word's Tools menu.

The global add-ins are crucial. HTML.Dot creates the HTML authoring mode's toolbars and menus, and HTML.WLL holds the programming code that manipulates HTML files.

How *Not* to Create HTML Templates

At some point you'll probably want to create your own HTML templates that incorporate text fonts, color schemes, and backgrounds that are specific to your company. Unfortunately, Word won't let you base a template on an HTML file. And because of the relative complexity of the HTML template architecture, you should *not* create HTML templates by opening HTML.Dot, customizing it, and saving it under a different name.

The template you create that way will contain all of HTML.Dot's macros and menu and toolbar customizations. When a user creates a new document based on your template, Word will determine that the document type is HTML and that the document's template is *not* HTML.Dot, and it will load HTML.Dot as a global add-in. All of HTML.Dot's menu customizations and all of your new template's menu customizations will go into effect. And because your template's customizations are the same as those of HTML.Dot, the result will be an interface in which your menu items and toolbar buttons are repeated twice.

How to Create HTML Templates

To create a custom HTML template, build it out of a Word template following these steps:

1. Create a new Word template based on the Normal template. (From the File menu, choose New, click the General tab, and select Blank Document.) In the Create New option group on the lower right of the New dialog box, select Template and click OK.

2. Make any formatting changes you'd like—redefine styles, add a background, and add boilerplate text and graphics.

3. Save the document as a Word document template. Don't close it.

4. Open the document's Properties dialog box, and select the Custom tab. (See Figure 9-18.)

5. In the Name field, type HTML. Specify its property type as Yes Or No, and make sure the Yes value is selected. Click the Add button. The property will appear in the list of custom properties. Click OK.

6. Save the template again, and close it.

Figure 9-18
The Properties dialog box for customizing an HTML template.

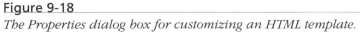

Hyperlink Styles

Whether you create HTML files or post Word documents on your intranet, Word's built-in features will go a long way toward optimizing your text's appearance online. The styles in HTML.Dot, Word's default template for HTML files, have larger font sizes than those in Word document templates, and when you view Word documents online, Word performs a "virtual" scaling-up of document's text.

Two new styles available in Word 97 and designed especially for online viewing are the Hyperlink and FollowedHyperlink styles (select Style from the Format menu). The two hyperlink styles take on the font of the paragraph the hyperlink is situated in, and by default add an underline and blue font color for hyperlinks and an underline and violet font color for followed hyperlinks. The underline and the colors reflect the current standard for the Internet, but you might want to customize them and create your company's own hyperlink look. If you're creating custom Word and HTML templates, it's a good idea to make the two hyperlink styles part of your design.

When you convert a Word document to HTML, the hyperlink styles remain. In HTML source, they take on the HREF tag. When you edit your HTML file in Word's HTML authoring mode, you can change the Hyperlink and FollowedHyperlink style attributes to customize your HTML file's appearance.

Word will store the template in the default template location, which under standard installations will be Program Files\Microsoft Office\Templates. Saving it in that folder, it will show up under the General tab in the New dialog box. Since you'll want it to appear under the Web Pages tab with the Web Page Wizard and the other Web page templates, move it to the Microsoft Office\Templates\Web Pages folder.

Posting Word Documents Online

Up to this point we've focused on using Word to create and edit HTML files. But there are many compelling reasons to take a different approach and to post your file on the intranet as a Word document rather than converting it to HTML:

- Users are viewing the document in Word, with Word's full native functionality.

- You can take advantage of Word 97's new Online Layout and Document Map display options to effectively present long documents in Internet Explorer.

- You can exploit extra features in Word's hyperlink fields and make use of other Word fields that are especially handy for online documents.

- You can run Word macros in Internet Explorer.

- Your document will retain the graphic and text formatting features that get lost when documents become HTML files.

- Data-driven OLE objects, such as graphs and charts, will remain functional in Internet Explorer.

- Your users can edit documents on your intranet using Word's collaborative editing utilities. Word incorporates powerful tracking and revision marking features to manage and catalog their changes.

In this section you'll learn about Word 97's new features for online documents and get some ideas on how to best use the traditional Word utilities on your intranet.

Online Layout View

Online Layout is a new display option in Word that optimizes your document's appearance for viewing and reading onscreen rather than printed out. Switch to Online Layout by selecting it from the View menu.

Online Layout view scales up the appearance of text (although it doesn't actually resize the font) so that at most 66 characters appear on each line. The document appears with equal narrow right and left margins, and your text rewraps to fit the screen.

Online Layout view won't display headers, footers, or page breaks, but it will display all of Word's special formats and objects, such as tables, drawings, and WordArt. In addition, it shows the page's background. The types of backgrounds you can use in Word documents—gradients, patterns, tiled images, and pictures as well as textures—are more varied than the backgrounds that HTML allows. So in a sense, because of its ability to display both HTML and Word features, online layout is the richest of Word's view

options. Figure 9-19 shows some of the background effects you can choose
from by selecting Fill Effects from the Background option of the Format menu.

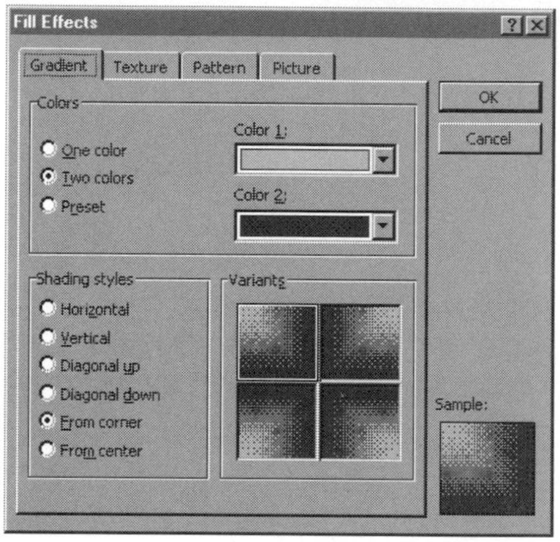

Figure 9-19

The Fill Effects dialog box.

NOTE Although Online Layout view defaults to wrapping text so it fits the screen, that setting is actually an option. You can switch word wrapping on and off by selecting Options in the Tools menu, then choosing the View tab and checking or unchecking the Wrap To Window box.

Document Map

Document Map is another new display option in Word 97, and it is so easy
to use, powerful, and handy that it alone should make you want to post your
Word documents online. To display the document map, click the Document
Map button on the Standard toolbar or choose it from the View menu.

The map is a narrow window on the left side of the screen (you can
change its width to suit your taste) that displays your documents' headings
in outline form. You can scroll down through the headings and get an overview of the document's structure. The document map shown in Figure 9-20
shows the options available in the shortcut menu.

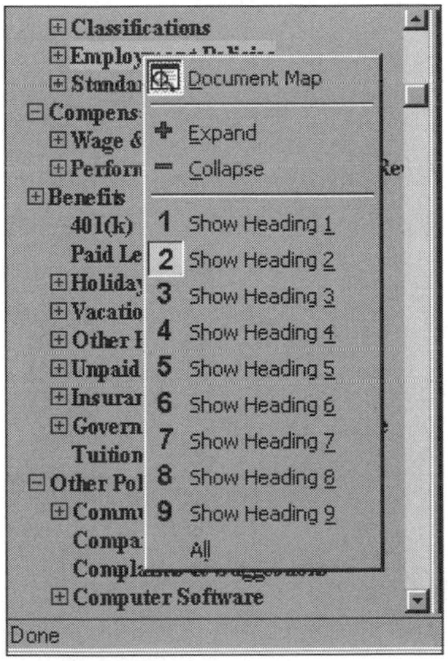

Figure 9-20

The context menu for the Document Map, shown here for the MMA Employee Manual.

Document Map is more than just a new name for Word's old Outline view, however. Here are some of the reasons why:

- You use Document Map simultaneously with other view modes. You can combine it with Online Layout, Normal, and Page Layout views.

- Better yet, the map's headings act like hyperlinks: you click on one, and Word will take you to that heading's place in your document.

- You can control the Document Map's display to show more or less detail. Click the expand or collapse button to the left of the heading.

- Using the context menu, you can hide the Document Map (the top item in the menu), incrementally expand or collapse the heading displays, choose a specific heading level (1 through 9) as the lowest level to display, or choose All at the bottom of the menu to show every available heading level.

Document Map style

You can to some extent control the text formatting in the Document Map by redefining the Document Map style. The style's default definition is 10 point Tahoma (a new font specifically designed for ease of reading online), with a dark blue background that highlights a heading when you click it . You can change the background color as well as the font's size, typeface, and color. For example, you might want to change the background color so that it picks up a color in your page layout.

To modify the Document Map style, choose Style from the Format menu and make changes as you would with any Word style. Modify the background color with the style's Shading property.

TIP
If the background you choose for your Document Map style is a dark one, keep the style's text color on Auto. That way, the text color will change from black to white when the heading is highlighted.

The Select Browse Object Toolbox

The vertical scrollbar has a useful feature for moving through online documents: the Select Browse Object Toolbox. To display the toolbox, click the small Select Browse Object button near the bottom of the scrollbar. Here's what you'll see:

Using the Select Browse Object Toolbox, you can open the Find and Replace dialog box to the Go To and Find tabs, and you can browse through your document object by object—that is, by page, section, footnote, table, graphic, field, and so on.

Word's Fields Online

When you post your Word documents online in their native form, you'll have all of Word's fields available and fully functional. Some fields, such as the field that displays the current page number, won't be good candidates for inclusion in your document; but several others, such as the FileName, UserName, and Date fields, might be useful. This section will focus on two fields that you can use especially effectively online: Hyperlink and Cross Reference.

Advanced work with hyperlink fields

You already know a lot about hyperlinks and hyperlink fields in Word. All hyperlink fields are structured with Word's traditional field brackets ("{" and "}"), the field name ("HYPERLINK"), and the link's destination. Within that structure, though, are some variations you might want to take advantage of.

In a Word document, you can insert hyperlinks using the Field dialog box. To insert the field this way, select Field from the Insert menu and choose the Hyperlink field, as shown in Figure 9-21. Enter the name of the hyperlink's destination in the text box.

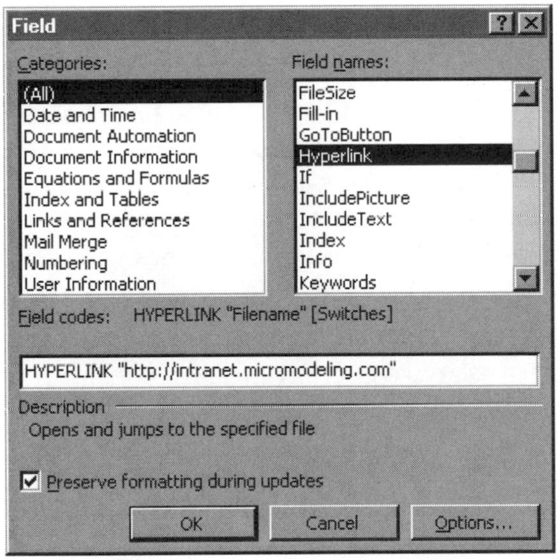

Figure 9-21
The Field dialog box.

Click the Options button to see the list of switches shown in the Field Options dialog box in Figure 9-22.

301

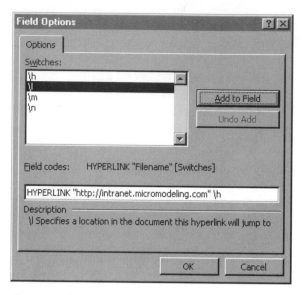

Figure 9-22

The Field Options dialog box.

The Field Options dialog box lets you add some special behaviors in the form of field *switches* to your hyperlink fields. The dialog box supplies a description of each switch as you click on it. Add one or more switches with the Add To Field button, and then click OK to exit the Field Options dialog box. Click OK again to exit the Field dialog box.

As you can see in Figure 9-22, you can use four switches with your hyperlink fields:

🌐 \h prevents the destination file from being added to the History list in Internet Explorer. This switch works only in a Word document viewed online; it won't work in an HTML file.

🌐 \l indicates a specific location in the destination where this hyperlink will jump. Type the range name after the switch. This switch will also work in HTML files.

🌐 \m lets you add coordinates so the link goes to a specific area of an HTML image map. This switch also translates well into HTML files.

🌐 \n opens the destination file in a new window. This switch works only in Word documents viewed online, not in HTML files. The hyperlink's destination will open in a new instance of Internet Explorer.

Cross references

Cross references are a common element in long business documents, and Word's cross referencing capabilities are powerful. You can insert a cross reference to various kinds of objects on your page—such as headings, bookmarks, equations, figures, and tables—and have the reference display specific information about the object, such as its text or page number, or just the words "Above" or "Below."

Word 97 offers you the option of inserting cross reference fields as hyperlinks. To insert a cross reference hyperlink, choose Cross Reference from the Insert menu, and select the object and reference information. Make sure the Insert As Hyperlink box is checked, then click on the Insert button. Figure 9-23 shows an example of cross references to headings.

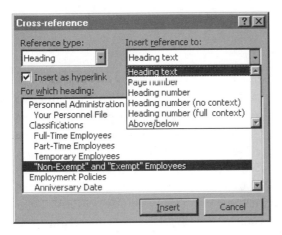

Figure 9-23

Cross-references dialog box showing options available for cross references to headings.

The cross reference hyperlinks won't survive a conversion to HTML, but they will work very effectively in Word documents posted on your intranet.

Text Effects

Two advanced text effects that work well online are animated text and WordArt.

- **Animated text.** Word 97 has a selection of animated text formats that make the text appear to move or flash. To add animated effects to selected text, select Font on the Format menu, click the

Animation tab, and then click the effect you want in the Animations box. This text is animated with the Sparkle Text animation:

Celebrating Birthdays

- 🌐 **WordArt.** WordArt is part of Office's drawing package. From its button on the Drawing toolbar, you can choose from several different effects for your text from the WordArt Gallery. Here is an example:

Collaborative Editing

You can exploit Word's ability to track editing changes made to your intranet documents. For example, you might want to post a draft policy statement and solicit suggestions from your intranet users. As a user makes changes to the document—right within Internet Explorer—Word will record those changes and display them, in a different text color and format for each user. The user can save and close the document as he or she would in Word. Later, an administrator can review the changes and accept or reject them.

There are three steps to preparing your document for collaborative editing:

1. **Turn on the tracking.** Select Track Changes from the Tools menu, then click Highlight Changes. Check all three check boxes in the Highlight Changes dialog box, as shown here:

Highlight Changes	? X
☑ Track changes while editing	
☑ Highlight changes on screen	
☑ Highlight changes in printed document	
OK	Cancel	Options...

2. **Set the Colors.** Click the Options button. In the Track Changes dialog box, make sure the colors for each change are set to By

Author. That way, Word will mark the first eight editors' changes with unique text colors. Close out of the dialog boxes.

3. **Password protect the document.** Now protect the document with a password so that only you can make the final decision to accept or reject users' changes. To protect the document, select Protect Document from the Tools menu, click the Tracked Changes option, and type your password. Now save the document.

Your document is ready to post. When the time comes to finalize users' changes, open the document in either Word or Internet Explorer and unprotect it. Then open the Accept Or Reject Changes dialog box from Tools/ Track Changes. This dialog box is shown in Figure 9-24.

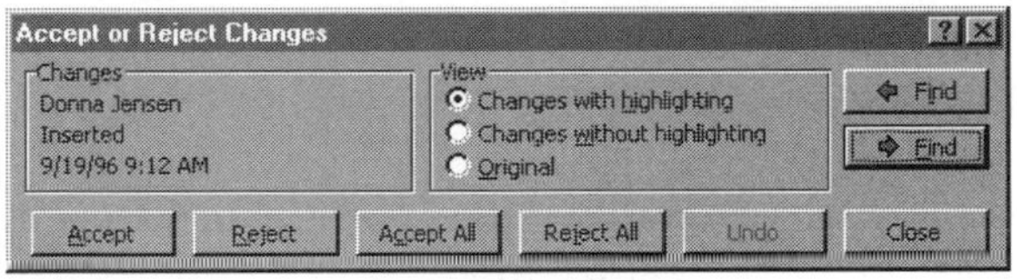

Figure 9-24

The Accept Or Reject Changes dialog box.

Similar to the old Revisions dialog box, the Accept Or Reject Changes dialog box lets you browse through the document revision by revision; for each revision, it will display the name of the user who made it and the time it was made.

So review the changes, accepting or rejecting them, and then save your document.

Posting VBA Routines with Your Documents

One of the revolutionary changes in Word 97 is its switch to the Visual Basic for Applications (VBA) programming language. Your Word macros are now actually VBA subroutines. A second and related change is that you can now store macros in individual documents in addition to keeping them in templates. This means that Word documents are completely transportable—you no longer need to distribute templates with your documents for their macros to function. The icing on the cake is that Word macros can run within Internet Explorer, so the possibilities for smart interactive documents on your intranet are virtually limitless.

You might consider starting with macros that optimize your Word document's display online, handling such tasks as opening the Document Map and making sure Word Wrapping is turned on. In the next section, you'll find sample code to manipulate these and other settings.

You can add Macrobutton fields to your online documents. A Macrobutton field will appear as text (or even as a graphic) in your document and will run any macro you specify when the user clicks it.

Automating Your Web Page Building with Word VBA

In the first section of this chapter you took a tour of Word's intranet features from a user's perspective. In this section you'll learn about using Word's programming language, VBA, to automate intranet objects. The section covers automating hyperlinks and backgrounds, running macros on HTML markup in Word, and using VBA on documents that you post online in their native format.

At the beginning of this chapter we talked about the three faces of Word: its interfaces as a document editor, HTML file editor, and plain-text HTML markup editor. Bear in mind as you work with Word VBA that VBA code is not designed to run in all three modes. Here's a brief summary of some of the differences in each mode and strategies for working with them.

 Your richest programming environment is with native Word documents. The entirety of the object model is functional there. In general, code pertaining to objects that are unavailable in HTML, such as shapes or cross reference fields, won't work in Word's HTML authoring mode.

 Hyperlink code will run in Word documents and HTML files, but only the code using hyperlink collections on documents and text ranges. You can work with shape objects and their hyperlinks only if your document is in native Word format.

 Remember that you can store macros in individual Word documents but not in HTML files.

 HTML markup is the most basic editing mode. Although you can run macros there, you should stick to very elementary procedures, such as the search-and-replace sample in this section.

NOTE The object model information and the VBA code examples in this chapter assume you're familiar with the general Office 97 object model as it pertains to intranet objects. See Chapter 8 for details on the Office 97 object model.

Controlling Hyperlinks Through Code

In Word you have quite a few choices for how to control your hyperlinks through code. You can use Hyperlinks collections, individual Hyperlink objects, or various other VBA features.

Hyperlinks collections in Word

In the Word object model, the Documents collection consists of all currently open documents. In turn, each of the open documents in the collection contains a Hyperlinks collection.

A major advance in Word 97 over previous versions of Word is the concept of *range*. A range is a specific portion of a document. Ranges within documents can also contain their own Hyperlinks collections.

You can specify ranges in a few different ways:

- By their location, such as the document's first paragraph or its last section
- By their object type, such as a table
- By the current selection in the active document
- By using a bookmark to create a named range

For example, if you want to return a count of all the hyperlinks in the main body of the active document, you would query one of Word's built in ranges, the Content range, which contains the main story of the document, and use this line of code:

```
ActiveDocument.Content.Hyperlinks.Count
```

If you want to narrow the search, use a custom range. The following line of code returns the count of hyperlinks in the first paragraph of the active document:

```
ActiveDocument.Paragraphs(1).Range.Hyperlinks.Count
```

This line counts the hyperlinks in a named range of text:

```
ActiveDocument.Bookmarks("BookmarkName").Range.Hyperlinks.Count
```

CHAPTER 9

This line returns the count of hyperlinks in the range made up of the currently selected text:

```
Selection.Range.Hyperlinks.Count
```

Finally, this line returns the hyperlinks contained in the second table in the document:

```
ActiveDocument.Tables(2).Range.Hyperlinks.Count
```

You can use the Parent property of a Hyperlinks collection to return the name of the document or range containing the collection.

Adding a hyperlink to the collection   The real work you'll be doing with the Hyperlinks collection will most likely consist of iterating through the collection and capturing specific information about each of its members, such as their destination file and their display content, or using the collection's Add method to insert hyperlinks programmatically.

The hyperlink field's location in your document or range is given by the Add method's Anchor argument. The trick about using the Anchor argument in Word is that it determines not only the placement of the hyperlink but also the hyperlink's display text. Once the hyperlink is inserted, you can capture its display text by using the Hyperlink object's Name property; but that property is read-only. So the anchor is your only chance to set a link's text programmatically. If the anchor you specify contains no text and it isn't a shape, the hyperlink's display text will be the same as the link's destination, for example, "http://intranet.micromodeling.com/".

The following code example will clarify the techniques to use in inserting hyperlinks and determining their display text programmatically. The first routine inserts an empty paragraph after the first paragraph in the active document and fills the paragraph with a little informative text. It then selects the text and formats the selection as a hyperlink. The second routine repeats the process, but instead of selecting the text, it just moves the selection point to the end of the paragraph.

```
Sub FirstAddAHyperlink()
'/Insert a paragraph after the first paragraph.
ActiveDocument.Paragraphs(1).Range.InsertParagraphAfter
'/Put a line of text in the new paragraph.
ActiveDocument.Paragraphs(2).Range.InsertBefore _
    "Click here to see our home page."
'/Select just the line of text, not its paragraph mark.
ActiveDocument.Paragraphs(2).Range.Select
Selection.SetRange Start:=Selection.Start, End:=Selection.End - 1
```

```
'/Add the hyperlink.
ActiveDocument.Hyperlinks.Add Anchor:=Selection.Range, _
    Address:="http://intranet.micromodeling.com"
End Sub

Sub ThenAddAnother()
'/Insert the paragraph and text again.
ActiveDocument.Paragraphs(1).Range.InsertParagraphAfter
ActiveDocument.Paragraphs(2).Range.InsertBefore _
    "Click here to see our home page: "
ActiveDocument.Paragraphs(2).Range.Select
'/This time, select nothing. Just place the cursor at the end of the
'/paragraph.
Selection.SetRange Start:=Selection.End - 1, End:=Selection.End - 1
'/Add the hyperlink.
ActiveDocument.Hyperlinks.Add Anchor:=Selection.Range, _
    Address:="http://intranet.micromodeling.com"
End Sub
```

This is what you'll see as a result of each routine:

> Click here to see our home page.
>
> Click here to see our home page: http://intranet.micromodeling.com

The first routine created the top line of text, which combines the instructions and the hyperlink, and the second routine created the bottom line, where the hyperlink display text is the same as its address.

If your hyperlink is jumping to a named range within the active file, you can leave the Address property blank. This code adds a hyperlink that jumps to the bookmark "TopOfFile" in the active document:

```
ActiveDocument.Hyperlinks.Add Anchor:=Selection.Range, Address:="", _
    SubAddress:="TopOfFile"
```

Working with individual Hyperlink objects

In Word, the Hyperlink object has a special property, ExtraInfoRequired, and method, PasteSpecial, that you might want to use.

ExtraInfoRequired property   This property returns a Boolean True if extra information is required for the specified hyperlink. Extra information can be specified using the ExtraInfo argument with the Follow or FollowHyperlink methods. The return value is implicitly set by the Follow method, becoming True when Follow includes a string in its ExtraInfo argument.

PasteSpecial method   This method pastes the contents of the clipboard into another document or location as a hyperlink. For example, the code below copies the selection, then creates a new document and inserts the clipboard content as a hyperlink.

```
Selection.Copy
Documents.Add.Activate
Selection.PasteSpecial Link:=True, DataType:=wdPasteHyperlink
```

Hyperlinks and shapes

A Hyperlink object can also exist as a property of a shape. In Word, there are many kinds of objects that go by the name "shape": simple lines and figures; complex "autoshapes," such as callouts and flowcharts; and special text effects called WordArt, OLE objects, and pictures. You can attach hyperlinks to shape objects such as WordArt and callouts, as shown here:

You can refer to Word's built-in shapes as members of a document's Shapes collection, such as "ActiveDocument.Shapes(1)", or you can refer to certain Word shapes by name—for example, the code line "Active-Document.Shapes("Ellipse 1")". Keep in mind that Shape objects are available only to Word documents, not to HTML files.

You get information about a shape's hyperlink by querying the shape's Hyperlink property. This line of code, for example, returns the first shape's hyperlink's target file:

```
MsgBox ActiveDocument.Shapes(1).Hyperlink.Address
```

If a hyperlink is anchored to a range, you can programmatically select the hyperlink by selecting its Range property, like this:

```
ActiveDocument.Hyperlinks(1).Range.Select
```

But if the hyperlink is anchored to a shape, you can select the hyperlink only by selecting the shape. And here you would use the complement of the shape's Hyperlink property: the hyperlink's Shape property.

```
ActiveDocument.Hyperlinks(1).Shape.Select
```

You should always query the hyperlink type before working with a hyperlink's Shape or Range property in Word, because the Range property will trigger an error if the hyperlink is anchored to a shape, and the Shape property will trigger an error if the hyperlink is anchored to a range. For example, the following routine captures the Type property of all the hyperlinks in the active document, and if it finds a hyperlink attached to a shape, selects the shape and informs the user:

```
Dim objHyperlink As Object
Dim objShape As Object
For Each objHyperlink In ActiveDocument.Hyperlinks
    If objHyperlink.Type <> msoHyperlinkRange Then
        Set objShape = objHyperlink.Shape
        objShape.Select
        MsgBox "This shape has a hyperlink."
    End If
Next
```

Other VBA hyperlink features

Word's object model provides developers with a few other handy commands for working with hyperlinks.

BrowseExtraFileTypes property   BrowseExtraFileTypes is a property of the Application object. With it, you can return or set the default application for opening hyperlinked HTML files. To have an HTML file open in Word instead of Internet Explorer when a user clicks on the hyperlink to the file, make sure the BrowseExtraFileTypes property includes the string "text/html". If you want the HTML file to open in Internet Explorer, set the property to "text/plain".

This example captures the current hyperlink file types that will open in Word:

```
Msgbox Application.BrowseExtraFileTypes
```

To have hyperlinked HTML files open in Word, use this line of code:

```
Application.BrowseExtraFileTypes = "text/html"
```

Otherwise, this line ensures that HTML files will open in Internet Explorer:

```
Application.BrowseExtraFileTypes = "text/plain"
```

The BrowseExtraFileTypes property has nothing to do with whether or not you can open HTML files in Word—you can always do that. It only sets the default viewer for HTML files that are hyperlink targets.

NOTE   There is no user-interface access to the BrowseExtraFileTypes setting. To work with it, you must use the VBA code.

311

IgnoreInternetAndFileAddresses property IgnoreInternetAndFile-Addresses is a property of the Options object. It determines whether Word's spell checker will ignore file name extensions, e-mail addresses, UNC paths, and Internet addresses. The property, a read/write Boolean, is the equivalent of the Ignore Internet And File Addresses option on the Spelling & Grammar tab in the Options dialog box. (See Figure 9-25.)

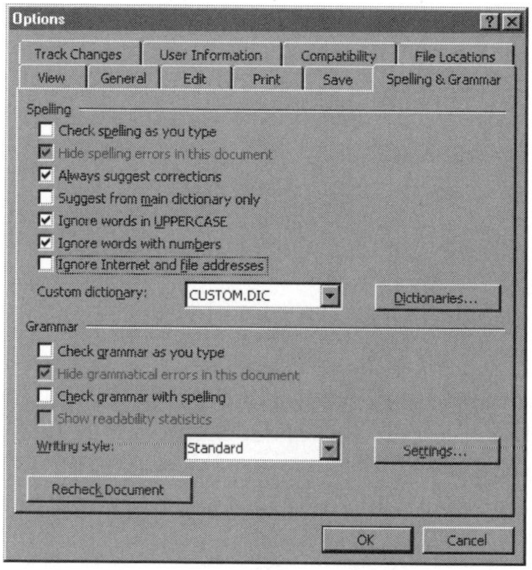

Figure 9-25
Word's Options dialog box.

The following line of code turns off spell checking for files and intranet (as well as Internet) addresses:

```
Options.IgnoreInternetAndFileAddresses = True
```

DisplayScreenTips property DisplayScreenTips is a property of the Application object. In Word, Screen Tips are context-sensitive automatic pop-ups that display the contents of footnotes, endnotes, comments, and hyperlinks as the mouse passes over the references to them in a document. Here is an example of a hyperlink and its screen tip:

The property takes a read/write Boolean value. This example sets the screen tips to display:

```
Application.DisplayScreenTips = True
```

Automating Backgrounds

Word VBA gives you several commands to control the background fill for your online files, whether you're working with Word documents or HTML files. Even within Online Layout view, for example, you can show or hide the document's background. This line displays the active document's background:

```
ActiveDocument.Background.Fill.Visible = msoTrue
```

You can also programmatically control the background's fill colors, textures, gradients, patterns, and clip art or other images. They're all options within the background's Fill property.

The following routine creates a light-to-dark cyan starburst gradient for the active document. Note that the colors are given in RGB values for more universal interpretability.

```
Sub FillTheBackground()
With ActiveDocument.Background.Fill
    .Visible = msoTrue
    .ForeColor.RGB = RGB(204, 255, 255)
    .BackColor.RGB = RGB(51, 204, 204)
    .TwoColorGradient msoGradientFromCenter, 1
End With
End Sub
```

Using HTML Macros in Word

One of the reasons Word is an intriguing choice for HTML file editing is that you can use Word VBA commands to help you build your HTML files. You will face limitations, though, in your ability to customize Word's HTML-specific utilities. When Word creates an HTML file, it loads HTML.WLL as a global add-in. The HTML utilities that appear on the Word menus and toolbars call routines in the WLL.

For example, to insert a video clip, you call the WLL file's "HTMLInsertVideo" routine. The Word VBA line that makes the call is this:

```
Run MacroName:="HTMLInsertVideo"
```

Although you can't affect the code in the WLL's routines, you can create Word VBA routines that perform custom tasks, make the call to the WLL's routines, and then proceed with other custom tasks.

313

9

C
H
A
P
T
E
R

Using VBA on HTML markup

There's no reason not to take full advantage of Word VBA when you edit HTML source text. You can create, record, and run VBA routines when you're in HTML Source view just as you can in Word's standard document view. And although you can't save your VBA macros within HTML files, you can save them in the Word templates attached to HTML files.

When you save a file as HTML, Word attaches it to the HTML template. You should save VBA routines in that template if you want to use them on HTML files in Word's standard "document" interface. When you view an HTML file's source, the text you're viewing is attached to the template HTMLView.Dot. Macros that you want to run on HTML source can be stored in that template.

For example, here's a simple VBA routine designed just for HTML source. It searches through the tags and changes all Heading 2 styles to Heading 3. Then it calls the Save routine in HTMLView.Dot.

```
With ActiveDocument.Content.Find
    .Text = "H2>"
    .Replacement.Text = "H3>"
    .Execute Replace:=wdReplaceAll, Forward:=True
End With
Application.Run "HTMLViewFileSave"
```

Optimizing Documents for Online Viewing

If you have Word documents that you plan to post on your intranet in native form—that is, without converting them to HTML—Word's VBA object model has several commands that will help you format them so they're attractive and readable online.

Online viewing properties

You can programmatically change the view to Online Layout by applying the appropriate Word constant (a member of the wdViewType family) to the active window's View property. This line of code switches to Online Layout view:

```
ActiveWindow.View.Type = wdOnlineView
```

When you display documents in Online Layout view, you'll also want to attend to some details of text formatting to ensure optimal readability. You should always set the text to wrap to the window width rather than letting it flow off the right edge of the screen. Turn on text wrapping by setting the View object's WrapToWindow property to True with this line of code:

```
ActiveWindow.View.WrapToWindow = True
```

You might also want to increase the size of smaller fonts in the document. To do this, use another View property, EnlargeFontsLessThan. The EnlargeFontsLessThan property can return and set a point-size value that sets the lower bound for text to display in its "real" size. Any text whose point size is smaller than the value you set will display larger than it is. This code, for example, scales up the display of any text smaller than 11 points:

```
ActiveWindow.View.EnlargeFontsLessThan = 11
```

What makes EnlargeFontsLessThan an attractive tool is that it has no real effect on the text. Its enlargement is only virtual, and the document will still print and display the text in non-online views in its true small size.

Document Map property

The DocumentMap property is a read-write Boolean property of the active window. This example displays the document map for the active document:

```
ActiveDocument.ActiveWindow.DocumentMap = True
```

Another property of the active window that affects the document map is DocumentMapPercentWidth. Use DocumentMapPercentWidth to query and set the relative amount of horizontal space the map takes up onscreen. For example, this line returns the percentage (as a 32-bit integer):

```
nPercent = ActiveDocument.ActiveWindow.DocumentMapPercentWidth
```

This line sets the document map's width to equal half the screen width:

```
ActiveDocument.ActiveWindow.DocumentMapPercentWidth – 50
```

NOTE
You can return the percentage width without the document map being visible, but if you set the width while the map isn't visible, Word will display the map and apply your new setting.

Building the MMA Intranet

As a Word developer, you specialize in automating documents—automating their creation, their interaction with other applications, and their formatting. As a Word *intranet* developer, you must also make decisions about how Word documents interact with your company's intranet—whether you post them in their native Word format or as HTML files, with or without form controls. You can apply your understanding of all the techniques you've learned about in this chapter to make those decisions and implement them.

CHAPTER 9

In this section we'll put some of Word's features to work and prepare two Word documents for posting on MMA's intranet. The first document, the MMA Employee Manual, is going on the intranet in its native Word form. We'll use some formatting and VBA techniques to optimize its appearance. The second document is MMA's employee newsletter. We receive that file from its editor as a Word document, and our job is to convert it to HTML.

The MMA Employee Manual Online

If anything, Word 97's object model and new utilities offer an embarrassment of riches. Features such as AutoFormatting for hyperlinks and the Document Map work so well out of the box that there's little you can do programming-wise to improve on them. Your main job when you post a document online is to exploit those utilities to optimize the document's appearance.

We've done four things to make the Employee Manual more appealing online:

- Changed the document map style so it's smaller than the default, because our headings are a little too long to show up well

- Added a tasteful background

- Written and run a VBA routine to convert the manual's cross references to hyperlinks

- Added a VBA routine to the document that optimizes its appearance in Internet Explorer

We'll look at the last two actions here.

Replacing cross references with hyperlinks

The MMA Employee Manual was written in an older version of Word, and it includes a lot of cross references. They'll be retained in Internet Explorer, but we wanted to use them as hyperlinks. We could go two ways here: we could replace each cross reference with a hyperlinking cross reference field, or we could simply replace each cross reference with a hyperlink. We decided to do the latter. One of the reasons we chose that tack is that a routine that makes such a substitution is handier: we can then use it later in documents we plan to convert to HTML.

This down-and-dirty routine examines all the fields in the document, and when it comes upon a cross reference (denoted by the Word constant wdFieldRef), it edits the contents of the field, replacing the text "REF" with "HYPERLINK." That replacement changes the field to a hyperlink field. The routine also cleans out the REF field's "\h" switch, which in a cross-reference field indicates a bookmarked range, and replaces it with an "\l" switch, which is a hyperlink field's indicator of a bookmarked range. Note that in hyperlink fields the "\l" switch must appear immediately after the word "HYPERLINK", whereas in the REF field the "\h" switch can appear anywhere. The routine accommodates that requirement.

```
Sub SwitchFields()
Dim objField As Object
'/View the field codes so that the content of the fields can be
'/edited.
ActiveDocument.ActiveWindow.View.ShowFieldCodes = True
'/Iterate through the Fields collection in the document.
For Each objField In ActiveDocument.Fields
    If objField.Type = wdFieldRef Then
        objField.Select
        '/Replace the field's text to convert it to a hyperlink
        '/with an \l switch.
        With Selection.Range.Find
            .Text = " REF "
            .Replacement.Text = " HYPERLINK \l "
            .Execute Replace:=wdReplaceOne
        End With
        '/Get rid of the REF field's \h switch.
        With Selection.Range.Find
            .Text = " \h "
            .Replacement.Text = " "
            .Execute Replace:=wdReplaceOne
        End With
        '/Apply hyperlink style to the field.
        Selection.Range.Style = wdStyleHyperlink
    End If
Next
'/Switch the view to display field results.
ActiveDocument.ActiveWindow.View.ShowFieldCodes = False
End Sub
```

Optimizing the manual's appearance

Earlier in this chapter we pointed out some settings you'll want to use to make your online documents look their best. Some other general settings are also important to consider. For example, you will probably *not* want your intranet users to see bookmarks, field codes, or the squiggly lines Word uses to indicate possible spelling and grammar errors, but you *will* want them to see screen tips, animated text, and graphics. The following routine switches to Online Layout view and incorporates the various settings that you should control for the best-looking online presentation of your Word document.

```
Private Sub Document_Open()
With ActiveWindow
    .DisplayScreenTips = True
    .DocumentMap = True
    .DocumentMapPercentWidth = 35
    With .View
        .Type = wdOnlineView
        .WrapToWindow = True
        .EnlargeFontsLessThan = 11
        .ShowAnimation = True
        .ShowPicturePlaceHolders = False
        .ShowFieldCodes = False
        .ShowBookmarks = False
    End With
End With
With ActiveDocument.Background.Fill
    .Visible = msoTrue
End With
With Options
    .CheckSpellingAsYouType = False
    .CheckGrammarAsYouType = False
End With
End Sub
```

Figure 9-26 shows the MMA Employee Manual in Internet Explorer after the online view routine has been run.

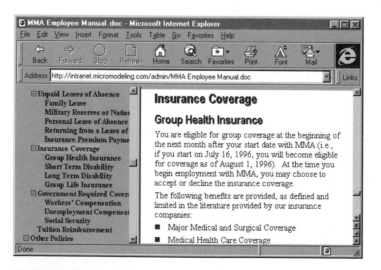

Figure 9-26

MMA Employee Manual in Internet Explorer.

Where and how to store the routine

By default, Internet Explorer will open Word documents with the display settings the user specified when he or she last viewed the document. Because we want the manual to display the way we designed it, we use the routine on the preceding page as a document event—specifically the Open event.

The VBA Document_Open event replaces WordBasic's AutoOpen macro. We keep the routine attached to the Employee Manual rather than in a template. That way, the Manual will always look the way we want it to when opened. The drawback is that users who have Word's automatic virus checking routine turned on will see a warning message whenever they open the manual in Internet Explorer. If you want to avoid that, you can store the routine in a template or add-in and run it on the document before you post it. If your intranet users change their view settings for the document, it's their loss.

Neither solution is inherently better than the other, and you should choose the one that suits your priorities.

NOTE You can protect your online documents from user revisions in any number of ways on the server side or within the document itself. We don't user Word's built-in write protection options. Instead, we store the Manual in a protected area of the intranet server.

MMA's Newsletter in HTML

There's one task that Word programming professionals constantly find themselves facing: trying to work out fast, automated processes to update older documents so that they can be used on newer platforms. And if the intranet doesn't represent a new platform, nothing does. Viewed in this light, our job of converting MMA's employee newsletter from Word document to HTML serves as a case study in migration.

Like most business documents, MMA's newsletter is somewhat long, is segmented by headings of various hierarchical levels, and starts out with a table of contents. Such a document won't translate smoothly into HTML. The table of contents won't survive conversion to HTML, and Word's document map isn't available for HTML files. In addition, you'll lose other mainstays of paper documents. For example, cross-references aren't supported by HTML, and you won't be able to separate thematic portions of your documents with page breaks.

The routines in this section overcome those losses and automate substitutions that are more appropriate for HTML presentation. You might want to combine any or all of these routines, along with the routine above that converts cross references into hyperlinks, into one megaconverter utility. We've left them distinct here so you can pick and choose.

The template

We use a custom Word template, EMPNEWS.DOT, for our document. The template has customized basic text styles and a background. It also contains some VBA routines that help convert the document to HTML:

- **SwitchFields,** the macro we described above, replaces cross references with hyperlinks.

- **MakeHyperlinkTOC** builds a table of contents at the top of the document.

- **AddBanner** is a little routine that inserts a prefab banner at the top of the newsletter.

- **PseudoPageBreaks** inserts dividing lines a la page breaks above the headings.

- **ChangeDocBullets,** a simple routine, formats bulleted text with fancy graphic HTML bullets.

Remember, we run all the macros except ChangeDocBullets *before* we convert the Word document to HTML. Also, we run SwitchFields first, before the other macros have added to the number of fields in the document.

Building a hyperlink table of contents

In previous versions of Word, if you wanted to impose a hierarchical structure on a document and see that structure reflected in Word's Outline view, you had to employ Word's built-in heading styles. There was some discrepancy between outlining and tables of contents: you had to use heading styles for outlines, but you could use your own styles to construct tables of contents. In Word 97, outlining has caught up. Now you can use the Paragraph dialog box to specify styles of your choice to appear in your outline, as shown in Figure 9-27. This dialog box is invoked by selecting Paragraph from the Format menu.

The MakeHyperlinkTOC routine we're about to build takes advantage of Word's new outlining flexibility. It creates a hyperlink "table of contents" at the top of the newsletter and bases the entries in that table of contents on the styles we specify as our outline styles. So before running the routine on your own document, decide which styles you want to appear in your table of contents, and format paragraph settings of those styles with the outline level you want.

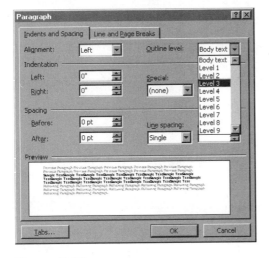

Figure 9-27
Outline levels defined in Word's Paragraph dialog box.

The routine uses Word's wdOutlineLevel constants and iterates through the newsletter's Paragraphs collection, recording information about the outline-level paragraphs it comes upon. It stores the information—the paragraph's text, its outline level, and the bookmark name the routine assigns to it—in a two-dimensional array. Then at the top of the document, it generates the table of contents out of the array. It uses Word's TOC 1 and TOC 2 styles to build the table of contents. In our custom newsletter template, we redefined those styles so that they're extra large and stand out online.

One note: the routine concerns itself only with outline levels 1 and 2. That criterion is set in this line of the routine:

```
If .OutlineLevel <= wdOutlineLevel2 Then
```

If you want to build the table of contents with more or fewer outline levels or start from a level other than 1, you'll need to edit that line.

```
Sub MakeHyperlinkTOC()
Dim objPara As Paragraph
Dim objHyperlinkRange As Range
ReDim sHeadList(2, 0) As String
Dim sBMarkName As String
Dim nIndex As Long
Dim nHeadCount As Integer
'/Initialize count of heading paragraphs.
```

(continued)

321

```
nHeadCount = -1
'/A heading may be the first paragraph.
'/Avoid bookmarking the first paragraph by inserting an
'/empty Normal-style paragraph at the top of the document.
ActiveDocument.Content.InsertBefore vbCr
ActiveDocument.Paragraphs(1).Style = wdStyleNormal
'/Examine each paragraph in the document.
'/If it's an outline heading, capture its level and its text
'/content.
'/Then assign it a bookmark name.
For Each objPara In ActiveDocument.Paragraphs
    With objPara
        '/Only look at outline levels 1 and 2
        If .OutlineLevel <= wdOutlineLevel2 Then
            nHeadCount = nHeadCount + 1
            ReDim Preserve sHeadList(2, nHeadCount)
            '/Record the heading level for formatting later
            '/in the table of contents.
            sHeadList(0, nHeadCount) = .OutlineLevel
            '/Record the text content of the heading.
            sHeadList(1, nHeadCount) = .Range
            '/Assign a bookmark name for the heading.
            sBMarkName = "bkmk" & LTrim$(Str$(nHeadCount))
            sHeadList(2, nHeadCount) = sBMarkName
            ActiveDocument.Bookmarks.Add Name:=sBMarkName, _
                Range:=.Range
        End If
    End With
Next

'/Create the hyperlink table of contents at the top of the document.
With ActiveDocument
    For nIndex = 0 To nHeadCount
        '/Insert a paragraph with the heading's text to be
        '/the first "TOC" entry.
        Set objHyperlinkRange = .Paragraphs(nIndex + 1).Range
        objHyperlinkRange.InsertBefore _
            sHeadList(1, nIndex)
        '/Make the paragraph a hyperlink pointing to
        '/the appropriate bookmark.
        objHyperlinkRange.SetRange Start:=objHyperlinkRange.Start, _
            End:=objHyperlinkRange.End - 2
        .Hyperlinks.Add Anchor:=objHyperlinkRange, _
            Address:="", SubAddress:=sHeadList(2, nIndex)
        '/A little aesthetics: apply the appropriate TOC 1,
        '/TOC 2, or TOC 3 style to the paragraph to give
        '/a hierarchical appearance.
        .Paragraphs(nIndex + 1).Style = _
            "TOC" & Str$(sHeadList(0, nIndex))
```

```
    Next
    '/Finally, insert "Contents" in Heading 1 style at the
    '/top of the document for a "title" effect.
    .Content.InsertBefore "Contents" & vbCr
    .Paragraphs(1).Style = wdStyleHeading1
End With
End Sub
```

Figure 9-28 shows the MMA Newsletter's HTML "table of contents."

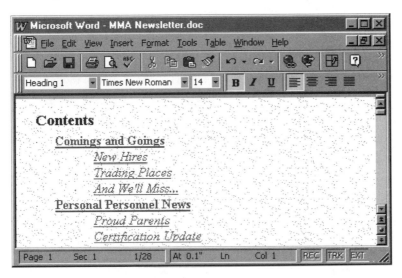

Figure 9-28

MMA Newsletter with HTML table of contents.

Creating virtual page breaks with horizontal rules and hyperlinks

Another enhancement is the insertion of visual breaks in the document that match its thematic breaks. The following routine seeks out headings in the document and inserts horizontal rules (the intranet equivalent of page breaks) above them. In addition, above each horizontal rule it inserts a hyperlink with the display text "Back to Top"; when clicked, this takes the user to a bookmark in the first paragraph of the file.

The routine could have been written more succinctly if it started from the bottom of the document and worked up toward the top. The nCounter incrementing that skips over each heading above which the line and hyperlink have just been placed would not have been necessary. But in the routine's current form, reading down from the top of the file, it can easily be folded into the hyperlink table of contents routine shown in the preceding section.

323

The anchoring of the horizontal rule is important. If it is anchored to the "Back to Top" hyperlink's paragraph, it will wind up, when the document is converted to HTML, *above* the hyperlink line. Therefore, it is anchored to the paragraph below the hyperlink—specifically, to the top of the paragraph below the hyperlink—and when the document is converted, everything appears in the right place.

```
Sub PseudoPageBreaks()
Dim objPara As Paragraph
Dim objHyperlinkRange As Range
Dim nCounter As Integer
Dim objShape As Object
nCounter = 0
'/Add the bookmark that the "Back to Top" hyperlinks will jump to.
ActiveDocument.Bookmarks.Add Name:="TopOfFile", _
    Range:=ActiveDocument.Paragraphs(1).Range

'/Go through each paragraph.
'/The routine skips the first heading it finds, assuming
'/that that heading is at or near the top of the file.
For Each objPara In ActiveDocument.Paragraphs
    nCounter = nCounter + 1
    '/Only look at outline level 1
    If objPara.OutlineLevel <= wdOutlineLevel1 And nCounter > 1 Then
        '/Add the text for the hyperlink and anchor the hyperlink
        '/to it.
        objPara.Range.InsertBefore "Back to Top" & vbCr
        With ActiveDocument.Paragraphs(nCounter)
            .Style = wdStyleNormal
            Set objHyperlinkRange = .Range
        End With
        objHyperlinkRange.SetRange Start:=objHyperlinkRange.Start, _
            End:=objHyperlinkRange.End - 1
        ActiveDocument.Hyperlinks.Add _
            Anchor:=objHyperlinkRange, _
            Address:="", SubAddress:="TopOfFile"
        '/Insert the horizontal rule.
        Set objShape = ActiveDocument.Shapes.AddLine _
            (0, 0, 450, 0, objPara.Range)
        With objShape.Line
            .Weight = 3#
            .DashStyle = msoLineSolid
        End With
        '/Increment the counter again to skip over the current
        '/objPara paragraph.
        nCounter = nCounter + 1
    End If
Next
```

```
'/Finally, put a horizontal rule and hyperlink after the
'/last paragraph in the document.
With ActiveDocument
    .Content.InsertParagraphAfter
    .Content.InsertAfter "Back to Top"
    .Hyperlinks.Add Anchor:=ActiveDocument.Paragraphs.Last.Range, _
        Address:="", SubAddress:="TopOfFile"
    .Content.InsertParagraphAfter
    Set objShape = .Shapes.AddLine _
        (0, 0, 450, 0, .Paragraphs.Last.Range)
    With objShape.Line
        .Weight = 3#
        .DashStyle = msoLineSolid
    End With
End With
End Sub
```

Figure 9-29 shows the horizontal lines and hyperlinks above level 1 headings inserted by the PseudoPageBreaks routine.

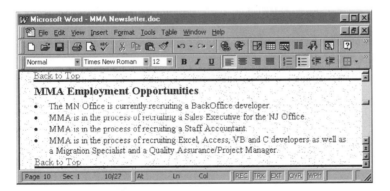

Figure 9-29

Horizontal lines and hyperlinks added by the PseudoPageBreaks routine.

An extra touch

You can see the results of the MakeHyperlinkTOC routine on the sample company newsletter on the CD that ships with this book. If you use the routine on your own company newsletter, you might want to add a banner above the table of contents. The banner might simply be a graphic logo, or it might be more complex. For example, you might want to insert hyperlinks to some Microsoft FrontPage WebBot components that will open a newsletter archive, search through back issues, or perform other tasks.

A good technique for handling this situation is to store the boilerplate banner text and graphics as AutoText in Word and then just insert the AutoText rather than going through all the VBA code involved in adding to the Hyperlinks collection. If you want, you can also store graphic elements along with the hyperlinks. Figure 9-30 shows the MMA Newsletter with an AutoText banner.

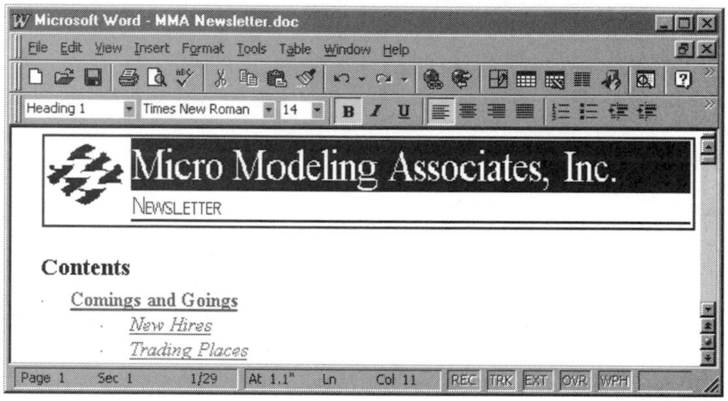

Figure 9-30

MMA Newsletter with AutoText banner.

Our banner is just a graphic with the newsletter logo, stored in the newsletter template as a piece of AutoText called "NewsLogo" (you can't store AutoText in documents). Although inserting the AutoText is easy to do manually, you can also use this code, which adds a new paragraph at the top of your document and inserts the AutoText:

```
Sub AddBanner()
'/Inserts a paragraph and AutoText at the top of the file.
With ActiveDocument
    .Content.InsertParagraphBefore
    .Paragraphs(1).Style = wdStyleNormal
End With
AttachedTemplate.AutoTextEntries("NewsLogo").Insert _
    Where:=ActiveDocument.Paragraphs(1).Range, RichText:=True
End Sub
```

After a final review, the document can be converted to HTML.

After conversion

After you convert your document to HTML, you can still run macros stored in your custom template. We run a simple routine that converts all bullets from the insertion point through the end of the document to fancy HTML bullets. (We usually position the cursor after the file's table of contents, since those paragraphs are also bulleted and we don't want them to be fancy.)

This is the routine, stored in our newsletter template and run on the new HTML file:

```
Sub ChangeDocBullets()
'/This sub changes all the bullets from the insertion point
'/to the end of the the document to fancy HTML bullets
'/of your choice.
'/Run this sub AFTER you've converted the document to HTML.
Dim objPara As Object
Dim objRange As Range
Dim nContinue As Integer

Application.Run MacroName:="HTML.HTML1.FormatBulletsAndNumbering"
nContinue = MsgBox("Apply this bullet to all bulleted paragraphs" & _
    " in the rest of the document?", vbYesNo, "MMA")
If nContinue = vbYes Then
    Set objRange = ActiveDocument.Range(Start:=Selection.Start, _
        End:=ActiveDocument.Content.End)
    For Each objPara In objRange.ListParagraphs
        If objPara.Range.ListFormat.ListType = wdListBullet Then
            objPara.Range.Select
            '/Call the FormatBulletDefault macro twice.
            '/The first call removes the existing bullet.
            '/The second call inserts the new bullet.
            Application.Run MacroName: _
                ="HTML.HTML1.FormatBulletDefault"
            Application.Run MacroName: _
                ="HTML.HTML1.FormatBulletDefault"
        End If
    Next
End If
End Sub
```

Figure 9-31 shows how the MMA Newsletter looks in HTML after its bullets have been fancied up.

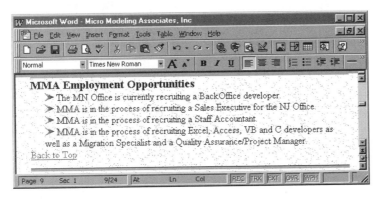

Figure 9-31

MMA Newsletter with customized bullets.

Going Forward

As you can tell by now, Word's powers are broad and varied when it comes to intranet development. This chapter has given you only a taste of the features available. Your best move now is to experiment and push the limits of what Word can do, as a programming tool as well as an editing and design tool. Happy exploring!

CHAPTER 10

Microsoft
Excel 97

Ken Heft

The value of a corporate intranet lies in its ability to make data readily available to the masses. An intranet provides one central location where your employees can turn for information. In some cases, all an employee needs is access to information such as a corporate phone list or an old annual report. In other cases, access to data is only half the picture; what is more important is the capability to transform raw data into meaningful information. So how can Microsoft Excel help you do this? It will integrate with your other documents and serve as a front end to your internal databases and the Internet.

By integration, we mean that your existing Microsoft Excel spreadsheets can be treated the same as any other Microsoft Office or Web document. Your existing Excel documents can be ported to your intranet as-is, or they can be converted to HTML using built-in features. You can move between Excel spreadsheets and other Office 97 documents as easily as you can move between

Web sites. You and your co-workers can even collaborate on a spreadsheet, keeping track of each other's changes and the document's entire history.

As a front end, Microsoft Excel has always been a great tool for analyzing data. It has very robust charting, scenario management, optimization, and reporting capabilities. You can filter your data to locate the information most important to you. You can use pivot tables to create complex custom reports that are unique to your needs. Microsoft Excel 97 has expanded on its abilities of the past by enhancing these features and adding a whole series of intranet-specific features. You can retrieve and post data to back-end databases on your intranet and even get stock quotes from the Internet.

This chapter will show you how Microsoft Excel 97 can help build your intranet site. We will go through all of the new Internet/intranet features of the product and also touch on some of Excel's more powerful data analysis capabilities. All of this will be done while continuing to build an intranet site for Micro Modeling Associates.

Integration and Microsoft Excel 97

When Microsoft talked about integration in the past, it was talking about very specific areas: consistency among products, Object Linking and Embedding (OLE), and Visual Basic for Applications (VBA). Consistency now means that if you want to copy a chart from your Microsoft Excel document, you use the same menu commands and shortcut keys that you would use to copy a sentence in Microsoft Word. OLE means that you can then take that copied chart and either link it or embed it into a Word document, allowing you to have a document that is always up to date. Integrated VBA means that you no longer have to learn three different programming languages if you want to programmatically control Word, Excel, and Microsoft Access. In Office 97, these integration concepts have become even more powerful.

In addition to these techniques, Office 97 offers some entirely new concepts in integration. The most important ones are integrated exploration tools, compatibility with HTML, and collaborative editing.

Getting Around: The Microsoft Web Toolbar and Hyperlinks

In Microsoft Office 97 you can move easily between a Microsoft Excel spreadsheet, a Word document, and a Web page. In the past, you could not view these three different document types (XLS, DOC, and HTML) under the same roof. Now they are usable, viewable, and accessible, sharing common tools for interaction.

The first common tool is the Web toolbar. As you saw earlier in this book, the Web toolbar provides a simple browser-like interface that allows you to move forward and backward among Office and/or HTML documents. These documents can be created in any tool, as long as the user has a copy of Office 97 (or the Office 97 viewers) on his or her machine.

The second tool is hyperlinks. You put hyperlinks in your Office documents to let users jump quickly to another document. The destination document can be a Microsoft Excel spreadsheet, Web page, Microsoft Access form, Word document, and so on. Although we discussed each of these tools earlier in this book, let's talk specifically about how Excel handles these situations.

You can put hyperlinks practically anywhere in Microsoft Excel. Start using hyperlinks instead of code whenever you need to provide exploration tools for users. Put hyperlinks in cells to create a table of contents. Put a hyperlink behind a Details command button to jump a user from a graph to a separate sheet of supporting data. Hyperlinks can be displayed in cells, as pictures, as command buttons, as WordArt images, and the like. Using hyperlinks provides a consistent way to move within an application and between applications.

When creating hyperlinks in Microsoft Excel, you have two options. You can use the standard Insert Hyperlink command or Excel's Hyperlink formula.

Insert Hyperlink command

The Insert Hyperlink command is the standard way to insert hyperlinks throughout the Office family. To use this command in Microsoft Excel, select the cell or other object you want to contain the hyperlink, and then select Hyperlink from the Insert menu and fill in the appropriate information in the Insert Hyperlink dialog box. If your hyperlink's destination is another Microsoft Excel spreadsheet, you can use this command to specify both the spreadsheet name and the desired location within the spreadsheet. Enter this location as a range name, sheet name, or an A1-style cell reference. For help in selecting a location within another spreadsheet, choose the Browse button for a list of sheet names and range names.

Tips and tricks for creating hyperlinks

If you want to create a hyperlink from a cell or range in one Microsoft Excel spreadsheet to a cell or range in another (or to a location within the same Excel spreadsheet or even to a Word document or Microsoft PowerPoint presentation), you can take advantage of some built-in shortcuts. One shortcut is to choose the source cell or range and select the Copy command. Then choose the cell or range you want to contain the hyperlink and select the Paste As Hyperlink command from the Edit menu. (Make sure you have saved the file first, otherwise the Paste As Hyperlink option will not be available.)

CHAPTER
10

This will place the hyperlink in your selected cell. You can now go back and edit the text in this cell and the hyperlink will remain intact. By default the text should appear underlined and in blue, indicating a hyperlink. Once you click this hyperlink, it will turn purple automatically.

Another shortcut option is to drag and drop. Select the source cell or range, point to the border of the selection, and drag the selection using your right mouse button. When you reach the area you want to contain the hyperlink, let go of the right mouse button and select the Create Hyperlink Here command from the shortcut menu that appears.

TIP

If the two locations are on different sheets, drag your selection toward the sheet tabs at the bottom of the screen. Hold down the Alt key as you drag your selection over the correct sheet tab, and then let go of the Alt key and go to the area you want to contain the hyperlink on the new sheet.

Maintaining hyperlinks

Once you have inserted hyperlinks into your document, you need to know how to modify them. Hyperlinks in Microsoft Excel are a little tricky: there's no way to click a cell or an object containing a hyperlink without jumping to the destination. If you want just to see what the hyperlink's destination is, hold the cursor over the hyperlink—a ToolTip will appear. If you need to change any of the attributes of the cell containing the hyperlink (font, borders, and so on), you'll have to select a nearby cell that doesn't contain any hyperlinks and then move around with the arrow keys.

If you need to make changes to the hyperlink, all of the hyperlink commands can be found by right-clicking over the cell or object containing the hyperlink and selecting the Hyperlink command from the shortcut menu. The commands for maintaining hyperlinks include Open, Open In New Window, Copy Hyperlink, Add To Favorites, Edit Hyperlink, and Select Hyperlink. You can use the Edit Hyperlink command to change the destination document or delete the hyperlink altogether.

Hyperlinks in VBA

If you want to write code to maintain your hyperlinks, you should read up on the Hyperlink object in on-line Help. This object has properties and methods to let you control all of the maintenance tasks mentioned above (Delete, AddToFavorites, and so forth). There are a few tricks to referring to individual hyperlinks in Microsoft Excel.

To refer to a hyperlink in a cell, you can use the Hyperlinks method of the Worksheet object or the Range object. The only reason to use the

Hyperlinks method of the Worksheet object is if you want to iterate through all of the hyperlinks in a sheet. For example, the following code would correct all of the hyperlinks on a sheet that were pointing to www.mma.com and redirect them to www.micromodeling.com.

```
Const OLD_NAME = "http://www.mma.com/"
Const NEW_NAME = "http://www.micromodeling.com/"
Dim objCurLink As Hyperlink

For Each objCurLink In Worksheets("Sheet1").Hyperlinks
    If objCurLink.Address = OLD_NAME Then
        objCurLink.Address = NEW_NAME
    End If
Next objCurLink
```

When you want to refer to a specific worksheet in code, you can refer to the sheet's name, as found on the sheet tabs (for example, Worksheets("Sheet1")). However, there is no similar way to refer to a specific hyperlink, because a hyperlink's "name" is the same as its destination. To refer to a specific hyperlink, the trick is to use the Hyperlinks method of the Range object, since you usually know which cell contains a hyperlink but not the hyperlink's name. To refer to a hyperlink behind an object such as a rectangle, use the Hyperlink method of the Shapes object. You use the Hyperlink (singular) method instead of the Hyperlinks (plural) method because a shape can have only a single hyperlink. Here is an example of each method:

```
Worksheets("Sheet1").Range("B5").Hyperlinks(1).AddToFavorites
Worksheets("Sheet1").Shapes("WordArt 5").Hyperlink.Follow
```

Hyperlink formula

Another hyperlink option within Microsoft Excel is the Hyperlink formula. Why would you choose to use a formula instead of the Insert Hyperlink command? Customization! You can dynamically change the destination of a hyperlink by modifying the contents of cells in your spreadsheet.

The Hyperlink formula takes two arguments. The first argument is the destination, whether it is a Microsoft Excel spreadsheet, Web document, or other location. The second argument is the text that you want to appear in the cell. You can enter or edit a Hyperlink formula by using the Hyperlink dialog box shown in Figure 10-1. Select the cell or object you want to apply the formula to, then click the Edit Formula button on the Formula toolbar. Select Hyperlink from the drop-down list, and enter the Link Location and the Friendly Name for the hyperlink.

CHAPTER 10

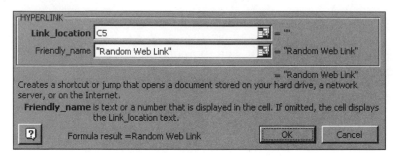

Figure 10-1

Hyperlink formula dialog box.

NOTE

You might be wondering if you can specify a destination within a document. The answer is yes—but the syntax can get confusing. The easiest way to get started is to use the function wizard and get help on the Hyperlink function. The Help file contains many examples of linking to specific locations in Microsoft Excel spreadsheets.

The good thing about the Hyperlink formula is that both of the arguments can be cell references. Therefore, you can dynamically change either the hyperlink destination or the text that appears in the cell by changing the corresponding cell value. In the sample file HL.XLS you will see examples of hyperlinks created with the Hyperlink formula. The Dynamic Links worksheet in the example contains a button, which randomly selects Web sites from a predefined list. By clicking the button, your Microsoft Excel spreadsheet becomes a guide for selecting random Web sites, as shown in Figure 10-2.

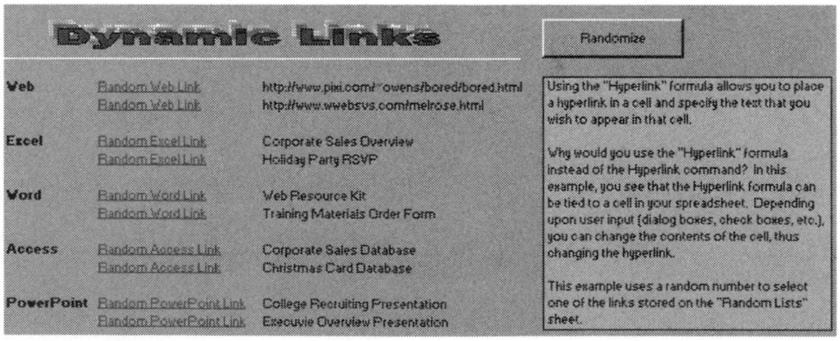

Figure 10-2

Sample random Web sites accessed by the Hyperlink formula.

NOTE
Hyperlinks created with the Microsoft Excel formula are completely different from hyperlinks created with the Insert Hyperlink command. They are treated as Excel formulas and are not considered Hyperlink objects. Therefore, these hyperlink formulas do not have the same commands available for maintenance (such as Edit or Add To Favorites), nor can you use the same programming techniques with them.

Compatibility with HTML

The quickest way for an application to become obsolete these days is to overlook HTML support. The HTML file format is quickly becoming a popular way of storing data. The files are small, you can edit them in Notepad, and they are platform-independent by design. As you might have guessed, Microsoft Excel 97 offers top-notch support for HTML.

How do you choose whether to post your documents in HTML or .XLS format? Ask yourself a few questions: Do all of your intranet users have Microsoft Excel 97 or the Excel 97 viewer on their desktops? Is the Microsoft Excel application providing value in reading your document, or are users just going to browse it? Is file size an important issue?

If you decide that your document needs to be an HTML document, you now have to choose an HTML editor. With Office 97, Microsoft FrontPage and Notepad are no longer your only options. Microsoft Word, PowerPoint, Access, and Excel are all user-friendly, familiar applications for creating HTML documents. So how do you choose which application to use? It depends on the document. If you're creating a document with a lot of tables, formulas, and special formatting, you should use Microsoft Excel. Microsoft Excel 97 has built-in features to help you create a document and convert it to HTML.

Saving as HTML

Microsoft Excel 97 ships with the Internet Assistant Wizard add-in. This add-in allows you to save your Excel spreadsheet as an HTML document. To use the wizard, select the Save As HTML command from the File menu. This will guide you through several steps in which you can choose specific charts and/or data ranges to export to HTML and also format your HTML document to have the look and feel you want. The Save As HTML command will also let you export charts and data to an existing HTML document, making it one of the easier ways to add a table to a Web document.

TIP
If Save As HTML is not an option on your File menu, make sure the Internet Assistant Wizard add-in is installed and selected under Add-Ins in the Tools menu.

CHAPTER 10

Opening HTML documents

Going the other way, opening an HTML document in Microsoft Excel is as easy as using the File Open command. HTML documents now appear as one of the file types you can import. Microsoft Excel is especially strong at opening HTML documents that contain tables, and it does a pretty good job with standard Web documents. When Excel imports your HTML file, it tries to maintain the file's Web look by hiding gridlines and merging cells where appropriate. It also imports hyperlinks and retains document formatting whenever possible. To get an idea of the types of conversions Excel performs, try opening the file HTML_TAGS.HTM on the CD in Microsoft Internet Explorer and then in Microsoft Excel. (This file is also available in the Microsoft Excel Web Connectivity Kit, included on the CD.)

Using special tags

When Web browsers read HTML files, they look for HTML tags, which provide instructions on everything from font size to table definitions. If the browser comes to a tag it doesn't understand, it simply ignores it.

Microsoft Excel 97 takes advantage of this fact by providing support for four HTML tags that ordinary Web browsers, such as Internet Explorer, will ignore. These tags are FORMULA, STYLE, FILTER, and CROSSTAB. As the names suggest, these tags can be used to spice up ordinary HTML files when you open them within Excel. They give you the ability to distribute a file that all of your users can view, regardless of platform, while giving extra features to the people who use Excel 97.

The easiest way to use these tags is to take your existing Microsoft Excel spreadsheet and save it as an HTML file, as explained earlier in this chapter. In future releases of Microsoft Excel, saving as HTML might automatically insert these special tags, but for now you will need to go into an editor such as WordPad to edit the exported HTML file. Here is an example of the FILTER and STYLE tags being used in a standard HTML file (the italicized portions are Microsoft Excel's HTML extensions):

```
<TR>
<TD FILTER="(ALL)">Name</TD>
<TD FILTER="Washington, DC">OfficeLocation</TD>
<TD FILTER="(ALL)">Client</TD>
<TD FILTER="(ALL)">ProjectSize</TD>
</TR>

<TR>
<TD>Donna Jensen</TD>
<TD>Washington, DC</TD>
<TD>The Wine Cellar</TD>
```

```
<TD STYLE="vnd.ms-excel.numberformat:$#,##0" ALIGN="right">
997375</TD>
</TR>
```

Internet Explorer will ignore the special FILTER and STYLE tags, showing a standard table with four columns of unformatted sales data. When you open the same HTML file in Microsoft Excel, you see the same four columns of data. However, the second column (Office Location) displays records only from Washington, D.C., and the fourth column (Project Size) is formatted as a whole-dollar currency.

Take a look at the XLFILTER.HTM and XLPIVOT.HTM files in your browser and then in Microsoft Excel. View the source code either in Internet Explorer or Notepad to see how the tags were implemented. Both of these HTML files were created by exporting the file XLHTML.XLS to HTML and editing the results in Notepad.

Collaborative Editing

Very often, several people need to contribute to a document or an analysis. A corporate budget cycle often requires multiple individuals or departments to add their numbers independently. Using Microsoft Excel 97, you can share your document with others, edit it simultaneously, reject and accept changes, and track its editing history.

To set up your spreadsheet for collaborative editing, select Share Workbook from the Tools menu to bring up the Share Workbook dialog box. You can change the options in this dialog box so that multiple users can edit your spreadsheet at the same time. By default, you won't see changes made by other users right away, but by changing the Update Changes section on the Advanced tab of this dialog box, you can see the changes at intervals that you determine.

Once your spreadsheet is shared, it might be very important to track the spreadsheet's history. Who changed what? When? You can find out this information by using the Track Changes option on the Tools menu. This option will allow you to invoke the Select Changes To Accept Or Reject dialog box, so you can accept or reject changes made by other users and even view the entire editing history of your document in an AutoFiltered table.

Microsoft Excel 97 and External Data

So now that you know the basics of Microsoft Excel 97's integration capabilities, it's time to start communicating with external data sources. The first question is, Where is the data you want? Even though an Excel spreadsheet can now include up to 65,536 rows, there's a good chance that your corporate data is stored elsewhere. Excel can communicate with any ODBC-compliant databases on your hard drive, network, or intranet. In Excel 97, you can even access data from remote sources on the Internet. Depending on where your data lives, you'll use different data access techniques.

Retrieving Data

You have several options for how to retrieve external data and put it into your Microsoft Excel 97 spreadsheet. The most common and user-friendly options are the Get External Data command for accessing data on your hard drive or corporate network, and Web queries for retrieving data from the Internet. Although other techniques for retrieving data are available, the majority of our discussion will center on these two methods.

Local and network data

To retrieve data from local and network databases, use the Get External Data option on Microsoft Excel's Data menu. By "local data," we mean not only the data sitting on your machine, but any data that you can access through an ODBC data source: Microsoft Access, SQL Server, Oracle, and so on. The data might be on your hard drive or sitting on a network server in another city. This is the traditional means of data access in Microsoft Excel. Point Excel to an ODBC data source, and you can access the data, filter it, and perform other such tasks by using Microsoft Query. For a more detailed example of accessing ODBC data, refer to the Corporate Sales Overview demonstration later in this chapter.

To access ODBC data, choose the Get External Data option from the Data menu. Select the Create New Query command. This launches Microsoft Query, a separate application, which prompts you to select an ODBC data source with the Choose Data Source dialog box. After Microsoft Query has connected to your database, you are guided through a series of steps in which you select the fields you want to retrieve, add any criteria, and set the sort order. Query automatically handles tasks such as joining tables and creating the proper SQL statement needed to retrieve your data. It also has a feature that lets you preview data while adding fields and setting criteria, as shown in Figure 10-3.

TIP If your only reason for retrieving external data is to create a pivot table, you can do this directly by selecting Pivot Table Report from the Data menu. When the Pivot Table Wizard dialog box appears, choose External Data Source. You will be prompted to create a query as explained in this section.

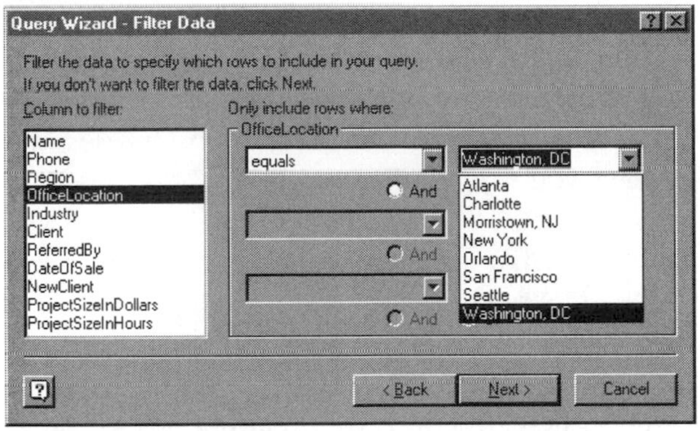

Figure 10-3

Previewing data in Microsoft Query.

After you have created your query, Microsoft Excel asks you where to put the data. Selecting Return Data To Microsoft Excel gives you options for how the data should be inserted. Should it overwrite existing cells? Move them out of the way? Do something else? After inserting the data, you can now treat it as if it were native Excel data. You can filter it, create charts or pivot tables based on it, and so on. If you want to update the data to reflect changes in your back-end database, highlight any of the cells in the query table and choose the Refresh Data option from the Data menu.

NOTE The downside of using Get External Data occurs when you need to control the process programmatically. A lot of overhead is associated with these queries, because they require the use of a separate application, Microsoft Query. If you are planning to use code to handle your external data, you should consider the ODBC add-in, data access objects (DAO), or the ODBC API. These methods are much closer to the underlying ODBC libraries that perform the actual data access and are therefore much faster. It's a trade-off, though—these methods are non-visual and require more programming skills.

Internet data

The concept of Internet data is pretty straightforward. Wouldn't it be great if Microsoft Excel could go out to the Internet and download the latest stock prices from a real-time Internet site? Yes, it would. Well, guess what. You can do this in Excel 97.

To pull data from the Internet, select the Run Web Query command from the Get External Data option of the Data menu. When prompted for a query file, select an .IQY file, located in the Program Files\Microsoft Office\Queries directory. Microsoft Excel ships with four predefined Web queries. Three of the queries allow you to access stock quotes and market data from PC Quote, Inc. The fourth query, Get More Web Queries.iqy, retrieves a Web page that allows you to download additional queries with various information.

Select one of the PC Quote .IQY files and follow the prompts. Microsoft Excel then goes out to the Internet, retrieves the latest stock information, and stores that information in your spreadsheet. If you want to refresh the data, just choose the Refresh Data command. It's that easy!

So what exactly is going on here? Technically speaking, it's a simple process. The .IQY file that you are "running" is a text file that gives Microsoft Excel the URL address of a certain Web page. If that Web page takes parameters, the .IQY file lists those parameters and specifies whether Excel should use the GET or POST method when calling the page. These are the two ways in which standard HTML forms send data.

On the server, the Web page referenced by the .IQY file handles the parameters and generates an HTML page, which is then transferred to the client machine. Once the file is on your machine, Microsoft Excel opens the HTML page and imports the data to your spreadsheet, in the location you specified.

The Web queries in Microsoft Excel have several nice features. First, you don't have to hard-code the parameters passed to the server. When you specify a destination range for a Web query, click the Parameters button on the Returning External Data To Microsoft Excel dialog box. The dialog box that will appear (Figure 10-4) allows you to choose whether Excel prompts you for the parameters (such as stock symbols), you hard-code the parameters, or the parameters are linked to cells in your spreadsheet.

Another nice feature is that .IQY files are very straightforward. This means you can create your own .IQY file to retrieve data from a Web site other than the few included with Microsoft Excel 97. If this Web site takes parameters, you can specify how those parameters should be set. For more information on setting up .IQY files, refer to the QUERIES.XLS file, which has examples of retrieving data from Alta Vista and PC Quote, using GET, POST, and a variety of parameter options.

NOTE As you might have guessed, you could modify a Web query so that it returns data from your corporate intranet into your spreadsheet. For more information, refer to the Microsoft Excel Web Connectivity Kit included on the CD, or go to:

http://www.microsoft.com/excel/webquery.

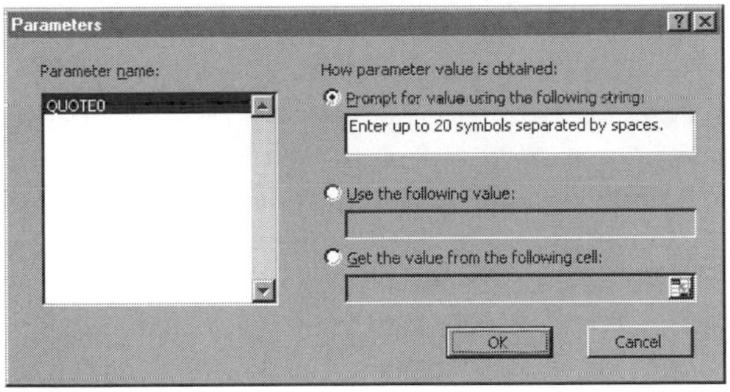

Figure 10-4

Parameters dialog box for the Multiple Stock Quotes by PC Quote, Inc.iqy query.

Sending Data

When you explore the Internet, you often come to Web sites that ask you to submit information, as part of a customer survey or site registration form. After you enter information into the text boxes provided, you click a button to submit your information to the server.

Behind the scenes, several things are happening. The document you are viewing is a special type of HTML document called a *form*. It uses standard HTML form components such as text boxes, radio buttons, and command buttons. After you fill out the information on the Web page, you click the Submit button. This button acts like a hyperlink, but it is calling a special type of Web page, called a *script*. The script then reads data that is "Posted" by the HTML form and inserts the data into the database.

How does Microsoft Excel fit into this equation? Well, you can use Excel to create the equivalent of an HTML form. Instead of entering information into text boxes and radio buttons, you can use the cells in an Excel spreadsheet. This method has several advantages. First, most people find it easier to create an Excel spreadsheet than to create an HTML form. Second, you are not limited to the few HTML form components; you can choose from all of Excel's form controls and ActiveX controls. Third, you have a lot more control over the look of your Excel spreadsheet. You can lay out your form exactly the way you want to, unconstrained by HTML's limitations.

Microsoft Excel 97 introduces two new ways to send data: Web Forms and the Template Wizard. A Web Form is Excel's equivalent of an HTML form, using the same HTTP protocol to send data to the server. The Template Wizard is similar, but it sends data to back-end databases using ODBC. Both of these options are intended for sending single records to a back-end database. If your application requires that you send large amounts of data or if speed is a significant factor, you should consider the ODBC add-in, data access objects (DAO), or the ODBC API.

Designing your data access screen

When designing your data access screen, you need to devote significant time and thought to the user interface. Be sure to provide visual cues such as colored cells or step-by-step instructions so that your users know exactly where to enter data. When you are done laying out your form, there should be a one-to-one correspondence between cells in your spreadsheet and the fields in the back-end database you want to update. These cells must all be located on the same worksheet. Figure 10-5 is a sample of a well-designed data access screen available in the file RSVPFORM.XLS.

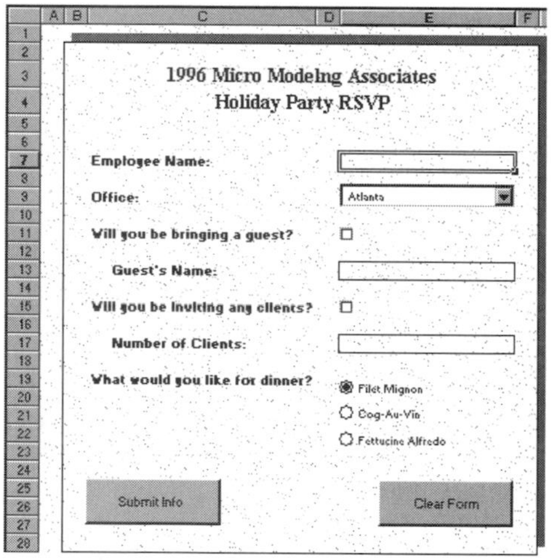

Figure 10-5

MMA Holiday Party RSVP data access screen.

Web forms

Web forms use HTTP, the data transfer method of the Internet, to "Post" information to your Internet/intranet server. A Web form relies on an Internet Database Connector (.IDC) or Perl (.PL) server-side script to read your post and send your data to a back-end database. Once you know the location of this script file, select the Wizard command from the Tools menu and pick the Web Form option.

NOTE If Wizard/Web Form is not an option on your Tools menu, make sure the Web Form Wizard add-in is installed and selected under Tools/Add-Ins.

The Web Form Wizard walks you through the step of mapping your spreadsheet cells to database fields. (See Figure 10-6.) Well, this isn't exactly true. . . . What you're really doing is mapping spreadsheet cells to parameters understood by your IDC or Perl file. These files will do the actual sending of data to specific fields in your back-end database.

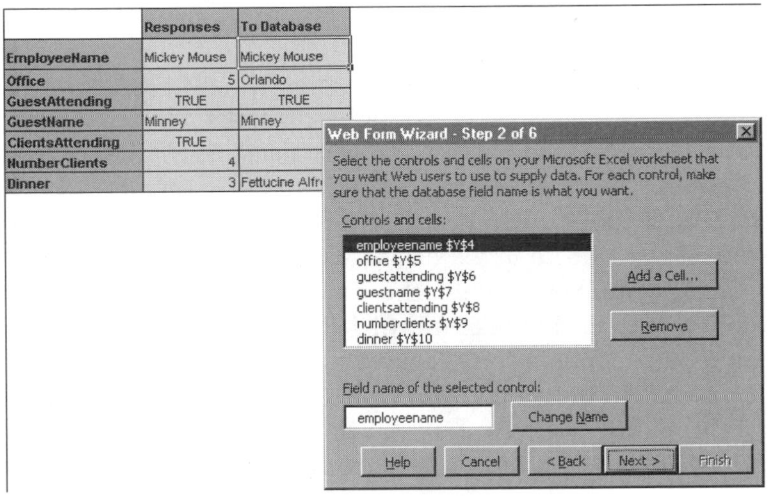

Figure 10-6
Using the Web Form Wizard to map cells to a database.

The wizard then prompts you for the type of server-side script you are using, the file location, and what type of confirmation message you want to

Using Form Controls in Your Data Access Screen

If you want to include form controls such as list boxes and option buttons in your spreadsheet, use the Cell Link property to tie the control's results to a cell on your spreadsheet. Depending on the control, this return value might not be the same value you want to store in your database. You might need another cell to "translate" the value to one that will be useful. For example, when you link a list box to a cell, the returned value is not the text of the selected item but its index number. If you want to store the text in your database, you will need to use a separate cell to look up the correct value. For example, if cell B2 is linked to a list box whose input range is called ListBoxInput, you would use the formula INDEX(ListBoxInput, "B2") to get the selected text.

be displayed after the data is sent. When the wizard is completed, a Submit Info button is added to your spreadsheet. This button is the equivalent of a Submit button on a standard HTML form. Click it to send your data to the server.

The file RSVPFORM.XLS shows an example of a Microsoft Excel–based Web form that allows employees to RSVP to the Micro Modeling holiday party over the intranet.

Template Wizard

The Template Wizard add-in creates a template that links selected cells in your spreadsheet to fields in your back-end ODBC database. Each time you enter information in a workbook based on this template, you are also entering information in a new record in your database. Each workbook is associated with a single record in the database. So if you save your workbook and reopen it later, you can edit the corresponding record in your database. However, deleting the workbook will have no effect on the record—you cannot delete a database record from within Microsoft Excel.

To create a data entry template, select the Template Wizard command from the Data menu. The wizard guides you through the process of naming your template, selecting a back-end database (any ODBC-compliant database), and, as shown in Figure 10-7, mapping cells in your spreadsheet

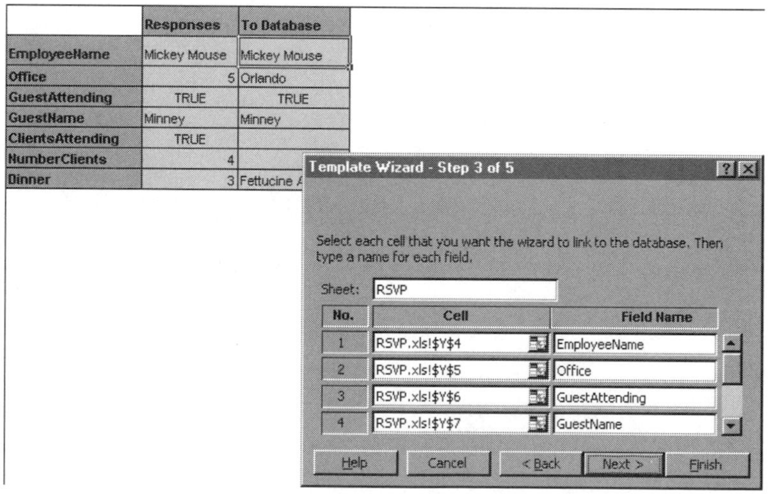

Figure 10-7
Using the Template Wizard to map fields to a database.

to the corresponding database fields. Once you have done this, you can begin an editing session simply by choosing the File New command. Your new template should appear in the list of options; if it does not, move it to the Templates subdirectory of your Microsoft Office directory.

NOTE If Template Wizard is not an option on your Data menu, make sure the Template Wizard With Data Tracking add-in is installed and selected under Tools/Add-Ins.

Building Your Intranet

In this section you'll apply the concepts you learned about earlier in the chapter to MMA's sample intranet site. You'll create two Microsoft Excel–based applications: the Corporate Sales Overview (CORPSALE.XLS) and a Competitive Analysis (COMPANAL.XLS). Both are executive information systems (EIS), designed to give corporate-wide data in a concise format. The rest of the chapter will focus on the meat of these applications, including some details about how they were constructed. Step-by-step formatting isn't discussed unless it's particularly interesting.

Corporate Sales Overview

The Corporate Sales Overview provides several reports and charts showing how Micro Modeling's sales force is performing around the country. The data comes from a Microsoft Access 97 database and is retrieved directly into a pivot table, using the Pivot Table Wizard and Microsoft Query. This data drives several pivot table reports and charts, keeping all of the information up to date. You can explore the report using hyperlinks, which make it very user-friendly. Figure 10-8 shows the main menu of this application.

Before you open the CORPSALE.XLS file on the companion CD, you need to create a DSN, called Corporate Sales Overview, to the CORPSALE.MDB database. For details on how to do this, see the README.TXT file on the companion CD.

Behind the scenes, the main components of this application are data access, pivot tables, charts, hyperlinks, and VBA code.

MICRO
MODELING
ASSOCIATES INC

Sales Force Totals by Office

Industry Sales by Region

Client Hours by Year

MMA Competitive Analysis

Corporate Sales Overview

Figure 10-8

Main menu of Corporate Sales Overview.

Data access

The Corporate Sales Overview is based on data stored in a Microsoft Access 97 database called CORPSALE.MDB. It resides on the server and consists of a series of tables and a single query. The tables contain information about Micro Modeling's salespeople, office locations, clients, industries, sales by dollars, and so on. The most important table, which stores information about every piece of business closed by any MMA salesperson, is called Sales. As the tables are normalized, the data in the Sales table uses codes for a lot of fields. The salesperson might be 23, while the office location is 5. A query called qsSales (qs indicates a Select Query) brings it all together in a readable format.

This query contains too much information to be useful in an EIS environment. So you'll want to retrieve this data into Microsoft Excel to make use of pivot tables and charts. Because this database contains hundreds of records and because all of the users on Micro Modeling's intranet have access to Excel and ODBC, we're going to use Microsoft Query to retrieve our data (as opposed to Web Queries). Because we need this data only for building pivot tables, we will retrieve it directly through the Pivot Table Report command instead of using the Get External Data command.

Pivot tables

The first pivot table shows MMA's sales by office. To set it up, use the PivotTable Report command on the Data menu to start the PivotTable Wizard. In the first step, select External Data Source as your data source. In step two, you are prompted to get the data using Microsoft Query. The process is identical to the one outlined earlier for using the Get External Data command.

Your first step after clicking the Get Data button is to choose a data source. If you don't have one set up for the Corporate Sales database, select New Data Source from the list and follow the prompts from the Create New Data Source dialog box (shown in Figure 10-9) to build a new data source for this application.

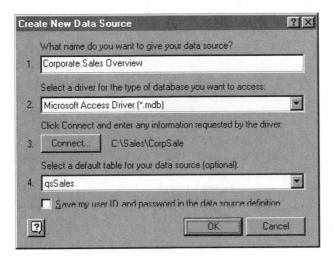

Figure 10-9

Create New Data Source dialog box.

Once Microsoft Query has connected to your database, you will be prompted to select the fields to include in your query. You want to retrieve all of the fields from the qsSales query, so you have a lot of options for pivoting in the future. The next steps prompt you to specify filtering criteria and a sort order, neither of which we need. In the final step, you are prompted to save your query as a .DQY file. This is a good idea if you think you may use this query, or a similar one, in the future. When you're all done creating your query, click the Finish button to return to the Pivot Table Wizard. Click the Next button to move on to step three, where you will construct your Pivot Table. Figure 10-10 shows how to construct a pivot table showing the sales force's sales by office.

The Corporate Sales Overview has two other pivot tables based on the same data. Instead of going through the same steps and connecting to the same database two more times, you can base the other pivot tables on this first pivot table. When you start your next pivot table, choose Another PivotTable as your data source and pick the first pivot table you created from the list. (See Figure 10-11.) You can then use the wizard to choose an appropriate layout for your new report.

10
CHAPTER

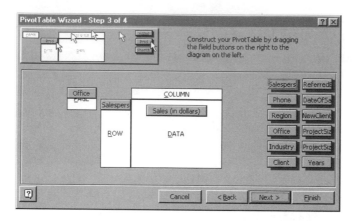

Figure 10-10

Pivot Table Wizard - Step 3 of 4 dialog box.

Figure 10-11

Using another pivot table as your data source.

Charts

Pivot tables are very powerful tools for analyzing data, but the truth is that all most users really want to see is pictures. If you have the chance to summarize data in a chart, do it! Wouldn't it be great if we could base our charts on these pivot tables, updating the charts automatically when the user switches views? This is exactly the functionality included in the Corporate Sales Overview, as Figure 10-12 illustrates.

Creating a chart is easy. Just select the range of data you want to graph and use the Chart Wizard to walk you through the process of selecting a design and creating your axes, legend, and titles. The problem is that your chart has to be based on a static data range. In other words, if you lay out your chart while San Francisco is the active office location, you will be plotting

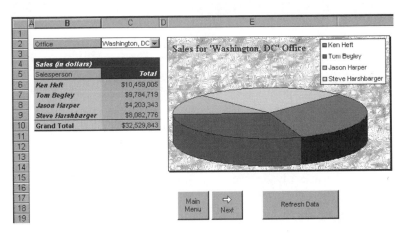

Figure 10-12
A pivot table and its corresponding dynamic chart.

three records, one for each salesperson. When you later change the "page" and pick the Washington, D.C., office, *only the first three salespeople will be graphed*, even though Washington, D.C., has *four* salespeople. How do you work around this problem? Unfortunately, the answer is the dreaded word... CODE! We'll discuss this example further in the "VBA Code" section on page 357.

Hyperlinks

If you're planning on including your Microsoft Excel spreadsheet as part of your intranet site, you should consider offering hyperlinks for getting around. If a user clicks a hyperlink to get to your spreadsheet, you want to include a mechanism to move from the spreadsheet to the next logical location. In this case, an executive of MMA might want to go from the Corporate Sales Overview to the Competitive Analysis. Therefore, use the Insert Hyperlink dialog box to insert a hyperlink to this spreadsheet on the main menu.

You'll also want to include hyperlinks for moving between the different sheets of the Corporate Sales Overview. Your users shouldn't have to stop and think, "I'm in a Microsoft Excel document now. I must have to select this sheet tab to get to the next page." You should keep with the Web functionality. To move from one report to another, just click the hyperlink. The Corporate Sales Overview includes hyperlinks on the main menu, as well as hyperlinked images. The Previous, Main Menu, and Next buttons you see throughout the report are actually bitmaps with hyperlinks, just like those you'd see at the bottom of a Web page.

VBA code

Yes, this application does have some code behind it. The good news is that the concepts behind the code are very straightforward, even if the code itself gets a little tricky in spots. At the core of the code are two routines: RefreshPivotData and RedefineChartSource.

RefreshPivotData gets called by the Refresh Data button you see in the report. It refreshes the current pivot table so that it reflects the most recent cut of data from the Microsoft Access database. It contains only two lines of code and was written by the Microsoft Excel macro recorder. As the code suggests, you must be in a pivot table to refresh it.

```
ActiveSheet.Range("StartPivot").Select
ActiveSheet.PivotTables(1).RefreshTable
```

RedefineChartSource is called each time one of the worksheets containing a pivot table is activated. The routine redefines the chart source so that it reflects all of the data, even if the size of the data has changed. The routine has two parts. The first part calculates the new range that needs to be graphed (stored in rngChartSource). The second part redefines the chart so it points to this range. Here's a sample:

```
'Set rngChartSource to the current range of data to be charted.
Set rngChartSource = ActiveSheet.Range(rngPivotStart, rngPivotEnd)

'Name the new chart data source.
sSourceName = ActiveSheet.Name & "!GraphSource"
rngChartSource.Name = sSourceName

'Set the chart's source property to the newly defined range.
ActiveSheet.ChartObjects(1).Chart.ChartWizard  Source:=sSourceName
```

Finishing touches

So, now that we've examined the nuts and bolts of the Corporate Data Overview, here's a quick peek at some of the finishing touches you can use to dress up the application.

🌐 **Transparent images.** If you use images such as logos in your application, use the Set Transparent Color tool to make your logo's background invisible. (Select Set Transparent Color on the Picture toolbar.)

🌐 **AutoFormat.** If you use the AutoFormat command of the Format menu on a pivot table, Microsoft Excel applies predefined formatting to the pivot table. The best part is that the formatting "sticks," updating automatically even when the report's size changes.

🌐 **WordArt.** With Office 97, WordArt is fully integrated into Microsoft Excel and the other Office applications. Create images using the WordArt toolbar. Edit them using the Drawing toolbar. Shadows, 3-D, and fill effects are just some of the possibilities.

Competitive Analysis

The Competitive Analysis spreadsheet uses live stock market data to track MMA's performance against its toughest competitors. The interface is a single form that allows a user to choose from a list of competitors and chart types. When you click Graph It, Microsoft Excel grabs the latest market information for the selected companies/composites. The results are then displayed in a graph. Figure 10-13 shows the main screen of the Competitive Analysis spreadsheet.

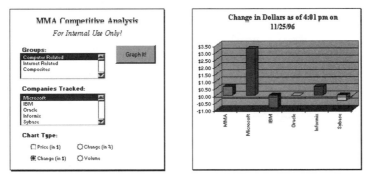

Figure 10-13

Main screen of the Competitive Analysis spreadsheet.

Behind the scenes, the main components of this application are form controls, Web queries, charts, and VBA code. The application's file name is COMPANAL.XLS.

Application structure

The Competitive Analysis application contains two worksheets: the main EIS, which is visible to the user (CompetitiveAnalysis); and another worksheet that contains information used behind the scenes (ControlCenter). The application has one module, which contains VBA routines for requerying the Web, formatting the data, updating the chart, and repopulating the company list box.

Working with ActiveX Controls

If your Microsoft Excel 97 application does not need to be viewed within a browser, ActiveX controls are the way to go. But here's a trick you should know about when working with these controls. ActiveX controls actually have two names. Let's say you insert an ActiveX list box into your spreadsheet. The first name is the one you assign to your list box using the Properties dialog box (for example, lstGroups). This is the name you will use when writing any VBA code concerning the control's functionality, such as setting its ListIndex property. The second name comes in because Microsoft Excel doesn't really see a list box—it sees an embedded object. If you were writing any code concerning the embedded object's properties, such as border style or position on the screen, you would refer to this name. This name is assigned through the standard Microsoft Excel "name box," located to the left of the formula bar. Figure 10-14 shows how these two names appear on the screen.

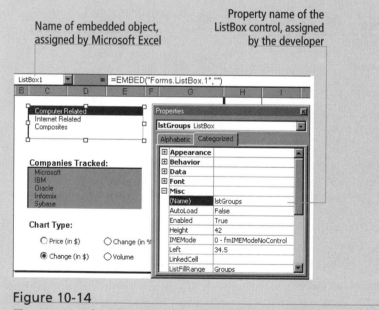

Figure 10-14

Two names of an ActiveX control (ListBox1 and lstGroups).

Microsoft Excel forms vs. ActiveX controls

In Microsoft Excel 97, you have two sets of controls you can use when designing your application. Your first choice is the traditional Excel Forms toolbar, which includes common controls, such as a list box, an option button, and a check box. Your new choice is to use the Control Toolbox, a collection of ActiveX controls. Using the new ActiveX controls will give you much more control over both the look of your controls and the code behind them, because ActiveX controls can respond to multiple events.

If that were the end of the story, the decision about whether to use Microsoft Excel forms or ActiveX controls would be very easy. However, you'll find a major limitation with using ActiveX controls in Microsoft Excel 97. If you try to view an Excel spreadsheet containing ActiveX controls from within Internet Explorer, your controls will not work. You'll get an error message when the spreadsheet opens, and you won't be able to interact with the controls (that is, select list items, click buttons, and so on). This limitation is true only in Microsoft Excel 97, not in the other Office 97 applications.

If you plan on viewing your spreadsheet from a browser, you should choose Microsoft Excel's standard form controls. For this reason, the list boxes, option buttons, and command button on the main sheet of the Competitive Analysis demonstration are standard Excel form controls.

Web queries

The Competitive Analysis application must perform a Web query to get the latest market data for the currently selected companies or composites. The Web query used is the Multiple Stock Quotes by PC Quote, Inc.iqy file included with Microsoft Excel 97, which queries against PC Quote's Web site.

Before the Web query gets run, the Competitive Analysis application must set a parameter listing which stock symbols to update. If the user has selected the Computer Related group, then a VBA routine runs, concatenating the symbols for Microsoft and others into a parameter list that the Web query can understand (for example, MSFT IBM ORCL IFMX SYBS). The symbols associated with each company are stored in tables on the ControlCenter worksheet, as shown in Figure 10-15, out of view of the user.

This VBA routine then passes the parameter to the PC Quote Web query and tells it to refresh. The results are returned to a predefined Raw Data range on the ControlCenter worksheet, as shown in Figure 10-16.

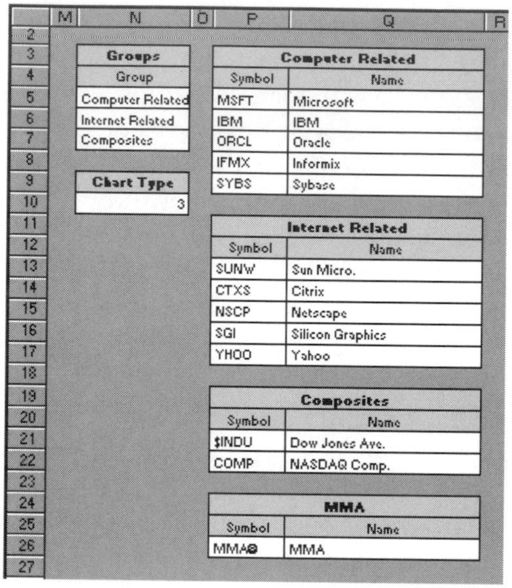

Figure 10-15

Tables of companies and their stock symbols.

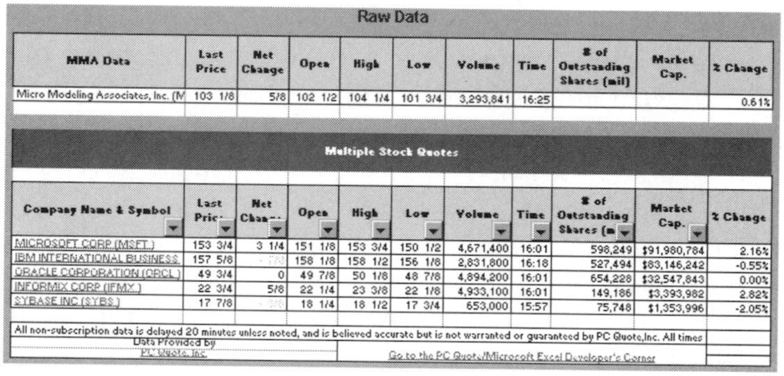

Figure 10-16

Raw data returned by the Web query.

Charts

Four charts are available to the executive using the Competitive Analysis spreadsheet. Each chart is derived from the same raw data returned by the Web query but uses different columns of data. Each chart also has unique components, such as its title, axis labeling, and chart style.

The first problem arises in organizing the data. Because our sample company, Micro Modeling, doesn't really have a publicly traded stock, we can't look up its stock value. Therefore, hard-coded numbers are used for this demonstration. It would be much easier to chart the data if it were all centrally located, with proper number formats, field names, and in the proper order. A VBA routine, FormatRawData, is used to organize all of the data into a FormattedArea range, as shown in Figure 10-17.

								# of Outstanding		
Name	Close	Change ($)	Open	High	Low	Volume	Time	Shares (mil)	Market Cap.	Change (%)
MMA	$ 103.13	$ 0.63	$ 102.50	$ 104.25	$ 101.75	3,293,841	4:25 PM			0.61%
Microsoft	$ 153.75	$ 3.25	$ 151.13	$ 153.75	$ 150.50	4,671,400	4:01 PM	598,249	$91,980,783.75	2.16%
IBM	$ 157.63	$ (0.88)	$ 158.13	$ 158.50	$ 156.13	2,831,800	4:18 PM	527,494	$83,146,241.75	-0.55%
Oracle	$ 49.75	$ -	$ 49.88	$ 50.13	$ 48.88	4,894,200	4:01 PM	654,228	$32,547,843.00	0.00%
Informix	$ 22.75	$ 0.63	$ 22.25	$ 23.38	$ 22.13	4,933,100	4:01 PM	149,186	$3,393,981.50	2.82%
Sybase	$ 17.88	$ (0.38)	$ 18.25	$ 18.50	$ 17.75	653,000	3:57 PM	75,748	$1,353,995.50	-2.05%

Formatted Data

Figure 10-17

Formatted data, ready for charting.

The VBA code then changes several aspects of the chart, such as its source, chart title, and so on. The chart's title is calculated by reading the time and date of the returned stock quotes. For the Volume Chart, the title might be "Volume as of 4:21 pm on 9/13/96."

VBA code

Four main routines control the Competitive Analysis application: RepopulateListBox, RequeryData, FormatRawData, and UpdateChart.

RepopulateListBox   The list of companies tracked is linked to a range called CurrentNames. As a user switches between Computer Related, Internet Related, and Composites, the list of companies tracked must reflect this switch. The VBA routine RepopulateListBox redefines the range CurrentNames to point to the names associated with the current group.

RequeryData   After selecting a group and a chart type, click the Graph It button. This button calls three VBA routines. The first is RequeryData. It constructs the necessary PC Quote parameter, using the current list of stock symbols, and then refreshes the query table.

You must first set the parameters of the query using the SetParam method. This method takes two arguments. The first argument tells the query whether to prompt the user for the parameter, use a hard-coded value, or use the value in a range. A hard-coded value is represented by xlConstant. The second argument is the corresponding prompt, hard-coded value, or cell reference. The variable sParameter contains the formatted parameter (for example, MSFT, IBM, ORCL, IFMX, SYBS).

```
With Worksheets("ControlCenter").Range("RawDataStart").QueryTable
    .Parameters(1).SetParam xlConstant, sParameter
    .Refresh False
End With
```

After setting the parameter, the next statement refreshes the data using the Refresh method of QueryTable. This method takes a single argument, which indicates whether or not your code should continue to run while the query tries to update. In some cases, it is beneficial to have a query run in the background. Your code can continue to run without having to wait for the query to finish executing. However, in this case, our code depends on the query having been executed successfully. Therefore, we set this argument to False.

FormatRawData   After the raw data is retrieved into the control center, the FormatRawData routine copies all of the MMA and competitor data to a central location where it can be graphed more easily. The code includes a lot of standard range manipulation (Offset, Resize, and so on), and one line that redefines a range name, called FormattedArea, to point to the entire data range.

UpdateChart   The last routine to run is the UpdateChart routine. This routine changes many aspects of the chart to match the selected chart type. It sets the chart title, changes the source data range, and so forth. This code shows how the Price chart is created:

```
With Worksheets("CompetitiveAnalysis").ChartObjects(1).Chart
    .ChartWizard Source:=rngSource
    .ChartType = xlCylinderCol
    .Axes(xlSeries).TickLabelPosition = xlNone
    .Axes(xlValue).TickLabels.NumberFormat = "$#,##0"
    .ChartTitle.Text = "Prices as of " & sDate
End With
```

More finishing touches

Another application is completed…almost. Here are a few finishing touches that will make the Competitive Analysis look great:

🌐 **Background image.** Use the Format/Sheet/Background command to select an image that sits behind your data. Some samples are in the ClipArt\Backgrounds subfolder of Microsoft Office.

🌐 **Fill effects.** No longer are you limited to solids and stripes when formatting drawing objects and charts. With fill effects, you have gradients, textures, patterns, and pictures to choose from. Four new ways for people (other than you) to create ugly user interfaces!

CHAPTER 11

Microsoft Access 97

Ken Heft

Microsoft Access 97 is truly versatile when it comes to your intranet. It is a relational database, a development environment, an HTML editor, and a Web publisher all rolled into one application. It fully integrates with the rest of the products in the Microsoft Office suite, both in its HTML support and its hyperlink capabilities.

First and foremost, though, Microsoft Access is a relational database. You can use Microsoft Access simply to store your data, even if you retrieve the data through tools such as Microsoft Excel or an HTML browser. Microsoft Access can import and link to data from many external data sources, including ODBC databases and HTML files.

As a development environment, Microsoft Access is very powerful. It includes full Visual Basic for Applications (VBA) support and has a rich set of form-designing capabilities, including support for ActiveX. Although Microsoft Access does not yet support the common Visual Basic Environment (VBE) or Forms[3], its environment shares many of the same new editing features, including a Locals window, Auto List Members, Auto Quick Info, and Auto Data Tips.

As an HTML editor and Web publisher, Microsoft Access is very strong. You can export your tables, queries, forms, and reports to HTML. You can publish your entire database to a Web site, automatically including a switchboard-like home page. But the most impressive Web publishing capability of Microsoft Access is its dynamic Web page creation. You can export your forms and queries to .HTX/.IDC or .ASP format, two formats designed to create dynamic Web pages. So instead of running a query locally in Microsoft Access, you can click on a Web page that goes out to the server, runs the query, and returns the results to a new HTML document created just for you.

Microsoft Access 97 also includes wizards that let you export your entire database to the World Wide Web. Figure 11-1 shows a home page that Microsoft Access generated automatically to help move around in various Web-based tables, queries, forms, and reports.

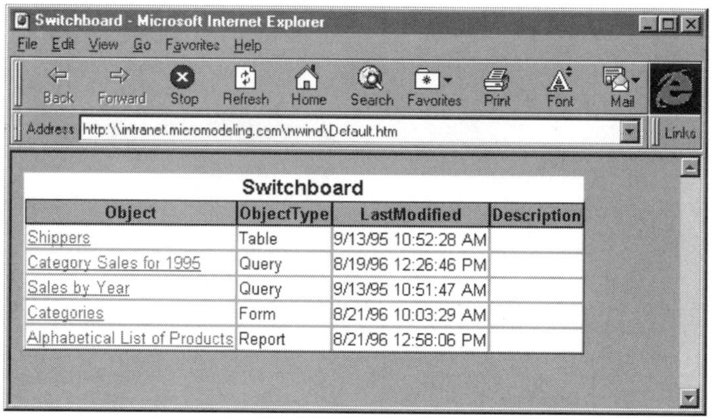

Figure 11-1

HTML switchboard generated by Microsoft Access.

To tie it all together, Microsoft Access includes support for hyperlinks. You can store hyperlink addresses (to locations such as Web pages and e-mail addresses) directly in a Microsoft Access table. You can create hyperlinks that jump to Microsoft Access tables, queries, forms, reports, macros, and modules. Finally, you can create hyperlinks for labels, images, and command buttons throughout your user interface. With the release of Microsoft Office 97, Microsoft Access has added an impressive list of features with the intranet in mind. This chapter will attempt to touch on all of them, while continuing to build Micro Modeling's sample intranet site.

Hyperlinks

Microsoft Access 97 includes thorough support for hyperlinks. Microsoft Access tables support the Hyperlink data type, a way to store URL, e-mail, and many other types of Internet/intranet addresses. Microsoft Access forms and queries recognize the Hyperlink data type and display the corresponding data as live hyperlinks.

Your hyperlinks do not have to be stored in tables, however. You can create them manually in the user interface to help users move through your application. For example, place a hyperlink behind a command button on a form to preview a Microsoft Access report without using or writing any code.

When Size Matters: Microsoft Access vs. SQL Server

In this book, two different Microsoft databases, Microsoft Access and SQL Server, are discussed. As we are focusing on the intranet capabilities of each product, you're probably asking yourself, "Which one should we use?" Here is a quick comparison of the products:

- Microsoft Access is a great relational database for workgroups/departments. SQL Server is more suited to organizations.

- Microsoft Access can be used as a data source for your local intranet, provided your group is relatively small. SQL Server can be used as the back-end database for your corporate Internet site.

- Microsoft Access can efficiently store tens of thousands of records. SQL Server can be used to store hundreds of thousands or even millions of records.

- Microsoft Access is designed with ease of use as a priority. Users can quickly develop personal databases. SQL Server comes with a suite of development tools but requires a certain degree of database administration and programming ability.

- SQL Server should be used if you are doing transaction processing and require features like fault tolerance and transaction roll-back.

- Microsoft Access and SQL Server both have impressive Internet/intranet capabilities in their latest releases.

Any of the Microsoft Access components (tables, forms, queries, reports, macros, and modules) can be the destination of a hyperlink—even when called from another application. But you're not limited to Microsoft Access components. Your hyperlinks can jump anywhere, from a Microsoft Excel range to the Microsoft Web site.

Using the Hyperlink Data Type

In Microsoft Access 97 tables, Hyperlink is now a valid data type, just as text or number. A hyperlink can be a standard World Wide Web address (for example, http://www.microsoft.com) or the location of an Office document (for example, C:\My Documents\sample.xls). In addition to these protocols, the Hyperlink data type can accept almost every protocol you can think of, including ftp, gopher, mailto (e-mail), pnm (Real Audio), and mms (Microsoft Media Server). Once you have created a table with at least one hyperlink field, you need to learn the different ways to enter valid hyperlinks into your table.

One option is to type the address directly. This works well for shorter and more common addresses, but it is sometimes difficult to remember the entire document address and subaddress. Luckily, you have a few more options to help you out. You can use the Insert Hyperlink or Edit Hyperlink commands to create and modify hyperlinks to any valid location. For hyperlinks to other Office documents, you can also choose from a variety of copy and paste options.

Entering a hyperlink manually

The first way to enter a hyperlink address is to type it directly into your table, query, or form field. The address can contain up to three parts, using the syntax displaytext#address#subaddress. For example, if you want to enter a hyperlink to Microsoft's home page but don't want to display the entire HTTP address, you would enter "Microsoft Home Page#http://www. microsoft.com.#". If you then bind a form to this table, only the display text portion of the hyperlink (Microsoft Home Page) would be displayed.

The subaddress portion of the hyperlink address can be used to specify a location within a document—a bookmark in an HTML file or a Microsoft Word document, a range in a Microsoft Excel spreadsheet, and so on. In the Microsoft Home Page example, there is no need to specify a subaddress, so this portion is left out. However, you should always include two pound (#) symbols as placeholders, even if you are leaving out sections of the hyperlink address. Each of the three portions of the hyperlink address can contain up to 2,048 characters.

Storing E-Mail Addresses as Hyperlinks

If you want to include an "e-mail address" field in your database, the syntax to use is mailto:e-mail address. This produces an SMTP e-mail address, the default for the Internet. If your internal mail system does not support SMTP, you can override it by specifying mailto: addressformat:e-mailaddress. For example, if your mail system uses MHS, a valid hyperlink would be mailto:[mhs:webmaster@micro-modeling.com]. Microsoft Access will automatically create a friendlier "display name" that includes only the e-mail address (for example, webmaster@micromodeling.com).

When you click the hyperlink, your default Internet mail client will launch. If you want to change your default Internet mail client, use the View Options command in Internet Explorer and change the application found in the Mail text box on the Programs tab.

Using the Insert Hyperlinks command

Select the Hyperlink command from the Microsoft Access Insert menu when you are entering data into a hyperlink field in a table, query, or form. The dialog box will let you choose both an address and a subaddress (but not a display name). When you click OK, Microsoft Access converts your information to the displayname#address#subaddress format. To change the display name, you will have to press F2 to edit the field. You should now see the entire hyperlink address (for example, #http://www.microsoft.com/#). Now you can type a display name before the address and modify either of the remaining sections. If the field is too small to see, you can also zoom it by pressing Shift-F2; but make sure to do this after pressing F2 to enter edit mode. You can edit the display name by clicking on the field with your right mouse button, selecting Hyperlink, and then clicking in the text box next to Display Text. If you want to edit an existing hyperlink in a table or a form, click on the field with your right mouse button and select Hyperlink and then Edit Hyperlink from the shortcut menu.

Inserting hyperlinks in other ways

If your destination document is an Office 97 document, there are a few shortcuts you can use to enter a hyperlink address. Select the portion of your Office document that you want to be your destination, and use the Copy command. Then select the hyperlink field, and choose the Paste As Hyperlink command from the Edit menu. Another option is to drag and drop with your right mouse button. In either case, if you need to edit the display name, address, or subaddress created in the hyperlink field, follow the same steps listed in the previous section.

TIP These methods for creating hyperlinks will not work if you are trying to go from one location in a Microsoft Access database to another.

Using queries, forms, and reports

Once you've created your Web page, e-mail address, or other hyperlink field in your Microsoft Access table, how are your queries, forms, and reports going to interpret them? Here's how:

- 🌐 **Queries.** Hyperlink fields that are included in queries will be displayed just as they are in a table. The field will show the display name portion of the hyperlink, and the hyperlink will be live. Add/edit hyperlinks using the methods discussed in the previous sections.

- 🌐 **Forms.** If you use the Form Wizard, the display name from your hyperlink fields will automatically appear in your form as data-bound text boxes. Without the Form Wizard, just add a text box (or combo box) manually and set its Control Source property to the hyperlink field in your table or query. There are no additional properties to set; being bound to a hyperlink field is enough. Add/edit hyperlinks using the methods discussed in the previous sections.

- 🌐 **Reports.** If your report has a hyperlink field in its layout, the display name will print. There is no way to click on a hyperlink in a report; but if you output the report to HTML or another external format, the hyperlink will export intact.

Including Hyperlinks in the User Interface

So far, we have seen some examples of creating data-bound hyperlinks in Microsoft Access. But what if you want to include your logo on a switchboard form and you want that logo to be a hyperlink to your company's Web site? This type of hyperlink is not bound to any data; it is simply inserted into a form at design time. Labels, images, and command buttons can all be hyperlinks in your form.

To put a hyperlink label in your form, start by putting your form in Design view. You can then take any of the following steps:

 Use the Insert Hyperlink command to select a hyperlink address and subaddress.

 Use Copy and Paste to paste an existing hyperlink from another location, such as a Web page.

Use Copy and Paste As Hyperlink or drag and drop to create a hyperlink to a particular location in another Office 97 document.

Each of these methods will automatically create a label that acts as a live hyperlink. If you later need to edit the hyperlink, click the hyperlink with your right mouse button and select the Hyperlink command. To modify the text that appears in the label, change the label's Caption property.

NOTE
You can insert hyperlinks into your Microsoft Access reports using the same methods explained above. However, the hyperlinks will have no effect within Microsoft Access. When you preview your report, you cannot click on the hyperlinks. The benefit of adding hyperlinks to your report is that these hyperlinks will work when you export your report to HTML. We will discuss exporting reports to HTML later in this chapter.

You can also turn standard images and command buttons into hyperlinks. To do this, start by inserting the control (image or command button) into your form at design time. Once the image or command button is on your form, bring up the properties of the control by using the Properties command on the View menu. Click once in the Hyperlink Address field on the Format tab, and then click the Build button located to the right of this property. (It appears as three baseline dots: ...) Enter the destination document's address and subaddress in the standard Insert Hyperlink dialog box that appears. Microsoft Access then sets the control's Hyperlink Address and Hyperlink SubAddress properties.

When you move the mouse over a hyperlinked image, the mouse will turn into a "hand" icon. This is your only visual cue that the image is a hyperlink. For a command button, the same hand icon appears, and the caption of the button will appear underlined and blue or purple by default. To modify the text that appears in the command button, change the command button's Caption property.

11 CHAPTER

When you set the HyperlinkAddress property of either of these controls, you are in effect telling Microsoft Access to perform an action when the user clicks the control. However, this does not replace the Click event. The Click event will still occur, but after the hyperlink is activated.

Using Microsoft Access Components as Hyperlink Destinations

Tables, forms, queries, reports, macros, and modules in Microsoft Access can all be the target of hyperlinks. You can jump to these Microsoft Access components both from within Microsoft Access and from external applications. Tables will open in Datasheet view, forms will open in Form view, queries will execute, reports will open in Preview mode, macros will run, and modules will open in Design view. To say it another way, whatever happens when you double-click an object will occur when you hyperlink to it.

To build a hyperlink to a Microsoft Access object, use the standard Insert Hyperlinks dialog box and start by specifying the .MDB file name under Link To File Or URL. If you want to create a hyperlink within the same Microsoft Access database, leave this field blank.

To specify a location within the Microsoft Access database, use the format "object type name" in the Named Location In File text box. Valid object type values are Table, Form, Query, Report, Macro, and Module. For example, to create a hyperlink to the Employees table, you would set the named location to "Table Employees." Although you can omit the object type, it gets confusing if you have multiple objects with the same name (for example, a form and a table both named "Employees").

Although you can hyperlink to a table, query, and the like, there is no way to specify where in that object you want to go. If you want to open the table and select the 500th record, you cannot do this with hyperlinks.

Referring to Hyperlinks Through Code

You can refer to hyperlinks in code in slightly different ways, depending on whether or not the hyperlink comes from a hyperlink field in a table. For hyperlinks not stored in a table, such as hyperlinks behind labels, command buttons, and images, you refer to the Hyperlink property of the object. The resulting Hyperlink object has two properties, Address and SubAddress; and two methods, Follow and AddToFavorites. Here is an example:

```
With Forms!Employees.Command1.Hyperlink
    .Address = "http://www.microsoft.com"
    .AddToFavorites
End With
```

When dealing with command buttons and labels, it is easy to keep the parts of a hyperlink straight. The visible portion is stored in the Caption property, the file name or URL is stored in the HyperlinkAddress property, and the location within the document is stored in the HyperlinkSubAddress property.

All of this information is stored together, however, when dealing with hyperlinks stored in tables. In the table, query, and bound form, the value of a hyperlink has the syntax "displaytext#address#subaddress". Chances are that this is not the syntax you want to see when you refer to the value of a text box or field.

To specify the portion of a hyperlink that you want to retrieve, use the HyperlinkPart function. This function takes two arguments: the hyperlink and a constant indicating the portion of the hyperlink that you want. Valid constants for the second argument are acDisplayedValue, acDisplayText, acAddress, and acSubAddress. The constants acDisplayText, acAddress, and acSubAddress correspond to the three parts of a hyperlink address. The value acDisplayedValue is the value displayed on the screen—this can be the display text, address, or subaddress, depending on which parts of the hyperlink address are left blank. For example, if the hyperlink address is "#http://www.micromodeling.com#", then acDisplayText and acSubAddress would each return a blank string; acDisplayedValue and acAddress would return the HTTP address.

Here is an example of using the HyperlinkPart function:

```
Dim rsEmployees As Recordset
    Set rsEmployees = _
        CurrentDB.OpenRecordset("Select * From Employees")
    MsgBox "e-mail address:  " & _
        HyperlinkPart(rsEmployees("EMail"), acDisplayedValue) & _
        chr$(10) "Home Page: & _
        HyperlinkPart(rsEmployees("HomePage"), acAddress)
```

11 CHAPTER

You can also use the HyperlinkPart function directly in queries, from both Microsoft Access and external data sources. The following SQL statement would retrieve only the home page address from the corresponding field:

```
SELECT CompanyName, HyperlinkPart(HomePage,2) As URLAddress
FROM Companies
```

NOTE You have to use the numeric equivalent of the acAddress constant when using SQL. The values for acDisplayedValue, acDisplayText, acAddress, and acSubaddress are 0, 1, 2, and 3, respectively.

Linking and Importing External Data

Your Microsoft Access database can easily incorporate data from external data sources. Two mechanisms for doing this are available: linking (attaching) and importing. You can link and import from a variety of external data sources, including any ODBC data source (SQL Server, Oracle, and so on), HTML files, or even other Microsoft Access databases.

Getting Data from the Internet via FTP/HTTP

The data you want to link to or import is not always sitting on your hard drive. With this in mind, Microsoft Access 97 allows you a number of ways for reaching your data, including HTTP and FTP over the Internet. Although these methods are not usually the quickest ways of retrieving data, they might be your only options depending on your network structure.

Your data options with FTP and HTTP are limited to file types such as HTML, dBASE, Microsoft FoxPro, and text files (consult the Microsoft Access Help files for a full list). You cannot import or link to other Microsoft Access tables or to ODBC data sources over the Internet.

To import or link using HTTP or FTP, select the Get External Data command from the File menu. Choose either Import or Link Tables, depending on the option you want. In the Look In list box, select the Internet Locations (FTP) option.

You can then select from the available list of FTP sites or double-click Add/Modify FTP Locations to create a new FTP site. If your document is on the Web, you can type the URL (for example, http://www.micromodeling.com/salesdta.HTM) in the File Name box, as shown in Figure 11-2.

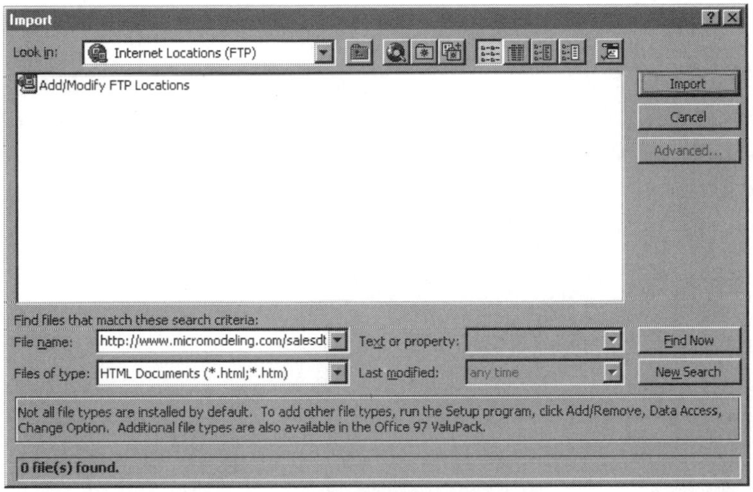

Figure 11-2

Importing an HTML file via the Internet.

If you need to browse the Web in order to locate your document, many Microsoft Access 97 dialog boxes contain a Search The Web button (a globe icon) that launches your Web browser and opens your default Internet search page. To use this feature, select the Import Or Link Tables command and click the Search The Web button at the top of the dialog box. This will launch Internet Explorer and let you browse for the Internet/intranet document you want to incorporate in your database. Once you find that document, you should copy the location to the clipboard, return to Microsoft Access, repeat the Import Or Link Tables command, and paste in the document location.

Using HTML

In addition to traditional data sources such as SQL Server and dBASE, Microsoft Access 97 allows you to import and link to data from HTML documents or .HTX templates. Start by using the File/Get External Data command to select a valid HTML file and clicking either Import or Link Tables. This will bring up the Import HTML Wizard or the Link HTML Wizard.

NOTE
Linking to an HTML document is read-only. You cannot use Microsoft Access to modify an existing HTML table.

CHAPTER 11

These wizards are very similar to the other import/link wizards you would see when connecting to SQL Server, dBASE, and so on. They guide you through the process of selecting a destination table and specifying formatting information for each field and also provide other assistance. Figure 11-3 shows you the second step of the Import HTML Wizard, where you are asked to specify the destination for the data. After you have completed the wizard, your new data will be brought into Microsoft Access.

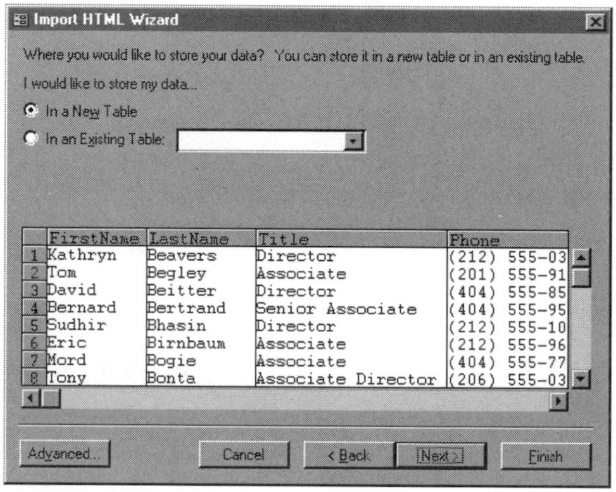

Figure 11-3

Import HTML Wizard.

If you import your data, you will see no difference between your new data and data in existing tables. If you link your data, your new table(s) will have arrows to the left of them, indicating a link. You will also see a different icon, indicating the type of database that you are linking to. Figure 11-4 shows a Microsoft Access database with links to several external data sources.

Linking and Importing Using Code

To automate the task of importing or linking data into your Microsoft Access database, you need to learn a few VBA commands: TransferDatabase, TransferSpreadsheet, and TransferText. TransferDatabase allows you to import or link from other Microsoft Access databases, Microsoft FoxPro, dBASE, and any ODBC data source; TransferSpreadsheet works for Microsoft Excel or Lotus; and TransferText is for standard text files and HTML.

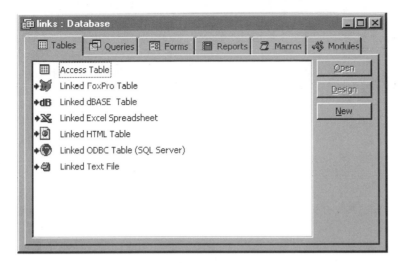

Figure 11-4
Tables linked to external databases.

All of these are methods of the omnipresent DoCmd object in Microsoft Access and are translations of Access macros. For example, here is the syntax for using TransferDatabase:

```
DoCmd.TransferDatabase [TransferType], DatabaseType, _
    DatabaseName[, ObjectType], Source, _
    Destination[, StructureOnly][, SaveLoginID]
```

For help on the acceptable values for each of the TransferDatabase arguments, create a new macro, select the TransferDatabase action, and look at the bottom of your macro window. You will see the same argument list as shown in the example syntax above and can choose from a list of acceptable values for each argument. Here is an example of using the TransferDatabase method to import data from an SQL Server table:

```
DoCmd.TransferDatabase TransferType:=acImport, _
    DatabaseType:="ODBC Database", _
    DatabaseName:="ODBC;DSN=SQLExample;UID=Admin;PWD=password;", _
    ObjectType:=acTable, _
    Source:="Pubs", _
    Destination:="SQLPubs", _
    StructureOnly:=False, _
    SaveLoginID:=False
```

Another way to link to an external database is to use Data Access Objects (DAO) and the Connect method. This way of linking can be used

11 CHAPTER

in place of TransferDatabase, TransferSpreadsheet, and TransferText, since it can link to any external data source. To use the Connect method, you must first create a reference to a table in your database. The following example uses DAO to link to the same SQL Server table as the preceding Transfer-Database example:

```
Dim db As Database
Dim td As TableDef
Set db = CurrentDb()
Set td = db.CreateTableDef("SQLPubs")
td.Connect = "ODBC;DSN=SQLExample;UID=Admin;PWD=password"
td.SourceTableName = "Pubs"
db.TableDefs.Append td
```

You should use the Connect method whenever you are linking to external data sources through code. It is much more direct than the Transfer methods because it uses DAO directly instead of manipulating a questionable DoCmd object. It can also be used for linking to any data source, whereas the DoCmd object has three separate methods, depending on the type of data you are linking to. As for importing data, your only option is to use the DoCmd object with the Transfer methods.

Saving in Web Format

By far, the most powerful intranet feature of Microsoft Access 97 is its ability to publish tables, forms, queries, and reports as Web pages. There are two broad categories of Web pages on the intranet/Internet: static and dynamic.

When you access static HTML pages, it's like calling the movie theater and listening to a recorded message of what movies are playing. If you're not sure what you want to see and your schedule is flexible, the recorded message is great. But if you're interested only in what time the new Van Damme movie is playing, you still have to hear about all fourteen movies and the ten times throughout the day that they are showing. If someone forgets to update the message, you might even be listening to last week's schedule. It's not until someone physically tapes a new message with all the movies and all the times that the recording will be different when you call.

When you use dynamic HTML pages, it's like dialing the automated movie hotline. You punch in your zip code and the first three letters of the movie you want to see, and the recorded voice on the other end of the phone gives you the nearest locations and times at which your movie is playing.

Now it's time to convert this analogy to Microsoft Access–speak. The recorded message in the first scenario is a static HTML page. It is created by taking a snapshot of data in your database. This snapshot can be an entire table, the results of a query or report, or a Datasheet view of a form. In all of these cases, the current cut of data is exported to HTML and then disconnected entirely from the database. If the database changes in the future, you have to export your data again—just as you have to re-record the message when the movie lineups change.

With the automated movie hotline in the second scenario, you have a dynamic Web of pages. A common scenario might be a table, a query, and a form all tied together. The form lets you enter information, which then gets passed to the query as a parameter. The query gets the latest data from the table and returns the data you requested. If the database changes in the future, your form sees the changes immediately—just as the automated movie hotline knows at 8:01 that it should no longer be telling you about the 8:00 showing of your movie.

Publishing Static Web Pages

In some cases, a static HTML page is all you need. For example, consider a Microsoft Access query that gets the names of your company's ten most profitable products of 1995. Whether you run this query today or in the year 2000, your results will be the same. For this type of situation, you would use the abilities of Microsoft Access to create a static HTML page showing the results of this query.

You can export tables, forms (in Datasheet view), queries, and reports as static HTML documents. Each table, form, and query will export as a single HTML file. Each page of your report will be a separate HTML file. You can export any amount of data, from a single record to an entire database, at the same time. With the Publish To The Web Wizard, you can even create a "home page" that automatically moves you from table to form to query to report on the intranet.

Here are some other reasons for using static pages:

- 🌐 **Reports.** If you have to export a Microsoft Access report to the Web, static HTML is your only noncoding option.

- 🌐 **Hyperlinks:** If you want your hyperlink data fields to export as live hyperlinks, you must use static HTML (or modify the exported files).

Exporting a single component

To export a single table, form, query, or report as a static HTML file, highlight the object and select the Save As/Export command from the File menu (or the right mouse button shortcut menu). When prompted, select the

External File Or Database option and click OK to bring up a Save As dialog box like the one shown in Figure 11-5. Then choose HTML Documents as the Save As Type, and pick a location and filename for your export file. Keep in mind that the location you pick for your exported HTML file cannot be a URL; it must be on your local machine or network.

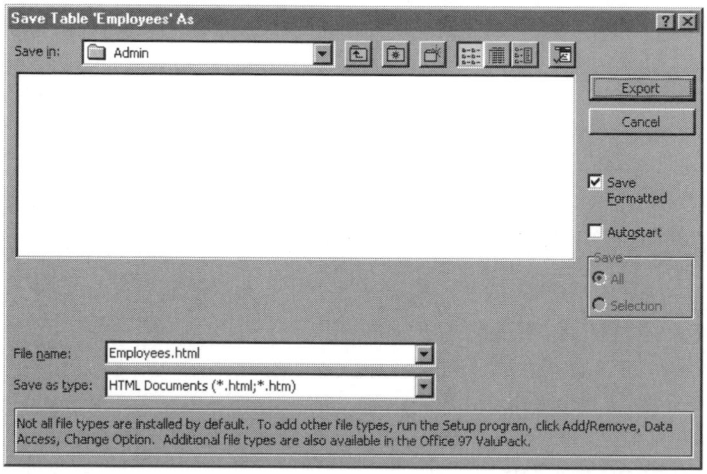

Figure 11-5
Exporting a table to an HTML file.

For tables and queries, the Save As dialog box gives the option to Save Formatted. If you save the formatting, Microsoft Access will try to mimic the cell color, borders, and fonts that you set up in Datasheet view. By default, this format is a table with white cells, light gray borders, and the Arial font. You probably didn't even know you could change this—but you can, by using the Format Cells and Format Font commands when you're in Datasheet view. If you choose not to save the formatting, Microsoft Access will create an HTML file with a basic table—no special formatting. For reports and forms, saving the formatting is automatic.

TIP If you want to see the generated HTML file immediately, choose the Autostart option. The exported file will be displayed automatically in your default browser.

If you are saving the formatting, after you click the Export button the next dialog box (shown in Figure 11-6) will prompt you for an HTML template.

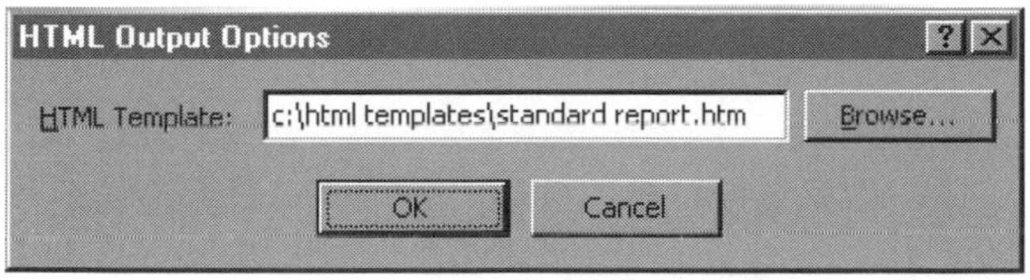

Figure 11-6

HTML Output Options dialog box for specifying an HTML template.

You can specify an HTML template to give your Microsoft Access–generated documents the same look and feel as your other intranet documents. You can specify backgrounds, logos, fonts, and so on. Refer to the "Using a Predefined Template" section later in this chapter for a clearer picture. If you do not specify an HTML template, you will get a basic HTML document, with no extra formatting. After clicking OK, your HTML file(s) will be waiting in the directory that you specified.

Exporting selected records

At times you won't want to export all your data to HTML—just certain records. To export a portion of your data, select the records in Datasheet view (tables, queries, or forms only—you can't export a portion of a report). Choose the Save As/Export command from the File menu, select HTML Document as the file type, make sure the Save Formatted box is checked, and then click the Save Selection option button. This will save only the selected record(s) to HTML.

Using the Publish To The Web Wizard

If you want to create HTML files for more than one component at a time, the Publish To The Web Wizard is the way to go. To start the wizard, select

---

Exporting Reports to HTML

If you export a report to HTML, you will get a separate HTML file for each page of the report. Each HTML page actually contains a separate HTML table for each record in your report. This cannot be changed.

Microsoft Access automatically generates hyperlinks for moving between the pages. The format of these hyperlinks is stored internally in Microsoft Access. If you want to change the look of these hyperlinks (perhaps using graphics instead of text), you can do this by using an HTML template. We will discuss HTML templates later in this chapter.

CHAPTER 11

the Save As HTML command from the File menu. The dialog box shown in Figure 11-7 will appear.

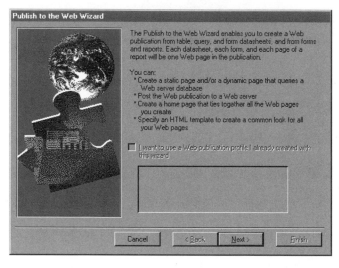

Figure 11-7

Opening window of the Publish To The Web Wizard.

The easiest way to go through the Wizard is to do an example. Let's use the Northwind Traders sample application, Northwind.mdb, that comes with Microsoft Access (Program Files\Microsoft Office\Office\Samples\ Northwind.mdb).

Start the Wizard, and click Next to advance to the second step. In this step we're going to select the components to export: the Shippers table, Category Sales For 1995 and Sales By Year queries, the Categories form, and the Alphabetical List Of Products report. Figure 11-8 shows the All Objects tab of the Publish To The Web Wizard, where you can view all the objects at once and select the items you want to export.

Click the Next button. We're going to skip over some templates for now, so click Next again. For the time being, we're going to export all of these files as static, so make sure the Static HTML option is checked, as shown in Figure 11-9, and click Next.

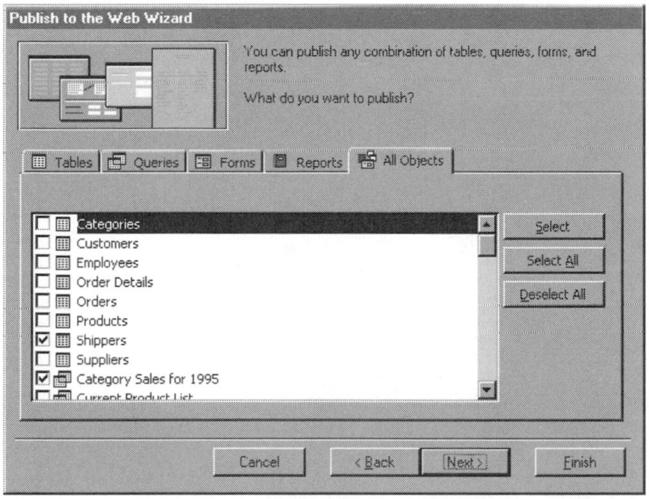

Figure 11-8

Selecting components to export in the Publish To The Web Wizard.

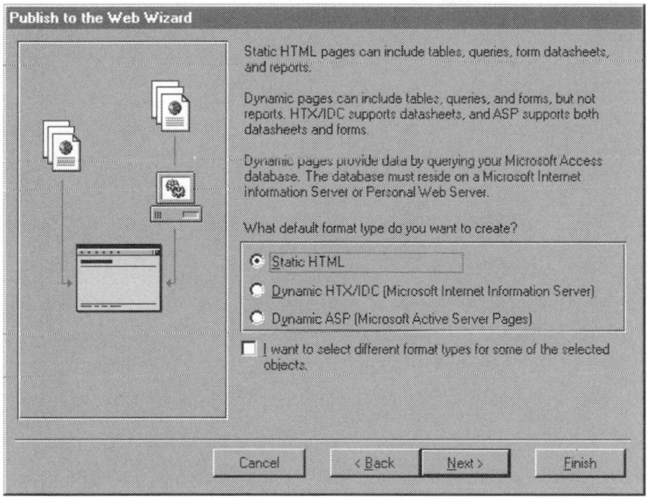

Figure 11-9

Selecting an HTML format (static or dynamic).

Select a directory in which Microsoft Access should store your HTML files, and click Next. Check the Yes, I Want To Create A Home Page box, and give that home page a name (Default is fine). Your Wizard window should look like the one shown in Figure 11-10. Click Next.

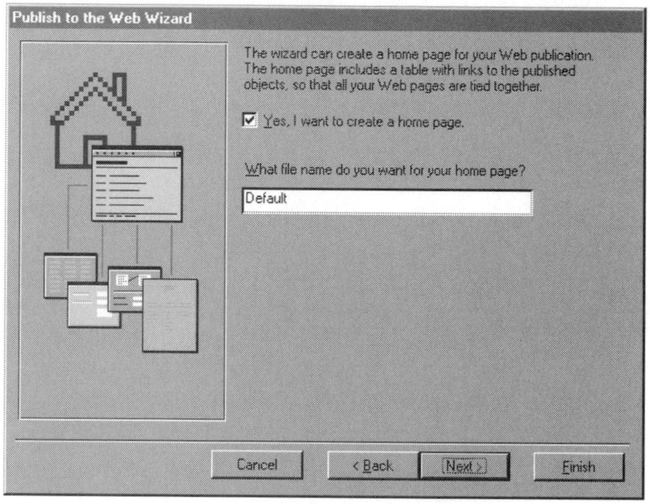

Figure 11-10

Specifying a home page in the Publish To The Web Wizard.

Finally, select the Yes option to save the profile you have just created, enter a name for the profile (for example, Northwind Export Sample), and click Finish.

Microsoft Access will prompt you for a Beginning Date and an End Date for the Sales By Year query. Enter 1/1/96 and 3/31/96 for these parameters. Remember that your exported HTML is static—only the matching records will be exported.

When Microsoft Access is done, launch Internet Explorer and use the File/Open command to open the home page you just created (for example, DEFAULT.HTML). Try roaming around the different pages and see what you think. Look at the Alphabetical List Of Products. Notice the exploration tools (First, Next) you get for free.

Microsoft Access does a pretty good job of creating static Web pages. You might have treated a few elements differently—logos, titles, and so on. We'll show you how to do this type of fine-tuning later in the chapter by using HTML templates.

Publishing static pages through code

To export your Microsoft Access tables, forms, queries, and reports as static HTML, you must use the OutputTo method of the DoCmd object. This method will export only one entire component at a time—there is no VBA equivalent to the Publish To The Web Wizard or the Export Selection Only option.

The OutputTo method is a VBA equivalent of the OutputTo action found in Microsoft Access macros. Here is the syntax for OutputTo:

```
DoCmd.OutputTo ObjectType[, ObjectName][, OutputFormat] _
    [, OutputFile][, AutoStart][, TemplateFile]
```

The easiest way to learn the correct syntax is to look at the macro arguments and descriptions when building your statement.

For the OutputFormat argument, you will want to use "HTML (*.HTML)" to create static HTML pages. The following statement exports the Alphabetical List Of Products report as a series of HTML files. Note that you specify only a single file—Microsoft Access will automatically create one HTML file per report page.

```
DoCmd.OutputTo ObjectType:=acOutputReport, _
    ObjectName:="Alphabetical List of Products", _
    OutputFormat:="HTML (*.HTML)", _
    OutputFile:="c:\temp\Alphabetical List of Products.HTM", _
    AutoStart:=True, TemplateFile:=""
```

If you want to send your static HTML file as an attachment in an e-mail message, use the SendObject method of the DoCmd object. The following example exports the Northwind Traders Employees table and places it as an HTML attachment in an e-mail message. Because we don't specify a recipient, this statement will create an e-mail message and leave you to fill in the blanks and send the message.

```
DoCmd.SendObject ObjectType:=acSendTable, ObjectName:="Employees", _
    OutputFormat:="HTML (*.HTML)", _
    Subject:="Northwind Employee List", _
    MessageText:="For your approval..."
```

Figure 11-11 shows how your e-mail message box will look in Microsoft Outlook with the HTML Employees table attachment that we specified in the above code.

11 CHAPTER

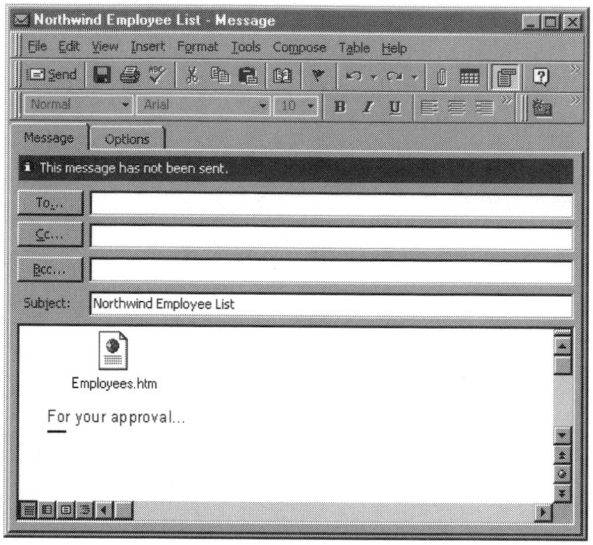

Figure 11-11

Sending an HTML table via e-mail.

Publishing Dynamic Web Pages

In the previous section, we exported a portion of the Northwind Traders sample application as static HTML. This was fine for an example, but let's think again about the Sales By Year query. Remember that we had to enter a beginning date and an ending date before we could export the data. Wouldn't it be great if the exported HTML page could also prompt for this information?

The Microsoft Access Publish To The Web Wizard will do all of this and more. We can use the same command we used to produce a static HTML

Publish To The Web Wizard

When you want to create a report in Microsoft Access, it is likely that you'll use the Report Wizard to get started. Then you'll probably need to go back and modify the finished report. You can expect the same from the Publish To The Web Wizard. The Wizard will guide you through the process of exporting your database to Web format. However, you'll probably need to go into the exported files and do some fine-tuning. We'll do some of this later in the chapter when we build our sample intranet site.

version of a table to create an intricate web of forms, queries, and tables that cross the client/server line. It will produce HTML pages that prompt the user for information and retrieve the most recent data from Microsoft Access, all without any code on your part.

With dynamic HTML pages, you get two advantages: interaction with the data and accuracy.

Dynamic Web formats

Microsoft Access 97 can export to two different dynamic Web formats, .HTX/.IDC and .ASP. We will discuss these options in more detail later in this book, so for now, here is just an overview.

The .HTX/.IDC format   HTX/.IDC is a term for the two file formats used with the Internet Database Connector (IDC). The IDC is a library that comes with the Microsoft Internet Information Server (IIS) that handles communications between the intranet/Internet server and back-end data-bases. From your browser, you request an .IDC file instead of an HTML file (for example, http://www.samplesite.com/getrec.IDC?Name=Ken). This .IDC file contains information about the data being requested. It lists the ODBC data source name, user name, and password; the SQL statement to execute, which can include parameters; and the location of the corresponding .HTX file.

When you request an .IDC file, the corresponding SQL statement is executed and the results are merged with the .HTX file. The .HTX file is another text file, an HTML template. It contains placeholders for the data (like merge fields in a Word document) and other formatting information that is used to create your dynamic Web page. Once the data and the .HTX files are merged, the results are sent back to the user and displayed in the browser. If you view the source HTML on the client, there are no traces of the .HTX or .IDC files.

The .ASP format   The file format .ASP (Active Server Pages) is the file format for the ActiveX Server Framework (ASF). The ASF is an extension for the IIS 3.0, which allows you to do server-side scripting. ASF is the server-side equivalent of Visual Basic, Scripting Edition (VBScript). VBScript is a client-side scripting language that has limited power by design. It needs to be able to automate necessary tasks without having the ability to damage a user's machine. ASF is a server-side scripting language that is much more powerful than VBScript. It can access components anywhere on the server machine, create objects, access data, and so on. Because ASF does not affect the client machine, there is no need to limit its power.

11
CHAPTER

Microsoft Access–generated .ASP files use ActiveX Data Objects (ADO)—a data access technique similar to Remote Data Objects—to communicate with back-end databases. The .ASP files can do more than just run a query. They can iterate through the records, create conditional formatting, and take full control over the resulting Web page. Once the script has finished processing, the results are returned to the user and displayed in the browser. If you view the source HTML on the client, there are no traces of the .ASP file.

Choosing a dynamic format (HTX/IDC vs. ASP) So, which technique should you use when outputting your Microsoft Access objects? First, make sure that both the Internet Database Connector (IDC) and ActiveX Server Framework (ASF) are installed on your IIS machine. IDC ships with IIS 1.0, 2.0, and 3.0. ASF ships with IIS 3.0 only.

If you have both IDC and ASF installed, then ASF is the way to go. It can support Microsoft Access forms. If you export a Microsoft Access form using HTX/IDC, you will just get a table. If you use ASP, you get an HTML form that mimics your Microsoft Access form, complete with exploration controls and editing capabilities. Second, ASP files use a much more robust scripting language. A single file supports the creation of objects and VBScript code. In the future, expect ASP to replace HTX/IDC.

NOTE .HTX/.IDC and .ASP files are just text files. If you understand Visual Basic and HTML, you'll be able to read through any of these files and make sense of them. You should start by opening sample .IDC, .HTX, and .ASP files in a text editor.

General rules for exporting dynamic HTML pages

When you want to create dynamic Web pages, you can use either the Save As/Export command to export a single component or the Publish To The Web Wizard to export multiple components at the same time. Either way, you'll have to supply the same information, such as ODBC connection information. In this section we'll be doing all of our examples using the Save As/Export command. We'll be doing a more involved example of the Publish To The Web Wizard when we continue building our sample intranet site at the end of this chapter.

TIP It's a good idea to move your database to a server and make a system DSN for it before you begin exporting dynamic Web pages. This topic is discussed later in this chapter.

When you enter an .IDC or .ASP file as your URL in Internet Explorer, you don't want the browser to display the text file, you want it to execute. Therefore, you must place these files in a directory that has been set up to handle this need. Issues such as this are all part of setting up a proper directory structure in IIS.

Exporting to .HTX/.IDC To export your table, form (in Datasheet view), or query to .HTX/.IDC format, select the component and choose the Save As/Export command from the File menu (or the right mouse button short-cut menu). Select the External File Or Database option, click OK, and then select "Microsoft IIS 1-2 (*.htx;*.idc)" from the Save As Type list. In Figure 11-12 you'll see the Save Query 'Sales By Year' As dialog box. Pick a name and location on your local machine, and click the Export button.

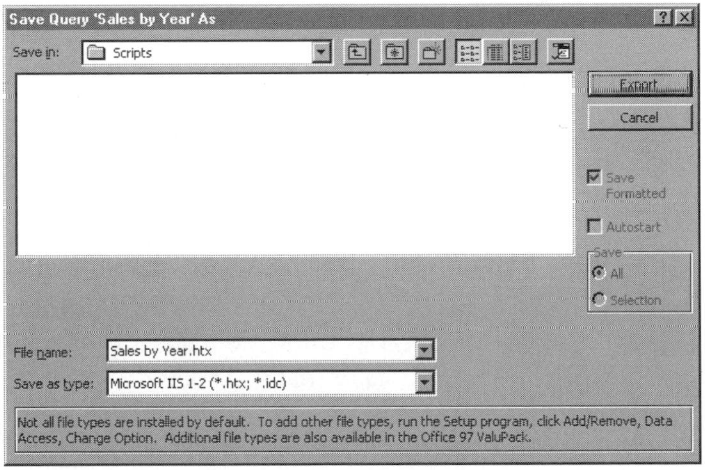

Figure 11-12

Exporting a file to HTX/IDC format.

You cannot export .HTX/.IDC files directly to your Web server using HTTP. You must save them locally and then copy the files to your server.

In the HTX/IDC Output Options dialog box, you can specify an HTML template along with the ODBC data source, user ID, and password that will be used *on the server* to connect to your back-end database. (See Figure 11-13.) It's important to remember that the ODBC data source must be set up on the server machine, either by using IIS's remote administrative tools or by way of the control panel on the IIS machine.

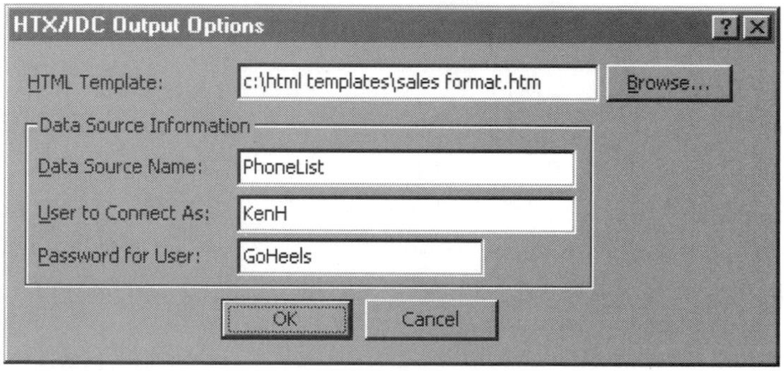

HTX/IDC Output Options

HTML Template: c:\html templates\sales format.htm   Browse...

Data Source Information

Data Source Name: PhoneList

User to Connect As: KenH

Password for User: GoHeels

OK   Cancel

Figure 11-13

Output options for HTX/IDC files.

Microsoft Access will then create both an .HTX and .IDC file of the same name in the directory you specified. If your query or form requires parameters, Microsoft Access will also create an .HTM file for entering values for your parameters. You can then move or copy these files to the appropriate location on your server. Remember that these files refer to each other. The .HTM file refers to the .IDC file, which refers to the .HTX file. They are expected to be in the same directory and with the same name. You might find that you need to change these filenames or that you want to put all of your scripts in a separate directory. If this is the case, you will have to go back and edit the exported .HTM and/or .IDC files to reflect your changes.

Exporting to .ASP   To export your table, form, or query to .ASP format, you select the component and choose the Save As/Export command from the File menu or from the shortcut menu you get by clicking your right mouse button on the object. Select the External File Or Database option, click OK, and then select "Microsoft Active Server Pages (*.asp)" from the Save As Type list. Pick a name and location on your local machine, and click the Export button.

You cannot export .ASP files directly to your Web server using HTTP. You must save them locally and then copy the files to your server. However, you can export these pages directly if you have set up the system DSN and use regular file copy instead of Web protocols.

In the Microsoft Active Server Pages Output Options dialog box, you can specify an HTML template, the ODBC data source, user ID, and password that will be used *on the server* to connect to your back-end database, the URL where the .ASP file will reside on the server, and the number of minutes a session should wait before timing out. (See Figure 11-14.) Note that specifying the URL has no effect when exporting a single component.

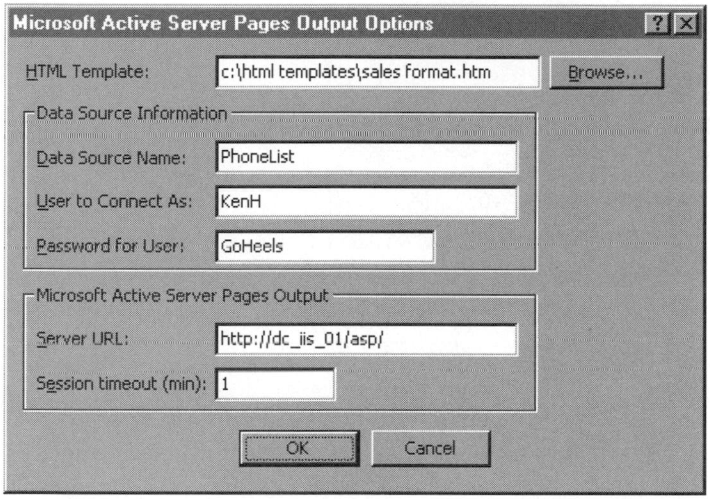

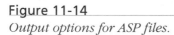

Figure 11-14
Output options for ASP files.

Microsoft Access will then create an .ASP file in the local directory you specified. If your query or form requires parameters, Microsoft Access will create a separate .HTM file for entering values for those parameters. You can then move or copy these files to the appropriate location on your server. Remember that this location must be set up to handle .ASP files.

CHAPTER
11

NOTE
You can set the defaults for the HTML template, ODBC connection information, and so on by using the Options command on the Tools menu and selecting the Hyperlinks/HTML tab, as shown here:

Tables

When you talk about exporting a table as a dynamic HTML page, you are really talking about exporting a query. Let's clear up any confusion by doing an example. If you want to export the Shippers table, you can export it either statically or dynamically. Exporting it statically would take a snapshot of the data and save it as HTML code. Exporting it dynamically saves a query that says "Select * From Shippers". This is dynamic because each time you run the query, you get the latest results.

Using .HTX/.IDC and .ASP will produce the same results. However, if you export to .ASP format, you automatically have the option of adding a filter later. Let's say you exported the Shippers table to both .HTX/.IDC and .ASP and copied them to http://Intra_Svr/Sample/. To use .HTX/.IDC, you would enter an address of http://Intra_Svr/Sample/Shippers.IDC. This would select everything from the Shippers table and display it in an HTML table.

To use .ASP, you would enter an address of http://Intra_Svr/Sample/Shippers.ASP to select everything from the table; or you could filter the selection by adding "?Param='Company Name'&Data='Speedy Express'" to the end of the address. The syntax is ...ASP?Param=*fieldname*&Data=*criteria*.

Queries

When exporting queries from your Microsoft Access database, you get different results depending on whether or not your query takes parameters. If it does not, your results will be identical to those you get when exporting a table.

If your query does take parameters, Microsoft Access will prompt you to enter values for those parameters when it exports the query. You can leave the parameters blank because they are ignored when creating dynamic Web pages. Microsoft Access will automatically create an .HTM page that will allow you to enter parameter values in the future. The .HTM page created by exporting to .HTX/.IDC will be identical in appearance to the one created by exporting to .ASP. Behind the scenes, the code in the .HTM files is different, since the files make calls to different server-side scripts.

To get a feel for exporting a query with parameters, try exporting the Sales By Year query from the Northwind Traders sample file to either .HTX/ .IDC or .ASP format. Take a look at the Sales By Year.HTM file that gets produced. Figure 11-15 shows the Sales By Year HTML page, generated by Microsoft Access, running in Internet Explorer.

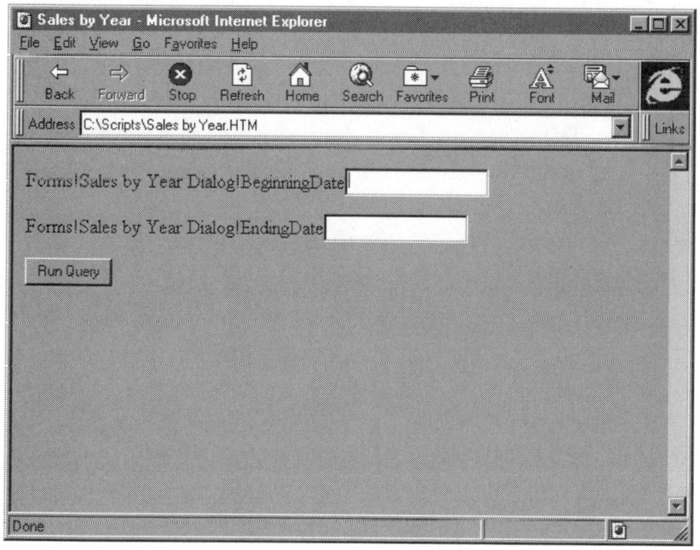

Figure 11-15

Dynamic HTML page generated by Microsoft Access.

11 CHAPTER

Use the Parameters command on the Query menu to define all the parameters in your query. If you do not do this, Microsoft Access will export your parameters with surrounding brackets, which will not work in HTML.

Forms

When exporting forms as dynamic Web pages, the format you choose plays a huge role. The results will look just like the Datasheet view of the form. If the form requires parameters, an .HTM front end will be created automatically. The process for exporting your form as .HTX/.IDC is identical to that for exporting a query.

If you choose the .ASP format, you have a choice of exporting the form as a Datasheet or as a Web form. If the form you are exporting is currently in Datasheet view or if its Default View property is Datasheet, Microsoft Access will export it as a Datasheet. In all other cases, Microsoft Access will export your form as a Web form.

If you choose to export your form in Datasheet view, the process will be identical to that for exporting a query. If you export your form as a Web form, Microsoft Access will try to create a Web form with the same look and feel as your Microsoft Access form, including the same layout, exploration controls, and so on. It will do this by using ActiveX controls and setting their properties. Microsoft Access accomplishes this by creating two .ASP files: one that contains the form definition and one that contains the data access components. The files refer to each other, so if you rename them you have to edit the files.

Here are some details about how Microsoft Access handles the translation from Microsoft Access Form to HTML Form:

- All forms are exported as single forms.
- All VBA code in the form is ignored.
- When data is exported, its data formatting (currency, commas, and so forth) is ignored.
- For hyperlinks, command buttons and labels that have their HyperlinkAddress and/or HyperlinkSubAddress properties set will be exported with the links intact. Text boxes containing data-bound hyperlinks will display the text of the link, but the link cannot be followed.
- Rectangles, lines, page breaks, object frames, tab controls, image controls, and the Picture property of a form are not supported.

For an example of exporting a form to .ASP, try the Customers form in the Northwind Traders sample database. Figures 11-16 and 11-17 show the Customers form as it appears in Microsoft Access and Internet Explorer.

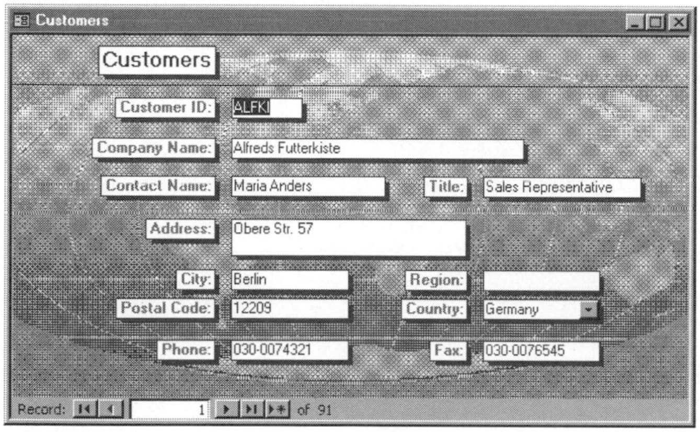

Figure 11-16
Customers form in Microsoft Access.

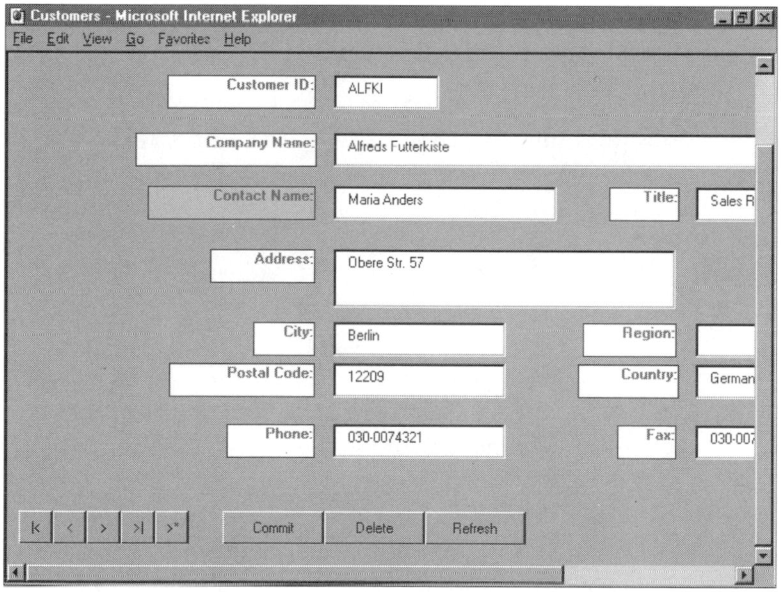

Figure 11-17
Customers form in Internet Explorer.

Reports

Reports cannot be generated dynamically in either .HTX/.IDC or .ASP. This might be because .HTX/.IDC and .ASP are used to generate single HTML files. Reports generate one HTML file per report page. If you must have a dynamic report, you might consider creating a query that simulates the look of your report and exporting it as a dynamic Web page. Your other option is to use code to run the desired report and export it to HTML on demand.

Publishing dynamic pages through code

To export your Microsoft Access tables, forms, and queries as dynamic HTML files, you use the same process that you used for exporting static HTML files. The syntax is DoCmd.OutputTo (or use the OutputTo action in a macro). The two acceptable OutputFormat options for dynamic Web pages are acFormatIIS and acFormatASP. Here is an example of exporting a Microsoft Access form to .ASP format:

```
DoCmd.OutputTo ObjectType:=acOutputForm, _
    ObjectName:="Customers", _
    OutputFormat:=acFormatASP, _
    OutputFile:="C:\temp\customers.ASP", _
    TemplateFile:=""
```

NOTE Unlike static Web pages, there is no way to send .IDC or .ASP files as e-mail attachments with the SendObject method. This is because .IDC and .ASP files must be on the server in order to run. If you want to distribute these pages, you should really be sending a shortcut to the server-side file.

Using a Predefined Template

Now that we have discussed exporting tables, queries, forms, and reports as Web pages, let's get into some design issues. You might have noticed some inconsistencies between the format Microsoft Access uses when creating Web pages and the formats you use for the rest of your intranet documents. For example, you might want to add a logo, contact information, background images, and so on. You can accomplish all of this fine-tuning using HTML templates.

An HTML template starts off as an HTML file that you create using Microsoft FrontPage or other editor of choice. Your page would contain all of the common components that you want to include in your exported pages. If you want all of your pages to have the same style, your template should include a reference to the appropriate cascading style sheet.

In terms of layout, you'll probably want certain design elements to appear before the data and others to appear after it. The question you're probably asking is, "How is Microsoft Access going to merge the data with my HTML template?" The answer is by using special HTML tags that only Microsoft Access recognizes. They act as placeholders, just as merge fields do in Microsoft Word. When Microsoft Access merges data with your HTML template, it replaces the placeholders with the corresponding data. Here is a list of those HTML placeholders and the data that replaces them:

HTML Placeholder	Replacement
<!--AccessTemplate_Title-->	Name of the exported object
<!--AccessTemplate_FirstPage-->	URL of the first page of a report
<!--AccessTemplate_PreviousPage-->	URL of the previous page of a report
<!--AccessTemplate_NextPage-->	URL of the next page of a report
<!--AccessTemplate_LastPage-->	URL of the last page of a report
<!--AccessTemplate_PageNumber-->	Current page number within a report

As you can see, most of these tags refer to exploring within a report. This is very helpful, since reports can include many HTML files, one for each page of the report. If you do not select an HTML template when exporting your report, Microsoft Access will automatically create standard text hyperlinks for First, Last, Next, and Previous pages. By using these tags in a custom template, you can mimic or enhance Access's hyperlinks. For example, you can include images instead of text for exploration hyperlinks. The body of the report will be inserted between the HTML tags <BODY> and </BODY>.

Here are some other notes to keep in mind when using Microsoft Access–specific HTML placeholder tags in a custom template:

- You can use each tag only once in a template. Any additional instances of the tag will be ignored.

- The tags relating to reports will produce either a URL address or a pound sign (#) if the tag is not applicable. For example, the tag <!--Microsoft AccessTemplate_FirstPage--> will be replaced with a # when you are on the first HTML page of a report.

- To use the report-related tags in hyperlinks, use syntax such as the following:

```
<A HREF="<!--Microsoft AccessTemplate_FirstPage-->">
First</A>
```

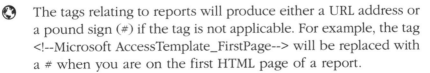

CHAPTER 11

If you want, you can substitute a graphic or other object for the text "First."

🌐 Your entire report will be exported to HTML, including any report headers and footers and the like. Use the headers and footers to include information such as the number of pages in the report (something for which there is no HTML placeholder).

🌐 Unfortunately, the report-related tags are replaced with values even if you are exporting a table, query, or form. In these cases, the page number will be 1 and the other tags will be filled with the pound sign. For this reason, you will probably want to have different templates for different Microsoft Access components (or at least a separate template for your reports).

The following template uses a style sheet, background image, logos, and custom exploration tools to give an exported report a completely different look.

```
<HTML>
<HEAD><TITLE><!--AccessTemplate_Title--></TITLE>
<LINK REL="STYLESHEET" TYPE="text/css" HREF="mma.css">
</HEAD>

<IMG ALIGN=LEFT SRC="pulsemma.gif">
<IMG ALIGN=RIGHT SRC="pulsemma.gif">
<CENTER><H1>Micro Modeling Associates - For Internal Use Only</H1>
</CENTER>
<P><BR><BR><CENTER><IMG SRC="waveline.gif"></CENTER></P>
<BODY BACKGROUND="brick.gif">
</BODY>
<P><CENTER><IMG SRC="waveline.gif"></CENTER></P>
<CENTER>
<A HREF = "<!--AccessTemplate_FirstPage-->">
<IMG SRC="first.bmp"></A>
<A HREF = "<!--AccessTemplate_PreviousPage-->">
<IMG SRC="prev.bmp"></A>
<A HREF = "<!--AccessTemplate_NextPage-->">
<IMG SRC="next.bmp"></A>
<A HREF = "<!--AccessTemplate_LastPage-->">
<IMG SRC="last.bmp"></A>
<P><B>Page <!--AccessTemplate_PageNumber--></B></CENTER></P>
<I>For further information, contact the
<A HREF = "mailto:webmaster@micromodeling.com">webmaster</A></I>
</HTML>
```

A report exported using this template will look like the one shown in Figure 11-18.

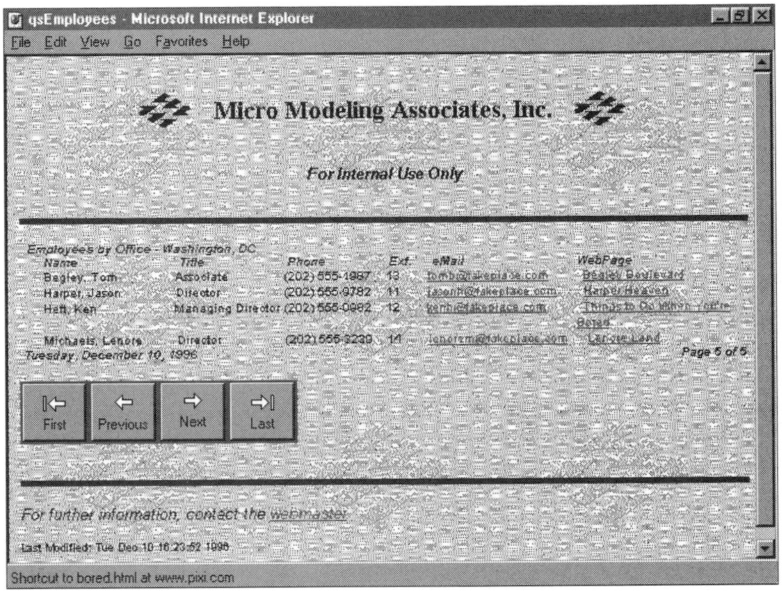

Figure 11-18

HTML report created with a template.

Troubleshooting

In theory, publishing your Microsoft Access database to the Web should be very straightforward. You just pick the elements you want to export, pick static or dynamic, click a few buttons, and you're done. Don't expect to be

Changing the HTML Table Properties

Unfortunately, templates and style sheets have no effect on the HTML table that Microsoft Access creates when exporting your data. This style is determined by the properties of your Datasheet. Using the Format menu, you can change the background color, font, border color, and other attributes of the Datasheet. Microsoft Access will then try to keep these attributes when it exports your data to HTML. However, there is no way to change the background color of the exported table to clear. This leads to your other option, going into an HTML editor and changing the table properties after the file is exported. The tag that you are looking for is <TABLE BGCOLOR=...>, which should be toward the top of the HTML page. Remove the BGCOLOR= argument and you will have a clear table. You can take similar steps for the table borders.

11 CHAPTER

quite that lucky when trying a real-life example! You have to think of the wizards as a starting point. It's no different than the Microsoft Access Report Wizard or Form Wizard. You use the wizards to give you ideas and to eliminate a lot of the tedious work. But you're going to have to make some changes to the exported files. In this section you'll see a few of the quirks that you have to fix when publishing your database. This is by no means a complete listing!

HTML table formatting

When you export your table, query, and/or form, Microsoft Access automatically creates a table. The table will probably have gray borders and a white background. The easiest way to change this is to manually edit the HTML table's BGCOLOR, BORDER, and/or BORDERCOLOR.

Parameter queries

If you try to export a Microsoft Access query that includes parameters, you will have problems unless you define every parameter that your query uses. The problems will be in the form of .HTM, .ASP, and/or .IDC files, where field names are surrounded by brackets. To fix the problem, return to your Microsoft Access query and use the Parameters command on the Query menu to define your parameters.

Using wildcards in criteria

If your Microsoft Access query includes an expression such as "Like 'H*'", you will have problems if you export it using .HTX/.IDC or .ASP. The reason is that the * wildcard is specific to Microsoft Access and the Microsoft Jet engine. If your .IDC or .ASP file is using the Like expression, you must edit the file and change the * to %. This is straightforward in an .IDC file but gets a little tricky if your exported file is an .ASP file, because the % sign has a different meaning. To include a literal percentage sign, you must use two percentage signs in ASP. In ASP, your change would look like this:

Before:

```
Like 'H*'
```

After:

```
Like 'H%%'
```

Exporting hyperlinks

If your table, query, form, or report includes data coming from a hyperlink field, keep in mind the following points:

 When you enter hyperlink addresses manually (in the format displayname#address#subaddress), make sure you always include two pound (#) signs, even if you leave one or more sections blank. If you don't include two pound signs, you'll have problems when you export.

- You cannot use the HyperlinkPart function when exporting to a dynamic Web page. If your query uses the HyperlinkPart function, this function will cause errors when you export it to HTX/IDC or ASP. This is because HyperlinkPart is a Microsoft Access–specific function and is not available in standard SQL.

- A side effect of not having the HyperlinkPart function is that there is no way to export hyperlinks to a dynamic Web page. If your table, query, or form includes hyperlink data, it will export as standard text when you publish it to HTX/IDC or ASP. The text will appear blue and underlined, but it will not be a hyperlink. Not only will it export as text, but you will see the entire field. This means that the Web Page column might look like "Microsoft#http://www.microsoft.com#". There is no way to select only the display name.

Reports

When you export a report to static HTML (your only Web option), Microsoft Access creates what appears to be a single table containing your report data. However, if you look at the HTML, you will see that each row of the report is actually its own table. Although this is good for formatting, you will find that editing these reports in HTML can be quite challenging.

Internet Replication

A powerful feature of Microsoft Access is the ability to keep multiple copies of a database synchronized. For example, imagine that your corporate sales data is stored on your network. Several salespeople in your office need to access and update the data in that database. However, a lot of the updates need to be made on laptops, unconnected to the network. How do the different salespeople keep their data in synch while they are all making independent changes offline?

Using replication, these salespeople can each store a local "replica" of the original "design master" database. When they make changes offline, they can synchronize their replica with the design master the next time they come to the office. Microsoft Access will update the data stored on the master and also send any structural changes back to the replica. This is a simple view of replication, but the general idea is what's important for this discussion.

CHAPTER 11

Because the Internet is really just another network, it makes sense that in Microsoft Access 97 you can now synchronize replicas and design servers across the Internet. This means that a salesperson traveling across the country doesn't ever have to come back to the office to update the corporate database—he or she can just connect via the Internet. For more information about synchronizing databases over the Internet, look up Replication in the Microsoft Access online Help.

Building Your Intranet

In continuing to build the Micro Modeling sample intranet site, we are going to use Microsoft Access 97 to create a supercharged intranet phone list. This phone list is going to include utilities to view the employee list in a variety of ways, as well as the ability to add new employees. Figure 11-19 shows a list of all Micro Modeling employees in Washington, D.C.

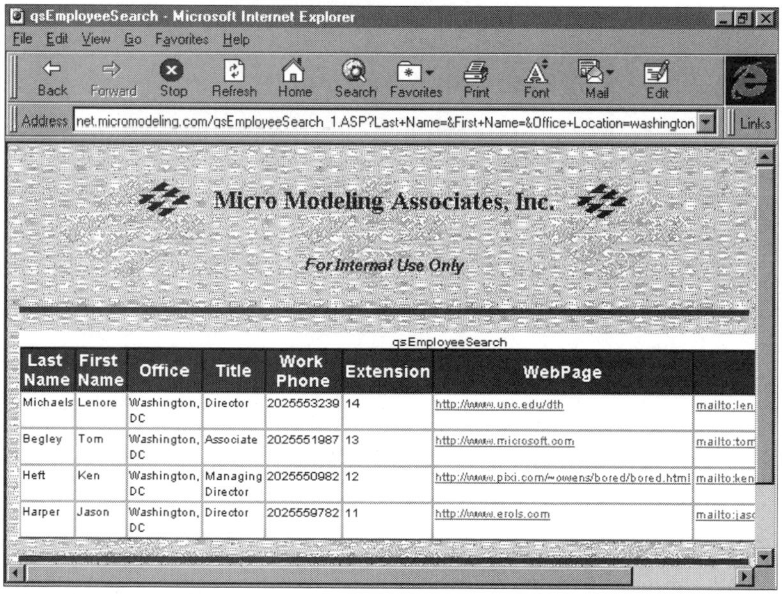

Figure 11-19

Micro Modeling employees in Washington, D.C.

In order to run the PHONLIST.MDB and NORTHWIND.MDB examples described in this chapter (and contained in the Chapter11 folder on the companion CD), you must first establish two ODBC DSNs: PhoneList and nwind. See the README.TXT file on the CD for details on establishing a DSN.

Creating the Database

This demonstration uses the Microsoft Access 97 database PHONLIST.MDB (found on the companion CD). This database stores information about Micro Modeling's employees. It includes everything from name and office to e-mail address and a picture. The data is normalized and stored in three tables: Employees, Offices, and Titles.

Tables

The Employees table is the main table in the database. It stores name, phone number, and several other informational fields. It includes two hyperlink fields, e-mail and Web page. The e-mail addresses take the following form: heftk@micromodeling.com#mailto:heftk@micromodeling.com#.

This way, the display name leaves out the "mailto", which is unnecessary on the screen but necessary when actually following the hyperlink. Notice the # at the end of the hyperlink. This is essential for a clean export to HTML.

There are also corresponding fields containing the static e-mail and Web page addresses. These fields are used to create dynamic hyperlinks in our HTML pages.

To dynamically create pictures in our HTML pages, there is a "PhotographLocation" field that includes the path to an employee's picture.

The Offices and Titles tables are lookup tables used to normalize the Employees table.

Queries

The database has five select queries. Here's a quick run through them:

 qsEmployees provides the same information as the Employees table except that it includes the names of office locations and employee titles instead of ID numbers. This is a simple select query.

- **qs5YearEmployees** retrieves the full name and number of years with the company for all employees with five years or more of service. This is a simple select query with hard-coded criteria.

- **qsEmployeeCount** totals the number of employees for each of Micro Modeling's office locations. This is a simple select query with grouping.

- **qsEmployeeOffice** retrieves information for all the employees in a specified office location. This is a parameter query that uses the Like expression to let you specify as much of the office location as you know. (For example, "Chi" will return employees in the Chicago office.)

- **qsEmployeeSearch** retrieves information for employees who match the criteria you enter. You can specify as much as you know about first name, last name, and/or office location. This is a parameter query that uses the Like expression for three different parameters.

Forms

There are three forms, which are used to view and edit information in the three tables. Coincidentally, they are named Employees, Offices, and Titles.

Report

There is only one report, Employees. This report displays all of MMA's employees, grouped by office, one office per page.

Creating the Template

When you publish your database to the Web, you want the entire Web site to have the same look and feel. To accomplish this, Microsoft Access lets you use an HTML template that will be merged with data to create formatted pages. For this example, we are going to use two different templates: one to be used with Microsoft Access reports (MMARPT.HTM) and one to be used with tables, queries, and forms (MMASTD.HTM). The templates are identical except that the one for reports includes exploration buttons for maneuvering between the different pages of the report.

The templates include some Microsoft Access–specific HTML tags that are used to merge the data and also include a reference to an HTML style sheet. Here is some sample code and output from the standard template:

```
<html>

<head>
<title><!--Microsoft AccessTemplate_Title--></title>
<link rel="STYLESHEET" type="text/css" href="mmastyle.css">
<meta name="FORMATTER" content="Microsoft FrontPage 1.1">
</head>

<body BACKGROUND="MMABKg.jpg" width=800 BGCOLOR="#A0C0C0">
```

Figure 11-20 shows how this standard template looks.

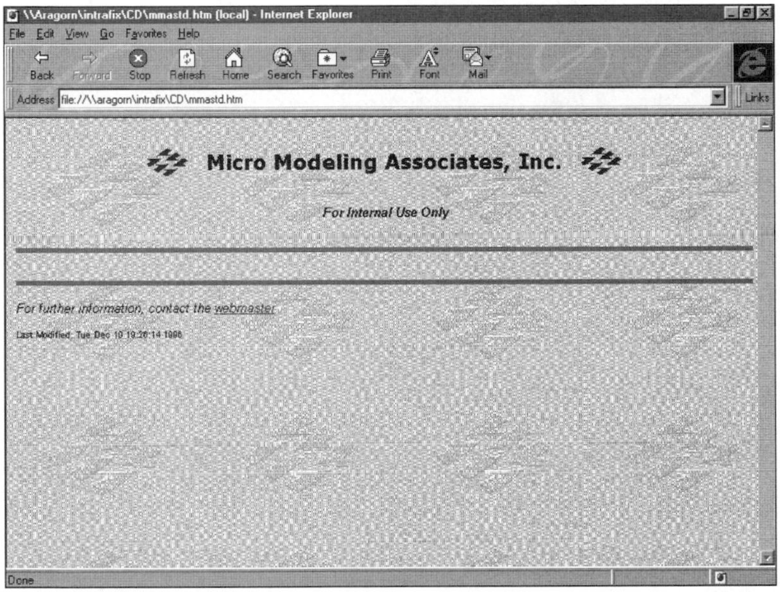

Figure 11-20

Standard HTML Template for MMA.

Exporting the Database to the Web

To export the database to the Web, you have two options—you can move the database to your intranet server now or move the exported files later. If you have access to the server machine and the machine has Microsoft Access 97 installed, it will be easier to move the database first.

To export the database, follow these steps:

1. Select the Save As HTML command from the File menu while the Phone List database is open. This will launch the Publish To The

Web Wizard. Read through the instructions in the first window, and then click the Next button.

2. The next window will prompt you to select which database components you want to publish to the Web. Select the Offices and Titles tables, all of the queries, the Employees form, and the Employees report before clicking the Next button.

3. The next window prompts you to select an HTML template. Make sure the I Want To Select Different Templates For Some Of The Selected Objects check box is checked, and then click Next.

4. Select all of the tables, queries, and forms. Then click the Browse button and find the standard HTML template (MMASTD.HTM). Select the report, assign the report template (MMARPT.HTM) to it. Your window should look like the figure below. Click Next.

Publish to the Web Wizard

Select one or more objects from the list and then browse to find the HTML document you want to use as a template.

Object	HTML template to use
Table: Offices	C:\Templates\mmastd.htm
Table: Titles	C:\Templates\mmastd.htm
Query: qs5YearEmployees	C:\Templates\mmastd.htm
Query: qsEmployeeCount	C:\Templates\mmastd.htm
Query: qsEmployeeOffice	C:\Templates\mmastd.htm
Query: qsEmployees	C:\Templates\mmastd.htm
Query: qsEmployeeSearch	C:\Templates\mmastd.htm
Form: Employees	C:\Templates\mmastd.htm
Report: Employees	C:\Templates\mmarpt.htm

Cancel   < Back   Next >   Finish

5. The next window asks you to choose a format type. When choosing between HTML format types, make sure the I Want To Select Different Format Types For Some Of The Selected Objects check box is checked, and then click Next.

6. We want to use each of the different format types: static HTML, HTX/IDC, and ASP. Generally, you would choose only static HTML if your data were not going to change or if speed is an important issue. You would choose only HTX/IDC if you were running an older version of IIS. However, for this example, we

want to use all three format types. Use the following picture as a guideline to picking format types, and then click Next.

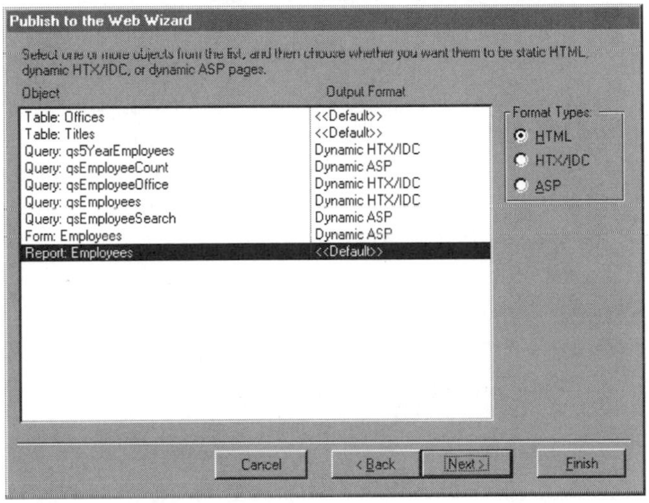

7. On the next window, specify the requested information about your intranet server, including the name of the data source that exists on the server. The Server URL should be the location on the server where you plan on saving the exported files, as shown here:

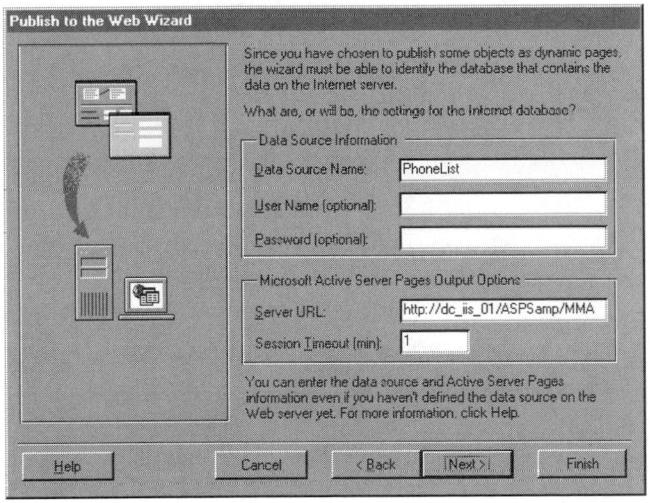

8. Click Next to select a location where you want to store the exported files locally. Note that unless you are currently on the server machine, you cannot save the files directly to the intranet server.

CHAPTER
11

9. Click Next, make sure the Yes, I Want To Create a Home Page check box is selected, and specify a name for your home page (for example, Default).

10. Click Next to get to the final page, where you can save your profile for the future.

11. Click the Finish button to have Microsoft Access publish your database to the Web. You will get several prompts along the way, as Microsoft Access asks you for parameter values. Just click OK through all of these dialog boxes, because these parameter values will not be saved in the exported files.

Making It Work

The exported Web pages will not work just yet. If you did not run the Publish To The Web Wizard on your server, the first thing you need to do is copy the exported files to your server. Make sure your directory is set up to handle HTML, HTX/IDC, and ASP files (it should be marked as Execute and Read). Also double-check that you have a data source created on the server and that it is pointing to the correct database. Finally, make certain that you copy over any extraneous files, such as style sheets and bitmaps used by your HTML template. For this sample application, you'll need the following support files:

- **FIRST.BMP, LAST.BMP, NEXT.BMP, PREV.BMP.** Exploration button graphics
- **MMASTYLE.CSS.** MMA's cascading style sheet
- **MMABKG.JPG.** Background graphic
- **PULSEMMA.GIF.** Animated GIF file with the MMA logo

Now give it a try by opening Internet Explorer and pointing to the Default.HTM home page that you placed on your intranet server. You should see the Web page shown in Figure 11-21.

Try clicking the different objects and see what happens. You should find that most of the tables, queries, forms, and reports work as-is. They look pretty good, too. However, a few objects don't work as advertised, specifically qsEmployeeOffice and qsEmployeeSearch. Clicking these objects will bring you to an HTML form that lets you enter parameter values. When you then click the Run Query button, Internet Explorer will return an error message, indicating that there is a problem with the "LIKE predicate."

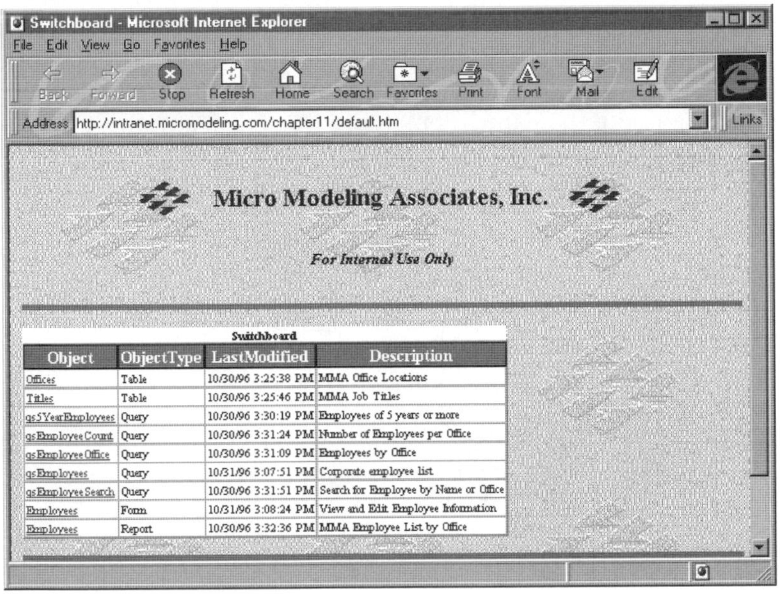

Figure 11-21

Default switchboard created by the Publish To The Web Wizard.

These queries need to be modified because they are parameter queries that use the Like expression. Furthermore, qsEmployeeSearch needs to be modified so that the query runs each time you refresh the Web page, a feature that doesn't come automatically with wizard-generated pages.

qsEmployeeOffice

In the qsEmployeeOffice query, you need to change the exported files so that they properly create an SQL statement using the Like expression. In Microsoft Access, the query contains the expression "Like [Office Location] & "*". Unfortunately, the meaning gets lost in the export and is translated as "Like '%Office Location%' & '%%'". This is fairly close but needs a minor adjustment. In the file QSEMPLOYEEOFFICE_1.IDC, you need to make the following change by editing the file in a text editor such as Notepad.

Before:

```
+WHERE (((Offices.Office) Like '%Office Location%' & '%%'))
```

%Office Location% gets the incoming "Office Location" parameter.
%% is how you create a literal percentage sign (%).
If "Chicago" were passed, the expression would be "Like 'Chicago%'".

After:

```
+WHERE (((Offices.Office) Like '%Office Location%%'))
```

If "Chicago" were passed, the expression would be "Like 'Chicago%'".

qsEmployeeSearch

The qsEmployeeSearch query has three parameters, each using the Like expression. In theory, the fix is identical to the one you just performed in qsEmployeeOffice. However, this query uses an ASP file instead of IDC. You need to make the following changes to QSEMPLOYEESEARCH_1.ASP to clean up the problems resulting from the use of wildcard characters. They are all found within the "sql=" expression that defines the SQL statement:

Before:

```
Like '" & Request.QueryString("Last Name") & "' & '*')
Like '" & Request.QueryString("First Name") & "' & '*')
Like '" & Request.QueryString("Office Location") & "' & '*')
```

After:

```
Like '" & Request.QueryString("LastName") & "%%')
Like '" & Request.QueryString("FirstName") & "%%')
Like '" & Request.QueryString("OfficeLocation") & "%%')
```

Another problem with the file QSEMPLOYEESEARCH_1.ASP is that it checks for a current Internet Explorer session before rerunning the query. This is fine for a standard query, where the data shouldn't change during the course of a session. But in this situation it means that if you use the Back button to enter new parameters and then hit Run Query again, the results will not be updated. Therefore, we need to remove this session-checking code.

Before:

```
<%
Session.timeout = 1
If IsObject(Session("PhoneList_conn")) Then
    Set conn = Session("PhoneList_conn")
Else
    Set conn = Server.CreateObject("ADODB.Connection")
    conn.open "PhoneList","",""
    Session("PhoneList_conn") = conn
End If
%>
<%
If IsObject(Session("qsEmployeeSearch_rs")) And
    Not (cstr(Param) <> "" And cstr(Data) <> "") Then
    Set rs = Session("qsEmployeeSearch_rs")
```

```
Else
    sql=...
End If
%>
```

After:

```
<%
    Session.timeout=1
    Set conn = Server.CreateObject("ADODB.Connection")
    conn.open "PhoneList","",""
    Set Session("PhoneList_conn") = conn
    sql=...
%>
```

Making It Look Nice

After these few changes, our Web site is now working smoothly. In this next section, we are going to make a few changes to clean up the application and make it look a little bit nicer.

qsEmployees

When you view the results of the qsEmployees query, you will notice that the Web page link and e-mail link fields come back as static text, not as hyperlinks. This is because the results are generated dynamically by an IDC file. If we want the resulting hyperlinks to be live, we need to take an extra step and add the hyperlink information to the QSEMPLOYEES_1.HTX file.

The fields eMail and WebPage contain the text of the URL addresses to which we want to hyperlink. So what we want to do is to surround that text with the "<A>" tag, which creates a hyperlink. The syntax for a link is "<A HREF=*URL address*>". We can get the URL by referring to the fields using the syntax recognized by the HTX file. For example, placing "<%eMail%>" inside an HTX file will translate to the current value of the eMail field. Putting it all together, the following code will display the current e-mail address as a live hyperlink:

```
<a href=<%eMail%>><%eMail%></a>
```

Here is the step-by-step code for creating live hyperlinks in the eMail and WebPage fields:

Before:

```
<TD BORDERCOLOR=#c0c0c0 ><FONT SIZE=2 FACE="Arial"
COLOR=#000000><%eMail%><BR></FONT></TD>
<TD BORDERCOLOR=#c0c0c0 ><FONT SIZE=2 FACE="Arial"
COLOR=#000000><%WebPage%><BR></FONT></TD>
```

11 CHAPTER

After:

```
<TD BORDERCOLOR=#c0c0c0 ><FONT SIZE=2 FACE="Arial" COLOR=#000000>
<a href=<%eMail%>><%eMail%></a><BR></FONT></TD>
<TD BORDERCOLOR=#c0c0c0 ><FONT SIZE=2 FACE="Arial" COLOR=#000000>
<a href=<%WebPage%>><%WebPage%></a><BR></FONT></TD>
```

The qsEmployees query returns information about all of the employees in MMA worldwide. But this query contains a lot of extraneous information. We can strip out the last three columns, photograph location, Web page link, and e-mail link to make a better looking table. Instead of redesigning the Microsoft Access query, let's do it directly in the IDC and HTX files.

QSEMPLOYEES_1.IDC   Here is the code for IDC files:

Before:

```
SQLStatement:SELECT [LastName] & ', ' & [FirstName] AS Name,
Titles.Title, Employees.Phone, Employees.Extension,
Employees.DateHired, Offices.Office, Employees.eMail,
Employees.WebPage, Employees.PhotographLocation,
Employees.WebPageLink, Employees.eMailLink
```

After:

```
SQLStatement:SELECT [LastName] & ', ' & [FirstName] AS Name,
Titles.Title, Employees.Phone, Employees.Extension,
Employees.DateHired, Offices.Office, Employees.eMail,
Employees.WebPage
```

QSEMPLOYEES_1.HTX   Here is the code for HTX files:

Remove the following lines from the Table Header definition:

```
<TH BGCOLOR=#c0c0c0 BORDERCOLOR=#000000 ><FONT SIZE=2 FACE="Arial"
COLOR=#000000>PhotographLocation</FONT></TH>
<TH BGCOLOR=#c0c0c0 BORDERCOLOR=#000000 ><FONT SIZE=2 FACE="Arial"
COLOR=#000000>WebPageLink</FONT></TH>
<TH BGCOLOR=#c0c0c0 BORDERCOLOR=#000000 ><FONT SIZE=2 FACE="Arial"
COLOR=#000000>eMailLink</FONT></TH>
```

Remove the following lines from the Table Definition:

```
<TD BORDERCOLOR=#c0c0c0 ><FONT SIZE=2 FACE="Arial"
COLOR=#000000><%PhotographLocation%><BR></FONT></TD>
<TD BORDERCOLOR=#c0c0c0 ><U><FONT SIZE=2 FACE="Arial"
COLOR=#0000ff><%WebPageLink%><BR></FONT></U></TD>
<TD BORDERCOLOR=#c0c0c0 ><U><FONT SIZE=2 FACE="Arial"
COLOR=#0000ff><%eMailLink%><BR></FONT></U></TD>
```

qsEmployeeSearch

The qsEmployeeSearch query has the same problem that the qsEmployees query had: the e-mail address and Web page fields are coming back as static text. To correct the situation, we are going to use the same technique of adding a hyperlink in code. The difference is that the qsEmployeeSearch query uses an ASP file instead of an HTX file, so the syntax is slightly different. The following example shows how you get the value of the WebPage field in an HTX file and in an ASP file.

HTX:

```
<%WebPage%>
```

ASP:

```
<%=rs.Fields("WebPage").Value%>
```

So to convert the Web page field to a hyperlink, you would use the following syntax:

```
<A HREF=<%=rs.Fields("WebPage").Value%>>
<%=Server.HTMLEncode(rs.Fields("WebPage").Value)%>
</a>
```

Here are the changes that need to be made to the file QSEMPLOYEESEARCH_1.ASP:

Before:

```
<TD BORDERCOLOR=#c0c0c0 ><FONT SIZE=2 FACE="Arial"
COLOR=#000000><%=Server.HTMLEncode(rs.Fields("WebPage").Value)%><BR>
</FONT></TD>
<TD BORDERCOLOR=#c0c0c0 ><FONT SIZE=2 FACE="Arial"
COLOR=#000000><%=Server.HTMLEncode(rs.Fields("eMail").Value)%><BR>
</FONT></TD>
```

After:

```
<TD BORDERCOLOR=#c0c0c0 ><FONT SIZE=2 FACE="Arial" COLOR=#000000>
<A HREF=<%=rs.Fields("WebPage").Value%>>
<%=Server.HTMLEncode(rs.Fields("WebPage").Value)%></a><BR>
</FONT></TD>
<TD BORDERCOLOR=#c0c0c0 ><FONT SIZE=2 FACE="Arial" COLOR=#000000>
<A HREF=<%=rs.Fields("eMail").Value%>>
<%=Server.HTMLEncode(rs.Fields("eMail").Value)%></A><BR>
</FONT></TD>
```

From here, you can continue making changes to colors, border styles, and so on. You can add more graphics, use a frame layout, or whatever you want. Microsoft Access 97 takes care of the hard part, providing the tools for dynamic data access via HTML.

CHAPTER 12

Creating Web Slide Shows with Microsoft PowerPoint 97

Donna Jensen

As a developer, you might be less familiar with Microsoft PowerPoint than with the other Microsoft Office applications, probably because the previous versions of the product had very limited programmability. PowerPoint 97, now fully automatable, is a wonderful tool for creating both paper-based and on-screen presentations. PowerPoint presentations are obvious aids for face-to-face meetings, but they are also useful and interesting ways for offering information on your intranet in an animated multimedia format.

Microsoft PowerPoint 97 brings a lot of new features into play—features that run the gamut from fancy graphic animations to the Visual Basic for Applications (VBA) programming language. Although the new features reside in such different facets of the application, many of them represent a move in one general direction: helping you create PowerPoint presentations that interact dynamically with the users viewing them.

In this chapter we'll look at many of those new features and the things you'll need to know as you use them to create your intranet. Here are some of the topics we'll cover:

- The different formats you can use for presenting slide shows online and the ramifications of choosing one format over another

- PowerPoint's new multimedia and animation features that make presentations more interactive

- Aspects of creating and working with hyperlinks that are unique to PowerPoint

- PowerPoint VBA and its uses for creating intranet shows

Finally, we'll put many of the features together and build MMA's Mission Statement for our company intranet. The completed Mission Statement, part of which is shown in Figure 12-1, includes such PowerPoint features as animated charts, Action Buttons, and an animated template. The MMA Mission Statement is in the PowerPoint presentation MISSION.PPS in the Chapter12 folder on this book's companion CD.

Figure 12-1

MMA's Mission Statement presented in a PowerPoint presentation.

Posting Online Presentations

As a PowerPoint intranet developer, you have a choice of four formats for posting a presentation online:

🌐 Post it as a PowerPoint slide show. The slide show file type is new in PowerPoint 97. Presentations you save as slide shows will still be PowerPoint files, but they'll have a .PPS extension. What's special about this type of file is that it will open—whether in PowerPoint or in Microsoft Internet Explorer—as a running slide show. Your presentation's online audience doesn't have to do anything to start the show running. The slide show will be completely functional, since it is, after all, a real PowerPoint slide show. Keep in mind that when opened in Internet Explorer, the .PPS file will open and run the slide show inside Internet Explorer's window, not in PowerPoint's traditional full-screen display.

🌐 Post it as a PowerPoint presentation file, that is, a "regular" PowerPoint file with a .PPT extension. These PowerPoint files open in Internet Explorer in slide show mode inside Internet Explorer's window. There's no major reason to take this approach, but if you want to post a PowerPoint file online for others to view and then download and work on in PowerPoint, Internet Explorer will certainly let you do so—and it will retain all the file's functionality and formatting.

🌐 Run the presentation through PowerPoint's Save As HTML Wizard and post the resulting HTML files.

🌐 Run the presentation through the Save As HTML Wizard and generate a PowerPoint animation for posting to your intranet. The animation file (another new file type, with a .PPZ extension) is essentially a movie of your slide show. Your audience doesn't need to have PowerPoint or the PowerPoint viewer to run it, but they do need to have the PowerPoint Animation Player—a free Internet browser extension available on the Microsoft Web site at http://www.microsoft.com/powerpoint/internet/player/—installed.

In this chapter we'll go into the details involved in each option. We'll also explore the relationship between PowerPoint and HTML. But first we'll focus on techniques for posting your PowerPoint files online without converting them to HTML.

CHAPTER 12

Getting Started with Microsoft PowerPoint

Don't be nervous about using PowerPoint, even if you're a novice at preparing presentations or have not worked with PowerPoint before. PowerPoint ships with tools to help users who haven't composed presentations or who are unfamiliar with PowerPoint to get started quickly.

PowerPoint's Templates for Online Viewing

The most powerful of the tools is the AutoContent Wizard, which makes it possible for users with virtually no PowerPoint skills to create intranet-ready presentations.

Building intranet presentations with the AutoContent Wizard

The AutoContent Wizard takes users in an organized, step-by-step fashion through the process of designing an intranet presentation, inserting standard boilerplate information, and formatting the file appropriately for intranet viewing. You can launch the wizard by choosing New from the File menu and then selecting AutoContent Wizard on the Presentations tab.

Ready-made online presentations

PowerPoint also ships with online versions of its presentation templates that have basic exploration buttons built in. Like the AutoContent Wizard, they're under the Presentations tab in the New Presentation dialog box, as shown in Figure 12-2.

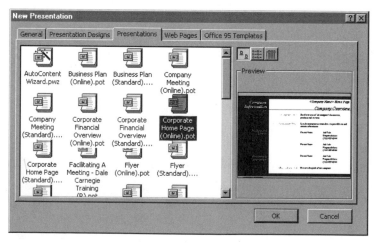

Figure 12-2

Presentation templates available from the New Presentation dialog box.

PowerPoint templates come in both online and standard formats. The online versions have preformatted graphic buttons with navigational Action Settings already defined.

You can save presentations as HTML or post them as PowerPoint presentation or slide show files. On an intranet, where you can guarantee that your audience has either PowerPoint or the PowerPoint viewer installed, it's best to post the online presentations as a presentation or slide show (that is, in PowerPoint's .PPT or .PPS formats). They'll have the best appearance and their exploration buttons won't be redundant with the buttons the Save As HTML Wizard creates (see the "Saving as HTML" section later in the chapter for information on this wizard).

NOTE PowerPoint's template set also includes ten new templates that contain animated graphics. We used one called high voltage, located on the Presentation Designs tab of the New Presentation dialog box, for our Mission Statement on our intranet.

Action Settings

In PowerPoint, Action Settings are events you can apply to objects and text on your slides. Hyperlinks are a type of Action Setting; that is, a hyperlink jump is one kind of activity triggered by a mouse move or a mouse click on a graphic or text object. To set the Action Settings for an object, select the object, and then select Action Settings on the Slide Show menu to open the Action Settings dialog box. (See Figure 12-3.) In the sample shown in Figure 12-3, the hyperlink will go to the last slide in the presentation and accompany the jump with an applause sound byte. Other Action Settings include running a program or macro and playing a sound.

Action Buttons

PowerPoint's new Action Buttons give users more power to drive the presentation themselves. The buttons are three-dimensional and resemble traditional Microsoft Windows toolbar buttons. You can use Action Buttons, available on the Slide Show menu, by placing them on a slide and associating Action Settings with them.

ActiveX Controls

You can add ActiveX controls to your slides and VBA routines to automate them. As do the other Office 97 applications, PowerPoint comes with the ActiveX Control Toolbox, which makes it easy to create and use the controls.

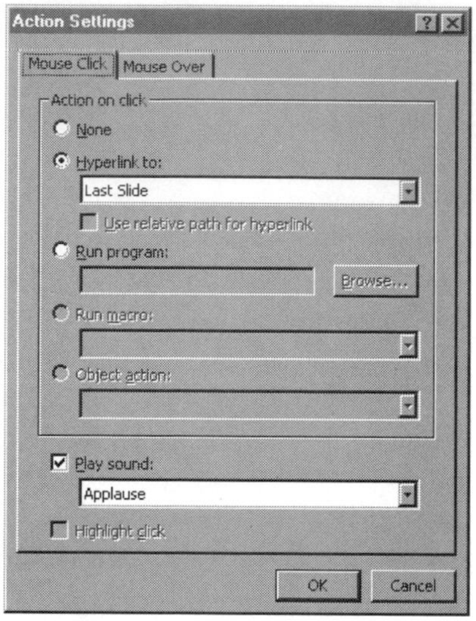

Figure 12-3

Mouse Click tab on the Action Settings dialog box.

When deciding whether to use ActiveX controls in a presentation you're preparing for your intranet, bear in mind that the controls will display and function perfectly in Internet Explorer when they're placed in presentations and slide shows (.PPT and .PPS files that are posted to your intranet), but they won't survive your presentation's conversion to HTML, and they won't be included in a PowerPoint animation file.

Posting PowerPoint Files on Your Intranet

You can save your presentation as a slide show so that the show will immediately start running when users open the presentation. To save your presentation as a slide show, select Save As from the File menu, and then choose PowerPoint Show (*.PPS) from the Save As Type list. PowerPoint will save the presentation with a .PPS extension.

In some ways, the slide show is the optimal PowerPoint online mode, since all your Action Settings, animations, multimedia effects, and VBA routines will function and your users won't have to trigger the show manually. You, as the show's designer, can also still work on the file—adding and changing text and graphics just as you would a .PPT presentation file. The slide show doesn't become inert, as it will when you save it as an animation, or

.PPZ, file. (See the section "Saving as a PowerPoint Animation" later in the chapter for information on animation files.)

Maximizing a Minimal Display

Remember, though, that your slide show file won't open in a full-screen display. Instead, it will open inside Internet Explorer's window. Here are a couple tricks you can use to spruce up the appearance of your slide show:

 Change the dimensions of your slides. The Internet Explorer window space is about twice as wide as it is high, so an extra long landscape slide will fill up the window space more evenly.

 Use a slide layout with a black background. That way, only you will know when a slide's space ends and Internet Explorer's window space begins.

Your intranet users can also use the option under Internet Explorer's Browse menu to switch the show to full-screen display. When we were planning our intranet, we wanted our show to be viewed in full-screen display. So our first slide just prompts the viewer to choose Full Screen from the Browse menu. The Mission Statement proper begins with the second slide.

If you're going to take the approach we did, it doesn't matter whether you post your online presentation in .PPT or .PPS format. Either choice will do. But we decided to post our file as a slide show (.PPS format) so that users who download it and run it in PowerPoint will initially see it in its slide-show view mode.

Setting Up a Slide Show, Part 1

When you're planning your show, you'll also need to think about PowerPoint's setup options and their role in your show's appearance and behavior.

PowerPoint's native viewing options

You can set your slide show to run in one of three basic view modes in PowerPoint:

 Speaker mode (Presented By A Speaker), the traditional full-screen look with PowerPoint's standard exploration controls in the lower left corner of the screen.

 Window or **Browse mode** (Browsed By An Individual), which runs the show inside an application window—whether the application is PowerPoint or Internet Explorer—and adds a Browse menu to the application's menu bar. The Browse menu contains

12 CHAPTER

exploration commands and shortcut keys that help users who are unfamiliar with PowerPoint's standard controls to run the show.

🌐 **Kiosk mode** (Browsed At A Kiosk), which hides PowerPoint's standard exploration controls and runs the show in full-screen view with *only* the show's Action Buttons and Action Settings available. (This means that users won't be able to move through the show using PowerPoint's traditional mouse-clicking, page-up/page-down, and spacebar methods; the show will loop continuously unless the user exits it.)

Choose a view mode in the Set Up Show dialog box under the Slide Show menu. The dialog box, which is shown in Figure 12-4, also lets you specify whether to run the show with or without narrations and animation, to run all or only some of the presentation's slides, and to set the default method by which slides are advanced—either manually or by using timings.

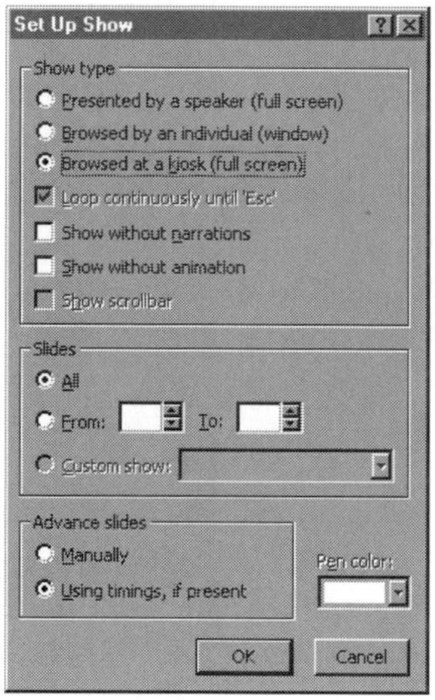

Figure 12-4

Designating Kiosk mode in the Set Up Show dialog box.

PowerPoint viewed through Internet Explorer

In all three PowerPoint viewing modes, all of PowerPoint's Action Settings, Action Buttons, VBA routines, animations, and multimedia effects are fully functional. But when you view the file in Internet Explorer, you should be aware of a few wrinkles:

🌐 Even though Speaker mode and Kiosk mode will run the show in full-screen view in PowerPoint, in Internet Explorer all three view modes will launch the show within Internet Explorer's window and display the Browse menu. In other words, regardless of the display mode you've saved your .PPT or .PPS file in, in Internet Explorer the show will initially run in the Window or Browse display mode.

Adding Comments to Online Presentations

The new Comments feature is in some ways PowerPoint's own version of collaborative editing: users can add comment notes to a presentation within PowerPoint as they view it, and other users can then see those notes and add their own notes to them.

PowerPoint has a new Reviewing toolbar, which pops open whenever a user adds a comment. Using the toolbar, users can choose to view the presentation with or without the comments.

The comment notes are flexible and easily handle many "commentators." You can toggle the comments' visibility or customize their appearance using all the colors and callout shapes available in Office Art. Figure 12-5 shows an example of a comment added to a presentation via the Reviewing toolbar.

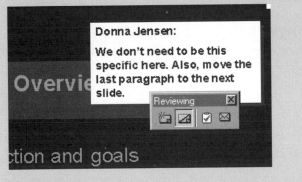

Figure 12-5
Comment added to a PowerPoint presentation via the Reviewing toolbar.

CHAPTER 12

Once in Window or Browse mode, however, your audience will see an option to run the show full screen. Here's where your users will see a difference between files you've saved in Speaker versus Kiosk mode. In Speaker mode, PowerPoint's traditional exploration controls will appear in the lower-left corner of the slide:

In Kiosk mode, the exploration controls won't appear; the only way the user can move through the show is via PowerPoint's Action Buttons—which you, the developer, must program in advance.

Finally, and most important, much of your decision about which display mode to use boils down to the role you want mouse-clicking to play in the show. This issue is closely bound up with PowerPoint's Action Settings, so we'll take it up again later in the chapter (in the "Setting Up a Slide Show, Part 2" section), after you've had a grounding in the basics of Action Buttons and Action Settings.

Converting Presentations to HTML

PowerPoint presentations work well with HTML. You can convert presentations into HTML files very easily, and you'll find that PowerPoint can accommodate a variety of formats and levels of information you might want to retain after the conversion. For example, you can have your converted presentation display in HTML frames, and you can choose whether to include any notes that accompany the presentation in the set of HTML files that PowerPoint generates.

Saving as HTML

When you save your presentation in HTML format, PowerPoint launches the Save As HTML Wizard to step you through the process. The Wizard records all your preferences for the HTML files.

You have the option of using a framed layout style, which will show your slide's headings in an outline down the left side of the screen.

You can choose graphics formats for saving graphics—.GIF, .JPG, or PowerPoint animation. You can also set the sizing and resolution for the graphics.

420

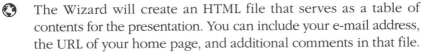

The Wizard will create an HTML file that serves as a table of contents for the presentation. You can include your e-mail address, the URL of your home page, and additional comments in that file.

The Wizard will add browser buttons to the HTML pages. You'll have the option of defaulting to the browser's colors or creating custom colors.

The Wizard will create a folder with all of the files that make up your presentation and prompt you to choose the location of that folder.

Finally, if you want, you can name and save all the options you've chosen in the Wizard so that you can apply them to other presentations you convert.

The conversion will preserve all of your presentation's Action Settings and hyperlinks. If any of your graphics are animated, choose PowerPoint Animation as your graphic format and, assuming that your users have Power-Point Animation Player installed, Internet Explorer will faithfully reproduce your animations. If the users do not have PowerPoint Animation Player installed, they will be prompted to download it from Microsoft's Web site.

If you edit a PowerPoint presentation while the presentation is open in Internet Explorer, your changes won't take effect until you've closed and restarted Internet Explorer.

How PowerPoint Handles the Conversion

PowerPoint creates an HTML presentation out of your PowerPoint file by generating several files for each slide, which it stores in the folder you specified in the wizard. Each slide itself becomes a numbered graphic file. The first slide image becomes IMG001.GIF (or IMG001.JPG if you've chosen that graphic format), and the succeeding slides increment up from there. The exploration buttons you specified in the wizard go into the folder as graphic files; for example, the Forward button becomes NEXT.GIF. PowerPoint also generates a text-only HTML file for each slide, which contains no images or exploration buttons. The text-only version of your first slide is stored in your folder as TSLD001.HTM. Finally, PowerPoint creates a text-only table of contents for the show, which it names INDEX.HTM.

Regardless of which options you choose in the wizard, PowerPoint will create all of those files and use the same nomenclature for the filenames. But the theme has a few variations.

CHAPTER 12

Standard layouts

If you have chosen the standard layout, PowerPoint won't display the presentation with frames. It generates HTML pages out of the exploration buttons and the slide .GIF or .JPG images. PowerPoint uses the same incremental numbering system for those files. The HTML file that displays IMG001.GIF and the exploration buttons is saved as SLD001.HTM, and so on. You can use either INDEX.HTM or SLD001.HTM as your presentation's starting page.

Framed layouts

If you've chosen a framed layout, the file architecture is somewhat different. PowerPoint still generates a graphic image and a text-only HTML file for each slide. But it does not compose graphic HTML files out of exploration buttons and images; instead the graphic HTML pages contain just the graphic slide images. They are named IMG001.HTM, and so forth. Figure 12-6 shows a sample result of saving your presentation as HTML and employing the framed layout view option.

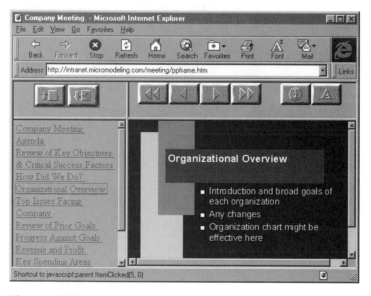

Figure 12-6

A PowerPoint framed layout HTML page viewed in Internet Explorer.

One of the files created for framed screen layout is PPFRAME.HTM. That's the file you should specify as your startup page. The exploration buttons (top right frame) exist in the NAVBTN.HTM file, and the buttons (top left frame) to expand or condense the heading outline display are in the SIZEBTN.HTM file. The heading outline frame will display either

OUTLINEC.HTM or OUTLINEE.HTM, depending on the user's button choice in SIZEBTN.HTM.

Saving as a PowerPoint Animation

When you save your presentation as HTML and choose PowerPoint Animation as your graphic type, PowerPoint will generate the various .GIF, .JPG, and HTML files based on your selections in the Wizard. It will also add an animation file with a .PPZ extension. The file is named PRES0.PPZ by default, but you can rename it. (If you do, however, you'll have to edit references to it in the source text of your HTML files that include it.)

Including notes

If you've elected to include slide notes in the converted presentation, PowerPoint will generate notes HTML pages and add them to your folder. Each slide will have its own notes HTML file, and they too are named incrementally—NOTE001.HTM and so on.

> **TIP**
>
> If you select the Download Original Presentation option in the HTML Wizard, PowerPoint will place a copy of your presentation (that is, the .PPT file) in the folder along with your HTML and .GIF files. It's a handy way to keep an archived copy of your source presentation.

The PowerPoint Animation Player

When you save your presentation in PowerPoint Animation format, PowerPoint will create a single self-contained animation file out of your presentation. The animation file is almost fully functional—all your Action Settings, Action Buttons, and hyperlinks will still work, and so will your custom-animated graphics and charts. The only things you'll lose are ActiveX controls and VBA routines that had been stored in your presentation file. Always keep in mind that PowerPoint will convert your *whole* presentation to one animation file.

You have several options for exploiting your animation file.

 You can save an entire slide show as a single animation file and post it online. That's the easiest way to use and distribute the file.

 You can save just one slide or just one animated graphic image as your PowerPoint animation file. Then you can include the animation in a presentation you post online in native PowerPoint (.PPT) or PowerPoint slide show (.PPS) format.

 Alternatively, you can embed the animation file into an HTML file—regardless of what application created the HTML file. That way, users can view the animation automatically when they link to the HTML page in Internet Explorer, or they can trigger it with a click on a button on the HTML page.

> **NOTE**
>
> Your PowerPoint animation file will always display inside Internet Explorer's window, even if the PowerPoint file from which you created it was set for full-screen viewing.

Importing HTML Text

Remember the old days, when PowerPoint touted its ability to import Word outlines as the building blocks of new presentations? The idea was that much of the time PowerPoint presentations were created from information that started out in a Word document. With PowerPoint 97, you can exploit the information in HTML files to build your presentation in the same way you used to take advantage of Word information. On top of that, if you've used PowerPoint's outline-importing feature before, you'll notice that in PowerPoint 97 it's significantly smarter, more effective, and easier to use.

Animated Banners

PowerPoint ships with animated banners you can experiment with and use on your own Web site. They're located in the New Presentations dialog box under the Web Pages tab, and they're intended for users who want to create animated objects to use as headings in their HTML files. If you save one of the banners as HTML and choose PowerPoint Animation as your graphic type, PowerPoint will build a .PPZ file out of the banner and embed it in an HTML file. Then you can use any HTML source editing utility to add text or other graphics to the page.

The animation file is an embedded object in HTML source and is tagged in this general format:

```
<OBJECT CLASSID="clsid:EFBD14F0-6BFB-11CF-9177-00805F8813FF"
WIDTH=640 HEIGHT=480>
<PARAM NAME="File" VALUE="pres0.ppz">
<EMBED WIDTH=640 HEIGHT=480 SRC="pres0.ppz"> </EMBED>
</OBJECT>
```

If you have an existing HTML page and want to embed the .PPZ file in it, you can do so, but you'll have to type in the tag yourself.

When you open an HTML file within PowerPoint, PowerPoint creates a new presentation file and parses the text into multiple slides. PowerPoint retains all text formatting and treats each paragraph from the HTML file as the title of a slide. As soon as you open the file, PowerPoint switches to Outline view, in which you can demote the paragraphs that shouldn't be titles. PowerPoint will also retain any hyperlinks in the file. Figure 12-7 shows a section of MMA's Employee Newsletter, EMPNEWS.HTM (located in the Chapter9 folder on the companion CD), in PowerPoint. When you demote slide titles, such as the selected paragraphs in the picture, they become text within the preceding slide.

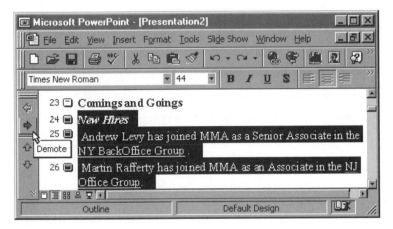

Figure 12-7

Select the slides to be demoted in Outline view.

Using Graphics and Multimedia Features

PowerPoint 97 has dramatically expanded the kinds of sound and motion effects you can add to slides. In addition to sound and video files, you can record narrations and add custom-composed soundtracks to your presentation. You can also create sophisticated animated graphics. Let's take a look at the new and more powerful effects available in PowerPoint 97.

Animations

If you're familiar with previous versions of PowerPoint, you know about adding animated effects to text and objects. In PowerPoint 97, those effects are housed under the Slide Show menu's cascading Preset Animation menu.

You'll probably recognize many of the effects: Flying, Camera, and so on are still there. Some significant improvements have been made as well. For example, you can now apply different animations to the different text areas on your slide. And the selection of built-in animations is larger.

But the big news in animation is custom-animated graphics and animated charts.

> **NOTE**
> PowerPoint has also optimized nonanimated graphics for intranet viewing. You can now save graphics to .JPG, .WMF, .EPS, .PICT, and .GIF formats.

Custom Animations

With Custom Animations, you can build a picture out of several different objects and animate each of the objects separately. The objects can move in various ways, but you can set timings for their animation so that one object can wait for another object to finish moving before it starts its own motion. You can incorporate movie, sound, and OLE objects in your animated graphic, and you can specify how they interact with the other animated objects.

To set up the animations, insert or draw the graphics on your slide, and then select Custom Animation from the Slide Show menu. The dialog box will help you "program" each graphic's behavior.

For more details and a real-world example of a Custom Animation, see the "Building the MMA Intranet" section later in this chapter.

Animated charts

You can create custom-animated charts from virtually all of PowerPoint's available chart types. You can also incorporate them into your custom animated graphics. Insert the chart in your slide, and then open the Custom Animation dialog box, shown in Figure 12-8.

For charts, animation means the way the chart elements draw themselves on the page. For example, in the chart sample in Figure 12-8, the elements appear one at a time, each building upward from the x-axis baseline. We've chosen to have the chart's legend and grid draw themselves in a Wipe Up pattern also.

Multimedia Sound Options

In PowerPoint 97, you're still able to add sound effects, such as applause and drumrolls, to your slide shows. But you can also exploit two new features—narration and custom soundtracks—that can make your presentation more informative and livelier for users running it in your intranet.

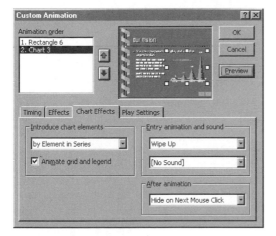

Figure 12-8

Animation settings for the cone chart in MMA's Mission Statement.

Virtual narrator

You might want to record a voice-over and keep it with your presentation when you post it online. PowerPoint saves the narration as a .WAV file so that you can attach it as you would any sound file to the presentation as a whole or to selected slides. Choose Record Narration from the Slide Show menu to choose audio quality and recording settings.

TIP

The Office 97 CD comes with an add-in that will convert your narration .WAV files to the Progressive Network RealAudio format.

Custom soundtracks

You can add customized background music to your presentation with the Custom Soundtrack add-in, available in the MusicTrk folder of the ValuPack folder on the Office or PowerPoint CD-ROM. Although you need to have this add-in installed to create the soundtrack for your presentation, the track becomes part of the slide show once you save your file, and any of the show's viewers who have a soundcard on their PCs will hear it. Figure 12-9 shows the Custom Soundtrack dialog box.

12 CHAPTER

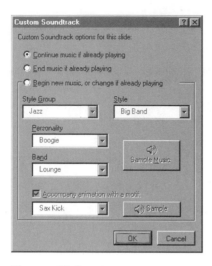

Figure 12-9

Custom Soundtrack dialog box showing settings for music that plays in MMA's Mission Statement.

After you've installed the add-in, click the Custom Soundtrack item at the bottom of the Slide Show menu. Mix elements in the lists to arrange the sound you want, and click the Sample button to hear the result. If you're choosing to continue the music from the previous slide, as is done in Figure 12-9, the style options are visible but not changeable.

The soundtrack operates on a slide-by-slide basis. You can't add it in one step to a whole presentation, and you can't apply it to a slide master. But the feature is pretty smart: if you set a soundtrack to start on slide 1, the Custom Soundtrack dialog box's default setting for slide 2 will be to continue that soundtrack. The slide-at-a-time model gives you a lot of flexibility. You can literally have a different soundtrack for every slide in your presentation.

PowerPoint will actually compose the music for you—you just specify the criteria in the Custom Soundtrack dialog box. Believe it or not, each time the presentation is viewed, PowerPoint composes a brand-new, unique soundtrack, again matching all your specifications for musical style, tempo, and instrumentation. You can also have the soundtrack perform riffs when an animation runs, and many of the soundtracks will add little wrap-up riffs when the slide show ends.

Movies and Sounds

To insert a video clip in a slide, choose one of the options from the cascading Movies And Sounds menu you'll find under the Insert menu. (See Figure 12-10.) You can select a file from the Microsoft Clip Gallery (Movie From Gallery, Sound From Gallery) or browse for a file (Movie From File, Sound From File). Office 97 ships with several movie and sound clips you can use.

Figure 12-10

Insert menu's Movies And Sounds options.

Performance Optimization

As you read about all these movie and animation features, you're probably thinking unkind thoughts about the speed at which all these features load and run in a slide show. But Microsoft has made major improvements in PowerPoint's performance:

- PowerPoint automatically compresses graphics and whole presentations. The presentations are decompressed when you open them. PowerPoint also stores .JPG files in their compressed size.

- PowerPoint now loads and saves files incrementally. In past releases, PowerPoint loaded the entire presentation into memory, then displayed the first slide. In PowerPoint 97, the first slide is displayed as soon as the first slide is loaded into memory. The result is that if you have a file with multiple slides, you will see the first slide on the screen and be able to start working in it much sooner than you could in previous releases.

- Movie support is built in, so video clips will play without any delay.

After you insert the movie or sound in your slide, you can customize its behavior with Action Settings and Custom Animations, as you would with any slide object. With movies you also have special Custom Animation options (under the Custom Animation dialog box's Play Settings tab) that dictate how the movie will interact with other animations on the slide.

Alternatively, you can insert the movie as an OLE object, by choosing Object from the Insert menu, selecting Video Clip, and then browsing for the clip you want to add. The video clip object will accept Action Settings and custom animations just as a movie object does, but your options will reflect the object's embedded OLE status. Specifically, you'll be able to do the following if you insert the movie as an OLE object:

- 🌐 You'll be able to select Play, Open, and Edit Action Settings for the object, which will launch Media Player. If you choose the Play setting, your audience will have the advantage of using Media Player's play controls to move ahead or back or to stop the movie.

- 🌐 You'll have access to Timing and Effects Custom Animation settings for the object, but you won't be able to exploit the advanced multimedia Play Settings options.

Setting Up a Slide Show, Part 2

Earlier in the chapter we talked about the three display modes your slide show can run in and the basic differences in their appearance. To recap: In Internet Explorer, whichever display mode you choose for your show—Speaker, Kiosk, or Window—the show will launch in Window mode. If the user chooses to view the show full screen, the show will switch to full-screen view and at that point run in Speaker mode (where clicking and PowerPoint's traditional exploration tools are available) or in Kiosk mode (where no clicking is available and the only way to move through the show is with Action Buttons and Action Settings).

Now we're going to focus on the final and most important aspect of your decision: the role you want mouse-clicking to play in the show. Here are the breakdowns in mouse-click response:

- 🌐 The crucial fact about Kiosk mode is that *no* mouse-clicking has any effect except mouse clicks associated with Action Settings. This means that not only will mouse-clicking on the screen not advance to the next slide (as it will in Speaker mode), but mouse-clicking on custom animations that you've set up to launch in response to mouse clicks will have no effect. Therefore, if you use Kiosk mode, you *must* set up all your custom animations to launch automatically.

🌐 If you use Window or Speaker mode, how you set the Slide Transition also affects mouse-clicking. The On Mouse Click check box in the Slide Transition dialog box, shown here, enables and disables all mouse-clicking in the show, not just clicking to advance slides:

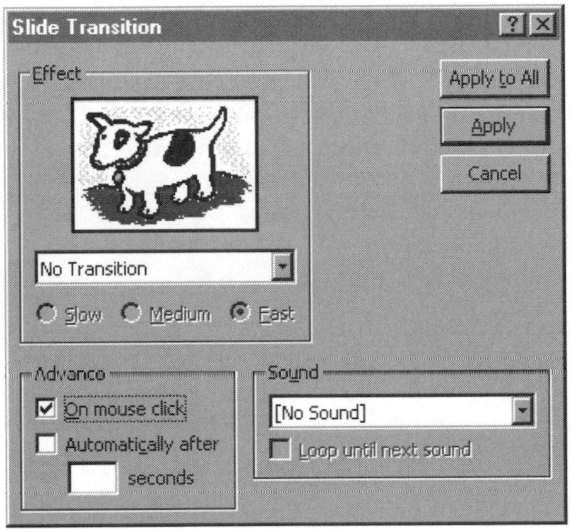

🌐 If you check the On Mouse Click check box, your slides will advance when the user clicks anywhere on the screen. So far so good. But if the slide has a Custom Animation on it—whether it's an animated graphic, movie, or chart—the click will cause the animation to run, regardless of where on the screen the user clicks.

🌐 If you uncheck the On Mouse Click check box, your slides will not advance when the user clicks anywhere on the screen. Keep in mind that your custom animations will not run from a mouse click, so you must be sure to set them to run automatically.

The bottom line is that either the mouse click has no power or it has completely indiscriminate power. For our intranet, we didn't like either option. We didn't want mouse clicks to advance our slides—we wanted to reserve that power for our Action Buttons. But we did want users to be able to click on specific hot spots in our slides and run custom animations. Our solution was to attach a VBA routine to our hot spots as an Action Setting to run the animations. (For more details, see the "Animating the Charts, Movie, and Map" section later in the chapter.)

CHAPTER 12

Working with Hyperlinks

You can create a hyperlink in PowerPoint in four ways:

- 🌐 Drag and drop from another slide or Office file
- 🌐 Use the Office Insert Hyperlink dialog box
- 🌐 Paste a selection as a hyperlink
- 🌐 Define an Action Setting for selected text or graphics

Chapter 8 covered the first three options, all of which are common features shared among PowerPoint, Word, Microsoft Excel, and Microsoft Access. In this chapter, we'll concentrate on the techniques for using PowerPoint's Action Settings to work with hyperlinks.

Hyperlinks as Action Settings

You can insert a hyperlink by assigning it as a selection's Action Setting. The result is the same as if you had used Office's Insert Hyperlink dialog box: a hyperlink to the file or location that you specify.

NOTE If you select a text area on a slide by clicking its boundary and apply a hyperlink to it, all the paragraphs in the text area will become hyperlinks.

To create a hyperlink within PowerPoint's Action Setting paradigm, select the text or object you want to format as a hyperlink. Then choose Actions Settings from the Slide Show menu.

What's intriguing about hyperlinks in PowerPoint is that any object or text on your slide can have *two* hyperlinks. You can set one hyperlink that activates when the mouse clicks on the object and another hyperlink that will be triggered when the mouse passes over the object. Use the Action Settings dialog box's two tabs—Mouse Click and Mouse Over—to set the two hyperlinks. Under either tab, click the Hyperlink To option, and then choose a destination for the link from the list. Your destination can be a specific slide, presentation, URL, or Office file. Needless to say, you don't want to use the Mouse Over Action Setting to launch major events since users can so easily and unintentionally trigger it. Some examples of appropriate uses for Mouse Over are playing a sound, flashing a highlight, or running a harmless VBA routine, such as one that does little more than display a message box.

PowerPoint will respond to your destination selection. If you select Hyperlink To a URL, for example, you'll be prompted to type in the address, as shown in Figure 12-11. If you select Hyperlink To a Slide, you'll see a list of available slides, as in Figure 12-12.

Figure 12-11

Hyperlink To URL dialog box.

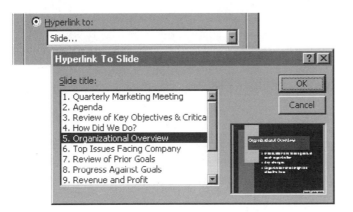

Figure 12-12

Hyperlink To Slide dialog box.

NOTE If you select a graphic object on your slide to which you want to attach a hyperlink, the Insert Hyperlink menu item will bring you to the Action Settings dialog box instead of to the Office Insert Hyperlink dialog box.

Hyperlinks on graphics

When you format a graphic object as a hyperlink, its appearance doesn't change. Instead, it prompts users by displaying the mouse pointer as a hand whenever the mouse passes over the object. You can augment the effect with an extra option in the Action Settings dialog box that's available only for

CHAPTER 12

graphic objects: Highlight Click. You can have PowerPoint highlight the object, either as the user clicks on it, or, if the Action Setting is Mouse Over, as the mouse moves over it. In addition to livening up your slides, the highlighting acts as a good visual cue for users that the object triggers an event. Keep in mind that you must select an action for the object before the highlight option is available. (The action can be any Action Setting: hyperlink, program, sound, and so on.)

TIP You can make image maps (that is, invisible hot spots) on your slides by creating shapes that have no fill and no line and then associating Action Settings with them.

Editing Hyperlinks

Because your hyperlinks are active only in Slide Show mode, editing the display text is straightforward: just type over it. Beware of deleting all of a hyperlink's text because that will also delete the hyperlink. If you want to change the hyperlink's destination or its behavior as an Action Setting, select the hyperlink and open the Insert Hyperlink or Action Settings dialog box. You can access these via the Insert and Slide Show menus, respectively, or you can position your cursor in the hyperlink, click with the right mouse button, and select Hyperlink on the shortcut menu.

Customizing a hyperlink's appearance

Your hyperlink's appearance is part of your slide's color scheme, so it will vary depending on the presentation template you choose. You won't see the standard blue and violet text colors in every presentation.

You can change the color for hyperlinks and followed hyperlinks. Select Slide Color Scheme from the Format menu, and click the Custom tab. As you'll notice in Figure 12-13, the list of colors and the screen elements they apply to contain two items that are new in PowerPoint 97: Accent And Hyperlink and Accent And Followed Hyperlink.

Select the item you want to change, and then click the Change Color button. The Office color palette opens, and from there you can choose or mix a new color.

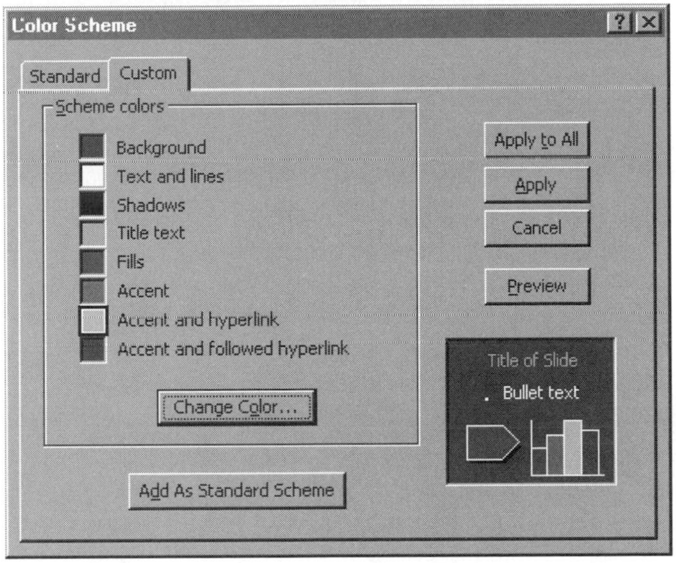

Figure 12-13

Color Scheme dialog box for working with your presentation's color scheme.

The trick to working with a hyperlink's color is to understand the scope of your changes.

- The smallest unit you can customize is the slide. If you apply a new color scheme, all hyperlinks on the slide will take on the new scheme.

- You can customize the hyperlinks for just your title slide by changing the Title Master color scheme. You can specify a different color for those hyperlinks in your non-Title slides by changing the Slide Master color scheme.

- You can change all the hyperlinks in the presentation by changing the color in a slide or a master and then clicking the Apply To All button in the Color Scheme dialog box. Your Title and non-Title slides will take on the new color, as will all new slides you add to the presentation.

- Finally, you can change future presentations by changing the presentation template. If you do change a template, you can apply its new scheme to any existing presentation based on it by choosing Apply Design from the Format menu.

435

NOTE
Inserting hyperlinks in your presentation has its advantages and disadvantages. On the up side, you don't have to work only in Slide View mode to insert your hyperlinks. You can add hyperlinks (and the full range of Action Settings, for that matter) to your slide text while you're in Outline view. On the down side, however, you can insert hyperlinks only on slides: you can't insert hyperlinks on notes pages, and you can't insert hyperlinks that jump *to* notes pages.

Action Buttons

PowerPoint's new Action Buttons give users more power to drive the presentation. The buttons are three-dimensional and resemble traditional Windows toolbar buttons. When the user clicks an Action Button, it takes on a pushed-in appearance.

You can use Action Buttons by placing them on a slide and associating Action Settings with them. To add a button, choose Action Buttons from the Slide Show menu. (As shown in Figure 12-14, the palette of buttons you'll see is a tear-off menu.) Click one of the buttons on the Action Buttons menu, and your insertion point will become a crosshair. Drag in the area of the slide where you want to position the button, and the Action Settings dialog box will open automatically to allow you to customize the button's behavior. As you move your mouse pointer over each button in the Action Buttons menu, a ToolTip will suggest a usage for the button. However, this is just a suggested usage; you can use any button to trigger any kind of action.

Figure 12-14
Action Buttons menu showing a ToolTip with a suggested use for a button.

The first Action Button on the menu is blank, and you can draw or insert your own graphic or text on it. The other buttons have common icons; when you insert one of them in your slide, the Action Settings dialog box will open with a suggested use for that button. For example, if you insert the Sound Action Button, the Action Settings dialog box will initially display with the Play Sound control checked and the Applause sound byte selected.

PowerPoint formats your Action Buttons' colors to match the color scheme of your presentation. You can change the button color by right-clicking the button and choosing Format AutoShape from the shortcut menu.

Keep in mind that those Action Buttons that use exploration icons are most handy for PowerPoint presentations and slide shows that you post online. They could be redundant in presentations you convert to HTML since the Save As HTML Wizard will automatically add exploration tools to your slides.

Running a Custom Slide Show

You can vastly increase the intelligence and responsiveness of your presentation by using custom shows, a new feature in PowerPoint 97. Create a custom show by selecting Custom Shows from the Slide Show menu and clicking New to bring up the Define Custom Show dialog box, shown in Figure 12-15. Select any specific slides from your current presentation, dictate the order in which they display, and give the show a name.

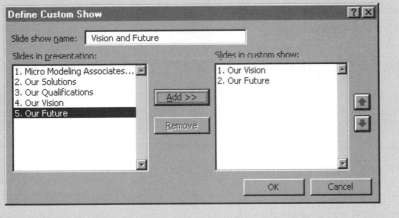

Figure 12-15
Define Custom Show dialog box.

Your custom show can skip, reorder, or repeat slides depending on users' actions as they view the presentation. For example, you can have a Skip To The End button that runs a custom show consisting of just the concluding slides in your presentation. You can launch a custom

(continued)

Running a Custom Slide Show *(continued)*

show using the Custom Show Action Settings, or you can write a PowerPoint VBA routine to specify and run custom shows. Some defined custom shows are listed in Figure 12-16.

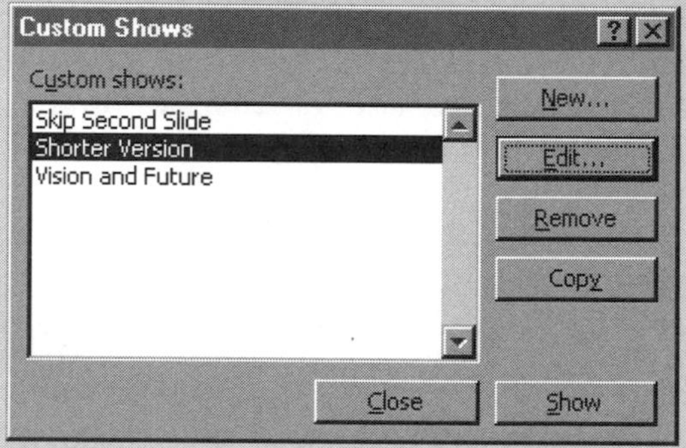

Figure 12-16

Custom Show dialog box showing defined custom shows.

The next section includes information on using VBA to define and launch custom shows.

Intranet Programming in PowerPoint

PowerPoint has grown up. The Office 97 edition is fully programmable and exploits the common Office programming language, Visual Basic for Applications (VBA). The object model is extensive. All of the standard objects that can make up a presentation are represented, and the exposed properties and methods will give you a great deal of control over them.

You can record, create, and save macros in presentations and in presentation templates. For posting presentations and slide shows on your intranet, you'll want to keep the VBA routines with the presentation itself; routines attached to a template won't run on your intranet in presentations based on the template.

In this section we'll survey those aspects of the object model you might find handiest for creating intranet content in PowerPoint.

NOTE The object model information and the VBA code examples in this chapter assume you're familiar with the general Microsoft Office 97 object model as it pertains to intranet objects. Refer to Chapter 8 for details on the Office 97 object model.

Hyperlinks Collections

In PowerPoint, the Hyperlinks collection is a property of a slide, master slide, or specified group of slides called a SlideRange. The general syntax to access the collection is

Presentation.SlideObject[Slides.Count or named slide object].Hyperlinks

For example, this routine iterates through all the slides in the active presentation, reporting the title text of each slide (notice how far down you have to drill to return the text), the number of hyperlinks in the slide, and each hyperlink's address.

```
Dim objHyperlink As Object
Dim objSlide As Object
Dim sSlidename As String
Dim nHCount As Integer
'/Loop through each slide in the presentation.
For Each objSlide In ActivePresentation.Slides
    sMsg = ""
    With objSlide
        '/Return the title text for the slide.
        sSlidename = .Shapes.Title.TextFrame.TextRange.Text
        nHCount = .Hyperlinks.Count
        '/Concatenate the addresses of the slide's hyperlinks.
        For Each objHyperlink In .Hyperlinks
            sMsg = sMsg + objHyperlink.Address + vbCr
        Next
    End With
    MsgBox sSlidename & vbCr _
        & nHCount & " hyperlinks" & vbCr _
        & sMsg
Next
```

This routine returns the message shown in Figure 12-17 for the first slide in MMA's Mission Statement. That slide has an Action Button with a hyperlink to MMA's intranet home page, and the routine has captured that hyperlink.

439

```
Microsoft PowerPoint                    ☒

Micro Modeling Associates, Inc.  Mission Statement
1 hyperlinks
http://intranet.micromodeling.com/

                ┌─────────────┐
                │     OK      │
                └─────────────┘
```

Figure 12-17

Message box invoked through a VBA routine run against MMA's Mission Statement.

If you run the query routine on a presentation like the MMA Mission Statement, you'll notice a couple of things that aren't apparent to the end user:

🌐 Hyperlinks placed in a master aren't counted among the slide's collection.

🌐 Action Settings that hyperlink to generic locations within the active presentation, such as Next Slide, don't show up in the Hyperlinks collection.

Hyperlinks in masters

Hyperlinks in masters are members of that master's collection. The PowerPoint object model includes a TitleMaster object and a SlideMaster object, and you should work with those objects when you're querying or manipulating hyperlinks in masters.

The two master objects are properties of the presentation. The following code reports the number of hyperlinks in the title and slide masters:

```
MsgBox ActivePresentation.TitleMaster.Hyperlinks.Count
MsgBox ActivePresentation.SlideMaster.Hyperlinks.Count
```

Hyperlinks that aren't hyperlinks

As for the intrapresentation hyperlinks that don't appear in the Hyperlinks collection, those aren't considered to be hyperlinks in the PowerPoint object model, even though they appear in the list of hyperlinks in the Action Settings dialog box. The Action Settings that fall into the not-really-hyperlinks category include such entries as Next Slide, First Slide, and End Show. They may not be programmatically "real" hyperlinks, but as a PowerPoint developer you'll need to work with them, and we'll talk about them in the next section.

Creating Hyperlinks

Although PowerPoint has a Hyperlinks collection and all individual hyperlinks are members of a Hyperlinks collection, you don't create a hyperlink programmatically by adding it to the Hyperlinks collection, as you would in Microsoft Excel and Word. Instead, you create a hyperlink by specifying the hyperlink as an object's Action Setting.

About the ActionSetting objects

As you've seen, every shape or text range on a slide can register two events: the left mouse button clicking on it and the mouse passing over it. Those two events make up the ActionSettings collection. In the PowerPoint object model, the ActionSettings collection is a property of shape and text objects. The two members of the collection are the ActionSetting objects, and you refer to them programmatically by their assigned numerical constants: ppMouseClick and ppMouseOver.

So when you work with hyperlinks, you must start off by referencing either or both of the ActionSettings properties of the object. For example, the code

```
ActiveWindow.Selection.TextRange.ActionSettings(ppMouseClick) [...]
```

refers to what happens when a selected text string is clicked, and

```
ActiveWindow.Selection.ShapeRange.ActionSettings(ppMouseOver) [...]
```

refers to what happens when a selected shape is passed over.

Each ActionSetting object takes several properties, but you'll probably use these three more than the others:

🌐 **Hyperlink** property, which includes such standard Office properties as Address, SubAddress, and Type.

🌐 **SoundEffect** property, which lets you accompany the Action Setting with a .WAV file or, if you don't want to include a sound effect, assigns a value represented by the constant ppSoundNone to the action.

🌐 **AnimateAction** property, which takes an Office Boolean constant of msoTrue or msoFalse. If you set the property to True, the object will flash when its action occurs.

This example adds a hyperlink as the first shape's mouse-click Action Setting and specifies values for the three common properties:

```
With _
ActivePresentation.Slides(1).Shapes(1).ActionSettings(ppMouseClick)
    .Action = ppActionHyperlink
    .Hyperlink.Address = "intranet.micromodeling.com"
    .SoundEffect.Type = ppSoundNone
    .AnimateAction = msoFalse
End With
```

CHAPTER
12

The line ".Action = ppActionHyperlink" is optional. As soon as you specify any attribute of a Hyperlink object, as we did above with the statement ".Hyperlink.Address", PowerPoint assumes the Action Setting is a hyperlink.

The next example adds a hyperlink to the second shape, but this time we use the sound effect and animation properties. Note that when you use a sound effect file, you don't have to use the SoundEffect Type property, as you did in the example above, but you must use the ImportFromFile property to refer to the .WAV file.

```
With _
ActivePresentation.Slides(1).Shapes(2).ActionSettings(ppMouseClick)
    .Hyperlink.Address = "intranet.micromodeling.com"
    .SoundEffect.ImportFromFile
        "c:\Windows\Media\Office97\APPLAUSE.WAV"
    .AnimateAction = msoTrue
End With
```

Nonhyperlink Action Settings

Those navigational Action Settings that work like hyperlinks but don't appear in the Hyperlinks collection are built-in PowerPoint behaviors and exist in the object model as constants, members of the ppActionType family. They break down as follows:

Action Setting	PowerPoint VBA Constant
Next Slide	ppActionNextSlide
Previous Slide	ppActionPreviousSlide
First Slide	ppActionFirstSlide
Last Slide	ppActionLastSlide
Last Slide Viewed	ppActionLastSlideViewed
End Show	ppActionEndShow
Custom Show	ppActionNamedSlideShow
No Action	ppActionNone

You can work with Action Settings programmatically by specifying one of the constants as the ActionSetting type and adding, if you want, sound effects and animation. For example, the following routine uses the ppActionNone and ppActionNextSlide to have the selected shape play a drumroll and flash when the mouse moves over it, and jump to the next slide and applaud when the user clicks on it:

```
With ActiveWindow.Selection.ShapeRange
    With .ActionSettings(ppMouseOver)
        .Action = ppActionNone
        .SoundEffect.ImportFromFile
            "c:\Windows\Media\Office97\DRUMROLL.WAV"
        .AnimateAction = msoTrue
    End With
    With .ActionSettings(ppMouseClick)
        .Action = ppActionNextSlide
        .SoundEffect.ImportFromFile
            "c:\Windows\Media\Office97\APPLAUSE.WAV"
        .AnimateAction = msoTrue
    End With
End With
```

> Although you can apply the AnimateAction property to a text box on your slide, you can't apply it to selected text within the text box. On top of that, the shape you apply the property to must have a background fill or your users won't see any flashing effect.

The Hyperlink Object

Once you've assigned a hyperlink to an object, the hyperlink becomes a member of your file's or range's Hyperlinks collection, just as it does throughout the Office 97 suite. But in PowerPoint the hyperlink also becomes a property of an object's Action Settings. You can query a shape or text object, specify whether to return its mouse-click or mouse-over Action Setting, and then query the type of action that Action Setting carries out. Refer to the Action Setting by its VBA ppActionType constant. A hyperlink on the object will return a value equal to the ppActionHyperlink constant.

The following routine examines the first shape in the presentation, querying both its mouse-click and mouse-over Action Settings. If the action type of either one is a hyperlink, the routine returns the hyperlink's address.

```
Sub QueryShape()
With ActivePresentation.Slides(1).Shapes(1)
    '/Look at the mouse click action.
    With .ActionSettings(ppMouseClick)
        If .Action = ppActionHyperlink Then
            MsgBox "Mouse click: " & .Hyperlink.Address
        End If
```

(continued)

443

12
CHAPTER

```
        End With
        '/Look at the mouse over action.
        With .ActionSettings(ppMouseOver)
            If .Action = ppActionHyperlink Then
                MsgBox "Mouse over: " & .Hyperlink.Address
            End If
        End With
    End With
End Sub
```

> **NOTE**
> If your routine iterates through all the hyperlinks in a collection, PowerPoint will return the hyperlinks object by object, in the order you created the objects on the slide (or, for PowerPoint's preformatted slides, starting with the title area and then the text area(s)). For each individual object, PowerPoint will return first the mouse-click hyperlink and then the mouse-over hyperlink.

Hyperlinking to Named Locations

If you use either of PowerPoint's user interface tools to insert hyperlinks (the Insert Hyperlink dialog box or the Action Settings dialog box), you can create a hyperlink to a named location in a file. You face an important limitation, however: the named location can be only in a PowerPoint file—it cannot, for example, be a cell range in Microsoft Excel or a bookmark in Word.

You can get around that limitation with PowerPoint VBA. Add a hyperlink Action Setting to any file and specify the named location as the hyperlink's SubAddress property. For example, this code adds a hyperlink to a special section in MMA's Employee Manual, a Word document that's on the company intranet site:

```
With ActiveWindow.Selection.TextRange _
    .ActionSettings(ppMouseClick).Hyperlink
    .Address = _
        "intranet.micromodeling.com/admin/Manual.doc"
    .SubAddress = "SpecialBenefitsNote"
End With
```

> **NOTE**
> A named location in a PowerPoint file can be only a slide, not a graphic or other location within the slide.

Hyperlinks for hackers

Some apparent hyperlinks that move you around within the active presentation are, from the point of view of PowerPoint's object model, really just unique internal Action Settings. (See the "Nonhyperlink Action Settings" section earlier in the chapter for more information on them.) But if you want, you can work with those Action Settings programmatically as true hyperlinks. For example, you've seen how you can make a selected shape a hyperlink to the first slide in the presentation by using the ppActionFirstSlide action type on the shape, like this:

```
ActiveWindow.Selection.ShapeRange.ActionSettings(ppMouseClick) _
.Action = ppActionFirstSlide
```

With PowerPoint VBA, you can create a hyperlink by using the title of the first slide as a named range and specifying that title as the hyperlink's SubAddress property. As with Office 97 in general, you can leave the address property blank if the link is within the current file. This code, using a "true" hyperlink, accomplishes the same thing as the preceding sample:

```
With ActiveWindow.Selection.ShapeRange _
    .ActionSettings(ppMouseClick).Hyperlink
    .Address = ""
    .SubAddress = "Mission Statement"
End With
```

The second method doesn't work any better than the first, but since it's basically the same as the syntax across Office, it's more transportable. In addition, it makes any routines you use that query the Hyperlinks collections in your presentation more effective.

VBA and Action Buttons

You can control Action Buttons with PowerPoint VBA, adding them to slides, remapping their actions, and removing them. In the PowerPoint object model, Action Buttons are AutoShapes and are properties of the Shape object on the slide. Specify what kind of button you want to create or work with using one of the msoAutoShapeType constants:

- msoShapeActionButtonBackorPrevious
- msoShapeActionButtonBeginning
- msoShapeActionButtonCustom
- msoShapeActionButtonDocument
- msoShapeActionButtonEnd
- msoShapeActionButtonForwardorNext

- msoShapeActionButtonHelp
- msoShapeActionButtonHome
- msoShapeActionButtonInformation
- msoShapeActionButtonMovie
- msoShapeActionButtonReturn
- msoShapeActionButtonSound

To create a new button on a slide, use the AddShape method and specify the type of button you want to create, its location in points from the left and top edges of the slide, and its width and height in points.

For example, this routine adds a custom button to the lower right corner of the slide master, sets it to run a custom slide show, and inserts the word "Summary" as the button's display text.

```
Sub AddAButton()
Dim objShape As Object
'/Insert the custom button.
Set objShape = _
    ActivePresentation.SlideMaster.Shapes.AddShape _
    (msoShapeActionButtonCustom, 600, 462, 120, 48)
'/Define the button's action.
With objShape.ActionSettings(ppMouseClick)
    .Action = ppActionNamedSlideShow
    .SlideShowName = "Shorter Summary"
    .SoundEffect.Type = ppSoundNone
    .AnimateAction = msoTrue
End With
'/Add some display text and format it.
With objShape.TextFrame.TextRange
    .Text = "Summary"
    With .Font
        .Name = "Times New Roman"
        .Size = 18
        .Bold = msoTrue
    End With
End With
End Sub
```

You can remap a button's action by writing to those Action Settings you want to change. For example, you can go through a presentation looking for buttons that play a certain sound and replacing the sound with another one. This routine does that (except that it limits itself to the current slide), iterating through all the shapes and looking for one whose AutoShapeType is msoShapeActionButtonSound. When it finds the button, the routine queries the sound the button plays and then, if appropriate, substitutes a new sound.

```
Sub RemapSound()
Dim objShape As Object
For Each objShape In ActiveWindow.Selection.SlideRange.Shapes
    If objShape.AutoShapeType = msoShapeActionButtonSound Then
        With objShape.ActionSettings(ppMouseClick).SoundEffect
            If .Name = "CLAP.WAV" Then
                .Name = "APPLAUSE.WAV"
            End If
        End With
    End If
Next
End Sub
```

Running and setting custom slide shows

You can make presentations more responsive to users by having PowerPoint VBA specify and run custom slide shows on the fly. For example, you might want to include a button at the beginning of the show that branches to a custom show containing a less-detailed version of your presentation, or have a later button show a different version of a custom Summary show depending on the user's preferences.

Remap the Action Button to run the different custom slide show by iterating through the Shapes collection by AutoShapeType, locating the Action Button that has the current show as its Action Setting's SlideShowName property, and writing the new show to that property.

To run a custom show using VBA, write to the presentation's SlideShowSettings object, passing it the slide show's name and the slide setup you want to use, and then running it. For example, this code runs a custom show called "Vision and Future":

```
With ActivePresentation.SlideShowSettings
    .RangeType = ppShowNamedSlideShow
    .SlideShowName = "Vision and Future"
    .ShowType = ppShowTypeKiosk
    .LoopUntilStopped = msoFalse
    .Run
End With
```

NOTE If you choose Kiosk mode in the Set Up Show dialog box, your show will loop continuously unless the user exits it. You can't change the setting in the dialog box, but you can change it programmatically. In the custom show code sample, the show will run in Kiosk mode, but the LoopUntilStopped = False property will limit its play to one showing.

With PowerPoint VBA you can also create new custom slide shows. Define an array of the slides that will make up the show, and then use the Add method on the NamedSlideShows property of the SlideShowSettings object in your presentation, passing a name for the show and the slide array as the method's arguments.

> **NOTE** The Link To Custom Show dialog box is invoked when you select Custom Show from the Hyperlink To list in the Action Settings dialog box. It includes a Show And Return check box that, when checked, causes the presentation to return to the current slide and resume the main show after the custom show runs. Unfortunately, there's currently no VBA equivalent to the check box. The main show will always resume at the current slide.

Automating Animations

You can use VBA to animate the objects on a slide. Although animation is a creative act and requires a human touch, in some instances you might want to have animation settings that respond to users' preferences as they are viewing your presentation. Or you might want to quickly set up animations in a "batch process" across several slides.

To animate shapes and text boxes, use the AnimationSettings object. Then specify its properties, such as EntryEffect and AdvanceMode, to create the animation you want. For example, the following routine goes through each shape on the currently active slide and animates it so that it flies in from the left of the screen and then disappears. The shapes will fly in at one-second intervals. Note the heavy use of enumerated constants to specify the actions.

```
ActiveWindow.Selection.SlideRange.Shapes.SelectAll
With ActiveWindow.Selection.ShapeRange.AnimationSettings
    .Animate = msoTrue
    .EntryEffect = ppEffectFlyFromLeft
    '/Specify the animation to begin automatically at one-second
    '/intervals.
    '/To have animations triggered by mouse clicks,
    '/set the AdvanceMode to ppAdvanceOnClick.
    .AdvanceMode = ppAdvanceOnTime
    .AdvanceTime = 1
    .AnimateBackground = msoTrue
    .AfterEffect = ppAfterEffectHide
End With
```

Chart animations

Charts in your presentation also use the AnimationSettings object and its properties. But with charts you can use an additional property, ChartUnitEffect, which specifies how to animate the elements in the chart—by category, series, or individual elements. The property can take any of the ppChartUnitEffect constants.

Working with charts programmatically requires a little care. Charts embedded in your slides become members of the Shapes collection. As you iterate through the collection, your only clue that a shape might be a chart is if its Type property is equal to the msoEmbeddedOLEObject constant. Several kinds of embedded objects are not weeded out by the Type property, so you also need to test the shapes' OLEFormat.Object.Application.Name property for the string "Microsoft Graph."

And here's a further wrinkle: your routine might try to animate a chart in a way that isn't appropriate. For example, you can't animate an area chart by category, so if you set the ChartUnitEffect property to ppAnimateByCategory your routine will generate an error. In the following sample we avoid that problem by skipping over the offending line. Any charts that we skip because they can't handle animation by category will still have a checkerboard animation, but the chart elements will appear all at once rather than by category.

```
Sub SetUpCharts()
On Error Resume Next
Dim objSlide As Object
Dim objShape As Object
For Each objSlide In ActivePresentation.Slides
    For Each objShape In objSlide.Shapes
        If objShape.Type = msoEmbeddedOLEObject Then
            If InStr(mobjShape.OLEFormat.Object.Application.Name, _
            "Microsoft Graph") > 0 Then
                With objShape.AnimationSettings
                    .Animate = msoTrue
                    .EntryEffect = ppEffectCheckerboardAcross
                    .AdvanceMode = ppAdvanceOnTime
                    .AdvanceTime = 1
                    .ChartUnitEffect = ppAnimateByCategory
                    '/The next line animates the grids and legend.
                    .AnimateBackground = msoTrue
                End With
            End If
        End If
    Next
Next
End Sub
```

Building the MMA Intranet

In MMA's intranet, the company's Mission Statement is presented as a Power-Point slide show. The show's main design goals are to hold the user's interest and to coax him or her into taking an active role in the show. To those ends, we used PowerPoint's new animation and sound features extensively.

The Template and the File

We chose the animated template "high voltage.pot" for the Mission Statement and customized its text and slide background. We decided to post the file as a slide show (in .PPS format) on our intranet using the Kiosk view mode so that we could present the show full screen with optimal graphic appearance regardless of users' screen display modes and at the same time exploit PowerPoint VBA in the show.

The Action Buttons

We used several Action Buttons on the show. Each slide has a Next and Back set of buttons, which we added to the slide master. The last slide in the show has a slightly different button set: we included a custom button that runs the End Show Action Setting to exit the slide show, and we placed a Back To Start button on top of the slide master's Next button.

As you can see in Figure 12-18, the first slide has three buttons, all of which are in the slide itself, not in the master.

Figure 12-18

The three buttons on the Mission Statement's first slide.

The first button has a hyperlink Action Setting that jumps to MMA's intranet home page. Next, the information button runs a helpful little VBA routine and lets users jump to Microsoft's PowerPoint Internet site if they wish. Finally, the third button performs a Next Slide Action Setting.

VBA Routine in the File

Although the MMA Mission Statement is a fairly short slide show, we took advantage of VBA automation to have the show display and behave the way we wanted it to. We added the ALittleInfo routine to the show. When triggered by the information button on the title screen, the ALittleInfo routine displays some information about PowerPoint and the show.

A little information

ALittleInfo is a simple routine that displays a message and offers to link the user to Microsoft's PowerPoint Web page. Note that it employs the Office standard FollowHyperlink method:

```
Sub ALittleInfo()
Dim nContinue As Integer
nContinue = MsgBox("PowerPoint 97 demo, created 10/96." _
    & vbCr & "PowerPoint can do amazing things!" _
    & vbCr & "Do you want to check out the PowerPoint Web site?", _
    vbYesNo + vbExclamation, "It's Showtime")
If nContinue = vbYes Then
    ActivePresentation.FollowHyperlink _
    Address:="http://www.microsoft.com/powerpoint", _
    NewWindow:=False, _
    AddHistory:=True
End If
End Sub
```

The Movie

The second slide in the show contains an .AVI file recorded with Microsoft's MS Camcorder and embedded in the presentation.

TIP

When you insert an .AVI file into a slide, PowerPoint inserts the file as a link. You can see the link's location by looking under More Options in the Custom Animation dialog box. When the slide show runs, PowerPoint looks for the .AVI file in the link's location. It will then look for the file in the PowerPoint application's folder. For our intranet, we stored our .AVI file with our slide show.

The Movie Button

PowerPoint includes an Action Button that you can use to play an .AVI file. We didn't use the button for aesthetic reasons, but you might find it appropriate for your site.

To get the button (or any Action Button or object, for that matter) to play a movie, insert a slide containing the movie. In the Action Settings dialog box, set the Movie Button to hyperlink to the movie's slide. Then, in the Custom Animations dialog box, select the movie object and set it to animate automatically. Now go to the Play Settings tab and set the movie's animation to follow the animation order.

12 CHAPTER

You can specify how movie, sound, and OLE objects interact with the other animated objects in the Custom Animation dialog box's Play Settings tab. In Figure 12-19, you'll notice that the animation settings for the .AVI file on our slide are straightforward. The movie plays once and then hides. If you click the More Options button, you can choose to have the movie loop indefinitely.

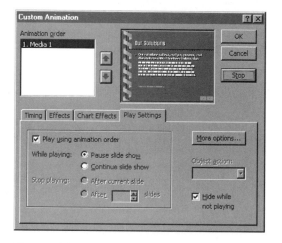

Figure 12-19

Play Settings for a Custom Animation.

The Animated Charts

The Mission Statement uses two animated charts: a three-dimensional pie, which builds its shapes in a checkerboard pattern; and a cone, which uses a Wipe Up animation style to give the illusion of the shapes building upward.

The animations are triggered automatically. We have our text labels ("Skill Sets" for the pie and "MMA Employees" for the cone) appear in a checkerboard pattern and then display the charts. On the pie chart, we also take advantage of MSGraph's new option to use gradient backgrounds in a chart's plot area.

The Animated Map

The animated map on the Mission Statement's last slide contains twenty-two shapes. Eighteen of the shapes are four-point stars that indicate cities on the map.

When you create an animated graphic like the map, the best strategy is to start by placing all the objects you'll want to animate in their final positions on your slide. It's usually a good idea to start with the background picture first and build the others on top of it. For example, we put in the map of the United States first and then placed the stars on it. Once everything's in place, you can set up the sequence of events in the Custom Animations dialog box. In Figure 12-20, all the four-point stars on the map are set to appear automatically, one immediately following another.

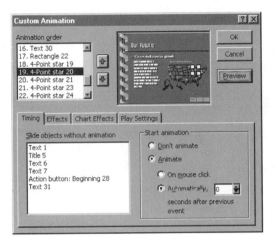

Figure 12-20
Setting the Timing in the Custom Animation dialog box.

The whole animation starts automatically with the Text1 object after five seconds. To animate the "Pending Offices" and "And Maybe Some Day" text, we used a custom checkerboard animation that builds text from the left word by word. All of the stars on the map use Zoom Out as their entry animation effect, as shown in Figure 12-21, so they flash brightly when they appear.

TIP

Lots of shapes can have the same automation. You can use VBA to automate batches of shapes quickly. You can also select multiple shapes in the Custom Animation dialog box and apply the same settings to them all at once.

The Custom Soundtrack

The custom soundtrack was very easy to set up. We chose a cool jazz sound and added some saxophone riffs to play whenever the user starts an animation. The same track continues throughout the slide show.

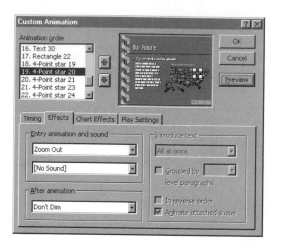

Figure 12-21

Setting Animation Effects to make stars flash.

Combining Your Talents

Let's face it: PowerPoint is fun. With its new graphic and multimedia features, it's more enjoyable to work with than ever. And now, with VBA backing it up, PowerPoint has brains. As you develop long, complex slide shows, you'll find ample opportunity to exploit VBA and PowerPoint's custom shows to handle the branchings among them, thereby letting users control the course and content of shows. You'll be able to import and display data in captivating ways and to create custom animations on the fly. As a PowerPoint intranet developer, you have the opportunity—and the challenge—to combine sophisticated graphic design, Visual Basic programming, and interactive responsiveness in ways that were unimaginable before.

CHAPTER

13

Microsoft Outlook 97

Ken Heft

Microsoft Outlook, the newest addition to the Microsoft Office family, is a supercharged e-mail client. Although Outlook might not play a big role within your intranet, it will certainly be an important tool for developing your intranet and managing it in the future. Outlook 97 handles information at both the individual and organizational levels.

For individuals, Outlook includes all the tools you'll need to keep your daily life organized: e-mail client, calendar, contact list, task list, journal, and even electronic sticky notes. When important messages arrive in your Inbox, you can use Outlook to take action on them immediately. You can log the receipt of the e-mail in your Journal, schedule a meeting with your co-workers (after checking the time against their existing appointments), assign your office manager the task of ordering donuts, and then leave yourself an electronic reminder to make follow-up phone calls later in the day. If you're using Outlook in conjunction with Microsoft Exchange Server, you can take action

Do You Need Microsoft Exchange Server?

Many of Outlook's features are client-based. This means that you can use these features even if your company does not use Microsoft Exchange Server on the back end. However, a few Outlook tools will not run unless you have Exchange Server, including these:

- **The Inbox Assistant and Out Of Office Assistant.** These tools react automatically to incoming e-mail based on a set of rules that you create.

- **Public folders.** Public folders are folders stored on the server. They are used to share information (documents, messages, forms, and so on) throughout your organization.

- **Security.** Security has been a major issue with e-mail (especially Internet e-mail). You've probably heard a horror story or two about someone's e-mail message getting intercepted and modified on the way to its recipient. Outlook and Exchange Server combine to prevent this problem by using digital signatures and sealed messages.

- **Scheduled deliveries.** When you send an e-mail message, you might not want it delivered right away. Scheduled deliveries let you specify the day and time you want a message sent.

- **Delegate Access.** Delegate Access gives others the ability to access your Inbox in the same way you might delegate to a co-worker the job of filtering your paper mail or signing your name on letters.

- **Log in via the Internet.** Using Outlook and Exchange Server, you can connect to your mail server directly through the Internet, bypassing the need for Remote Access. This way, you can check e-mail, schedules, and so on from across the world at a reduced cost.

- **Accessing Outlook with a browser.** If you are running Exchange Server 4.5 or later, you have the ability to access public folders containing e-mail messages, read and send e-mail, and schedule appointments directly from Internet Explorer or your other Web browser of choice.

on a new e-mail message even before you read it *and* even when you're out of the office!

At the organizational level, Outlook is a powerful way of sharing information. Using Microsoft Exchange Server, you can share e-mail messages, contact lists, schedules, electronic forms, Office documents, Web shortcuts, and most anything else you can imagine through the use of public folders. Whether you want to create a corporate phone list or central location for submitting software bug reports, public folders are the way to go.

One of the most powerful features of Outlook 97 is customization. You can change the font and colors in your e-mail addresses to lend a friendly tone to your communications. If you don't like seeing the subject and time for your incoming e-mail, you can remove them from your view and replace them with different fields. If you don't like the look of the standard e-mail form, you can create your own custom form. If you want your Journal to create a log entry automatically when you open an Office document, just set the appropriate Journal options.

Outlook is well integrated with the rest of Office 97 and with the Web. You can create hyperlinks in your e-mail messages or create an e-mail message from a Web page. You can use Microsoft Excel spreadsheets and Microsoft Word documents as electronic forms for submitting information. And through its object model, you can automate Outlook from any of the other Office 97 applications.

In this chapter we'll highlight the Outlook features you can use to effectively manage both your personal tasks and your corporate communications. We'll also build a sample intranet site that uses a combination of public folders, custom forms, and shared documents to give employees at Micro Modeling an easy way to distribute information.

The Outlook Bar

The Outlook Bar, shown in Figure 13-1, is the main way to move around the Outlook user interface. Located at the left of the screen, it contains shortcuts that point to the different Outlook components. To help organize all your shortcuts, the Outlook Bar is split into several groups. The Outlook group is the primary exploration point, guiding you through Outlook's main components: Inbox, Calendar, Contacts, Tasks, Journal, Notes, and Deleted Items. You can also add your own items and groups to the Outlook bar, such

Figure 13-1

The Outlook Bar.

as shortcuts to your favorite public folders or groups like Projects and Status Reports shown in Figure 13-1. There is no way to launch an application from the Outlook Bar.

Inbox

The Inbox is where you go when you want to deal with e-mail: sending, receiving, reviewing, and so on. All your new e-mail arrives via the Inbox. When you click Inbox, you'll see a list of all your new mail items, along with icons indicating what type of action you have performed against each item (for example, a reply or a forward), whether it contains an attachment, and so on. As we'll discuss later in this chapter, you can change many aspects of the Inbox's appearance, including the fields you see and their order on the screen.

While in your Inbox, click the Folder List button on the toolbar to display a list of folders that are available to you. You will see built-in folders such as Outbox and Sent Items in addition to any personal folders you create and any public folders that have been set up for your group on the server. You can open the Folder List from within any group or view, not just from your Inbox, and it will remain open until you close it.

All the usual tools are available, including reply, forward, cc, bcc (blind carbon copy), and so on. But here are a few highlights of Outlook 97 and e-mail that you might not know about:

- 🌐 **AutoNameCheck.** When entering names in e-mail address fields, Outlook automatically tries to resolve all the names you enter with the Address Book. Resolved names are underlined and aliases are replaced by full names.

- 🌐 **Hyperlinks.** If you enter a Web address or other valid URL in the body of your e-mail, Outlook automatically converts it to a live hyperlink. You can even include hyperlinks to other Outlook components using the syntax Outlook://*item* to open a folder (for example, Outlook://Big Project/Status Reports/Phase 1 would open the Phase 1 folder) or Outlook://~*subject* to open an individual item (for example, Outlook://Big Project/Status Reports/Phase 1/~RE: Draft).

- 🌐 **Send mail to public folders.** Outlook and Exchange Server work together to allow you to send e-mail messages to public folders as well as to individuals. This doesn't happen automatically—an administrator on the server must set it up.

- 🌐 **Message recall.** Have you ever accidentally hit the Send button and embarrassed yourself? Just open the Sent Items folder, double-click on your sent message, and then choose the Recall This Message command from the Tools menu. If the recipient is running Outlook and the message is still in his or her Inbox, you might be able to keep your job! Unfortunately, this command won't work with Internet e-mail. :-(

- 🌐 **Voting buttons.** If you want to poll a group of people and receive a simple yes or no answer, use voting buttons to automate the process. Create a new message, and click the Options tab. Select the Use Voting Buttons option, and pick from choices like "Yes;No" or your own custom options. Then send the message. As other Outlook users receive your message and choose an answer from the voting buttons toolbar, you will get replies in your Inbox, and your original e-mail (now found in the Sent Items

13 CHAPTER

folder by default) will automatically tally the results in a Tracking tab, as shown here:

🌐 **Delivery and tracking options.** When you send an e-mail message, click the Options tab if you want to specify that the message should not be sent until a certain time or date. You can also indicate that your message should be removed from the recipient's Inbox if it hasn't been read by a certain time or date.

🌐 **Message flags.** You can use message flags when reading e-mail to leave yourself reminders. For example, you can create a flag that reminds you to respond to or follow up on a particular item by a certain date or time. Outlook will then display a message if you have not completed the task by that date or time. From within an open message, choose Message Flag from the Edit menu (or click the Message Flag button on the toolbar). You can also set message flags in messages you're sending to others as reminders for them.

🌐 **AutoSignature.** Do you find that you always want to add your name, title, company, phone number, and/or favorite Bon-Jovi quote to the end of every e-mail message you send? If so, this command on the Tools menu will save you a lot of typing.

Calendar

Use the Calendar to help plan your daily schedule, set up meetings with co-workers, and review your outstanding tasks. Before using the Calendar, you might need a quick Outlook vocabulary lesson to understand the difference between appointments, meetings, and events, three separate activities in Outlook-speak. An *appointment* is an activity that involves scheduling just yourself. A *meeting* involves scheduling and coordinating with other people. An *event* is an activity, such as a birthday party, that you need to schedule but that does not, by default, appear as "busy time." Now that we've got that straight, here are some highlights of the Calendar:

- **Day, week, and month.** Use the toolbar to toggle between viewing one day at a time, the current week, or even an entire month.

- **Plan recurring activities.** Use the New Recurring Appointment, New Recurring Event, and New Recurring Meeting commands in the Calendar menu to schedule those activities that occur daily, weekly, or on any sort of regular basis.

- **Plan a meeting.** The Plan A Meeting command on the Calendar menu allows you to view other people's schedules when trying to set a meeting time (as shown below). Unavailable time periods will be displayed as either Tentative, Busy, or Out Of Office. Use the AutoPick feature to have Outlook pick a mutually agreeable meeting time, based on the schedules of the people you are inviting.

NOTE For you to open other people's schedules, the schedules must be made available to you. Likewise, if you want people to be able to see your schedule, you must share it. To share your Calendar, click the Calendar icon in your Outlook Bar with your right mouse button. Select Properties, and go to the Permissions tab. Under Permissions you can give different rights to different people, allowing read-only or read/write access to your schedule. To give everyone access to your schedule, change the permissions of the default user.

Contacts

Use Outlook's Contact manager to store the vital statistics for all your important contacts. You can set up a contact list for your personal contacts or create a shared contact list in a public folder. Each entry within a contact list can store standard pieces of information, such as addresses and phone numbers, and can also include e-mail addresses, Web addresses, nineteen different phone numbers, birthdays (which will automatically trigger a reminder on the day), and custom fields for any other information you might need. You can also print contact lists. Figure 13-2 shows a sample contact list in Print Preview.

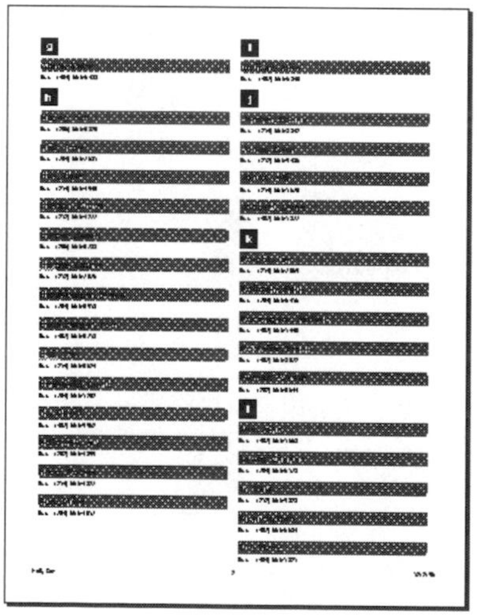

Figure 13-2

Print Preview of a contact list in Outlook.

Importing and Exporting Your Contact List

You might already have an external database, such as Microsoft Access, that stores your contact information. Well, good news: you don't have to retype your contact list in Outlook. Just choose the File/Import And Export command and follow the steps in the Import And Export Wizard to select a table and map the fields from database table to Outlook contacts. You can import and export to a variety of data formats (for example, Microsoft Excel and dBASE) and with any of the different Outlook components (Inbox, Tasks, and so on). The following illustration shows how you go about mapping fields from a Microsoft Access table to your contacts list via the Map Custom Fields dialog box in the Import And Export Wizard:

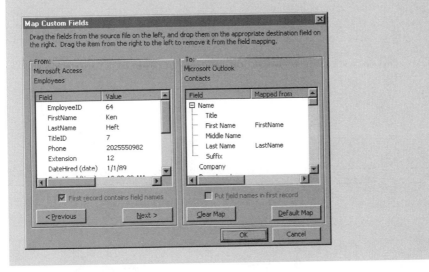

Your Outlook contacts can be displayed in a phone list grid or as electronic address cards. Select a contact and choose from toolbar buttons that let you dial the person on the phone (as shown in Figure 13-3), send him a new e-mail message, invite him to a meeting, or explore his Web page.

CHAPTER
13

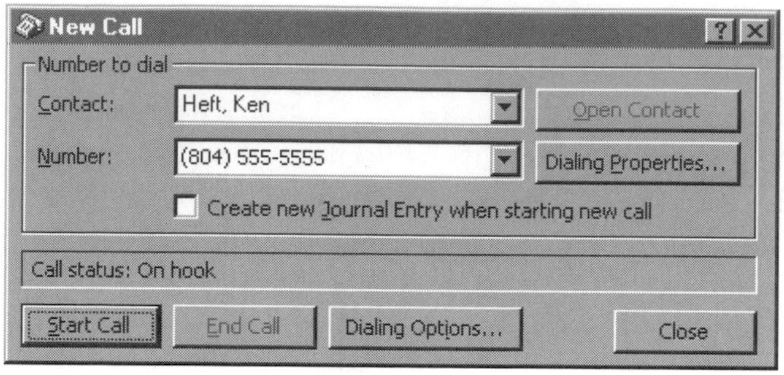

Figure 13-3

Using AutoDial to call a selected contact.

Tasks

Use Tasks to manage your to-do list electronically. When you create a task, you can specify that it occurs just once or you can specify that it is recurring by clicking the Recurrence button on the toolbar of the open task. For recurring tasks, you can indicate that the task occurs once a day, once a week, and so on. For tasks that aren't quite that regular, you can select an interval that is dependent on the task's completion date. Figure 13-4 shows a recurring task that occurs every Friday for ten weeks.

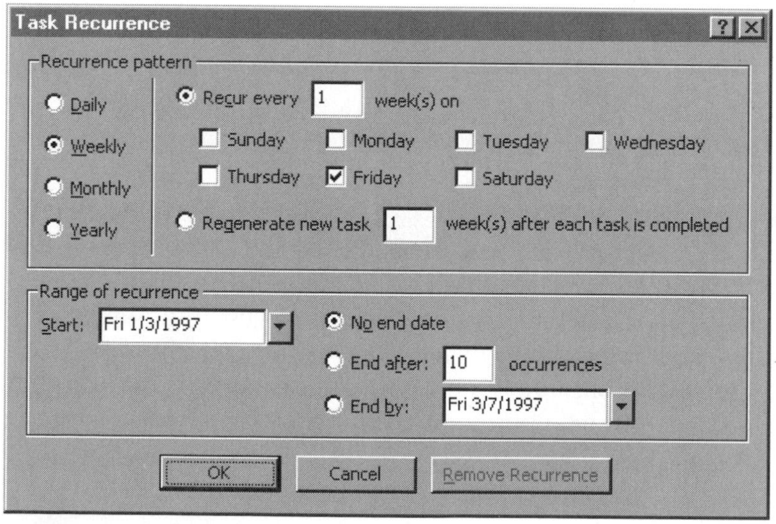

Figure 13-4

Specifying the details of a recurring task in the Task Recurrence dialog box.

In your task, you enter a subject, due date, status, and other relevant information. This allows you to track the progress of your task through completion. You can have Outlook remind you when your task is due or when other important milestones are to occur. If your schedule is looking busy, use the Assign Task command on the toolbar to pawn the work off on a co-worker. If your co-worker accepts the task (she can decline or reassign it) and completes it, Outlook can automatically send you a status report.

Journal

The Outlook Journal is a central location for logging all of your important activities. You can set up your Journal so that it automatically records activities such as scheduled meetings, modifications to Office 97 documents, and sending e-mail to contacts. To specify your Journal settings, select Options from the Outlook Tools menu. Click the Journal tab, and then select the options you want. You can also enter journal items manually for activities such as phone calls, written correspondence, package deliveries, or any other correspondence you want to log.

The Journal is Microsoft's attempt to help people who need to account for their time and also to solve a common user problem: "Where did it go?" People lose files and phone numbers, forget where Web pages are, and so on. When looking for a document, a lot of people don't think, "I know it's in the C:\Projects\Big Client folder"; rather, they recall, "I know I was working on it Thursday morning." This is where the Journal can help. By setting Journal options, you can automatically log Office 97 activities such as opening documents. Figure 13-5 on the next page shows you the kinds of options you can set in the Option dialog box on the Journal tab to track events.

To review your activities, just look in the Journal under the appropriate day and open an entry. You will see not only the time you opened each file but how long you worked on it and even a shortcut to it! Figure 13-6 on the following page shows you what yours truly was doing the week of October 7, 1996.

Using the Outlook object model, you can integrate your custom application with the Journal. Maybe you'd like the Journal to log each time a user installs your application or receives an error message. We'll do an example of creating a Journal entry through code later in this chapter.

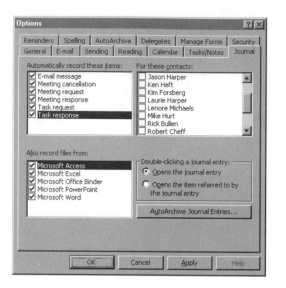

Figure 13-5

Setting options to automatically track events in the Journal.

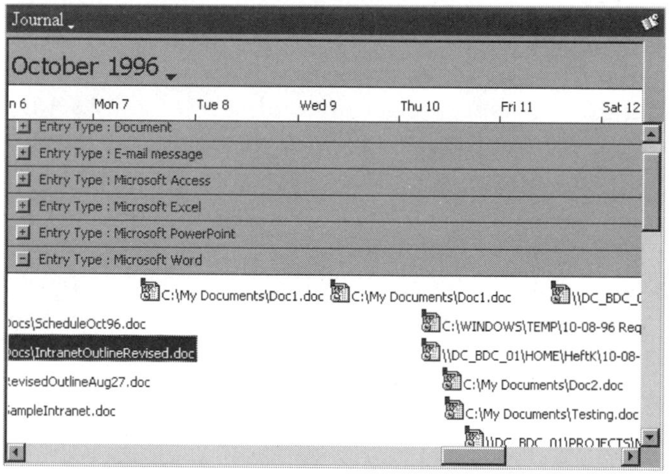

Figure 13-6

Timeline view of Word documents in the Journal.

Notes

Outlook Notes are free-form notes that you can use in the same way you use sticky tags to clutter your office. You can insert notes into e-mail messages and other Outlook items. You can even color-code your notes to add some organization, but that takes the fun out of it. Basically, Notes are electronic reminders that help to save trees.

Integration

Now that you know the basics of Outlook, let's talk about the fun stuff. Outlook was designed to be a completely integrated environment. You can drag and drop between any two places within Outlook and get the results you would expect. In Microsoft-speak, this describes the AutoCreate feature. Let's follow an example to see how AutoCreate works.

You open Outlook and get a message from a client who says his company just ran out of money. Obviously, you need to take immediate action. The first thing you do is log the receipt of the client's e-mail message in your Journal. To do this, highlight the e-mail message in your Inbox and drag it to the Journal on your Outlook Bar. Outlook AutoCreate creates a new Journal entry with the subject and other information already filled in. It also includes the original e-mail message as an attachment. When you save the entry, it will appear in your Journal under the "E-mail message" entry type.

Next you need to schedule a meeting about this e-mail with some of your co-workers. Do this by dragging the e-mail message onto the Calendar on your Outlook bar. Outlook fills in all of the information it can for an appointment. You then click the Meeting Planner tab in the Appointment dialog box, supply your co-workers' names, view their schedules, select a meeting time, and finally send out invitations to the meeting.

Of course, if you're having a meeting you'll need to have cookies. So drag the e-mail message to the Tasks on your Outlook Bar. Outlook creates a new task that you can modify (change the subject to "We need cookies to discuss this e-mail") and then assign to your office manager by using the Assign Task command on the Task menu.

Finally, you might want to leave yourself a reminder to get an overhead projector for the meeting. So drag the e-mail to the Notes on your Outlook Bar. Outlook brings the text of the e-mail into the new note. Add a line at the top saying "Order Projector" and you're done.

We won't go through every possible combination of drag and drop between the different Outlook components (there are thirty), but here are a few highlights:

🌐 **Log your phone calls.** Drag a contact into the Journal when you make a call, and Outlook creates a new Phone Call Journal entry. You can even use the Start Timer button to log the start time, stop time, and duration of your call.

🌐 **Inform co-workers about important phone calls and meetings.** Drag a Journal entry into the Inbox to automatically create an e-mail message that includes information such as the time and length of the meeting, phone call, or other journal item. Any notes you have entered on the item in the Journal will be included as well.

🌐 **Create a to-do list for an upcoming meeting.** Drag a Scheduled Meeting into Tasks, and Outlook will create a task with the due date and reminder set up automatically, as shown in Figure 13-7. Assign the task to a co-worker if you'd like.

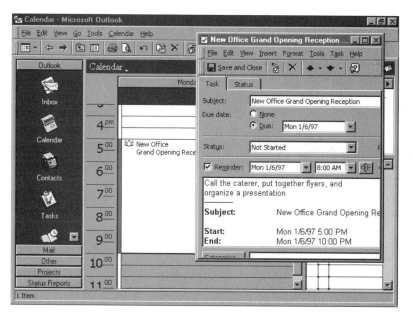

Figure 13-7

Drag a meeting onto the Tasks group to create a new task.

The Six Degrees of Customization

Before we get into the intricate details of how to modify everything you just learned, let's do a broad overview of things you can customize in Outlook 97. Some of these techniques are very simple (1 through 3), whereas others require programming skills and a lot of patience (4, 5, and especially 6):

1. **Customizing your view.** You can change the fields that you see, the order in which they appear, and the style of presentation in

470

an Outlook folder using only the View menu. If you also need to add a custom field or two (for example, "Requires Action?"), you can add the field and edit its value without even opening the item.

2. **Sharing Outlook items.** If you want to create a shared contact list, schedule, task list, journal, or note list, you can do so without any development effort by creating a new item in a public folder.

3. **Use Office documents as forms.** If you already have a Word document or Microsoft Excel spreadsheet that you use as a form, you can include it in an Outlook public folder and you can use it in place of an Outlook form, which gives you some powerful features.

4. **Customize Outlook forms.** Outlook forms are completely customizable. Pick the form you want to start with (for example, an e-mail message or an appointment item), switch to Design view (Tools/Design Outlook Form), and then you're free to revamp the look of your form.

5. **Add ActiveX controls to forms.** With the ActiveX control toolbox, you can add any installed ActiveX control to your Outlook form, including anything from a list box to a movie.

6. **Add VBScript to forms.** Now it starts getting a little trickier. We won't discuss VBScript (Visual Basic, Scripting Edition) in this chapter, but it is currently the language of choice for Outlook forms. Create a script to add additional functionality to your forms.

A Customized View

So far, we've focused on the different components of Outlook: Inbox, Calendar, Contacts, Tasks, Journal, and Notes. Now let's talk about customizing these components to work the way you want. Using the View menu, you can change almost all aspects of Outlook's presentation, from the sort order to the way your data is organized.

Current View

The Current View command controls the way your data is displayed in Outlook. For example, when you look at your Inbox, you are looking at the Messages With AutoPreview view by default. This view includes certain fields and displays a single row for each e-mail message and the first three lines of the message. You can change the current view so that your messages are grouped by sender, displayed graphically in a timeline, or only unread messages are displayed. Change the current view in your calendar to switch between a 1-day view and a 31-day wall-calendar view. The view options change from Inbox to Calendar to Tasks. You can even create your own custom views using the Define Views command on the View menu.

Show Fields

Use the Show Fields command to modify which fields and columns are displayed in your current view. You can change the order of the fields, remove the ones you don't want to see, and add new ones. Maybe you don't care about when an e-mail was received but do care about its size. You can use the Show Fields command to make such modifications.

When we discuss creating custom forms in Outlook, we'll discuss creating user-defined fields. Maybe you have a public folder that deals with projects. Using the Show Fields command, you can create a custom field called Project Name and then give users the ability to change its value.

Group By Box

If you've worked in Microsoft Excel, you are used to the idea of a pivot table. A *pivot table* is a custom report that lets you dynamically change the way data is presented to you. The Group By Box command in Outlook follows a similar concept. Let's say you're looking at your Journal. Your view is set up to organize your Journal entries by Type or by Contact. But what if you want to break it down further, organizing by both type and contact? This is where grouping can come in.

Go to your Journal and select Entry List as your current view. Select the Group By Box command on the View menu. This toggles a group-by box, which appears above your entry list. You can now use drag and drop to create column headers for your table. Drag the Entry Type heading to the Group By box and you will see your Journal items collapse to a handful of entry types. Next drag the Contact heading to the box, to the right of the Entry Type. You won't see any changes right away, but if you expand one of the entry types (by clicking the plus sign next to it), you should see a list of collapsed contacts. You can then expand and collapse the appropriate items, change the group-by columns (equivalent to pivoting in Microsoft Excel), and so on. Figure 13-8 shows an example of grouping in a Journal.

You can use the Group By box to "pivot" your view in any of the Outlook components. You can even use it when you're looking at My Computer to create an ordered view of folders on your hard drive, as shown in Figure 13-9.

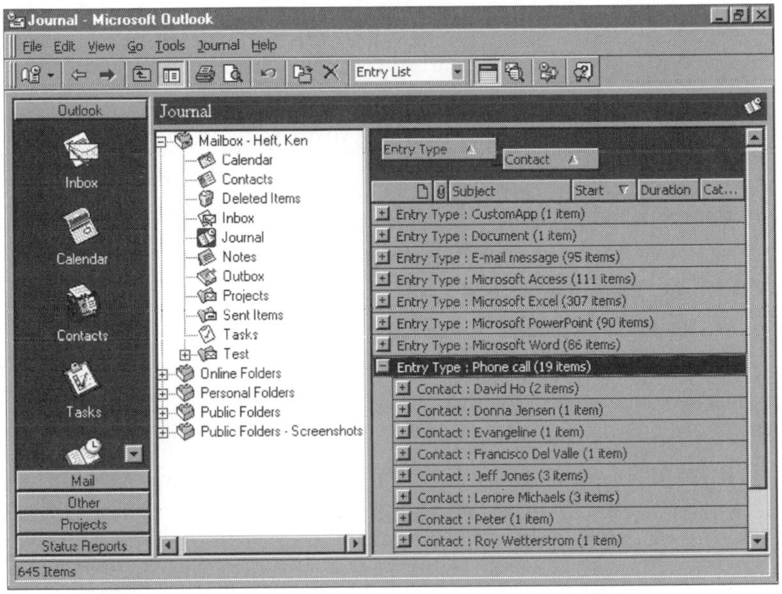

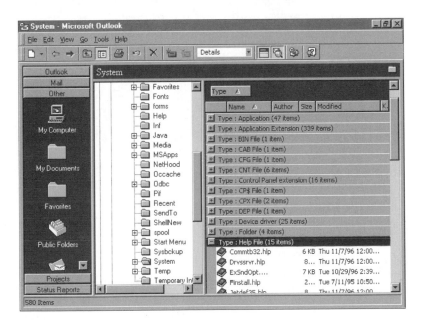

Figure 13-8

Grouping Journal entries by Entry Type and Contact.

Figure 13-9

My Computer grouped by file type.

Other Ways to Customize Your View

Many other tools are available for changing the way you view your Outlook data. When you customize your view, it is specific to your machine. Therefore, you can change the view for everything from your Inbox to a public folder. Here are some of the other commands found on the View menu:

- **Define Views.** Once you've set up a view exactly how you like it, you might want to save it with the Define Views command. It will then be available as a view option in the future.

- **Format Columns.** Use the Format Columns command to change the look of your columns. You can change such aspects as the column's width, alignment, and format of any fields in your current view.

- **Sort, Filter.** Sorting and filtering can be used to arrange your data and/or select the records you want to see.

Adding a Custom Field to an Item

Suppose you have a folder in which you store outstanding issues for a project. At a glance, you'd like to know the status of each issue, even though there's no easy way to store this information in an e-mail message. What you can do is use the Show Fields command to pick a field to show (for example, Status from the All Task Fields group) and then use the Format View command to Allow In-Cell Editing. You'll be able to read and write to that custom field directly in your folder, as shown in Figure 13-10.

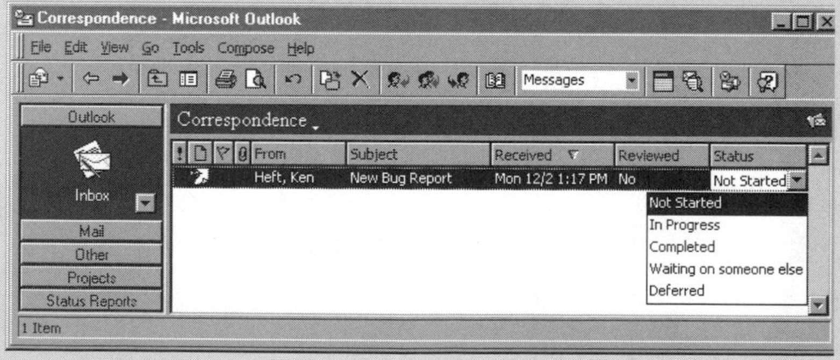

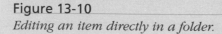

Figure 13-10

Editing an item directly in a folder.

- **Format View.** Format View changes things such as font and grid-line color in your current view. It also allows you to edit items directly in a folder and can modify the AutoPreview behavior of e-mail messages.

- **Field Chooser.** The Field Chooser is another way to add fields to your current view. It is very similar to the Show Fields command but allows you to use drag and drop to position fields in your current view.

- **AutoPreview.** AutoPreview allows you to view the first three lines of messages in a particular folder. You can use the Format View command to control whether AutoPreview will affect all messages or just the unread ones.

- **Folder List.** Viewing the Folder List allows you to see all of your Outlook folders at the same time. It looks very similar to Windows Explorer and is easier to use than the Outlook Bar for things like public folders.

Public Folders

So far, we've focused on the best ways for you to organize your personal workload. Now you're ready to take everything you've learned and apply it at the intranet level. With public folders, you can create folders that are seen by everyone connected to the same Exchange Server. Of course, everyone's first question is, "What if I don't want *everybody* to be able to use my folders?" With Exchange Server security, you can specify which users have which rights and to which public folders.

Public folders can contain everything from e-mail messages to contact lists, calendars, and even Office documents. These folders will be completely independent from your other folders. So you could create a separate public folder for each project that your company or department is working on. Each public folder could be accessed only by the people working on the project and could contain project-specific items such as proposals (Word documents), client contacts (Outlook Contacts), and correspondence logs (Outlook Journal and/or e-mail folders).

Public folders can serve a variety of needs. You can set up a public folder as a knowledge base, where people "post" questions and answers. You can use them as a central location for storing Office, Web, and other documents that need to be shared. And you can also use Outlook public folders to share schedules, contact lists, task lists, journal items, and notes among your group.

TIP

If you want to share information with only a few selected individuals, you can use shared private folders as an alternative to public folders. You can do this by right-clicking on the folder you want to share and selecting the Properties command. Then select the Permissions tab and set up the permissions for the appropriate people. Users will now be able to view your e-mail, contacts, and so on by using the File/Open Special Folder command, selecting Exchange Server Folder, and entering your name and the name of the shared folder.

Creating a Public Folder

To create a public folder, you must have the proper rights. If you have the proper rights, you can select an existing public folder from the folder list (for example, All Public Folders), click on it with your right mouse button, and select the Create Subfolder command. In the Create New Folder dialog box, which is shown in Figure 13-11, you give your public folder a name, select the type of item that you want to place in the folder (for example, an appointment, a contact, or a message), and click OK.

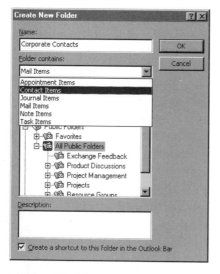

Figure 13-11

Creating a new public folder.

To assign privileges to your newly created public folder, right-click on the folder, choose Properties, go to the Permissions tab, and assign permissions to the appropriate people. Although you can control people's privileges in your folder, you cannot hide a folder from certain users.

If you don't have the rights to create a public folder, ask your administrator to create one for you and to make you the folder owner. Then you can have full control over that folder and its subfolders.

Accessing a Public Folder

Once you've created your public folder, you need to let people know about the folder and show them how to access it. Here are a few ways to introduce your public folder:

🌐 **Send a shortcut.** Create a new e-mail message. From the Outlook folder list, select the public folder and drag it into the body of your e-mail message. If you can't see the e-mail message when you have focus on the Outlook window, you can drag the folder to the e-mail message icon on the Windows 95 or Windows NT taskbar and the message will appear. This will attach an .XNK file that the recipient can then double-click to view the public folder contents.

🌐 **Create a hyperlink.** Use the syntax Outlook://*folder location* to create a hyperlink from a Web page, Office 97 document, or other location. The following example is a hyperlink to a public folder named Office 97:

```
Outlook://Public Folders/All Public Folders/Office 97
```

That takes care of letting people know about new public folders. Now here are a few ways that you can access your favorite public folder more easily:

🌐 **Add To Favorites.** In the folder list, you should see a folder called Public Folders that has two subfolders, Favorites and All Public Folders. The Favorites folder can be a very small subset, containing only those folders you use regularly. One advantage of using the Favorites folder is that Outlook automatically puts a number next to each of your favorites, telling you how many unread items are in that folder. To add a folder to your favorites, select the folder and then use the File/Folder/Add To Public Folder Favorites command.

- **Create a shortcut on the Outlook Bar.** Getting around in the folder list can sometimes be overwhelming. You can simplify the process by creating a shortcut to a public folder on the Outlook Bar. To do this, select a folder, click on it with your right mouse button, and choose the Add To Outlook Bar command. You can also select the folder and drag it to the Outlook Bar.

- **Create a shortcut on your desktop.** If you access a public folder frequently, you might want to have it available directly on your desktop. You can add a shortcut to your desktop by selecting the folder from the folder list and dragging it onto the desktop.

Contributing to a Public Folder

Now that you can create, access, and read items in a public folder, you probably need to know how to contribute to one. After all, the idea of a public folder is that it is a place for people to share information. The way to contribute depends on the type of public folder you're in. As you might remember, public folders are set up for different reasons, including threaded conversations (discussion groups), shared documents, and shared Outlook components.

Threaded conversations

One of the main draws of the Internet is that it offers a worldwide community that can share its common interests. Whereas you might be used to a small town in which only two or three people share a hobby, the Internet might have hundreds or thousands of people who discuss this hobby regularly via newsgroups. There are over 10,000 newsgroups, ranging from comp.lang.c++ to alt.tv.dinosaurs.barney.die.die.die.

The key feature of these newsgroups is the idea of a threaded conversation. If you post a message in the Howard Stern newsgroup asking when his new movie is coming out, someone can reply to you in the same "thread." If another person is interested in the topic, he or she can read through the entire thread, following the flow of the conversation.

When using Outlook with Microsoft Exchange Server, you have the ability to set up public folders that behave in the same way as Internet newsgroups or bulletin boards do. For example, you might start a public folder where people can share tips and tricks, ask questions, and learn more about how people use a certain software package. Here's how it works:

- **Post a new message.** If you want to start a discussion or just share some information with others in a public folder, select that folder and choose the New Post In This Folder command from the Compose menu. Enter a subject, type a message, attach any necessary files, and then click the Post button to add your message to the folder.

NOTE When you say that you want to Post a new message in this folder, Outlook will use the default form for that public folder. Later in this chapter we'll talk about how you can customize this form. If you want to use a form other than the default form, you have two options. If the form you want to use is specific to a folder, it will appear at the bottom of the Compose menu when you are in that folder. For other custom forms, use the Choose Form command on the Compose menu to select from a list of custom forms.

- **Respond to an existing post.** If you are reading through the posts in a public folder and you want to reply to one, open the post and click the Post Reply button. You can then type your reply in the new "discussion" item. You'll notice that the field named Conversation gets filled in automatically. This is how Outlook keeps track of the different conversations. When you're done responding, click the Post button to add your message to the thread.

- **Responding and forwarding via mail.** You might want to take action on a post you see in a public folder, but not publicly. You can send your response directly to someone by opening the post and using the Reply or Forward buttons to send messages via e-mail.

- **Changing your view to see conversations.** By default, when you look at a public folder you will see a standard list of posts sorted by date. If you change the current view to By Conversation Topic, as shown in the illustration at the top of the next page, you might find the folder much more useful. Changing to the By Conversation Topic view will sort the items by topic, telling you how many items are in the conversation along with how many of those are unread.

13
CHAPTER

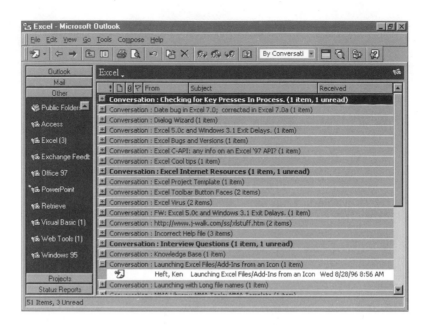

 Other options. Just because your public folder is set up for discussions doesn't mean you are limited to standard posts. Your public folder can include custom forms set up to facilitate the discussion. It can also include standard e-mail messages, Microsoft Excel spreadsheets, and other documents.

NOTE If you want to send an e-mail message to a public folder instead of using a post, create a new e-mail, click the To button, and look for the public folder name(s) in the address list. Provided your administrator has exposed the names to the address list, they will be available.

Shared documents

In your corporation, many documents are important to all employees. You might have an employee manual, annual report, various expense reports and other forms, project summaries, marketing materials, and so on. One way to ensure that all employees have easy access to these shared documents and that the versions are always the most current is to include them in a public folder.

A public folder can include any type of file, not just messages and posts. Office 97 documents, Web shortcuts, executables, and the like are all fair game. When you double-click on the item in Outlook, the appropriate application will be launched (for example, Word or Internet Explorer) and your document will appear. If your document was created using Outlook, it will appear as a mix between a mail message and an Office document. You will have the editing tools of the Office application (for example, Word's Format menu) along with Outlook components such as the Reply and Forward buttons.

Office 97 documents offer an added measure of integration. You can use the Properties command on the File menu to specify many properties of your document, from title and subject to language and custom properties you create. These properties can be linked to data within the document, including bookmarks in Word and ranges in Microsoft Excel. When you then share that document using Outlook public folders, you can display those properties directly in the view, as shown in Figure 13-12.

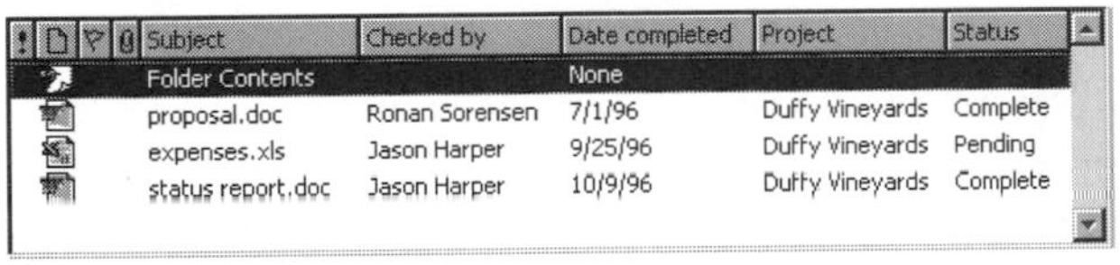

Figure 13-12
Outlook displaying Office Document properties.

Here are some methods for placing documents into your public folders:

🌐 **Create the document with Outlook.** Use the File/New/Office Document command to create a new Microsoft Excel, Word, or PowerPoint item. Using this method provides the greatest degree of integration with Outlook features.

🌐 **Drag and drop.** Find the documents you want to include in Windows Explorer and then drag them to the corresponding public folder in Outlook.

🌐 **Send to.** If you're trying to share a document created with Office 97, you can do so directly from the application. Suppose you are in a Word 97 document. Choose the Send To command from the File menu, select Exchange Folder, and then pick the folder you want to send to. This functionality is available in Word 97, Excel 97, and PowerPoint 97.

Calendars, contact lists, journal items, task lists, and notes

When you create a new public folder, you or your administrator must specify what type of information that folder will hold. In the previous sections, we discussed messages, posts, and documents—all of which fall under the category Mail Items. However, you can also choose Appointment Items, Contact Items, Journal Items, Note Items, or Task Items. When you create a folder of one of these types, Outlook will create a new calendar, contact list, or other item. This new folder will be completely separate from your default Calendar, Contacts, and so on that sit on your Outlook Bar.

Now let's talk about the uses for a public folder containing Outlook items. Suppose you want to create a single shared contact list for your entire company. You could do this by creating a public folder that stores an Outlook contact list. You or your administrator would create a new public folder that stores Contact Items and call it Corporate Contacts. By setting its permissions, you would specify who gets to see the contact list and who gets to update it. Employees would then see these contacts directly in their Outlook address book and use the contact list to send e-mail and faxes. Another idea is to create a public folder that stores an Outlook task list. You could then create a to-do list that is specific to one project or department.

With shared Outlook items, you can use the same techniques for creating tasks, scheduling appointments, and e-mailing contacts for both yourself and a project, department, or company. Here are some guidelines for creating Calendar Schedules, Contact Lists, Journal Items, Task Lists, and Notes in a public folder.

Adding a contact list to your Address Book   Suppose your project has a special contact list, separate from your default contact list. If you plan on sending e-mail or faxes to these contacts, it is very helpful to have the information available in an address book. Here are the steps for adding a contact list to your Address Book:

1. Make sure the Outlook Address Book is in your Services list. Select the Services command on the Tools menu. If Outlook Address Book is not on the list, click the Add button to include it in your profile. This will prompt you to restart Outlook.

2. From the folder list, right-click on the contact list that you want to add to your address book. Choose the Properties command.

3. Select the Outlook Address Book tab, shown in Figure 13-13, make sure the Show This Folder As An E-Mail Address Book check box is checked, and give a name to your book. Now, the next time you look in your Address Book, this contact list will be available.

Using a Journal in a public folder   You might want to add a Journal to your public folder to create a correspondence log for your project. However, your actions will not be recorded automatically in this Journal. Only

Figure 13-13
Adding your contact list to the Outlook Address Book.

your default Journal can store information automatically. This means that each time you send an e-mail message, save changes to an important document, and so on you must remember to enter a journal item manually. One alternative is to write code that creates journal items for you. We'll discuss the necessary code later in this chapter.

You do still have the ability to use drag and drop in a shared Journal. For example, if you call one of the contacts in your project, you can drag that contact into the Journal you are storing in the same public folder. This way, you can log the call, along with its duration, so that everyone involved on the project can see.

NOTE If you create a public folder that includes its own contact list and Journal, these items are unrelated. In other words, if Outlook is set up to log e-mail to your contacts, even if you use contacts from the public folder, it will still log them in your default Journal, not in the Journal stored in that public folder. The only way to log correspondence with these contacts is by dragging and dropping or manually entering the journal item.

Customized Outlook Forms

Whenever you choose to send an e-mail message, you get the same message form. It prompts you to enter recipients, cc addresses, subject, and so on. If you choose to create a task, appointment, or other Outlook item, you get a different form to fill out. Have you started wondering if there's a way to customize these forms? Well, as you might have guessed from the title of this section, the answer is yes.

You can customize the way mail messages, tasks, journal items, and so on appear on the screen. You can redesign the form by adding and removing fields, creating your own user-defined fields, and adding graphics, ActiveX controls, or even code. You can then save and publish these forms so that they can be used in the future. You can make it so that anyone who posts a message to a public folder will be using your custom form.

Forms do not have to be created using Outlook. If you have existing documents that you have created in Office, such as an expense report in Microsoft Excel or a proposal template in Word, you can use these as forms as well.

Forms Included with Outlook

Every time you create a new item in Outlook, it is based on a form. In addition to the standard appointment, contact, journal entry, message, note, post, and task forms, there are several sample forms that come on the Office 97 CD. To install these sample files, read the Help file (VALUPK8.HLP) that is found on the CD in the VALUPACK folder. Run the Help file and select Microsoft Office Templates, Forms, And Wizards. You can also use Outlook's Help menu and select Microsoft On The Web/Free Stuff to download the samples from the Web.

The sample forms include Classified Ads, Sales Tracking, Training Management, Vacation Request, and While You Were Out. To get an idea of how these forms work, let's look at the Sales Tracking sample form.

For the sake of this example, you're a salesperson. You spend a lot of time talking to people at different companies, making cold calls, scheduling appointments, and closing business deals. You need to know if other salespeople have contacts at these companies so that you don't overlap. And you would like to have a record of all correspondence with your contacts that can be shared among salespeople. The Sales Tracking form was designed for just these purposes.

When you contact a new company, you would go to the Sales Tracking public folder and select New Account from the Compose menu. This takes you to the Sales Tracking New Account form shown in Figure 13-14. You

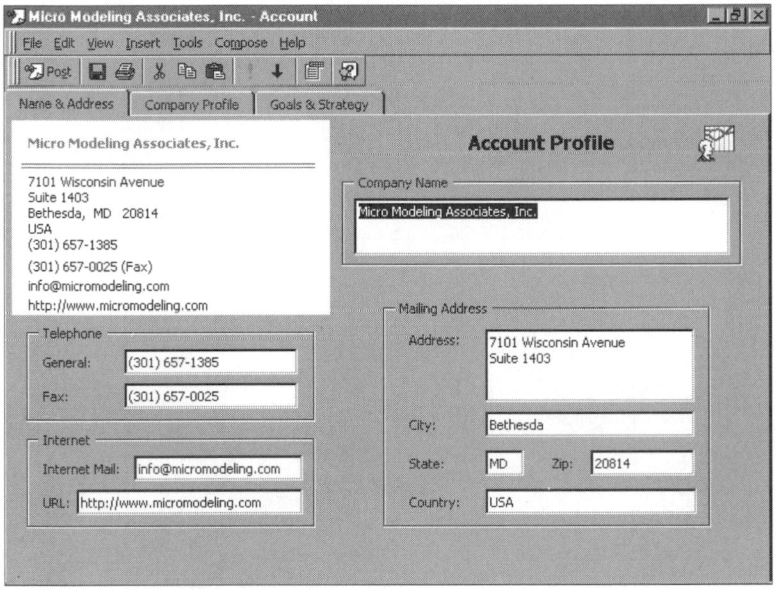

Figure 13-14

Composing a new account with the Sales Tracking form.

would then enter information such as the company name, phone number, and profile into a custom form. When you're done, you save the form to the public folder using the Post button.

In the future, whenever you are dealing with that company, you would open the posted message. This takes you to the Read page for the New Account form. It looks different from the form you used to enter the information, just as e-mail messages look different depending on whether you are reading or composing them. At the top of the form are five buttons: Contact, Opportunity, Action Item, Contact Report, and Response. An example of an existing account that has been opened from the posted account message is shown in Figure 13-15.

These five buttons appear instead of the standard Post Reply, Reply, and Forward buttons that you might be used to seeing. If you click one of these buttons, such as Contact, you will jump to a new form to enter the appropriate information.

Once you enter all the information and post your responses, you can then select from custom views such as Contacts By Account or Action Items By Contact to view your sales tracking information. Figure 13-16 shows Sales Tracking viewed by Contacts By Account.

CHAPTER 13

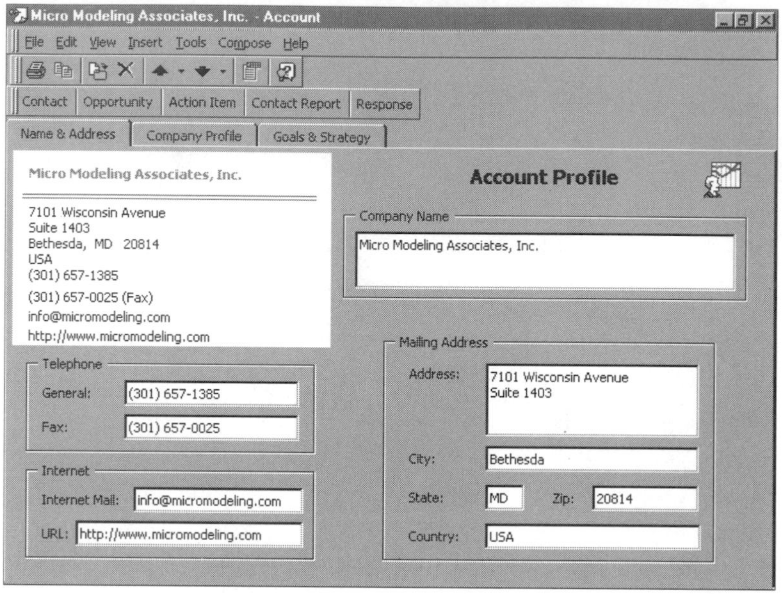

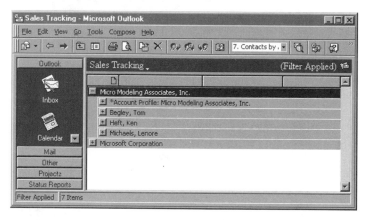

Figure 13-15

Reading an existing account.

Figure 13-16

Viewing contact information with a custom view.

Using Office Documents as Outlook Forms

In Outlook, you can create two types of custom forms. You can use the Outlook development environment to create a custom Outlook form, or you can customize Word documents, Microsoft Excel spreadsheets, or PowerPoint presentations and "wrap" them in Outlook.

Let's clarify this idea with an example. Suppose your current expense reporting system is done in Microsoft Excel. This makes sense, since Excel has built-in abilities that handle complex formatting, formulas, and tables. In your system, you might fill out your expense reports in Excel, send them as attachments to the proper person, who saves the file, opens it in Excel, reviews it, and so on. The problem is that the reviewer has no way of quickly glancing at a group of expense reports to find information. Each e-mail will show up with a subject and an attachment that needs to be opened separately.

By bringing this Microsoft Excel spreadsheet into Outlook, you can "promote" certain properties of the spreadsheet. For example, you might have cells that store the employee name, date, social security number, and total expense amount. When you post this "form" to an Outlook folder, you can view these fields just as easily as you view From, To, and Subject.

The benefit of using an Office document such as Microsoft Excel is that because you already know how to customize these documents there is no learning curve. But, as it is an imperfect world, you will experience problems and limitations along the way.

Creating a new Office document form

Depending on how you create your Office document form, you will get very different results. The most integrated way to create an Office document is to choose the New command from Outlook's File menu and select Office Document from the list of item choices. You can then select from Microsoft Excel Worksheet, Microsoft Excel Chart, Microsoft Word Document, and Microsoft PowerPoint Presentation. We'll call this approach the *integrated Office document*.

The problem with an integrated Office document is that it doesn't allow you to use any existing Office templates that you might have. Because you always have to use the File/New command, there is no way to open an existing document and convert it to an Office document that Outlook will integrate with. The alternative is to drag an existing Word document, Excel spreadsheet, or PowerPoint presentation directly into a public folder. You can also use the File/Send To/Exchange Folder command to send an Office document to a folder directly from the application. Either of these actions will produce what we'll call a *nonintegrated Office document*.

Integrated vs. nonintegrated Office document forms

So, what are the advantages of creating an integrated Office document form? Let's think back to the Microsoft Excel expense-reporting example. If you created this expense report in the standard, nonintegrated way, to create a new one you would launch Excel, create a new spreadsheet, and fill out your expenses. You would then either use the Send To command or save the spreadsheet and drag it to a public folder. When someone needs to review it, the user would double-click the item to open it in Excel, make changes to it, and then either save it under a different filename or use the Send To command to accept or reject the expenses.

If the expense sheet were integrated, you would create a new report by going to the proper public folder and selecting New Expense Report from the Compose menu. This would launch a window that contained a blend of Microsoft Excel and Outlook menus. You would be allowed to edit cells, formatting, and formulas as if you were in Microsoft Excel; but you could also use Outlook commands such as Post, Reply, and Forward. If you wanted to add your own custom actions, you could do so by opening your form in Outlook Design View. In other words, your Excel spreadsheet would inherit all the behavior of an Outlook form.

Those are the advantages of creating integrated Office document forms. Now for the disadvantages. First, the only way to convert an existing Office document to an integrated Office document form is to use the File/New/ Office Document command and then cut and paste from your original document to the new one. No conversion utilities are currently available. Second, there is no way to create a new integrated Office document based on an existing one. You cannot save an Office document as an Outlook template, only as an Office template (*.DOT, *.XLT, *.POT). And Outlook does not see these as valid templates for creating new forms.

Using Office document properties in Outlook

Whether you use an integrated or a nonintegrated Office document, you can still promote properties from your document to an Outlook view. The way you do this is through the Properties command on the File menu of an Office 97 application such as Microsoft Excel. Every document has a set of properties that you can set values for. Along with built-in properties such as Title, Subject, and Date Completed, you can create your own custom properties.

You can assign values to these properties in one of two ways. Using the File/Properties dialog box, you can enter hard-coded values manually. This is the way to enter information such as Subject and Author. You can also link the value of a field to data in your document. In Word, you can bind a field to the value entered in a bookmark (which can also be a form field). In Microsoft Excel, you can use values inside of named ranges. To bind a field to data in your document, select the Custom tab in the File/ Properties dialog box and make sure the Link To Content check box is checked. You can then choose from the linkable items in the Source drop-down box, as shown in Figure 13-17.

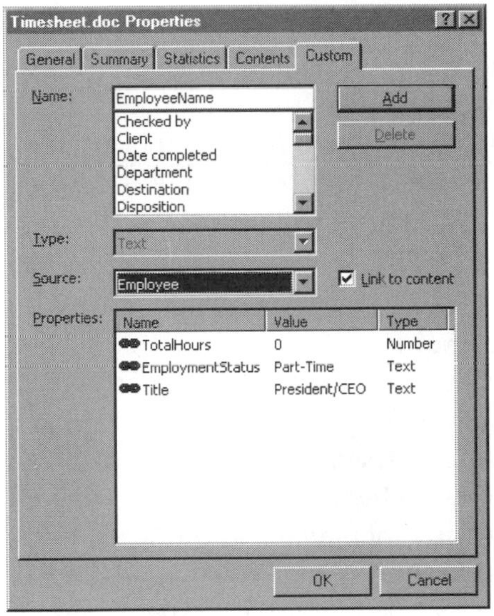

Figure 13-17

Binding properties to data in your Office document.

When you then post your document to a folder, these custom properties will be available for you to include in a view. Use the Show Fields command on the View menu, and select User-Defined Fields In Folder from the Select Available Fields From drop-down list. You can combine standard Outlook fields such as Size and Received with your custom document properties.

> **NOTE** Although you can view your Office document properties from Outlook, there is no way to set them directly from Outlook. You have to double-click on the item and change the property through the File/Properties dialog box.

Saving Office document forms

Once you've created your Office document form, you need to be able to access it in the future. If you chose the nonintegrated solution, you will save your Office documents as standard documents. Microsoft Excel spreadsheets will be saved as .XLS files, and so on.

If you chose the integrated method of using Office document forms, you have another option. You can use Outlook's Publish command to publish your form to a folder. This way, you can create a new instance of your Office document form by selecting it from the Compose menu. To learn more about publishing forms, read the "Publishing your form" section on page 494.

13
CHAPTER

How to Customize Outlook Forms

If you decide to create a custom Outlook form, you don't really start from scratch. The first step is to select an existing form to use as a starting point. Select the Choose Form command from the Compose menu, and pick a form that you'd like to modify. (The standard forms will be listed under Application Forms.) Keep in mind that you can change all aspects of the form once you start. Click OK, and you should be viewing your form. Select Design Outlook Form from the Tools menu, and you're ready to start.

The Outlook forms design environment

When you are designing an Outlook form, you might recognize the environment as being Visual Basic–like. You will find a grid, property windows, layout commands, and other user-friendly design features. On the Form menu, you can toggle the Control Toolbox, which is used to insert ActiveX controls on your form, just as you would in other Microsoft products. However, the environment is not quite the same as that you would find in Microsoft Excel 97, Word 97, PowerPoint 97, or Visual Basic 5.0.

In terms of technology, Outlook 97 uses Microsoft Forms. This is the standard environment for creating forms, adding ActiveX controls, and so on. However, Outlook does not use the standard Visual Basic Environment (VBE), nor does it support Visual Basic for Applications (VBA). If you want to add code to your form, you are stuck with VBScript, a subset of Visual Basic that is used mainly in HTML. There is also no debugger, so you are left to enter your script in a Notepad-like code window.

Creating the look of your form

There isn't enough room in this chapter to give you an in-depth guide to creating Outlook forms, but we'll at least point out some of the basics. You can customize all aspects of the form. You can add, remove, and rename the tabs that appear across the top of your form. You can even change the icon that appears next to your item when it is posted to a folder.

When it comes to adding controls, most of your controls will be bound to Outlook fields. Think of it as if you are designing a Microsoft Access form based on a table. You choose the fields you want to display and then drag them onto the form. It works the same way in Outlook. Use the Field Chooser to select the field you want, and then drag it onto your Outlook form. If a field doesn't exist for the data you want to track, you can create a new field by using the New button on the Field Chooser. Figure 13-18 shows an Outlook form in Design view.

Keep in mind when you are designing your form that you are actually designing two different forms, the Compose Page and the Read Page.

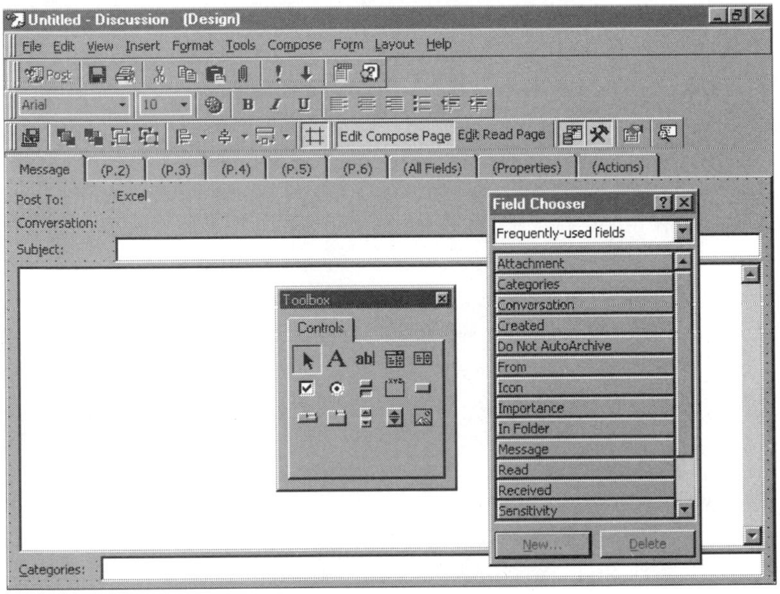

Figure 13-18
The Outlook form design environment.

To toggle between the two views, click the Edit Compose Page or Edit Read Page toolbar button. A typical difference between these two views is to have certain text boxes enabled in the Compose Page but read-only in the Read Page. Think of a standard e-mail message. When you compose the message, you can enter information such as the To, Cc, and Subject. When you read an e-mail message, all of this information is grayed out and uneditable. If you decide that the Compose Page and Read Page should be exactly the same, you can toggle the Separate Read Layout command on the Form menu.

If you want to add code to your form, use the View Code command on the Form menu to open the Script Editor. From there, you're pretty much on your own. You can turn to the Microsoft Web site or a variety of other Internet sites for documentation on VBScript.

Adding actions to your form

Earlier in this section, we talked about the Sales Tracking form for Outlook included with the Office 97 ValuPack. This form includes custom buttons such as Contact and Opportunity instead of the standard Post Reply, Reply, and Forward.

In fact, you can access these custom actions directly from the public folder. Let's say you're in your Sales Tracking public folder looking at a post for Microsoft's account profile. If you click on that item with your right mouse button, Contact, Opportunity, and the other custom actions are all available as commands on your shortcut menu.

The way to modify the actions associated with your form is to look at your form in Design view and go to the Actions tab. If your form is based on a Post, the list will have three entries: Reply, Forward, and Reply To Folder. If you look through the columns, you can see what effects each action will have. For example, the Forward action will create a new form based on the Message form (a standard e-mail message). The subject will be prefixed by FW, and the recipient list will be cleared so that you can enter a new list of recipients for the forwarded message.

If you want to disable any of these built-in actions, just set their enabled property to No. If you want to add a new action, click the New button at the bottom of the form to bring up the Form Action Properties dialog box. From here you can specify the action name, form to use (either standard or custom), and various other characteristics, as shown in Figure 13-19. When you publish your form, the new actions will appear on a special command bar at the top of your form.

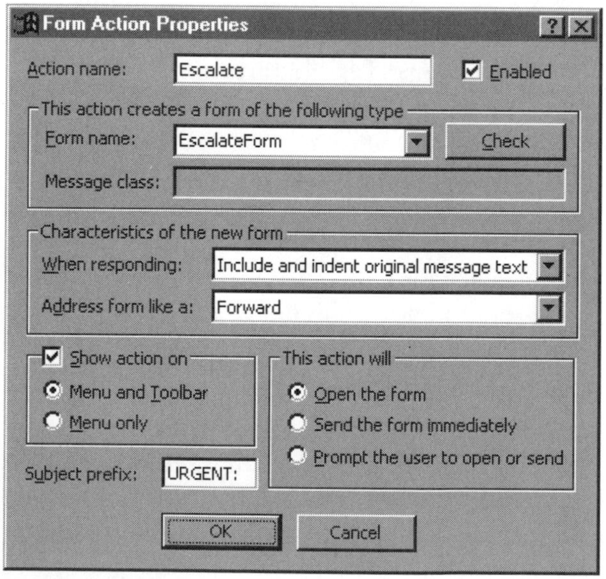

Figure 13-19

Creating a custom action for your form.

Saving and publishing forms

Once you create your form, you need to store it so that it can be used again in the future. You can store your form in two ways: by saving it as a template or by publishing it.

Saving your form as a template   Saving your form as a template is similar to saving a template in Word or Microsoft Excel. You are giving yourself a blueprint so that you can use this form again. If you find yourself sending the same basic e-mail message to a lot of people, you might fill out part of an e-mail message, including addressing information and a file attachment, and save it as a template. You can also customize a form (such as a message or an appointment) and save it as a template for future use. You can even move this template to your intranet or the Internet to create new forms via hyperlinks from Microsoft Internet Explorer or another Office document.

To save a form as a template, you use the Save As command on the File menu and choose Outlook Template (*.oft) as the Save As Type, as shown in Figure 13-20. To see these templates in the future, you should store the template in the Microsoft Office/Templates/Outlook folder or in a subfolder of it (for example, Microsoft Office/Templates/Outlook/Personal). You can use the Save As command from Design view of a custom form, from inside a form you are composing, or after selecting a message, journal entry, and so on from the Outlook window.

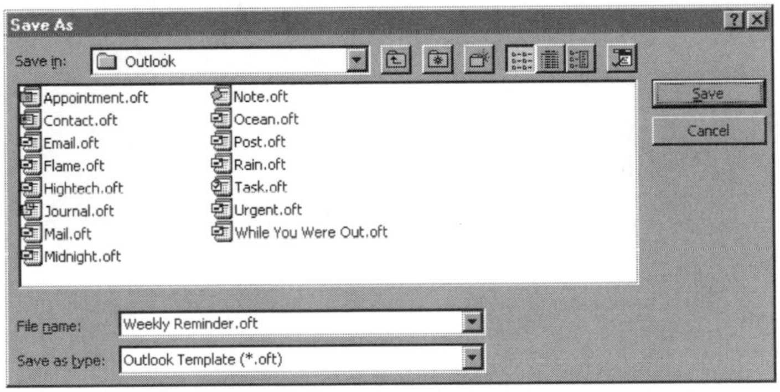

Figure 13-20
Saving an Outlook template.

To create an item based on a template, select the Choose Template command from the Compose menu. This will show you a list of custom templates that includes both templates you have created and some sample templates that ship with Outlook.

CHAPTER 13

Another way to create an item based on a template is to create a hyperlink to the template file. This hyperlink can be in an Office document or a browser such as Internet Explorer, provided the user has Outlook installed on his or her machine. For example, this hyperlink would create a new form based on the "MMA" template stored on Micro Modeling's intranet:

<http://intranet.micromodeling.com/mma.oft>

NOTE If you are saving a custom form as a template, you need to make sure to save the form definition with the item. You do this in Design view by clicking the Properties tab and checking the Save Form Definition With Item check box. By doing this, Outlook will store the form definition with the item you are sending. This enables the Outlook recipient to view the form even if his or her machine doesn't have the Outlook template.

Publishing your form   Earlier in this chapter, we talked about creating public folders. Suppose we set up a public folder to track software bugs (features) during the development process. Each time a user finds a bug, he or she needs to report certain pieces of information, such as the operating system and what was being attempted. So you create a custom form that allows a user to enter this information quickly and completely. But how do we bind the form to the public folder so that each time a user tries to post to that public folder, he or she gets the custom form? This is where publishing comes in. Here's how you publish a form to a folder (public or private):

1. Open a form in Design view, and choose the Publish Form As command from the File menu.

2. Name your form. The name of the class gets filled in automatically.

3. Click the Publish In button to invoke the Set Library To dialog box, shown in Figure 13-21.

4. Choose the Folder Forms Library option, select the proper folder, and click OK.

5. Click the Publish button.

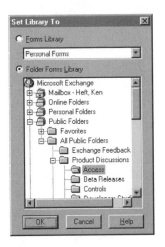

Figure 13-21

Publishing a form to a public folder.

Now when you select that public folder and go to the Compose menu, you should see a command at the bottom of the menu to create a new instance of your custom form. You can publish multiple forms to a public folder and choose which one should be the default. To choose the default form for a public folder, click on the folder with your right mouse button, choose the Properties command, and then select the General tab, shown in Figure 13-22 on the next page. Modify the When Posting To This Folder, Use entry to change the default form. In the future, any time you are in this folder and use the New Post In This Folder command on the Compose menu, you will see the custom form.

TIP
When you use the Publish command, you don't have to specify a folder to publish to. Instead, you can choose the Forms Library, which allows you to publish a new Personal Form or Organizational Form (if you are an administrator). A Personal Form is stored in your personal mailbox and is accessible only to you, whereas an Organizational Form is stored on the server and is available to everyone. In the future, you create new instances of these forms with the Choose Form command on the Compose menu from anywhere in Outlook.

CHAPTER 13

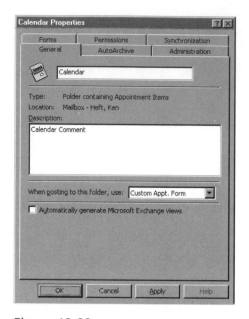

Figure 13-22

Selecting the default form for a public folder.

Rules

When new e-mail arrives, you sometimes know how to handle it without even opening the message, just by seeing who sent it or by its subject. For example, if the subject includes the words "Bake Sale," you might delete it without looking every time. If the subject includes the name of a project that you used to work on, you might want to send it to the new project manager automatically.

What if you're out of the office and unable to dial in to get your e-mail (a foreign concept for many people)? Can you really afford to let your e-mail accumulate in your Inbox? If you take this to the next level, picture a public folder that is set up to facilitate user discussions on a software product. Depending on the subject, you might want to have certain messages sent automatically to different technical experts.

Can you think of some rules that could be used to forward the right e-mail to the right people? If you can, then there are several commands that are perfect for you. For the individual, the Inbox Assistant and Out Of Office Assistant, both of which are accessed from the Tools menu, are designed to automate your Inbox. For a public folder, the corresponding command is the Folder Assistant.

NOTE To use the Inbox Assistant, Out Of Office Assistant, and Folder Assistant, you must be running Outlook with Exchange Server. You also must have the Inbox Assistant add-in loaded.

The Inbox Assistant

You use the Inbox Assistant to create rules for handling e-mail messages that arrive in your Inbox. For each rule, you specify criteria along with the action(s) to take. If you create multiple rules, they will be applied in the order that you indicate.

Criteria can include a list of senders, words to look for in the subject or message body, or a list of recipients. If you click the Advanced option in the Edit Rule dialog box, you can set options for everything from the date received to whether or not the message had an attachment.

Once you've identified the messages, you have to specify the action(s) to take. Actions include displaying an alert, deleting, moving, copying, forwarding, and replying. You can specify that multiple actions take place. Figure 13-23 shows a rule that *replies* to the user, telling her the message is being forwarded to the proper person; *forwards* all messages about training to the right person; and *deletes* the message. To set the text of your reply, you create a template and save it, using the Template button.

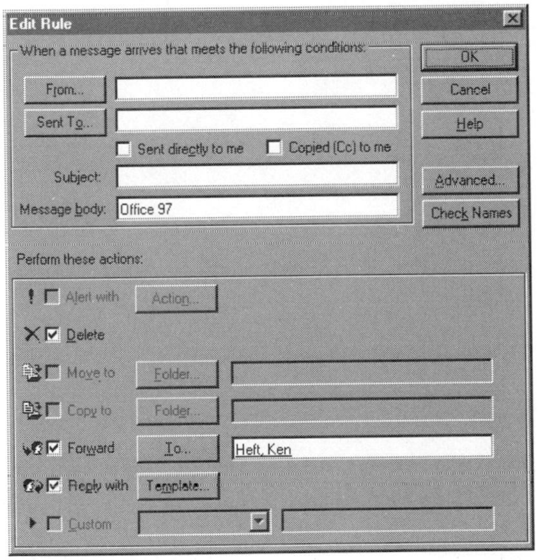

Figure 13-23

Editing a rule with the Inbox Assistant.

Out Of Office Assistant

You can use the Out Of Office Assistant to handle incoming e-mail when you are out of the office. If you'll be unable to respond to e-mail for a time, you should use this assistant to alert people to this fact.

You enable the Out Of Office Assistant by choosing the command and selecting the I Am Currently Out Of The Office option, as shown in Figure 13-24. You then specify the message that you would like to use to automatically reply to people the first time they send you a message. You will still continue to receive messages, but you will be alerting people that you are not in the office. If you want to do more than just reply, you can specify rules for handling incoming e-mail in the same way you do with the Inbox Assistant.

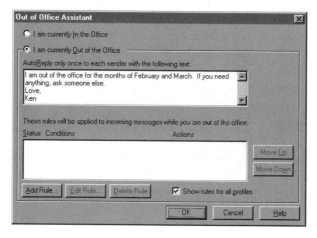

Figure 13-24

Setting up e-mail rules using the Out Of Office Assistant.

Folder Assistant

The Folder Assistant allows a public folder owner to create or modify rules for that folder. To access the Folder Assistant, select a public folder from the folder list and click on it with your right mouse button. Select Properties, choose the Administration tab, and click the Folder Assistant button. The process for creating rules is the same as it is with the Inbox Assistant or Out Of Office Assistant.

The Outlook Object Model

So are you thinking, "All this is great, but now how do I automate it through code?" Luckily, Outlook has a full object model that can be implemented anywhere . . . except from Outlook. Outlook is not a VBA host. Therefore, if you want to automate Outlook, you need to open Visual Basic, Microsoft Excel 97, or another Office 97 application. You can then create a reference to the Microsoft Outlook 8.0 Object Model and scroll through it using the Object Browser, shown in Figure 13-25.

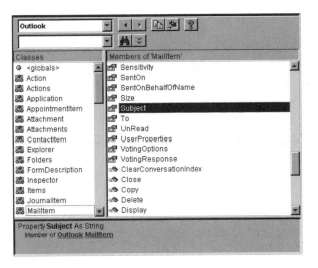

Figure 13-25
The Visual Basic 5 Object Browser showing the Outlook object model.

Overview

The Outlook Object model contains all the tools you'll need to access data in Outlook. It was designed to let you create new e-mail messages, appointments, contacts, and so on and to access the data in existing items. If your goal is to manipulate views and change the Outlook user interface, the object model provides little help. If you're looking for more help in using the Outlook object model, the Office 97 CD includes a Help file named

VBAOUTL.HLP. This file ships as part of the ValuPack, in the MOREHELP folder (or it can be installed by following instructions under the Additional Help Files section of the ValuPack Help file).

The Main Players

Here is a quick guide to the most important objects, properties, and methods you'll need to get started automating Outlook:

- **Outlook.Application.** This object expression is how you create a connection to Outlook. From VBA, use the code

```
CreateObject(Outlook.Application)
```

to create a new instance of Outlook.

- ***Application*.CreateItem(*Item Type*).** Use the CreateItem method to create a new appointment, contact, and so on. The constants you need are olAppointmentItem, olContactItem, olJournalItem, olMailItem, olNoteItem, olPostItem, and olTaskItem.

- **AppointmentItem, ContactItem, JournalItem, and so on.** These are the actual Outlook item objects. These objects have properties such as Subject, Body, and many other data-related values.

- **NameSpace.** This is the central object in Outlook for referencing existing folders and items. To get to the NameSpace object, you use this syntax: *Application*.GetNameSpace("MAPI").

- **Folders and items properties.** These properties can be used to move from the NameSpace to the specific Outlook item you want, either MAPIFolder or one of the item types (for example, ApplicationItem or MailItem). You can refer to individual folders and items either with index numbers or case-sensitive names. The following example moves to an e-mail called Follow-Up in the Sent Items folder:

```
Dim objOutlook as Object
Dim objNS as NameSpace

Set objOutlook = CreateObject("Outlook.Application")
Set objNS = objOutlook.GetNamespace("MAPI")
objNS.Folders("Mailbox - Heft, Ken").Folders("Sent Items") _
    .Items("Follow-Up").Display
```

NOTE Here is a note for you object model purists. Even though Folders is listed as a property, it is behaving like a method in this example. When you say objNS.Folders("Mailbox - Heft, Ken"), you are really using a method that returns a single MAPIFolder object. Also note that you can use the Folders "property" both on a NameSpace object and on a MAPIFolder object. This is the way to move through multiple levels of Outlook folders.

🌐 **GetDefaultFolder.** From the preceding example, you can see that moving to the Sent Items folder looks pretty difficult because it depends on the person's name. An easier way to get to the default Inbox, Outbox, Sent Items folder, and so on is to use the GetDefaultFolder method of the NameSpace object. The following example shows the number of unread e-mail messages in a user's Inbox:

```
MsgBox "You have " & _
    objNS.GetDefaultFolder(olFolderInbox).UnReadItemCount & _
    " unread e-mail(s) in your Inbox."
```

Example

Suppose you are creating a setup program for a custom application. The setup program creates a text file that acts as a log file and contains information about the success or failure of the installation. A nice feature would be to have your setup program automatically log itself in the Outlook *Journal*, indicating the time and duration of the installation and containing a shortcut to the setup log file. Here's how you'd do it:

```
Sub CreateJournalEntry()

Dim objOutlook As Object
Dim objNewJournalEntry As JournalItem
Dim objAttachments As Attachments

Set objOutlook = CreateObject("Outlook.Application")
Set objNewJournalEntry = objOutlook.CreateItem(olJournalItem)
```

(continued)

```
With objNewJournalEntry
    .Type = "CustomApp"
    .Subject = "Installation"
    .StartTimer
End With

'Code to install application and create log file.

Set myAttachments = objNewJournalEntry.Attachments
myAttachments.Add "C:\install log.txt"
'More .Add statements could be used to create multiple attachments.

objNewJournalEntry.StopTimer
objNewJournalEntry.Save

End Sub
```

Web Browsers and the Internet

Most of the features we've discussed so far rely on all parties having the Outlook client installed on their desktops. However, this is not always the case in a larger corporation. Some employees might be using Windows 95 and Outlook, whereas others might have Windows 3.1 or even an Apple. In this section, we'll discuss some intranet and Internet abilities of Outlook, both for the Outlook-only and for mixed-platform corporations.

Using Outlook over the Internet

When you're using Outlook with an Internet connection, a few issues arise. What happens when you send a form or an appointment request to an Internet recipient? Is there any way to connect to an Exchange Server directly using the Internet instead of having to use Remote Access?

Sending Outlook components to Internet recipients

In this chapter, we've talked a lot about forms, appointments, e-mail, tasks, contacts, and notes. Outlook makes it very easy to send these items around the office. Just create a new meeting, invite your co-workers, and wait for responses. It's all very user-friendly and has a consistent look. But what if one of the parties you want to invite can be reached only with Internet mail?

Although sending attachments via Internet mail can sometimes be unreliable, your Outlook forms, appointments, e-mail messages, and so on will all arrive intact as long as you follow a few rules. First, all recipients must be using Outlook. This rule actually has nothing to do with the Internet. Even if you send a form over your intranet to a co-worker who doesn't have

Outlook installed, he or she won't be able to see the form either. Second, if you create a custom form, make sure to save the form definition with the item. (We discussed this earlier in the chapter.) Basically, when you check this option, Outlook stores the form definition with the form, so the recipient will be able to see the same form on his or her machine.

Connecting to Exchange Server via the Internet

Another capability you have with Outlook is that you can connect to your back-end Exchange Server via the Internet. This means that no matter where you are in the world, you can connect to the Internet, point to your corporate Exchange Server, and access your Inbox, public folders, and so on as if you were in the office.

Of course, plenty of server-side issues will come up when you do this. It's not magic. For one, you have to worry about security and firewalls. But if you decide connecting to your Exchange Server via the Internet is a feature you want, you must expose your server to the Internet and assign it a name. Then you would type in the Internet address of your server (for example, exchange.micromodeling.com) when listing the location of your Exchange Server in your Outlook profile. Outlook can then find the server over the Internet and display your mailbox.

Accessing E-mail, Appointments, and Public Folders with a Browser

If you're running Exchange Server 4.5 or later, you have the ability to read and send e-mail and appointment items and view public folders (containing e-mail messages) directly from a Web browser. With the Web Service feature included in Exchange Server 4.5, you can access these items even if you don't have Outlook or Exchange Client installed on your desktop. If your company is in a mixed environment, it means that all employees can access their e-mail, even if they are on a Macintosh or Windows 3.1 system.

NOTE If you do have Outlook installed on your machine, you can access Outlook folders and forms from a Web page in a Web browser just by using hyperlinks such as *outlook://folder name* or *http://formname.oft*. Although this solution requires Outlook, it does not require Exchange Server.

The Web Service also provides for another scenario. What if you have an internal public folder that you think would be valuable to individuals outside your company? Perhaps you have a public folder set up to handle wish lists or suggestions. You could use Exchange Server's security to grant

13
CHAPTER

permission to certain clients, expose the Exchange Server to the Internet, and let your clients access the public folder via the Internet. They could then view existing e-mail messages in the public folder and create their own, all through HTML and a Web browser.

Really Cool Things in Outlook

Where should we start? Here are a few of the cool Outlook features that you won't be able to live without once you experience them:

- 🌐 **Date recognition.** Anywhere you have to type a date in Outlook (for example, a start time for a new appointment or a due date for a task), type an expression in everyday language. "Tomorrow," "Next Thursday," "First Monday in Sept," and "Cinco de Mayo" all work perfectly.

- 🌐 **Birthday and anniversary reminders.** When you set up a contact person, you can include personal information such as a birthday or anniversary date. When you open Outlook on that day, you will see a reminder message alerting you about the special day.

- 🌐 **Print your contact list.** Your contacts will automatically print alphabetically and be grouped by letter if you choose the Address Cards or Detailed Address Cards view. Your list of contacts comes out formatted and looking sharp.

- 🌐 **Web history.** Create a shortcut to your Internet Explorer HISTORY folder to view your Web surfing experiences in Outlook. In Windows Explorer, select the HISTORY subfolder of the Windows folder. Right-click on the HISTORY folder and choose Create Shortcut. A shortcut to the HISTORY folder is created in your Windows folder. Drag this shortcut to the Favorites folder in the Other group in the Outlook Bar. To see a list of URLs in the HISTORY folder from Outlook, open the Favorites folder and double-click on the History shortcut.

Sample Application

Micro Modeling is a software development company. It creates custom applications for various clients. Each application is actually part of a project, which includes consulting, custom development, training, and other services. For each project, MMA needs to maintain similar pieces of information.

A new project form that indicates the vital statistics for the project—such as name, manager, and description—has to be filled out. Many other documents are also associated with the project, such as proposals, meeting notes, and technical documentation. A project timeline includes milestones, due dates, and scheduled meetings. All of this information needs to be readily accessible by both the project team and management.

In our sample application, you will examine an Outlook-based project management system that includes all of the above information and more.

Overview

To make all of the project information accessible, it will be stored inside of Outlook public folders. At the highest level will be a public folder named "MMA Projects." This folder will initially contain a folder named "Template." The Template folder contains all the subfolders and items that you want to copy each time MMA starts a new project.

Now we need some way to create a new project from within Outlook. To do this, we will create a Visual Basic application that prompts you for some project details and then creates a new project in Outlook based on the Template folder. Ideally, you could launch this executable directly from the Outlook Bar, in the same way you launch My Computer. However, Outlook does not provide this functionality. The next best thing is to create a shortcut to the directory containing the executable and put it on the Outlook Bar—not a bad compromise.

Finally, we'd like a way to get a quick summary of all MMA's projects. We can do this by automating Outlook and reading information from documents stored in our public folders. To make this information accessible in and out of the office, we will present this information as an HTML document, viewable by any browser. To do this, we will use Microsoft Active Server Pages to create a dynamic, server-side Web page.

The Template

The Template folder is a blueprint for creating public folders for new projects. It contains a Project Initiation Form, bug list, project calendar, documents, issues, mail, and status reports. The documents included in these folders are a combination of Outlook items and Office 97 documents.

Getting started

To start things off, you have to create the folder structure on the server. This must be done by an administrator who has the rights to create new public folders. The command to create a new folder is Create Subfolder and is found under the Folder command on the File menu.

13 CHAPTER

As you can see in Figure 13-26, the Template folder contains six items. Four of them, Bug List, Documents, Mail, and Status Reports, are all standard mail folders. Issues and Project Calendar are Outlook items—a task list and a calendar. To create these two special folders, you use the same Create Subfolder command, but make sure to specify that the folders contain Task Items and Appointment Items, respectively. Figure 13-27 shows how you would create the Project Calendar folder.

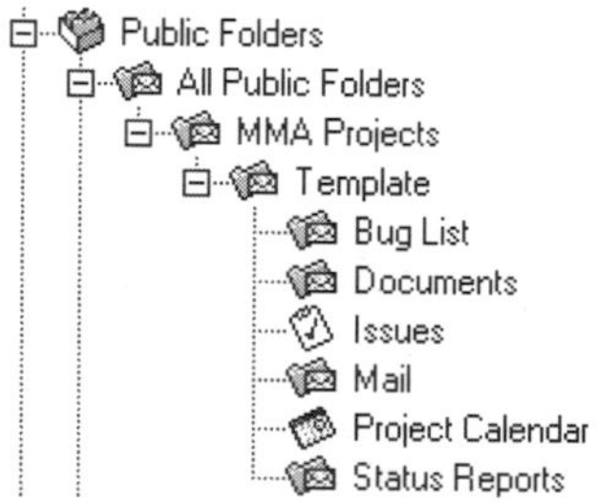

Figure 13-26

Structure of the Project Manager's public folders.

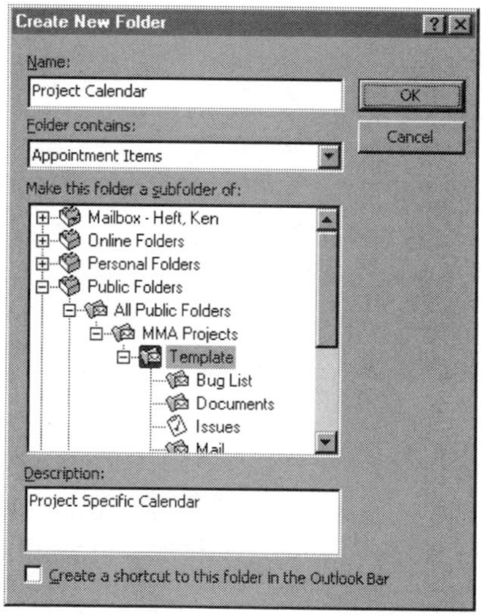

Figure 13-27

Creating a Project Calendar folder.

Project initiation form

Every time MMA starts a new project, a Project Initiation Form must be filled out. This form includes information such as the project name, start date, and description. As the project continues, this form can be updated, giving its status and providing more detailed documentation if necessary. The form is a customized Outlook form that is posted to the root directory of a project.

Creating the form   Here is a guide to getting started designing the Project Initiation Form:

1. In Outlook's folder list, highlight the Template public folder under MMA Projects.

2. Select New Post In This Folder from the Compose menu.

3. Select Design Outlook Form from the Tools menu.

4. On the Form menu, look to see if there is a check mark next to Separate Read Layout. If there is, select this command to toggle the check mark off. Click Yes when prompted to discard changes to the read layouts. This enables you to use the same custom form to compose and view posts.

Designing the form   Now that you have entered "design mode" in your custom form, you can start adding controls, setting properties, and creating the look you want. The easiest way to start is by removing all the controls on the form that you don't need. In this case, you can remove all the controls except the Post To label and the In Folder label (Template) found at the top of the form.

Follow these steps to add the Project Name label and text box:

1. Make sure the Field Chooser and Control Toolbox are visible. If they are not, select them from the Form menu.

2. Click the New button on the Field Chooser. Then for its name type "ProjectName", leave the type and format as text, and click OK.

3. Drag the ProjectName field from the Field Chooser to your Outlook form, underneath the existing fields. This will give you a label and text box.

4. Click the ProjectName text box with your right mouse button. Select the Properties command and then the Value tab of the dialog box. Notice that ProjectName was automatically selected as the field. This link will be very important later.

CHAPTER 13

Follow similar steps to create new fields and controls for StartDate, ProjectOwner, ProjectStatus, Funded, and ProjectDescription. For Funded, set up the field so that it stores Yes/No values instead of text. For ProjectStatus, there are a few tricks we need to use to add option buttons. The completed form is shown here:

Here is a guide to setting up the Project Status option buttons on your Outlook form.

1. Create a new field called "ProjectStatus" to store text values.

2. Use the Toolbox to create a new frame on your form. Set the Caption in the frame's Properties dialog box to "Status". Inside that frame, place three option buttons.

3. View the properties of the first option button. On the Display tab, enter the caption you want displayed next to the option button; in this case we'll use "Green". On the Value tab, click the Choose Field button and select the ProjectStatus field from the User Defined Fields In Folder, as shown at the top of the next page:

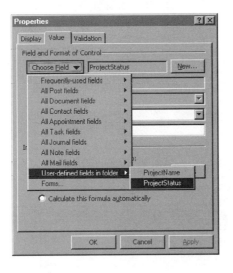

4. In the Value text box, enter the value that you want to store when that option is selected. You might choose for the value to be the same as the caption or you might want to use codes for automation. For example, if your options are Green, Amber, and Red, you can use those text values or you might choose codes, such as 1, 2, and 3.

Your form should be almost complete. The last control to talk about is the bitmap. You insert the bitmap using the Image control on the Toolbox. Select the Image control, click on the form, and then drag the image onto your form. Select the Advanced Properties command from the control's shortcut menu. Here you can set the Picture property along with other options such as PictureSizeMode and SpecialEffect.

One last step before we're done. When you are designing the form, you can also decide what actions users can take with the form. For example, you might want to let users forward the form to another person but not be able to post a reply to the folder. You might even want to take a custom action. You can change the default actions by clicking the Actions tab (the right-most tab) on your form in Design view.

CHAPTER 13

For this example, we want users to have the ability to either reply to the person who created the project initiation form or forward the form to someone else. However, we don't want users to reply to the folder. To do this, you need to find the Reply To Folder action and set its enabled property to No, as shown in Figure 13-28.

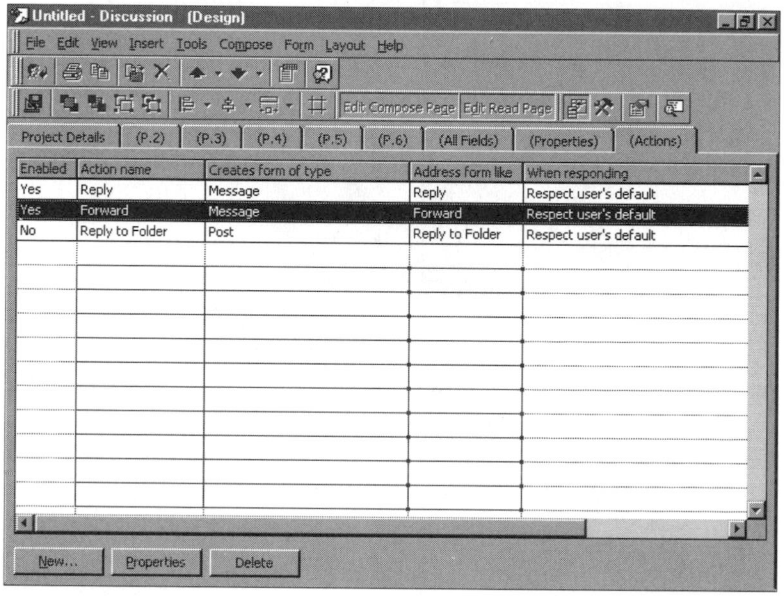

Figure 13-28

Enabling and disabling actions in an Outlook form.

Tips and tricks for designing forms   Here are a few tips and tricks that can keep you from pulling out all of your hair while designing your first Outlook form:

- 🌐 **The Escape key: stay away from it!** If you are accustomed to using the Escape key to make dialog boxes go away, try to get away from this habit. Depending on when you hit the Escape key, Outlook will often think you want to close your form.

- 🌐 **Resize With Form property.** An Outlook form will always be resizeable. With that in mind, consider how you want your form to look when it resizes. With the Properties dialog box, you can set or clear the Resize With Form check box for each control on the form. The one exception is the Message field. There is no way to prevent this field from resizing with the form.

- ⊕ **MultiLine property.** If you want users to be able to type multiple lines of text in a text box, don't forget the MultiLine and WordWrap properties, found in the Advanced Properties of a text box.

- ⊕ **Accelerator keys.** Outlook forms support accelerator keys for keyboard access. Use an ampersand (&) in front of the proper letter in the control's caption property.

- ⊕ **Tab order.** Use the Advanced Properties of controls to set the TabIndex property.

- ⊕ **Initial values.** Use the Value tab of the Properties dialog box to set the initial value of each control. This is especially important for option buttons and check boxes.

- ⊕ **Formulas.** When you assign an initial value to a field, it can be based on a formula. Just choose the Edit button on the Value tab of the Properties dialog box for help building a custom formula. For example, if you want the Start Date text box to display today's date, set its initial value to *Date( )*.

- ⊕ **Form title.** To change the text that appears on your form's title bar, use the Properties tab of the form and change the Form Caption property.

Saving and publishing the form   Now that you've finished designing your form, it's time to save and implement it. To do this, select Publish Form As from the File menu. Because you want to make this form specific to a folder, click the Publish In button to bring up the Set Library To dialog box. By doing this you can be sure you are publishing to the proper folder, which in this case is the Template folder. (See Figure 13-29.) Give your form a name (for example, Project Initiation Form), and publish it. If you want to use this form as a base for creating other forms, you could also save this file out as a template, using the Save or Save As commands from the File menu.

Now when you return to Outlook and go to the Template public folder, you'll be able to create a new Project Initiation Form using the Compose menu. However, if you create a new post by clicking the toolbar button or using the New Post In This Folder command on the Compose menu, you'll still get a standard Outlook post. To fix this, you need to change the properties of the Template folder, setting its When Posting To This Folder, Use property to your custom form, as shown in Figure 13-30.

CHAPTER 13

Figure 13-29

Publishing a custom Outlook form to the Template folder.

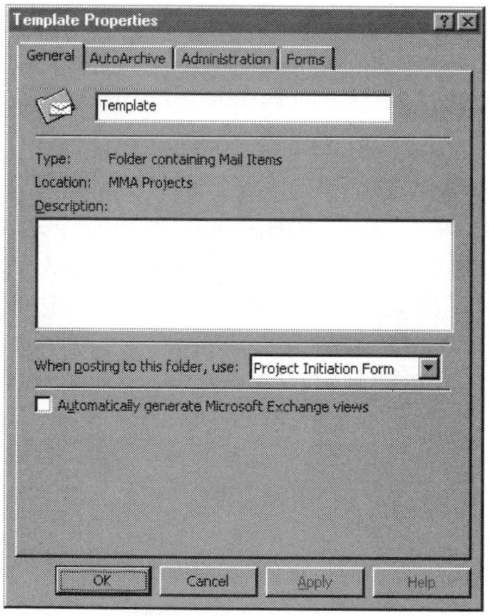

Figure 13-30

Setting the default form for a custom folder.

Changing the view   So you've created your custom Outlook form to store the overall status of your project. The only trouble is that when you open the folder and look at the item from within your Outlook window, the

512

only information you see is the sender, subject, and so on. If you want to find any of the useful information, you have to double-click on the object to open the form. Wouldn't it be nice if you could view information such as the project name, status, and start date directly from the Outlook window? Why, yes it would, and Outlook lets you! Another nice touch would be if you could change some of this information directly from the window, without ever launching the form. This is also possible in Outlook.

Here's what you need to do to change the view for the Template folder so that you can get the most information at a glance:

1. Select the Template folder in Outlook and choose the Show Fields command from the View menu.

2. Remove all the existing fields from the right side of the dialog box.

3. Under Select Available Fields From, select User-Defined Fields In Folder.

4. Add all the Available Fields to the right side of the dialog box. Change the order so that they appear as follows (top to bottom): ProjectStatus, ProjectName, StartDate, ProjectOwner, Project-Description, and Funded. Click OK.

5. Resize the column headings so that all the fields are legible.

6. Select Format View from the View menu. Make sure the Allow In-Cell Editing check box is checked, and then click OK. This will allow you to make changes to any of the visible fields without ever launching the form. To make changes, just click on a field and type a new value. To launch the form, double-click.

7. Select Define Views from the View menu. Make sure the <Current View Settings> record is selected, and click the Copy button.

8. Give a name to your new view (for example, Project View), select the This Folder, Visible To Everyone option, and click OK. Click OK when prompted to make modifications, and then click Close to return to Outlook.

By saving your customized view, you now have an easy way of switching between this view and other Outlook views by using the Current View tool on the standard toolbar. Choose Message Timeline from the list of current views to see another example. Then choose Project View to return to your customized settings. Notice that you can now type in a new start date or project description without launching the form.

CHAPTER 13

Bug list

The bug list is a public folder that serves as a central location for storing information about known bugs in a particular application. When someone finds a bug, he or she creates a new bug report and posts it to this folder. Developers can review the list of bugs, assign priorities to them, research them, and update their statuses. Observers can then look over the bugs and see what progress has been made.

The Bug List folder is a standard folder created as a subfolder of the Template folder. It contains Mail Items. When you post to this folder, you will be using a custom Outlook Bug Report form, as shown in Figure 13-31.

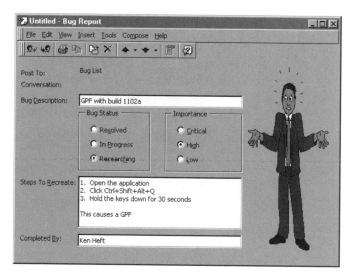

Figure 13-31

Custom Bug Report form.

To create the custom Bug Report form, you follow the same steps you did to create the Project Initiation form. After you complete the form, you can create a custom view that shows the name of the person who found the bug, the bug status, importance, and description. Also make sure that the Bug Report is the default form used for posting to the Bug List folder.

Project calendar

For every project, it is very important to keep track of the project's timeline. Staying on top of your timeline is crucial not only for organizing the future (meetings, deadlines, and so on) but also for documenting the past. Keeping an accurate calendar can help you remember details such as when important meetings took place and when different project versions were released.

To insert a new calendar that is specific to a folder, you select that folder, create a new subfolder (for example, Project Calendar), and indicate that the folder should hold Appointment Items, as we did earlier. You can then use this calendar to schedule appointments, enter due dates, and use any of the other features of a standard Outlook calendar.

Documents

Outlook can store not only forms, messages, and appointments but also a variety of file types. In the Documents subfolder, we want to store all the documents related to the current project. These "documents" can be Word documents, Microsoft Excel spreadsheets, Outlook messages, and so on. You might find that having one folder for all your project documents is not sufficient. You might then switch to a system of subfolders and use one for internal communications and another for client communications. You could break it down even further, based on the purpose of the document. Whatever you want to do to support your corporate structure, Outlook can be very flexible.

Issues

The Issues folder is really just an Outlook task list. By putting it within a project, you can create a list of project-specific tasks, assign them to the proper people, and have a well-documented list of assignments. Again, the idea is to have all the project information centrally located.

Mail

The Mail folder is basically an inbox for an individual project. It is set up to store mail items related to the project. The idea is that all communications about a project should be public. So if you wanted to ask one of the developers a question, you would send it to the public folder and he or she would then respond via the public folder. This way, all members of the project team can benefit from the questions and answers.

The only trick to the Mail folder is to get the folder listed in Outlook's global Address Book. This is a step that must be handled on the server side by an administrator. Our sample application could automatically send an e-mail request to the administrator to add the new folder to the address list each time a new project is created.

Status report

For every project, a weekly meeting is held to discuss the project's status. Out of this meeting, a status report is filled out and kept on record. The Status Report folder provides an online way to complete this form and share the information with the rest of the project team.

The Status Report form, shown in Figure 13-32, is another customized Outlook form. The only new feature of this form is that it includes multiple tabs. To include multiple tabs in your form, follow these steps:

1. In form Design view, click on a new tab (for example, "(P.2)"). Then select Display This Page from the Form menu.

2. Choose the Rename Page command from the Form menu to give a new name to the tab.

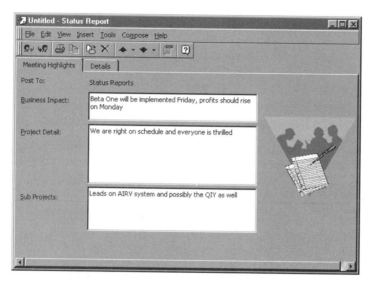

Figure 13-32

Custom Status Report form.

Creating New Projects

So we've set up the default project. The blueprint contains the folder structure we need, the custom forms we want to use, and the correct views defined in each folder. Now, how do we create a new project? One answer would be to copy the Template folder and go back to fine-tune it to the individual project. But, wouldn't it be nice if we could automate this process? That way, you could fill in the name of the project and through automation the folder structure would get copied, the names already filled in, a project initiation form created, and so on.

Overview

Outlook provides an object model, which allows you to automate it from any Automation client. (Note, however, that Outlook is not an Automation client.) For this demonstration, we're going to choose Visual Basic 4.0 – 32 bit. Here are the basic steps we need to follow:

1. Collect the necessary information from the user (project name, owner, and so on).

2. Establish a connection to Outlook.

3. Copy the Template folder structure to a new folder and rename the folders appropriately.

4. Create a project initiation form with the proper information filled in.

In order to complete these four tasks in our project, we take advantage of Visual Basic class modules. For this project we created a class named "MMAProjectMgr", that acts as a project manager "object." This class/object contains properties and methods that allow us to manipulate it. For example, we use the NewProject method of the MMAProjectMgr object to create a new project. We use the object's properties to get and set project attributes, such as ProjectManager or StartDate. In the next section, we'll examine some of the sample code.

The Visual Basic application

The Visual Basic application (MMA NEW PROJECT.VBP, available in the VB CODE subfolder of the Chapter13 folder on the companion CD) consists of three pieces: a form, a module, and a class module. When you launch the Visual Basic application, you are running Sub Main in the module. This routine creates an instance of the MMAProjectMgr object and then calls its method that displays the main form (ShowMe).

```
Sub Main()

    Dim objNew As New MMAProjectMgr

    objNew.ShowMe
    objNew.NewProject

End Sub
```

13
C
H
A
P
T
E
R

The form, shown in Figure 13-33, collects all the information from the user. It contains standard labels, text boxes, and check boxes. There are only two pieces of code behind the form: a routine to set a default start date and a routine behind the OK button that checks to make sure all fields were filled out.

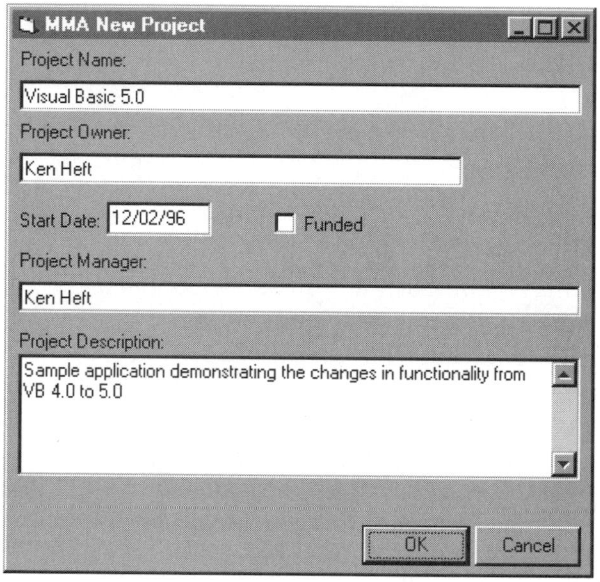

Figure 13-33

Collecting project information with a VB form.

When you click the OK button, the application needs to take this information and apply it in Outlook. The NewProject method accomplishes this in several steps. The first step is to connect to the Outlook object.

To take advantage of Visual Basic's early binding, we first create a reference to the Microsoft Outlook 8.0 Object Library using the References dialog box. Then we write some code to establish a connection to the Outlook Application and NameSpace objects. The NameSpace object is a central object for accessing existing mail items.

```
Dim objOut As Outlook.Application
Dim objName As Outlook.NameSpace
Dim objTemplateFolder As Outlook.MAPIFolder
Dim objNewFolder As Outlook.MAPIFolder
Dim objItem As Object

On Error GoTo NewProject_Err
```

```
'Create Outlook object.
Set objOut = CreateObject("outlook.application.8")
Set objName = objOut.GetNamespace("MAPI")
```

Once we are connected to the Outlook object, we can copy the existing Template folder along with its subfolders, creating the new project.

```
'Create a reference to the Template folder.

Set objTemplateFolder = _
    objName.Folders("Public Folders") _
    .Folders("All Public Folders") _
    .Folders("MMA Projects").Folders("Template")

'Copy the Template folder to a new directory.

Set objNewFolder = objTemplateFolder _
    .CopyTo(objName.Folders("Public Folders") _
    .Folders("All Public Folders"). _
    .Folders("MMA Projects"))
```

We then make some changes to the new project. First we edit the project initiation form so that it reflects the current project. Then we rename the Mail folder so that it also reflects the name of the current project.

```
'Edit the Project Description post in the folder.
Set objItem = objNewFolder.Items(1)

With objItem
    'Change the user-defined properties.
    .UserProperties("ProjectName").Value = ProjectName
    .UserProperties("StartDate").Value = StartDate
    .UserProperties("ProjectOwner").Value = ProjectOwner
    .UserProperties("ProjectDescription").Value = Description
    .UserProperties("ProjectStatus").Value = "New"
    .UserProperties("Funded").Value = Funded
    .Save
End With

'Rename Mail folder.
objNewFolder.Folders("Mail").Name = ProjectName & " Mail"
```

Summarizing the Projects

Another piece of this Outlook solution involves the intranet. Executives at Micro Modeling need a way to quickly gather information about the status of all projects. They don't want to go to Outlook and look at the status report

13 CHAPTER

for each project. They want a quick "at a glance" view that gives them the whole picture. To build this report, we're going to create a dynamic Web page that reads the information directly from Outlook and presents it in HTML.

Overview

Active Server Pages (ASP) provides a way for creating such dynamic Web pages. It is a Visual Basic–like scripting language that provides a bridge between HTML and your server applications, such as databases or Outlook. When an executive wants to get the latest project information, she would request the ASP file from the server—just as she would request any HTML page—by typing in the address. When the ASP file is executed, it establishes a connection to Outlook, reads the information out of the status reports, and summarizes it into an HTML page. That page will include not only the summary data but also hyperlinks back to Outlook, should someone want to get more detailed information.

The Active Server Pages

The first part of the ASP file (PROJECTS.ASP in the HTML subfolder of the Chapter13 folder on the companion CD) establishes a connection to the Outlook application and to the public folder "MMA Projects." The syntax "<% %>" indicates that the contents should be executed instead of displayed as text.

```
<% Set objOut = Server.CreateObject("Outlook.Application.8")
   Set objName = objOut.Getnamespace("MAPI")
   Set objFolder = objName.folders("Public Folders") _
       .Folders("All Public Folders").Folders("MMA Projects") %>
```

The code then loops through all the subfolders found in the "MMA Projects" folder. For each folder other than the template, various pieces of information need to be read from the status report and displayed in HTML.

```
nCount = objFolder.Folders.count
For nCtr = 1 to nCount%>
    <%If objFolder.Folders(Cint(nCtr)).Name <> "Template" THEN%>

    <!-- Code to read status report info-->

    <%End if%>
<%Next%>
```

The following line of code shows an example of reading the "StartDate" property from the current status report:

```
<%=objFolder.Folders(cint(nCtr)).items(1) _
    .UserProperties("StartDate").value%>
```

To put it all together, here is a section of code that displays the name of the current project as a hyperlink back to Outlook and displays the words "Start Date" followed by the current project's start date:

```
<TR><TD><P>
<A HREF="outlook://public folders/all public folders/mma projects/
<%=objFolder.Folders(cint(nCtr)).Name%>">
<%=objFolder.Folders(cint(nCtr)).Name%></A>
<B>Start Date: </B>
<%=objFolder.Folders(cint(nCtr)).items(1) _
.UserProperties("StartDate").value%>
```

Figure 13-34 shows what it all looks like when you put it together.

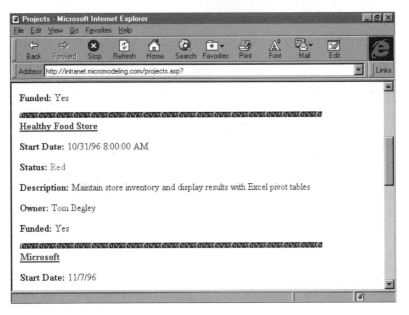

Figure 13-34
Active Server Pages Web page that reports project status.

Putting It All Together

So far, we've covered how to create each component of MMA's Outlook-based Project Management system. We discussed how to set up a project template on your Exchange Server, create custom forms and views, write a Visual Basic application that creates a new project, and design an HTML-based information system that summarizes the current projects. In this section we'll put it all together and distribute the application.

13
CHAPTER

The Outlook Bar

This Outlook-based solution has three distinct components: public folders, a Visual Basic application, and an intranet Web page. To keep these components organized, we can use the Outlook Bar. In this new group, we want to have shortcuts to the public folders, to the Visual Basic executable, and to the intranet page. Here are the steps you need to take to create these shortcuts:

1. Add a new group to your Outlook Bar using the Add To Outlook Bar command on the File menu. Select the MMA Projects folder.

2. Click on the Other group, select My Computer, and locate the folder containing your Visual Basic executable. You might want to create a special folder on your network that contains only this file.

3. Drag the folder containing the Visual Basic application onto the Outlook Bar. (Note that you cannot place an executable directly on the Outlook Bar.)

4. Create a shortcut to the ASP file you created on the intranet server.

5. Place the shortcut in its own folder and drag this folder onto the Outlook Bar.

You now have a central way to launch all of the components of the MMA Project Manager solution!

Distributing your application internally

Now that you've organized your public folders and created the proper views and custom forms, how are you going to distribute your solution? Internally, there is nothing to distribute. This is a server-side solution that will be available automatically to your users when they log on to Exchange Server. They will immediately have access to the public folders, custom forms, and views. The only missing element is a customized Outlook Bar. Unfortunately, there is no way to customize a user's Outlook Bar through files on the server or even through code.

The intranet Web site (ASP file) and Visual Basic application will also be stored on the server. Your users might need to run a Visual Basic setup program to get the run-time files associated with the application. Otherwise, your application is all on the server.

Distributing your application externally

If you wanted to distribute your application externally, say to a client, the easiest way is via personal folder files (.PST files). The idea is that you export your entire Outlook directory structure (folders, forms, views, messages, and so on) to a single file. The client would then import the file and your application would be transferred. However, accomplishing this transfer is a little trickier than you might expect.

The problem is that the standard Import And Export command on the File menu *will not work with custom forms*. This option will copy the folders, messages, and posts, but your custom views and forms will be left behind during the export process. Similarly, using the Import command for an existing .PST file will leave behind any custom forms that were included as part of the file.

Importing and exporting without custom forms

With that last disclaimer out of the way, there might be times when you want to do a simple import/export of messages; perhaps you want to archive your Inbox or your correspondence with a particular client. To export your messages, you would choose the Import And Export command from the File menu. This will start the Import And Export Wizard, which is shown in Figure 13-35. Choose the Export To A Personal Folder File (.PST) option, and click Next. Make sure the correct folder is selected, optionally check the Include Subfolders check box, and click Next. Then select a file location and click Finish to kick off the export process. To import the file later, you would use the same wizard.

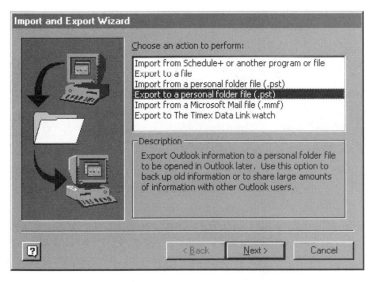

Figure 13-35

Importing and exporting with custom forms.

In the case of the MMA Project public folder and subfolder structure, we have many custom views and forms that we need to include in the .PST file. To perform this type of an export, we need to follow a different set of steps. The basic idea is that you need to add a blank personal folder to your current Outlook profile and then copy or move folders into it. Here are the step-by-step instructions for exporting a .PST file with custom forms:

1. Complete all of the forms, permissions, defaults, and so on for your MMA Project or other folder structure while the folder is still under All Public Folders.

2. Choose the Services command from the Tools menu.

3. Click the Add button.

4. Select Personal Folders from the list of Available Information Services, and click the OK button.

5. Select a path and a filename for your *new* .PST file. Do not choose an existing .PST file from this dialog box. Click the Open button to open this new folder.

6. Give your folder a friendly name (such as "Transfer"), and click OK. You should now see your new personal folder in your Outlook Folder List.

7. Copy the root folder ("MMA Projects") from the All Public Folders folder to the new folder you have created ("Transfer").

8. Return to the Services command on the Tools menu, select your new public folder ("Transfer"), and click Remove. This removes the .PST file from your Outlook folder—it does not delete the file.

You have now successfully exported your .PST file, complete with custom forms, views, and so on. You can now distribute the file to your client or other external user. But what do they need to do to import your .PST file? Just use the Import command? Unfortunately, the answer is no. Here are the step-by-step instructions for importing a .PST file that contains custom forms:

1. Choose the Services command from the Tools menu.

2. Click the Add button.

3. Select Personal Folders from the list of available information services, and click the OK button.

4. Select the path and a filename for your *existing* .PST file that you want to import. Click the Open button to open this folder.

5. Give your folder a friendly name (such as "Transfer"), and click OK. You should now see your new personal folder in your Outlook Folder List.

At this point, you have successfully imported the .PST file. However, you might have noticed that you could not import the file so that it appears with the rest of your Public Folders. Sticking with the names used in this example, you now have a Transfer folder that contains your MMA Projects folder and subfolders. You don't care about the Transfer folder; what you want is MMA Projects. Highlight the MMA Projects folder, click with your right mouse button, and choose the Copy "MMA Projects" command. When prompted, choose the All Public Folders folder as your destination. This will complete the transfer process, as well as our example!

CHAPTER 13

CHAPTER 14

Web Site Search

Francisco DelValle,

Jeffrey M. Jones, and Donna Jensen

Depending on its configuration, your intranet might be comprised of several servers that contain documents relevant to a specific business process.

Your intranet might have a Human Resource server, an Accounting server, and a Product information server distributed across the company at various sites, or it might have a single server containing all the documents available across it. With a browser, users can hyperlink their way to the documents they seek, regardless of where those documents are stored. Searching provides an easier way for users seeking specific information to locate that information without having to follow hyperlinks from page to page. Using a search page, users can specify criteria to search for, initiate a search, and be presented with the relevant document result set. The user can then determine which of those documents to look at.

You should choose a search mechanism for your intranet based on the intranet's size and potential for growth. For a small, one-server intranet, your

CHAPTER
14

best bet might be to use either the Search WebBot component, which is included with Microsoft FrontPage 97, or Microsoft's Web Find Fast utility, which ships with Microsoft Office 97. This type of search mechanism is easy to configure and quick to implement. For larger, distributed intranets, you would want to implement the more powerful search capabilities provided by Microsoft Index Server.

In this chapter you'll find out how to set up a search mechanism across an intranet using either the FrontPage Search WebBot, Web Find Fast, or Microsoft Index Server. Although we'll examine all three technologies, we'll focus primarily on Index Server, which is an add-on module for the Microsoft Internet Information Server (IIS). You'll learn how Index Server processes requests for information, what specific files the administrator must create before the user can begin searching, and finally, how to create a simple HTML search page. This search page will interact with Index Server to return an HTML page consisting of links (and other properties) to documents—HTML-based *and* Office documents—that are found to match specified criteria.

The FrontPage Search WebBot

The FrontPage Search WebBot is a lightweight text search engine for searching just the current Web. Essentially, the page containing the search input form calls the _VTI_BIN/SHTML.DLL, which generates the search results. The configuration options are pretty much limited to those available in the WebBot Search Component Properties dialog box, as shown in Figure 14-1.

Here's a brief summary of what you can and can't do:

- You can change the input and button labels and the width of the text box; you can't add buttons or inputs, and you can't change the alignment of form options on the page.

- You can search all directories on your Web or in a single discussion group; you can't limit your search to one or more directories.

- You can include score, file date, and file size with the search results; you can't add other parameters or reconfigure how results display.

The FrontPage Search WebBot is limited in its customization capabilities and search range. Implementing such a limited search mechanism across a large intranet is not beneficial; a large intranet requires a search mechanism that can comb all servers across it to locate documents. When we discuss Index Server, you'll see that it can provide greater search flexibility and customization to your searches.

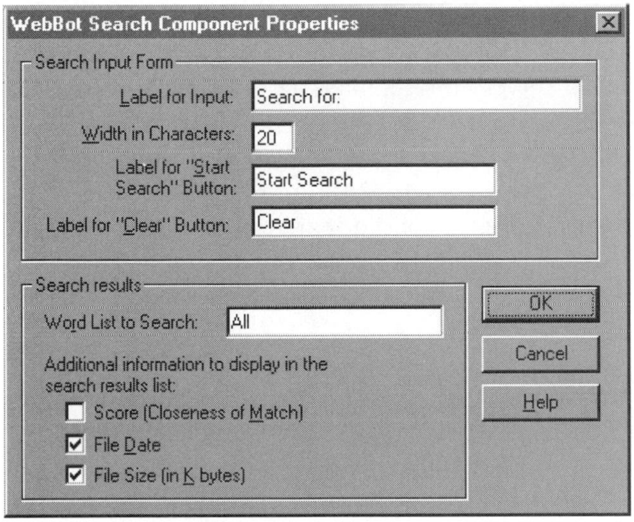

Figure 14-1
FrontPage WebBot Search Component Properties dialog box.

NOTE

If you publish your FrontPage Web to a server with IIS version 2.0 or later installed and the Index Server installed, the server automatically replaces the Search WebBot functionality with the Index Server. Ultimately, you'll be glad for the free upgrade: the Index Server lets you create far more sophisticated queries and even enables you to hide specific folders and files. Also, the Index Server uses a different page to display return results; if your search page is named FILENAME.HTM, the Index Server results page will be the file named FILENAME.HTM0.HTX in the _VTI_MAP folder. Refer to the "Microsoft Index Server" section later in this chapter for more information.

Web Find Fast

Web Find Fast is a new search utility specifically designed for intranets. It ships with Microsoft Office 97 as part of the Office Server Pack on the Office 97 CD.

You might already be familiar with the Find Fast utilities of Microsoft Windows 95, which create indexes of files and allow users to conduct full-text searches through the indexes. Web Find Fast represents another flavor of Find Fast, performing the same kind of indexing and searching. But whereas the older forms of Find Fast run on the user's local drive or on Microsoft NT servers and exploit the File Open dialog box as their interface, Web Find Fast runs on Web servers and its interface is an HTML page that you can set as your intranet's default search page.

Your intranet users can enter their search criteria on Web Find Fast's query page in Microsoft Internet Explorer. Web Find Fast will then generate a second HTML file with the results of the search. When the user clicks the name of a found document on the results page, the document will open. If the document is a Microsoft Office file, the Office application will open inside Internet Explorer.

Installing Web Find Fast

Install Web Find Fast on your Web server only. Its Setup utility is on the Office 97 CD, in the Server Pack ("SRVPACK") folder. You'll find several documents in the folder and in its WEBADMIN and WEBSRCH subfolders that will take you through the setup process and help you use and administer Web Find Fast:

🌐 **README.TXT.** Up-to-date configuration information and setup instructions.

System Requirements

Web Find Fast uses indexes created by the Find Fast NT service running on Windows NT Server or Windows NT Workstation. You must configure the Windows NT server or workstation as an HTTP server using Web server software, such as Internet Information Server (IIS). To run Web Find Fast, you'll need:

🌐 Windows NT Server or Workstation 3.51 and Service Pack 5 (or later), or Windows NT Server or Workstation 4.0 (or later)

🌐 An installed Web server, such as IIS

🌐 A Web browser, such as Internet Explorer 3.0

To run the Web Find Fast Remote Administration Tool, which will be described later in this chapter, you'll need:

🌐 Windows NT Server 4.0 (or later)

🌐 An NTFS partition on which to install the remote administration tool

🌐 Microsoft Internet Information Server 2.0 (or later)

- **WEBADHLP.HTM.** The main documentation for Web Find Fast, covering setup, configuration, and administration. The file also contains a list of frequently asked questions.
- **SRCHWIZ1-4.HTM.** A tutorial for creating a Web Find Fast index.
- **ADMNWIZ1-4.HTM.** A tutorial for creating a Web Find Fast index using either the Find Fast dialog box or the remote Web Find Fast Administration Tool.

After you've installed Web Find Fast on your server, you can customize it to run on your intranet.

TIP If you install Office 97 on your Web server after installing Web Find Fast, you must be careful to avoid replacing Web Find Fast with the less powerful single-user Find Fast. When you run the Office Setup program, choose Custom installation; under the Office Tools option, clear the Find Fast check box.

Running Web Find Fast on Your Intranet

To run Web Find Fast on your intranet, you need to create and customize the utility's three basic components:

1. An index of files on your intranet. The Web Find Fast engine searches the index for files that meet the criteria set by the user.

2. A query page, an HTML file located on your Web server that submits the user's search criteria. Office 97 ships with a sample query page that you can customize.

3. A results page, another HTML file that displays the names and descriptions of files that match the user's search criteria. Office 97 also ships with a sample results page for you to customize.

Creating Indexes

Web Find Fast can search indexes that cover multiple drives and folders. It also lets you create multiple indexes. Properly managing the scope of a Web Find Fast index is the key to building the most useful indexes for your intranet.

You can work with Web Find Fast indexes directly on your Web server through the server's Control Panel. To create an index, follow these steps:

1. In the Windows NT Control Panel, double-click the Find Fast icon.

2. On the Index menu, choose Create Index, which displays the Create Index dialog box. Then click Browse and select the drive

14 CHAPTER

or folder to index. Web Find Fast will index the files in that location and in its nested subfolders.

3. In the Create Index dialog box, click Web Options and in the Web Options dialog box enter any additional search folders and a unique user-friendly name for the index.

4. Click OK in both the Web Options dialog box and the Create Index dialog box.

Web Find Fast will generate the index. By default, all Microsoft Office files, HTML files, and other files that Office applications can convert will be included in the index. You can change this default by selecting an option available from the Of Type drop-down list in the Create Index dialog box. Web Find Fast can generate an index that covers 100 megabytes worth of files in about one hour.

Setting index defaults

When you create an index, you can set four important options:

- ⊕ **Continue to update automatically.** By default, Web Find Fast will update the index every two hours. You can change the time interval, or you can disable updating entirely.

- ⊕ **Speed up property display.** Web Find Fast can create a separate index for document properties such as Title and Author. If document properties are indexed, Web Find Fast will display them on the results page. Indexing the properties substantially increases the index file size.

- ⊕ **Enable phrase searching.** With Enable Phrase Searching checked, Web Find Fast can locate contiguous strings of letters and punctuation. Be aware that under this option, indexes increase in size to about 5 to 30 percent of your document collection and take longer to create.

- ⊕ **Include relevance information for Web searching.** Web Find Fast utilizes relevance ranking to help the user select the most helpful document from the list of returned documents on the results page. Documents in which the search terms are repeated more frequently appear on the results page above documents that have fewer occurrences of the search terms. Unusual words, such as "thermodynamics," are ranked higher than more common words, such as "hot." This option substantially increases the index file size, but it also allows Web Find Fast to return documents that are more likely to be relevant to the user. This is especially handy when the user is searching a collection of hundreds or thousands of documents.

Modifying indexes

Once an index is created, you can easily modify it and add or remove folders from its range by double-clicking the Find Fast icon in the Control Panel. Use the Update Index command on the Index menu to make your changes. You can also create new indexes or delete unneeded ones.

Using the Web Find Fast Administration Tool to work with indexes

You can use the Control Panel's Find Fast icon to manipulate your indexes only if you're actually working on your Web server machine. Alternatively, you can use the Web Find Fast Administration Tool, which allows for remote administration of your indexes and query and results pages from any computer connected to your server. The Web Find Fast Administration Tool consists of a set of HTML files you work with through Internet Explorer either directly on the server or remotely from any client machine.

To work with an index using the Web Find Fast Administration Tool, open WEBSRCHW.HTM from the folder into which it was installed on your Web server in Internet Explorer. Then click Create Or Modify Indexes. The HTML files will take you through the process of creating, modifying, or deleting indexes and can also display information about your current indexes.

Monitoring your index

You can check the status of your index by looking at the Find Fast indexer log by double-clicking the Find Fast Control Panel icon and choosing Show Indexer Log from the Index menu. (You can also open FFASTLOG.TXT in the WINDOWS\SYSTEM32 folder.) The log contains a record of all Find Fast sessions and records changes made to all your current indexes.

After you generate an index, it is ready to be used for Web searching. Your next step is to provide your users with an entry to the index by creating and implementing query pages.

Customizing a Web Find Fast Query Page

Web Find Fast ships with two default query pages:

- 🌐 QUERY.HTM for simple queries, as shown in Figure 14-2
- 🌐 QUERYADV.HTM for advanced queries, as shown in Figure 14-3

14
CHAPTER

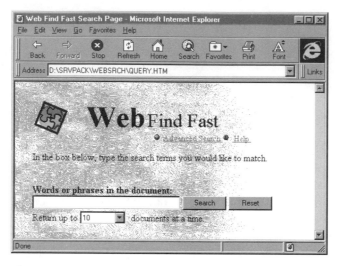

Figure 14-2

The simple query HTML page included with Web Find Fast.

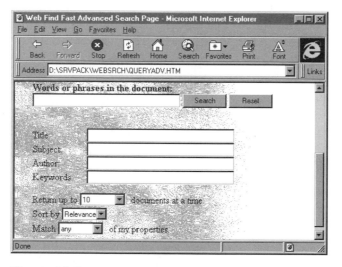

Figure 14-3

The bottom part of the advanced query HTML page included with Web Find Fast.

The advanced query page allows users to search for file properties and to control the sorting of any found files. The two pages contain hyperlinks to each other.

To make your query pages usable on your intranet, you must add some custom information to them, such as the default index to be searched. You do this by editing the query page HTML code. On your Web server, open QUERY.HTM in a text editor, and specify these values:

 The index name. Replace the empty VALUE string in the following tag with the friendly name you gave the index when you created it:

```
<INPUT TYPE = "hidden" NAME = "Index" VALUE = "">
```

 The path to the results page. If you create a customized results page somewhere other than the default location, you must specify its path in this tag:

```
<INPUT TYPE = "hidden" NAME = "Template" VALUE =
"C:\wwwroot\results.htm">
```

 The virtual path to GIF files. Replace the empty VALUE string with the HTTP path to the Web Find Fast GIF files and other GIF files you've added to the query or results page, such as your company logo.

```
<INPUT TYPE = "hidden" NAME = "Gif" VALUE = "">
```

 The sort order. In the results page, returned documents can be sorted. This feature works correctly only if you included relevance information when you created the index:

```
<INPUT TYPE = "hidden" NAME = "SortBy" VALUE =
"Relevance">
```

 The protocol. You can specify the protocol you want to use for document links in the results page. In the following tag, specify HTTP or File:

```
<INPUT TYPE = "hidden" NAME = "Protocol" VALUE = "HTTP">
```

QUERY.HTM does contain additional values that may be relevant to your situation. Where appropriate specify these additional values.

When you're done, save QUERY.HTM, and then edit QUERYADV.HTM (the advanced query page) in the same way. You can copy QUERY.HTM and then customize it to create any number of query pages to search different indexes. Or you can use more advanced HTML tags such as the Select tag to let your users choose among different indexes in a single custom query page. WEBADHLP.HTM, the main documentation file for Web Find Fast, contains sample HTML source using the Select tag to create a drop-down list of indexes in a single query page. Also, check out the Frequently Asked Questions section of WEBADHLP.HTM. It has some good information on when to use the HTTP or File protocol when creating an index.

Customizing the Results Page

You don't need to edit the default results page that ships with Web Find Fast, RESULTS.HTM, before it can be used. However, you can edit it in the same way you edited the query pages. Check out WEBADHLP.HTM for a list of the tags in RESULTS.HTM that you can customize. Web Find Fast looks for those tags in RESULTS.HTM, and if it finds them there, it inserts the appropriate information every time it generates a results page.

Setting Up Your Query Page as the Web Search Page

Finally, you'll want your customized query page to be the default search page on your intranet. An easy way to distribute the query page URL to your users is to include it in an e-mail message. In the message, instruct the recipients to display the page and then set it as their default search page. Alternatively, you can specify the query page as the default search page yourself using Office 97 System Policies. To learn more about setting System Policies, see the resource kits for Windows 95, NT 4.0, or Office 97.

Generating Web Find Fast Page View

A Web Find Fast Page View is a collection of pages of hyperlinks to documents that have certain properties in common. The documents must be included in the current index before they can appear in a Web Find Fast Page View.

You can create a Web Find Fast Page View that contains hyperlinks to all indexed documents that have properties matching the criteria you specify. You can create up to three levels of groupings. For example, you can create a Web Find Fast page that includes hyperlinks to all indexed documents written by your organization's president (Author property) about new business opportunities (Subject property) grouped by title (Title property).

After you create a Web Find Fast Page View, you can distribute the URL for its start page (or a hyperlink to it) to your intranet users. They then have a single location to browse, by whatever levels of groupings you have defined.

536

To create a Web Find Fast Page View, open the Web Find Fast Administration Tool, WEBSRCHW.HTM, and click Generate Web Find Fast Page Views. Enter the appropriate values, including the index name and the properties by which you want the documents to be grouped. Then click Generate. Using your criteria, Web Find Fast Page View generates a series of linked HTML documents.

Microsoft Index Server

Microsoft Index Server is an add-on module to Microsoft Internet Information Server (IIS) and Microsoft Peer Web Services (PWS). Index Server provides end users with the ability to index and search the full text and properties of documents residing on intranets as well as any drive accessible through a uniform naming convention (UNC) path. Searchable documents can be either *HTML-based* or *formatted,* such as those created using Microsoft Word or Microsoft Excel.

Index Server is very similar to the Internet Database Connector (IDC), which is available in IIS and PWS. IDC is a mechanism to access data in ODBC-compatible databases from an HTML page. IDC converts an HTML query into an ODBC-compatible query, which is then passed to a data source that returns a result set. IDC then converts the result set into an HTML page that is displayed on the user's screen. You'll find more information about the workings of IDC and about how to implement it in Chapter 16, but in the sections that follow you'll learn how Index Server is used in a way that is very much like IDC.

Hardware, Space, and Software Requirements

On Microsoft Windows NT Server, Index Server requires the following minimum hardware:

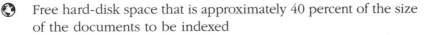 486/25 MHz or higher, or Pentium/Pentium PRO processor

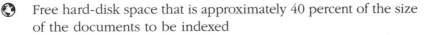 Free hard-disk space that is approximately 40 percent of the size of the documents to be indexed

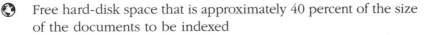 16 MB of memory (RAM)

Because Index Server can index documents in several languages, disk space for program files is dependent on the number of languages installed. The average disk space required for program files is between 3 and 12 megabytes. Disk space required for indexes depends on the size of the document body (the corpus) and the type of documents. Generally, the amount of disk space required is 40 percent of the size of the corpus.

14

CHAPTER

To run Index Server, you'll also need either Windows NT Server version 4.0 running Internet Information Server version 2.0 or later or Windows NT Workstation version 4.0 running Peer Web Services.

NOTE This chapter assumes that Index Server is installed on a Windows NT server (version 4.0) running Internet Information Server (version 2.0 or later). It further assumes that you're familiar with HTML and FrontPage 97. Although Internet Information Server and Peer Web Services ship with Windows NT Server version 4.0 and Workstation version 4.0, respectively, Index Server is a separate product. As of this writing, Index Server can be downloaded for free (except for connect time charges) from, you guessed it, http://www.microsoft.com.

How Index Server Works

Now that we know what Index Server is and what's required to install it, let's examine how it integrates with IIS to provide search capabilities to an intranet.

Query processing

Typically, an administrator creates a search page where users can define the criteria they are looking for. An Internet data query file and a results HTML extension file (discussed in the "Using Index Server on Our Intranet" section later in this chapter) are also created by the administrator and are used by Index Server to process the query. These two files are internal to Index Server and are used with the entered criteria to define the three elements of a query: scope, restriction, and result set.

Scope A scope identifies a corpus, or body of documents, to be searched. Scopes are specified as a path on a physical volume such as C:\docs. The site administrator specifies this path, also called a virtual root, using the Internet Service Manager (discussed on the next page). Each virtual path points to a collection of documents on the server. There can be specific paths for managing specific groups of documents.

Restriction A restriction provides a means by which a set of words or phrases can be merged, weighted for ranking, and used to query the corpus. Index Server provides the ability to search for multiple words and phrases within documents, for words and phrases near other words and phrases, and for free-text queries. You might use the standard comparison operators (=, >, <, >=, <=, and !=) in queries as well as Boolean operators

(AND, OR, and NOT) and parentheses. Index Server supports queries containing simple wildcards (for example, "bus*" will return "busy," "busing," "busboy," and so on) or that match inflected and base forms of words (for example, "run**" is expanded to "runtime," "running," "ran," and so on).

In addition to querying the content of documents, users can query their properties. These properties can include file size, creation and modification dates, file name, author, and others. Clients can also query all ActiveX properties, including custom properties in Microsoft Office documents.

Result set A result set is a list of found documents returned by the engine after executing a query. It can be returned sorted according to any document property, including relevance ranking.

For efficiency, an administrator can limit the maximum number of hits returned to the client. Thus a result set of 200 hits can be returned to the client in 10 pages of 20 hits each, allowing the user to go to the next page if she doesn't see what she needs. The Internet data query file specifies the number of hits returned per page.

In addition to returning document properties, Index Server can also return document abstracts, which briefly summarize the content of a document. Abstracts consist of a few lines of the found document and are produced automatically by Index Server. They are useful when looking through a long list of results to quickly determine if a document should be retrieved.

Integration with Internet Information Server

In order to search for documents, Index Server needs to know where documents are located—and this is where the integration with IIS comes in. IIS provides a mechanism to establish virtual directories (paths) to locate documents for indexing. These paths are set up in IIS via the Microsoft Internet Service Manager utility. The directory setup in the WWW Service Properties dialog box of the Internet Service Manager is shown in Figure 14-4.

The Internet Service Manager allows an administrator to configure any of the services that IIS provides (WWW, FTP, and Gopher) and add paths as necessary for searches to be effective and efficient. In addition to local and networked directories, the Internet Service Manager allows an administrator to include a virtual directory into the corpus. Thus a site on another server on your intranet or on the Internet can become part of the searchable corpus. An administrator can also establish a default document for directories, allow users the ability to browse directories, and grant read and execute rights on documents in a specific directory.

CHAPTER
14

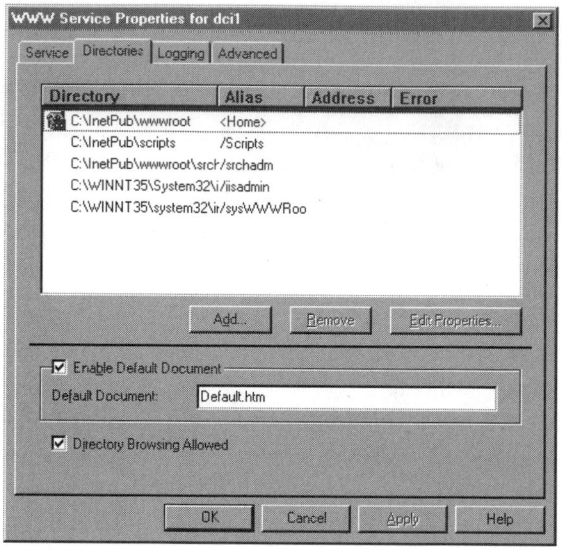

Figure 14-4

Internet Service Manager directory setup for the WWW service.

Filtering, merging, and indexing

Once paths are established, Index Server identifies documents and begins a process of filtering, merging, and indexing. This three-step process constantly works to take many smaller indexes and create one large master index that Index Server uses to locate documents.

Index Server filters documents by extracting document file data and inserting it into content indexes. To do this, Index Server uses a process called the CiDaemon process, which receives a list of documents and filters the documents by identifying the correct filter and word-breaker DLLs associated with a specific document in the list. These filters separate documents into words (keys) and create word lists that supply data for indexes. The filtering process involves three steps:

1. The filter DLL "recognizes" a document format and is capable of extracting text and properties from documents using the IFilter ActiveX interface. The CiDaemon process uses this interface to extract text from a document. The locations of filter DLLs are stored in the Registry in the \HKEY_LOCAL_MACHINE\Software\ Classes tree. Editing the Registry is a good way to avoid filtering documents with no useful content.

540

2. The word-breaker DLL parses the text and textual properties returned by the filter DLL into words. This DLL is language dependent.

3. Noise words (also called Stop Words) are words common to everyday speech (for example, "a," "are," "the"). Because including them would produce a very large index, noise words are removed from the extracted data. The remaining words are stored in the index.

Once filtering occurs, Index Server begins creating indexes. The indexing process begins as many small word lists that constantly merge to eventually become one large master index. There are three types of indexes and merges:

- **Word lists and shadow merges.** Word lists are small indexes that reside in memory and contain data for a small number of documents. Once the number of word lists exceeds the MaxWordLists setting in the Registry, the word lists are merged into a shadow index. A shadow merge combines multiple word lists and shadow indexes into a single shadow index. It is usually performed to free up memory.

- **Shadow indexes and master merges.** A shadow index is created by merging word lists and other shadow indexes into a single index. Multiple shadow indexes can exist. A master merge combines all shadow indexes and the current master index (if any) to create a new master index and free up disk space.

- **Master index and annealing merges.** A master index contains the indexed data for a large number of documents. An annealing merge is a special kind of shadow merge performed when the system is idle for a certain amount of time and the total number of shadow indexes and master indexes exceeds the MaxIdealIndexes setting in the Registry.

Indexes are controlled on each virtual path that, in turn, is created on a set of directories and their children. Indexes, by default, are incrementally refreshed. On setup, the administrator determines a drive on which Index Server's indexes will reside (usually C:). The drive chosen will require as much available space as possible because all indexes created for all specified virtual paths will be stored there. The indexes can be approximately

CHAPTER 14

40 percent of the size of the corpus. Once Index Server is installed, all operations are automatic—including updates, index creation, and optimization.

Language support

Index Server provides the ability to index documents in seven languages: Dutch, English (U.S. and International), French, German, Italian, Spanish, and Swedish. Because all index information is stored as Unicode characters and all queries are converted to Unicode before processing, Index Server can dynamically load and unload language-specific utilities and modules for retrieving multilingual documents.

Administration

Administration of Index Server is performed via HTML pages. Using the main administration page, an administrator might see the number of query hits and misses, update the indexing of virtual roots known to the server, and force a scan of all or selected virtual roots. Figure 14-5 shows the Index Server Administration page, ADMIN.HTM.

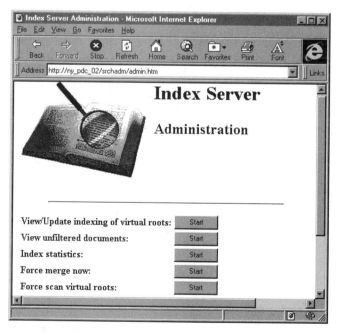

Figure 14-5

The Index Server Administration page.

Scanning

The process of inventorying the virtual roots to determine which documents should be indexed is called scanning. In a full scan, all the documents in the directories that are inventoried are added to the list of documents to be filtered. A full scan is performed the first time a directory is added to the list of indexed directories and also as part of recovery if a serious error occurs. In an incremental scan, only those documents modified since the last filtering are added to the list of documents to be filtered. On startup of Index Server, an incremental scan is performed on all the indexed directories to determine which files were modified when it was not running.

Using Index Server on Our Intranet

Now that you know how Index Server works, let's find out how to implement it to provide search capabilities for our sample intranet. We'll start by creating a simple search screen using Microsoft FrontPage 97 and move on to creating an Internet data query file and an HTML extension file using a text editor.

Index Server works on the client/server principle: a client makes a request of the server; the server processes that request and returns the results back to the client. We've already spoken about how the server aspect of this equation works; it's time to talk about the client side. In this section we'll look at how to build a search form using HTML and how to write simple but effective scripts that Index Server will use to perform our searches and display the results.

To use Index Server, you need to create three files: the query page itself, the Internet data query file (the .IDQ file), and the HTML extension file (the .HTX file). These files work together to provide the query's scope, restriction, and result set. It is a good idea to maintain search pages in a WWWROOT subdirectory and .IDQ and .HTX files in a SCRIPTS subdirectory.

The search form, .IDQ, and .HTX files used in this chapter are in the Chapter14 folder on the companion CD.

Creating the Search Page

We used Microsoft FrontPage 97 to create our search page (see Figure 14-6), which contains a form that consists of a caption, a text box for entering criteria, and two push buttons that will either submit the query or clear the contents of the textbox.

14
CHAPTER

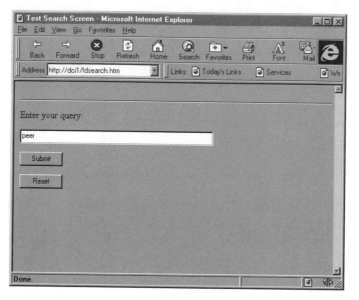

Figure 14-6

A simple query search page.

The HTML code to create this form is shown here:

```
<!DOCTYPE HTML PUBLIC "-//IETF//DTD HTML//EN">
<html>
<head>
<meta http-equiv="Content-Type"
content="text/html; charset=iso-8859-1">
<meta name="AUTHOR" content="Francisco DelValle Jr.">
<meta name="GENERATOR" content="Microsoft FrontPage 2.0">
<title>Test Search Screen</title>
</head>
<body>
<hr>
<form action="/scripts/pdcdemo.idq" method="POST">
    <p>Enter your query:</p>
    <p><input type="text" size="60" maxlength="100"
    name="Restriction"></p>
    <p><input type="submit" name="B1"></p>
    <p><input type="reset" name="B2"></p>
</form>
</body>
</html>
```

Specifying the Scope of the Query

You can see that we assigned a path and an .IDQ filename to the Action property of the form. The Action property will call the .IDQ file when the Submit button is clicked. The criteria we type in the text box will be passed to the .IDQ file that uses the text as a restriction for our query.

The .IDQ file provides scope for queries. Through this file we can determine which columns to display, whether to search subdirectories, and what directory to search. In addition, we can limit the number of returned documents, set the number of results to display on a page, specify which HTML extension file to use for displaying our results, set which columns to use to sort the results, and specify what sort order should be used.

Although more variables could be used, those listed in our sample .IDQ file below are more important for our discussion. All of the available variables are listed in the Microsoft Index Server Guide. The Microsoft Index Server Guide is a set of HTML files that gets installed in the SRCHADM\HELP directory when Index Server is installed.

The .IDQ file provides the framework in which the query will work. Let's look at our simple .IDQ file:

```
[QUERY]
'What columns should display in result page
CiColumns=filename,size,rank,characterization,vpath,doctitle,write
'Tell Index Server how deep to search
CiFlags=DEEP
'What to search for
CiRestriction=%Restriction%
'Limit number of results to return from a query
CiMaxRecordsInResultSet=150
'Limit number of results to display on a page
CiMaxRecordsPerPage=30
'Define search start directory
CiScope=/
'HTML extension file (htx) to use
CiTemplate=/scripts/spdcl.htx
'Column names to use in sorting and the order
CiSort=rank[d]
'Location of index
CiCatalog=c:\
```

Because we can provide different scope for each search we allow, a separate .IDQ file is required for each search form in our intranet. In this way, a search for "Products" can be scoped differently than a search for "Employee Manual."

Formatting the Result Set

When the form is submitted and Index Server finds documents matching our criteria, the .HTX file is used to format an HTML result page, complete with hyperlinks to each result list document if appropriate. Returned documents can also be displayed as text and/or images that might not take the user to another document (for example, to display a listing of employees and their telephone extensions).

Let's look at the contents of our simple .HTX file:

```
<HTML>
<TITLE>Search Results for "<%CiRestriction%>"</TITLE>
<BODY>
    <%begindetail%>
        <%if CiCurrentRecordNumber EQ 1 %>
            <b>Documents found matching your criteria:
            <%CiMatchedRecordCount%></b>
            <hr>
            <p>
        <%endif%>
        <%if CiCurrentRecordNumber EQ CiFirstRecordNumber%>
            Documents <%CiFirstRecordNumber%> to
            <%CiLastRecordNumber%>
            matching the query "<%CiRestriction%>" are displayed
            below.
            <p>
        <%endif%>
        <a href=<%vpath%>> <%vpath%></a> Size: <%size%> Ranking:
        <%rank%><p>
        <%characterization%></p>
    <%enddetail%>
    <P>
    <%if CiLastRecordNumber EQ 0%>
        No Documents matching: "<%CiRestriction%>".
    <%endif%>
    <%if CiLastRecordNumber LT CiMatchedRecordCount%>
        <FORM ACTION="\scripts\pdcdemo.idq?" METHOD="POST">
        <INPUT TYPE="HIDDEN"
            NAME="CiBookmark"
            VALUE="<%CiBookmark%>">
```

```
      <INPUT TYPE="HIDDEN"
          NAME="CiBookmarkSkipCount"
          VALUE="<%CiMaxRecordsPerPage%>">
      <INPUT TYPE="HIDDEN"
          NAME="CiMaxRecordsPerPage"
          VALUE="<%CiMaxRecordsPerPage%>">           '
      <INPUT TYPE="HIDDEN"
          NAME="CiRestriction"
          VALUE="<%CiRestriction%>">
      <INPUT TYPE="HIDDEN"
          NAME="CiScope"
          VALUE="<%CiScope%>">
      <INPUT TYPE="SUBMIT" VALUE="Next page">
      </FORM>
   <%endif%>
</BODY>
</HTML>
```

Now let's go over how this .HTX file works:

1. We start with setting a title for our result form.

2. We next determine if we've returned any documents. If we didn't, we skip the <%begindetail%> section and notify the user.

3. If documents are found, we determine our position in the result set. If we're on the first row, we inform the user of the number of documents found.

4. Next we inform the user of how many documents we're returning on this page (1 to 10; 15 to 20; and so on).

5. We then create a hyperlink for each document returned.

6. If there are more records to be displayed, we create a push button at the bottom of the form that allows the user to retrieve the next set of documents in our result set. To do this, we created a form element that contains hidden text boxes to hold the necessary parameters to reissue our query.

Figure 14-7 shows the results of a query. For a full explanation of the variables used in this file, consult the Index Server Guide installed with the Index Server in the SRCHADM\HELP directory.

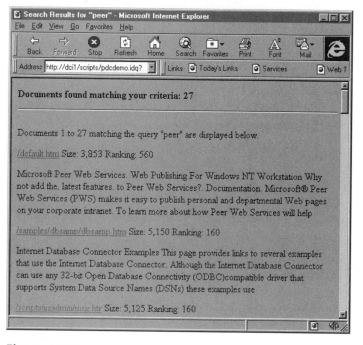

Figure 14-7

The results of our query.

15

CHAPTER

Extending Internet Information Server

Ronan Sorensen

You can extend the capability of Microsoft Internet Information Server (IIS) in many ways to deliver powerful distributed intranet systems. The most exciting ways are very recent innovations based on the Component Object Model (COM) that Microsoft invented. In this chapter, we'll examine how you can take your intranet to a higher level of capability and sophistication by using CGI, ISAPI, Active Server Pages, DCOM, and Transaction Server.

Here are the three main reasons you'd want to extend IIS:

1. To customize the response sent back to an Internet browser, allowing you to exploit the richer capabilities of advanced browsers such as Microsoft Internet Explorer 3.0 and Netscape Navigator 3.0 while still providing support for simple browsers that run on 16-bit operating systems such as Microsoft Windows 3.1.

2. To provide a programming language that can receive information from a client, process it, and send back a response.

CHAPTER 15

3. To integrate the functionality of IIS with existing applications, such as databases or components, that encapsulate business logic.

CGI, ISAPI, and Active Server Pages enable you to extend IIS using all three of the reasons above, whereas DCOM and Transaction Server only use the reason of integrating the functionality of IIS with other applications.

CGI

CGI (Common Gateway Interface) is the most mature and widely used specification for creating executable programs that run on your Web server. CGI scripts are typically written in the C language, but you can also write them in languages such as Perl, Unix Shell, and AppleScript. Remote users can start these executables by filling out an HTML form or by simply requesting a URL from your server like this:

http://www.micromodeling.com/cgi-bin/myprog.exe?arg1+arg2+arg3

This URL will cause the executable "myprog.exe" to run on the Web server at www.micromodeling.com, and it will be passed the arguments arg1, arg2, and arg3. As you can see from the following example, the CGI program itself can be quite simple to write:

```c
#include <stdio.h>
#include <stdlib.h>
#include <string.h>
char * getenv(const char * env);
void main(int argc, char *argv[])
{
    //Get the environment variable QUERY_STRING
    const char *strq = getenv("QUERY_STRING");
    //Extract the two numbers
    if(strq == NULL) strq = "var1=0&var2=0";
    int n1 = strcspn(strq, "=")+1;
    double dls = atof(strq+n1);
    double drs = atof(strq+(strcspn(strq+n1, "=")+1+n1));
    //Multiply the numbers and send back the answer
    //You need to print a content type and a blank line
    printf("Content-Type: text/html\r\n\r\n");
    printf("<html><body><BR>");
    printf("<H1>This is a very simple cgi app</H1>");
    printf("<FORM ACTION=\"http://www.micromodeling.com/");
    printf("scripts/Test.exe\" METHOD=GET>");
    printf("Multiply numbers :");
    printf("<input type=text size=8 name=\"number1\" ");
    printf("value=%f>", dls);
```

```
    printf("<input type=text size=8 name=\"number2\" ");
    printf("value=%f>", drs);
    printf("<input type=submit value=\"Calculate\">");
    printf("<input type=text size=10 value=%f>", dls*drs);
    printf("</FORM>");
    printf("</body></html>");
}
```

To run this CGI program, you can use the following HTML code:

```
<html><body><BR>
<H1>This is a very simple cgi app</H1>
<FORM ACTION=http://www.micromodeling.com/scripts/Test.exe
METHOD=GET>
Multiply numbers :
<input type=text size=8 name=number1 value = 0>
<input type=text size=8 name=number2 value = 0>
<input type=submit value=Calculate>
<input type=text size=10 value = 0>
</FORM>
</body></html>
```

This CGI program demonstrates how to extract two numbers from a form using the environment variable QUERY_STRING, multiply them, and send back an HTML page with the result. You might have noticed the similarity between CGI and console programs; although they use the same input and output functions, the printf() function writes to an HTML page rather than to the screen. The program sends an HTTP header (Content-Type:) to the browser, informing it what type of data is being sent so that the browser can handle it correctly. You can include other header information here also; however, you must send back a Content-Type header even if you do not send back data. When you're finished with your headers, you must insert a blank line and then begin your HTML code. One of the main tasks of CGI, ISAPI, and Active Server Pages is to pass on environment variables to your program. An environment variable is information about the client request that the server maintains in memory. Information on the CGI specification, available at the World Wide Web Consortium Web site (found at http://www.w3.org/pub/WWW/CGI/), lists and explains the following environment variables:

```
AUTH_TYPE
CONTENT_LENGTH
CONTENT_TYPE
GATEWAY_INTERFACE
HTTP_*
```

(continued)

CHAPTER 15

```
PATH_INFO
PATH_TRANSLATED
QUERY_STRING
REMOTE_ADDR
REMOTE_HOST
REMOTE_IDENT
REMOTE_USER
REQUEST_METHOD
SCRIPT_NAME
SERVER_NAME
SERVER_PORT
SERVER_PROTOCOL
SERVER_SOFTWARE
```

HTTP_* is used for variables that are specific to requests made with HTTP, such as the HTTP headers received from the client. One very useful environment variable is the HTTP_USER_AGENT; it informs your program which browser the client is using. This knowledge enables you to respond to all types of browsers but also provides more sophisticated responses for advanced browsers such as Microsoft Internet Explorer 3.0 and Netscape Navigator 3.0. The QUERY_STRING environment variable refers to the data following the "?" in the URL, which the browser sends to the server. Because our form example above uses the GET method, the FORM ACTION URL

http://www.micromodeling.com/scripts/Test.exe

will be appended with "?", followed by the form variables. So if a user inputs the numbers 3.45 and 6.45 and then presses the Calculate button, the following URL, which has been broken into two lines, is sent to the server:

http://www.micromodeling.com/scripts/
Test.exe?number1=3.45&number2=6.45&=0

The function getenv("QUERY_STRING") strips everything beyond the "?" and returns the string "number1=3.45&number2=6.45&=0". From this, we have extracted the two numbers for our multiplication and then sent back HTML code displaying the result. The CGI specification also allows the use of the POST method in a form instead of the GET method. If we had used the POST method in our example above, we would have gotten the length of our data from the CONTENT_LENGTH environment variable and then read it in from the standard input stream, stdin.

CGI is a simple and powerful mechanism for extending IIS. It can be programmed in many languages; it provides a way to customize your response for different browser types; and because it can be programmed in C, it is a very portable and expansive gateway to other applications.

ISAPI

ISAPI (Internet Server Application Programming Interface) is a high-performance alternative to CGI. We need ISAPI because CGI scales very poorly. Every time a client connects to a CGI application, a separate instance of the program is brought into memory. If you have hundreds of clients hitting your site, you will have hundreds of instances of your program loaded into memory. Each call will be slower because of the performance hit of loading the CGI application and the passing of environment variables across memory address spaces. An ISAPI application, on the other hand, is a runtime dynamic-link library (DLL) in the same memory address space as the HTTP server; therefore, all the resources within the HTTP server can easily be made available to it. More important, an ISAPI DLL needs to be loaded only once for all clients accessing it. This requires that your ISAPI application be multithread-safe because multiple requests from different clients can be received simultaneously. For each client, a new thread can be spawned, or better, your application can create a pool of threads and use synchronization objects to allow your clients to share them.

Although ISAPI is more complex than CGI, it is still a relatively short API. ISAPI has two necessary entry points that it must export: GetExtensionVersion and HttpExtensionProc. When the HTTP server loads an ISAPI application, it calls the function named GetExtensionVersion (HSE_VERSION_INFO *pVer*), which retrieves the version number of the specification on which the DLL extension is based. The second necessary entry point for an ISAPI designed application is HttpExtensionProc (EXTENSION_CONTROL_BLOCK *pECB*). This function is similar to the main function in CGI, and it is called for each request. It is passed the EXTENSION_CONTROL_BLOCK data structure, which is shown here:

```
typedef struct _EXTENSION_CONTROL_BLOCK {
    DWORD     cbSize;
    DWORD     dwVersion;
    HCONN     ConnID;
    DWORD     dwHttpStatusCode;
    CHAR      lpszLogData[HSE_LOG_BUFFER_LEN];
    LPSTR     lpszMethod;
    LPSTR     lpszQueryString;
    LPSTR     lpszPathInfo;
    LPSTR     lpszPathTranslated;
    DWORD     cbTotalBytes;
    DWORD     cbAvailable;
```

(continued)

15
CHAPTER

```
LPBYTE      lpbData;
LPSTR       lpszContentType;

BOOL ( WINAPI * GetServerVariable )
    ( HCONN        hConn,
      LPSTR        lpszVariableName,
      LPVOID       lpvBuffer,
      LPDWORD      lpdwSize );

BOOL ( WINAPI * WriteClient )
    ( HCONN        ConnID,
      LPVOID       Buffer,
      LPDWORD      lpdwBytes,
      DWORD        dwReserved );

BOOL ( WINAPI * ReadClient )
    ( HCONN        ConnID,
      LPVOID       lpvBuffer,
      LPDWORD      lpdwSize );

BOOL ( WINAPI * ServerSupportFunction )
    ( HCONN        hConn,
      DWORD        dwHSERRequest,
      LPVOID       lpvBuffer,
      LPDWORD      lpdwSize,
      LPDWORD      lpdwDataType );

} EXTENSION_CONTROL_BLOCK, *LPEXTENSION_CONTROL_BLOCK;
```

This structure contains member variables that hold the most commonly needed information for a request. You can get additional information through its callback functions. In fact, you can get all CGI variables with the member function GetServerVariable, which is equivalent to getenv( ) in CGI . The member function ReadClient serves the same purpose as stdin in CGI, allowing you to read in data from an HTML form that uses the POST method. It places the data into a buffer supplied by the caller and will block the thread until the data is available. ReadClient is required for reading in data that is not in the lpData member variable, that is, for data greater than 48 KB. The WriteClient is equivalent to stdout in CGI, allowing the server to optimize writes to improve performance. Finally, the ServerSupportFunction callback provides some general-purpose functions as well as functions that are specific to HTTP server implementation, such as URL redirection, session management, and response headers.

You can call an ISAPI program in the same way you call a CGI program. For example, http://www.micromodeling/MyISA.dll? will ask the Micro Modeling Web server to run the DLL MyISA. Writing ISAPI applications is made easier with Visual C++ 4.2. This development tool includes an ISAPI Extension Wizard (see Figure 15-1) that will generate a generic ISAPI application for you. It uses the Microsoft Foundation Class (MFC) libraries, which wrap most of ISAPI in two classes: CHttpServer and CHttpServerContext.

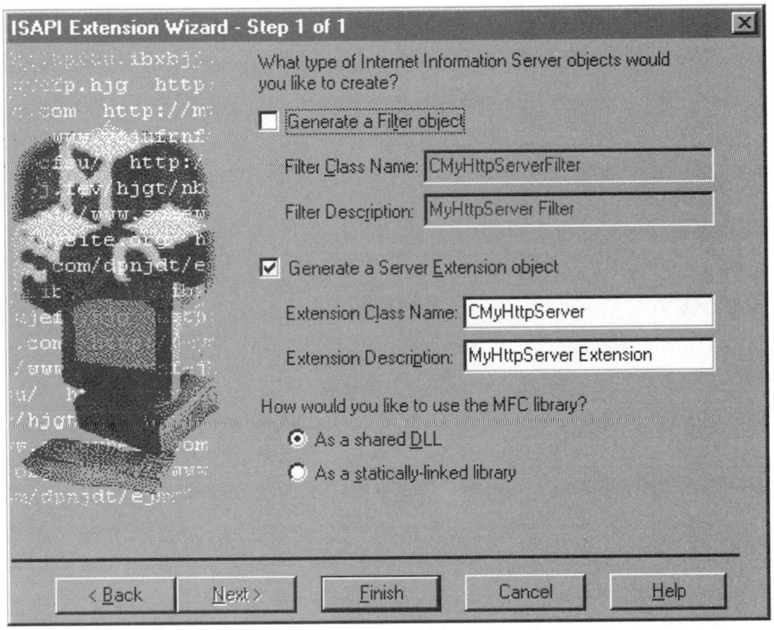

Figure 15-1
Visual C++ ISAPI Extension Wizard.

The generic default handler for an MFC ISAPI application is as follows:

```
void CMyHttpServer::Default(CHttpServerContext* pCtxt)
{
    StartContent(pCtxt);
    WriteTitle(pCtxt);
    *pCtxt << _T("This default message was produced by the
        Internet");
    *pCtxt << _T(" Server DLL Wizard. Edit your
        CMyHttpServer::Default()");
    *pCtxt << _T(" implementation to change it.\r\n");
    EndContent(pCtxt);
}
```

Another way to extend IIS is through ISAPI filters. This is a totally new concept in Web server extensions—there is no CGI-like counterpart. ISAPI filters provide the capability of intercepting specific server events before the server itself handles them. A filter is loaded when the Web service starts,

CHAPTER 15

and it tells the server what sort of event notifications it is interested in. If these events occur, the filter has the options of processing the events, passing them on to other filters, or sending them back to the server after it has dealt with them. You can use ISAPI filters, for example, to improve the logging capabilities of your Web server or to provide custom authentication techniques to enhance security. The API for filters is very similar to that for ISAPI applications. You can also create ISAPI Filters with the Visual C++ ISAPI Extension Wizard. Most of its API is wrapped in the MFC classes CHttpFilter and CHttpFilterContext.

Active Server Pages

Now that you understand the difference between CGI and ISAPI, we can examine the role of the Active Server Pages (ASP), code name "Denali." This new technology performs very similar tasks to CGI and ISAPI, but it is much easier to use because it is coded in a script language such as Visual Basic Scripting Edition (VBScript) or JavaScript. ASP is in fact an ISAPI application that, as we know, runs in the same memory address space as IIS. It loads and caches precompiled script files in memory and compiles them at run time using an interpreter such as the VBScript DLL. It will scale better than CGI and might be faster, but it cannot be as fast as an ISAPI application written in C because it uses a run-time interpreted language.

So why would you want to use ASP? One of the main reasons is that it simplifies the maintenance of a Web site. Theoretically speaking, you could port all HTML code to compiled C code in an ISAPI DLL. This would enable your Web server to respond quickly to requests without having to load any HTML files. However, maintenance would be very difficult because even if you wanted to make a minor change to a Web page you would have to recompile and link your ISAPI DLL and restart your server to load it. Also, every Web page designer would have to be trained to write ISAPI applications in C. A Web site that is changed frequently will encourage people to come back to it, and ASP provides an easy and powerful way to do this for scripts as well as for HTML code.

ASP is very content-centric and is completely integrated with your HTML files. In fact, if you change the file extension of an HTML file to .ASP, the file will automatically become an Active Server Page file. All ActiveX Server files consist of straight ASCII text coded to be HTML or script. The following is an ASP version of the multiplication CGI form sample we wrote above:

```
<HTML><BODY><BR>
<H1>This is a very simple ASP app</H1>
<%num1 =Request.QueryString("number1")%>
```

```
<%num2 =Request.QueryString("number2")%>
<FORM ACTION=http://www.micromodeling.com/denali/Test.asp
METHOD=GET>
Multiply numbers :
<input type=text size=8 name=number1 value = <%=num1%>>
<input type=text size=8 name=number2 value = <%=num2%>>
<input type=submit value=Calculate>
<input type=text size=8 name=result value = <%=num1*num2%>>
</FORM>
</BODY></HTML>
```

You'll notice that script code and HTML code are in the same file. The script code is between the tags <% and %> and does not get sent back to the browser. If you place = after the <% tag, the result of the script is sent back. The Request object is the way that ASP gets access to the environment variable QUERY_STRING. It has five associated collections: QueryString, Form, Cookies, ClientCertificate, and ServerVariables. The following syntax gives you access to the information in the Request object:

```
Request.CollectionName(variablename)
```

All the environment variables you could access with CGI can be accessed with ASP using the Request collection ServerVariables. This one line of code,

```
<%=Request.ServerVariables("ALL_HTTP")%>
```

revealed the following information to my ASP program:

```
HTTP_ACCEPT:image/gif, image/x-xbitmap, image/jpeg, image/pjpeg, */*
HTTP_ACCEPT_LANGUAGE:en
HTTP_HOST:207.42.56.1
HTTP_REFERER:http://207.42.56.1/denali/atest.asp
HTTP_UA_PIXELS:1024x768
HTTP_UA_COLOR:color8
HTTP_UA_OS:Windows 95
HTTP_UA_CPU:x86
HTTP_USER_AGENT:Mozilla/2.0 (compatible; MSIE 3.0; Windows 95)
HTTP_COOKIE:DENALISESSIONID=MSSVIGDLYLSQKQUL
```

This informs my program what MIME types my browser will accept, the referring page that brought me to the site, the version of the browser I'm using, the operating system I'm using, and the configuration of my desktop. The cookie at the end of the list above is an identification token that is sent to the client browser and is stored on the client's hard drive. This can be used to track a user during many URL requests in a Web application. The Request object Cookies collection can be used to retrieve the information stored in the cookie.

559

ASP uses a Response object to set the value of a Cookie. The following code will set a cookie with the value of "BuyItem=sugar":

```
<%Response.Cookies("cookie")("BuyItem")= ("sugar")%>
```

You could use this technique to gather a list of items a user might buy while visiting your site. The Response object, in general, is the equivalent of the WriteClient in ISAPI or the stdout in CGI. You can use it to add HTTP headers, to redirect users to other URLs, and even to add a string to the end of a Web server log file using its AppendToLog method. You can find the syntax for all the ASP functions in the online documentation that comes with the product.

ASP extends IIS in a very natural and powerful way with two additional objects: the Application object and the Session object. An Active Server Page application consists of all the directories and files under a virtual directory on the Web server. Therefore, if you have an Active Server Page application at the URL

http://www.micromodeling.com/MyASP

all users accessing files in, or beyond, the directory "MyASP" will be able to share resources through the Application object. This allows you to store common information that is available to all users accessing the application. For example, the following piece of code will create a real-time discussion application that all users can participate in to share their views on ASP:

```
<HTML>
<BODY>
<H1> Join the discussion on ASP here !</H1>
<%Application("comments")=Application("comments") & _
"<BR>" & Request.QueryString("Name") & "   -   " & _
Request.QueryString("Comment")%>
<FORM  ACTION=http://www.micromodeling.com/denali/discuss.asp
METHOD=GET>
<input type=submit value="Add Comment"><BR>
<input type=text size=11 name=Name value =
<%=Request.QueryString("Name")%>>Name<BR>
<input type=text size=60 name=Comment value = "">Comment<BR>
</FORM>
<%=Application("comments")%>
</BODY>
</HTML>
```

The Session object is similar to the Application object except that it is used to manage state information for a single user during his or her activity within your Web site. You can keep information about this user in memory even if he or she moves off to others sites and then returns again to yours. A session automatically starts when a new user goes to one of your application pages. It will end automatically if the user does not refresh or connect to another page in your application within the time-out value set for your session. You can also abandon a session early with the code <%Session.Abandon%> or set the time-out value to any specified number of minutes. For example, you could abandon a session after thirty minutes with the code <%Session.Timeout=30%>.

You initialize the Application and Session objects in a file called GLOBAL.ASA. Each ASP application can have only one such file, and it is located in its root directory. The GLOBAL.ASA file contains the following code to handle OnStart and OnEnd events for Application and Session objects:

```
<SCRIPT LANGUAGE=VBScript RUNAT=Server>
    SUB Application_OnStart
    END SUB
</SCRIPT>
<SCRIPT LANGUAGE=VBScript RUNAT=Server>
    SUB Application_OnEnd
    END SUB
</SCRIPT>
<SCRIPT LANGUAGE=VBScript RUNAT=Server>
    SUB Session_OnStart
    END SUB
</SCRIPT>
<SCRIPT LANGUAGE=VBScript RUNAT=Server>
    SUB Session_OnEnd
    END SUB
</SCRIPT>
```

The desired implementation for these events will depend on your application. If you modify the code in this file, you must restart IIS for it to take effect.

NOTE

You probably noticed that we specify the script language to be VBScript. However, you can write ASP in JavaScript, or another compatible scripting language, by using the <SCRIPT LANGUAGE=JScript RUNAT=Server> and </SCRIPT> tags instead of <% and %>.

Active Server Pages also has COM capabilities, and as you'll see in the next section, this is perhaps its greatest feature.

CHAPTER 15

DCOM and Transaction Server

To extend the capability of Internet Information Server to deliver powerful distributed systems for an intranet or the Internet, we must go beyond the design methodology of CGI and ISAPI. To meet the demands of mission-critical transactional systems running on an intranet, we must apply the principles of object-oriented technology, transaction processing, and distributed computing. On the client side, the Internet browser has been extended with COM-based ActiveX controls and Java applets. The Component Object Model (COM) is also being applied to extend the Internet Information Server in an extremely powerful way.

COM is an object-based programming model designed to allow components written by different vendors to interoperate easily in a well-known and consistent manner. As software development becomes increasingly complex, with lines of code measuring in the millions, it's not realistic to incorporate this functionality into CGI or ISAPI applications. Competitive pressures within a very dynamic industry have also spurred the need for rapid application development. Such speed and efficiency can be achieved only through software reuse and integration, which is why COM was designed.

COM is an industry standard, compatible with other standards such as C++, Java, Basic, and COBOL. It is not a new programming language but rather a cross-platform object system model that can be implemented using existing languages. COM is a fully published and open specification that was refined through an open process forum in which major independent software vendors participated. It is a standard that is widely adopted and will be in use for many years. By building COM on a binary standard, Microsoft has made it very easy for it to be adopted by new programming languages and technologies that will emerge in the future. The COM-based systems of today will be able to evolve and grow and to cooperate with the more sophisticated systems of tomorrow.

COM allows you to apply the concept of reuse to the application level. Using COM, you are able to *easily* extract and reuse pieces of functionality within various applications and tie the results into an integrated whole. For example, you can combine the calculation engine of Microsoft Excel with a database in Microsoft Access and produce reports in Microsoft Word. If a piece of functionality is not present in these applications, you can develop another COM component and plug it in to complete the solution. Although the opportunities for reuse through COM today are great, they will grow more dramatically over the next few years as the software industry more firmly embraces this technology.

Active Server Pages (ASP) uses COM in its ActiveX Server Components and ships with the following COM components, which are fully documented with the product:

- 🌐 Database Access Component
- 🌐 File Access Component
- 🌐 Ad Rotator Component
- 🌐 Browser Capabilities Component
- 🌐 Content Linking Component

These components allow you to do standard tasks such as access databases, read and write to files, or publish advertisements. The following piece of code comes with ASP and uses the Database Access Component to retrieve information from a database:

```
<HTML>
<HEAD><TITLE>ActiveX Data Object (ADO)</TITLE></HEAD>
<BODY BGCOLOR=#FFFFFF>
<H3>ActiveX Data Object (ADO)</H3>
<%
Set Conn = Server.CreateObject("ADODB.Connection")
Conn.Open "ADOSamples"
Set RS = Conn.Execute("SELECT * FROM Orders")
%>
<P>
<TABLE BORDER=1>
<TR>
<% For i = 0 to RS.Fields.Count - 1 %>
    <TD><B><%= RS(i).Name %></B></TD>
<% Next %>
</TR>
<% Do While Not RS.EOF %>
    <TR>
    <% For i = 0 to RS.Fields.Count - 1 %>
        <TD VALIGN=TOP><%= RS(i) %></TD>
    <% Next %>
    </TR>
    <%
    RS.MoveNext
Loop
RS.Close
Conn.Close
%>
</TABLE>
</BODY>
</HTML>
```

15 CHAPTER

You can use this same technique to connect to your own COM components or any of the thousands of third-party COM components currently available. ASP combines the ease of maintenance of a scripting language with the power of a system object component technology.

COM is given distributed capabilities with DCOM. This essentially means that everything you could do on the server with COM you can now do across your intranet with DCOM. Because it is language independent and works natively with Internet technologies such as TCP/IP, ActiveX, Java, and the HTTP protocol, it is a very powerful and expansive way to extend IIS for the Internet as well as for your intranet. Microsoft is openly licensing DCOM technology to other software companies so that it will run on all major operating systems. Software AG, Digital Equipment Corporation, Bristol, Main-Soft, Macromedia, and Metrowerks are working with Microsoft to port COM technologies to Unix, MVS, Macintosh, VAX, AS/400, and other operating systems. You can find the Internet Draft technical publication for DCOM at:

http://www.microsoft.com/oledev/olecom/dcomspec.txt

With DCOM, the browser can use ActiveX controls or Java applets to communicate directly with server components. You'll no longer have to pass environment variables through the HTTP server because you'll be able to pass them in through simple function calls from the browser's controls to the COM components on the server. These server components can also call back functions in the ActiveX controls in the browser, providing much richer two-way data communication capabilities. DCOM will enable this communication over any network transport, both connection-oriented and connectionless, including TCP/IP, UDP/IP, IPX/SPX, AppleTalk, and HTTP. As Internet-based computing enters all aspects of corporate life, the inherent integration capabilities of DCOM will enable the rapid creation of powerful distributed worldwide systems.

Distributing your application among many components on different servers introduces new complexities, however. You now have to provide threading support for groups of components that work together as a unit. You also have to be more concerned with fault tolerance because distributed systems tend to have less reliability, less availability, and higher failure rates. Real-life distributed systems will require more than the infrastructure for client/server computing provided by DCOM. Ways of controlling the integrity of client/server interactions are also needed. This is the domain of transaction processing. If you are selling products over the Internet, you need to ensure the integrity of all the elements in the transaction. This requires complete accuracy in processing inventory, orders, delivery, and billing. For example, you may have one DCOM component that handles orders and another that takes care of billing. Both these components must commit or abort together. Otherwise, you could have people being billed for goods they do not receive, or receiving goods for which no billing record exists. Transaction processing provides ways of treating groups of separate activities as single isolated atomic entities. Changes to any element will result in consistent changes throughout the atomic entity as a whole. Transaction processing also provides durability, ensuring that committed updates to managed resources such as databases survive system failures.

Microsoft has introduced Transaction Server, code name "Viper," to address these problems. Transaction Server combines the principles of component-based programming with the principles of transaction processing. It is built on the DCOM infrastructure but extends it by providing a server application framework that handles registration, process and thread management, context management, management and synchronization of shared resources, component-based security, and management tools for administering the distributed environment. Transaction Server imposes specific requirements on your COM components. They can only be DLLs, they must have a standard class factory, and they must only export interfaces that can be standard marshaled. Your Transaction Server components should not create threads. The Transaction Server framework itself manages server process pools and thread pools; its sophisticated locking protocols prevent deadlocks, race conditions, and starvation.

A Transaction Server application consists of the following elements:

- **Transaction Server Components.** These are the COM component DLLs that implement the business rules of your application.

- **Transaction Server Executive.** This DLL is loaded into the processes that host application components. It provides run-time services such as thread and context management.

- **Application Server Processes.** These provide surrogate process environments where your DLL components will be loaded.

- **Resource Managers.** These are used to manage durable states, such as inventory, order, and billing information. They are the backbone of transaction processing and help provide the ACID properties.

The ACID Properties

ACID is an acronym for Atomicity, Consistency, Isolation, and Durability coined by Haerder and Reuter. The Transaction Server documentation describes the ACID properties as follows:

- **Atomicity** ensures that all the updates completed under a specific transaction are committed (and made durable) or that they get aborted and rolled back to their previous state.

- **Consistency** means that a transaction is a correct transformation of the system state, preserving the state invariants.

- **Isolation** protects concurrent transactions from seeing each other's partial and uncommitted results, which might create inconsistencies in the application state. Resource managers use transaction-based synchronization protocols to isolate the uncommitted work of active transactions.

- **Durability** means that committed updates to managed resources (such as a database record) survive failures, including communication failures, process failures, and server system failures. Transaction logging even allows you to recover the durable state after disk media failures.

- **Resource Dispensers.** These are similar to resource managers, but they manage only nondurable shared state on behalf of the components.

- **Microsoft Distributed Transaction Coordinator.** This is a system service that coordinates transactions that span multiple resource managers. It implements a two-phase commit protocol ensuring that the transaction outcome of commit or abort is consistent across all resource managers involved in the transaction.

Transaction Server components can be loaded directly into IIS or into the client browser process space. Its integration of transaction-processing technology with DCOM makes it the most powerful and exciting way of extending the Microsoft Internet Information Server.

CHAPTER 16

Integration with Microsoft SQL Server

David C. Ho and Paul Li

Microsoft SQL Server 6.5 is a relational database engine designed to support multiple users who are querying and performing transactions against large databases. SQL Server integrates easily with Microsoft Internet Information Server and gives you the ability to publish data to your intranet and Internet applications. SQL Server also offers a number of features that are important in mission-critical environments, including online backup and restore capabilities, automatic recovery, and robust security. SQL Server features Transact-SQL, an enhanced version of SQL, which allows for the programming of business rules and logic through stored procedures, triggers, and rules. All in all, SQL Server is a good choice (over Microsoft Access) for large multiuser database applications and the *right* choice for transaction processing or other mission-critical applications.

CHAPTER 16

Client/Server Application Architectures

Business applications that work with Microsoft SQL Server databases are usually written in languages such as Visual Basic and use DB-Library or Open Database Connectivity (ODBC) to send commands to and receive results from SQL Server. These client/server applications typically reside on users' workstations and communicate with the database server via a local area network (LAN) or a wide area network (WAN). Client/server database applications can be structured in a number of different ways, including these:

- Splitting the business logic between the back-end database server and the front-end client is known as a two-tiered client/server architecture. A *thin* client is a front-end application that contains mostly just the presentation logic (that is, user interface) and has very little or no business logic. A *fat* client stores business logic and interface on the client machine. A fat server, then, is a database server that contains most of the business rules and logic.

- A three-tiered client/server architecture is one in which the logic resides on a separate server between the front end and the back end.

You can develop Web-based solutions with Microsoft SQL Server in a number of ways, with the browser acting as a universal client environment. In this chapter, we'll be covering the SQL Server Web Assistant, a wizard-like tool that comes with Microsoft SQL Server 6.5, and the Internet Database Connector (IDC), which is part of the Internet Information Server.

Advantages of Web-Based Solutions

Having an HTML-based application instead of a traditional client/server application working with SQL Server offers several advantages:

- The application will work on all the various platforms a Web browser supports, so many database connectivity issues go away. If users can run a Web browser, they can run the application.

- Distribution and installation problems also go away because all a user needs is a working browser and the URL for the application.

Many maintenance issues are resolved—once you put the updated HTML application on the Web server, you won't have to worry about users working off older versions of the application.

 Providing a Web-based solution also allows users to access the application through the Internet if they are not connected to your LAN or WAN.

Microsoft SQL Server Web Assistant

The SQL Server Web Assistant comes with Microsoft SQL Server 6.5 and can be used to automatically publish SQL data in HTML format. It works on a "push" model—data is published, or *pushed,* at scheduled times or when there is a change to the data on SQL Server. In the push model, a client using a browser cannot dynamically query the database. This model works well for publishing lists of information such as a company directory or, as in our example at the end of the chapter, a project list.

Querying the Database

Using the SQL Server Web Assistant, you can query the database in three ways:

 Build a query from a database hierarchy. Graphically drill down and select the database, table(s), and column(s) you want to display. One disadvantage to using this method is that the table column names, which might be somewhat arcane, will be used as the column headings in the resultant Web page.

 Type in a SQL query. In this option, enter SQL statements in the Type Your Query text area in the dialog box. We will use this option in our example.

 Use a query in a stored procedure. For some organizations, stored procedures are the only way to get at the data.

Scheduling

SQL Server is very flexible in scheduling the publication of data. You can publish now, later at a specified date and time, on certain days of the week, or on a regular basis. You can also choose to publish every time data in the affected table(s) has changed, although this option is not recommended for applications with heavy transaction volumes. Later in the chapter, we'll show the Scheduling screen for the SQL Server Web Assistant.

16
CHAPTER

Publishing

The SQL Server Web Assistant also allows you to include URL links and reference texts in the resulting Web page. You can format your results using an HTML template file or specify some formatting preferences if you're not using a template file.

The Long Way Works, Too

Everything you can do with the SQL Server Web Assistant you can also do manually in Microsoft SQL Server 6.5. Three stored procedures are used to manage the publication of information from SQL Server onto HTML pages: sp_dropwebtask, sp_makewebtask, and sp_runwebtask. Refer to the SQL Server documentation for more information on how to use these procedures.

Handling Dynamic Requests

The SQL Server Web Assistant is limited in that clients cannot dynamically specify criteria for what data to publish and they cannot update data in the database. To handle these types of requests, the user would need the ability to enter data and/or select options and pass it back to the server. This can be accomplished with HTML forms.

The browser takes the data in the form, concatenates it into a single string, and then sends it to the server. On the server, a process parses the string to form the SQL statement and passes it to SQL Server for execution. SQL Server processes the query and returns the result to the process. The process then takes the result, creates an HTML page, and passes it back to the client Web browser. This "gateway" process between SQL Server and the client Web browser is traditionally a Common Gateway Interface (CGI) application. With Microsoft Internet Information Server, ISAPI (Internet Server Application Programming Interface) can also be used to write a DLL to talk to the database. Writing either a CGI application or an ISAPI DLL is rather technically involved, however, and we won't cover that subject here. (See Chapter 15 for more information on ISAPI.) Fortunately, Microsoft provides an easier alternative to these methods for handling dynamic SQL Server requests: the Internet Database Connector (IDC).

IDC and the Pull Model

The core of IDC is a dynamic-link library (DLL) named HTTPODBC.DLL that is itself an ISAPI application. IDC communicates with SQL Server via 32-bit ODBC. (In fact, IDC works with any database product that has a 32-bit ODBC-compatible driver and is not limited to just Microsoft SQL Server.) Requests from clients come in with a URL that specifies a file with an .IDC

> ### SQL Server Licensing for Internet/Intranet
>
> You'll need to purchase the SQL Server Internet Connector license (not to be confused with the Internet Database Connector) if you're going to connect SQL Server to IIS or any other Web server, even though you might be using IDC or a third-party product to communicate with SQL Server. The license allows an unlimited number of intranet or Internet connections to a single SQL Server.

extension residing on Internet Information Server (IIS). The .IDC files specify the ODBC data source, SQL Server logon information, the HTML template file, and the SQL statement to be executed. IIS calls HTTPODBC.DLL, which in turn executes the SQL call resulting from substituting the parameters in the SQL statement in the IDC file with the values coming in from the HTTP header. When the results come back, IDC then merges them with an HTML template file and sends this page to the client. Because IDC allows clients (users) to retrieve information directly from SQL Server on demand, it is said to be based on the *pull* model.

SNA Server and the AS/400

With an installed base of over 300,000 machines, the IBM AS/400 is still a critical component of many organizations' information systems, housing everything from accounting systems to a specialized line of business applications. Many companies port, or "stage," data from these applications onto servers for further analysis and reporting—setting up SQL databases and developing solutions like those described in this chapter. Although porting data from AS/400 to servers is certainly an option, it is by no means the only one.

SNA Server, part of Microsoft's BackOffice family, is Microsoft's PC gateway to the AS/400. SNA Server provides a single connection to an AS/400 for an entire workgroup—managing access, security, and traffic flow. With SNA Server, PCs can access existing AS/400 applications via terminal emulation. Better yet, SNA server turns an AS/400 database into just another ODBC data source, and the AS/400 into a database server. Any application that can use an ODBC data source can get at data from an AS/400 DB2 database through SNA Server.

The AS/400 and Intranets

One method of utilizing the capabilities of AS/400 on an intranet is to use it with an SNA Server.

16
CHAPTER

Browser emulation and more

Using SNA Server and a third-party product such as Simware's Salvo, you can dynamically convert an AS/400 terminal stream to HTML. This means that users can access existing AS/400 applications directly through their browsers. At first glance, this doesn't seem to buy much since the resulting Web page looks pretty much like the original terminal-based application. Looking further, however, this approach has some real benefits:

🌐 Stream conversion can go one step further than emulation; it can take the information from the terminal output and populate HTML controls with it. In other words, it is possible to create a user-friendly front end to these legacy systems using HTML pages.

🌐 Access to the AS/400 can theoretically extend to any user with a Web browser. You'll need to take security measures on your intranet and network to restrict access to these legacy systems as required.

SNA Server and Internet Information Server

Microsoft Internet Information Server also provides a powerful link between the Web browser and legacy AS/400 data via IDC. As mentioned above, IDC works with any database product that has a 32-bit ODBC-compatible driver, and SNA Server provides that driver for the AS/400. So if your back-end data store happens to be an AS/400, you can still get at the data and create the same kinds of applications mentioned here.

Building Sample Web Pages That Utilize SQL Server

In this chapter, we'll be publishing information from as well as inputting information into a database using the SQL Server Web Assistant and IDC. The database, named MMA, contains client and project information. This database has two tables: Clients and Projects. The Clients table captures the name and address of each client, and the Projects table captures the name, description, estimated project cost, start date, and end date of each project. Projects can be active (ProjectStatus = 'A'), not yet active (ProjectStatus = 'N'), or completed (ProjectStatus = 'C'). The fields for these two tables are as follows:

Clients Table
ClientID
ClientName
ClientAddress
ClientCity
ClientState
ClientZip

Projects Table
ProjectID
ProjectName
ProjectDesc
ClientID
ProjectStatus
ProjectEstCost
ProjectStartDate
ProjectEndDate

Creating the MMA Database

To create the database in Microsoft SQL Server, follow the steps below. If necessary, consult Online Help or SQL Server Books Online for more information.

1. Using SQL Enterprise Manager, create two storage devices: one for data and the other for log.

2. Create a database named MMA using the devices created in step 1.

3. Using the graphical query utility ISQL/W, load and execute the PROJECT.SQL script file on the companion CD to create the Clients and Projects tables.

4. Copy the CLIENTS.BCP and PROJECTS.BCP files, which contain sample data for the two tables, from the companion CD to your hard disk. Load the sample data into the database by executing the bulk copy program twice at an MS-DOS command session as shown below. (Because of length restrictions, these two commands are printed here on four lines.) Substitute [server] with your actual server name. If you have a password for your system admin account, specify it after the -P option.

    ```
    C:\bcp mma..clients in clients.bcp -c -Usa -P -S[server]
        /r\n -t~~
    C:\bcp mma..projects in projects.bcp -c -Usa -P -S[server]
        /r\n -t~~
    ```

Note that all samples in this chapter are in the Chapter16 folder on the companion CD.

Using the Web Assistant

In the following example, we'll be using the SQL Server Web Assistant to set up the periodic updating (for example, 10 p.m. every 2 days) of a Web page containing the list of active projects from the MMA database.

16 CHAPTER

1. Start the SQL Server Web Assistant. The SQL Server Web Assistant - Login screen will display.

2. Enter the SQL Server Name, Login ID, and Password. In our example, we'll be using the system administrator account 'sa'. If you're running the SQL Server Web Assistant from the same server hosting SQL Server, you could type in *(local)* for server name. If you're using integrated or mixed security, you don't have to enter a login ID and password. You should, however, check the box next to Use Windows NT Security To Log In Instead Of Entering A Login ID And/Or A Password. After filling in the information, click the Next button to go to the next screen.

3. Enter the query as free-form text in the Web Assistant Query screen, as shown below. This query can be copied from the file QUERY.TXT, available on the companion CD. Select MMA from the database drop-down list, and click Next.

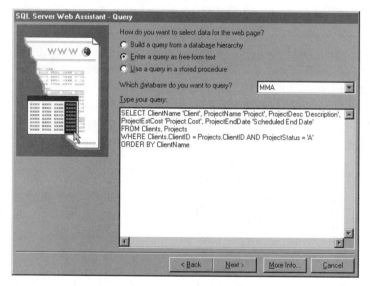

4. In the Scheduling screen, specify when to publish the information. In our example, we chose to publish On A Regular Basis, at 10 p.m. every 2 days, as shown in the dialog box at the top of the next page. Click Next when done.

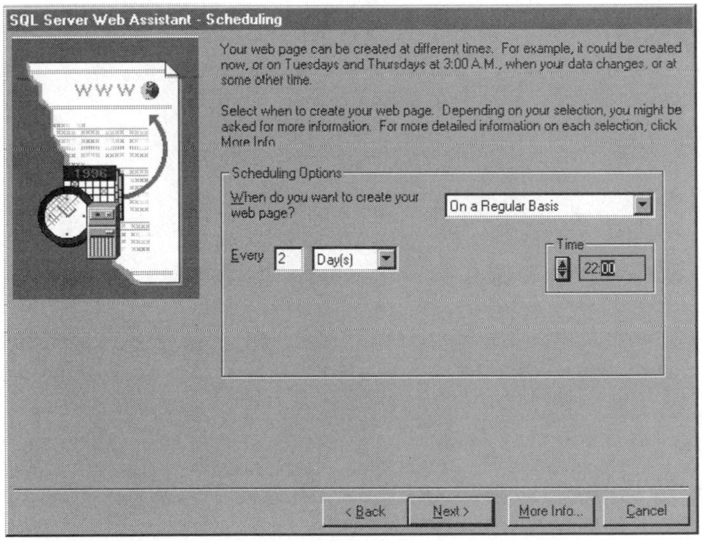

5. Specify the filename and title of the resultant Web page as well as the title for the query results in the File Options screen, as shown below. You can also specify an HTML template file to format your results. An example of how the template file is formatted is shown later in this chapter. Click Next when done.

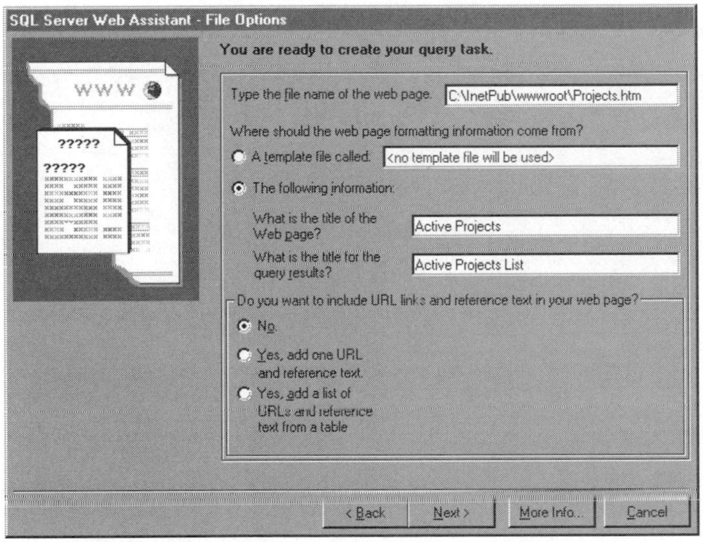

6. The last screen of the SQL Server Web Assistant, the Formatting screen shown at the top of the next page, allows you to specify a number of formatting options.

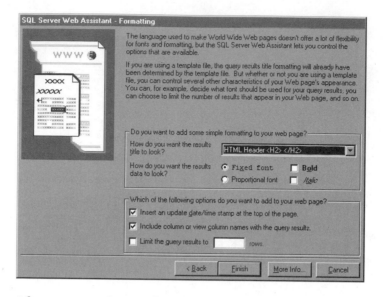

After you specify your formatting options, click the Finish button. The SQL Server Web Assistant will create a task in the SQL Executive that you can view by double-clicking the SQL Executive icon for the server in the SQL Enterprise Manager. After the task is executed, view the published Web page with your Web browser. (Figure 16-1 shows a sample of the resulting Web Page.)

Figure 16-1

Active Projects List generated from SQL Server Web Assistant.

Using IDC

Before we can go on to some examples using IDC and the pull model, we must properly configure your server. Just follow these steps:

1. First we must create an ODBC system data source. Be aware that if you are using Windows NT 3.51 or a different version of ODBC, these steps may be different. In Windows NT 4.0, double-click the ODBC icon in the Control Panel window, which displays the ODBC Data Source Administrator, as shown here:

   Click the System DSN tab, and click the Add button. Select the SQL Server driver, and click Finish. In the ODBC SQL Server Setup dialog box, enter a Data Source Name of *MMA*, along with other setup information, as shown at the top of the next page.

   When you are finished, click OK in the ODBC SQL Server Setup dialog box, and click OK in the ODBC Data Source Administrator to complete the system data source setup.

CHAPTER 16

ODBC SQL Server Setup

Data Source Name: MMA
Description: Sample SQL Server database
Server: (local)
Network Address: (Default)
Network Library: (Default)

☐ Use Trusted Connection

Login
Database Name: MMA
Language Name: (Default)

☑ Generate Stored Procedure for Prepared Statement
☑ Use ANSI Quoted Identifiers
☑ Use ANSI Nulls, Padding and Warnings

Translation
☐ Convert OEM to ANSI characters

2. Next we need to create a virtual directory named MMA with Execute permissions. First, create a directory named MMA on your server. Start the Internet Service Manager, select the WWW computer icon, and choose Service Properties from the Properties menu. In the WWW Service Properties dialog box, click the Directories tab.

WWW Service Properties for mspls2

Service | Directories | Logging | Advanced

Directory	Alias	Address	Error
C:\InetPub\wwwroot	<Home>		
C:\inetpub\ASPSamp	/ASPSamp		
C:\inetpub\ASPSamp\Ad	/AdvWorks		
C:\InetPub\Intrafix	/Intrafix		
C:\InetPub\scripts	/Scripts		
C:\InetPub\scripts\Sampl	/Scripts/sample		
C:\InetPub\scripts\srchac	/Scripts/srchac		
C:\InetPub\wwwroot_vti/	_vti_bin		

☑ Enable Default Document
Default Document: Default.htm

☐ Directory Browsing Allowed

Click the Add button, specify the MMA directory, enter MMA for the Alias, and check the Execute permissions, as shown below. When done, click OK in the Directory Properties and WWW Service Properties dialog boxes.

3. Finally, copy all of the files including the Images directory in the Chapter16 directory from the companion CD except for the BCP, SQL, and TXT files into the MMA directory you just created.

IDC Example 1: Selecting Specific Client Information

In this first of three IDC examples, we're going to get all the client information and put it into an HTML table. The IDC file contains the necessary information such as data source, SQL Server user name, HTX file (HTML template file to view result set from the query), and SQL statement. Listing 16-1 and Listing 16-2 show the entire contents of CLIENTS.IDC and CLIENTS.HTX. The result set will be populated within the <%begindetail%> and <%enddetail%> tags of the HTX file. Data for each of the fields will be substituted for field names enclosed by <% and %>, for example, <%ClientName%>, as shown here in this code snippet:

```
<%begindetail%>
    <%If CurrentRecord EQ 0 %><tr>
        <!Fill in Column header text>
        <th><font size="2"><b>Client</b></font></th>
        <th><font size="2"><b>Address</b></font></th>
        <th><font size="2"><b>City</b></font></th>
```

(continued)

581

```
      <th><font size="2"><b>State</b></font></th>
      <th><font size="2"><b>Zip</b></font></th>
      </tr>
  <%endif%><tr>
  <!Fill in client information from result set>
  <td><%ClientName%></td>
  <td><%ClientAddress%></td>
  <td><%ClientCity%></td>
  <td><%ClientState%></td>
  <td><%ClientZip%></td>
  </tr>
<%enddetail%><tr>
```

To see how this works, start Microsoft Internet Explorer 3.0 and go to the following address:

http://[IIS server name]/mma/default.htm

Figure 16-2 shows the default page for the MMA IDC examples. Click the Client Information Query link and IDC will return the list of clients using the template CLIENTS.HTX, as shown in Figure 16-3.

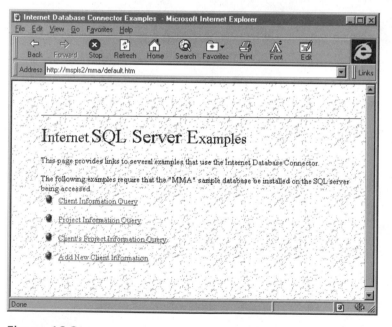

Figure 16-2

Default page for MMA IDC examples.

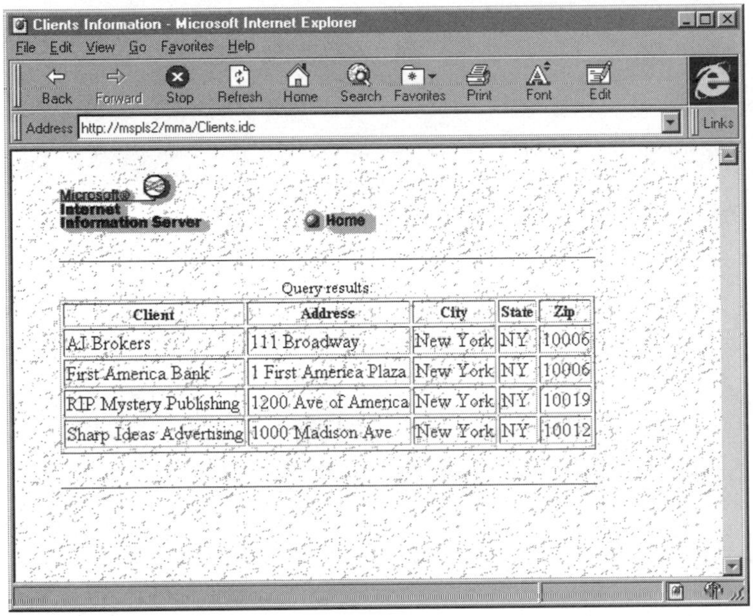

Figure 16-3

Result set in a tabular format from the Client Information Query.

```
Datasource: MMA
Username: sa
Template: Clients.htx
SQLStatement:
+SELECT ClientName, ClientAddress, ClientCity, ClientState,
+ClientZip
+FROM MMA.dbo.Clients
```

Listing 16-1

CLIENTS.IDC

```
<html>
<head>
<title>Clients Information</title>
</head>
```

Listing 16-2

CLIENTS.HTX

(continued)

583

Listing 16-2 *(continued)*

```
<BODY BACKGROUND="images/backgrnd.gif">
<BODY BGCOLOR="FFFFFF">
<table>
   <tr>
   <td><img src="images\SPACE.gif" alt=" " align="top"
   width="21" height="27"></td>
   <td><a href="db_mh.map" ismap><img src="images\db_mh.gif"
   alt=" " align="top" border="0" width="350" height="54"
   ismap></a></td>
   </tr>
   <tr>
   <td> </td>
   <td> <hr>
   <p> </p>
   <p> <font size="2"> </font> </p>
   <p align="center"><font size="2"> </font> </p>
   <div align="center"><center><table border="1">
   <caption align="top"><font size="2">Query results:</font>
   </caption>
   <%begindetail%>
      <%if CurrentRecord EQ 0 %>
          <tr>
          <th><font size="2"><b>Client</b></font></th>
          <th><font size="2"><b>Address</b></font></th>
          <th><font size="2"><b>City</b></font></th>
          <th><font size="2"><b>State</b></font></th>
          <th><font size="2"><b>Zip</b></font></th>
          </tr>
      <%endif%>
      <tr>
      <td><%ClientName%></td>
      <td><%ClientAddress%></td>
      <td><%ClientCity%></td>
      <td><%ClientState%></td>
      <td><%ClientZip%></td>
      </tr>
   <%enddetail%>
   <tr>
   <td><font size="2"> </font></td>
   </tr>
   </table>
```

Listing 16-2 *(continued)*

```
    </center></div>
    <p><font size="2"> <%if CurrentRecord EQ 0 %>
    <b><i>Sorry, no client.</i></b>
    <%endif%></font> </p>
    <hr>
    </td>
    </tr>
</table>
</body>
</html>
```

IDC Example 2: Developing Projects for a Specific Client

In the second example, we want to specify a client and get back all the projects related to that client. Click the Client's Project Information Query link on the home page. IDC will retrieve all the client names in the Clients table and populate the combo box in the HTX file, as shown in Figure 16-4. Listing 16-3 and Listing 16-4 show the files CPROJ.IDC and CPROJ.HTX used to create this page. Select a client and click the Query button. This will send the selected client to the CPROJINF.IDC file referenced in the CPROJ.HTX file, as shown in the code snippet below. IDC will query for the project information related to the client and return the results as shown in Figure 16-5. Listing 16-5 and Listing 16-6 show the files CPROJINF.IDC and CPROJINF.HTX used to create this page.

```
<form method="POST" Action="cprojinf.idc">
    <p><select Name="CName">
        <%begindetail%>
            <!Set combo value to client id and display client name>
            <option value="<%ClientID%>"><%ClientName%></option>
        <%enddetail%>
    </select></p>
</form>
```

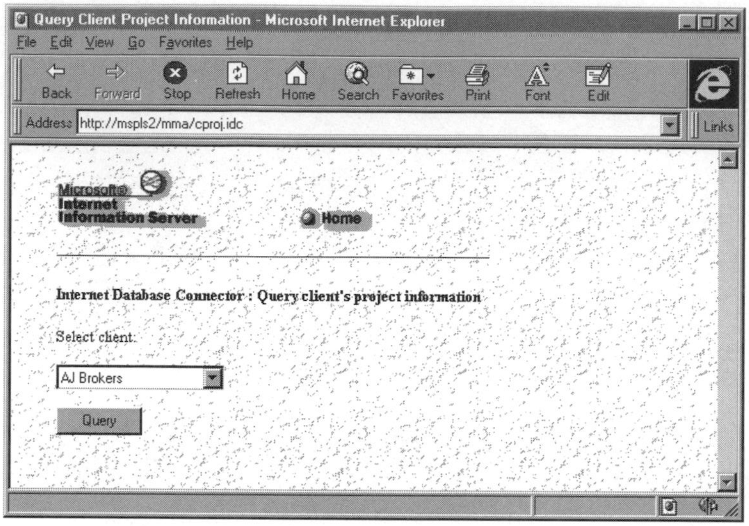

Figure 16-4

Query by client.

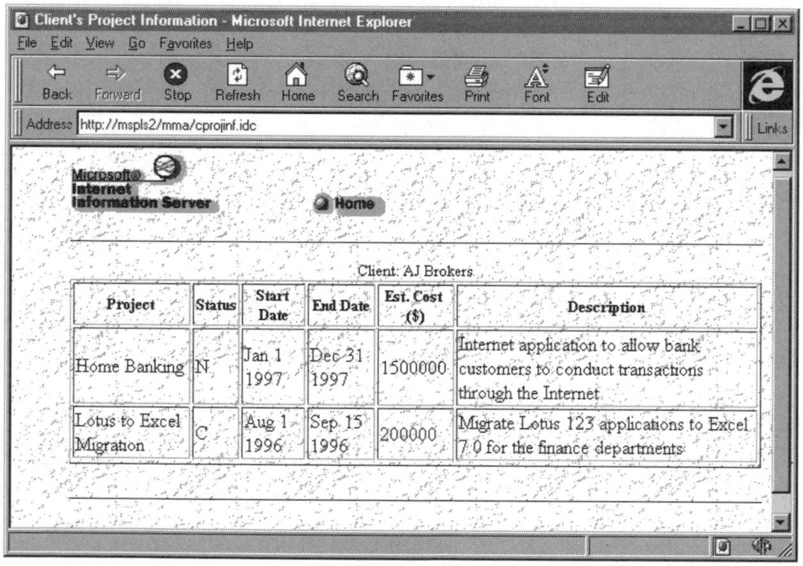

Figure 16-5

All projects for the selected client AJ Brokers.

```
Datasource: MMA
Username: sa
Template: cproj.htx
SQLStatement:
+SELECT ClientID, ClientName
+FROM MMA.dbo.Clients
```

Listing 16-3

CPROJ.IDC

```
<html>
<head>
<title>Query Client Project Information</title>
</head>
<BODY BACKGROUND="images/backgrnd.gif">
<BODY BGCOLOR="FFFFFF">
<table>
    <tr>
    <td><img src="images\SPACE.gif" alt=" " align="top"
    width="21" height="27"></td>
    <td><a href="db_mh.map" ismap><img
    src="images\db_mh.gif" alt=" " align="top" border="0"
    width="350" height="54" ismap></a></td>
    </tr>
    <tr>
    <td> </td>
    <td> <hr>
    <p> </p>
    <p> </p>
    <p> </p>
    <h2 align="center"><font size="2">Internet Database
    Connector: Query client's project information</font> </h2>
    <p><font size="2">Select client:</font> </p>
    <form method="POST" Action="cprojinf.idc">
        <p><select Name="CName">
            <%begindetail%>
                <option value="<%ClientID%>"><%ClientName%>
                </option>
            <%enddetail%>
```

Listing 16-4

CPROJ.HTX

(continued)

587

16
C
H
A
P
T
E
R

Listing 16-4 *(continued)*

```
        </select></p>
    </form>
    <p> </p>
    <p> </p>
    <p> </p>
    <input type="submit" value="Query">
    </td>
    </tr>
</table>
</body>
</html>
```

```
Datasource: MMA
Username: sa
Template: cprojinf.htx
SQLStatement:
+SELECT ClientName, ProjectName, ProjectStatus,
+convert(char(12),ProjectStartDate) ProjectStartDate,
+convert(char(12),ProjectEndDate) ProjectEndDate,
+ProjectEstCost, ProjectDesc
+FROM MMA.dbo.Projects Projects, MMA.dbo.Clients Clients
+WHERE Projects.ClientID = Clients.ClientID AND
+(Clients.ClientID=convert(int,'%CName%'))
```

Listing 16-5
CPROJINF.IDC

```
<html>
<head>
<title>Client's Project Information</title>
</head>
<BODY BACKGROUND="images/backgrnd.gif">
<BODY BGCOLOR="FFFFFF">
<table>
    <tr>
    <td><img src="images\SPACE.gif" alt=" " align="top"
    width="32" height="32"></td>
    <td><a href="db_mh.map" ismap><img src="images\db_mh.gif"
```

Listing 16-6
CPROJINF.HTX

(continued)

Listing 16-6 *(continued)*

```
    alt=" " align="top" border="0" width="350" height="54"
    ismap></a></td>
    </tr>
    <tr>
    <td> </td>
    <td> <hr>
    <p> </p>
    <p> <font size="2"> </font> </p>
    <p align="center"><font size="2"> </font> </p>
    <div align="center"><center><table border="1">
    <caption align="top"><font size="2">Client:
    <%ClientName%></font></caption>
    <%begindetail%>
        <%if CurrentRecord EQ 0 %>
            <tr>
            <th><font size="2"><b>Project</b></font></th>
            <th><font size="2"><b>Status</b></font></th>
            <th><font size="2"><b>Start Date</b></font></th>
            <th><font size="2"><b>End Date</b></font></th>
            <th><font size="2"><b>Est. Cost ($)</b></font></th>
            <th><font size="2"><b>Description</b></font></th>
            </tr>
        <%endif%>
        <tr>
        <td><%ProjectName%></td>
        <td><%ProjectStatus%></td>
        <td><%ProjectStartDate%></td>
        <td><%ProjectEndDate%></td>
        <td><%ProjectEstCost%></td>
        <td><%ProjectDesc%></td>
        </tr>
    <%enddetail%>
    <tr>
    <td></td>
    </tr>
    </table>
    </center></div><p> </p>
    <p><font size="2"> <%if CurrentRecord EQ 0 %>
    <b><i>Sorry, no project.</i></b>
    <%endif%></font> </p>
    <hr>
    </td>
    </tr>
</table>
</body>
</html>
```

IDC Example 3: Adding a New Client to the Database

In this last example, we'll insert a new client into the MMA database and validate it against duplicate entry of client names. In addition, we want to make the client name a required field. The code below shows the SQL statement used to ensure that duplicate client names are not entered into the database.

```
'Query client name for duplicate name.
if exists (
    select * from MMA.dbo.Clients
    where ClientName='%Name%'
    )
    select result='duplicate'
else
    'no duplicate name, insert entry
    INSERT INTO MMA.dbo.Clients
    (ClientName, ClientAddress, ClientCity, ClientState,
    ClientZip)
    VALUES('%Name%', '%Address%', '%City%', '%State%',
    '%Zip%');
```

Click the Add New Client Information link on the home page. This will bring you to the client data entry page. Figure 16-6 shows this data entry page with some sample client information already entered. Listing 16-7 shows the code to create this page. After you fill in the client information, click the Submit button. This will submit the data for insertion into the Clients table. Figure 16-7 shows the page displayed when the client's information has been successfully inserted into the MMA database. Listing 16-8 and Listing 16-9 show the files INSCLINT.IDC and INSCLINT.HTX used to insert the information and display a confirmation.

```
<html>
<head>
<title>New Client</title>
</head>

<body background="images\backgrnd.gif" bgcolor="#FFFFFF">

<table>
    <tr>
        <td><img src="images\SPACE.gif" alt=" " align="top"
        width="21" height="27"></td>
```

Listing 16-7

INSCLINT.HTM

(continued on page 592)

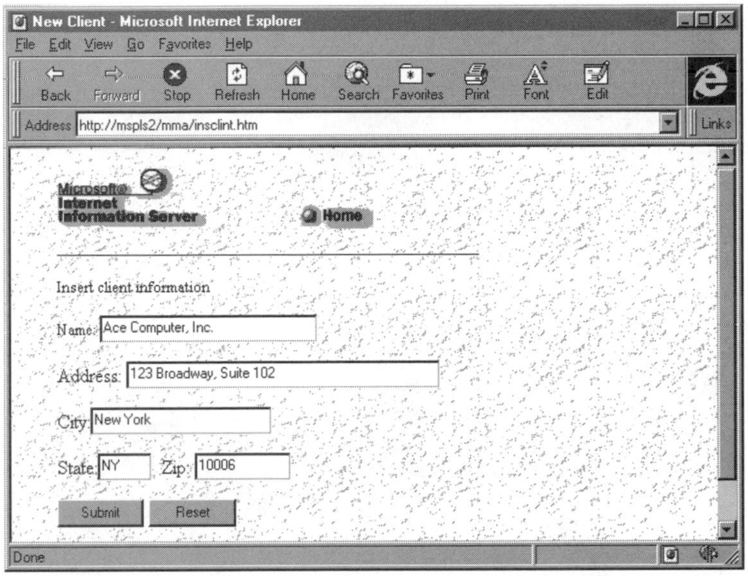

Figure 16-6
Client data entry page.

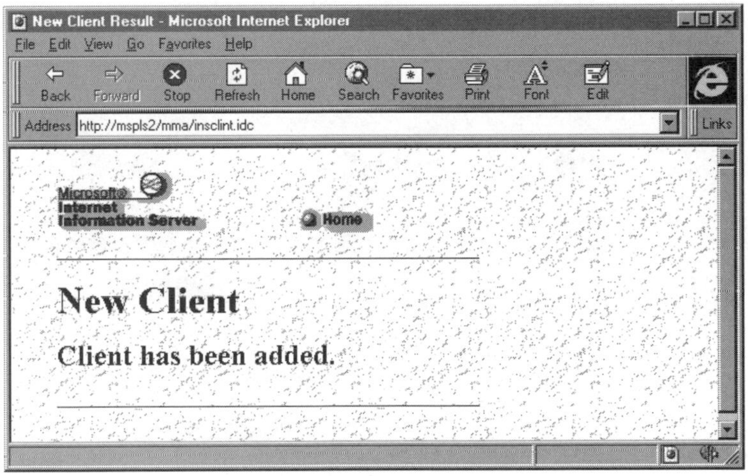

Figure 16-7
Confirmation page displayed when the client's information has been successfully inserted into the database.

Listing 16-7 *(continued)*

```
            <td><a href="db_mh.map" ismap><img
            src="images\db_mh.gif" alt=" " align="top" border="0"
            width="350" height="54" ismap></a></td>
    </tr>
    <tr>
        <td> </td>
        <td> <hr>
        <p> </p>
        <p><font size="2">Insert client information</font> </p>
        <form action="insclint.idc" method="POST">
            <p><font size="2">
            Name: </font><input type="text" size="32"
            maxlength="50"
            name="Name"></p>
            <p>Address: <input type="text" size="48"
            maxlength="100"
            name="Address"></p>
            <p>City: <input type="text" size="26"
            maxlength="30"
            name="City"> </p>
            <p>State: <input type="text" size="5" maxlength="2"
            name="State">
            Zip: <input type="text" size="12" maxlength="5"
            name="Zip"></p>
        </form>
        <p> </p>
        <p> </p>
        <p> <input type="submit" value="Submit"> <input
        type="reset"
        value="Reset"></p>
        <p> </p>
        </td>
        <td> </td>
    </tr>
</table>
</body>
</html>
```

```
Datasource: MMA
Username: sa
Template: insclint.htx
RequiredParameters: Name
SQLStatement:
+if exists (
+    select * from MMA.dbo.Clients
+    where ClientName='%Name%'
+    )
+    select result='duplicate'
+else
+    INSERT INTO MMA.dbo.Clients
+    (ClientName, ClientAddress, ClientCity, ClientState,
+    ClientZip)
+    VALUES('%Name%', '%Address%', '%City%', '%State%',
+    '%Zip%');
```

Listing 16-8
INSCLINT.IDC

```
<html>
<title>New Client Result</title>
<BODY BACKGROUND="images/backgrnd.gif">
<BODY BGCOLOR="FFFFFF">
<TABLE>
    <TR>
    <TD><IMG SRC="images/SPACE.gif" ALIGN="top" ALT=" "></TD>
    <TD><A HREF="db_mh.map"><IMG SRC="images/db_mh.gif" ismap
    BORDER=0 ALIGN="top" ALT=" "></A></TD>
    </TR>
    <tr>
    <TD></TD>
    <TD>
    <hr>
    <h1>New Client</h1>
    <%begindetail%>
    <%enddetail%>
```

Listing 16-9
INSCLINT.HTX

(continued)

Listing 16-9 *(continued)*

```
    <%if CurrentRecord EQ 0 %>
        <h2>Client has been added.</h2>
    <%else%>
        <h2><I><%idc.ClientName%></I> is already registered.</h2>
    <%endif%>
    <hr>
    </td>
    </tr>
</table>
</body>
</html>
```

CHAPTER

17

Web Administration

Jeffrey M. Jones and Rick Bullen

Web authoring can be heaven or hell, but Web administration is definitely purgatory (when it isn't limbo!). If you think your work is over once your site is up and running, think again—it's only just begun! Not only will you keep doing everything you're already doing, but you'll also be called on to revise and update existing material, set or reconfigure passwords and other security features, add and remove proxies and other servers, customize .INI files and other environment settings, initiate version control, provide a project plan, assure quality control . . . everything short of securing the blessings of happiness for yourself and yours for posterity!

Because Web administration is something of a mixed bag, this chapter will cover different features of various tools, including Microsoft FrontPage Explorer (passwords and proxies), Microsoft FrontPage Server Administrator (server configuration), and Microsoft Visual SourceSafe (version control). Bear with us; sooner or later something in here is bound to come in real handy.

CHAPTER

17

FrontPage Administration

As we just mentioned, your tasks as a Web administrator will involve everything from doing your basic Web housekeeping chores to ensuring your intranet's security. In the following sections, you'll get a rundown of your duties as Keeper of the Web.

General Web Maintenance Features

Here's a quick review of Microsoft FrontPage Explorer features and commands that are particularly relevant to the problems of Web maintenance:

- **Adding and importing.** Choose Import from the FrontPage Explorer File menu to add selected pages or folders to the active Web. You can also import files by choosing New from the FrontPage Explorer File menu, selecting FrontPage Web and then Import Web Wizard, and making sure that you've checked the Add To The Current Web option.

- **Project management and tasking.** Choose Add To Do Task from the Edit menu to create a Task List entry linked to your currently selected page. You can also choose the command from the FrontPage Editor menu to create an entry linked to the open page. To view the Task list, choose Show To Do List from the Tools menu in either the FrontPage Explorer or the FrontPage Editor. Clicking the Add button in the FrontPage To Do List dialog box creates only an *unlinked* entry. The FrontPage To Do List dialog box is a simple but effective project manager, and once you create a linked entry, you can click the Do Task button in the FrontPage To Do List dialog box to open the page in the FrontPage Editor. Unlinked entries won't tell you anything about the relevant source page, so they're really useful only for more general tasks.

- **Verifying hyperlinks.** Choose Verify Hyperlinks from the FrontPage Explorer's Tools menu to find and fix broken internal and external hyperlinks.

- **Updating hyperlinks.** Choose Recalculate Hyperlinks from the FrontPage Explorer's Tools menu to update the indexes used by the FrontPage Search WebBot component. If you use the WebBot, you should *always* recalculate hyperlinks whenever you (or any other author) edit your intranet; if you don't, sooner or later your search pages will embarrass you with invalid page references.

Maintaining FrontPage Discussion Groups with the FrontPage Explorer

FrontPage Discussion Group Webs—such as MMA's Developer Knowledge Base—maintain user postings as separate numbered .HTM files in a special hidden directory. At some point, you'll need to purge old entries. To do so, select the files in the FrontPage Explorer Folder view, right-click with the mouse, and choose Delete. Once you recalculate links, FrontPage will automatically update the Next and Previous jumps in the page headers.

Unfortunately, FrontPage is less successful at updating the Contents list, which is generated in the TOCPROTO.HTM page in the threaded message subfolder. You should always open this page in the FrontPage Editor after deleting messages and refreshing hyperlinks; in most cases you'll probably see some deleted pages still listed. Use FrontPage Editor commands to delete these entries from the page manually.

Another limitation is that FrontPage doesn't reset the file counter the server uses to generate the sequentially numbered threaded message filenames. If you've received n files in a discussion group and delete them all, the first new message will be numbered $n+1$, not 1.

Administration Privileges and Security

FrontPage provides two basic kinds of Web-level security:

- 🌐 Password-based security for specified logon IDs
- 🌐 IP address-based security for specified computers

NOTE
FrontPage permissions can be set only at the Web level. Use network or server permissions to restrict access at the folder or file level; as a workaround, you could also create a restricted Web for one or more pages.

Both kinds of security allow three ranges of access: browse, author, and administer.

CHAPTER
17

Browse access

Users have read-only (or "browse") access to the Web. They won't be able to launch the FrontPage Explorer (unless they know an author or administrator's ID and password); and if browse access is limited to registered users, they'll have to supply their password even to view the Web in their browser.

NOTE Although the FrontPage Editor includes a Registration WebBot that creates a form for end-user self-registration, this functionality doesn't work with Microsoft Internet Information Server or Personal Web Servers.

Author access

Authors have read/write (or "browse and author") access to the Web. They'll be able to launch the FrontPage Explorer and FrontPage Editor, and add or delete pages, but they won't be able to create or delete Webs or establish Web permissions (again, unless they know an administrator's ID and password).

Administer access

Administrators have full access to the Web and can establish permissions for other administrators as well as for authors and users.

NOTE The FrontPage server automatically assigns Webmaster rights over the <ROOT WEB> as part of the FrontPage server setup. The FrontPage Server Webmaster, in turn, confers authority to all other Web-level Webmasters. You *can* have more than one <ROOT WEB> level Webmaster, and you *must* have at least one. See the "FrontPage Server Administration" section (page 619) for more information.

If you're logged on to the Web as an administrator, choose Permissions from the Front Page Explorer Tools menu. If you are in the <ROOT WEB>, you'll see a dialog box with two tabs, Users and Computers.

Users tab   Click the Users tab, shown in Figure 17-1, to set permissions based on IDs and passwords. Create individual IDs for maximum security since each ID has a separate password that can be changed by the user once he or she has logged on. Otherwise, you can use generic group IDs, such as "author."

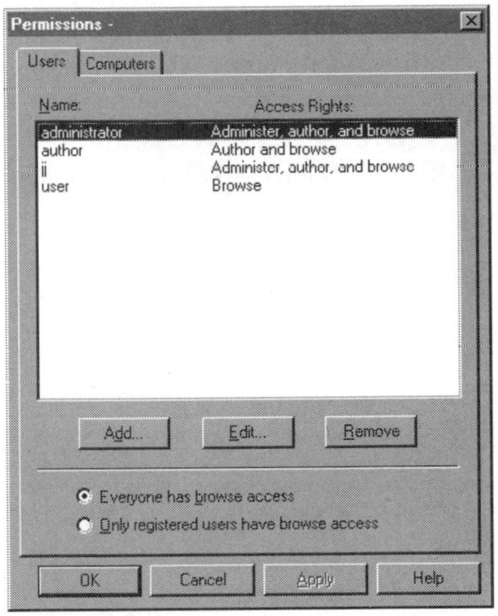

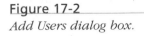

Figure 17-1

Users tab in the Permissions dialog box.

Click the Add button to enter a new ID and password, and assign the degree of access in the Add Users dialog box, shown in Figure 17-2. IDs cannot contain spaces, tabs, or colons. Keep in mind that IDs and passwords are both case-sensitive.

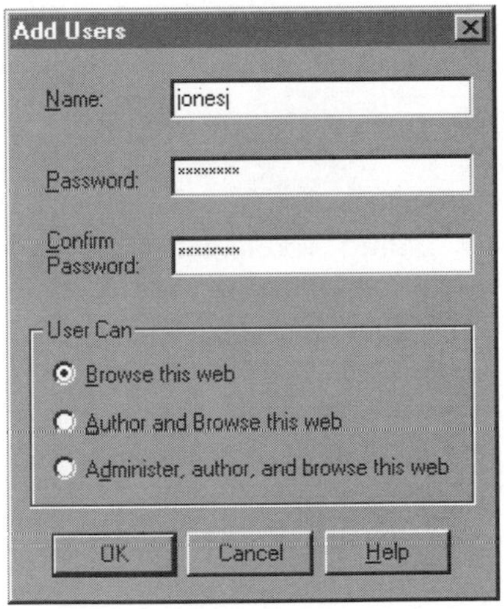

Figure 17-2

Add Users dialog box.

Click the Edit button in the Users tab to *reassign* rights (you cannot change the ID or password with this feature) and the Remove button to delete the selected ID. The radio buttons at the bottom of the tab apply or remove browse permissions; if only registered users have browse access, the user will have to enter a valid ID and password in order to open the Web in Internet Explorer (or any other browser, for that matter).

Computers tab Click the Computers tab, shown in Figure 17-3, to set permissions based on IP address.

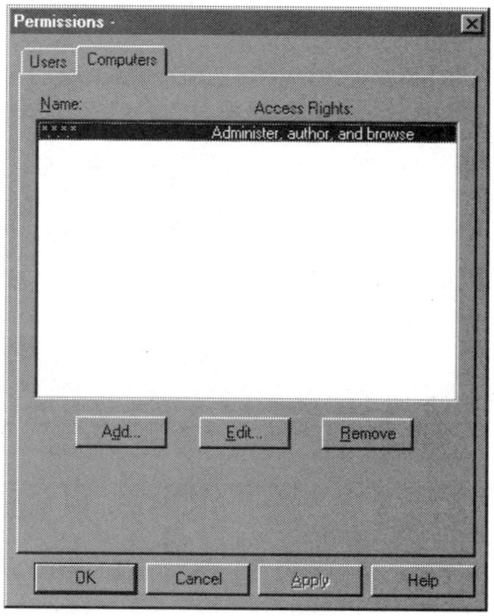

Figure 17-3
Set IP address permissions on the Computers tab.

Since this method of assigning permissions is automatic and depends entirely on identifying individual machines by address, you might be tempted to use it for maximum security. Just be aware that you'll need to work closely with your network administrator in order to implement it. Some networks assign static IP addresses, unique to each user's PC. If your company has such a network, you can target individual machines with confidence (though you'll have to keep abreast of changes—and you'll never know for sure who's actually *using* the PC). Other networks (like Micro Modeling's) use a server to assign addresses dynamically. Such servers can also identify exceptions, which are addresses permanently assigned to one PC, as well as scopes, which are groups of PCs assigned to unique address ranges. Be aware that users with dial-up access are usually given dynamic IP addresses as well.

Click the Add button to enter a new IP address and assign its degree of access in the Add Computer dialog box, shown in Figure 17-4.

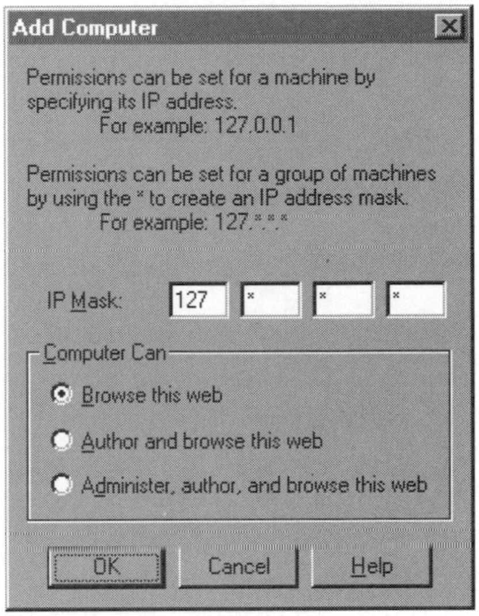

Figure 17-4
Add Computer dialog box.

The most useful aspect of this feature involves IP masks—the FrontPage term for IP ranges or "scopes." Assuming your network administrator has established IP address scoping (say at the department level), you can use asterisk wildcards instead of numbers to designate an address range. The remaining commands on the Computers tab (Edit, Remove) correspond to the User Permissions functionality: you can edit the degree of access rights assigned to an address or address mask, but you can't change the address itself.

Unique Web permissions

Permissions assigned to the <ROOT WEB> are automatically applied to all FrontPage sub-Webs on your server unless you specifically remove them. The Permissions dialog box in a sub-Web contains an additional Settings tab, shown in Figure 17-5, which lets you apply <ROOT WEB> permissions or create unique permissions for the sub-Web. Be aware that if you select the Use Unique Permissions For This Web option, *all* permissions are automatically removed; if you want to apply any unique permissions to a sub-Web, you must explicitly select them.

CHAPTER 17

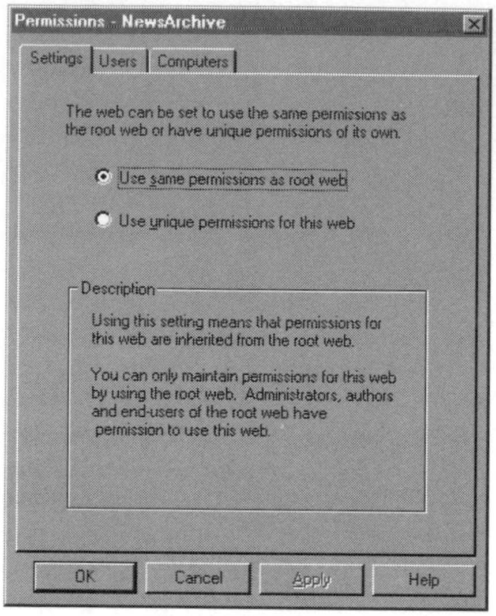

Figure 17-5

Settings tab of the Permissions dialog box for a sub-Web.

Changing passwords

Web administrators and authors can change their own passwords by choosing
Change Password from the FrontPage Explorer Tools menu and then entering the old and new passwords in the Change Password dialog box, as shown
in Figure 17-6.

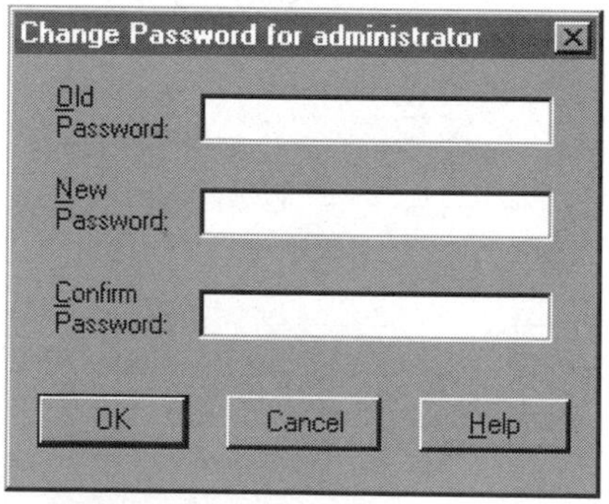

Figure 17-6

Change Password dialog box.

This command only lets you change the password associated with the logon name. Because you can only launch the FrontPage Explorer with a name and password at the author level or above, you can't use this command to change passwords for names that only have browse access. If you want to change these passwords, the easiest way will probably be to delete the existing permission and add a new one.

Is your socket secure?

FrontPage includes several rather cryptic references to "SSL" (for example, the Connect Using SSL option in the Open FrontPage Web dialog box). SSL is an acronym for Secure Socket Layer, a low-level protocol that encrypts TCP/IP transmissions between client and server. Because both FrontPage and IIS support SSL, you can choose this option to establish a secure transmission channel between FrontPage components and your servers. Whether you need SSL is another matter, since presumably you or your Network Administrator will have already enabled robust network and firewall security, and SSL provides relatively weak encryption. Because SSL involves encryption and decryption of each transmission, expect a performance hit as well.

Firewalls and Proxy Servers

Firewall is the generic name for all mechanisms that interrupt and monitor TCP/IP transactions to prevent access by unauthorized users. Firewalls are typically used to protect internal networks from outsiders. They generally use some combination of these strategies: *packet filters,* in which a router filters out unauthorized IP packets in the transaction; *application gateways,* in which a proxy outside the network establishes connections to the outside for specified applications according to specified rules; and *circuit-level gateways,* which are generic gateways that don't need to be separately configured for each client application.

A proxy server is a second, independent server that effectively "represents" the actual server in all TCP/IP transmissions. Requests to the designated server are in fact received by the proxy, which can therefore deny unauthorized requests while preventing any direct access to the actual server and its data. Proxy servers use a central cache as their data repository. The initial request for server data causes a copy of the data to be stored in the proxy cache; the cached copy is then returned to the server. And because additional requests are processed directly from the cache, proxy servers also reduce main-server traffic.

Proxies and firewalls are hardly trivial; but if you have a proxy server, FrontPage makes it easy to use. Simply choose Options from the FrontPage Explorer Tools menu, click the Proxies tab, and enter the proxy server in the HTTP Proxy input box, using the syntax *hostname:port*. The Proxies tab includes two input boxes, both of which accept whatever you type in the box. However, only the HTTP Proxy input has any effect on FrontPage functionality (and only if the host name is valid); the list of hosts *without* proxy is really just a place to record other hosts for which there is currently no connection. In the example in Figure 17-7, you'll see we only listed a nonproxy host, and, somewhat redundantly, checked the option not to use a proxy server for internal URLs.

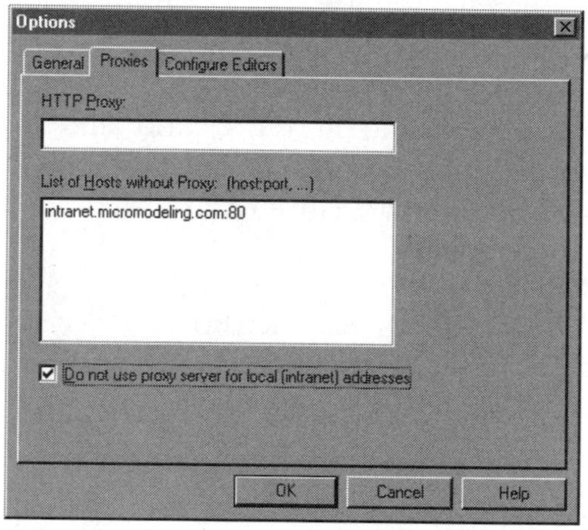

Figure 17-7

Proxies tab in the Options dialog box.

If you define a proxy, your FrontPage server will use it for all URLs unless you check the Do Not Use Proxy Server For Local (Intranet) Addresses option, in which case the proxy will be used only for Internet addresses. However, a word of caution. Because there's no validation, there's nothing to prevent you from entering an invalid proxy. If you make a mistake and have not limited proxies to external addresses, the FrontPage Explorer will try to use the invalid proxy to open the Web . . . and won't be able to. As visions of pink slips dance in your head, it occurs to you that the setting must be retained somewhere, and you can use the Windows Explorer to search for recently modified files. Sure enough, there in your WINDOWS folder is FPEXPLOR.INI. Just look for the

```
HTTP_Proxy=
```

line in the

```
[Proxy Information]
```

section and remove the offending entry. Which brings us back to . . .

.INI Files and Other Good Stuff

FrontPage might call them .CNF files—and Microsoft Windows 95 might have eliminated many of them—but in our book, a text file with editable environment settings that are interpreted at run time is still an .INI file. The FrontPage server relies on several such files, all in the FRONTPAGE WEBS\SERVER\CONF folder; and if you ever have to start poking around there, you'll thank the FrontPage development team for their forethought. The files are not only extensively annotated but also come with their own generic backup files. (They're the files with the .ORG extensions, though the circumstances under which you'd need to make use of them are almost too grisly to contemplate.)

Because the files *are* so well annotated, we'll do little more than reprint them as is. Heed the warnings at the top, though, and silly as it might sound, *always, always* make a backup copy before you start changing a .CNF file. *ALWAYS!*

The HTTPD.CNF file

The HTTPD.CNF file establishes your principal server configurations. It's written during setup and rewritten whenever you run the FrontPage Server Administration tool. You're better off modifying this file through the interface, but in case you want to see what it does, have a look:

```
# -FrontPage- version=2.0
#-----------------------------------------------------------------
#
#    HTTPD.CNF
#
# Main server configuration for the FrontPage Personal Web Server
#
# This is the main server configuration file. It is best to
# leave the directives in this file in the order they are in, or
# things may not go the way you'd like.
#
# Do NOT simply read the instructions in here without understanding
# what they do, if you are unsure consult the online docs.
#
# Server configuration commands are similar to those for the NCSA
# server version 1.3R.  If you have questions please see the online
# documentation at http://hoohoo.ncsa.uiuc.edu
#
```

(continued)

CHAPTER 17

```
# NOTE: path defaults are relative to the server's installation
#       directory (ServerRoot). Paths should be given in Unix
#       format (using '/').
#
#-------------------------------------------------------------------

# ServerRoot: The directory the server's config, error, and log
# files are kept in. This should be specified on the startup command
# line.
#
# Format: ServerRoot <path>
#
ServerRoot c:/frontpage\ webs/server/

# Port: The port the standalone listens to. 80 is the network
# standard.
#
Port 80

# Timeout: The timeout applied to all network operations. It's the
# maximum time for a network send or receive, and the maximum time
# that a CGI script is allowed to take.  The default is 20 minutes
# (1200 seconds).
#
# Format: Timeout nn     (seconds)
#
# Timeout 1200

# ServerAdmin: Your address, where problems with the server should
# be e-mailed.
#
# Format: ServerAdmin <email addr>
#
# ServerAdmin www-admin

# ErrorLog: The location of the error log file. If this does not
# start with / or a drive spec (recommended!), ServerRoot is
# prepended to it.

# Format: ErrorLog <path/file>
#
# ErrorLog logs/error.log

# TransferLog: The location of the transfer log file. If this does
# not start with / or a drive spec (recommended!), ServerRoot is
# prepended to it.

# Format: TransferLog <path/file>
```

```
#
# TransferLog logs/access.log

# ServerName allows you to set a host name which is sent back to
# clients for
# your server if it's different than the one the program would get
# (i.e. use
# "www" instead of the host's real name). Make sure your DNS is set
# up to alias the name to your system!
#
# Format: ServerName <domain name>
#
# no default

# Command line template for CGI WinExec
# Uncomment next line for shorter form of command line
ShellWinCmdTempl ~p ~v ~a
```

If you do make manual edits to this file, remember that you must close and relaunch your Personal Web Server before they take effect.

The SRM.CNF file

The SRM.CNF file establishes your server resource configurations: things like the document layout, the default name of your home page, the name of the folder-level access files, and so forth.

```
# -FrontPage- version=2.0
#--------------------------------------------------------------------
#
#    SRM.CNF
#
# Server resource configuration for the FrontPage Personal Web
# Server
#
# The settings in this file control the document layout and name
# specs that your server makes visible to users. The values in the
# comments are the defaults built into the server.
#
# Server configuration commands are similar to those for the NCSA
# server version 1.3R.  If you have questions please see the online
# documentation at http://hoohoo.ncsa.uiuc.edu
#
# NOTE: path defaults are relative to the server's installation
#       directory (ServerRoot). Paths should be given in Unix
#       format (using '/').
#
#--------------------------------------------------------------------
```

(continued)

17
CHAPTER

```
#
# DocumentRoot: The directory out of which you will serve your
# documents. By default, all requests are taken from this directory,
# but aliases may be used to point to other locations.
#

DocumentRoot c:/frontpage\ webs/content
# DirectoryIndex: Name of the file to use as a pre-written HTML
# directory index. This document, if present, will be opened when
# the server receives a request containing a URL for the directory,
# instead of generating a directory index.
#
# DirectoryIndex index.htm

# AccessFileName: The name of the file to look for in each directory
# for access control information. This file should have a name which
# is blocked from appearing in server-generated indexes!
#
# AccessFileName #haccess.ctl

# UserDir is not supported on Windows
UserDir DISABLED

# =========================
# Aliasing and Redirection
# =========================
#
# Redirect allows you to tell clients about documents which used to
# exist in
# your server's namespace, but do not anymore. This allows you to
# tell the
# clients where to look for the relocated document.
#
# Format: Redirect fakename url
#

# Aliases: Add here as many aliases as you need, up to 20. One
# useful alias to have is one for the path to the icons used for the
# server-generated directory indexes. The paths given below in the
# AddIcon statements are relative.
#
# Format: Alias fakename realname
#

# ScriptAlias: This controls which directories contain DOS server
#              scripts.
#
```

610

```
# Format: ScriptAlias fakename realname
#

#ScriptAlias /cgi-dos/ c:/frontpage\ webs/content/cgi-dos/
# WinScriptAlias: This controls which directories contain Windows
#                 server scripts.
#
# Format: WinScriptAlias fakename realname
#

#WinScriptAlias /cgi-win/  c:/frontpage\ webs/content/cgi-win/
# =========================
# MIME Content Type Control
# =========================
#
# DefaultType is the default MIME type for documents which the
# server cannot find the type of from filename extensions.
#
# DefaultType text/html
DefaultType text/plain

# AddType allows you to tweak MIME.TYP without actually editing it,
# or to make certain files to be certain types.
#
# Format: AddType type/subtype ext1
#

# ReadmeName is the name of the README file the server will look for
# by default.  The server will first look for name.htm, include it
# if found, and it will then look for name.txt and include it as
# plaintext if found.
# NOTE: Do not include an explicit extension, it is an error.
#
# Format: ReadmeName name
#
ReadmeName #readme

# ==============================
# AUTOMATIC DIRECTORY INDEXING
# ==============================
#
# The server generates a directory index if there is no file in the
# directory whose name matches DirectoryIndex.
#
# FancyIndexing: Whether you want fancy directory indexing or
# standard
```

(continued)

CHAPTER

17

```
#
# FancyIndexing on

# IconsAreLinks: Whether the icons in a fancy index are links as
# well as the file names.
#
# IconsAreLinks off

# AddIcon tells the server which icon to show for different files or
# filename extensions. In preparation for the upcoming Chicago
# version, you should
# include explicit 3 character truncations for 4-character endings.
# Don't rely on the DOS underpinnings to silently truncate for you.
#
AddIcon /icons/text.gif      .html  .htm   .txt   .ini
AddIcon /icons/image.gif     .gif   .jpg   .jpe   .jpeg   .xbm
.tiff  .tif   .pic   .pict   .bmp
AddIcon /icons/sound.gif     .au    .wav   .snd
AddIcon /icons/movie.gif     .mpg   .mpe   .mpeg
AddIcon /icons/binary.gif    .bin   .exe   .bat   .dll
AddIcon /icons/back.gif      ..
AddIcon /icons/menu.gif      ^^DIRECTORY^^
AddIcon /icons/dblank.gif       ^^BLANKICON^^

# DefaultIcon is which icon to show for files which do not have an
# icon explicitly set.
#
DefaultIcon /icons/unknown.gif

# AddDescription allows you to place a short description after a file
# in server-generated indexes. A better place for these are in
# individual "#haccess.ctl" files in individual directories.
#
# Format: AddDescription "description" filename
#

# IndexIgnore is a set of filenames which directory indexing should
# ignore
# Here, I've disabled display of our readme and access control
# files, plus anything that starts with a "~", which I use for
# annotation HTML documents. I also have disabled some common editor
# backup file names.
# Match is on file NAME.EXT only, and the usual * and ? meta-chars
# apply.
#
# WARNING: Be sure to set an ignore for your access control
```

Administration

```
# file(s)!!
#
# Format: IndexIgnore name1 name2...
#
IndexIgnore  ~* *.bak *.{* #readme.htm #haccess.ctl

#

## END ##
Alias /icons/ c:/frontpage\ webs/server/icons/
WinScriptAlias /cgi-bin/imagemap/ c:/frontpage\ webs/content/cgi-bin/
imagemap.exe/
WinScriptAlias /cgi-bin/htimage/ c:/frontpage\
webs/content/cgi-bin/htimage.exe/
WinScriptAlias /_vti_bin/_vti_adm/ c:/frontpage\
webs/content/_vti_bin/_vti_adm/
WinScriptAlias /_vti_bin/_vti_aut/ c:/frontpage\
webs/content/_vti_bin/_vti_aut/
WinScriptAlias /_vti_bin/ c:/frontpage\ webs/content/_vti_bin/
WinScriptAlias /cgi-bin/ c:/frontpage\ webs/content/cgi-bin/
WinScriptAlias /mmastuff/_vti_bin/_vti_adm/ c:/frontpage\
webs/content/mmastuff/_vti_bin/_vti_adm/
WinScriptAlias /mmastuff/_vti_bin/_vti_aut/ c:/frontpage\
webs/content/mmastuff/_vti_bin/_vti_aut/
WinScriptAlias /mmastuff/_vti_bin/ c:/frontpage\
webs/content/mmastuff/_vti_bin/
```

If you set the Fancy Indexing option to ON and *don't* have what FrontPage calls the DirectoryIndex page (and you and I call the Home page), the FrontPage server generates a more elaborate FTP-style index like the one shown in Figure 17-8 at the top of the next page.

You can even assign your own .GIF file icons by extension type if you so desire.

The MIME.TYP file

Web servers respond to requests by sending files back to the client. In the case of a typical Web page, this file will probably include graphics as well as text and is increasingly likely to include audio, video, and other formats. Now, the server doesn't really care about the nature of the data—but the client certainly does, and the standards known as MIME (for Multipurpose Internet Mail Extensions) establish recognized data formats through file extensions.

17 CHAPTER

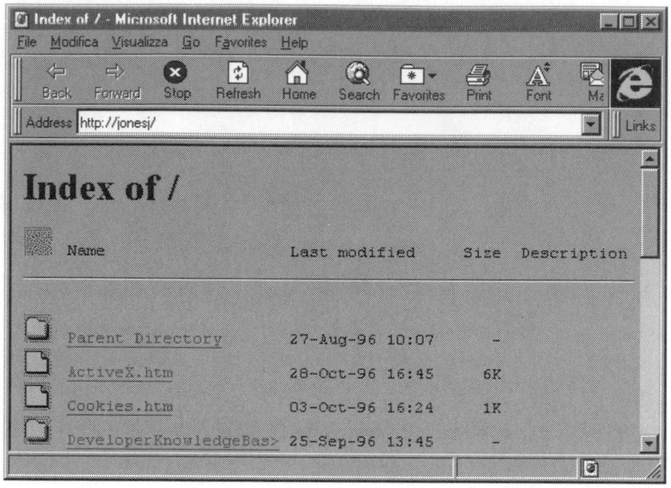

Figure 17-8
Fancy indexing page.

The MIME.TYP file is just the list of these associations maintained by your FrontPage server—line after line of MIME type and associated extension. Here's a brief sample:

```
application/activemessage
application/andrew-inset
application/applefile
application/atomicmail
application/dca-rft
application/dec-dx
application/mac-binhex40
application/macwriteii
application/news-message-id
application/news-transmission
application/octet-stream      bin
application/oda               oda
application/pdf               pdf
application/postscript        ai eps ps
application/remote-printing
application/rtf               rtf
application/slate
application/mif               mif
application/wita
application/wordperfect5.1
```

```
application/x-csh            csh
application/x-dvi            dvi
application/x-hdf            hdf
application/x-latex          latex ltx
```

We have no idea what latex files do, although our imaginations run wild.

The ACCESS.CNF file

The ACCESS.CNF file controls who gets access to your personal FrontPage server. Because you're probably not using this server to host your intranet, you probably won't need to change this file, either. The file is based on concepts developed for the original NCSA HTTPD server, in which server directories and their access limits are specified sequentially. For example, the following statements would deny server access to all users (probably not such a great idea):

```
<Directory c:/frontpage\ webs/server>
<Limit GET>
deny from all
</Limit>
</Directory>
```

One reason this file is tricky to use is that all statements are interpreted sequentially. For example, the following modification would first deny all access and then *allow* access from any host name that contains the string ".micromodeling.com":

```
<Directory c:/frontpage\ webs/server>
<Limit GET>
order deny,allow
deny from all
allow from *.micromodeling.com
</Limit>
</Directory>
```

Because sequence alone determines the logic by which access is evaluated, changing the third line to read

```
order allow,deny
```

would mean that global access would be denied *after* limited access was allowed—again freezing out all users.

CHAPTER 17

In any event, here's the ACCESS.CNF file from our sample Web site:

```
#------------------------------------------------------------------
#
#   ACCESS.CNF
#
# Global access configuration for the FrontPage Personal Web Server
#
# This is the server global access configuration file. It is best to
# leave the directives in this file in the order they are in, or
# things may not go the way you'd like.
#
# Do NOT simply read the instructions in here without understanding
# what they do, if you are unsure consult the online docs.
#
# Server configuration commands are similar to those for the NCSA
# server version 1.3R.  If you have questions please see the online
# documentation at http://hoohoo.ncsa.uiuc.edu
#
#------------------------------------------------------------------
#
# The following access configuration establishes unrestricted access
# to the server's document tree. There is no default access config,
# so _something_ must be present and correct for the server to
# operate.
#
# This should be changed to whatever you set ServerRoot to.
#
<Directory c:/frontpage\ webs/server>
Options Indexes
</Directory>

## This should be changed to whatever you set DocumentRoot to.
#
#
#<Directory c:/frontpage\ webs/content/>
## This may also be "None", "All", or "Indexes"
#
#Options Indexes
#
## This controls which options the #HACCESS.CTL files in directories
## can override. Can also be "None", or any combination of
## "Options", "FileInfo", "AuthConfig", and "Limit"
#
#AllowOverride All
#
## Controls who can get stuff from this server.
```

```
#
#<Limit GET>
#order allow,deny
#allow from all
#</Limit>
#
#</Directory>

# You may place any other directories you wish to have access
# information for after this one.
```

The #HACCESS.CTL file, incidentally, is the access control file that appears in each Web directory. It establishes the limits of the GET, POST, and PUT methods used in HTML forms and provides the paths of your FrontPage server password files. Here's a sample from our Web site:

```
# -FrontPage-

IndexIgnore #haccess.ctl */.??* *~ *# */HEADER* */README* */_vti*

<Limit GET POST>
order deny,allow
deny from all
allow from all
</Limit>
<Limit 1 PUT>
order deny,allow
deny from all
</Limit>
AuthName jj
AuthUserFile c:/frontpage\ webs/content/_vti_pvt/service.pwd
AuthGroupFile c:/frontpage\ webs/content/_vti_pvt/service.grp
```

The #HTACCESS.CTL files

You've probably noticed that FrontPage also writes an #HTACCESS.CTL file to every Web folder. This file supplements the server access file by providing access control at the Web folder level. Here's what the default version looks like:

```
# -FrontPage-

IndexIgnore #haccess.ctl */.??* *~ *# */HEADER* */README* */_vti*

<Limit GET>
order deny,allow
deny from all
```

(continued)

617

```
allow from all
</Limit>
<Limit POST PUT>
order deny,allow
deny from all
</Limit>
AuthName default_realm
AuthUserFile d:/frontpage\ webs/content/_vti_pvt/service.pwd
AuthGroupFile d:/frontpage\ webs/content/_vti_pvt/service.grp
```

These files are read—and the directives they contain are loaded—whenever a browser requests a file from the directory in which they are stored. If you maintain self-extracting .ZIP files for download, for example, you might move them to a special subfolder and add a statement changing the MIME type associated with the .EXE extension so that the browser won't think they're applications. When working with #HTACCESS.CTL files, just be very careful that you debug your changes thoroughly. (And save them to the appropriate Web folder!)

Server logs

In any active session, the FrontPage server writes messages to two files located in the FRONTPAGE WEBS\SERVER\LOGS folder—ACCESS_LOG and ERROR_LOG. After a while these files grow rather large, in which case there's every reason to open them in a text editor and get rid of all that ancient history. The HTTPD.PID file contains a session ID number, written anew each time you launch the server. Try as we might, we just can't think of a single good reason to diddle with this file.

FrontPage .INI files

Historically, at any rate, FrontPage documentation has sometimes been a little skimpy. So for the sake of completeness, you might want to look at the two .INI files for FrontPage itself, both of which can be found in the Windows folder: FRONTPG.INI and FPEXPLOR.INI.

Now Start Recycling!

Web authoring is, among other things, a great way to fill up all that pesky empty space on your extra-large hard disk. (After all, that's why you bought one, isn't it?) Bad enough that all the applications are memory hogs; bad enough that your Recycle Bin quickly becomes bloated with discarded graphics while your Temporary Internet Cache balloons out with download .HTML, .JPEG, and .GIF files. Did you know that FrontPage has its *own* temporary file subfolder?

First make sure that you're not running any FrontPage components (Server, Editor, or Explorer). Then, using the Windows Explorer or some such utility, locate the Temp subfolder of your Microsoft FrontPage folder on your hard disk. Around here, it's typically:

```
C:\PROGRAM FILES\MICROSOFT FRONTPAGE\TEMP
```

You can delete anything you find there.

FrontPage Server Administration

The FrontPage Personal Web Server has a separate Server Administrator that comes in two flavors: FPSRVWIN.EXE is Windows-compatible, and FPSRVADM.EXE is the command line version (which lets you do everything from an MS-DOS prompt, either directly or through batch file statements). Because the online documentation is quite good and because we don't expect you to use the Server to host your intranet anyway, we'll only give you a brief overview of what this utility does.

When you launch the Windows version, you'll see a dialog box similar to the one shown in Figure 17-9.

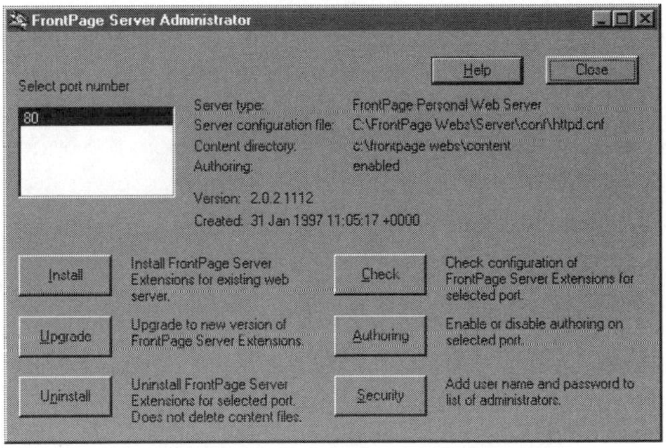

Figure 17-9

FrontPage Server Administrator dialog box.

Four of the buttons run processes for installing, upgrading, checking, and uninstalling the FrontPage Server Extensions, which are programs and scripts you need to make FrontPage work on a server. For example, you'd

17 CHAPTER

use these commands to install the Server Extensions on the IIS server (which means that you also have to install FrontPage on the IIS server). In fact, even the FrontPage server needs the extensions, so you might want to think of this tool as a FrontPage *Server Extensions* Administrator.

🌐 The Select Port Number list shows the ports on which you have the Server Extensions installed. You must always select a port before performing any of the remaining operations. If you already have Server Extensions running on a port and want to change the port *number*, you must first uninstall the extensions from the current port, change the port number (in the case of the FrontPage server, by changing the value of the Port line of the HTTPD.CNF file), and then reinstall the Server Extensions on the new port and restart the server.

🌐 Click the Authoring button to enable or disable authoring on the active port.

🌐 Click the Security button to add new server administrator names and passwords for the active port.

Command Line Version

The Command Line version of the FrontPage Server Administrator contains additional functionality and can be run from the MS-DOS prompt or in batch mode. Command statements use switches and variables to express specific command options. For instance, the following example (taken from the online Help file) would install the root FrontPage Web for an Apache server configured for multihosting, with the server configuration file

```
/usr/local/www/t8148/conf/httpd.conf
```

and the Server Extensions installed for the host name

```
cy.vermeer.com.
```

```
fpsrvadm -o install -u username -pw password
      -r /usr/local/www/t8148/vermeer
      -t apache
      -s /usr/local/www/t8148/conf/httpd.conf
      -m cy.vermeer.com
```

Table 17-1 lists command line switches, syntax, and functionality.

Table 17-1   Command Line Switches.

Switch and Syntax	Function
-h, -help	Displays a help screen giving command line usage.
-o *operation_type* −operation *operation_type*	Specifies the operation to be performed. Operation_type must be one of these: install, upgrade, uninstall, check, recalc, enable, disable, security, putfile, recalcfile.
-p *port* -port *port*	Specifies the port number. Port must be between 1 and 32767. For a multihosting configuration, port is given as hostname:port. If more than one server is listening on the same port, give the port as hostname:port or ipaddress:port.
-w *webname* -web *webname*	Specifies the name of the FrontPage Web. For the root FrontPage Web, use "".
-r *front_page_root_directory* -root *front_page_root_directory*	Specifies the name of the directory where the FrontPage Server Extensions are installed.
-t *server_type* -type *server_type*	Specifies the server type. Server_type must be one of these: ncsa, ncsa-manual-restart, apache, apache-manual-restart, cern, cern-manual-restart, netscape, netscape-manual-restart.
-s *server_config_file* −servconf *server_config_file*	Specifies the server configuration filename. By default, the server configuration file is located under the directory where the server is installed, at a location that depends on the server. For NCSA or Apache, it's conf/httpd.conf For CERN, it's config/httpd.conf For Netscape, it's config/magnus.conf

(continued)

17
CHAPTER

Table 17-1 *(continued)*

-m *hostname* –multihost *hostname*	Specifies the hostname for a multi-hosting server configuration. This is required if you are installing the FrontPage Server Extensions to a server that is configured for multihosting; that is, the server will respond to more than one host name. The hostname parameter might be either a fully qualified domain name or a four-part numeric Internet address.
-u *username* –username *username*	Specifies the administrator user name. Required on install or security operations.
-pw *password* –password *password*	Specifies the administrator password. Required on install or security operations.
-i *internet_address* –ipaddress *internet_address*	Specifies allowable Internet addresses for administrators. FrontPage will not accept the administrator username and password unless the client's address matches this Internet address pattern. This is a four-part numeric Internet address, where the wildcard * can be used in each part.
-d *destination_URL* –destination *destination_URL*	The destination URL for a document in some FrontPage Web on the server machine. The URL is relative to the FrontPage Web specified with the -web switch.
-f *filename* –filename *filename*	Specifies the full path name for a file on the server machine.

Document Management with Visual SourceSafe

If your intranet is successful, and we can't think of any reason why it shouldn't be, it will attract content providers from all over your firm wanting to set up Web sites for departments, projects, products, offices, and so on. Your intranet could become the repository of choice for hundreds or perhaps thousands of corporate publications contributed by many people. These people will want to share graphics, create sample pages that need evaluation, and deploy final versions of these to their production Webs, all the while keeping their environment under some degree of orderly control.

This section discusses how Microsoft's version control product, Visual SourceSafe, can be used for this purpose in your firm.

What Is Version Control?

Version control has traditionally been the concern of programmers who have to support one version of a program while they are developing the next version of it and of multiple programmers who are working on one program simultaneously. As a consequence, version control software has been in use for many years by application development organizations. Basically, a version control product supplies three sets of services to its users: library, history, and security. We'll discuss these services below using Microsoft Visual SourceSafe 5.0 as a context.

Library services

These entail providing a stable, structured repository for documents, with a table of contents, a check out/check in service, and protection against inadvertent deletion. Visual SourceSafe implements a special database structure that presents the Windows Explorer–like user interface shown in Figure 17-10.

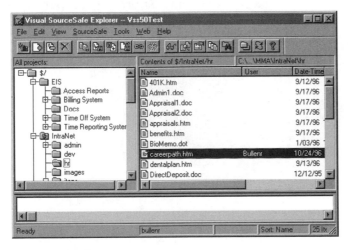

Figure 17-10

Visual SourceSafe 5.0.

The project hierarchy is clearly shown on the left-hand side. The documents are listed on the right-hand side, including the user ID of the user who has the document checked out at the present time. Visual SourceSafe allows only one person to have the document checked out at a time (generally), so write access to each document is mediated in an orderly way. People who have only read access to documents might have copies of those

17
CHAPTER

documents in working folders on their local hard drives, but Visual SourceSafe automatically makes those copies read-only, thereby calling attention to the fact that the person possessing the copy has only read access at that time.

Because Visual SourceSafe uses a proprietary database structure, the normal file delete command does not apply. Visual SourceSafe has a "delete" command, but it is automatically reversible, without the need for a special "recycle bin" such as the one used in Windows 95.

Visual SourceSafe's project hierarchy is a natural fit to the structure of an organization that might want to build an intranet and to the hierarchy of Webs that an organization might build with FrontPage. The designer of a new Web simply adds a "project folder" to the proper place on the left-hand side of the file structure in Visual SourceSafe.

A perennial question when dealing with a rapidly changing documentation environment is, What changed when that document was last updated? Visual SourceSafe automatically requests that the person checking in a document supply a comment on changes that were made. The Check In dialog box shown in Figure 17-11 provides a Comment text box for this purpose.

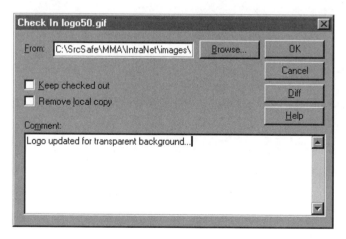

Figure 17-11

Check In dialog box.

Since Visual SourceSafe has the ability to produce reports, you could easily review these comments by generating a report that lists all the comments on recently changed documents.

The library function in Visual Source Safe is not limited to storing source-coded files. You might store DLLs, Microsoft Word or Microsoft Excel documents, .HTM files, graphics, and so on.

History services

If it did nothing more than keep track of and report on who currently has write access to a document, Visual SourceSafe would be useful. But it does more. For example, in a development project it is often necessary to archive and be able to restore a historical version of a project, including source code files, test scripts, and so on. Visual SourceSafe maintains these historical versions of files automatically, without any action required by the user checking in the updated version of a file. In addition, Visual SourceSafe allows all of the files in a folder to be "labeled" with a user-defined string, such as "Version 2.1a." This project-wide, comprehensive labeling is what makes it possible to subsequently delve into the accumulated history of a project and restore the particular, labeled version.

Visual SourceSafe maintains what's called a "reverse delta" history. Instead of storing version 1, then the change to version 2, it stores version n, then the change to version n-1, and so on. In this way it takes no time at all to get the current version, whereas a historical retrieval (not done very frequently) takes a little longer because of the need to apply a series of reverse deltas.

Because Visual SourceSafe has the accumulated history for a file, it can, through reports, tell you who made changes and what the changes were, assuming your updaters are conscientious about their check-in comments. In addition, it can compare any two versions, so if the comment isn't descriptive, you can see the change visually. This facility is available only for text files, such as Visual Basic source code and HTML.

In addition to tracking changes at the file level, where text might be edited, added to, or deleted from a file, Visual SourceSafe tracks changes to projects, noting files that were added or removed. Because deletes of files are reversible (as mentioned above), historical projects can be restored even if files were deleted.

Security services

The Visual SourceSafe Admin application allows an administrator to grant rights to users of a project at five levels:

- No rights
- Read-only access
- The above, plus check in/check out access
- The above, plus add, rename, and delete access
- The above, plus destroy rights

The ability to destroy is the ability to perform an irreversible delete, something an administrator can control.

17 CHAPTER

I've had quite a bit of experience with the security control system in Visual SourceSafe and have some comments on its operation. First, my experience is that the administrator should extend destroy rights to key participants in a project so someone will be available who can perform this special function in those cases when it is critical to do it. Second, since rights propagate downward, you should have the default right be "no access" instead of the factory-supplied Read/Check In/Check Out/Add. Finally, bear in mind that "Add" means both add a file, a right that most of your content providers will need, and add a project (that is, folder), a function that is considered administrative in many organizations.

Setup of Visual SourceSafe

Visual SourceSafe has a number of components that are discussed in this section. Be prepared to do a little work to get Visual SourceSafe set up properly in your environment.

The Visual SourceSafe database

The Visual SourceSafe database should reside on a network or shared folder where it will be accessible to all who will need it. Your initial empty database will be set up the first time you do a server install. The database structure consists primarily of a SRCSAFE.INI file, a USERS.TXT file, a DATA directory, and a USERS directory. (There is also a TEMP directory, which we recommend you put on your users' local hard drives.)

You might create any number of Visual SourceSafe databases for different projects, Webs, departments, whatever. This practice makes it easier to back up and restore databases in the event of problems. Also, hardware outages that affect the availability of Visual SourceSafe databases will affect fewer people if multiple databases are located in different locations on your network. It is a simple matter to create (and tuck away for general use) an empty database. In fact, this technique is recommended if you have standard project structures, templates, or other files you want all Visual SourceSafe users to share on their projects. Just create a template database, and then use it to initialize new projects.

Administrator setup tasks

The administrator program is automatically installed in the Visual SourceSafe client directory and added to your Start menu when a client install is performed. It might also be useful to make an icon for it on your desktop. The following list describes some of the setup tasks the administrator should perform.

1. Your first responsibility is to create users. Give each appropriate rights in appropriate projects. You will find it less work to maintain looser control over the security of your database, but you might find that the chaos that results is unacceptable. Each organization is likely to approach this differently.

2. Define shadow folders as required. Shadow folders are global system folders in which Visual SourceSafe automatically places the latest version of a file every time it is updated. These are useful as directories for testing tools and as repositories for documents referred to by shortcuts in mail messages.

3. Define your Web projects. Use the Web Projects and Web tabs on the SourceSafe Options dialog box, available by selecting Options from the Tools menu, to specify which folders in your Visual SourceSafe database are to be treated as Web sites. This enables the Web-oriented client workstation commands for these projects.

Client setup and working folders

Each user should run Visual SourceSafe from a shared network directory or from a local install. If your users plan to use the Visual SourceSafe VB or C++ integration, they *must* do local installs.

The next step after installation is to associate working folders with Visual SourceSafe projects. Remember that the Visual SourceSafe database is a repository in a proprietary format. To view or modify a file, it must be extracted from the repository. The location to which this extraction is done is referred to as the client's working folder, generally located on the client workstation. We recommend that every user of a Visual SourceSafe project structure his or her working folders in the same way. This makes maintenance and debugging tasks easier.

Shadow folders

Working folders are user-specific. Every user has one for each project, and they are almost always located on the user's local hard drive. Shadow folders are global system folders in which Visual SourceSafe automatically places the latest version of a file every time it is updated. Administrators must set up this facility.

17 CHAPTER

MMA uses shadow folders for two purposes in our environment. First, we use them as folders for test setups. The primary advantage of using them in this manner is that you get the shadow folders for a minimum of overhead. We tested our first intranet in this manner by shadowing our Web directly to the test Web server. The disadvantage of this method is that the shadow contains the latest version of each file, which might be unstable. What you really want is a *specific* version, selected by the developer, to be the one that is available for test. Visual SourceSafe supports this type of operation as well, through its project labeling feature, but this is not connected with shadow folders.

Our second use for shadow folders has been as a repository for documents that will be referred to in Mail messages and posts to Exchange public folders associated with the shadowed Visual SourceSafe projects. This gives project teams the combined benefits of Visual SourceSafe and Exchange for project management.

Integration setups

Some developer and end-user tools provide integrated user interfaces for Visual SourceSafe. These include Visual Basic, Visual C++, FrontPage, Visual FoxPro, Visual J++, and Microsoft Access 97. These integrated user interfaces give you the ability to connect to a remote Visual SourceSafe database and perform view, checkout, and check-in functions directly from the user interface.

According to late-breaking information, FrontPage 97 has tight integration with Visual SourceSafe, automatically performing Web page deployment and Visual SourceSafe database update in tandem.

RAS installations

Visual SourceSafe runs quite smoothly when operated via RAS. This might be a preferred mode of operation for a network administrator. In this case, install the Visual SourceSafe client on your remote workstation.

Visual SourceSafe Features for Webs

Visual SourceSafe features for Webs are included in the administrator and client portions of the product.

Administrator functions

Administrator functions for Webs are located on two tabs of the SourceSafe Options dialog box. Select Options from the Tools menu to bring up this dialog box.

Web Projects tab   The Visual SourceSafe administrator specifies that a Visual SourceSafe project is a Web project using this tab, shown in Figure 17-12. This enables the Web site–oriented commands discussed in the "User functions" section later in this chapter.

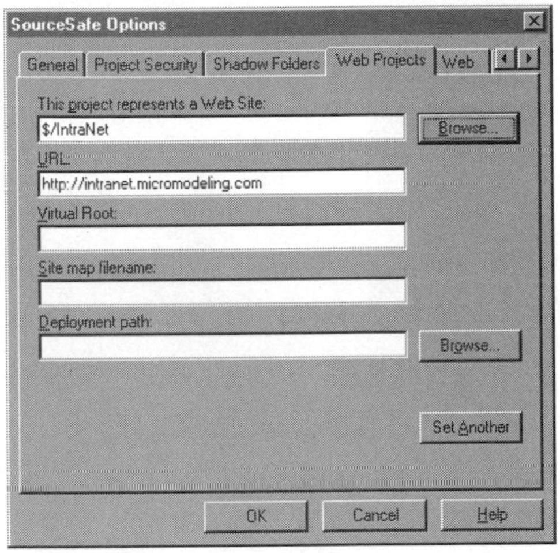

Figure 17-12
Web Projects tab of the SourceSafe Options dialog box.

The first input box accepts the name of the project that represents the Web site. You might type in the full project name or use the Browse button to select the project name using the project tree, which is shown in Figure 17-13.

You must give a URL or a virtual root for your server. In our example above, we included the URL for our intranet.

You might include a site map filename and a deployment path for your Web site. If you don't include a site map filename, Visual SourceSafe uses SITEMAP.HTM as the default. The deployment path is used with the Deploy Web command discussed a little later. Your deployment path might be a local or network path name or UNC name. Alternatively, it might be an FTP path in URL format. You can specify multiple deployment paths for the same Web site.

To remove the Web project designation, select the site project name, clear the URL and virtual root fields, and click OK.

CHAPTER 17

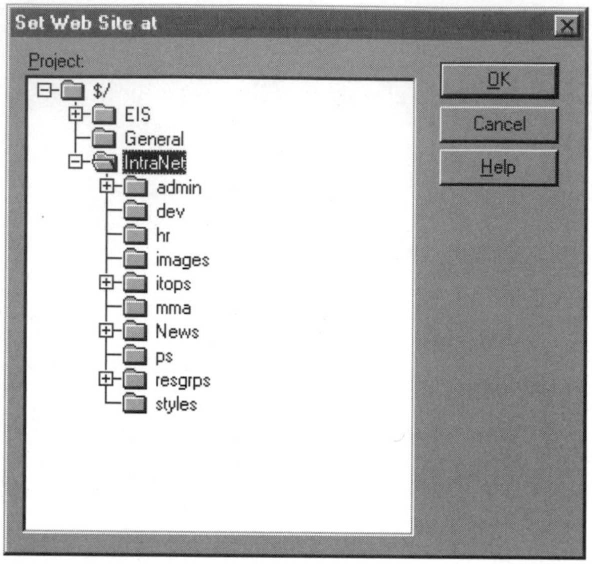

Figure 17-13
Set Web Site.

Web tab   On this tab, shown in Figure 17-14, you identify the proxy to be used when you deploy your Web through a firewall; servers that don't require a proxy because they are inside the firewall; and the default filename (other than DEFAULT.HTM, the "default" default) when checking URL folder references.

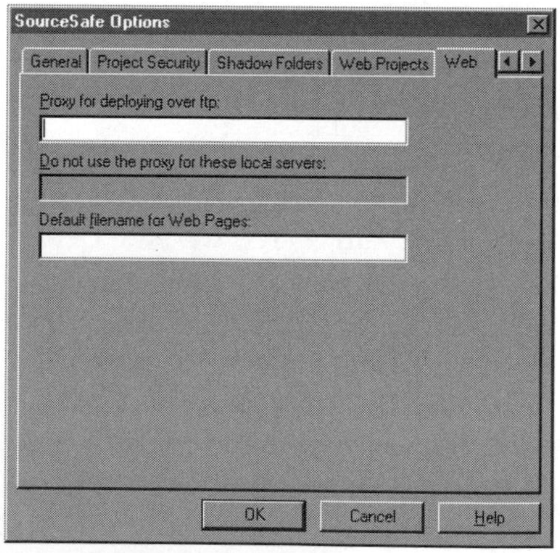

Figure 17-14
SourceSafe Options: Web tab.

User functions

The three user functions are located on the Web menu in the Visual SourceSafe client, as shown in Figure 17-15. These commands are enabled when you select a folder on the left-hand side of the Visual SourceSafe Explorer that has been designated by your administrator as a Web site using the Visual SourceSafe Administrator module.

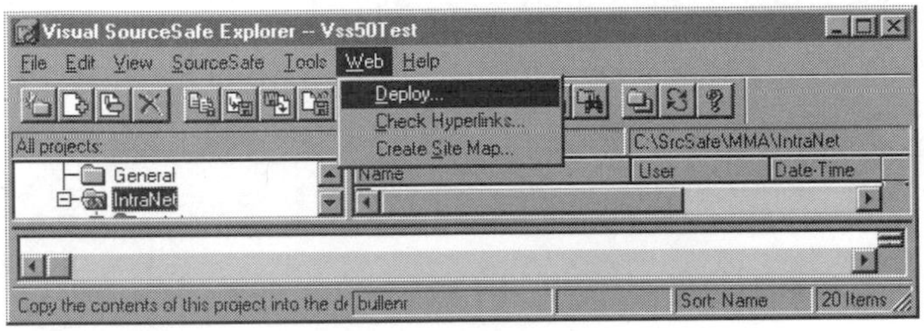

Figure 17-15
Visual SourceSafe Web menu.

Deploy... command   This command brings up the dialog box shown in Figure 17-16, from which you deploy a Web site project to one or more Web servers, specified by the Visual SourceSafe administrator in the Administrator module. The command is functionally the same as performing the Get Latest Version command on the SourceSafe menu, except that it has the ability to use FTP and deploy through firewalls.

Figure 17-16
Deploy dialog box.

Check Hyperlinks... command   This command brings up the dialog box shown in Figure 17-17 so you can inspect the links referred to in HTML <A HREF>, <IMG SRC>, and <OPTION VALUE> tags as well as links associated with image maps.

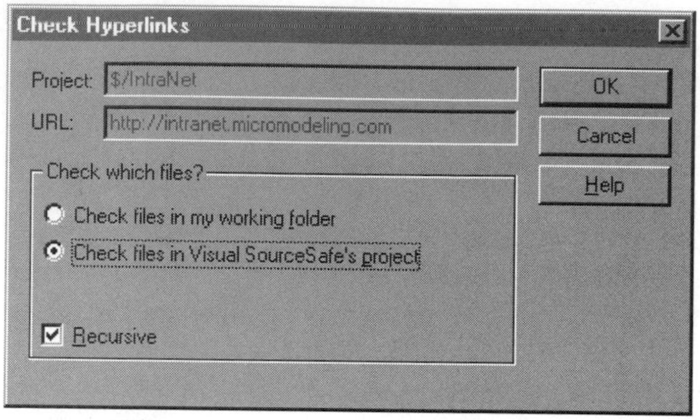

Figure 17-17

SourceSafe Check Hyperlinks dialog box.

When the check is complete, Visual SourceSafe displays the dialog box in Figure 17-18, which indicates the files that were checked, the list of invalid internal links, and the list of external links that were not checked.

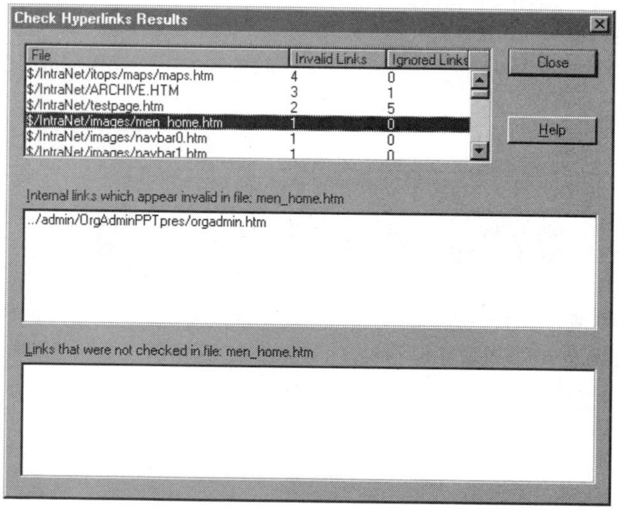

Figure 17-18

SourceSafe Check Hyperlinks Results dialog box.

Create Site Map command This command brings up the dialog box shown in Figure 17-19 and creates a list of the HTML files in your Web site as an HTML file itself. You identify the Web site for which you want the map to be produced.

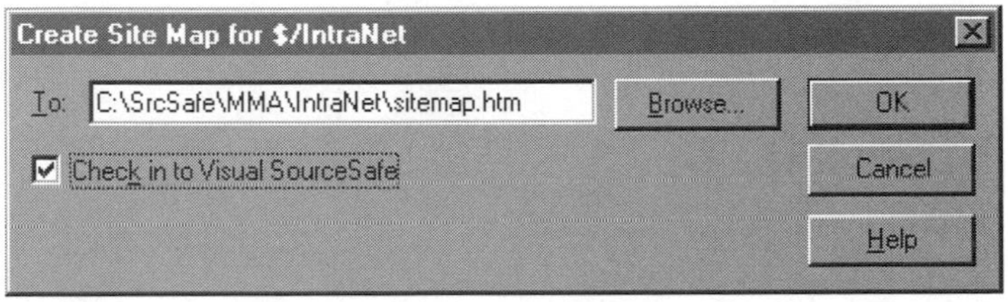

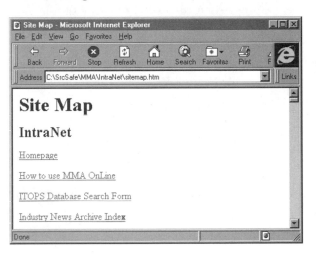

Figure 17-19

Create Site Map.

In Figure 17-20 you see what the basic map looks like within the browser, while Figure 17-21 shows you the same map in its native HTML form.

Figure 17-20

Site Map in Microsoft Internet Explorer.

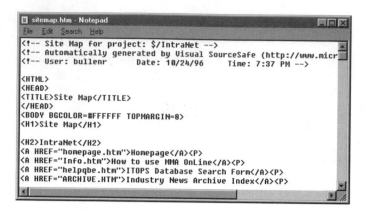

Figure 17-21

Site Map HTML code displayed in Notepad.

As you can see, this is very basic HTML and lacks aggressive formatting. You will probably want to add styles, horizontal rules, or even graphics to make the map more appealing when displayed on your site.

Visual SourceSafe, a tool widely used by VB and Visual C++ programmers for source code control and versioning, has come of age in Visual SourceSafe 5.0 with tools valuable to Web site content providers. Non-programming teams can now use this product to keep content organized and tracked since Visual SourceSafe has been updated for the benefit of Web site users.

CHAPTER 18

Putting It
All Together

Steve Harshbarger

Welcome to the final chapter of *Official Microsoft Intranet Solutions*! We've covered an amazing amount of material in this book. What is perhaps more amazing is that virtually none of the technology we've described even existed one year ago. And it is more than likely that significant new developments have arisen between the time we wrote this book and the time you are reading it! One ramification of this rapid pace of innovation is that many great ideas—many of which can be used to solve the same problem—are being developed in products concurrently. This applies not only across vendors (for example, Microsoft Internet Explorer vs. Netscape Navigator, or Microsoft ActiveX vs. Sun Microsystems Java) but within the suite of Microsoft tools as well. For example, in this book we've learned about no less than six Microsoft products to author HTML documents (FrontPage, Word, Power-Point, Excel, Access, and Notepad), two scripting languages (VBScript and JavaScript), and two methods of creating interactive Web-based database applications (ASP and HTX/IDC). With all of these choices, how do you begin selecting the right tools and architecture to build your intranet?

In this final chapter, we'll not only recap the major tools and their uses but also try to contrast similar ones and discuss how you might go about deciding which tool to use where. First we'll discuss how to build a solid framework for your intranet site. Then we'll talk about how to create and deliver content in the multitude of available formats including HTML and Microsoft Office documents. Next we'll look specifically at ways to integrate with relational databases. Finally we'll look at the tools available for building true applications on an intranet site. For even more information on the ever-evolving topic of intranet development, consult Appendix B.

Building an Intranet Site Framework

In the first few chapters, you learned how to use Microsoft FrontPage and Microsoft Internet Information Server to build a fully functional intranet Web site. The type of site you can build with these tools is similar to many sites you might see on the World Wide Web and is constructed almost entirely by using HTML. We recommend that this be your first step into the intranet. By keeping the tools you use to a minimum, you can focus your effort on designing a *framework* on which to build more sophisticated content and applications. And keeping this part of the site in HTML will ensure that the entry point and exploration is as fast as possible and available even to the lowest-common-denominator user base.

User Interface Considerations

From a user interface perspective, you should concentrate on designing a Home page that organizes content into a small set of logical categories that are targeted toward various constituents or functional areas in your user base. Keep the number of categories small, yet extendible—specific enough to be meaningful but general enough to allow you to add content beneath without having to add additional top-level categories.

You should also come up with a standard concept for the layout and style of your site at this point. A site with a consistent look and method of getting around will be perceived as higher quality by your users and will be easier for them to use. If you miss the opportunity to establish standards at the outset, every group that develops content and applications will likely do its own thing, which will lead to a site in disarray. And don't fall into the trap of thinking that all the content of an intranet will be developed centrally—one of the major reasons for building an intranet is to promote collaboration and sharing. A good site will inspire people to create useful contents—all you need to do is predefine a framework of standards for them to work within. Two concrete examples of ways to do this include using cascading style sheets (discussed in Chapter 4) and a shared exploration bar (discussed in Chapter 3).

Infrastructure Considerations

Concurrent with the user interface design, you must ensure that an adequate platform exists to both host and view your intranet site. On the hosting side, you'll need to put up one or more Microsoft Internet Information Servers, making sure you have adequate resources (disk space, server processing power, network bandwidth) to support your anticipated user load. Your networking or information systems staff can help with this aspect of the planning. Keep in mind, however, that if your intranet is successful, its use will expand greatly over time. For a review of the mechanics of installing and configuring Internet Information Server, refer to Chapter 5.

On the client side, you'll need to make sure that Microsoft Internet Explorer is available to all potential users of your site. Chapter 6 discusses how to customize the configuration and installation of Internet Explorer to make it behave a standard way in your organization. At the same time, you'll likely need to ensure that Microsoft Office is rolled out to users as well since much of the content and applications you'll build after the initial framework is built will rely on it.

Delivering Content: HTML and Office Documents

Once the basic framework is in place, the next step is to deliver substantial and meaningful content on your site. As you are well aware after reading this book, Internet Explorer allows you to choose from any number of document formats (thanks to ActiveX Document technology). These formats include both HTML (the traditional format of the Internet) and Office formats such as Microsoft Excel, Word, and PowerPoint (the likely format of your legacy corporate documents). Having a choice is a luxury. You can present information in the tool that presents it best. You can create information in the tool that creates it best. Or you can minimize effort and present information in the tool that it just happens to reside in today. This section will present some of the issues to consider when choosing document formats for posting on an intranet site. The details behind these concepts were presented in Chapters 8–12.

CHAPTER 18

Properties of HTML Documents

HTML documents are designed to be lightweight (small file size) and transfer quickly over a network (TCP/IP) connection. To meet this goal, an HTML document contains very little overhead associated with the file. If you look at the source code of an HTML document, you can see that there is very little beyond what is presented on the screen. If you compare the file size of an HTML document with a Word document containing the exact same text, you can see that the HTML document is significantly smaller. This makes an HTML document faster to download than an Office document when moving across a network. (The transfer itself is not faster—there are just fewer bytes to transfer.)

HTML is also platform independent. Because the browser reads the HTML, you don't have to worry if your users are on Windows, Macintosh, OS/2, UNIX, or any other platform, and you won't need any additional software to view the page. Because the browser takes care of understanding the HTML in the platform that the user wants it, it is easier to develop cross-platform pages in HTML. No matter what browser your user is running (from Internet Explorer to Netscape Navigator or even to a user-built browser), the HTML will be understood.

HTML is the native language of the Internet. The actual syntax of HTML is decided by an independent organization (the World Wide Web Consortium, or W^3) whose purpose is to keep HTML lightweight and platform independent while expanding it to meet new user needs. So if you have documents on your intranet that might also wind up on your Internet site, HTML is still the standard to use.

Properties of Office Documents

Unlike HTML, Office documents provide all the functionality built into the program that created them. For example, creating a page to sum up numbers and chart the results is relatively simple in Microsoft Excel. It would be much easier for you to include a hyperlink to this Excel document in your intranet than to try to create an HTML page with cells and an ActiveX graph control. As another example, Word provides a great feature called the document map, which makes moving around large documents easy. And PowerPoint provides a great format for presenting multimedia presentations that incorporate animation, video, narration, and other sound.

Another benefit of using Office documents is collaboration. Suppose several people are working on the same document. With Office's built-in collaborative features, you can share the document and all work on different sections at the same time. If security allows, you can make changes directly to an Office document and then the next user viewing the document from your intranet will see the changes you just made. Using HTML, it is nearly impossible for users to edit your pages.

Which Formats to Use: The Balanced Diet Approach

So, what formats should you use to post content? All of them, of course. The key is to use the right format for the task at hand. It is clear that the basic framework for your site should exist in HTML because of the superior speed with which it can be rendered. Beyond that, content can and *should* vary.

From a pure presentation standpoint, Office documents are very appropriate for many types of information. Use Microsoft Excel documents for financial, tabular, or graphic information, especially that information with which the user needs to interact. Managers would love to get monthly financial reports in a form that allows them to sort, analyze, and run what-if analyses. Use Word for large, complex, or highly formatted documents, especially those that need to be printed. HTML formatting comes nowhere near what Word can deliver, and Word's document map feature gets you intradocument navigation for free. And finally, use PowerPoint for anything that smacks of a presentation.

You likely have many legacy documents in Office format (employee manuals, for example). Whether they are better viewed in HTML or Office formats might be irrelevant if you don't have the time to convert them. In this case, a great benefit of using Internet Explorer as your browser is that you can simply post the existing document without converting it to HTML, and your users will be able to read it in their browsers.

Other documents probably belong in HTML. Assuming that your user base does have Office, the primary reason to use HTML over Office is speed. If the information you are presenting doesn't need the added functionality of an Office application, you should keep it in HTML. This will minimize the time necessary to render it and give your users a much more pleasant experience.

A Multitude of Capable Editors

For those documents you do deliver in HTML, you need to decide how to create them. As you can probably tell by now, if you want to create HTML pages, you have many choices of tools. You can use FrontPage, Word, Excel, PowerPoint, Access, or even Notepad. All of them can produce valid HTML files for your Web. So which one do you use?

Maybe this sounds a little heartless, but—who cares? All of them have strengths and weaknesses and all of them are capable of producing quality HTML files. So how do you decide? You should use all of them. Not at the same time, of course. But as you build an entire Web, you probably will need all of them.

First consider what you're trying to produce. If you're setting up your intranet site with hyperlinks and basic layout, FrontPage is your best bet. You can use FrontPage to set up the underlying framework of your entire intranet site. Right now, the other Office applications are not designed to manage a site.

If you're trying to create an HTML page, consider what will be on it. If it is full of tables and graphs, start with Microsoft Excel and then convert it to HTML. If it is an existing document or manual, start with Word. If you want your pages to be viewed as a slide show, use PowerPoint. And if you are trying to connect it to a database, use Microsoft Access.

Do you need your pages to be more dynamic? Do they need to include scripts? For client-side scripts (for example, VBScript), the FrontPage Editor might be easier, but Notepad still works. For server-side scripts (for example, ASP), Microsoft Access might be a good starting point, but then you're still left with Notepad to do your editing.

When choosing a tool to create HTML, you should select one that you are comfortable using. You don't generally need to learn a new tool just to produce an HTML document. As we said before, how you create HTML pages isn't a big deal. The important thing is that the tool you choose works for you.

HTML-On-The-Fly

Up to this point, we have implicitly assumed that your entire user base has Microsoft Office installed on their machines. This is what gives you the option of using Office documents on your intranet. But what if certain segments of your user community do not have Office? Should you forgo Office documents altogether? Fortunately, the answer is "no," thanks to a technology called HTML-On-The-Fly that supports users who cannot open Office documents in their browsers. After you install the ISAPI conversion filter for HTML-On-The-Fly on your IIS server, here's how it works.

When a user queries an intranet server requesting information, the server deciphers what information or address the browser is requesting and sends it back to the browser. When the browser requests this information from the server, it also provides the server with information about itself in the HTTP header file. The browser informs the server of the browser type and version. It also provides a return address, what pages were last modified, and what version of HTML you are using. The server then knows how to return the appropriate information to the requesting browser.

NOTE

For further details about what an HTTP header file contains, refer to Matthew Powell and Leon Braginski's article "HTTP Revealed" in the September 1996 issue of *Microsoft Interactive Developer* magazine.

What if the browser also told the server whether or not it could handle Office documents? Then if you click on a hyperlink to an Office document, the server would know whether to provide the requested information as an Office document or first convert it to HTML. HTML-On-The-Fly allows your server to provide this service.

When a browser requests an Office document from a server, the server can now find out whether the browser will know what to do with it. If it can handle it with either a viewer or an Office 97 application, the server will send back the Office document, which is opened in your browser. If your browser cannot handle an Office document, the server can convert your Office document into HTML and then pass back the data in HTML format for the browser to view. The server does this conversion by using the same Internet Assistant technology built into all the Office 97 products.

This process somewhat eliminates the need for developers having to worry about whether someone has Office 97 compatibility. You could argue that this would eliminate the need for HTML at all on your intranet, but be careful. Remember: speed is always a factor. Although HTML-On-The-Fly is better than receiving an error when you try to access an Office document that your machine cannot handle, it will be much slower than accessing a standard HTML file. The server has to open the file, convert it to HTML, and then send it to your browser. This takes time, and your users will have to wait for this process to complete before receiving the requested information. Again, a good rule of thumb is that if your document doesn't need the added functionality, author it in HTML.

Database Integration

Beyond the publishing of relatively self-contained document content, the next challenge to tackle is creating database-driven Web pages. These would integrate with various relational databases from departmental Microsoft Access databases to enterprise-wide SQL Server (or other) databases to host-based databases. A number of tools are available for creating such pages, but they can generally be classified into two categories: push model and pull model.

Push Model Database Integration

The push model is used to simply publish information in a database as HTML documents at specified intervals. Once published, the information is relatively static in that the user cannot perform queries on it; it is merely viewed. This approach makes sense for many applications.

SQL Server has a tool called the Web Assistant that also performs push model database publishing. It has the added advantage of being able to schedule publishing at predefined times or intervals or in response to certain events.

Push model database integration can be performed in several ways. In Microsoft Access, you can manually save any database object (such as a table, query, form, report, and so on) as HTML using the File Save As command. Getting a little more sophisticated, you can use the Microsoft Access Publish To The Web Wizard to save multiple objects as HTML at the same time. Note that the data does not necessarily need to reside in a Microsoft Access MDB file; these methods can work for data stored in linked SQL Server tables or tables in other databases that Microsoft Access can see through ODBC.

Pull Model Database Integration

The pull model is used to create interactive database applications in which the user can perform queries, get results, or even update the database. The two primary tools for accomplishing this are HTX/IDC (also called the Internet Database Connector) and ASP (Active Server Pages, or server-side scripting, which has other applications besides database integration). Both of these tools work with any ODBC data source (Microsoft Access, SQL Server, or otherwise), although the Microsoft Access Publish To The Web Wizard can generate much of the source code to get each technique to work.

HTX/IDC

HTX/IDC is a term for the two file formats used with the Internet Database Connector (IDC). From your browser, you request an .IDC file instead of an HTML file. This .IDC file contains information about the data being requested. It lists the ODBC data source name, user name, and password; the SQL statement to execute (which can include parameters); and the location of the corresponding .HTX file. When you request an .IDC file, the corresponding SQL statement is executed and the results are merged with the .HTX file. The .HTX file is another text file, an HTML template. It contains placeholders for the data (such as merge fields in a Word document) and other formatting information that is used to create your dynamic Web page. Once the data and the .HTX files are merged, the results are sent back to the user and displayed in the browser.

ASP

ASP is an extension for Internet Information Server that allows you to do server-side scripting. ASP is the server-side equivalent of VBScript, but it is much more powerful. It can access components anywhere on the server machine, create objects, access data, and so on. Because it does not affect the client machine, there is no need to limit its power. These scripts can use ADO (ActiveX Data Objects, a data access technique similar to Data Access Objects) to communicate with back-end databases. And they can do more than just run a query. They can iterate through the records, create conditional formatting, and take full control over the resulting Web page. Once the script has finished processing, the results are returned to the user and displayed in the browser.

Which should you use?

In general, ASP is the way to go. First, it can support forms. If you export a Microsoft Access form using HTX/IDC, you will just get a table. If you use ASP, you get an HTML form that mimics your Microsoft Access form, complete with exploration controls and editing capabilities. Second, ASP is a much more robust scripting language. In a single file, it supports the creation of objects and VBScript code. Going forward, ASP will likely replace HTX/IDC.

Other Application Development Tools

Perhaps the most sophisticated ways in which you'll use development tools will be to use them to build more interactive applications for your intranet site. In this area, the choices abound. You can write Office-based applications using Visual Basic for Applications (VBA). You can embed ActiveX controls and Java applets into your HTML pages and automate them with VBScript and JavaScript. You can use these same scripting languages to implement data validation, explore, or otherwise manipulate the browser or its content. As mentioned above, you can write server-side scripts that not only get data but provide custom content, run server processes, or integrate with other back-end applications, all without any regard to the browser in use. Finally, for the very technical at heart, you can write your own controls, objects, and server-side extensions and components in a number of languages, including Visual C++, Visual Basic, and Visual J++.

It would be impractical even to attempt to lay out exhaustive rules for applying these tools. Designers and developers have always had a choice of tools, and this continues to be the case with intranet development. With this said, we still need to point out a few relevant issues for deciding which tool to use. For detailed information on the following topics, refer to Chapters 6–12 and 15.

Office/VBA Development

Beyond delivering content, Office is a robust development platform with hundreds of exposed programmable objects and a professional development environment that includes the popular VBA programming language. This book barely touches on the capabilities and features of Office for the developer. Suffice it to say that you can build entire information retrieval, analysis, presentation, and publishing applications with Office and VBA. Your intranet can then function as a launch point for any number of these applications. One important technical point to note: Office applications running *in* the Internet Explorer browser window cannot display custom dialogs or use embedded ActiveX controls. For this reason, these applications are best spawned into their own window within the particular Office application in which they are hosted.

A Brief History of Java

Most of us have read article upon article about Java, JavaScript, JScript, Visual J++, and various other plays on the coffee bean. Where does this fit into your whole intranet solution? How does it compare with ActiveX, C++, VB, and VBScript? Let's first take a step back and look at what Java is.

HTML started out as a very static way of presenting information. As discussed earlier, it is fairly lightweight and has limited functionality. People wanted to be able to do more with the Internet. At the same time, Sun Microsystems, Inc. was creating a new development language that would run efficiently over a TCP/IP connection. This language was called Java and had immediate Internet implications since it was designed to work well over a network. It was a perfect match. Java came along as a language that was platform neutral just like HTML but had much more functionality. You could now develop small programs, or "applets," to run inside your HTML pages. A Java applet can be anything from a calculator to help you compute taxes to a sports ticker that gives you the latest scores. The big advantage is that Java applets give a whole new dimension to a static Web page. All of a sudden, Web pages can be dynamic.

Java has similarities to C++ and Visual Basic, but adds more Internet-related capabilities. Java looks a lot like C++ in syntax but was designed to be a 100 percent object-oriented language from the beginning (unlike C++, which was added to make C object oriented). When you create a Java applet, you compile it at development time into special machine-independent bytecode. Now for the great part—you can download and run this applet from virtually any type of machine and operating system (Windows, UNIX, OS/2, Macintosh). This is accomplished through what is called a Java virtual machine, a run-time interpreter that translates the bytecode into platform-specific instructions at run time. This virtual machine understands your applet and translates it into native code so that your machine can understand it. You might be asking, "Where is this virtual machine and how can I get one?" Actually, it is probably built into your browser. Microsoft, Netscape, and others have virtual machines incorporated into their browsers to interpret your Java code.

Because different operating systems use different browsers, your browser includes the correct virtual machine needed to interpret Java applets into the correct native code for your operating system. What that means to a developer is that when you write your Java applet and connect it to your HTML page, you don't have to worry about who is going to use it. The browser will interpret it correctly for the operating system your user is on.

Development Languages Compared

Now let's take a moment to distinguish between a few of these technologies. First concept: ActiveX is not a language—it's a set of technologies. So for this discussion, let's stick to languages. In the "full featured" language world, we basically have Visual Basic, Visual C++, and Java to contend with. In the scripting world, we have VBScript and JavaScript. As you're about to see, each language can be used to create different useful intranet tools, components, and applications.

Visual C++ is typically used to create high performance application components. The specific forms this can take are ActiveX controls that can run inside the browser; server applications in the form of ISAPI applications and filters; and server-side components, which are communicated with via DCOM (no browser or HTTP protocol involved).

Visual Basic is typically used to create ActiveX document applications (entire applications that can activate inside the browser) and server-side components, which are communicated with via DCOM (no browser or HTTP protocol involved).

VBScript is used in the browser to automate or connect objects (either ActiveX controls or Java applets), perform data validation, or manipulate the browser or its contents. Microsoft's Internet Explorer currently hosts VBScript, and as of this writing, Netscape has committed to doing so in a future release of Navigator. On the server side, a more capable version of VBScript (in the form of the Active Server Pages) can perform database integration and automate other objects on the server. The results of this code are always

18
CHAPTER

HTML, thereby eliminating the need for the browser to understand scripting languages of any kind.

JavaScript is used in the browser to automate or connect objects, perform data validation, or manipulate the browser or its contents. Both major browsers (Microsoft and Netscape) currently host JavaScript.

Applets and ActiveX Components Compared

We just learned that we can write ActiveX controls with C++ and applets with Java. They both are ways to run mini-applications inside the browser. So, what's the difference?

Java applets have the advantage of being able to run on any platform. This makes them a good choice for environments in which the client configuration cannot be controlled (for example, the Internet). They have the design feature of downloading each time they are run; that is, they are not permanently stored on the client machine. This could be an advantage or a disadvantage, depending on the situation. For example, Java applets will never take up disk space, and there is no potential for a version control problem. However, there will be time involved in downloading it over and over again. Finally, the Java language itself is in its infancy—therefore, the tools and experience base are in the process of maturing.

ActiveX controls currently run in Windows platforms. Support is expected in other platforms, but this is not in place today. Microsoft's recent move to turn ActiveX over to the industry will likely make multiplatform availability a reality. Unlike Java applets, ActiveX controls can be automatically downloaded and installed on client machines, removing the need to download over and over again. There are features of the download mechanism to handle versioning. And the experience base and developer tools are more mature.

APPENDIX

The FrontPage File/Folder Structure

Jeffrey M. Jones

This appendix, as its title indicates, contains an overview of the Microsoft FrontPage 97 file/folder structure. If you find this information whetting your appetite for more, press on to the technical documentation available from Microsoft's Web site. The documentation includes the FrontPage Software Development Kit (SDK) and knowledge base articles.

What *Is* All That Stuff?

FrontPage client-side applications—FrontPage Explorer, FrontPage Editor, and the helper utilities—are all installed under Windows in a common program folder. By default, they are in a subfolder of your PROGRAM FILES folder. The executables themselves are stored in the MICROSOFT FRONTPAGE\BIN subfolder.

The Personal Web Server and all Web contents are stored in another common folder. Again, by default, the Personal Web Server is in the FRONTPAGE WEBS\SERVER subfolder, and Web contents are in the

FRONTPAGE WEBS\CONTENT subfolder. Note, however, that the Personal Web Server, FrontPage Explorer, and FrontPage Editor all refer to the FRONTPAGE WEBS\CONTENT subfolder as <ROOT WEB> and will allow you to view only those Webs that are created in <ROOT WEB> or its sub-directories. This means that subfolders of FRONTPAGE WEBS\CONTENT are created for each new Web—but these subfolders are not to be confused with subdirectories that are created *within* <ROOT WEB>.

Things get even more interesting from this point on. Whenever FrontPage creates a Web, it automatically creates three folders (or directories) in each Web folder:

- A _PRIVATE folder is where you can store "hidden" Web pages, which won't appear in a FrontPage WebBot–generated table of contents (more about "hidden" folders in a moment).

- A CGI-BIN folder is where you store executable pages, such as CGI (Common Gateway Interface) scripts. By default, FrontPage installs two server-side image map processors in this folder: HTIMAGE.EXE (for CERN maps) and IMAGEMAP.EXE (for NCSA maps).

- An IMAGES folder is where you store all your .GIF and .JPG files. Because it's the default folder that FrontPage Editor uses for every Web page, however, you'll probably want to store your images there, too. Just remember that every Web subdirectory has its own IMAGES folder, so if you're planning to use subdirectories with your intranet, you'll either have to adjust URLs or create copies of image files in each subdirectory.

You can save pages to any of these three folders by using one of two methods:

- From FrontPage Editor's File menu, choose Save As, and enter the folder name and the file URL in the dialog box.

- From FrontPage Explorer's File menu, choose Export, and select the folder and enter the filename in the dialog box.

FrontPage also creates a private subfolder, _VTI_CNF, which you should *not* modify unless you're *absolutely* sure you know what you're doing. This folder contains an .HTM file for every corresponding Web page in the parent folder. The pages themselves contain data (in name/value pairs) that FrontPage uses to maintain your Web properly. If these files can't be located, FrontPage re-creates them as necessary.

> **NOTE**
>
> If you also see a folder named _VTI_SHM, it is left over from an installation of a previous version of FrontPage. It is not used in FrontPage 97, so go ahead and delete it.

A Few Simple Rules

If you're bound and determined, despite all intimidating warnings, to use another application such as WordPad to work with your FrontPage Web pages, at least keep in mind these rules:

- If you move or copy pages to FrontPage subfolders, you'll have to refresh your Web to see them in FrontPage Explorer, and you'll have to use the Recalculate Links command on the Tools menu in FrontPage Explorer before you can see them in the Table Of Contents page.

- Edits made directly to a file will not update the Modified By and Modified Date attributes of FrontPage, which are stored in the corresponding file in the _VTI_CNF folder.

- If you manually remove a page, remove all corresponding _VTI_CNF versions as well.

- Be sure the file permissions of any new or modified files are set so that the FrontPage Personal Web Server CGI scripts can modify them.

The Belly of the Beast

The file/folder structure of any FrontPage Web also includes a single instance of each of these folders, off <ROOT WEB>:

- **The _VTI_BIN folder.** This folder contains three CGI executables:
  - SHTML.EXE implements all browse-time behavior. (WebBot-generated forms, for example, all reference this URL.)
  - _VTI_ADM/ADMIN.EXE implements administrator operations such as Create Web, Change Permissions, and so forth.
  - _VTI_AUT/AUTHOR.EXE implements author operations.

🌐 **The _VTI_TXT folder.** For Webs that contain Search WebBot components, this folder contains text indices, stored as multiple files within the _VTI_TXT/DEFAULT.WTI subfolder.

🌐 ALL.* is the index for all text and HTML pages in the Web *except* those in subfolders that have an underscore as the first character of their names.

🌐 _DISCUSS.* is the index for all text and HTML pages in the discussion group named Discuss.

The text index is recalculated when you save a page to your Web and when you use the Recalculate Links command on the Tools menu in FrontPage Explorer. You can delete these files and folders if you don't want a text index, and FrontPage will not regenerate them.

🌐 **The _VTI_PVT folder.** This folder includes these elements:

🌐 _X_TODO.HTM, the Web's To Do list

🌐 _X_TODOH.HTM, the Web's To Do list history

🌐 ACCESS.CNF, which stores FrontPage Administrator permissions

🌐 BOTSINF.CNF and BOTS.CNF, which store information about any existing custom WebBots

🌐 DEPTODOC.BTR and DOCTODEP.BTR, Web-dependency databases

🌐 FRONTPG.LCK and SERVICE.LCK, the Master and Service lock files, which store any rwxd permissions for user accounts

🌐 SERVICE.CNF, which stores the Web's metainformation, including the values set by the Settings command on the FrontPage Explorer Tools menu

🌐 SERVICE.GRP, an NCSA-style group storage file used by Apache, NCSA, and FPPWS.

🌐 SERVICES.CNF, in <ROOT WEB>, which lists all sub-Webs on the server

🌐 SERVICES.ORG, which is a backup copy of SERVICES.CNF, ensuring that sub-Webs are automatically reconstructed after reinstallation

- SVCACL.CNF, which stores information about service access controls so that permissions are automatically reconstructed after reinstallation

- **The _VTI_LOG folder.** If you have enabled the logfile option, authoring operations will be stored in this folder in a file named AUTHOR.LOG.

Creating "Hidden" Pages and Directories

FrontPage considers any file or folder that has an underscore as the first character of its name to be "hidden." Hidden files and files in hidden folders such as _PRIVATE are ignored by FrontPage WebBots and therefore won't appear in your WebBot-generated Table Of Contents or Search Results pages. Hidden files and folders, however, do display by default in the FrontPage Explorer and FrontPage Editor. If you don't see them, choose Web Settings from the FrontPage Explorer Tools menu, choose the Advanced tab, and then check the Show Documents In Hidden Directories check box. You will then be prompted to refresh your Web.

You can create hidden pages in various ways:

- Export (or save) the page to the _PRIVATE folder.

- Create a file or folder with an underscore as the first character in its name (for example, _HIDDEN.HTM). Be aware, however, that the Search WebBot ignores the initial underscore in Web page filenames and reads all files that are not in hidden folders.

- Give the file a custom extension (for example, HIDDEN.HDN). If you use nonstandard file extensions, however, you won't be able to create links to them in the FrontPage Editor unless they are currently open.

Unfortunately, the use of the initial underscore to designate "hidden" files is *not* a property of the IIS server. If you publish your Web on an IIS 3.0 server, you'll have to use the Index Server to define hidden files.

APPENDIX
B

Where to Get More Information

Ken Heft

With the hyper-rapid pace of innovation in Internet and intranet tools, you will need to actively seek out additional information on the topics covered in this book as well as information on entirely new technologies that will inevitably be introduced. In this appendix we'll list some of the best resources we uncovered during our book-writing process. Some of these references might become outdated in the future, especially the Internet resources. We encourage you to check both the Microsoft (http:\\www.microsoft.com) and Micro Modeling Associates (http:\\www.micro-modeling.com) Web sites for an up-to-date listing of valuable links.

Books

🌐 *Microsoft Excel 97 Developer's Handbook* by Eric Wells and Steve Harshbarger (Microsoft Press, May 1997). This newly updated book is co-authored by Micro Modeling Director Steve Harshbarger. It is a thorough guide to advanced programming in Microsoft Excel 97 using VBA.

- *The Visual Basic Programmer's Guide to the Win32 API* by Daniel Appleman (Ziff-Davis Press, 1996). This is a good reference guide for making 32-bit API calls from Visual Basic and Visual Basic for Applications (VBA). One nice feature is that the entire text of the 1400+-page book is stored in a help file on the CD.

- *Build Your Own Web Site* by Louis Kahn and Laura Logan (Microsoft Press, 1996). Using this book, you can learn how to use Microsoft Windows NT Server and Microsoft Internet Information Server to build Internet and intranet sites.

- *HTML in Action* by Bruce Morris (Microsoft Press, 1996). This book contains techniques plus tips and tricks intermediate and advanced developers can use to create innovative Internet and intranet sites.

- *Introducing Microsoft FrontPage* by Kerry A. Lehto and W. Brett Polonsky (Microsoft Press, 1997). With this book, you'll learn the ins and outs of using Microsoft FrontPage to create great-looking Web pages and functional Web sites.

- *Inside Microsoft Visual Basic, Scripting Edition* by Scot Hillier (Microsoft Press, 1996). This book will help you put your knowledge of Visual Basic programming to work to create Internet applications using VBScript and ActiveX controls.

- *Microsoft Office 97 Developer's Handbook* by Christine Solomon (Microsoft Press, April 1997). This book is for a hybrid audience of information specialists and corporate developers and covers how to use Microsoft Office 97 applications to generate business solutions. It includes a chapter that discusses how a well-structured intranet can help alleviate "information overload" in your office.

Magazines

- *Microsoft Interactive Developer.* Fawcette Technical Publications (www.microsoft.com/mind). This is by far the best-written, most thorough guide to Internet and intranet development there is. It includes both broad concept discussions and technical code samples. We cannot recommend this magazine and its corresponding Web site enough.

- *Visual Basic Programmer's Journal.* Fawcette Technical Publications (www.windx.com). This is a great resource for tips and tricks of Visual Basic programming. You can either subscribe to the print magazine or to the CD edition, which includes demos, shareware, and a searchable database of information.

 Access/Visual Basic Advisor. Advisor Publications (www.advisor.com/av.htm).

 BackOffice Magazine. PennWell Publishing Company (www.backoffice.com).

Internet Resources

🌐 *Microsoft Interactive Developer.* www.microsoft.com/mind. This is the Web site that accompanies the MIND magazine. It includes a majority of the articles for each month, along with downloadable sample code. You can also subscribe to the print magazine from the Web site.

🌐 *Avatar—The Interactive Developers' Online Magazine.* www.avatarmag.com. An online magazine from Fawcette Technical Publications. It includes a combination of news, tips and tricks, and sample code on various emerging technologies.

🌐 *Microsoft.* The Microsoft site is itself a maze that includes a lot of incredibly useful information. Here's a guide to some of our favorite sites within the site.

🌐 *The Microsoft Developer Network Online.* www.microsoft.com/msdn. This is the central location for developer information on the Microsoft Web site (formerly known as "For Developers Only"). Check this site often!

🌐 *The Microsoft Site Builder Workshop.* www.microsoft.com/workshop. This site has all the latest news about Microsoft Internet technologies.

🌐 *Office 97.* www.microsoft.com/office/office97 and/or www.microsoft.com/msoffice.

🌐 *Microsoft Product Downloads.* www.microsoft.com/msdownload. This is the central location for all Microsoft downloadable software.

🌐 *Microsoft Technical Support.* www.microsoft.com/support/. This is a central resource for downloading patches, troubleshooting, and searching online knowledge bases.

APPENDIX B

- *Internet Explorer.* www.microsoft.com/ie. This is the main page for Internet Explorer information. Follow the link to the "How-To" guide for an in-depth look at Internet Explorer issues and capabilities.

- *Internet Explorer 4.0.* www.microsoft.com/ie/ie40. This is a guide to Internet Explorer 4.0.

- *Carl & Gary's Visual Basic Home Page.* www.apexsc.com/vb/. This great Visual Basic site includes a well-organized assortment of links, code samples, and other technical information.

- *The Spreadsheet Page.* www.j-walk.com/ss/index.html. John Walkenbach of Jwalk & Associates develops this site. It has a great deal of useful information about Microsoft Excel, including sample code, downloads, and other tips and tricks.

- *Beyond... The Black Stump.* www.werple.net.au/~lions/index.html. This site is an amazing collection of links (over 6000), including those to many hot programming topics and valuable shareware.

- *C|Net NEWS.COM.* www.news.com. c|net was one of the early leaders on the Internet. They not only maintain an excellent Web site (www.cnet.com), but they also have a weekly television series and this spin-off site at www.news.com. This is a great resource for daily news, including the latest information and rumors about Internet and intranet technologies, Microsoft news, and the like.

- *The Development Exchange.* www.windx.com. This is the main site of Fawcette Technical Publications. It includes information on their publications (MIND and VBPJ) along with many technical resources.

- *Microsoft Systems Journal.* www.msj.com. This is the companion site to the *Microsoft Systems Journal* monthly magazine. It includes source code and many tools for Windows developers.

- *Jumbo.* www.jumbo.com. This collection of over 93,000 shareware and freeware applications includes typical shareware apps and also source code, debuggers, and so on.

- *World Wide Web of Windows.* www.intersource.com/~rpurcell. This site features a long list of various Windows-related links.

Etcetera

 CompuServe. Although Microsoft is no longer directly involved in doing technical support via CompuServe, there is still a very strong user community. Try going to the following areas for sample code and answers to your questions:

- Go INETRES for Internet Resources
- Go BASLAN for Basic Languages and Visual Basic
- Go IBMFF for the PC file finder, when you are searching for a particular file to download, such as a .DLL or a software patch
- Go MICROSOFT for the Microsoft connection (not as good as their Web site, but not bad either)

Microsoft newsgroups. msnews.microsoft.com. This is the premier location for getting your questions answered by Microsoft. Post a question in the appropriate newsgroup (for example, microsoft.public.excel.programming, microsoft.public.vb.ole). You can generally expect an answer to your question within a day or two.

Microsoft Developer Network. This is a CD subscription service that Microsoft offers. It ships quarterly and contains hundreds of technical articles, sample code, software patches, and online documentation.

APPENDIX B

Index

A

<A> tag, 114, 124, 192, 407
AboutBox method, 231
accelerator keys, 511
Access, 17–18, 163, 253, 255, 562
  building your intranet with, 398–99
  Corporate Sales Overview and, 348, 352
  Excel and, 332, 340, 348, 352
  Internet replication and, 397–98
  linking/importing data with, 267, 370–74
  publishing static Web pages with, 375–82
  troubleshooting, 395–97
Access Report Wizard, 396
ACID properties, 566
Action Buttons, 267, 418, 423, 431, 436–38,
  445–48, 450–51
Action Settings, 414, 420–21, 423, 430, 432–34,
  442–43, 445, 447
Action Settings dialog box, 415–16, 433–34,
  436, 448
ActiveMovie, 187, 257
ActiveX, 13, 25, 92, 255, 471, 490, 540
  Access and, 361, 383–84, 390
  basic description of, 227–51
  control object model, 231–32
  Control Menu, 232
  Control Pad, 228, 232–48
  creating dynamic pages with, 205–51
  custom Wizards and, 52
  demo page, 240, 246, 249
  Document container, 183–86
  download time and, 83
  dynamic file formats and, 383–84
  Excel and, 343, 354, 355–56
  frames and, 125
  HTML forms and, 288
  IIS and, 553, 562–64
  Internet Explorer and, 15, 16, 183–86, 191,
    195
  PowerPoint and, 19, 415–16
  Server extension, 228
  Server Framework (ASF), 207, 383, 384
ActiveX Control Toolbox, 415–16
Add Banner routine, 320
Add button, 32, 75, 95, 101, 107, 158, 213
Add Editor Association dialog box, 96
AddHistory argument, 264
AddItem method, 231, 244–45
Add method, 262, 308
Add/Modify FTP Locations dialog box, 260
address argument, 262
Address history list, 258
Add Task button, 39, 41
AddToFavorites method, 264–66, 369
Add To The Current Web option, 111
administrator permissions, 53, 138–39, 166
ADO (ActiveX Data Objects), 384
Advanced tab, 43, 91, 105, 115, 173–74, 188,
  339
Alchemy Mindworks Web page, 122
alignment, of cells, 104
Alignment property, 237
ALittleInfo routine, 450–51
Alta Vista search engine, 342
ALT+F4 (Shut Down command), 113
ampersand (&), 218, 511
anchor argument, 262, 308
Anchor object, 192
AnimateAction property, 441, 443
Animated Button control, 230
animation(s), 122, 291, 303
  animated maps, 452–53
  Animation Player and, 19, 413, 421, 423–24

animation(s) *(continued)*
 automating, 448–49
 for charts, 411, 426, 449–50, 452
 Custom Animations, 426, 430, 451–53
 PowerPoint and, 412, 416, 418, 420–21,
  423–26, 429, 448–50
 soundtracks for, 429
AnimationSettings object, 449
anniversary reminders, 504
API (Application Programming Interface),
 341, 344
Appearance tab, 118
AppendToLog method, 560
Apple, 502
AppleScript, 206, 552
Application object, 312
appointments, 463, 503–4
appVersion property, 226
Archie browser, 68
ARCHIVE directory, 112
Archive page, 50
arrays, 215
Article Post form, 48
Articles tab, 159
AS/400 (IBM), 573–74
ASCII (American Standard Code for Informa-
 tion Interchange), 61, 77, 127,
 129–130, 246, 558
ASF (ActiveX Server Framework), 207, 383, 384
ASP (Active Server Pages), 383–92, 396–97,
 402, 404, 406, 409, 505, 520–21, 522,
 558–61, 563
asterisk (*), 130
atomicity, 566
attributes, 74–76, 83, 88
 Extended, 91, 95, 101, 103, 106, 133, 213
 frame, 128
 style sheets and, 99, 100
auditing, 166
authentication, 178–79
Author permissions, 53
Authors group, 175
AutoCorrect dialog box, 271–72
AutoContent Wizard, 414
AutoCreate, 469
AutoFormat command, 352–53
AutoFormat tab, 271
AutoFormatting, 271–72, 292, 316
AutoNameCheck, 461

AutoOpen macro, 318
AutoSignature, 462
AutoText, 325–26
AVI files, 83, 122, 451–52

B

<B> tag, 287
B1_OnClick event procedure, 212
Back button, 8, 60, 137, 258, 450
background(s)
 automating, 313
 effects, creating, 274–75
 PowerPoint and, 417
 in Word, 271–75, 298, 313
Background button, 274
Background tab, 90, 92, 119
BackOffice, 10, 20–21, 574
backslash (\), 24, 37
BackStyle property, 239
Back To Top link, 101, 109, 323–24
backup documents, 291–92
banners, animated, 424
<BASE> tag, 88
<BASEFONT> tag, 94
Base Location, 88
Basic, 562
Behavior list, 286
Bibliography Template, 52, 61, 66
birthday reminders, 504
bitmaps, 123, 274, 351, 404
<BLINK> tag, 83
<BLOCKQUOTE> tag, 70, 97
BMP files, 123, 274, 351, 404
<BODY> tag, 47, 70, 79, 90–92, 94, 99, 106–7,
 109–11, 213–14, 393
Boilerplate Page Template, 88–93
boldface font, 124
Bonus Pack, 10–14
bookmarks, 93, 307, 364. *See also* links
borders, 73, 75

 tag, 287
braces ({}), 301
Break mode, 195
Browse button, 92, 118, 139, 160
BrowseExtraFileTypes property, 311
Browse mode, 417–18, 420

browser(s). *See also* Internet Explorer
    browser; Netscape Navigator browser
  Archie browser, 68
  basic description of, 8–9
  blank cells and, 78
  emulation, 575
  IIS and, 551
  Lynx browser, 68
  Mosaic browser, 134
  Outlook and, 458, 502–4
  previewing your work with, 68–69, 92–93,
    100, 101, 104, 110, 131
Browser button, 104
Browser Capabilities Component, 563
BtnLoad_Click event procedure, 249
BtnMenu Object, 244–45
Bug List, 48, 505–6, 514
Bug Reports, 48
Build button, 367
bullets, 54, 280–81, 284, 285, 327
Busy property, 200
By Conversation Topic view, 479

C

caches, 188–89
Calendar, 459, 463–64, 472, 481–82, 505–6,
    514–15
callouts, 310
Camera effect, 426
Caption property, 367
cascading style sheet, 94–101, 110, 123, 404
Category menu, 156
CD Auto-Run screen, 188
CD-ROM drives, 164
cell(s)
  alignment of, 104
  backgrounds, 79, 83
  blank, 78
  merged, 79
  padding, 117
  placing links in, 332–33
  spacing, 117
  width, 117
Cell Link property, 345
Cell Properties dialog box, 78, 104, 132
ChangeDocBullets routine, 320
charts, 230, 350–51, 356–57
  animated, 411, 426, 449–50, 452

Chart Wizard and, 350–51
ChartUnitEffect property, 449
Check Spelling dialog box, 41
child Webs, 38
Choose Data Source dialog box, 340
Choose Directory dialog box, 139
Choose Form command, 479
Choose Technique dialog box, 127
CHR() function, 217
CHttpServer class, 557
CHttpServerContext class, 557
CID (CompuServe Internet Dialer), 256
CiDaemon process, 540
<CITE> tag, 97
CLASS attribute, 77, 103
CLASSID attribute, 230
Clear button, 82
Clear method, 231, 245
Click event, 240, 368
client/server paradigm, 25
client-side validation, 219–24
clip art, 117, 160, 313, 358
Clip Art tab, 117
Clipboard, 256, 271
CodeBase property, 237
Code pane, 245
Code View, 242–46
collaborative editing, 266–67, 304–5, 339
colon (:), 103
color(s), 144, 419
  background, 88, 90, 92, 119–20, 123, 150,
    274–75, 300, 313, 395
  exploration bar and, 116, 119–20
  font, 285, 286, 296
  hyperlink, 88, 90, 120, 123, 296
  menus and, 123
  palette settings, 116
  RGB color, 116, 120, 238, 313
  schemes, 47, 49, 434–37
  text, 88, 150, 304–5
Color dialog box, 120
Color Scheme dialog box, 435
columns, 291, 292, 473
COM (Component Object Model), 551, 561–66
Comic Chat, 187
comments, 44, 61, 93, 99, 124, 291–92, 312,
    419
Comments form, 61
<COMMENT> tag, 208
Comment WebBot, 60

compatibility, with HTML, 337–39
Competitive Analysis (MMA), 347, 351, 353–59
Compose menu
    Choose Form command, 479, 495
    New Expense Report command, 488
    New Post In This Folder command, 495, 511
    Publish command, 489
Compose Page, 490–91
compressed files, 132
CompuServe, 164, 256
Configuration title, 43
configuration variables, 30, 47
Configure Editors tab, 44, 95–96
Confirmation Field WebBot, 81, 159, 160, 223
Confirmation form, 49–52, 62, 149, 151, 159, 217
Confirmation page, 149, 156–60
connection timeouts, 171
Connect method, 373, 374
consistency, 566
constants, 369, 441–42, 445–46
contact lists, 471–72, 481–82, 504
Contacts, 459, 464–66
CONTENT attribute, 89
Content frame, 105, 118–19, 124–25, 127, 146, 160–61
Content Linking Component, 563
Contents page, 118, 119, 142
Context menu
    Horizontal Line Properties command, 72
    Table Properties command, 74
Continue With Next Document dialog box, 42
ControlCenter, 353, 355
Control Panel, 165, 166, 533, 579
Control Toolbox, 288, 355, 490
conversion
    of presentations to HTML, 420–25
    from HTML to Word format, 292–93
    from Word format to HTML, 290–94, 326
cookies, 224–25
Copy Child Webs option, 180
Copy command, 365
copying
    links, 333, 365–67, 432
    with the Publish command, 38
Copy method, 264
Copy Web command, 38

copyright notices, 47
Corporate Presence Wizard, 11, 29–33, 45–47
Corporate Sales Overview (MMA), 340, 347–53
Create Hyperlink command, 124
Create Hyperlink dialog box, 132–33, 160
CreateItem method, 500
Create New Data Source dialog box, 349
Create New Folder dialog box, 476
Create New Option group, 295
Create New Query command, 340
cross references, 291, 292, 303, 316–17
<CROSSTAB> tag, 338
Current option, 71
Current View command, 471–72
Custom Animations, 426, 430, 451–53
Custom Animations dialog box, 451–53
custom Wizards, 52–53
Customers form, 391
Customer Support Template, 47–48
Custom Show dialog box, 438
Custom Soundtrack dialog box, 427–28
Custom tab, 434
Cut method, 264

D

DAO (data access objects), 341, 344, 373
Database Access Component, 563
Database Connector Wizard, 52, 60
Database Results Template, 62
databases, 19. *See also* Access
    creating, 399–400
    Template Wizard and, 346–47
Data menu, 340–41
    Pivot Table Report command, 340
    Template Wizard command, 346–47
Datasheet view, 368, 375, 376, 390
date(s)
    in footers, 103
    recognition, 504
dBASE, 370, 371, 372
DblClick method, 246
DCOM, 551, 552, 562–66
DDE (Dynamic Data Exchange), 186
Decrease Indent button, 70
Default Document setting, 172, 174
Default Hyperlink Location box, 118
Default Target Frame, 88, 107–8

Default View property, 390
Define Custom Show dialog box, 437
Deleted Items, 459
Delete method, 264
deleting
  default HTML tags, 97
  e-mail messages, 497
  graphics, 62
  routines, 213
  templates, 112
  Webs, 35
deliveries, scheduled, 458
Desktop shortcut icons, 478
Developer Knowledge Base, 50–51, 88, 136,
    147–61
DHCP (Dynamic Host Configuration
    Protocol), 165, 173
Dim statement, 212, 246
directories, 9, 34–35. *See also* folders
  FrontPage and, 30, 31
  hidden, 43
  importing/exporting, 37–38
  <ROOT WEB> directory, 30, 38, 44, 53,
    59, 88, 92, 102, 112, 116, 128, 141,
    146, 151, 153, 160, 180, 181
  slash marks and, 24
  structure of, 53–55
  virtual, 172
Directories tab, 172, 174
Directory Browsing Allowed setting, 172
Directory of Press Releases Template, 52, 62
<DIR> tag, 70
Discussions page, 48, 50, 70
Discussion tab, 158–59
Discussion WebBot, 148
Discussion Wizard, 45, 48–49, 148–49, 150–52
DisplayScreenTips property, 312–13
DLLs (dynamic link libraries), 206, 540, 541,
    555, 556, 558, 572
DNS (Domain Name System), 26, 28, 167
DoCmd object, 373, 374, 381
document(s)
  basic description of, 8
  default format for, 8
  sharing, 480–82
Document Close event, 265
Document Map, 18, 267, 297–300, 305, 316
Document object, 191
Document Properties dialog box, 290
Documents folder, 515

domain names, 26, 28, 167
Download page, 48, 132–36
download time, 83
drag and drop, 481, 483
Drawing objects, 291
Drawing toolbar, 353
Drop-Down Menu Properties dialog box, 156
durability, 566
Dynamic Links worksheet, 336
dynamic Web pages, 205–51, 374–75, 379,
    382–92

E

Easter eggs, 250
Edit menu, 44, 249
  Image Properties command, 118
  Insert ActiveX Control command, 234
  InsertHTML Layout command, 249
  Paste As Hyperlink command, 333, 365–66
  Properties command, 151
Editor (FrontPage), 12–13, 24–25, 28, 32, 36,
    44, 141, 146
  ActiveX and, 234
  basic description of, 56–85
  building custom Web pages with, 57
  creating space and, 124
  creating templates and, 88–93
  creating dynamic pages and, 208, 209
  download pages and, 147, 155, 156–60
  exploration bar and, 120
  footers and, 103
  frames and, 127
  image maps and, 115
  importing HTML and, 67
  launching, 59
  Page Wizards, 59–65
  saving master templates and, 109–11
  script shells and, 106–8
  style sheets and, 99, 101
  Templates, 59–65
EIS (executive information systems), 347–59
Element object, 192
e-mail. *See also* Outlook
  accessing, with a browser, 503–4
  addresses, 30, 365
  delivering user feedback as, 61
  HTML attachments to, 381
  links, 47, 103, 365, 407–9

e-mail *(continued)*
  messages, deleting, 497
  messages, recalling, 461
  rules, 496–98
embedded objects, 282
Employee Directory Template, 52, 62
Employment Opportunities Template, 52, 62
Empty Folder button, 188
Empty Web Template dialog box, 138–39
endnotes, 291, 312
EnlargeFontsLessThan property, 314
EntryEffect property, 448
error(s), 122, 213, 311
  download pages and, 151–52
  FAT system and, 177
  HTML tags and, 70
  IIS and, 177–79
  Internet Explorer and, 188
  operator, 188
  server, 132
  slash marks and, 24
  spelling/grammar, 317
Errors tab, 151–52
Escape key, 510
events, 463
Excel, 17–20, 132, 154, 253, 255, 372
  basic description of, 331–59
  building your intranet with, 347–59
  collaborative editing in, 266–67
  external data and, 339–47
  file objects and, 265–66
  hyperlinks and, 261–65
  integration and, 332–39
  Internet Explorer and, 184
  IIS and, 562
  Outlook and, 481, 486–87, 488, 489
  Web Connectivity Kit, 338, 342
Excel Forms toolbar, 355
Exchange Server, 457–58, 461, 475, 522
  basic description of, 20, 21
  browsers and, 503–4
  connection to, via to Internet, 503
  public folders and, 478
Explain Results button, 28
exploration bar, 114, 116–20, 125, 128
Explorer (FrontPage), 24–33, 44–53, 58, 60, 119
  creating the Industry News archive and, 138–41

download pages and, 132–36, 147, 151–56
editing Web settings with, 42
global text operations and, 40–42
IIS and, 178, 180
image maps and, 115
launching, 59
maintaining your Web with, 39–44
recalculating hyperlinks with, 110
saving pages and, 65, 111
style sheets and, 97
toolkit, 35–44
Export button, 376, 386
Export command, 37–38
exporting
  databases, 401–4
  dynamic HTML pages, 384–88
  forms, 390–91
  links, 396–97
  reports, 377, 397
  selected records, 377
  single components, 375–77
Extended Attributes, 91, 95, 101, 103, 106–7, 133, 213–14
Extended Attributes dialog box, 74–75, 101, 106, 107, 213–14
Extended button, 74, 101, 103, 132
ExtraInfo argument, 264
ExtraInfoRequired property, 309–10

F

FAQs (Frequently Asked Questions), 48, 52, 63
FAT system, 177, 179
Favorites folder, 8
Favorites list, 188, 258
Feedback Form Template, 31, 46, 52, 63, 148
field(s), 273–74, 291–92, 297, 301–3, 306
  adding custom, 473
  codes, changing, 274
  editing, 273–74
  storing links as, 272–74
Field Chooser, 490
Field dialog box, 301
Field Options dialog box, 301–2
file(s). *See also* file extensions
  formats, 134, 383–84, 413, 414
  names, 9, 38, 92, 421

file(s) *(continued)*
  opening, 259
  posting, 266–67
  saving, 259
file extensions
  .CSS, 95
  .EXE, 132
  .HTML, 543
  .PPS, 413
  .PPT, 413
  .PPZ, 413
  .ZIP, 132
File menu, 29, 35–38, 43, 45, 59–60
  Folder command, 505
  Get External Data command, 370
  Import And Export command, 523
  Import command, 151
  New command, 119, 127, 150, 276, 295,
    414, 487
  Open command, 71
  Page Properties command, 88, 90, 92, 106,
    107, 117, 123, 213
  Preview In Browser command, 68–69, 92–
    93, 110
  Properties command, 289, 488
  Publish Form As command, 494, 511
  Publish FrontPage Web command, 180
  Save As command, 108, 416
  Save As/Export command, 375, 377, 386
  Save As HTML command, 266, 290, 378, 401
  Save As Word Document command, 292
  Save command, 110
  Send To command, 481, 487
File/Open dialog box, 260, 261, 530
File property, 313
fill effects, 298, 359
Fill Effects dialog box, 298
filtering, 473, 540
<FILTER> tag, 338–39
Find And Replace dialog box, 300
Find dialog box, 41
Find tab, 300
Finish button, 404
firewalls, 43–44
flag variables, 221–22
Flying effect, 426
Folder Assistant, 496–97, 498
folders. *See also* directories
  moving Web pages between, 36, 37, 152–56

  public folders, 458, 461, 475–83, 497, 503–4,
    505–16, 523–25
  storing templates in, 66
Folder View, 33–35, 37, 88, 90, 141, 152
FollowHyperlink method, 265, 451
Follow method, 264, 369
fonts, 73, 83, 376, 395
  boldface font, 124
  frames and, 129
  menus and, 124
  style sheets and, 94–95, 97–98, 101
  Word and, 284–89
<FONT SIZE> tag, 67, 93
footers, 47, 50–51, 54, 103, 153, 159, 291
  adding, 102–5
  creating, 91
  importing, 151
footnotes, 291, 312
foreign language support, 542
form(s), 287–89
  Access and, 361–62, 366–67, 390–91, 400
  adding actions to, 491–92
  definition of, 343
  Excel and, 343–47
  exporting, 390–91
  inserting hyperlink labels in, 366–67
  integrated vs. nonintegrated, 487–88
  Outlook and, 471, 484–96
  publishing, 489, 494, 511
  saving, 511
  titles, 511
  using Office documents as, 486–89
Format Cells command, 376
Format Font command, 376
Format menu, 298, 395
  Apple Design command, 435
  AutoFormat command, 352–53
  Background command, 274
  Paragraph command, 101
  Slide Color Scheme command, 434
  Style command, 300
FormatRawData routine, 357, 358
Format tab, 367
Formatting toolbar, 285, 286
Format toolbar, 70
Format View command, 473
Form Page Wizard, 60, 148–49
Form Properties dialog box, 158, 177
Form property, 510

<FORM> tag, 209, 289
formulas, 338, 511
<FORMULA> tag, 338
Form Wizard, 52, 345
Forward button, 258
forward slash (/), 24, 37, 217–18
FoxPro, 372
frame(s), 49–50, 125–31, 137–38, 150
    contents, evaluation/updating, 214–16
    PowerPoint and, 422–23
    target, 91, 146–47, 160
    working with, 79–81
FRAME attribute, 74–75
Frame object, 190–91
framesets, 61, 69, 79–81
<FRAMESET> tag, 61, 79–81
Frames Wizard, 11, 52, 60–61, 69, 79, 125–31
From A Wizard Or Template option, 29
From Location button, 71
FrontPage. See also Editor (FrontPage);
        Explorer (FrontPage)
    basic description of, 10–14, 23–55
    building Webs with, 23–55, 86–161
    creating dynamic pages and, 213, 223,
        234–36, 239
    defaults, 72–73
    extensions, installation of, 168–69
    maintaining Webs with, 39–44
    online Help, 71
    principle components of, 24–25
    Server Administrator, 27
    Server Extensions, 26–27
    Setup, 68–69
    Software Development Kit (SDK), 12, 51, 112
    verification tests, 40
FTP (File Transfer Protocol), 166–67, 170–72,
        174, 180
    Access and, 370–71
    Office 97 and, 253, 255–56, 259–61
    sites, interacting with, 259–61

G

General tab, 43, 91, 106, 107, 295
Generator tag, 279
GetDefaultFolder method, 501
getenv( ) function, 556
GetExtensionVersion function, 555

GET method, 342, 554
GetObject function, 200–201
GetServerVariable function, 556
Getting Started With Microsoft FrontPage
        dialog box, 29, 43, 59, 138
GIF Construction Set, 122
GIF files, 117, 121–23, 140, 195, 282, 404,
        420, 422–23, 426, 535
Glossary Of Terms Template, 52, 63
Go button, 258, 259
Go To tab, 300
Gopher, 166–67, 170–72, 256
Gradient control, 230
graphics. See also images
    bitmaps, 123, 274, 351, 404
    clip art, 117, 160, 313, 358
    deleting, 62
    design considerations for, 54, 113–14
    exploration bar and, 116–18
    GIF files, 117, 121–23, 140, 195, 282, 404,
        420, 422–23, 426, 535
    hyperlinks on, 433–34
    logos, 46–47, 62, 122, 123, 352, 394, 404
    PowerPoint and, 420–23, 425–31, 433–34
    referenced, importing files with, 141
    saving, 62
    style options for, 47
    ToolTips and, 121–22
    Word and, 270, 274, 282, 284, 292
Group By Box command, 472
Guest Book Template, 52, 63, 148
GUI (graphical user interface), 55, 121, 250

H

"hand" icon, 367
hard drive space, 164
hardware, 164
headers, 47, 50–51, 54, 69–70, 151, 154, 159–60,
        216, 291
<HEAD> tag, 67, 84, 89, 98–99
HEIGHT attribute, 123
"Hello, World" routines, 208, 210
Help, 27, 53, 334, 336, 575
Help Desk, 53
Help menu, 27
History folder, 8, 504
History list, 302
History object, 191

Horizontal Line Properties dialog box, 72–73, 281–82

horizontal lines, 72–73, 94, 281–82, 284, 286, 323–25

host names, 26, 28

Hot List Template, 52, 63

hot spots, 114–15, 137. *See also* links

HREF attribute, 99, 160, 215, 233

<HR> tag, 94

HTML (Hypertext Markup Language)
 basic description of, 8
 Consortium standards, 84
 converting, to Word, 292–93
 converting Word documents to, 290–92, 293
 encoding options, 289–90
 extending, 74–76
 familiarity with, importance of, 58
 format, compatibility with, 337–39
 function of, 68
 IIS and, 558–59
 intranet tools and, 10–21
 Microsoft guide for, 58–59
 tags, child, 94
 tags, nested, 77

HTML Editing View, 244

HTML Layout Control, 187, 232–33, 247–51

HTML Markup WebBot, 74–76, 123, 137, 142, 219–20

HTTP (Hypertext Transfer Protocol), 10, 25, 27, 71, 146, 160
 Access and, 364, 369–71
 basic description of, 7
 converting URLs with, 109
 cookies and, 224
 download pages and, 135
 Excel and, 343, 344
 IIS and, 553, 554, 555, 560, 564
 Internet Explorer and, 188
 Office 97 and, 253, 256
 parameters, 207
 Submit button and, 153
 Web site searches and, 530, 535

https protocol, 257

hyperdocuments, 52, 63, 136–38

hyperlink(s). *See also* URLs (uniform resource locators)
 Access and, 19, 267, 363–74, 375
 adding, to the exploration bar, 118–20

AutoFormatting, 271–72, 292, 316

basic description of, 4, 7, 33–35

broken, 24–25, 39, 152–53, 155–56

changing cross references to, 292

collections, 261–65, 307–9, 439–50

controlling, through code, 307–13

copying, 333, 365–67, 432

creating, 323–25, 333–34, 440–43

customizing the appearance of, 434–35

default target frames and, 107

dragging and dropping, 256, 271, 334, 367

editing, 434–36

e-mail, 47, 103, 365, 407–9

entering, manually, 364–65

Excel and, 332–37, 351

fields, 301–3

hot spots, 114–15, 137

in hyperdocuments, 136–38

in the Marketing Catalog, 136–38

inserting, 271

maintaining, 334

in menus, 122–25

to named locations, 444–45

objects, 263–65, 309–11, 443–44

Office 97 and, 253, 255–59, 261–65

Outlook and, 461, 476, 494

pasting clipboard contents as, 256, 271

PowerPoint and, 414, 421, 423, 432–36, 440–45

to ranges, 255–56

recalculating/updating, 24–25, 39, 91–92, 143, 152–56

referring to, through code, 368–70

replacing cross references with, 316–17

storage of, 272–73, 365

that are not links, 440

validating, 39–40, 110–11, 143–47, 152–53

Web site searches and, 534–35, 536

Word and, 270, 271–75, 292, 296, 301–17, 323–25

HyperlinkAddress property, 368–69, 390

Hyperlink data type, 363, 364–70

Hyperlink formula dialog box, 335–36

Hyperlink property, 369, 441

Hyperlinks method, 334–35

HyperlinkSubAddress property, 369, 390

Hyperlink To Slide dialog box, 433

Hyperlink To URL dialog box, 432–33

Hyperlink View, 33–34, 35

I

<I> tag, 287

IBM AS/400, 573–74

IDC (Internet Database Connector), 60, 345, 383–86, 388–90, 396–97, 402, 404–8, 537, 570, 572–94

IEAK (Microsoft Internet Explorer Administration Kit), 187–88, 194

<IFRAME> tag, 83

IHTMLDocument class, 195

IIS (Microsoft Internet Information Server), 25, 131–32
  Access and, 386, 402
  basic description of, 10, 20, 163–81
  configuring, 169–74
  creating dynamic pages and, 206
  extending, 551–94
  publishing your Web to, 180–81
  Server Extensions, 168–69
  setting up, requirements for, 164–66
  SQL Server and, 569, 573, 575
  troubleshooting, 178–79
  Web site searches and, 528, 530, 537, 539–40

Image Composer (Microsoft), 13–14, 113, 117, 122

image maps, 47, 53, 137
  client-side, 114–15
  Word and, 302

images, 11, 13–14. *See also* graphics; image maps
  background, 79, 358
  size recommendations for, 121–22
  transparent, 352

<IMG> tag, 66, 282

Immediate pane, 195

Import And Export Wizard, 465, 523

Import command, 37–38

import filters, 274

Import HTML Wizard, 371, 372

importing, 36–37, 39, 67, 424–25
  Contact lists, 465
  without custom forms, 523–24
  external data, with Access, 370–74
  files, into the Industry News archive, 139–41
  headers and footers, 151

Import Or Link Tables command, 371

Inbox, 458–59, 460–62, 471–72, 496–98

Inbox Assistant, 458, 496–98

Include Component Properties dialog box, 104

Included footer, 47, 50–51, 103, 151, 153, 159

Included header, 47, 50–51, 69–70, 151, 154, 159–60, 216

Include WebBot, 47, 54, 81, 100, 109, 111

indexes, 151, 154, 291, 528, 531–33, 537–48

IndexOf() function, 226

Index Server (Microsoft), 528, 537–48

Industry News archive, 136, 138–47

Information Request forms, 31–32

inheritance, 73

<INPUT> tag, 210, 240, 244, 289

Insert ActiveX Control dialog box, 234

Insert Action lists, 243–45

Insert Hyperlink command, 333, 337, 367

Insert Hyperlink dialog box, 255, 274, 275, 368, 444

Insert menu, 82, 284, 429
  Cross Reference command, 303
  Form Field command, 156
  Horizontal Line command, 72–73, 281
  Hyperlink command, 124, 132, 365
  Picture command, 282
  Script command, 208
  Scrolling Text command, 285
  WebBot Component command, 103

Insert Picture dialog box, 280–81

installation
  of the ActiveX Control Pad, 233
  of FrontPage, 26, 30, 168–69
  of the IIS, 166–69
  settings, in the IEAK, 188

Install button, 168

Instr() function, 217

Internet
  basic description of, 3–21
  servers and, 7–8

Internet Assistant Wizard, 337

Internet Content Template, 151

Internet Explorer browser, 31–32, 49–50, 68, 89–90, 107, 124, 318, 530
  Access and, 371, 380, 385, 391–92, 404, 406
  ActiveX controls and, 229–30
  Automation and, 193–202
  basic description of, 10, 14–16, 183–202
  cell formatting and, 116
  creating dynamic pages and, 206, 216–18, 224, 229–51
  customizing, for your intranet, 187–88

Internet Explorer browser *(continued)*
  download pages and, 135
  Excel and, 339, 355
  fonts and, 83
  frames and, 125, 128, 129
  graphics and, 122
  HTML forms and, 287
  IIS and, 164, 551, 554
  image maps and, 115
  Office 97 and, 258
  opening unknown file formats in, 134
  Page Template previewed in, 100, 101
  PowerPoint and, 417, 418–19, 424
  programming, 194–202
  scripting object model, 189–94, 196, 207
  style sheets and, 94
  tables and, 78–79
  ToolTips and, 121
  URLs and, 89
  Word and, 289–90, 297, 302, 305, 311, 318
Internet Mail, 187
Internet News, 187
Internet Service Manager, 166, 168–70, 175,
    177–78
Internet Studio, 113
intranet(s)
  basic description of, 3–21
  business needs and, 4–7
  components of, 7–9
  regular networks and, difference between,
    9–10
  tools, 10–21
IP addresses, 28, 43–44
  basic description of, 7
  domain names and, 26
  IIS and, 165
  preventing access to, 173
ISAPI (Internet Server Application Program-
    ming Interface), 20, 206–7, 551, 553,
    555–58, 560, 562, 572
isolation, 566
Issues folder, 515
ItemCount property, 231
IWebBrowser interface, 185

J

Java, 13, 21, 562, 564
  Applets, 206

creating dynamic pages and, 206, 225–26
  Internet Explorer and, 15, 185–86
JavaScript, 9, 13, 15, 83, 92, 558, 561
  dynamic pages and, 211, 226
  frames and, 128
  Internet Explorer and, 185, 189
JIT (just-in-time) compiler, 186
Journal, 459, 467–69, 481–83, 501–2, 566–68
JPG files, 117, 420, 422, 423, 426, 429
JustAButton object, 240–42

K

keyboard shortcuts, 37
keywords, for indexing URLs, 89
Kiosk mode, 188, 418, 419, 420, 430–31, 447,
    450
Knowledge Base, 50–51, 88, 136, 147–61

L

Label control, 230, 239
Label object, 237, 246
Label Object method, 246
labels, 230, 237, 239, 246, 366–67
language support, 542
Language tab, 43
LANs (local area networks), 256, 569
laptop computers, 25
Last Modified dates, 47
LCase( ) function, 216
Learning FrontPage Wizard, 45
Lecture Abstract Template, 52, 63
<LI> tag, 70, 76–77, 95
line(s)
  breaks, 124
  horizontal, 72–73, 94, 281–82, 284, 286,
    323–25
link(s). *See also* URLs (uniform resource
    locators)
  Access and, 19, 267, 363–74, 375
  adding, to the exploration bar, 118–20
  AutoFormatting, 271–72, 292, 316
  basic description of, 4, 7, 33–35
  broken, 24–25, 39, 152–53, 155–56
  changing cross references to, 292
  collections, 261–65, 307–9, 439–50
  controlling, through code, 307–13

link(s) *(continued)*
  copying, 333, 365–67, 432
  creating, 323–25, 333–34, 440–43
  customizing the appearance of, 434–35
  default target frames and, 107
  dragging and dropping, 256, 271, 334, 367
  editing, 434–36
  e-mail, 47, 103, 365, 407–9
  entering, manually, 364–65
  Excel and, 332–37, 351
  fields, 301–3
  hot spots, 114–15, 137
  in hyperdocuments, 136–38
  in the Marketing Catalog, 136–38
  inserting, 271
  maintaining, 334
  in menus, 122–25
  to named locations, 444–45
  objects, 263–65, 309–11, 443–44
  Office 97 and, 253, 255–59, 261–65
  Outlook and, 461, 476, 494
  pasting clipboard contents as, 256, 271
  PowerPoint and, 414, 421, 423, 432–36,
    440–45
  to ranges, 255–56
  recalculating/updating, 24–25, 39, 91–92,
    143, 152–56
  referring to, through code, 368–70
  replacing cross references with, 316–17
  storage of, 272–73, 365
  that are not links, 440
  validating, 39–40, 110–11, 143–47, 152–53
  Web site searches and, 534–35, 536
  Word and, 270, 271–75, 292, 296, 301–17,
    323–25
Link object, 192
<LINK> tag, 83, 98–99, 143
Link To Custom Show dialog box, 448
ListBoxInput range, 345
ListIndex property, 354
lists
  creating, 76–77
  style sheets and, 95
  of users, controlling, 176
List View, 186–87, 240
local hosts, 26, 28
location.href property, 216
Location object, 191
Logging tab, 173
logon, 178, 179, 261, 458

logos, 46–47, 62, 122, 123, 352, 394, 404. *See
  also* graphics; images
Loop list, 286
Lotus, 372
Lynx browser, 68

M

macro(s), 318, 373, 381, 392
  PowerPoint and, 415
  recorders, 352
  Word and, 276, 291, 293, 297, 305–6, 313–14,
    320
Mail folder, 515
mail merge, 291
Mailto links, 103, 257, 365
Make A Custom Grid option, 61, 127
MakeHyperlinkTOC routine, 320–23, 325
margins, 89–90, 138
Margins Tab, 90
Marketing Catalog, 88, 102, 136–38
Markup object, 99
Markup WebBot, 79
Marquee control, 230
marquees, 68, 83, 230, 285–87
<MARQUEE> tag, 68, 287
Media Player, 430
Meeting Agenda Template, 52, 63
meetings, 52, 63, 463, 469, 470
Members page, 50
Menu control, 230
MenuName variable, 245
menus. *See also* specific menus
  basic description of, 113–14, 122–25
  frames, 105, 124–25
  PopUp, 229–30, 236, 240–45
message flags, 462
meta information, 89
metafiles, 274
<META> tag, 84, 89, 279
method(s)
  AboutBox method, 231
  AddItem method, 231, 244–45
  Add method, 262, 308
  AddToFavorites method, 264–66, 369
  AppendToLog method, 560
  Clear method, 231, 245
  Connect method, 373, 374

method(s) *(continued)*
  Copy method, 264
  CreateItem method, 500
  Cut method, 264
  DblClick method, 246
  Delete method, 264
  FollowHyperlink method, 265, 451
  Follow method, 264, 369
  GetDefaultFolder method, 501
  GET method, 342, 554
  Hyperlinks method, 334–35
  Label Object method, 246
  MouseDown method, 246
  MouseUp method, 246
  NewProject method, 518
  OutputTo method, 381
  PasteSpecial method, 309, 310
  PopUp method, 231, 240
  POST method, 342, 554, 556
  Refresh method, 358
  RemoveItem method, 231
  Select method, 264
  SendObject method, 381
  ViewSource method, 195
  WriteLn method, 216–18
  Write method, 216–18
MFC (Microsoft Foundation Class) libraries, 557
microprocessors, 164, 537
Microsoft Access. *See* Access
Microsoft Excel. *See* Excel
Microsoft Exchange Server. *See* Exchange
    Server
Microsoft Foundation Class (MFC) libraries, 557
Microsoft FrontPage. *See* FrontPage
Microsoft Image Composer, 13–14, 113, 117,
    122
Microsoft Index Server, 528, 537–48
Microsoft Internet Information Server. *See* IIS
    (Microsoft Internet Information
    Server)
Microsoft Network (MSN), 164, 257
Microsoft Office. *See* Office
Microsoft Online Support, 179
Microsoft Outlook. *See* Outlook
Microsoft PowerPoint. *See* PowerPoint
Microsoft Query, 347, 348, 349
Microsoft SNA Server, 20–21, 573–74
Microsoft SQL Server. *See* SQL Server
Microsoft TCP/IP dialog box, 165

Microsoft Web site, 71, 164, 194, 196, 224,
    229, 233, 247, 280, 364, 421
Microsoft Word. *See* Word
MID() function, 218
MIDI (Musical Instrument Digital Interface), 257
MIME types, 559
MMA (Micro Modeling Associates)
  Competitive Analysis, 347, 351, 353–59
  Corporate Sales Overview, 340, 347–53
  Employee Manual, 298, 316–19, 444–45
  Holiday Party RSVP screen, 344–46
  Industry News, 122
  Newsletter, 319–27, 425
  Mission Statement, 412, 414, 417, 427,
      439–50, 452–53
  Online Frameset, 129
  OnLine Search, 146
mms protocol, 257
modular coding, 219
monitors, 164
Mosaic browser, 134
Most Recently Used file list, 108
MouseDown method, 246
MouseUp method, 246
Movie Button, 451
movies, 429–30, 451–52
Movies And Sounds menu, 429–30
Mozilla, 226
MS-DOS, 24, 27
MsgBox function, 208, 211–12
MSN (Microsoft Network), 164, 257
Multiline property, 511
multimedia, 8, 412. *See also* animation;
    graphics; images; sound
  PowerPoint and, 416, 418, 425–31
  video clips, 282–84, 313, 429–30
Multiple Stock Quotes, 355
My Computer, 472–73

N

NAME attribute, 89
Name property, 263, 308
names
  domain names, 26, 28, 167
  home page, 131
  host, 26, 28
  logon, 261
  Web, 29–30, 43, 46

NamedSlideShows property, 448
<NAME> tag, 132
Name/Value Pairs dialog box, 75, 106, 107
narration, 427
Navbar frame, 125
navigation buttons, 258
Navigation Ledge, 48
Navigator object, 191, 226
NCSA (National Center for Supercomputing
    Applications) tutorial, 59
Nested Three-Level Hierarchy option, 127
NetMeeting, 187
Netscape Navigator browser, 13, 15, 83, 94
    IIS and, 551, 554
    JavaScript and, 226
    opening unknown file formats in, 134
Network dialog box, 165
Network icon, 166
Network Test button, 27
New command, 29
New dialog box, 293
new-line characters, 216
New Page dialog box, 60, 67, 108–9, 143
New Page tab, 118
New Post In This Folder command, 479
NewProject method, 518
New Presentation dialog box, 414, 424
news archive, 88
news protocol, 257
Next button, 8, 137, 139, 349, 351, 403–4, 450
nNotAvail flag, 222
nntp protocol, 257
NoBigDeal routine, 208, 211
<NOFRAMES> tag, 79, 128
Normal Page, 52, 64, 88, 92, 96, 103, 116
Normal View, 298
Normal Web Template, 45, 60, 295
Northwind Traders, 378–80, 389, 391
Notepad, 25, 337, 339, 405
Notes, 459, 468–69, 481–82
Novice HTML tutorial, 58–59
nretVal variable, 221
NTFS (NT File System), 166, 174, 179

O

Object Browser, 196
<OBJECT> tag, 229, 232, 234, 236–38, 247

OCX controls, 228
ODBC (Open Database Connectivity), 60,
    163, 167, 173
    Access and, 361, 370, 372, 383–85, 387,
      388
    Excel and, 340–41, 343–44, 346, 348
    SQL Server and, 569, 572–73, 575, 579
Office, 11, 481, 486–89, 499–500, 529. See
    also Excel; Outlook; Powerpoint;
    Word
    ActiveX and, 184–85
    basic description of, 10, 17–20
    Binder application, 184
    file management with, 259–61
    files, posting, 266–67
    Internet Explorer and, 15, 16, 186–87
    Setup program, 256
    user-side Web page tools, 254–61
    Visual Basic and, 205
    Web object model, 261–66
Office Directory Template, 52, 64
Office Insert Hyperlink dialog box, 432
OLE (Object Linking and Embedding), 15,
    206, 227, 332, 517
    Internet Explorer and, 184, 196–97
    PowerPoint and, 426, 430, 452
    Word and, 282, 284, 290–91, 297, 310
<OL> tag, 95, 287
onBlur event, 192, 210
onChange event, 192, 210
onClick event, 192, 209, 210–11, 240, 243, 246
onFocus event, 192, 210
Online Support page, 188
Online Layout, 274, 297, 314
Online Layout View, 297–98, 313, 318
OnLoad attribute, 213–14, 244
Onload event, 107, 213–14
On Mouse Click check box, 431
onMouseMove event, 192
onMouseOver event, 192
onSelect event, 192, 210
Open FrontPage Web dialog box, 35–36
Option Explicit statement, 213–14
Options button, 301
Options dialog box, 96, 193
Options tab, 461–62
Oracle, 340, 370
Original option, 71
Other Texture button, 274
Our Human Resources page, 215

Out Of Office Assistant, 458, 496–98
Outbox folder, 460
Outline View, 53, 320, 436
Outlook, 17, 18
    basic description of, 457–525
    customization, 458, 470–75, 484–96
    integration of, 469–70
    Object Library, 518
    Object model, 499–502, 517
    rules, 496–98
Outlook bar, 459–69, 478, 482, 522
OutputFormat argument, 381
OutputTo macro, 392
OutputTo method, 381
Overview page, 118, 119, 128

P

<P> tag, 73, 94, 97, 100, 287
padding, 73
page breaks, 291, 323–25
Page Layout View, 298
Page Properties dialog box, 88–91, 106
Page Properties style sheet, 88–95, 111, 116–17,
    120, 141, 153, 158, 213–14
PaintShop Pro, 117, 122
Page Templates, 51–52
Page Wizards, 51–52
Paragraph Properties dialog box, 101
paragraphs, 73, 101
    center-aligning, 75
    indenting, 69–70
    line breaks at the end of, 124
    Word and, 280–81, 291, 292
parameters, 30, 42, 102–3, 207, 342–43, 387,
    396, 406
Parameters button, 342
Parameters dialog box, 343
Parameters tab, 42
<PARAM> tag, 230, 232, 236, 238–39, 247
password(s), 166, 179, 305, 576
    Access and, 385–86, 387
    changing, 43, 261
    FrontPage and, 26, 30, 43
    supplying, when creating new Webs, 138–39
PasteSpecial method, 309, 310
PC Quote, 17, 342–43, 355–57
Perl, 206, 345, 552
permissions, 53, 138–39, 166, 175, 176

Permissions dialog box, 175, 176
Personal Home Page Wizard, 52, 60, 61
Personal Web Server, 24–26, 28–32, 65, 81,
    110, 128, 131–32, 179
phone calls
    informing co-workers about, 470
    logging, 469
Pick A Template option, 61, 127
Pick Template Layout dialog box, 127
PICT files, 426
Picture property, 390
Pivot Table Report command, 348
pivot tables, 340, 347–50, 352–53, 472
Pivot Table Wizard, 340, 347–50
Pivot Table Wizard dialog box, 340
PopUp Menu object, 229, 240–42, 244–45
PopUp menus, 229–31, 236, 240–45
PopUp method, 231, 240
Port 80, 179
POST method, 342, 554, 556
Post Reply button, 479
pound sign (#), 393, 397
PowerPoint, 17–19, 253, 267. See also slide
    shows
    Animation Player, 19, 413, 421, 423–24
    building the MMA intranet with, 450–54
    file objects and, 265–66
    files, posting, on your intranet, 416–20
    getting started with, 414–16
    hyperlinks and, 261–65
    intranet programming in, 438–49
PowerPoint Viewer, 125
<PRE> tag, 216
presentations. See PowerPoint; slide shows
Preset Animation menu, 425
Press Release Template, 52, 64
Preview in Browser command, 71
Preview In Browser dialog box, 69
Previous button, 351
printing, contact lists, 504
Private statement, 246
procedures, definition of, 245
processors, 164, 537
Product Description Template, 52
Product or Event Registration Template, 52,
    64, 148
Products/Services page, 46
Programs menu, 169
Programs tab, 135
Project Calendar, 506, 514–15

Project Initiation Form, 505, 507–8
Projects and Status Reports, 460
Project Template, 45, 50–51
Project Web Template, 69–70
Properties button, 165, 236
Properties dialog box, 152, 259, 260, 295, 354
Properties menu, 168, 178–79
Properties Table Editor, 232
Properties table, 235, 236–38, 248
protocols
    Office 97 and, 256–57
    Web site searches and, 530, 535
Protocols tab, 165
Proxies tab, 43
PseudoPageBreaks routine, 320, 325
public folders, 458, 461, 475–83, 497, 503–4, 505–16, 523–25
Public statement, 246
Publish command, 38
Publish FrontPage Web dialog box, 180
Publish To The Web Wizard, 377–80, 381, 382, 384, 401–2
PWS (Peer Web Services), 537

Q

qsEmployeeCount query, 400
qsEmployeeOffice query, 400, 404, 405–6
qsEmployeeSearch query, 400, 404, 406–7, 409
qsEmployees query, 399, 407–8
qsYearEmployees query, 400
queries, 341–43, 355–56, 399–409, 533–36, 538–43, 545–48. *See also* SQL Server,
    Access and, 366, 389–90, 399–400
    parameter, 396
    SQL Server and, 571
quotation marks ("), 95

R

RAM (random-access memory), 164, 537
Range object, 334, 335
Range property, 263, 310
ranges, 255–56, 263, 310, 334–35
Read Page, 490–91
RealAudio, 257
Recycle Bin, 35

RedefineChartSource routine, 352
Redim statement, 246
References dialog box, 518
Refresh button, 258
Refresh Data button, 352
Refresh Data option, 341, 352
Refresh method, 358
RefreshPivotData routine, 352
Registration WebBot, 148, 149
Registry, 178, 194
Registry Editor, 178
REL attribute, 99
Remote Data Objects, 384
RemoveItem method, 231
Replace In FrontPage Web dialog box, 145
replication, Internet, 397–98
RepopulateListBox routine, 357
reports, 169, 366, 375, 392, 397, 400
Report View, 169
RequeryData routine, 357
Reset button, 210
restrictions, 538–39
result sets, 539, 546–48
results page, 536
Results tab, 177
Resume button, 39
Reviewing toolbar, 419
revision marks, 291
RGB (Red-Green-Blue) color, 116, 120, 238, 313
rlogin protocol, 257
<ROOT WEB> directory, 30, 38, 44, 53, 59, 88, 92, 102, 112, 116, 128, 141, 146, 151, 153, 160, 180, 181
Run Query button, 404, 406
Run Web Query command, 341

S

Save As command, 65–66
Save command, 65–66
Save As dialog box, 65, 96–97, 376
Save As/Export command, 384
Save As HTML Wizard, 413–14, 420–21
Save Results WebBot, 63, 147–48, 177
saving
    documents to FTP sites, 261
    files in HTML format, 337–38
    files to Web sites, 259

saving *(continued)*
  forms, 489, 511
  graphics, 62
  Normal pages, 96–97
  Office document forms, 489
  slide shows, 416
  templates, 91, 92, 108–12
  in Web format, 374–75
  Web pages back to the server, 71
scanning, 543
Scheduled Image WebBot, 82, 83
Scheduled Include WebBot, 82, 83
Schedule page, 50
scheduling, 458, 571, 576
scope, 538
Script dialog box, 208
scripting. *See also* VBScript (Visual Basic
    Scripting Edition); JavaScript
  basics, 9, 205–13, 239–47, 343
  object model, 189–94, 196, 207
Script object, 191
script shells, 105–8, 142
<SCRIPT> tag, 185, 208–9, 211, 213, 240
Script Wizard, 232, 234, 239–47
Script Wizard button, 239
scrollbars, 123, 125, 127, 137
scrolling text, 285–87
search-and-replace action, 306
Search form, 31, 39, 49, 50, 51, 53, 132, 136,
    151
search pages, 46, 48, 50, 52, 54, 64–65, 141,
    143, 187, 259, 543–44
Search WebBot, 82, 90, 123, 528–29
section breaks, 291
Section menu, 216
security, 171, 175–79, 458. *See also* passwords
  administrator permissions, 53, 138–39, 166
  firewalls, 43–44
Select Case structures, 212, 221–22
Select Changes To Accept Or Reject dialog
    box, 339
Select method, 264
<SELECT> tag, 192, 289
Seminar Schedule Template, 52, 65
SendObject method, 381
Sent Items folder, 460, 461–62, 500–501
server(s). *See also* IIS (Microsoft Internet
    Information Server)
  authentication, 178–79

basic description of, 7–8
  extensions, 26–27
  download pages and, 132–33
  proxy, 43–44
  use of the term web sites and, 23
Server Administrator, 27
Services Properties dialog box, 170–75, 177
Services tab, 166, 171
Set Library To dialog box, 494, 511
Settings button, 158, 188
Settings dialog box, 188
Settings For Discussion Form Handler dialog
    box, 159
Set Transparent Color tool, 352
Set Up Show dialog box, 418, 447
Shape object, 265
Shape property, 310
shapes, 265, 310–11
Share Workbook dialog box, 339
Shippers table, 388
shortcut(s)
  icons, 477–78
  keyboard, 37
Show And Return check box, 448
Show Documents In Hidden Directories box,
    91
Show Fields command, 472, 473
Show Only Web Toolbar button, 258
Shut Down command, 113
Skip To The End button, 437
slash (/), 24, 37, 217–18
Slide Show menu, 418, 425, 426–27
SlideShowName property, 447
slides shows. *See also* PowerPoint
  converting, to HTML, 420–25
  display settings for, 417
  file formats for, 413, 414
  running, 437–38, 447–48
  setting up, 417–20, 430–31
  view modes for, 417–19
SNA Server (Microsoft), 20–21, 573–74
Software Data Sheet Template, 52, 65
sorting, in Outlook, 473
sound, 83, 88
  custom soundtracks, 427–28, 453–54
  movies and, 429–30
  PowerPoint and, 415, 425, 426–28
  Word and, 282–84
SoundEffect property, 441, 442

Source option, 195
Source property, 195
spacing, 73, 76, 124
Speaker mode, 417, 419, 420, 430–31
spell checking, 40–41
Split button, 127
spreadsheets, 17–20, 77. *See also* Excel
    collaborative editing and, 266–67, 339
    hyperlinks and, 261–65
SQL Server, 20–21, 163, 340
    Access and, 363, 370–73, 383, 405–6
    handling dynamic requests with, 572–73
    integration with, 569–94
    sample Web pages that utilize, 574–75
Standard toolbar, 276, 298
Start button, 258
Start menu, 28, 169
Start page, 187, 259
static Web pages, 374, 375–82
Status page, 50
status reports, 505, 515–16, 519
<STRIKE> tag, 287
style(s)
    Document, 300
    hyperlink, 296
    Word and, 291, 296, 300
style sheets
    cascading style sheet, 94–101, 110, 123, 404
    Page Properties style sheet, 88–95, 111,
        116–17, 120, 141, 153, 158, 213–14
<STYLE> tag, 124, 143, 338–39
STYLSRC attribute, 109, 110
Submission form, 48, 50, 51, 149, 151, 152,
    154–60
Submit button, 153, 288
Substitution WebBot, 42, 54, 82, 159
Suggestions From Customers form, 48
Summary tab, 44
Sun Microsystems, 206
<SUP> tag, 287
Survey Form Template, 52, 65, 149
symbols
    & (ampersand), 218, 511
    * (asterisk), 130
    \ (backslash), 24, 37
    {} (braces), 301
    : (colon), 103
    / (forward slash), 24, 37, 217–18
    # (pound sign), 393, 397
    " (quotation marks), 95
    _ (underscore), 43
switches, 302
SwitchFields macro, 320
system requirements, 530, 537–38

T

Tab Index property, 511
table(s), 19, 399. *See also* Access; tables of
        contents
    creating, 77–79
    download pages and, 132–33
    exploration bar and, 117
    exporting, 388
    formats, 73, 396
    pivot tables, 340, 347–50, 352–53, 472
    properties, changing, 395
    style sheets and, 95
    Word and, 291, 292
Table menu
    Cell Properties command, 79, 104, 118,
        124, 132
    Insert Table command, 117
    Table Properties command, 74, 79
tables of contents, 50–55, 60–61, 138, 141–
        43, 233, 291
    form, 132, 152
    hyperlink, in Word, 320–22
    page, 31–32, 46, 48–49, 52
    regenerating, 39
Table of Contents WebBot, 61, 82, 90, 141, 148
Table Properties dialog box, 74–75, 78
<TABLE> tag, 74–75, 287, 395
tabs, 291
task lists, 481–82
Tasks, 459, 466
TCP/IP (Transfer Control Protocol/Internet
        Protocol), 7, 27–28,
164, 564
<TD> tag, 77–79, 95, 287
telnet protocol, 257
template(s), 36, 44–53, 98–100, 293–94
    Access and, 376–77, 380, 392–95, 400–401
    adding styled text to, 101
    animated, 412
    creating, basic description of, 88–93, 400–401
    customizing, 65–66
    hyperdocument, 137

template(s) *(continued)*
  Outlook and, 497, 505–16
  PowerPoint and, 412, 414–15, 450
  saving master page, 108–12
  Word and, 293–96, 320
Template Wizard, 343, 346–47
Temporary Internet Files group, 188
terminal emulation, 257
text
  aligning, 137
  animated, 303–4
  color, 88, 150, 304–5
  effects, 303–4
  formatting, 284–89
  global text operations, 40–42
  HTML tags for, 287
<TEXTAREA> tag, 289
Text Box Properties dialog box, 157
Text Box Validation dialog box, 157
textures, 274, 313
Texture tab, 274
<TH> tag, 78, 97, 132–33
threaded conversations, 50, 478–79
3-D buttons, 267
timeouts, connection, 171
Timer control, 201, 229–30
timestamps, 82, 83, 91, 103
Timestamp WebBot, 82, 83
title bar, 43
<TITLE> tag, 84, 287
titles, 29–30, 43, 46, 511
tN3270 protocol, 257
To Do list, 26, 30, 32, 39, 41, 47, 470
Toggle Field Code option, 272
toolbars, 113–22, 117–18, 149, 156, 160,
    288–89
ToolBox window, 250
Tools menu, 35, 39–40, 43, 239, 337, 345
  AutoCorrect command, 271
  Options command, 95
  Permissions command, 175, 176
  Protect Document command, 305
  Recalculate Hyperlinks command, 110,
    143, 152
  Recall This Message command, 461
  Services command, 524
  Share Workbook command, 339
  Validate Hyperlinks command, 110
  Verify Hyperlinks command, 111, 144–45,
    152–53

Web Settings command, 91, 105, 115
tool tips, 121–22, 334
<TR> tag, 77, 95, 97, 287
tracking, 304
Transaction Server, 551, 552, 561–66
TransferDatabase command, 372–74
TransferSpreadsheet command, 372, 374
TransferText command, 372, 374
troubleshooting, 178–79, 395–97
TrueScript, 20
<TT> tag, 98
TYPE attribute, 99
Type property, 263, 311, 449

U

<UL> tag, 76–77, 95, 287
UNC (uniform naming convention), 537
underlined text, 296
underscore (_), 43, 296
UNIX, 24, 174, 552
UpdateChart routine, 357, 358
URLs (uniform resource locators), 29–31, 39,
    43. *See also* links
  absolute, 55, 109, 110, 146
  converting, 109–10, 217
  download pages and, 132–35
  for frames, 127
  for images, 66
  hot spots and, 114–15
  invalid, 97
  relative, 55, 96–97, 99, 109, 110, 155, 160
  slash marks and, 24
  valid, 237
Use Voting Buttons option, 461
Usenet newsgroups, 257
UserAgent property, 226
User Manager, 175–76
User Name field, 178
User Registration Template, 52, 65, 149
Users tab, 175

V

validation, 149, 157, 219–24
value(s)
  initial, 511
  passing by, 224

Value property, 196
variables
    configuration, 160
    for modifying lists of users/groups, 176
    passing, 224
    redefining, 224
    system, 89
    user, 89
VBA (Microsoft Visual Basic for Applica-
        tions), 15, 19, 205–6, 261, 334–35
    Access and, 361, 381, 390
    automating Web page building with, 306–15
    Excel and, 332, 347, 351–53, 357–58
    PowerPoint and, 411–12, 418, 431, 438–51,
        453
    Web object model, 253
    Word and, 269, 271, 305–16, 318
VBScript (Visual Basic Scripting Edition), 9,
        13, 67, 83–84, 91–92, 111, 125
    dynamic pages and, 205–51, 233, 239,
        242–47
    IIS and, 20, 558, 561
    Internet Explorer and, 185, 189
    menus and, 114
    Outlook and, 471, 490
    script shells and, 105, 106, 107, 142–43
    style definitions and, 124
Verify button, 39, 144
Verify Hyperlink command, 39
Verify Hyperlinks dialog box, 39–40, 144–45
video clips, 282–84, 313, 429–30
View menu, 33–34, 76, 186–88, 193, 195, 298
    Define Views command, 474, 513
    Field Chooser command, 475
    Filter command, 473
    Folder List command, 475
    Format Columns command, 473
    Format View command, 475, 513
    Forms Toolbar command, 149
    HTML command, 69, 70, 110
    HTML Source command, 293
    Options command, 135
    Properties command, 367
    Refresh command, 71–72, 143
    Show Fields command, 489, 513
    Sort command, 473
View or Edit HTML window, 70, 71, 77, 83,
        109, 111, 120, 154, 209
View property, 314–15
ViewSource method, 195

virtual narrator, 427
Visual Basic, 13, 67, 112, 490, 505, 517–18,
        522, 569. See also VBA (Microsoft
        Visual Basic for Applications);
        VBScript (Visual Basic Scripting
        Edition)
    ActiveX and, 21, 247
    creating dynamic pages with, 205–51
    custom Wizards and, 52
    Enterprise Edition, 250–51
    Internet Explorer and, 15, 185, 194–201
    scripting basics for, 207–13
    script shells and, 105, 106
VRML (Virtual Reality Modeling Language), 113

W

W3C (World Wide Web Consortium), 99, 553
WANs (wide area networks), 569
watermarks, 88
Web(s)
    deleting, 35
    maintaining, 39–44
    names, 29–30, 43, 46
    problems opening, 178
    site searches, 527–48
    sub-, 138–39, 149, 150–52
    webs within, 53
    use of the term, 23
Web Assistant, 570, 571–73, 574–79
WebBots, 26, 34, 42, 53–55, 61, 67, 179. See
        also WebBots (listed by name)
    basic description of, 13, 81–83
    broken links and, 155–56
    download pages and, 158–59
    security and, 177
WebBots (listed by name). See also WebBots
    Comment WebBot, 60
    Confirmation Field WebBot, 81, 159, 160,
        223
    Discussion WebBot, 148
    HTML Markup WebBot, 74–76, 123, 137,
        142, 219–20
    Include WebBot, 47, 54, 81, 100, 109, 111
    Markup WebBot, 79
    Registration WebBot, 148, 149
    Save Results WebBot, 63, 147–48, 177
    Scheduled Image WebBot, 82, 83
    Scheduled Include WebBot, 82, 83

WebBots (continued)
    Search WebBot, 82, 90, 123, 528–29
    Substitution WebBot, 42, 54, 82, 159
    Table of Contents WebBot, 61, 82, 90, 141, 148
    Timestamp WebBot, 82, 83
Web Connectivity Kit, 338, 342
Web Find Fast, 528, 529–37
Web Form Wizard, 345
Web pages
    dynamic, 205–51, 374–75, 379, 382–92
    moving, between folders, 36, 37, 152–56
    static, 374, 375–82
    total size recommendations for, 114
    use of the term, 23
Web Page Wizard, 276–78
Web toolbar, 257–58, 275, 278, 332–37
Welcome page, 47
What's New page, 46–47, 52, 65
WIDTH attribute, 123
wildcard characters, 130, 396
Window mode, 417, 420, 430, 431
Window object, 190–92, 208, 215
Windows Explorer, 27, 35
    Internet Explorer and, 184, 186–87
    List View, 186–87, 240
Windows NT, 164, 166, 171, 187, 579
    File System (NTFS), 166, 174, 179
    Server, 20, 163
    Web site searches and, 530, 531, 537–38
Wizards
    Access Report Wizard, 396
    AutoContent Wizard, 414
    Chart Wizard, 350–51
    Corporate Presence Wizard, 11, 29–33, 45–47
    custom Wizards, 52–53
    Database Connector Wizard, 52, 60
    Discussion Wizard, 45, 48–49, 148–49, 150–52
    Form Page Wizard, 60, 148–49
    Form Wizard, 52, 345
    Frames Wizard, 11, 52, 60–61, 69, 79, 125–31
    Import and Export Wizard, 465, 523
    Import HTML Wizard, 371, 372
    Internet Assistant Wizard, 337
    Learning FrontPage Wizard, 45
    Personal Home Page Wizard, 52, 60, 61
    Pivot Table Wizard, 340, 347–50

Publish To The Web Wizard, 377–80, 381, 382, 384, 401–2
Save As HTML Wizard, 413–14, 420–21
Script Wizard, 232, 234, 239–47
Template Wizard, 343, 346–47
Web Form Wizard, 345
Web Page Wizard, 276–78
Word, 17, 18, 71, 253, 393, 481, 487
    building/editing HTML files in, 275–90
    creating Web documents with, 269–328
    design tools, 279–87
    Document Maps in, 267
    documents, posting, 296–306
    format, converting HTML format to, 292–93
    format, converting, to HTML format, 290–92, 326
    download pages and, 132
    Excel and, 332
    file objects and, 265–66
    Internet Explorer and, 184, 186–87
    IIS and, 562
    links and, 261–65
    style sheets and, 94, 95
    template architecture, 293–96
    three faces of, 270–71
WordArt, 255, 304, 310, 333, 353
WordPad, 27, 44, 232, 384
    editing style sheets with, 94–101
    frames and, 129–31
word wrap, 305, 314
Worksheet object, 334
WrapToWindow property, 314
write-ins, last minute, 215
WriteLn method, 216–18
Write method, 216–18
WWW Service, 166, 172, 174, 178–79, 539, 580–81
WWW Service Properties dialog box, 172, 179, 539, 580–81
WYSIWYG (What You See Is What You Get), 25, 68, 266, 270, 276

X

<XMP> tag, 98

Micro Modeling Associates,

Inc. (MMA), founded in 1989, is a leading Microsoft Solution Provider Partner with over 150 professionals in New York, New Jersey, Washington, D.C., Minneapolis/St. Paul, Chicago, Boston, and soon, San Francisco. We deliver custom desktop, departmental, client/server, Internet, intranet, and enterprise solutions to large organizations using the Microsoft suite of products, including Microsoft Office, BackOffice, Visual Basic, Visual C++, ActiveX, and other Web technologies. We are unique in our Microsoft focus and our heavy emphasis on application usability, data access, and reporting. While several of our employees are published authors, this is the first book we have authored as a firm. We can be reached at www.micromodeling.com.

The contributing authors for *Official Microsoft Intranet Solutions* are listed on the following two pages.

Tom Begley is a Managing Associate in Micro Modeling's Washington, D.C., office. He runs the DC Office Group and is responsible for application development, system design, and project management. He is a Microsoft Certified Solution Developer and holds a B.S. in mathematics from Fairfield University. He lives with his wife Cathy and their daughter Sabrina in Northern Virginia. Tom can be reached at begleyt@micromodeling.com.

Rick Bullen is a Director in MMA's New York office and has been in the computing field for more than thirty years. He has an A.B. in mathematics from Columbia College and an M.S. in management of technology from MIT. Rick manages MMA's internal systems group and believes that MMA's intranet will be the user interface of choice for many of its internal systems in coming years. He was a Sysop of a Bulletin Board System in pre-Internet days. His hobbies are stocks, jazz, and winter sports, three avocations well represented on the Internet. Rick can be reached at bullenr@micromodeling.com.

Francisco DelValle Jr. is a Senior Associate in Micro Modeling's New York BackOffice group. With over six years of experience, he specializes in the analysis, design, and development of client/server applications using Visual Basic and SQL Server. He has also written HTML home pages for individuals and corporations and developed client/server applications for state and local governments, nonprofit organizations, and performance rights societies. He attended Pace University, where he studied management information systems. Frank can be reached at delvallef@micromodeling.com.

Jason Harper is Micro Modeling's national Manager of Information Technology, with responsibility for all of MMA's network and communications infrastructure. He is a Microsoft Certified Systems Engineer and has been working with Microsoft Windows NT and BackOffice since its inception. Jason can be reached at harperj@micromodeling.com.

Steve Harshbarger is a Director at Micro Modeling Associates and manages MMA's Washington, D.C., consulting practice. He oversees a team of developers implementing business applications using the entire suite of Microsoft development tools. Steve recently co-authored *Microsoft Excel 97 Developer's Handbook* with Microsoft's Eric Wells. He is a frequent speaker at industry events such as VBITS and TechEd. Prior to joining MMA in 1994, Steve was a consultant at KPMG Peat Marwick and earned his degree in accounting information systems from Virgina Tech. Steve can be reached at harshbargers@micromodeling.com.

Ken Heft is a Senior Associate in MMA's Washington, D.C., office. He is a Microsoft Certified Solution Developer and Certified Trainer, dividing his time between Office development and developer training. Before MMA, Ken was doing Windows development for KPMG Peat Marwick. A 1992 graduate of the University of North Carolina at Chapel Hill, Ken spends his time out of the office running, seeing bands, and waiting patiently for the Howard Stern movie. Ken just completed his first marathon and his first book and is now planning to rediscover a social life. Ken can be reached at heftk@micromodeling.com.

David Ho is a Managing Associate who heads up the Client/Server Development Group in MMA's New York office. He has ten years of computer experience and holds a bachelor's degree in physics from N.Y.U. and a master's degree in computer science from the City College of the City University of New York. David lives in Long Island, New York, with his wife Diane and their children Amanda and Brandon. David can be reached at hod@micromodeling.com.

Donna Jensen is a Senior Associate in Micro Modeling's New York office, specializing in Office and Visual Basic development. She has developed publishing and presentation systems for many major financial institutions and law firms. Although the words "leisure time" haven't been in her vocabulary in recent months, she faintly remembers enjoying writing, reading, hiking, and woodworking. Future plans include convincing Roy to let her set up an MMA office in Barbados. Donna can be reached at jensend@micromodeling.com.

Jeffrey M. Jones, Senior Associate, is the MMA Webmaster, a senior Office developer, and team manager for all Micro Modeling's printed and online documentation. He is also the author of *70 Scenes of Halloween* and, most recently, the musical *J.P. Morgan Saves the Nation* with the late Jonathan Larson. Jeff can be reached at jonesj@micromodeling.com.

Paul Li is a Senior Associate in Micro Modeling's New York BackOffice group. He has designed and coded many large-scale applications using Visual Basic and Microsoft Access. Paul can be reached at lip@micromodeling.com.

Lenore Michaels is Micro Modeling's Director of Marketing and has project-managed and internally edited this book. Four years ago, she left the world of investment banking to join this (then) teeny 25-person company and has never looked back. Her husband Ken thanks MMA for giving her back her life, her sense of humor, and the time to bring their incredible son Julian into this world. Lenore has a B.S. from the Wharton School of the University of Pennsylvania. Lenore can be reached at michaelsl@micromodeling.com.

Peter Mueller is an Associate Director and runs MMA's New York Desktop Development Group. He is a Microsoft Certified Developer and Trainer and has a B.A. in accounting from Queens College. Peter can be reached at muellerp@micromodeling.com.

Ronan Sorensen is a Managing Associate in the OLE/ActiveX Component Group at Micro Modeling Associates in Washington, D.C. He specializes in developing Intranet components that integrate into Microsoft Office and BackOffice using C++, OLE, DCOM, and ActiveX technology. Ronan holds a baccalaureate in commerce from University College in Dublin, Ireland, and is a Microsoft Certified Professional in MFC and OLE. In addition to writing articles for technical publications, he is a regular speaker at software industry events. He has spoken at Tech-Ed, Developers Days, Software Development East, Visual C++ Teach, and the Windows NT Intranet Solutions Conference. Ronan is a co-founder of the Mid-Atlantic Visual C++ User Group and is vice president of the Association of Windows NT Systems Professionals. Ronan can be reached at sorensenr@micromodeling.com.

Brian Stanton is an Associate Technical Director in MMA's Advanced Technology group in New York. He has been involved with computers and programming since 1977 and thought he knew everything there was to know until this Internet thing came along and proceeded to turn everything on its rear. He does have a life outside of computers and technology, and enjoys watching his young daughter grow into a little person with each passing day. Brian can be reached at stantonb@micromodeling.com.

Roy Wetterstrom is the President and founder of Micro Modeling Associates. Roy moved from Minnesota to New York City seven years ago to found Micro Modeling. Roy now lives back in Minnesota with his wife Emily and son David and divides his time between the six (and counting) Micro Modeling offices. Roy can be reached at wetterstromr@micromodeling.com.

The manuscript for this book was prepared and submitted to Microsoft Press in electronic form. Text files were prepared using Microsoft Word for Windows 95. Pages were composed by VersaTech Associates using Adobe PageMaker 6.0 for Windows 95, with text in MSP Garamond and display type in Frutiger. Composed pages were delivered to the printer as electronic prepress files.

Cover Graphic Designer
Creative Department,
Microsoft Press Marketing

Cover Photo/Illustration
Robin Bartholick

Interior Graphic Designer
Kim Eggleston

Interior Graphic Artist
Travis Beaven

Principal Compositor
Sybil Ihrig, VersaTech Associates

Principal Proofreaders
Deborah O. Stockton
Lorraine Maloney

Indexer
Liz Cunningham

IMPORTANT—READ CAREFULLY BEFORE OPENING SOFTWARE PACKET(S). By opening the sealed packet(s) containing the software, you indicate your acceptance of the following Microsoft License Agreement.

MICROSOFT LICENSE AGREEMENT

(Book Companion CD)

This is a legal agreement between you (either an individual or an entity) and Microsoft Corporation. By opening the sealed software packet(s) you are agreeing to be bound by the terms of this agreement. If you do not agree to the terms of this agreement, promptly return the unopened software packet(s) and any accompanying written materials to the place you obtained them for a full refund.

MICROSOFT SOFTWARE LICENSE

1. GRANT OF LICENSE. Microsoft grants to you the right to use one copy of the Microsoft software program included with this book (the "SOFTWARE") on a single terminal connected to a single computer. The SOFTWARE is in "use" on a computer when it is loaded into the temporary memory (i.e., RAM) or installed into the permanent memory (e.g., hard disk, CD-ROM, or other storage device) of that computer. You may not network the SOFTWARE or otherwise use it on more than one computer or computer terminal at the same time.

2. COPYRIGHT. The SOFTWARE is owned by Microsoft or its suppliers and is protected by United States copyright laws and international treaty provisions. Therefore, you must treat the SOFTWARE like any other copyrighted material (e.g., a book or musical recording) except that you may either (a) make one copy of the SOFTWARE solely for backup or archival purposes, or (b) transfer the SOFTWARE to a single hard disk provided you keep the original solely for backup or archival purposes. You may not copy the written materials accompanying the SOFTWARE.

3. OTHER RESTRICTIONS. You may not rent or lease the SOFTWARE, but you may transfer the SOFTWARE and accompanying written materials on a permanent basis provided you retain no copies and the recipient agrees to the terms of this Agreement. You may not reverse engineer, decompile, or disassemble the SOFTWARE. If the SOFTWARE is an update or has been updated, any transfer must include the most recent update and all prior versions.

4. DUAL MEDIA SOFTWARE. If the SOFTWARE package contains more than one kind of disk (3.5", 5.25", and CD-ROM), then you may use only the disks appropriate for your single-user computer. You may not use the other disks on another computer or loan, rent, lease, or transfer them to another user except as part of the permanent transfer (as provided above) of all SOFTWARE and written materials.

5. SAMPLE CODE. If the SOFTWARE includes Sample Code, then Microsoft grants you a royalty-free right to reproduce and distribute the sample code of the SOFTWARE provided that you: (a) distribute the sample code only in conjunction with and as a part of your software product; (b) do not use Microsoft's or its authors' names, logos, or trademarks to market your software product; (c) include the copyright notice that appears on the SOFTWARE on your product label and as a part of the sign-on message for your software product; and (d) agree to indemnify, hold harmless, and defend Microsoft and its authors from and against any claims or lawsuits, including attorneys' fees, that arise or result from the use or distribution of your software product.

DISCLAIMER OF WARRANTY

The SOFTWARE (including instructions for its use) is provided "AS IS" WITHOUT WARRANTY OF ANY KIND. MICROSOFT FURTHER DISCLAIMS ALL IMPLIED WARRANTIES INCLUDING WITHOUT LIMITATION ANY IMPLIED WARRANTIES OF MERCHANTABILITY OR OF FITNESS FOR A PARTICULAR PURPOSE. THE ENTIRE RISK ARISING OUT OF THE USE OR PERFORMANCE OF THE SOFTWARE AND DOCUMENTATION REMAINS WITH YOU.

IN NO EVENT SHALL MICROSOFT, ITS AUTHORS, OR ANYONE ELSE INVOLVED IN THE CREATION, PRODUCTION, OR DELIVERY OF THE SOFTWARE BE LIABLE FOR ANY DAMAGES WHATSOEVER (INCLUDING, WITHOUT LIMITATION, DAMAGES FOR LOSS OF BUSINESS PROFITS, BUSINESS INTERRUPTION, LOSS OF BUSINESS INFORMATION, OR OTHER PECUNIARY LOSS) ARISING OUT OF THE USE OF OR INABILITY TO USE THE SOFTWARE OR DOCUMENTATION, EVEN IF MICROSOFT HAS BEEN ADVISED OF THE POSSIBILITY OF SUCH DAMAGES. BECAUSE SOME STATES/COUNTRIES DO NOT ALLOW THE EXCLUSION OR LIMITATION OF LIABILITY FOR CONSEQUENTIAL OR INCIDENTAL DAMAGES, THE ABOVE LIMITATION MAY NOT APPLY TO YOU.

U.S. GOVERNMENT RESTRICTED RIGHTS

The SOFTWARE and documentation are provided with RESTRICTED RIGHTS. Use, duplication, or disclosure by the Government is subject to restrictions as set forth in subparagraph (c)(1)(ii) of The Rights in Technical Data and Computer Software clause at DFARS 252.227-7013 or subparagraphs (c)(1) and (2) of the Commercial Computer Software — Restricted Rights 48 CFR 52.227-19, as applicable. Manufacturer is Microsoft Corporation, One Microsoft Way, Redmond, WA 98052-6399.

If you acquired this product in the United States, this Agreement is governed by the laws of the State of Washington. Should you have any questions concerning this Agreement, or if you desire to contact Microsoft Press for any reason, please write: Microsoft Press, One Microsoft Way, Redmond, WA 98052-6399.

Register Today!

Return this
Official Microsoft® Intranet Solutions
registration card for
a Microsoft Press® catalog

U.S. and Canada addresses only. Fill in information below and mail postage-free. Please mail only the bottom half of this page.

1-57231-509-1A   *OFFICIAL MICROSOFT® INTRANET SOLUTIONS*   *Owner Registration Card*

NAME

INSTITUTION OR COMPANY NAME

ADDRESS

CITY   STATE   ZIP

Microsoft ® *Press*
Quality Computer Books

For a free catalog of
Microsoft Press® products, call
1-800-MSPRESS